The
Edwardians

The
Edwardians

ROY HATTERSLEY

LITTLE, BROWN

A *Little, Brown* Book

First published in Great Britain in 2004
by Little, Brown

Copyright © Roy Hattersley 2004

The moral right of the author has been asserted.

A CIP catalogue record for this book
is available from the British Library.

ISBN 0 316 72537 4

Endpapers: (front) The House of Commons,
1895-1901, 'A Division Called', engraver unknown;
(back) The House of Commons, 1914, Leopold Braun.
Both courtesy of the Palace of Westminster Collection.

Typeset in Bembo by M Rules
Printed and bound in Great Britain by
Clays Ltd, St Ives plc

Little, Brown
An imprint of
Time Warner Book Group UK
Brettenham House
Lancaster Place
London WC2E 7EN

www.twbg.co.uk

CONTENTS

Part Four: 'Everybody Got Down off their Stilts'

Part Five: 'Full of Energy and Purpose'

ACKNOWLEDGEMENTS

The persistent myth depicts the Edwardian era as a long and leisurely afternoon. In fact, the years between Queen Victoria's death and the outbreak of the First World War were a watershed in British history – not an interlude that separated the old and new worlds, but the time when a modern nation was born. The Edwardians witnessed the world changing around them.

It has been my good fortune to read three unpublished diaries which illustrate life – in very different parts of society – during the turbulent thirteen years. I am deeply grateful to my three benefactors – the late Duke of Devonshire, for the diaries of his grandfather, Victor Cavendish, MP until 1908 and then 9th Duke; Gervald Frykman, for the diaries of his grandmother, Kate Jarvis (née Bedford), a children's nanny with the Crutchley family in Ascot; and Christine Glossop, for the diaries of Rowland Evans, her father – the schoolboy son of a Bradford Nonconformist minister and then an engineering apprentice in Leicester.

Will and Alison Parenti – pursuing on my behalf a legend about King Edward's coronation – found it confirmed in *Men, Women and Things*, the memoir of the 6th Duke of Portland. It proved to be a fascinating quarry.

Once again I am indebted to Anthony Howard, who read the manuscript and improved it by giving me his advice as a candid friend. Cynthia Shepherd typed numerous versions of the text – eliminating errors, correcting grammar and identifying contradictions as she did so. The book is better for their help. Its shortcomings are, of course, my sole responsibility.

INTRODUCTION

Hope and Glory

Between the death of Queen Victoria on 22 January 1901, and the outbreak of the Great War on 4 August 1914, a political and social revolution, accompanied and sustained by an explosion of intellectual and artistic energy, swept Britain into the modern world. Yet the Edwardian Age is constantly described as a long and sunlit afternoon, no more than a congenial bridging passage between the glories of the nineteenth century and the horrors of slaughter in France and Flanders. Charm is thought to have replaced energy in a nation, exhausted by the activity and achievement of Victorian Britain, gratefully at rest.

Much of the blame for the epic mistake lies with the King who gave the age its name. Edward VII personified benevolent self-indulgence. The Entente Cordiale, for which he took only partially deserved credit, came to represent more than a warmer friendship with France. It became the genial symbol of the age. Britain, history came to believe, was cordial in general.

In truth, Edwardian Britain teemed with the excitement of innovation and change. The King – either indulging his appetites at country house parties or attempting to impose his royal will on ministers – began his reign thinking that the old order would last for ever. Even he came to realise how the old world was disappearing around him. Only the years which followed the Second World War can compare with the speed and extent of Edwardian change.

The politicians, as politicians will, assumed that the new society would be built in Parliament. The introduction of the National Insurance Bill certainly established a novel principle of government – the State's responsibility for the welfare of its most vulnerable members. And the battle between Lords and Commons, which that bill precipitated, shifted the balance of power a little nearer to democracy. The House of Commons itself was becoming a professional legislature which no longer relied on *noblesse oblige* to motivate its Members. Class interests and rival ideologies were rippling the smooth surface of what had been a gentleman's Parliament. But those reforms were the direct result of changes in society outside Westminster and Whitehall.

A new political party talking of mass membership and demanding manhood suffrage had emerged from the factories and mines, the mills and docks of industrial Britain. The result was not the death of Liberal England but the evolution of progressive opinion within the Liberal Party (most strongly represented in Scotland and Wales) into the Labour Party. The radical spirit of the time was typified by two militant campaigns – Votes for Women and Home Rule for Ireland. Both of those demands were met because Edwardian militants battled for their causes in the streets. By 1914 there was no turning back. The war, so often said to have made Irish Home Rule and Votes for Women irresistible, postponed, not promoted, both reforms. The arguments were won in Edwardian Britain.

The new willingness to challenge authority – without which women would not have achieved even an extension to their franchise and Ireland would not have obtained its blemished freedom – was not confined to politics. The right of the Lord Chamberlain's office to censor plays was contested by the greatest playwrights of the day – men who were determined to redeem late-Victorian drama by demonstrating that thought and entertainment were not incompatible. Fiction enjoyed a decade of eclectic brilliance. A masterpiece – covering a spectrum that stretched from Henry James to D. H. Lawrence – was published in every Edwardian year. The Grafton Gallery in London's Dover Street, uncertain how to describe a new school of painting which it believed possessed the mark of genius, decided to call it Post-Impressionism.

The Church – at least the Church of England – would have

welcomed a period of calm, but it had to defend its immutable beliefs against a tide of unprecedented intellectual and scientific advances. Rutherford, in the dawn of nuclear physics, redefined the nature of matter. Moore promised a moral philosophy which both suited the mores of the age and stood much Christian teaching on its head. Russell even questioned the way in which the old world thought. They were the real spirit of the age, not Edward's 'Marlborough House Set' at the Henley Regatta, Ascot and the Eton versus Harrow match at Lord's.

Indeed sport — real sport, the true opiate of the Edwardian masses — changed as quickly as every other aspect of early twentieth-century life. The hard edge of professionalism began to alter the character of football and cricket, making the spectator who paid at the turnstile essential to a team's success. Boxing moved out of public-house yards into the big halls. But the Olympic Games in London maintained the British tradition of admiration for good losers. Queen Alexandra presented a trophy to the Italian athlete who collapsed just before he won the marathon.

The evidence of material progress was all around. The motor car — neither reliable nor accepted in 1900 — became so common that a new tax had to be levied to pay for the tarmacadam which was needed on the roads. The aeroplane — after a series of breathtaking trials and competitions — was accepted as the transport of the future. The turbine engine transformed merchant shipping and naval warfare — just in time. The Edwardians discovered that Britain's real enemy was not France but Germany.

Because of the Great War, progress was suspended and, in the slaughter which followed, the achievements of the century's early years were underrated and overlooked. But one irrefutable fact remains. The Land of Hope and Glory which was celebrated in Edward VII's 'Coronation Ode' was moving irresistibly into the modern world.

PART ONE

'Anxieties for England'

When the long day of Queen Victoria's funeral was over, Viscount Esher stood in the falling snow outside the Frogmore Mausoleum and, much to his own surprise, thought about the future rather than the past. He had, at royal request, supervised the Golden Jubilee Celebrations, so he felt part of the fifty-year imperial glory which those festivities symbolised. He believed, as did most of his contemporaries, that the victorious reign was an age of unsurpassed achievement. He also feared, like many of the mourners on that cold February day, that imperial greatness had died with the Queen.

Edward VII had never hidden his dissolute habits or disguised his louche ways. Victoria was the epitome of imperial greatness. Her son seemed to be the personification of the decadence which guarantees decline. The superstition was reinforced by statistics. The British economy, though still strong, was not expanding at the rate of its competitors. The British Army, which little boys were told had never lost a war, was losing its battle with the Boers.

It is unlikely that Esher thought much about the real state of the nation – the standard of living of the urban poor, the wages of agricultural labourers, the status of women and the quality of elementary education. But all over Britain working men and women had begun first to argue and then to agitate for a greater share of the wealth which was, they believed, the bequest of history. The Edwardian age became a social and economic revolution. Esher, the quintessential courtier with vested interests in the established order, was right to fear that a 'new regime, full of anxieties for England, had begun'.

CHAPTER 1

A Cloud Across the Sun

The King and the cortège were ready exactly as planned, at half past eleven. But it took more than two minutes for the Earl Marshal's message – relayed by twelve Hussar signallers along Buckingham Palace Road, down the Mall, up St James's and into Piccadilly – to reach the head of the column. To the officers of the headquarters' staff, who waited to give the order 'Slow March', the delay seemed much longer. They had fought in battles from Majuba Hill to Spion Kopje, but, on the morning of 2 February 1901, they were more nervous than raw recruits under fire for the first time. The procession which it was their duty to move off was part of the biggest parade of the armed forces that Britain had ever seen. Twenty thousand men were ready to march and another thirty thousand lined the route. But it was the occasion, not its size, which intimidated them. In the words of *The Times*, 'the day had come for the Army to pay its last tribute of devotion' to Queen Victoria.

The slow march across London was only one part of the royal obsequies. They had begun on the previous day. The Queen had died in Osborne House on the Isle of Wight. The first stage of her journey home – for the funeral service at Windsor and then to the Royal Mausoleum at Frogmore for the brief lying-in-state – provided an ideal opportunity to offer an appropriate tribute to the monarch 'who had been Ruler of a Worldwide Empire and Mistress of the Sea'.[1] Thirty British battleships and cruisers lined the route of the royal yacht *Alberta*, followed by the *Hohenzollern* bearing Victoria's grandson, the Kaiser of Germany. Three German 'ironclads', anchored alongside the cruisers which had been sent to pay the respects of France, Japan and Portugal, joined in the tribute. A Spanish frigate, hurrying across the Bay of Biscay to join the armada, lost steam and was replaced by a yacht which belonged to the Prince of Monaco. The memorial fleet stood in line for two days waiting to fire a vale-dictory salute as the cortège of the dead queen sailed by.

The railway companies, which had been the economic glory of Victorian Britain, accepted the task of bearing the body of the Queen from Portsmouth to London with appropriate solemnity. All adver-tisements on or about Victoria Station, where the coffin was to arrive, were removed or obscured. The platform along which it was to be carried was covered in blue cloth and a pavilion, to provide a moment's respite for the royal mourners, was built exactly opposite the place at which Edward VII would alight. The engine and most of the carriages – including the coach that carried the new king – were the property of the Brighton Company, but the body of the old Queen in its lead-lined coffin made the journey in a carriage which belonged to the Great Western Railway. It was provided at the special request of her son in tribute to the many happy journeys his mother had made in what had become the royal coach.

The inside of the carriage was no longer decorated in the famous chocolate and cream livery of 'God's Wonderful Railway'. Everything was white. The notion that a white funeral would proclaim a life of purity was put into Victoria's mind by Lord Tennyson during a rev-erential visit to Prince Albert's tomb in the Royal Mausoleum at Frogmore. The insistence that she should not be shrouded in black had been included in her detailed instructions about how her funeral should be conducted.

Queen Victoria had always taken funerals seriously, and she had left few details of her own last rites to the vagaries of her family and court. Her dresser had been given details of the contents of her coffin – the Prince Consort's dressing gown, her wedding veil, numerous bracelets and lockets, a cloth which had been embroidered by her dead daugh-ter and a photograph of John Brown to be held, together with a lock of his hair, in her left hand. The funeral itself had to be entirely military, with her coffin drawn through London on a gun carriage by eight horses which she instructed should be white or bay, not the usual sable.

Providence did not quite provide the weather that the Queen would have chosen. Snow was falling on the Isle of Wight when the royal yacht set sail for Portsmouth. Next day in London the early morning was bitterly cold, so the troops who lined the route were in greatcoat order. There were gusts of rain as the train, bearing Victoria's coffin, approached Victoria Station. By the time that the procession was ready to move off, the sky was a clear blue. It was, therefore, a good morning for marching soldiers who hate the heat. It was less congenial to the crowds of mourners who stood for hours along the route. But London was not in a mood to be prevented from saying farewell to the old Queen.

Almost two weeks had passed between the Queen's death on 22 January and the return to London in preparation for the funeral and lying-in-state. During those days, the Earl Marshal, the Lord Great Chamberlain, the Master of Horse, the Commander-in-Chief, Lord Esher (a family friend and Secretary to the Office of Works), numerous private secretaries, sundry bishops and assorted courtiers had contributed to making certain that nothing went wrong during two days of unique ceremony which began with a naval regatta and continued with a whole Army corps – more men than went to France in the British expeditionary forces in 1914 – marching through London. In general the arrangements were brilliantly successful. The careful planning, not to mention the presence of the Kaiser, the Kings of Greece and Portugal, five crown princes, fourteen princes, two grand dukes, one archduke, five dukes and most of their consorts, did not make for a spontaneous outpouring of emotion. However, there is no doubt that the whole nation was engulfed in genuine grief. Britain had lost a queen who had reigned for so long that nobody under the age of seventy – far beyond the average lifespan of the age could remember the time before she occupied the throne. The mourning was almost universal.

In London, Victor Cavendish, MP – nephew of the 8th Duke of Devonshire and heir presumptive to the title and to Chatsworth –

wrote in his diary, 'Everybody most depressed.' Cavendish had just been appointed government whip in the House of Commons and was therefore technically a member of the Court with the title of Treasurer of the Royal Household. His grief had to be publicly and properly expressed. 'When I woke this morning, found a note saying that there was to be a Privy Council Meeting at St James' Palace and that I was to attend. My uniform was not finished. So I hurried off to Sir F Ponsonby [the Queen's assistant private secretary] and asked him what I ought to do. He lent me a suit but it was much too big.'

Two hundred miles north in the town of Bradford, the Reverend Rowland Evans, minister of the Galington Baptist Church, spoke to the local newspaper about the rewards of sacrifice and service and prayed for the soul of the departed queen. His twelve-year-old son, also Rowland, seemed enthusiastic only about cricket and fretwork, a particularly Victorian form of handicraft. Perhaps the Reverend Evans thought that a new reign in a new century was an ideal time for his son to start a diary. The initial response was encouraging. Rowland wrote on the first page:

> Rowland Evans is my name
> England is my nation
> Bradford is my dwelling place
> The Lord is my salvation

All over Britain, curtains were drawn, in the traditional sign of shared mourning. Services were held in cathedrals and parish churches at or about the same time as the last rites were performed in the Chapel Royal at Windsor. The symbols of grief and the expressions of sorrow were, of course, at their greatest – and their most ingenious – in the capital. Mayfair families made, or arranged for their servants to make, wreaths of cypress and laurel which they hung from lamp-posts. Crossing sweepers in the Strand tied wisps of black rag to their brooms. Cabmen fastened ribbons to their whips.

As the funeral train steamed towards London, men and women from the farms of Hampshire and Surrey rushed to the side of the track. The platforms of the suburban stations through which it passed were crowded from the early morning. The Commissioner of

Metropolitan Police had insisted that the procession from Victoria to Paddington must be diverted past Buckingham Palace, up Constitution Hill and through Hyde Park rather than travel by the easiest and quickest route along Grosvenor Place. Unless the crowds could be spread over a longer distance some mourners would, he feared, be killed in the crush. It proved to be a wise precaution. Almost a million men and women travelled into London late on the night before or early on the morning of the funeral procession. A few had paid for vantage points in the shop windows or on the balconies of houses along the way. The rest hoped to find a spot where they could stand and see. Most of them were disappointed.

The crush was greatest in Hyde Park, part of the addition to the route which the Commissioner had hoped would avoid dangerous congestion on the pavements of the Mall and Piccadilly. At places the crowd was a hundred deep and, as it swayed forward, the soldiers who were lining the route pushed it back. An occasional coster offered tawdry mementos for sale and a few dozen pickpockets were apprehended by mourners and handed over to the police. But what was most noticeable about the crowd was its silent discipline.

There was a hushed intake of breath and the incredulous whisper, 'The Queen', as the head of the procession appeared. In an age of hats – silk for gentlemen, bowlers for prosperous clerks and respectable shopkeepers and flat caps for the rest – it was followed by a rustle as men lifted their arms to bare their heads. The sound which most of the mourners remembered was the tramp of marching feet. Even the bands – alternating Chopin's Funeral March and the Dead March from *Saul* – were subdued. There were, however, signs of life from the soldiers who lined the route. They should have stood to attention with arms reversed and heads bowed, but many of them risked punishment by raising their eyes to watch the coffin as the cortège passed.

The massed bands of the Household Cavalry at the head of the procession moved out in silence apart from the mournful sound of one drum, draped like the rest in black crêpe, beating out the rhythm of the slow march. Behind the band came four battalions of militia, volunteers and yeomanry, representatives of the colonial levees, officers and men of the Pay, Ordnance and Service Corps, six battalions of Infantry of the Line, four of foot guards, the Royal Regiments of Artillery and

the Engineers. Lancers, Dragoons and Hussars and finally the Horse
and Life Guards made up the last of the military contingent but not the
rearguard of the main parade. That honour properly fell to the Senior
Service – the Royal Navy and the Royal Marines. The sailors put the
Army, and the weather, to shame by scorning greatcoats and marching
into the February wind in shirt-sleeve order.

Four more bands, Engineers, Artillery, Marines and Foot Guards,
preceded the Court and Household. The Earl Marshal, as befitted his
age and seniority, rode. The rest were on foot. Victor Cavendish was
in the third rank. When, on 1 February, he received a telegram from
the Duke of Norfolk telling him that he 'had to walk in the procession' he was once more not properly prepared. His diary reveals his
anguish. 'Full dress coat. Had to borrow one. My own not finished.
Arthur Hill lent me his.' No doubt that night when he dined with
Lord Lansdowne, his father-in-law and Secretary of State for War, he
expressed his relief that the difficulties with clothes were resolved. If
so, he spoke too soon. On the day before the funeral procession,
although he 'thought satisfactory arrangements had been made,
Arthur Hill came round and asked for his uniform back. Tried to raise
another one. He was very nice about it.' Fortunately, the obliging
Arthur Hill found a minister who had chosen to sit on a stand rather
than march behind the coffin. So Victor Cavendish embarked, properly dressed, on a 'long, tiring day. But, on the whole, everything
went off very well.'

Cavendish was mistaken. According to the plan, the gun carriage
on which the coffin rested was to be drawn to the private funeral in
St George's Chapel in Windsor Castle by eight bays of the Royal
Horse Artillery, but the traces broke. An attendant equerry, Prince
Louis of Battenberg (one day to become First Sea Lord), suggested
that the job should be done by sailors. The Artillery – well represented at Court – argued, but the King, fearful of a fiasco, ordered the
Navy to take over. The communication cord was removed from the
royal train and employed as a hawser. As a result the most memorable
picture of the whole funeral – jolly tars in straw hats towing their sovereign to her eternal rest – was created.

During the week which followed, observers disagreed about the
mood that the funeral had created in the country. The *Daily Chronicle*

found 'everything shrouded in gloom', while Arnold Bennett – who had failed to find a place on the pavement from which he could see the procession – believed the crowd that obscured his view to be 'serene and cheerful. The people, on the whole, were not deeply moved, whatever the journalists may say.'[2] Henry Labouchere, MP – a republican but in his place in the Parliament stand – hated the 'furs and feathers' of the military. Even Field Marshal Lord Roberts, the Commander-in-Chief, had criticisms to make. In order to get the procession through London in the prescribed time, Chopin's Funeral March was played too quickly. Worse still, seats in the stands were changing hands through the initiative of an early manifestation of ticket touts. But the general judgement was that the grief, however expressed, was genuine. Indeed it was so intense and prolonged that the editors of national newspapers, the men who had described 'the sorrow of her people as her coffin was carried through their midst',[3] began to fear that the country had, in the words of *The Times*, 'turned aside from the stern tasks of everyday life by an excessive indulgence in the luxury of mourning'.[4] *The Economist* warned, 'We are not so prosperous that we can all succumb like widows in the protracted luxury of tears'[5] The *Westminster Gazette* compared the interment in the Royal Mausoleum at Frogmore to a burial at sea. 'The ship is slowed down when the body is committed to the deep, but once that has taken place there can be no waiting . . . Full steam ahead is today's order – just because it can be nothing else.'[6]

Bernard Shaw sought 'to interrupt the rapture of mourning in which the nation [was] enjoying its favourite festival – a funeral'. But the editor of the *Morning Leader*, to whom he wrote his complaint, felt unable to publish a letter which described the funeral as 'a total suspense of common sense'.[7] It was probably the scandalously scientific nature of Shaw's objections, rather than the absence of respect, that made them unsuitable for publication. 'To delay a burial for a fortnight, to hermetically seal up the remains in a leaden coffin' was, he insisted, both 'insanitary and superstitious . . . The Queen should have been either cremated or buried at once in a perishable coffin in a very shallow grave.'

The Queen's death – long anticipated but unexpected at the end – had left Great Britain insecure and uncertain and, in some extreme cases, incredulous. Some parish clerks refused to nail the notice of her death to their church doors because they could not believe that the terrible news it bore was true. Throughout most of her sixty-four glorious years, the British people had been told, by their politicians, their newspapers and their popular entertainers, that 'Victorian' was the adjective which symbolised the nation's industrial, commercial and military greatness. The Victorians' belief that they ruled the world had been underlined on 12 May 1876 when the Queen was declared Empress of India, and confirmed on 21 June 1887 when the crowned heads of Europe travelled to London to celebrate her Golden Jubilee. At first 'it seemed', wrote the *Daily Chronicle*, 'as though we had bidden farewell to an era, the greatness of which we can scarcely judge'.[8]

News of the Old Queen's death was received in wildly different ways in the various corners of the Empire on which the sun never set. The Irish nationalists could not resist using the occasion to repeat historic grievances. 'As the sovereign of Ireland, she was immensely forgetful of her obligations. No reign was more destructive for our people or more ruinous since the time of the Tudor queen.'[9] But the Boer prisoners, at the Greenall detention centre in South Africa, behaved with more decorum. They 'suspended their amusements for a period of mourning'.[10] A pro-Boer paper was less gracious. It used the prisoners' unexpected tribute to reiterate its opposition to the war. 'Her Majesty was, to them, the symbol of the country with which they are engaged in a deadly struggle. These prisoners do not know what has become of their farms, their wives or their children. Yet they desire to pay her memory the only mark of respect in their power . . . It is a signal proof that the Boers are the exact opposite of the barbarous and brutal savages they have been called in our Yellow Press.'[11]

Lord Curzon wrote from the governor's house in Calcutta with the news that the death of the Empress had moved all India. Victoria, in life, had exerted an 'overpowering effect on the imagination of the Asiatic'.[12] In the city itself, sweetmeat vendors closed their stalls on the Maidan during the day of the funeral and joined the vast throng of silent mourners. Curzon reported that messages of condolence had been painted on banners. 'We poor Musulmans from Sialdah grieving.'[13] The personal sorrow was to be matched by an unprecedented display of public respect. As the days passed, those two emotions were combined with visceral apprehension – fuelled by the recognition that the days of Victorian glory, as well as Victoria herself, had passed away for ever. *The Times* was particularly portentous.

At the close of the reign we find ourselves somewhat less secure of our position than we could desire and somewhat less abreast of the problems of the age than we ought to be considering the initial advantages we secured. Others have learned our lessons and bettered our instructions while we have been too easily content to rely upon the methods which were effective a generation or two ago. In this way the Victorian age is defined at its end as well as at its beginning. The command of natural forces which made us great and rich has been superseded by new discoveries and methods and we have to open what might be called a new chapter.[14]

There was much hard evidence to reinforce *The Times*'s warning. Agriculture was in decline. Between 1890 and 1900 the total acreage under wheat diminished by half a million acres. Britain's industries had continued to grow during the last decade of Queen Victoria's life but at nothing like the speed at which they had expanded during her first fifty years on the throne. It was the old staple industries – textiles, coal, steel and shipbuilding – which had fared the worst, not suffering an absolute decline but falling behind Germany.

By the turn of the century, Germany had begun to challenge more than Britain's European supremacy. It seemed that the Kaiser (Queen Victoria's grandson) and Admiral Tirpitz (his Navy minister) were not prepared to leave uncontested the worldwide maritime supremacy which Britain had enjoyed since 1805. In April 1898 the Bundestag passed the Navy Law which authorised the construction of twelve new battleships, ten new large cruisers and twenty-three small cruisers. Despite the ostentatious presence of the Kaiser at his grandmother's deathbed, and his conspicuous participation in the funeral, London did not think of Berlin as a friend.

Apprehensions about Germany had been increased by that nation's sympathetic attitude to the Boers. And the Boers' victories were undermining the self-confidence which came from an absolute belief in the invincibility of the British Army. The notion that the 'Soldiers of the Queen' had 'always won' was a myth. But the nineteenth-century defeats had all been converted, in popular imagination, into preludes to victory. The death of General Gordon had been avenged at Omdurman. The slaughter at Isandhlwana had been redeemed by the heroic defence of Rorke's Drift. Even the catastrophe of the Crimea had resulted, admittedly ten years later, in the Cardwell Army reforms. Popular opinion had taken it for granted that the might of empire would soon deal with an insurrection by Boer farmers, but the Boers had proved remarkably difficult to suppress. Lord Salisbury had no doubt that it was events in South Africa – the Boers' ingratitude and the generals' incompetence – which had been the eventual cause of Queen Victoria's death. On 22 January 1901, Britain had begun to worry about its place in the world.

Henry James, who did not always speak for England, articulated fears which were felt far beyond the boundaries of his fastidious circle. Suddenly Victoria, once the epitome of philistine materialism, became the symbol of a lost civilisation. He greeted the news of her terminal illness with what can only be called reluctant regret.

> The poor dear stricken Queen is *rapidly* dying . . . Blind, used up, utterly sickened and humiliated by the war . . . She is a very pathetic old monarchical figure . . . I fear that her death will have consequences for this country that no man can foresee. The Prince of Wales is a vulgarian . . . The wretched little 'Yorks' are less than nothing . . . The Queen's magnificent duration has held things beneficially together and prevented all sorts of accidents.

When it came, he found 'the old Queen's death . . . a real emotion' because England* had 'dropped to Edward . . . fat Edward . . . Edward the Caresser'. James's letter to Clare Benedict reflected an anxiety which encompassed far more of the country than the aesthetic elite.

---

*It is worth noting that, throughout the period, writers of undoubted intellectual quality often wrote 'England' when they meant Britain or the United Kingdom. They included A. J. Balfour, who was a Scotsman.

'I mourn the safe, motherly old middle class queen who held the nation warm under the folds of her big, hideous Scotch-plaid shawl . . . I felt her death far more than I should have expected. She was a sustaining symbol and the wild waters are upon us now.'[15]

The anxiety which Henry James felt was shared by most of the nation; but Lord Esher was both surprised and impressed by the dignity with which the new King balanced the glorious news of his accession with the mournful fact of his mother's death. Queen Alexandra had won the admiration of the Court by refusing permission for her regal title to be used until the funeral was over. The King himself had won high praise for an impromptu address to the first meeting of his Privy Council. Victor Cavendish, who did not formally attend but 'heard and saw everything' from just outside the audience chamber, judged that it was 'a wonderfully fine speech indeed'.[16] But, although Esher, rather to his surprise, began to grow impressed by Edward as a man, he was still dubious about him as a monarch. 'It may be my imagination but the sanctity of the throne has disappeared. The King is kind and debonair and not undignified – but too human.'

It was not only the King's character which concerned him. When the funeral was over, he stood outside the Frogmore Mausoleum in the falling snow and meditated on the historic moment he had witnessed. 'So ends the reign of the Queen. And I now feel for the first time that the new regime, so full of anxieties for England, has begun.'[17]

CHAPTER 2

The Spirit of the Age

Edward VII was born heir to the throne. But he was sixty before he succeeded his mother and became both King and Emperor. The long years of waiting had not been occupied in preparation. His father, the Prince Consort, had certainly tried to make the Prince of Wales a better man. However no one, least of all his mother, had thought of helping him to become a better king. No matter how much Queen Victoria talked of wanting to join her beloved Albert, the Court could not bring itself to contemplate her death. Indeed, they could barely believe that it would ever happen. In consequence, the education of her son and successor was badly neglected. Despite Victoria's retreat into near invisibility – the Widow of Windsor spent much of her time at Balmoral and Osborne House – the Prince of Wales did not preside at a Privy Council until 1898 when he was fifty-seven.

Admirers of the Prince of Wales, in his own lifetime and more recently, have argued that he would have willingly, indeed enthusiastically, served a proper apprenticeship. It is certainly true that attempts, notably by Gladstone, to find him appropriate employment were constantly frustrated by Queen Victoria herself. Disraeli had been the first prime minister to suggest that Edward live for a time in Ireland – a notion largely designed to demonstrate the Crown's affection for the Province. Her Majesty dismissed the suggestion in categoric language. 'Not to be thought of . . . Quite out of the question . . . Never to be considered'.[1] Gladstone revived the idea as a way of keeping a man whom he regarded as a middle-aged roué out of trouble. He invested the idea with a more exalted purpose and told the Cabinet that he felt a 'duty [to] make a resolute endeavour at improving the relations between the Monarchy and the Nation by framing a worthy mode of life (good public duties) for the Prince of Wales'.[2] No doubt the Grand Old Man also had in mind what he regarded as the Prince's obligation to earn some of the £100,000 a year he received from public funds. Whatever the reason, Ireland was proposed again. Before the Queen had an opportunity to veto the idea, Edward himself dismissed it. The Cabinet's preparation of a 'cut and dried plan' for his future was, he said, 'distasteful' to him and inappropriate to his status.

It was strong feelings about dignity – at least as much as a desire to understand the complications of statecraft – which kept the Prince of Wales in constant conflict with both his mother and a succession of prime ministers about his right to see Cabinet papers. The extent of his exclusion, and the deep offence it caused, was confirmed by a letter he wrote to Disraeli from Seville following the announcement that the Queen was to assume the title of Empress of India. 'As the Queen's eldest son, I think I have some right to feel annoyed that . . . the announcement of the addition to the Queen's titles should have been read by me in the newspapers instead of having received some information from the Prime Minister.'[3]

By the time of the Royal Titles Bill, Queen Victoria had agreed that her son could see a selection of official papers. But Disraeli had warned the Foreign Office that the Prince of Wales was indiscreet and urged caution in its decisions about which documents he should see. Victoria, as usual, endorsed Disraeli's judgement and, more unusually, copied his cunning. 'It would be best *not* to refuse to send any despatches to the Prince of Wales but to send such as were not very confidential . . .'[4] It was the papers that he was denied which he hoped to see as he prepared himself for what he believed to be the monarch's proper role in world affairs. His mother was not willing for him to anticipate her demise.

It was, however, his temperament, not his lack of training, which made the nation fear that Edward VII would become a thoroughly unsatisfactory king. *The Times* could not wait to set out the country's forebodings. On the day that the death of Queen Victoria was announced, it thundered its doubts about the character of the new monarch who had, in his youth, 'been importuned by temptation in its most seductive forms' and had no doubt prayed 'lead us not into temptation [with] a feeling akin to hopelessness'. It conceded that it was his private, not his public, life that gave cause for concern. He had 'never failed in his duty to the throne or to the nation'. *The Times* completed its strictures with a sanctimonious combination of praise and blame. 'We shall not pretend that there is nothing in his long career which those who respect and admire him would wish otherwise.'

The whole nation knew that, by temperament and conduct, the new King was quite the opposite of his mother, for whom reticence and propriety had been cardinal virtues. Edward loved pleasure and often found it in louche society. His inclinations had been revealed in a series of public scandals. On each occasion his involvement had been vicarious and he had escaped without anything being proved directly against him. But his reputation had suffered.

During the early weeks of 1870, Sir Charles Mordaunt petitioned for divorce, citing two of the Prince of Wales's friends, Lord Cole and Sir Frederic Johnstone, as co-respondents. Edward was subpoenaed as a witness at the trial and warned that his cross-examination would reveal that he had written to Lady Mordaunt and visited her on a number of occasions. The Queen's private secretary was assured that the trial judge would not allow 'any improper questions to be put by the Mordaunt counsel'[5] and the Prince of Wales protested his innocence to his wife and to his mother. The Lord Chancellor, who read the letters which had been submitted in evidence, concluded that 'no useful object' could be served by the subpoena[6] except to damage Edward with guilt by association. But the Prince, although certain that he must expect everything he said to be 'twisted and turned', decided that if he refused to appear it would be assumed that he 'shrank from answering these imputations'.[7] He decided to waive the royal prerogative and accept the subpoena.

The Prince of Wales survived his seven minutes in the witness box with dignity. But the Queen – with admirable understanding of the moral superiority of the inferior orders of society – feared that his 'intimate acquaintance with a young married woman being publicly proclaimed will show an amount of imprudence which cannot but damage him in the eyes of the middle and lower classes'.[8] Her fears were justified. After the trial, the Prince of Wales became the subject of lewd broadsheets sold for a penny on the streets of London and, for some weeks, he was hissed and booed when he appeared in public. When Lady Mordaunt was certified insane and committed to an institution, the suspicion that there was a conspiracy to silence her – because there was more to her husband's charges than His Royal Highness would admit – seemed, in many people's minds, to be confirmed. Mr Gladstone, at his most tactless, wrote to the Prince of Wales and reminded him of the consequences of a previous royal scandal. George IV's divorce from Queen Caroline had rocked the throne. 'The revival of circumstances only half a century old must tend rapidly to impair [the monarchy's strength] and might bring about its overthrow.'[9]

The Prince of Wales did not learn discretion. Six years after the embarrassment of the Mordaunt affair, he once more flaunted his close association with the disreputable element in Victorian society. Lord Aylesford cited the Marquis of Blandford as co-respondent in his divorce action. The Marquis's younger brother, Lord Randolph Churchill, asked Edward to use his influence to persuade Aylesford to drop the case on the grounds that His Royal Highness must take some responsibility for the situation. He had insisted on taking the wronged husband with him to India, even though he knew that the field would then be left clear for Blandford's adultery. When Edward refused to intervene, Lady Aylesford gave Lord Randolph letters which the Prince had written to her years before.

Randolph Churchill, never the subtlest of men, called upon the Prince of Wales with a not very cryptic message which amounted to the threat of blackmail. 'Being aware of peculiar and most grave matters affecting the case [of *Aylesford* v. *Aylesford*] he was anxious that His Royal Highness should give such advice to Lord Aylesford as to induce him not to proceed against his wife.' The Lord Chancellor was again consulted. His judgement was not much consolation. Even if the letters signified no more than a flirtation, they had been 'Written in a strain of undue familiarity' and 'must, when displayed to the public, be injurious and lowering to the writer'. Total disgrace was only avoided by Lord Aylesford agreeing, after immense pressure from his peers, to drop his action for divorce and Lord Randolph Churchill temporarily leaving the country. But the idea that the heir to the throne kept squalid company had been confirmed. His constant companions achieved the notoriety of a nickname. They became known as the 'Marlborough House Set' because of the frequency with which they visited the Prince's royal residence.

That idea was reinforced in 1891 when Lady Charles Beresford, wife of the MP for York who had left the House of Commons to resume his career in the Royal Navy, discovered a letter written to her husband by his mistress, 'Daisy' Brooke, an unconventional aristocrat who was soon to become the 'Red Countess' of Warwick. Beresford had abandoned politics in favour of the sea on the advice of the Prince of Wales, who adjudged that only a period of active service would end an infatuation which was becoming an embarrassment to his friends. Daisy Brooke's letter was written in such persuasive terms that Lady Charles feared that it would result in a resumption of the relationship and took legal advice about how its writer could be restrained.

Meanwhile, Daisy Brooke – who certainly had been the Prince of Wales's mistress and probably still was – asked Edward to retrieve the letter and return it to her. Foolishly he agreed. Lady Charles, a woman of spirit and independence, resented his intrusion into what she reasonably regarded as a private matter. And she told him so. The Prince retaliated by removing her from the Marlborough House visiting list, a penalty which so angered her husband that he demanded an explanation of the heir apparent's conduct. Affronted by the almost literal lese-majesty, Edward stood on his dignity and asserted his rights. Beresford responded with a letter of such ambiguity that he must have realised some people would take it to mean that improper and unwelcome advances had been made towards his wife: 'Sir, I cannot accept your letter as in any way an answer to my demand. Your Royal Highness's behaviour to Lady Charles Beresford having been a matter of common talk in the two years I have been away from the country on duty. I am Your Royal Highness's Obedient Servant Charles Beresford.'⋆

⋆When, years later, Edward attempted to effect a reconciliation by inviting Beresford to dinner, Lord Charles replied by telegram 'Very sorry. Can't come. Lies follow by post.' (*The World of Fashion*, R. Nevil, Chapter 5.)

No heir to the throne of a great empire – and certainly not one who anticipated following a monarch of such conspicuous propriety as Victoria – should have allowed himself to get into a position in which one of his future subjects thought such a letter appropriate. Once again, the Prince of Wales – although he had done nothing illegal or anything which could be proved to be in conflict with the canons of the Church of which he would one day be Supreme Governor – had associated himself with a tawdry dispute between dissolute aristocrats. Such squalid connections did his reputation far more damage than his much publicised association with Lillie Langtry. That affair was at least a liaison of the sort that was expected of the male members of the royal family.

Most of his adventures with other men's wives were kept from the wider British public, but in 1891, shortly after the Beresford affair had died down, a cause célèbre made so many headlines that there was hardly a family in England which did not realise that the Prince of Wales kept disreputable company. The scandal which revealed the unpalatable truth concerned gambling, not adultery, and came to be called the Tranby Croft Affair.

Tranby Croft was the East Riding home of Arthur Wilson, a self-made shipping magnate whom the Prince of Wales cultivated and exploited. In September 1890, Edward, at his own request, was Wilson's guest during Doncaster race week. The whole house was redecorated in anticipation of the royal visit and the other guests were carefully selected to suit the Prince's taste. Among them was Sir William Gordon-Cummings, a guards officer who had fought for Queen and country against the Zulus at Ulundi and the Egyptians at Tel-El-Kebir. After dinner, all the guests played baccarat – a card game described by the Attorney General during the litigation that followed as 'about the most unintelligent way of losing your money or getting someone else's I have ever heard of'. It was also illegal when played in public and, worse still in the eyes of many Englishmen, thought to be popular in France.

Baccarat had, during the years since (oppressed by his obesity) he had given up dancing, become an obsession with the Prince of Wales. He played, or wished to play, each evening and carried with him, wherever he went, a set of counters which were engraved with the

'Prince of Wales's Feathers'. Naturally Arthur Wilson arranged a game at Tranby Croft. For the first couple of evenings, Edward was kept amused without incident. Then, on 8 September, Gordon-Cummings was discovered to be cheating. The Prince had not noticed any irregularities and, when the misdemeanour was reported to him, was assured by the accused that the accusations were unjust. However, the evidence of five unequivocal witnesses was too strong to ignore. The Prince sat in judgement and the verdict was guilty. Gordon-Cummings was required to sign a declaration that he would never play cards again. The house party broke up after all the participants vowed never to speak of the shameful incident.

The secret was kept for almost four months. Then, on 27 December, Gordon-Cummings received a letter from Paris, telling him that he was forbidden to frequent the casino at Monte Carlo because he was regarded as a card sharp. He consulted the colonel of his regiment, who told him what he should have already known. Putting aside the evidence of the five witnesses, his agreement never to play cards again would be taken as proof of his guilt. Gordon-Cummings then made the crucial mistake of issuing a writ for slander against his accusers. They, of course, refused to retract their accusations.

The case came to court in June 1891 and attracted all the attention which has been accorded to society scandals down the ages. The *Pall Mall Gazette* reported that 'from an early hour, the gallery was besieged'. Sir Edward Clarke, QC (Solicitor-General but allowed, according to the practice in Victorian England, to take private briefs) represented Gordon-Cummings. His opening speech increased the prospect of massive press coverage. The plaintiff was a man whose sword had 'never been stained except with the blood of his country's foes' and 'had been a close friend of the Prince of Wales for twenty years'. To the consternation of the Queen and delight of the popular press, Edward himself was called as a witness for the defence. His evidence was not, in itself, helpful. He confirmed that, although he had seen nothing, he accepted the word of the plaintiff's accusers. But it was his presence, not his opinions, which caused the sensation. There were suggestions in society that the Prince wanted to destroy Gordon-Cummings because of their rivalry for the affections of Daisy Brooke.

And, before the case was concluded, Clarke was to imply that the accusations against his client had a sinister purpose. He spoke of 'dishonourable deeds done by men of character and done by them because they gave their honour as freely as they gave their lives to save the interests of a tottering dynasty or to conceal the foibles of a Prince'. Nobody was sure what he meant. The likelihood is that it was a piece of barrister's rhetoric which meant nothing. But it so alarmed the Queen that she complained to Lord Salisbury, the Prime Minister, about the conduct of his junior law officer.

Whatever the implication of Clarke's Delphic allegations, his speech failed to impress the jury, who found against Gordon-Cummings. *The Times* thundered that the plaintiff 'must leave the army, must leave his clubs and must no longer think of himself as a member of that society in which he has lived so long'. It was almost equally censorious about Edward. 'If the Prince of Wales is known to pursue on his private visits a certain round of questionable pleasures, the serious public who are, after all, the backbone of England, regret and resent it.' It added that it wished, 'for the sake of English society', that the Prince had also sworn never to play cards again. The *Daily Chronicle* was far more direct. 'It is enough to say that the readiness of the Prince of Wales to dispose of himself as a prize guest in rich but vulgar families where his tastes for the lowest form of gambling can be gratified even at the cost of dishonouring the proudest name in the country, has profoundly shocked, we may even say disgusted, the people who one day may be asked to submit to his rule.'

The *Chronicle*'s implication that the succession was not secure was, of course, absurd. But the reputation which the Tranby Croft Affair established remained with Edward right up to his accession. And men and women who had been brought up to believe that Victoria epitomised England's nineteenth-century greatness genuinely feared that her replacement by a man of such dubious character equally symbolised the end of English industrial and military supremacy.

The forebodings were reinforced – at least for the more superstitious of His Majesty's subjects – by what seemed to be an augury of doom. On 24 June 1902 Victor Cavendish wrote in his diary, 'Charles Montague came in at about 12 and said that there was a report that the Coronation was to be postponed owing to the King's illness.

Announced at 12.30 that it was necessary to do an operation. Great consternation.' Rowland Evans's father had already condemned the anticipated extravagance. 'He said that in Westminster Abbey on that day there will be millions and millions of pounds represented . . . And within half a mile's radius from the Abbey there will be people starving and with nowhere to sleep.' When the news of the postponement reached Bradford, Rowland Evans junior was at Park Avenue cricket ground watching the Australians beat Yorkshire by forty-four runs. He reacted calmly to both catastrophes and his comment on the King's Coronation was surprisingly commercial. 'Some millions will be lost on this. All decorations have been taken down and there will be no procession or anything else.'[10]

The King, much to his credit, had done his best to avoid the postponement. An appendicitis had been suspected almost a fortnight earlier but, perhaps foolishly, he had insisted on struggling on. His temporary absence from the public and social scene had been explained away by an announcement that he was suffering from lumbago. But when the pain intensified, his physician, Sir Francis Laking, concluded that it was time to take the advice of Sir Frederick Treves, Sergeant Surgeon to the King.

Treves had no doubt that the appendicitis, which he had confirmed twenty-four hours earlier, was at what he called 'an acute' stage. An immediate operation was essential. The alternative was peritonitis and almost certain death. But surgery – as well as requiring a postponement of the Coronation – carried its own risk. The uncrowned King might die under Sir Frederick's knife. Three Sergeant Surgeons served the monarch. Treves suggested that, before the lot was finally cast, another opinion should be obtained. He was particularly anxious to hear the diagnosis of the most senior of his colleagues. 'The King objected. He did not see the necessity of any further consultation. He said that he was ready and wished for the operation to be done at once. I pressed the need for such a consultation on public grounds and grounds of policy. He consented, whereupon I at once sent my carriage for the two gentlemen named. They were awaiting my message and came at once.'[11]

The Senior Sergeant was the seventy-five-year-old Lord Lister, the leader of the 'antiseptic revolution' which, he claimed, had transformed the prospect of a patient surviving surgery. In fact, the dramatic improvement in morbidity was the result of many causes – improved hospital sanitation, better nursing and new surgical techniques. But Lister received the credit and became a Victorian hero. To have operated on the King without him being consulted would have been a scandal. If the King had died during surgery, failure even to ask Lister's opinion would have been regarded as something approaching treason.

When the postponed Coronation was eventually held, the King celebrated his accession with the creation of the Order of Merit. Lister was one of the original recipients in an award ceremony which was held less than two months after the royal operation. His Majesty found some difficulty in getting the ribbon over Lord Lister's head. In the embarrassing moment which followed, the King said, 'Lord Lister, I know that if it had not been for you and your work I would not have been here today.'[12]

The King was overgenerous. Sir Frederick Treves recorded that during the consultation which preceded the operation, 'Lord Lister hesitated. While he did not oppose the operation, he said that the other alternative was to wait and to apply fomentation. I did not discuss this point with him but pressed him to say if he was prepared to *advise* delay and fomentation. He hesitated and at last said that he would not go to the length of *advising* that course.'[13]

Medicine had moved on since Lord Lister had begun to develop his theory of aseptic and antiseptic surgery. By 24 June 1902, he was part of a world which was past. The way in which his colleagues behaved at Buckingham Palace on that day was an early symbol of the new age's impatience with the old.

To loyal subjects who thought of the monarchy in mystical terms, the postponement of the Coronation – and the possibility that Edward VII would die without his anointment symbolising God's endorsement of his reign – was a spiritual catastrophe. For men and women of a more cynical persuasion, an illness related to the bowels seemed the inevitable result of the King's eating habits, to which they attributed his unusual size and shape. Both his chest and waist measured forty-eight inches.

Edward VII was not a great drinker. He enjoyed champagne and the occasional glass of port but preferred to 'join the ladies' in the drawing room rather than stay at table with the men. But he both smoked and ate to excess. The extent of his addiction to tobacco can be judged by his decision to 'ration' himself to one cigar and two cigarettes before breakfast. His gluttony was compounded, at least in so far as it affected his health, by the nature of the food that he enjoyed. Roast beef and Yorkshire pudding was his occasional light relief from richer and heavier food. His dinner (private as well as official) normally consisted of twelve courses. A typical entrée was *Cotelettes de bécassines à la Souvaroff* — snipe, boned and halved, stuffed with pâté de foie gras and mincemeat and served with truffles and Madeira sauce.[14]

The upper classes naturally followed his extravagant lead. Harold Nicolson claimed that 'no Edwardian meal was complete without ptarmigan,★ hot or cold'.[15] The Edwardians' uninhibited enjoyment of physical pleasure was an attitude to life which the King, at least, felt no obligation to disguise. When Sir Henry Campbell-Bannerman warned that deteriorating health would soon make it necessary for him to resign his office, the King replied that the announcement should be postponed until a date which would not require an early end to the royal holiday in Biarritz.

It would be wrong to suggest that Edward, Prince of Wales, had longed to spend his entire time studying state papers and performing official duties. But he did, throughout the long years of waiting, make periodic forays into public policy. Sometimes he thought it his duty to advise his mother. In 1885, when Gladstone resigned and a general election could not be held because of imminent constituency boundary redistribution, the Queen refused to travel south from Balmoral in order to discuss with ministers how an interim administration could be formed. Edward's telegram urging her speedy return to Windsor and duty was a model of both tact and responsibility. 'In present grave ministerial crisis your presence near London earnestly desired . . . Fear your position as sovereign might be weakened by your absence. Forgive me for saying this, but universal feeling is so strong I could not help telegraphing.'[16]

★A grouse with plumage which changed from grey in summer to white in winter.

The Prince's participation in the procedures of the House of Lords was less judicious but generally benign. On three occasions – 1879, 1882 and 1885 – he intervened in debates to support a change in the law which would allow a man to marry his deceased wife's sister. The espousal of such a cause is normally the result of friendship with someone who is affected by the proscription. But it seems that Edward simply regarded the law to be misconceived on that particular point. On the first occasion that he advocated the change, he presented a petition in its support drawn up by Norfolk farmers. On the third he endorsed a petition from London cabmen. The Lords rejected the proposal on all three occasions.

He spoke again in the House of Lords when, after much lobbying, he obtained a place on the Royal Commission on Housing the Working Classes, but he avoided controversy by confining his remarks to evidence of his good intentions. 'I have been much occupied in building houses for the poor and the working classes in and about the Sandringham Estate.' He attended eighteen of the Commission's thirty-eight meetings – remaining silent in most of them because of the dangers of becoming embroiled in controversy. The same fear prompted the Cabinet to decline the Prince's offer to serve on the Royal Commission on Labour Disputes. He did, however, become a member of the equally contentious Royal Commission on the Aged Poor. His main interest, he said, was to 'ascertain the grounds of the strong prejudices harboured by the aged poor against entering the workhouse'. It could be argued that his bewilderment at the objection to indoor relief confirmed the importance of his using membership of the Commission to remedy his ignorance. His unwillingness to sign either the majority report or the note of dissent confirmed that he recognised the need for the Heir Apparent to avoid becoming involved, even vicariously, in politics. When he became King, he ignored the golden rule. Time after time, his intrusions into his real political interest – foreign affairs – jeopardised the interests of the nation.

Although he attended only thirty-five of the forty-eight meetings held by the Royal Commission on the Aged Poor, in general he was moderately assiduous in the discharge of his royal duties. In the year before his accession, he made eighty-six public appearances. He also attended thirty-seven race meetings (no doubt encouraged by almost continuous success),* joined forty-five shooting parties and visited the theatre and opera on forty-eight occasions.[17] On other nights he dined with his friends, The Marlborough House set. Edward was essentially gregarious, an attribute which romantics believe represented the spirit of the age. He could not bear to be alone. So parties would be arranged at twenty-four hours' notice and at weekends he would descend on country houses where, although he was a welcome visitor, host and hostess trembled in fear that they would not meet his needs. Neither age nor elevation changed him. 'All Edwardian houses kept stores of things like ginger biscuits and aubergines and French patisseries and bath salts in case the King came. And come he did. He came over and over again. And on Monday morning other people would read of it in the *Morning Post*.'[18]

Taxing though the royal visits undoubtedly were, their cancellation caused even greater trauma. In the early weeks of 1903, Victor Cavendish braced himself for the King's arrival at Chatsworth. On 26 January he had his hair cut and tried on his Lord Lieutenant's uniform. 'Odd sort of clothes to have to put on in the middle of the day.' On 27 January he learned, with a mixture of pleasure and apprehension, that, as a yeomanry officer, he was 'to take command of the escort'. On Saturday 31 January he 'arrived at Chatsworth about 11.30. Great preparations going on'. The blow fell on 1 February. The King was too unwell to travel. 'A very large party, but it was a great blow that the King was unable to come and caused great consternation, not only in Chatsworth but all round the county [where] great preparations had been made.'

In some of the houses which the Prince of Wales visited, the preparations were of dubious respectability. The society within which the Prince of Wales moved took serial promiscuity for granted. In her novel *The Edwardians*, Vita Sackville-West, who grew up in that milieu, describes the good hostess's obligation to arrange house-party bedrooms in a way which accommodated irregular liaisons.

The name of each guest would be written on a card slipped into

---

*Royal victories included the Grand National, the Two Thousand Guineas, the Newmarket Stakes, the St Leger and the Derby with Diamond Jubilee and its brother Persimmon.

a tiny brass frame on the bedroom door. The question of the disposition of bedrooms always gave the duchess and her fellow hostesses cause for anxious thought. It was necessary to be tactful and, at the same time, discreet. The professional Lothario would be furious if he found himself by ladies who were all accompanied by their husbands.

Edward accepted the mores of his friends and cronies and shared their lifestyle, and took unscrupulous advantage of the hospitality which they thought it their loyal duty to provide.

By the time of his accession to the throne, Edward VII had more or less given up the capricious liaisons of his youth and middle age and settled down, in a manner of speaking, with Alice Keppel. Mrs Keppel, the daughter of an admiral and sister-in-law of a peer, was sufficiently well connected to justify her appearance at country houses which entertained royalty.* So after 27 February 1898 – the date of their first meeting and virtually instant mutual infatuation – hostesses who welcomed Edward to their houses had a clear view of how the bedrooms should be allocated. Proud as they were to entertain him, the demands imposed by his visits were colossal. When, two years after his coronation, he stayed with Lady Saville at Rofford Abbey, his entourage included a valet, a sergeant footman and a 'brusher', two equerries (who brought their own valets), two telephonists, two chauffeurs and an Arab boy to prepare his coffee. Had the Queen (rather than Mrs Keppel) accompanied him, space would have been needed below stairs for at least another six servants. Yet the King's demands were regarded as relatively modest. On his annual visit to Marienbad – where he spent a month taking the waters – he was satisfied with a suite of rooms in the Hotel Weimar. His mother – on her rare travels abroad – always rented the entire hotel and furnished it with favourite items of furniture from Balmoral and Osborne House which she sent on in advance of her arrival.

Sir Phillip Magnus, in his almost entirely uncritical biography of Edward VII, charted the course of a typical peripatetic year.[19] The

---

*Only two great houses refused to entertain Mrs Keppel: Welbeck and Hatfield.

pattern was preserved, in almost exactly the same form, throughout Edward's reign. Christmas and New Year were spent at Sandringham. The King then moved on to one of England's great houses for a week's shooting, after which brief pleasure duty called him back to London for the State Opening of Parliament held, in those days, at the beginning of the calendar year. At the beginning of March he left England for Paris and Biarritz and a cruise in the royal yacht, *Albert and Victoria*. He presided over the London season in May, moved to Windsor for Ascot in the middle of June and to Goodwood (where he usually stayed with the Duke of Richmond) at the end of the month. In August he again joined the royal yacht at Cowes for the Regatta. Then – when Queen Alexandra left for Denmark, to make her annual visit to her sister, the Dowager Empress of Russia – he visited Bohemia for his Marienbad cure. Back in England, he paused for a few days in London before travelling north, first for the Doncaster race week and then for shooting and stalking at Balmoral. During November and early December he moved, depending on how the fancy took him, between Buckingham Palace, Sandringham and Windsor.

King Edward's life of ostentatious pleasure was, to most of his subjects, in happy contrast to the near invisibility of his mother during the last years of her reign. After the pomp and pageantry of 1876 which celebrated her becoming Empress of India she was no longer a total recluse. But age combined with instinct to prevent a constant round of public engagements. Her son, on the other hand, became a consistently visible monarch. Newspaper pictures showed him at race meetings and picnicking with shooting parties. Pleasure was the fashion of the time and the idea of holidays was just beginning to catch the public imagination. The British people, from the intellectual middle classes who spent their springs with Baedeker in Florence and Rome to the cockney costermongers who hoped for a day in Margate with shrimps and whelks, were not in a mood to deny their King his own measure of happiness. Whether the newspapers reported that Edward VII had read the Speech from the Throne at the State Opening of Parliament – a tradition he revived after Queen Victoria had abandoned the greatest spectacle of the Westminster year – or described his elation at the victory of a horse in the Derby, a basically imperialistic people felt that they were, once again, ruled by a sovereign whose uninhibited extravagance reflected the glory of the Empire they had helped to build. It was not the general public who were worried about the King's social life. It was the Court and the political establishment. And they were not concerned by either the extent or the extravagance of the King's regular pleasures. Nor were they unduly alarmed by his amorous exploits. They were worried about the male company he kept.

During his scandalous middle age, Edward VII had seemed to seek the company of men with dubious reputations. As he grew older, he chose his companions with greater discretion. Many of the men with whom he shared his pleasures – racing, shooting and bridge – were in trade. Lord Iveagh was a brewer. Sir Blundell Maple made furniture. Baron Hirsch and Sir Ernest Cassel were bankers and, worse still in an openly anti-Semitic society, Jewish. The Kaiser, on hearing that the King and Sir Thomas Lipton were together at the Cowes Regatta, amused his family by announcing that the King of England had 'gone boating with his grocer'. Shortly after Edward's accession, young Winston Churchill, brother to the Duke of Marlborough and born in Blenheim Palace, spoke for the aristocracy. He was clearly much amused by his pun about Mrs Alice Keppel, who was more Edward's wife than his mistress. 'I am curious to know about the King . . . Will he sell his houses and scatter his Jews or will Reuben Sassoon be enshrined amid the crown jewels and other regalia? Will he become desperately serious . . . Will Mrs Keppel be appointed First Lady of the Bedchamber?'[20]

Winston Churchill regarded the King as rather vulgar. And the era to which he gave his name was, according to the old aristocracy, very much the same. The release from the conspicuous solemnity of Victorian England would have resulted in an explosion of hedonism whether or not it had been encouraged by the behaviour of the sovereign. Edward was the embodiment of a new age in which the old standards were despised and abandoned.

'The lavish expenditure and feverish pursuit of pleasure do not appeal to me any more than the restaurant life which did not exist in my day,' wrote the Countess of Cardigan and Lancaster. 'Money shouts while birth and breeding whisper.'[21] Lady Dorothy Neville was even more

categoric in her condemnation. 'Society today and society as I knew it
are two entirely different things. Indeed it may be questioned whether
society, as the word used to be understood, exists at all . . . Society
as it used to be – a somewhat exclusive body of people, all of them
distinguished for their rank, their intelligence or their wit – is no more.'

The new society, which the *ancien régime* deplored, held the view
that it was possible to maintain a tenuous relationship with respectability by the adoption of the most blatant double standards. The King's
definition of acceptable conduct provided a perfect illustration of that
moral ambivalence. He was not a hypocrite. He never sought to hide,
at least from members of his own circle, his weaknesses for women
and gambling. But, like the country over which he reigned, he
believed that it was possible to apply moral standards selectively.
Affection for rich *parvenus* was matched by an obsession for Court
protocol. His concern that the Countess of Torby – the morganatic
wife of Grand Duke Michael of Russia – should not sit on the
Duchesses' bench at Buckingham Palace balls was no worse than
ridiculous. But that a man with Edward's amorous history should tell
the Duke and Duchess of Marlborough that, were they to separate,
'they should not come to any dinner or evening party or private
entertainment at which either of Their Majesties was expected to be
present' illustrates the fascination with propriety which hid much
that was squalid in Edwardian Britain.

The King, though shrewd, was essentially superficial. To him
appearance was all. His concern about how things looked was illustrated by his obsession with the correct choice of dress and display of
decorations. He made an official complaint, through his principal
private secretary, to the First Lord of the Admiralty that Lord Charles
Beresford had failed to change into full dress uniform before wel-
coming the King of Greece aboard his flagship at Corfu. Beresford
had been a competitor for the favours of 'Daisy' Warwick and was a
public critic of naval policy as devised by Sir John Fisher, the First Sea
Lord and a royal crony. The King was not a man to forget old grudges
or overlook new offences against his friends. But his rebuke to Frederic
Ponsonby, his assistant private secretary, could be attributed only to an
almost deranged attachment to the rules (real or imaginary) of formal
etiquette. Ponsonby was forbidden to accompany his master to an art

exhibition because he was wearing a tailcoat. 'I thought,' said the King by way of reproach, 'everyone must know that a *short* jacket is always worn with a silk hat at a private view in the morning.'

Appearances were what counted when Edward VII considered the conduct of greater affairs. Morality was simply a matter of social form and constitutional expediency. The solemnity of the Coronation would not be compromised by the presence of a group of ladies – Sarah Bernhardt, Mrs Hartman, Lady Kilmorey, Mrs Arthur Paget and Mrs George Keppel – sitting in what wags, with an interest in the turf, called 'The King's Loose Box'. Their association with the King, although well understood within society, was kept out of the news-papers. So, at the moment of his anointment, there was no risk of a recurrence of the debilitating public scandal which had disfigured his early manhood.

The King, no less than his mother before him, regarded the Coronation as an event of mystical significance. He had no doubt about the imperial destiny of the country which he had been called by God to serve and lead. Edward Elgar disliked the words which A. C. Benson had set to his Pomp and Circumstance March to make part of the Coronation Ode. But the King himself was sure that Britain was the 'land of hope and glory' and that the whole world would benefit when its boundaries wider still were set. God who had made Britain mighty was not going to disturb the proper order of things because of an occasional adultery – though He would be righteously angry if the ceremony in which the Defender of the Faith pledged his fealty to the Established Church was not suitably organised. Fortunately, what appeared to be divine intervention averted a fiasco.

A couple of weeks before Coronation Day, the Duke of Rutland, the Master of Horse, had what he reasonably described as a 'remark-able dream'. In it, the State Coach, bearing King Edward to the Abbey, got stuck as it passed under the arch between Horse Guards Parade and Whitehall. It was only released when a Life Guard drew his sword and hacked the crown from the coach's roof. The Crown Equerry was, at first, unimpressed by the Duke's premonition. Eventually he was persuaded to compare the height of the coach and the clearance of the arch. Constant road repairs – tarmacadam heaped on tarmacadam – had so heightened the level of the ground that the

coach was two feet too high to pass through in safety. The level of the
road was reduced.

The King then, rightly or wrongly, decided that the Coronation
itself was not being properly organised and ordered that the preparations must, henceforth, be under the command of the Guards. The
first officer to take charge of a rehearsal, the splendidly named 'Polly'
Carew,* insisted on the participants 'numbering off' in proper military style. In respect for his age and rank, Lord Salisbury, the Prime
Minister, was designated number one.[22]

The Coronation, at least to the Court and King, was accepted as
confirmation that nothing had changed the natural order of society. As
long as the monarchy, and the state from which it was indivisible, was
not put at risk, the King could do what he liked. So the Countess of
Athlone happily explained to her family, 'Aunt Alex was renowned
for her beauty, very lovely with a gracious presence and a disposition
which endeared her to a public which worshipped her. But being
stone deaf and not mentally very bright she was not much of a companion for an intelligent man like Uncle Bertie.'[23] Had it ever become
public knowledge – or even a private certainty within the Court –
that Aunt Alex was having an affair with the Honourable Oliver
Montague, her niece would not have been so understanding.

The King certainly never agonised about the contradictions on
which his life was built. Indeed he did not notice that they existed. He
was a man of his time – an era in which many women who would
have been scandalised by female adultery were prepared to accept
with equanimity what Henry Wilcox in the Edwardian *Howards End*
regarded as the justification for his loose behaviour: 'I am a man and
I possess a man's vices.' To expect Edward VII even to think about the
paradoxes of his existence would have been, within the mores of his
time and circle, wholly unreasonable. Edward VII was not tormented
by guilt or doubt. Subtlety was not a feature of either the man or the
age to which he gave his name. Nor was he an intellectual. Indeed he
despised intellectual pursuits. Back in 1876, Mr Gladstone had

---

*Let us hope it was not 'Mad Carew' from the 'Green Eye of the Little Yellow
God' who 'for all his foolish pranks was worshipped in the ranks.'

suggested that Queen Victoria persuade her son 'to adopt the habit of reading'. He received a frank, but deeply disappointing reply. 'She has only to say that the POW has never been fond of reading and that from his earliest years it was impossible to get him to do so. Newspapers, and very rarely a novel, is all he ever reads.'[24] Forty years later – Edward dead and England allied to France in the war against Germany – A. J. Balfour was so irritated by the suggestion that the Entente Cordiale with France had been the achievement of the King rather than the Cabinet that he wrote to Lord Lansdowne (who had been Foreign Secretary in his government) to ask for a confirmation of his recollection. 'During the years when you and I were ministers, he never made an important suggestion of any sort on large questions of policy.'[25]

The implication of Balfour's demand was that the Prince of Wales did not possess the intellectual capacity to contribute much to the government's programme. Sir Charles Dilke, a friend, although a radical, made a more charitable assessment of the Heir Apparent's ability.

> The Prince is, of course, a very strong Conservative and a still stronger Jingo, readily agreeing to the Queen's politics and wanting to take everything if possible, but a good deal under the influence of the last person to talk to him. So he would sometimes reflect the Queen and sometimes reflect me, or Chamberlain or some other Liberal who had been shaking his head at him. He had more sense and more usage of the modern world than the Queen, but less real brain power. He is very sharp in a way – the Queen is not sharp at all, but she carries heavier metal, for her obstinacy constitutes the power of a king.[26]

Dilke claimed to have formed his 'more accurate impression' of the Prince of Wales during the reorganisation of Gladstone's second administration in 1882. Because Dilke had earlier supplied him with information about the inner workings of the government, Edward was determined that a place should be found for him in the Cabinet. The Queen would not contemplate a Republican becoming Chancellor of the Duchy of Lancaster – in her view a 'personal office'

within her gift – so the Prince tried to reorganise the whole government. He first suggested that Chamberlain should go to the Duchy and
Dilke become President of the Board of Trade. Chamberlain declined
with thanks. Then he proposed Dilke for the Admiralty. When that too
was rejected (by the prospective incumbent as well as the Prime
Minister), he reluctantly agreed to Dilke accepting the Presidency of the
Local Government Board – at the very bottom of the Cabinet ratings.

Interference – at once so detailed, so prejudiced and so determined – would have been improper if carried out by the sovereign.
For the Prince of Wales to behave in that way should have been
intolerable to ministers and, therefore, not tolerated. They accepted
the interference because, from time to time, Edward's unconstitutional
conduct assisted them. He helped persuade Rosebery to accept the
Foreign Office (for a second time) after he had initially decided to
give up politics, and he convinced the Queen that her cousin, the
Duke of Cambridge, should resign as Commander-in-Chief of
the Army after thirty-nine years in that appointment. Tolerating the
promotions and honours which the Prince of Wales demanded
should be awarded to his friends and favourites was a small price
to pay in return for his assistance in the pursuit of ministers' most
elusive objective – persuading the Old Queen to change her mind.

Original thought, on any subject, was not Edward VII's forte, but,
from time to time, he did try to influence government by attempting
to deflect it from the course which the Cabinet had set. In the early
years of his reign, disputes between the monarch and his Tory ministers more often concerned personalities than policies. The King
regarded the Army and Navy as royal fiefdoms and initially aspired to
sign all military and naval commissions personally. He blamed the
Army's failure swiftly to overcome the Boers on Lord Lansdowne
(Secretary of State for War at the time of the early defeats) and, to a
lesser extent, on St John Brodrick★ who succeeded him. Lansdowne's
promotion to the Foreign Office precipitated a series of head-on
conflicts. Most of them were the result of the King's conviction that
his royal birth and upbringing at Court had given him a particular

---

★According to the OUP Concise Dictionary of National Biography, Brodrick also
spelt his name Broderick.

talent for diplomacy, which transcended the Foreign Secretary's limited ability. That, when combined with the special relationship which he enjoyed with the sovereigns of the Great Powers, might have offered opportunities for beneficial international initiatives. The Kaiser was King Edward's nephew and Queen Alexandra was the Csar's aunt. But his status as 'uncle of Europe' did not equip him for the task of forging Britain's foreign policy, particularly when his *démarches* were directed at monarchs whose negotiations, unlike his own, were not constrained by the tedious interventions of politicians.

There was speculation at Court that 'Lansdowne may have become a little jealous at the King being supposed to run foreign policy'. One private secretary admitted, 'I always had the impression that if the King ever made a false move, Lansdowne, so far from defending him, would stand and look on.'[27] In fact, loyalty made him overlook the false moves the King did make. They began at the beginning of his reign, when he attended the funeral of his sister, the Dowager Empress of Germany. Lansdowne supplied him with briefing notes for any discussions he might have with the Kaiser on contentious subjects. The King handed them over to his nephew, who chose to represent them as official British policy. His error did not encourage subsequent foreign secretaries to believe that Lansdowne had been wrong to ignore the King's diplomatic talents.

When Edward came to the throne England was still an imperial oligarchy, in effect ruled by groups of aristocratic and mercantile families who were separated more by interests than by ideology. Less than half the adult population had the vote. The monarchy remained the cornerstone of the constitution, with powers which Edward's son and grandson would gradually lose. It was his destiny to preside over changes that culminated in a constitutional monarchy at the head of a pluralistic democracy. It was a role he rarely welcomed, sometimes resisted and occasionally refused to accept. A year into his reign, his patience, as well as his acceptance of a figurehead's role, was put to the test by a dispute over a source of constant conflict between the monarch and his ministers – the award of honours.

Lansdowne, wanting to detach Persia from Russia as part of 'the great game' of securing India's northern border, invited the Shah to London with the inducement that he was likely to be made a Knight of the Garter. The King rejected the suggestion out of hand, rightly claiming that the Foreign Secretary had pre-empted his prerogative and adding, with what at the time must have seemed equal justification, that the Shah was a Muslim and the Garter was an essentially Christian order of chivalry. Lansdowne, with the self-confidence of an Old Etonian who had gone on to be one of Jowett's star undergraduates at Victorian Balliol, suggested that the statutes of the Order be revised to accommodate religions other than Christianity and, on his own initiative, arranged for sample insignia to be made to demonstrate how easy it would be to dispense with the cross which decorated the Garter Star and replace it with the crescent of Islam. The King was on the royal yacht when he received Lansdowne's suggestion. He threw the letter and the picture it contained out of a porthole.

Meanwhile, the Shah made clear that he had been led to believe that the initials KG would soon follow his name and that nothing else would induce him to visit London, matching, in obduracy, the King's announcement that, on reflection, he was not prepared to award him any honour whatsoever. With the North-West Frontier in jeopardy, the Duke of Devonshire advised the King to accept his Foreign Secretary's advice. After much agonising about his obligations to the powers and his dignity as monarch, the King capitulated. But his relations with Foreign Office ministers were permanently impaired. When, in 1903, he set off on his tour of European capitals, he chose not to be accompanied by the Foreign Secretary. Instead Charles Hardinge – assistant permanent under-secretary and the diplomat who, in Bucharest, had negotiated the marriage between the Crown Prince of Romania and one of Queen Victoria's innumerable granddaughters – was given the constitutionally dubious title of Minister Plenipotentiary and the exacting task of constantly advising and occasionally restraining his monarch.

It was on the King's own initiative, enthusiastically endorsed by the Cabinet, that the President of France was informed that Edward VII, at the conclusion of a series of visits to his European relatives, would be happy to visit Paris on his way home from Rome. It was a difficult time in Anglo-French relations, but there is no doubt that Edward's exuberant style did a great deal to bring the countries closer together. His reception was initially cool. But during the interval of a performance of *L'Autre Danger* at the Théâtre français, he noticed Mlle

Jeanne Granier standing in the foyer. Pushing his way past the other members of the specially invited audience, he kissed her hand and said, 'I remember applauding you in London when you represented all the grace and spirit of France.' It was the sort of flamboyant gesture which was reported and appreciated. As a result his popularity began to grow. He was applauded at Longchamps and cheered on his way to the state banquet at the Élysée palace. On his way back to the British Embassy, he was mobbed by crowds chanting, '*Vive Edouard!*' The Ambassador attributed the success of the visit to 'the indefatigable readiness with which he adapted himself to the overcharged programme of functions',[28] and Hardinge reported to Lansdowne the King's invariable agreement — after a little arguing — to accept additional engagements which he 'knew to be irksome'.[29] So came about the triumph which, in its way, was the defining incident of Edward VII's brief reign — the Entente Cordiale. The genial picture of a pleasure-loving monarch charming the previously hostile French has become the paradigm of all that Edwardian England seemed to represent. Even Victor Cavendish, son-in-law of the snubbed Foreign Secretary, noted that the 'King has enjoyed an unusual success'; and up in Bradford, Rowland Evans recorded that 'The King has been cheered to the Echo in France.' The Parisians cried '*Vive Edouard!*' and England echoed, 'Good old Teddy.' Queen Victoria had clearly underestimated her son.

CHAPTER 3

The Powers Behind the Throne

From his very earliest interventions in politics and the processes of government, Edward was fortunate in being surrounded by men who – putting aside what they knew to be defects in his character – thought it their duty to protect as well as advise the future king. In part he made his own good fortune. He possessed a natural charm which, when he chose to employ it, won over critics of his lifestyle and doubters about his capabilities. And he unscrupulously cultivated those from whose help he believed he would benefit.

Even William Ewart Gladstone – always too candid in his advice for Victoria's taste – became a friend of sorts. When the Grand Old Man won his second term of office, and the Queen made plain that she would 'rather abdicate than have that half-mad fireball Prime Minister', it was her son who convinced her that neither Granville nor Hartington could be persuaded to usurp the Liberal Party leadership and that the rightful Prime Minister would not 'ruin everything and become a dictator'. With the Prince of Wales's authority, a message expressing hope of a reconciliation was sent to Granville in the knowledge that its contents would be passed on to Gladstone himself. Sensible people accepted that 'if the Queen would only look upon Mr Gladstone as a friend instead of as an enemy of Her Majesty and the Royal Family (which Prince Leopold delights in persuading her he is) she will find him all that she could wish'.[1] The Queen was infuriated by the doubts the message cast on both her judgement and the integrity of her younger son, but the Prince of Wales continued to cultivate Gladstone by sending him Christmas and birthday presents and inviting him to private dinner parties at Marlborough House.

Gladstone, classical scholar, part-time theologian and full-time prig, could never bring himself to approve of the louche prince. His attitude towards the Marlborough House Set is best exemplified by his arrival at a soirée at which Joe Chamberlain was already playing cards with His Royal Highness. 'Behold,' said the Grand Old Man, 'the apotheosis of the Birmingham screw manufacturer!' The Prince of Wales must have realised that only duty and deference reconciled Gladstone to his company. But he paid proper respect to the greatest of all British Prime Ministers – even when he had nothing more to gain by cultivating him. Much to Queen Victoria's fury, the Prince of Wales acted as one of the pall-bearers at Gladstone's funeral.

By the time of Edward VII's accession to the throne, Gladstone had been dead for three years and Rosebery – the friend whom the King had persuaded Gladstone to make Foreign Secretary and then talked out of premature retirement after the death of his wife – had first briefly won and then permanently lost the leadership of the Liberal Party. Salisbury, as austere as Gladstone but, despite his politics, less agreeable to the King, was His Majesty's First Minister. Because of his long apprenticeship, the new sovereign held strong and usually prejudiced views about all the great figures of Commons and Lords.

The first Cabinet of Edward VII's reign was made up of men who had grown old in the service of Queen Victoria. Lord Salisbury himself was Prime Minister for the third time. He was seventy-one. It was thirty-four years since he had first accepted the Seals of a Secretary of State. The Duke of Devonshire, Lord President of the Council and Leader of the Liberals within the Unionist Coalition,★ was sixty-eight. He had served as a junior minister in Lord Palmerston's government in 1863. The Chancellor of the Exchequer, Sir Michael Hicks Beach, was a mere sixty-four and his ministerial experience

---

★The Liberal Party was irrevocably divided by the Irish Home Rule Bill of 1886. Liberal opponents of Irish devolution – led by Chamberlain and the then Marquis of Hartington – eventually joined with the Conservatives in a 'Unionist coalition'.

stretched back for no more than a quarter of a century. His years in office had been interrupted by sudden blindness – a disability which mysteriously struck him down and then miraculously disappeared.

It was not only age which made Salisbury unsuitable to lead Britain into the twentieth century. He was instinctively in favour of allowing events to take their natural course. The result was splendid isolation abroad and masterly inactivity at home, a policy supported in his Cabinet as much by the Gladstonites who had deserted the Grand Old Man over Home Rule as by the Tories with whom they had made common cause. Few people doubted that the higher ranks of the government were in urgent need of new blood.

The two young Turks, A. J. Balfour and Joe Chamberlain, were both middle aged and each of them was handicapped by character weaknesses which were simultaneously attractive and destructive. It was assumed, on both sides of the House, that Balfour, Leader of the Commons and Salisbury's nephew, would succeed his uncle as Prime Minister. But his patrician view of government seemed increasingly outdated at a time when working men aspired to sit in Parliament. He had no doubt that the aristocracy had a duty to serve the nation and that no other class could adequately protect its interests, and he did not believe that men like him should demean themselves by struggling for office. His sister-in-law, Lady Frances Balfour, said that she had never met a politician who so lacked political ambition. 'Arthur's opportunities were all made for him. He did not push or pull himself into the Irish Secretaryship',[2] his first Cabinet appointment. But, once in Dublin Castle, he behaved with a brutality that caused his critics to change the sobriquet with which they characterised him from 'Pretty Fanny' to 'Bloody Balfour'.

The Duke of Devonshire, who had himself twice declined the premiership because he thought that honour required him to stand aside, judged that Balfour's only fault, 'if fault it could be called, [was] a sort of indolence and strong contempt for popularity – but his sense of duty [was] strong enough to overcome all this'.[3] That sense of duty encouraged him to return to the Cabinet as First Lord of the Admiralty in Lloyd George's Great War coalition, ten years after the government he led was defeated. When he died, Ramsay MacDonald, paying tribute to him in the House of Commons, caught his whole character in one brilliant sentence. 'He saw a great deal of life from afar.'[4]

Joseph Chamberlain, in sharp contrast, was a thruster. By the age of forty he had made his fortune and was ready to take Westminster and Whitehall by storm. In Birmingham, as mayor and leader of the Liberal caucus on the town council, he had bought the local gas works and used the profits to provide new sewers and fresh drinking water. He had served in Gladstone's government as President of the Board of Trade, but in 1886 he (like the Duke of Devonshire and Sir Michael Hicks Beach) left the government and party rather than support Irish Home Rule. Salisbury made him Colonial Secretary and he set about his task with such messianic fervour that Hicks Beach thought it necessary to remind his colleagues, 'I was an imperialist when Mr Chamberlain's politics did not go any further than Birmingham.'[5]

Chamberlain's imperial obsession – not confined to, but principally concerned with Africa – both complicated and complemented foreign, as well as colonial policy. The Victorian view of Britain's place in the world was succinctly expressed by George Curzon – in his time an Oxford undergraduate of such obvious merit that, when he failed to gain a first-class honours degree, the university changed what they assumed must be a deficient examination system. 'As long as we hold India, we are the greatest power in the world.'[6] It was generally assumed that, given half a chance, Russia would advance through Afghanistan and steal the jewel from the imperial crown. The extension south of the Russian strategic railway network added to the apprehension. Defence policy amounted to a reliance on naval supremacy to keep Great Britain safe and the maintenance of an army that could defend India against invasion. Diplomacy was increasingly addressed to the perceived need to construct alliances which detached the European powers from Russia.

Fear of Russia influenced Salisbury's judgement about Germany, a nation which, unlike most of his Cabinet colleagues, he believed would never make an alliance with Britain. The Kaiser, he told Curzon, 'is in mortal terror on account of that long undefended frontier of his on the Russian side. He will therefore never stand by us against Russia.'[7] Balfour described the risk in more cataclysmic language and (although he feared France more than Germany) regarded Russian imperial pretensions as a possible argument against making an alliance with Japan, the Czar's historic enemy. 'A quarrel with Russia anywhere about anything means the invasion of India and, if England were without allies, I doubt if it would be possible for France to resist joining the fray.'[8]

There were solid material reasons for maintaining British rule in India. Not once, during the whole reign of Queen Victoria, was Britain's balance of physical trade in surplus. The deficit on the United Kingdom's international account was more than made up by 'invisible exports' to the subcontinent. But to many Englishmen the ownership and control of the princely states had a significance which was more mystical than economic. Principal among the romantic imperialists was George Nathaniel Curzon – the 'most superior person' of the Balliol rhymes. While still at Eton he had heard Sir James Stephens (barrister and member of the India Council) describe 'British possessions in the Asian continent' as 'an empire more populous, more amazing and more benevolent than Rome' and he had swelled with pride at the notion that 'never was a goal sought with so much resolution and won with such merit and perseverance'.[9] Curzon was, perhaps, extreme in his views of Britain's Indian destiny – Lord George Hamilton, the Secretary of State for India, called him 'a regular jingo with Russia on the brain'[10] – but his obsessive determination to keep India British was the extreme form of a commonly held view. He took the admirably practical step of creating the North-West Frontier Province – from what amounted to a tribal wilderness – as a buffer against Afghanistan and its supposed Russian allies.

Despite the unanimous view that he was a man of almost unique ability, Curzon lay fallow through most of the years when Edward VII was served by a Liberal prime minister – consoled by his long affair with Elinor Glyn, a popular novelist. We possess a vignette of Curzon's character courtesy of *Halcyon*, the novel which Elinor Glyn regarded as her masterpiece. It was written in 1911, shortly after the relationship between politician and novelist had been resumed following a period of estrangement. The hero, John Deringham, was clearly a caricature of Curzon – Captain of the Oppidans at Eton, gilded undergraduate at Oxford, Member of Parliament and Under-Secretary of State for Foreign Affairs. But the recent reunion did not prevent Miss Glyn from describing the faults of her lover's doppel-gänger. Deringham possessed an 'insouciant arrogance' and a 'sublime belief in himself'. He thought women should be 'feminine, dainty, exquisite creatures' and made speeches in simple language so that 'uneducated clods' could follow his argument. Miss Glyn's judge-ment of Curzon's character was confirmed by the letter with which he thanked her for sending him a copy of *Halcyon*. It drew the author's attention to two spelling mistakes in the cover note.[11]

Genuine radicals rejected Curzon's imperial pretensions, but they too believed in the Anglo-Saxon obligation to bring good govern-ment to a savage people. John Morley, journalist, Liberal Cabinet minister and Gladstone's biographer, spoke even for progressive opin-ion when he confessed that he could 'not see how any Englishman, contrasting India as it is now with what it was and certainly would have been under any other conditions than British rule, could fail to see that we came and we stayed . . . in obedience . . . to the will of providence'.[12] Morley recognised the existence of 'a school of thought who (sic) say that we might walk out of India and that the Indians can manage their affairs better than we can'. But he went on to insist that 'Anyone who pictures to himself the anarchy, the bloody chaos which would follow might shrink from that decision.'[13]

That view, although shared by most of the political Establishment, did not hold good for the colonies in which the population was predominantly white. The Durham Report had proposed self-government for Canada in 1839. Almost fifty years later, in Adelaide, Lord Rosebery – soon to become, albeit for barely a year, Prime Minister and Liberal Leader – spoke of extending the same prin-ciple to other territories which were 'no longer colonies in the ordinary sense of the term'. Australia, he argued, was 'A country which has established itself as a nation. Its nationality is now, and will be henceforth, recognised by the world . . . But there is a further question: does the fact of your being a nation imply separation from Empire? God forbid! There is no need for any nation, however great, leaving the Empire because the Empire is a Commonwealth of nations.'[14]

The notion of Commonwealth was profoundly attractive as a means of avoiding the separation which had been the inevitable result of Westminster's aggressive rule in North America. But it was conceived as a constitutional settlement between people of the same race. India did not qualify. The Cape Colony was clearly British. The Transvaal was not. Resolving the differences between English-speaking and Afrikaans South Africa exposed both the inadequacy of the British Army and the incompetence of the Salisbury government.

The Liberal Opposition was in no position to take advantage of either the Tory Party's disarray or the obvious inadequacy of its moribund leadership. After Gladstone resigned the Liberal Party leadership in 1894 – rejecting the Navy estimates with the explanation that 'things are best done by those who believe in them' – there were two contenders for the succession: Lord Rosebery, the Foreign Secretary, and Sir William Harcourt, the Chancellor of the Exchequer. Nobody doubted that Harcourt was the more able man. Unfortunately the rest of the Cabinet found him personally intolerable. When Rosebery became Prime Minister, Harcourt demonstrated why he was so disliked. Knowing that the new government's survival depended on his support, he insisted on becoming both Chancellor and Leader of the House of Commons, being allowed to call Cabinet meetings on his own initiative and enjoying as much political patronage as the Prime Minister. Rosebery reacted to Harcourt's behaviour with a combination of patrician fury and aristocratic disdain, but he did not fight to assume full control of the government. His languid character did not allow such vulgar conduct.

Rosebery's reminiscences revealed his true attitude towards the demands and rewards of high office. 'There are,' he wrote, 'two supreme pleasures in life. One is ideal, the other is real. The ideal is when a man receives the seals of office from his Sovereign. The real pleasure comes when he hands them back.'[15] Rosebery's Eton tutor said that he 'sought the palm without the dust'.[16] That characteristic made him as much an anachronism as Balfour. He was accused of 'feeling about democracy as if he were holding a wolf by the ears', a view which he confirmed by an admission of the reluctance with which he accepted and continued to hold office. 'When I found myself in this evil-smelling bog, I was always trying to extricate myself. This is the secret of what people used to call my lost opportunities.'[17]

The Liberal Party lost office in 1895. Rosebery's brief residence in Downing Street was most notable for his two Derby winners, Ladas and Sir Visto, and a growing national enthusiasm for colonial expansion which followed the annexation of Matabeleland. Once the election was over and he was out of office, Rosebery announced that he was, and always had been, against Irish Home Rule. When, in 1896, Gladstone came out of retirement to demand that Britain intervene in the Balkans to protect the Armenians against Turkey, Rosebery announced that 'the last straw' had broken his will to lead the Liberal Party. He was still under fifty and his comparative youth, combined with his capricious temperament, made his erstwhile colleagues fear that it was only a matter of time before, being 'unduly attracted by the dramatic', he indulged in the 'pleasure of making some sort of fine gesture'. Its object, they assumed, would be a demonstration of his moral superiority over members of the official opposition.

Rosebery's successor as Liberal Leader was Sir Henry Campbell-Bannerman, a Scottish barrister whose jovial manner hid a fine mind and strong will. His father, who imported foreign goods into Scotland, had been Lord Provost of Glasgow. So Liberal politics was in his blood. He spent an undistinguished three years at Cambridge and failed to make an early mark on Parliament. After almost two decades as an MP he reached the Cabinet and, at his first meeting, was struck dumb by the proximity of Mr Gladstone. Born Campbell he added Bannerman as the condition of a rich uncle's legacy.

Ironically, he was the occasion, though not the cause, of the election which preceded his predecessor's ejection from office. When he was Secretary of State for War, he was accused of leaving the Army short of cordite, a smokeless explosive used in ammunitions. A snap vote, censoring the government, was unexpectedly carried by the House of Commons. Most of the Cabinet wanted to dissolve Parliament rather than resign, but Rosebery insisted on handing over the government to the Tories. Salisbury, able to choose the election date, went to the country at the moment which gave him greatest advantage. The Tories won a majority of one hundred and fifty-two.

At the time of Queen Victoria's funeral, it was taken for granted that the Liberal leadership would soon pass to Herbert Henry Asquith, Gladstone's Home Secretary and a man of universally admired intellect and probity. Asquith, born in Morley, a small West Riding woollen town, was a man of modest origins whose success was wholly the result of his extraordinary ability. He won a classical scholarship to Balliol, gained the anticipated First and, having been called to the Bar, affronted more traditional members of the legal Establishment by standing for Parliament, and winning the seat, before he took silk. His appointment as junior counsel for the plaintiff when Charles Stewart Parnell, the Irish Party leader, successfully sued *The Times* for libel, made him famous. From then Asquith ascended to the heights of political achievement without apparent effort, though no one who knew him doubted that his life was a victory for the vigorous application of a fine mind and highly developed conscience.

We learn much of the workings of Mr Asquith's mind – as well as the process of government before the Great War – from the extensive correspondence which he carried on with Miss Venetia Stanley, the youngest daughter of Lord Sheffield. It began in 1910 and increased in regularity, as well as volume, into and throughout his life as war leader. Miss Stanley was twenty-five when they met. Asquith was fifty-eight. The relationship was certainly emotional (although probably never physical) and it was carried on with a charming candour which would be impossible today. On most Friday afternoons throughout Asquith's premiership, the couple were driven round one of London's more picturesque suburbs or through Richmond Park. They lunched together in fashionable, though highly respectable, restaurants and Asquith called upon Miss Stanley at her parents' house in the early evenings. Occasionally they spent a weekend with Lord Sheffield in his house on Anglesey. Miss Stanley kept Asquith's letters. Asquith destroyed hers.[18]

Asquith, Sir William Harcourt, John Morley and Edward Grey were Campbell-Bannerman's Praetorian Guard – though, like the Roman originals, they were from time to time attracted by the idea of assassinating the leader whom it was their duty to protect. None of them thought that the Liberal Leader had the qualities which were essential to the successful conduct of the nation's business. The importance of the quartet, in terms of the Opposition's prospects of recovery, was the wide spectrum of Liberal opinion it represented. Asquith and Grey were Liberal imperialists and had doubts even about Home Rule.

Morley, crucially for the recovery of his party, proclaimed himself the heir to Gladstonian liberalism. He was far more radical than his mentor and hero. But he remained stubbornly attached to Irish Home Rule and Free Trade and attributed his 'advanced' views on domestic policy to his development of the Grand Old Man's 'Newcastle Programme' of social reform. Although a journalist by trade, he was a philosopher by inclination who, in his youth, had sat at the feet of George Meredith and John Stuart Mill. 'In such ideas as I have about political principles, the leader of my Federation was Mr Mill. He was a great and benign lamp of wisdom and humanity and I and others kindled our modest rush lights at that lamp.'[19] In the first turbulent decade of the twentieth century, the Liberal Party was fortunate to retain within its high command someone who maintained their beliefs in the first principles of radicalism, albeit guided by the sentimental misconception that Mill's essays on *Liberty*, *Representative Government* and *The Subjection of Women* had determined the programme of Gladstone's four administrations.

Morley was – like Harcourt and, to an extent, Campbell-Bannerman – part of the Liberal Party's illustrious past. The new Liberal Leader's poor health (combined with his constant concern for his chronically ill wife) added to the impression that a revival depended on the transfusion of new blood. Asquith – both the bridging passage between Gladstonian glories and the last great flowering of Liberalism and the architect of the final triumphs – was accepted as the man who could lead the recovery once Campbell-Bannerman could be decently dispatched to the House of Lords. But he needed followers of youth and vigour, men who, in the popular imagination, were clearly figures of the future. Fortunately, two such paragons were at hand. They were men of wildly different origins who were united in energy, ambition and self-confidence – though at the beginning of their parliamentary careers they were not even members of the same party.

Winston Churchill was a soldier and adventurer. His father, Lord

Randolph, Chancellor of the Exchequer at thirty-seven – had died
of syphilis before he was fifty. His son was similarly prodigious but
more sober. He was elected to the House of Commons – aged twenty-
six – a month after Queen Victoria's death, as the Conservative
Member of Parliament for Oldham. Just over three years later, on 29
May 1904, he crossed the floor of the House of Commons and
declared himself a Liberal, attributing his apostasy to the Conservatives'
abandonment of free trade* and his fear that the government's
immigration bill would exclude from Britain Jews who were seeking
asylum from persecution in Russia and Poland. After the Liberal election
victory of 1906, he became Under-Secretary for the Colonies† and
he remained a minister until November 1915, when he resigned the
office of Chancellor of the Duchy of Lancaster. Six months before, he
had been demoted from First Lord of the Admiralty, one of the most
prestigious appointments in the early twentieth-century ministry. His
fall had followed the tragic consequences of the allies' failed attempt
to open a second front against the Turks by invading the Dardanelles,
a disaster for which he was held solely responsible. It was generally
assumed that his political career was over. He was forty years of age.

In the closing years of Edward's reign, Churchill was to form a
glittering parliamentary partnership with a young Welsh MP of
diametrically different background and temperament. David Lloyd
George – a solicitor who was born in Manchester but adopted by his
uncle in the Principality – entered Parliament in 1890 as Member for
the Caernarvon Boroughs. His by-election victory, by eighteen votes,
so elated his supporters that they carried him home to Llanystumdwy
shoulder-high, where his wife complained that the noise they made
was likely to wake the baby. He at once made his name as a formidable, indeed ferocious back-bencher and became the champion of
Nonconformist demands for the disestablishment of the Church of
Wales. At the turn of the century he spent long parliamentary days and

---

*See Chapter 6, 'A Preference for Empire'.
†During his first week at the Colonial Office, he sent Lord Elgin, the Colonial
Secretary, a long memorandum which concluded, 'There, then, are my ideas on
colonial policy.' Elgin added to the foot of the last page, 'But not mine.'

nights enhancing his popular reputation by conduct which irritated his honourable friends almost as much as it infuriated his opponents.

Lloyd George was an irreconcilable opponent of the Boer War. Churchill, a retired cavalry officer who had fought at Omdurman, went to South Africa as a war correspondent and took such an intimate interest in the campaign that he was captured and imprisoned by the Boers. The unlikely partnership was destined to set Edwardian politics alight.

There were politicians whose company the King enjoyed – but his enjoyment was confined to occasions when they were companions at dinner, competitors at race meetings and opponents at baccarat. When he needed to deal with them as politicians he normally conducted his business through the intervention of a small group of men with whom he felt at home and who were, therefore, employed – initially as a result of private acquaintance – to act as a conduit between the sovereign and men whom he neither liked nor trusted. Edward certainly possessed distinct (some would say idiosyncratic) ideas about the prosecution of foreign policy. But his attempts to impose them on ministers were usually assisted (and sometimes frustrated) by the urbane advice of Arthur Hardinge.

The degree to which the King depended upon Hardinge was illustrated, during the 1903 tour of European capitals, by letters sent to their wives by both master and servant. The King told Queen Alexandra that Hardinge was 'invaluable in every respect'[20] and Hardinge wrote home with the joyous instruction, 'read all the King's speeches as they are all my composition. He is delighted with them and never changes a word.'[21] The work of the European tour completed, Hardinge returned to St Petersburg as Ambassador in 1904. To confirm the King's pleasure he was made a Privy Councillor and Knight Commander of both the Victorian Order and Saint Michael and Saint George. Two years later he became the permanent secretary of the Foreign Office and Head of the Diplomatic Service. Back in London he joined the group of advisers on whom the King was wise enough to rely. Perhaps there was something in the Hardinge genes which particularly equipped them for royal service. His son became principal private secretary to Edward VIII and warned his King that, if his determination to marry Mrs Simpson brought down the government and precipitated a general election, 'even those who would sympathise with Your Majesty as an individual would deeply resent the damage which would inevitably be done to the Crown'. Plain speaking of that order was a family characteristic. It saved Edward VII, though not his grandson, from innumerable acts of folly.

The difficulty of the tasks that Hardinge was expected to discharge and the delicacy with which he completed them is illustrated by a *démarche* which he was instructed to execute on behalf of the King early in his Russian accreditation.

> When you are received by the Emperor, pray express to him my earnest desire that the best and most desirable relations should be established between the two countries and that all important points should be discussed in the most amicable spirit and arranged as soon as possible . . . You can, at the same time, convey to him my hope that he may find himself able to grant a more liberal form of Government to his country.[22]

Not surprisingly, the King's increasing reliance on Hardinge began to agitate ministers. And Hardinge himself – appointed on merit Head of the Diplomatic Service and happy occasionally to occupy the unusual role of Minister Plenipotentiary – sometimes worried about the role to which the King had elevated him. 'Although I fully represented the Foreign Office, I had not the responsibility of a Member of the Cabinet.'[23] That was not the sort of nicety which worried the King, but, despite his extraordinary dependence on Hardinge, in November 1906 he was prepared – indeed he was anxious – for his favourite to leave his side and become Ambassador to Washington. Edward Grey, Foreign Secretary in the recently elected Liberal government, responded with great tact. The suggestion that Hardinge should represent Britain in America was 'the very best arrangement – for Washington. But what we shall gain there we shall lose here.'[24] The King continued to press his proposal, despite Hardinge's own preference for remaining in London.

It was not long before Grey began to regret that he had not accepted the King's suggestion. The relationship between sovereign and head of the diplomatic service was diminishing the role of the

Foreign Secretary. Special difficulties were arising when the King travelled abroad, always in the company – by royal command – of Hardinge. In the conversations which followed, the civil servant convinced the minister that he had no wish to exceed his authority – an act of humility he confirmed by seeing the King secretly rather than by broadcasting his many audiences in a way which would have bolstered his prestige. The idea of surreptitious meetings was proposed in a recklessly frank letter. 'I send you very privately these suggestions which I trust you will keep suitably to yourself.'[25] The plan was unhesitatingly accepted by another royal confidant, Francis Knollys, the King's principal private secretary.

Francis Knollys possessed the courtier's invaluable gift of speaking plainly in language which minimised offence. His father had been appointed treasurer to, and comptroller of, the Prince of Wales's household in 1862. Young Knollys, an unsettled soldier and reluctant civil servant, met Edward while assisting, more or less unofficially, in the comptroller's office. In 1870 he became private secretary to the Heir Apparent. Their relationship was cemented during the Tranby Croft 'baccarat scandal' and the weeks of embarrassment which surrounded the Mordaunt divorce case. Knollys gave calm and frank advice at a time when most of the Court was virtually incapacitated by a debilitating combination of disapproval and deference. After the election of Campbell-Bannerman in 1905, Knollys's Liberal inclinations and associations, never hidden from a basically Conservative Court, helped to improve the relations of the sovereign and his Cabinet. But his most important task was persuading Edward VII that he must step out from under the shadow of his mother's sixty-year reign. The King, so worldly and socially self-assured, could not forget Victoria's lack of confidence in his ability to take her place. During the public dispute with Benjamin Disraeli about the cost of the Prince of Wales's visit to India in 1875, Francis Knollys had been the vehicle for Edward's complaint that, despite his constant efforts to please his mother, he never enjoyed her approval or support. Knollys believed Victoria's lack of faith to be unjustified. He was rewarded by Edward boasting to him about small achievements in the manner of an uncertain schoolboy describing his successes to a sympathetic master.

Knollys was sixty-four when Edward succeeded to the throne, and had spent almost all of his adult life at Court. He had worked for the new King for so long that he understood how the royal mind worked and possessed the inestimable advantage of being able to speak for His Majesty without prior consultation and still represent the King's view in every detailed particular. Only once did his judgement fail him.

On 5 November 1909, Lloyd George's Finance Bill – which raised money to pay both for dreadnoughts and for the pensions that the Liberal government proposed – was rejected by the House of Lords by the substantial majority of 350 votes to 75. The result was a constitutional crisis which was only resolved by an Act of Parliament that curbed the power of the Upper House, and the threat to create enough new Liberal peers to guarantee the passage of whatever legislation Mr Asquith's government thought right to put to the House of Commons.*

By then a peer himself, Viscount Knollys (as he had become) had thought of voting with the Liberals. Cabinet ministers in the Commons had told him that they 'saw no harm in it' and he had come to the independent conclusion that 'it would be no bad thing if it were supposed (for it can only be supposition) that the King is opposed to the rejection of the budget'.[26] He honestly believed that by appearing in the division lobby he would be doing his 'best to prevent a disaster happening to the Constitution and, inadvertently, to the Monarchy'. The King took a different view and Knollys changed his mind.

The catastrophe which Knollys feared was averted by the Lords' capitulation. But only just. Knollys discovered that the Prime Minister was on the point of asking for guarantees about the creation of enough Liberal peers to carry the government's business in the House of Lords. Knollys's contact in the Cabinet, Richard Haldane, the Secretary of State for War who spoke with dubious authority for colleagues of different temperaments and attitudes, claimed to have told ministers that they were asking the sovereign for 'an abdication of his prerogative, not only on his behalf but on that of his successors'.[27]

---

*For an account of the Finance Bill's rejection and the conflict which followed see Chapter 8, 'Who Shall Rule?'.

Knollys thought it better not to excite the King by passing on that opinion. 'He is not over fond of the Cabinet as it is . . . It would be a mistake to set him further against them.' The man who had no scruples about heightening the conflict between the two Houses of Parliament was another Liberal, Reginald Brett, Viscount Esher.

Reginald Brett was a courtier who had served Queen Victoria and who was inherited by her son. He had begun his public life as private secretary to the Duke of Devonshire when (as the Marquis of Hartington) the eventual leader of the Liberal Unionists had been Gladstone's Secretary of State for War. Had he so wished, Esher could have enjoyed a distinguished parliamentary career of his own. He had been elected to Parliament in 1880 as Member for Penryn and Falmouth, but he was defeated at Plymouth in the general election of 1885 and gave up politics for ever. Too interested in public affairs — and too well connected — to abandon public service completely, he allowed Lord Rosebery (an old school friend) to persuade him to become Secretary to the Office of Works. He supervised the Diamond Jubilee celebrations with such success that he was invited to become permanent secretary to the War Office and Colonial Office in turn. He declined both offers.

Esher's mother had been a personal friend of Queen Victoria and there is no doubt he was regarded at Buckingham Palace as one of the family. Perhaps it was that special relationship which made him, after he had helped to organise the funeral, despondent about the nation's future under its new sovereign. It may be that, during the first year of Edward's reign, he adjusted his opinion about both the King's character and the country's prospects. Or he may have thought that Britain was in particular need of his talents. Whatever the reason, in 1902 he agreed — at the suggestion of Balfour, another old school friend — to serve on the Committee of Enquiry into the conduct of the South African war. At the end of each day's session, he wrote to the King describing the proceedings. Not surprisingly, when he published a minority report, 'the palace' was strongly in favour of its implementation. For the rest of his reign, Edward VII took it for granted that the War Office and Imperial Defence in general should be organised according to the prescription set out by Reginald Balliol Brett, Second Viscount Esher.

The Establishment both feared and resented Esher's elevation into
the role of most trusted and most assiduous adviser. Even Charles
Carrington, perhaps the King's closest friend, expressed surprise at the
extent of Esher's influence. 'He is an extraordinary man and has a
wonderful footing in Buckingham Palace. He seems to be able to run
about as he likes and must be a considerable nuisance to the household. He is a clever, unscrupulous man who might be dangerous
and he is not trusted by the general public who look upon him as an
intriguer.'[28] St John Brodrick – Secretary of State for War and the
man who suffered most from Esher's role in the Boer War Enquiry –
thought that 'it would be tedious to record the endless contretemps to
which this usurpation of power by an outsider gave rise.'[29] Esher's
power depended on the King's refusal to accept a diminished role –
the gradual reduction of the Crown to the position of constitutional
cipher. Edward possessed neither the sustained energy nor the incisive
intellect necessary to impress his will on governments. Esher – usually
supported, though sometimes frustrated, by Knollys and Hardinge –
helped the King postpone the reduction in stature which his son was
later to accept with bad grace.

Esher was also the crucial ally of the King's most controversial
adviser, Admiral Sir John Arbuthnot Fisher, an outspoken sailor who
persisted in expressing the view that Germany, not France, was the
potential enemy that Britain should fear. It was an opinion which he
held with such certainty that he told the King, not altogether humor-
ously, that the Kaiser's Grand Fleet should be 'Copenhagened'. By
that he meant that it should be taken by surprise and sunk without
warning, just as his hero Nelson had destroyed the Danes in the
Baltic. The King replied, 'My God, Fisher, you must be mad.'[30] But
usually the two men saw eye to eye. Both, though for different
reasons, were instinctively critical of the War Office. And Fisher
possessed an attribute which confirmed the King's admiration. He
was in constant conflict with Lord Charles Beresford, Commander-
in-Chief of the Fleet (when Fisher was First Sea Lord) and more
successful rival in love to Edward VII.

Fisher became First Sea Lord in May 1904. He immediately wrote
to Esher with the news, to which he added that Lord Selborne (the
First Lord of the Admiralty) was afraid of him.[31] Such silliness was

typical of a fundamentally serious sailor. Winston Churchill (who brought him out of retirement in 1914 and, despite his misgivings, persuaded the Cabinet to support the disastrous Gallipoli expedition) summed up Fisher's strengths and weaknesses. 'His genius was mainly that of a constructor, organiser and energiser. He cared little for the army and its fortunes. That was the affair of the War Office. He delighted to trample on the Treasury whenever spending money was concerned. To build warships of every kind, as many as possible and as fast as possible, was the message (and in my judgement the only message) which he carried to the Admiralty.'[32] Protocol was brushed aside and the First Sea Lord was asked to advise on the reorganisation of the War Office. As a result, an Army Board – on the model of the Board of Admiralty – replaced the Commander-in-Chief as the supreme military authority, and the Commander-in-Chief of the Army was relegated to a position subservient to Chief of the General Staff, a comparable appointment to First Sea Lord.

Fisher's memorial – for which he might not have qualified without royal patronage – was the reorganisation of the fleet.* But he also had moments of calm statesmanship to his credit. Seven months after his appointment as First Sea Lord, Russian battleships, mistaking it for the Japanese enemy, sank the Hull trawler fleet in the North Sea. There was an immediate outbreak of war fever, to which Fisher remained mercifully immune. The crucial ministerial meeting was called while he was in bed with influenza. When he heard that it was taking place, he rose, dressed, travelled to Downing Street and burst into the half-finished meeting. The First Sea Lord argued for patience, so it was difficult for ministers to disagree. The Russians apologised, offered compensation and war was averted. It was another ten years before the crowned heads of Europe were engaged, family to family, in bitter warfare, which only the House of Saxe-Coburg and Gotha (recently renamed Windsor) survived.

Edward fought a valiant rearguard action against the irresistible forces of increasing democracy. When, in the early summer of 1904, Balfour's Unionist government, so recently re-elected on a tide of

---

*See Epilogue, 'The Summer Ends in August'.

jingoism, divided and collapsed, Edward VII agreed with weary resignation that constitutional propriety required him to kiss hands with a self-confessed radical. 'I presume I shall have to send for Sir Henry Campbell-Bannerman.'[33] The acceptance of the inevitable was swiftly followed by the realisation that a government of personalities whom he disliked was probably to be preferred to a government with policies of which he disapproved. He was properly impressed by an administration which, with some justification, thought of itself as a ministry of all the talents. 'It is certainly a strong government with considerable brain power. Let us only hope that they will work for the good of the country and indeed the Empire. Sir E Grey will, I hope, follow in the footsteps of Lord Lansdowne in every respect.'[34]

Lansdowne's popularity increased after he left office. Change disturbed the King, so he would have been reluctant to accept new ministers of any sort, but the advent of Liberals caused him special problems. He had not abdicated what he believed to be his right to influence the choice of ministers and, in so doing, preserve the policies with which he agreed. R. B. Haldane would, he thought, 'make an excellent war minister', far better than St John Brodrick, his predecessor, who 'was hopeless'. Lord Carrington, a personal friend, became President of the Board of Agriculture. But one appointment, rumoured rather than proposed, caused consternation at the Court. There was a suggestion that John Burns – the first working man to hold Cabinet office and a figure of unimpeachably unimaginative attitudes and opinions – might become First Commissioner for Works, a ministry which gave him responsibility for the upkeep of the royal palaces. Francis Knollys, the principal private secretary, recorded His Majesty's opinion. 'It would almost be an insult to the King to propose Burns for the post – though, of course, he would not make any objection to his occupying some other office . . . if he is not actually a Republican, he is very nearly one.'[35]

Republican or not, John Burns had shown himself to be antipathetic to royal interests by voting in July 1901 against the Report of the Select Committee on Royal Incomes in the very bad company of James Keir Hardie, Henry Labouchere and the Irish Nationalists. The Civil List which the committee proposed had been highly generous. The basic vote of £470,000 a year was £85,000 more than Queen

Victoria had received and additional sums had been set aside for pensions, repairs to the royal estate and the upkeep of the royal yacht. There was to be a £70,000 annual allowance for the Prince of Wales, £18,000 for each of the princesses and the promise of a generous pension for Queen Alexandra in the event of her being widowed. The Report had been carried in the House of Commons by three hundred and seventy votes to sixty.

There was no instinctive antagonism between Edward VII and the Liberals. He had many Liberal friends. When the hugely proper radical Henry Campbell-Bannerman was replaced in Downing Street by the less progressive but more worldly Herbert Asquith, Mrs Keppel, who was an enthusiastic supporter of the party, was always a welcome guest at No. 10. After the King's death, Hardinge recorded her service to the nation in his private file.

> I would like to pay a tribute to her wonderful discretion and to the wonderful influence she always exercised upon the King. She never utilized her knowledge to her advantage or to that of her friends and I never heard her repeat an unkind word of anybody. There were one or two occasions when the King was in disagreement with the Foreign Office and I was able, through her, to advise the King with a view to the policy of the Foreign Office being accepted.[36]

Mrs Keppel certainly numbered among the King's advisers.

Despite that benign influence, the Liberal government persisted in pursuing policies which the King thought wild and extravagant. In foreign affairs and matters of defence he thought them neither better nor worse than their Tory predecessors. They too, in the royal opinion, underestimated what might have been achieved by personal diplomacy between the relations in the several courts of Europe, and the Cabinet (like all Cabinets) contained men who sought to impose limits on military and naval spending. Haldane disappointed earlier hopes by introducing military reforms which reduced the size of the standing army. European monarchs, including the Kaiser, the King's nephew, spoke of 'England in her present unprepared state'.[37] Edward was mortally afraid of being patronised. Haldane fell so far from grace that he was described by his sovereign as 'a damned radical lawyer and a German professor'.

Every item of that description was intended to be detrimental to Haldane's reputation to a greater or lesser degree. In the hierarchy of infamy, Haldane's racial origins took second place to his radical inclinations. Every time the government of which he was a member exhibited that attribute the King complained. It was his misfortune to be served by the first great radical government in British history, and no progressive policy was allowed to pass unchallenged. The King persisted in the belief that he was, if only vicariously, part of the process of government.

When the Liberals had attacked the Balfour government's decision to sanction the importation of 'indentured labour' into South Africa for work in the gold mines, the King expressed his 'great regret that so much heated opposition should have been shown to such a necessary measure as the Chinese Labour Bill'.[38] When Campbell-Bannerman suspended the Act's operation without notifying the King he caused great offence. The King's reaction was incredulous anger. He could barely believe that 'a reversal of the policy [could be] decided upon after so short an experience in office'.[39] But the rush to legislation continued. The King discovered that his government proposed to introduce a Trades Dispute Bill, which freed trade unions from legal liability for all their members' actions. He responded by instructing Knollys to tell the Prime Minister that 'the King trusts [that] it will not include a clause allowing what he thinks is rather absurdly described as peaceful picketing'.[40] Presented with the Education Bill, which made local education authorities responsible for the management of 'maintained schools' and provided a system for part-financing those which remained under the basic control of the churches, he asked, 'What can the government be thinking of in excluding teaching of religion in our schools? Do they wish to copy the French?'[41] He was beginning to share Knollys's fear that 'the old idea that the House of Commons was an assemblage of gentleman had quite passed away'.[42]

Lloyd George, 'The People's Budget', the emasculation of the House of Lords, the creation of a parliamentary Labour Party and the irresistible demand for women's suffrage were yet to come. So were a new view of the nation's obligation towards the poor and the decision eventually to partition a partly independent Ireland. There would be a revolt against censorship in the theatre, the acceptance that the motor car would eventually dominate our roads, the acquiescence to professionalism in sport and a growing scepticism about the power of prayer and the redemptive quality of faith. Although the King did not know it, the Edwardian era was to be a time of massive change.

CHAPTER 4

The Condition of England

These days, we think of Edwardian Britain as the time of the lotus eaters, the decade or more of prosperity and pleasure before the Armageddon of 1914. Happy cockneys spent Bank Holiday Mondays in Margate or at the funfair on Hampstead Heath. The metropolitan middle classes 'dressed' for dinner. In the provinces, clerks and shop-keepers worked hard and lived well. The aristocracy and the very rich hunted in winter, shot during the autumn and played tennis under the endless blue skies of spring and summer. All that happened. But Edward's reign began in a mood of national uncertainty. Victoria's death had disturbed the confidence that comes with continuity. The Boers seemed a match for the greatest empire the world had ever known. The King's illness meant that the Coronation was more an occasion for relief than rejoicing. And the men who set the nation's mood – the popular philosophers, the newspaper economists and the political observers – had decided, almost unanimously, that Britain was in moral and economic decline. They were wrong. But it took them some time to discover the nature of their error.

The most imaginative contemporary analysis of the pressures which created Edwardian Britain was provided by C. F. G. Masterman, Fellow of Christ's College, Cambridge, Liberal Member of Parliament and, for seven years, a minister in Asquith's government. Masterman was an unlucky politician. In 1912, after six years as a parliamentary secretary, he was promoted to Financial Secretary to the Treasury – an elevation which, by the rules of the day, was regarded as the acceptance of an Office of Profit Under the Crown and required him to resign his House of Commons seat and seek re-election. He lost the by-election, tried again and lost for a second time. It was the end of his ministerial career.

In May 1909 he published *The Condition of England*. At the time of its publication, the Liberal government, of which he was a member, was locked in mortal combat with the permanent Tory majority in the House of Lords. Added to the emergence of the Labour Party, the increasing militancy of the suffragist movement and the re-emergence of demands for Irish Home Rule, the battle between peers and people filled Masterman's mind with fear of conflict. *The Condition of England* consciously reflects the ideas set out by Matthew Arnold in *Culture and Anarchy*. Both men believed in the desperate need for a new 'Enlightenment'.

Like Arnold, Masterman wanted to unite the classes. He set out his own version of 'sweetness and light' and accepted the need to limit the powers and rights of the upper and middle classes (Conquerors and Suburbans – in place of Arnold's Philistines and Barbarians) if England was to achieve the general tranquillity for which he hoped. But he added a new dimension to the argument. The problem of British society was, Masterman contended, the mismatch between those parts of national life which were changing and those which were not.

By the standards of the early twentieth century *The Condition of England* was a 'best seller' throughout all the United Kingdom (England being taken to mean all of Britain). Masterman's diagnosis, if not his prescription, provides a commentary on Britain's life and times before the great changes which came about during the Edwardian social revolution. There is something of the William Cobbett in Masterman – a yearning for the Arcadian past of his imagination. But his analysis helps to reveal the reality of the Edwardian present with the clarity that comes from a combination of high intellect and deep sympathy.

It begins with a description of the country's own estimation of itself: 'We see ourselves painted as a civilisation in the vigour of early

manhood, possessing contentment still charged with ambition: a race
in England and Europe full of energy and of purpose, in which life for
the general has become more tolerable than ever before.' But he
noticed a change in the character of the middle classes, which he
observed was 'losing its religion [and] slowly or suddenly discovering
that it no longer believes in the existence of the God of its fathers or
in life beyond the grave'. However, the more secular qualities which
excited the world's admiration endured. 'It is the middle class whose
inexhaustible patience fills the observer with admiration and amazement as he beholds it waiting in the fog at a London terminus for
three hours beyond the advertised time and then raising a cheer, half
joyful half ironical, when the melancholy train at last emerges from
the darkness.'

It was from the character of the British people that Masterman
believed salvation would come. He rejected 'Mr Pinero's jibe' that
Britain was 'the suburb of the universe'. It was 'the locality whose
jolly, stupid, brave denizens may be utilized in every kind of hazardous
enterprise'.[1]

Other commentators predicted certain disaster. Rider Haggard –
having temporarily forsaken science fiction in favour of travel journalism – anticipated an imminent apocalypse. 'The impression left
upon my mind by my extensive wanderings is that English agriculture
seems to be fighting against the mills of God.'[2] Others forecast nothing worse than steady decline. A. L. Bowley – the most distinguished
statistician of the period – judged that real earnings had peaked during
the last years of Victoria's reign and then certainly ceased to grow and
in many cases had actually fallen. And many of the social surveys
published during the period described such depths of poverty and
such widespread illness that, fifty years on, two distinguished sociol-
ogists could write, 'It is no exaggeration to say that the opening of the
twentieth century saw malnutrition more rife in England than it had
been since the deaths of medieval and Tudor times.'[3] That was, in fact,
a gross exaggeration. But it is easy to understand, with hindsight, how
it came about.

A comparison of per capita income demonstrated that Great Britain
was the richest country in Europe, but the gap between the United
Kingdom and its main competitors was narrowing fast. In the twenty

years between 1893 and 1913 production of coal, pig iron and steel in the United Kingdom rose, respectively, by 75 per cent, 50 per cent and 131 per cent. In Germany the increase in output was 159 per cent, 287 per cent and 522 per cent and in the United States 210 per cent, 337 per cent and 715 per cent. United Kingdom exports of manufactured goods more than doubled. German manufactured exports trebled and America achieved a five-fold increase. British steel production rose, but German output rose so much more quickly that, by 1908, it was producing twice as much as Britain – a shattering psychological blow to the country to which Bessemer had come to perfect his new technique for 'converting' iron into steel. Germany subsidised its smelting plants and the reduced price of the raw material gave Soligen a competitive advantage over Sheffield, and Hamburg a head start against the Clyde. But cutlery and shipbuilding went steadily on. The problem with British industry was that its progress was too steady. Production and exports expanded in absolute terms but were in relative decline.

Alfred Marshall, the great economist of Edwardian Britain, attributed the decline to the complacency of the entrepreneurs who had inherited the companies which they owned and so badly ran. They were

content to follow mechanically the lead given by their fathers. They worked shorter hours and they exerted themselves less to obtain new practical ideas as their fathers would have done and thus a part of England's leadership was destroyed rapidly. In the nineties it became clear that, in future, Englishmen must take business as seriously as their grandfathers had done and as their American and German rivals were doing: that their training for business must be methodical, like that of their new rivals, and not merely practical on lines that had sufficed for the simpler world of two generations ago: and lastly that the time had passed at which they could afford merely to teach foreigners and not learn from them in return.*

---

*Marshall's memorandum, largely ignored by the government of the day, was published as a White Paper (No. 321) in 1908 when the Liberals had come to power.

The increasing gap between the technological progress of the competing economies was illustrated by a humiliation which was particularly painful to a seafaring nation. The Germans built ocean liners which won the Blue Riband of the Atlantic for three successive years. At least among the Establishment, anxiety about the speed of the competitor nations' economic progress was moderated by relief that the Mother Country had not descended to their level of commercial vulgarity. Masterman, without quite realising it, demonstrated the problem to which Alfred Marshall referred – the attitude which guaranteed that Britain would fall behind. 'Already in America one can detect a kind of disease of activity in people to whom "business" has become a necessary part of life. The general effect is of children with over-strung nerves, restless and aimless, now taking up a book, now a play thing, now roaming round the room in uncertain uneasiness.'

Anyone who wanted to take refuge in the certainty of Anglo-Saxon superiority could rely for comfort and a false sense of security on what, in Edwardian Britain, seemed to be Britain's indestructible asset. Invisible earnings – the commercial triumph of worldwide empire – kept Britain a mighty nation on which other countries, with more rapidly expanding manufacturing industry, still relied. Until 1914 world trade depended on the gold standard – in theory the inflow and outflow of bullion to compensate for deficits and surpluses on the balance of trade. In fact it was usually sterling – 'as good as gold' – with which the international books were balanced. For sterling to 'operate on equal terms with gold'[4] as a multinational currency, the pound had to be beyond speculation, depreciation and, in terms of transfer payments, short supply. Until 1914 all these conditions were amply met. Indeed throughout the Edwardian era sterling grew stronger as Britain's trading balance increased. Between 1901 and 1905 average annual net imports were valued at £471.5 million. Average net exports for the same period had a total value of £296.9 million. The consequent deficit on the balance of trade (£174.6 million) was easily offset by income from 'invisibles' – £116.6 million from services and £112.9 million from interest and dividends. The result was an average annual surplus of £49 million on current account and an accumulating balance abroad of £2,642 million. And the surplus grew. Between 1911 and 1913, the same pattern persisted –

deficit on physical trade was more than liquidated by surplus on the 'invisible' account. The result was an average surplus on current account of £206.1 million and an accumulated foreign balance of £3,990 million.[5]

That once apparently permanent guarantee of overall economic stability was liquidated by the First World War, although, since it depended on worldwide free trade, the growing enthusiasm for protection (including in Britain) jeopardised the role of sterling, and the international status which it gave to the United Kingdom, long before 1914. But the cost of war precipitated the catastrophe. By accelerating the great asset sale, Britain began to pay the price for investing abroad rather than in domestic industry and, in consequence, failing either to diversify or to modernise its basic staple trades. Textiles, coal mining, iron and steel and shipbuilding, on which it had over-relied since the early days of the industrial revolution, died during the second half of the twentieth century, but they were doomed fifty years earlier. In 1907 those four sectors of the economy produced 50 per cent of industrial output and employed 25 per cent of the working population. When they began to contract, so did the whole economy.[6]

Ironically, during the period when British industry was being overtaken by its United States competitors, American food exports to Britain began to decline. Canadian and Argentinian produce began to take its place. Grain and meat from the New World were still, despite transport costs, cheaper than anything grown and bred on the small home farms and by 1910 there were transatlantic suppliers who could even undercut the United States. So the decline in agriculture, at least in terms of numbers, continued. The 1901 census showed that, by the turn of the century, 77 per cent of the population of England and Wales lived in urban areas – 12 per cent more than in 1890.[7] A reduction in manpower is not necessarily the result of a reduction in output or the consequence of economic stagnation. But one sort of farming was the victim of a continuing depression. The great cereal farms of East Anglia were no longer prosperous and, in many cases, barely viable. But the position of agriculture as a whole was nothing like as gloomy as Rider Haggard made out. While some parts of the country were doing badly, others were doing well. It was the *idea* of rural England that perished during the reign of Edward VII. Masterman mourned its passing.

No one today would seek in the ruined villages and dwindling population the spirit of an 'England' four fifths of whose people have now crowded into the cities. The little red-roofed towns and hamlets, the labourer in the field at noontide or evening, the old English services in the old English village church now stands but as the historical survival of a once great and splendid past. Is 'England' then to be discovered in the feverish industrial energy of the manufacturing cities?

The collapse of agriculture was nothing like as great or universal as Masterman implied. Even within the hardest hit areas the prospects varied. Some of the wheat farms in the heavy clay-lands of Essex went out of business altogether, but in Norfolk, where prices had always been higher, the fall in grain prices was at least accommodated to a point at which the farmers struggled on, and some parts of the country took up more profitable types of farming. During the thirty years which preceded the First World War the acreage under crops in England and Wales fell from 24 to 19.5 million. Some farmers, who were willing to switch to produce in newly increased demand, were able to increase their income. Farms with easy access to rail links usually survived and prospered. Britain was eating more meat, more fruit and more vegetables. The price of bread was falling, but wages, by and large, were stable or actually showing a marginal increase.

A. L. Bowley contended that wages rose to a peak in 1900 and then fell away until economic recovery produced a second, though more modest, high point in 1907. Another decline then continued until the fear of world war stimulated production in 1913. On the other hand, the cost of living – at least according to Bowley – rose steadily throughout the period.[8] The consequent reduction in real wages was, according to many commentators, the cause of the industrial unrest which affected industry after 1909. However, later (and more sophisticated) work by C. H. Feinstein suggests that, on average, real wages were at worst static and, in many cases, showed a slight improvement. The strikes may have occurred in the unlucky industries. Or perhaps the workers *thought* that their standard of living was falling. But it is far more likely that the unrest was the result of changing attitudes. 'Hundreds of thousands [were] living below the poverty line, i.e.

without the means to buy enough to keep themselves physically healthy.'[9] Militancy was on the march. The stark reality of life in darkest Britain was brought home to an anxious nation by the discovery that 6,000 of the 20,000 men who volunteered to fight for Queen and country in South Africa were unfit even to be considered for military service.[10]

Masterman was at least as concerned with preserving social tranquillity as he was with the plight of the poor. He wrote of the 'huge and unexplored region which seems destined in the next half-century to progress towards articulate voice and to demand increasing power'. By that he meant the people whom Matthew Arnold called 'The Populance', a class which Masterman said would 'endure almost anything, in silence, until it become unendurable'. His fear was that the heroic stoicism would not survive the changes in the moral values that characterised the new century. He had observed with evident disapproval the conduct of 'that section of society which regards its possessions as a trinket, a plaything and, amid an atmosphere of triviality, is engaged in squandering its brief existence through every variety of passionate pleasure'. How long, he wondered, would 'the obscure multitudes, who labour with scanty return, be satisfied with what [to them] appears so improvident a bargain?' Masterman was not writing only about the desperately disadvantaged and the deeply dispossessed. He was anticipating the alienation of the whole working class. But at the turn of the century most commentators concentrated their criticism on the condition of the poor.

Attention on the extent of the problem was focused by the two historic surveys which revealed, in irrefutable statistical form, the way the poor lived. The first was Charles Booth's *Life and Labour of the People of London*, published over the fifteen years between 1889 and 1903. Booth could not resist the occasional moral judgement. Despite all the sentimental talk of family solidarity, only 30 per cent of London families took responsibility for grandparents. And when he extended his surveys to outside London, he noted that in Richmond, Yorkshire, 'filial duty was at a low ebb'.[11] But he did identify age and unemployment, rather than character weakness, as the chief cause of destitution. The second social survey, *Poverty, a Study in Town Life* (begun in 1889 and published in 1901), was, perhaps, even more important. Benjamin Seebohm Rowntree's examination of poverty in York disposed of the argument that Booth's principal survey proved only that poverty was endemic in the overcrowded capital. And it established, in the official mind, a distinction between 'primary' and 'secondary' poverty.

According to Rowntree, 9.91 per cent of the York population lived in 'primary poverty' and were unable to maintain 'merely physical efficiency' while 17.73 per cent lived in 'secondary poverty', able to 'meet physical efficiency, were it not for some other expenditure either useful or wasteful'. Compassion combined with the national interest. Over a quarter of the population were prevented, by their material condition, from making a proper contribution to the national economy.

Poverty was greatest in Edwardian Britain among the agricultural labourers. It was argued that living in the country – and therefore being able to supplement basic diets with local produce – enabled families to subsist satisfactorily on a lower wage than that which they would need in a town. The survey carried out by P. H. Mann during 1903 in Ridgemount, Bedfordshire, disproved that sentimental assumption. Rowntree, in his survey of York's poor, had set out the 'poverty line' at earnings of 21s 8d a week. Families which lived on less survived in profound deprivation. Because most farm workers occupied rent-free cottages, Mann adjusted that definition down to 18s 4d a week. Even at that reduced income level, 38.5 per cent of all the working-class families (41 per cent of the working-class population) lived in poverty.

Ridgemount proved to be typical. The 1906 *Earnings and Hours of Labour Enquiry* discovered that in England the average weekly earnings of agricultural labourers was 17s 6d. Horsemen and cattlemen did rather better. They received 18s 4d. In Wales, farm labourers earned more than their English counterparts: the average wage for all agricultural workers was 18s.

Maude Davies, writing in her *Life in an English Village* about Corsley in Wiltshire during the years 1905 to 1907, reported that 37 of the 220 households were living in 'secondary poverty', a condition for which she offered an unusual, but nevertheless significant, definition – 'all households whose income does not give 1/- per head above primary poverty, as well as those households where the income should be sufficient but where it is squandered and the members are obviously living in want'.[12] On that basis, her survey concluded that in Corsley, 12.7 per cent of households were in primary and 16.8 per cent in secondary poverty. Some of that total figure, 29.5 per cent in all, were old or sick. Amongst families in which the head of the household was employed – in fact the families of farm labourers – the number in poverty (primary and secondary) was 23 per cent.

The situation barely changed with the years. The first decade of the twentieth century is thought of as a period of progress. Yet *How the Labourer Lives*, a survey carried out during 1913, revealed that, with five exceptions (North Cumberland, Durham, Westmorland, Leicestershire and Derbyshire), the average earnings in every county in England and Wales were below the poverty line. Wages paid by farmers were too low to enable workers to maintain a state of 'physical efficiency' – with all the consequences of that condition.

It means that people have no right to be in touch with the great world outside the village by so much as taking a weekly news-paper. It means that the wise mother, when she is tempted to buy her children a pennyworth of cheap oranges will devolve the penny to flour instead. It means that the temptation to take the shortest journey should be strongly resisted. It means that toys and dolls and picture books, even of the cheapest quality, should not be purchased: that birthdays should be practically indistin-guishable from other days. It means that every natural longing for pleasure should be ignored or set aside. It means in short, a life without colour, space, or atmosphere that stifles and hems in the labourer's soul as in too many cases his cottage does his body.[13]

That describes not the condition of the unemployed but the state of the working poor. The extent of their social deprivation can be assessed against even the simple pleasures of Kate Jarvis, nursemaid to an admiral, and Rowland Evans, the teenage son of a Bradford Congregationalist Minister. On Monday 22 December 1902 young Rowland:

in the morning played football and also in the afternoon. At night borrowed 3d off Father and went to town to buy some presents . . . Bought 5 in all.

Father	1 ounce of Cigarettes	6d
Mother	an ornament	6d
Mabel	a purse	6d
Oliver	a picture book	3½d
Glyn and Bernard	a bagatelle board	6½d
		———
		2/4d

Neither farm labourers' children, nor farm labourers themselves, could afford such extravagance. They were even less likely to indulge themselves with the Christmas luxuries enjoyed by a child's nurse. At Christmas 1906 Kate received the typical utilitarian gifts of the thrifty working class. From 'Dear Mother, A Lovely Petticoat, Dear Father, stockings and a card and Gran 2 prs Bloomers'. Underclothes were not the habit of the very poor.

Despite the comforting myth about the farm labourer supplementing his income with vegetables grown in his own garden and eggs laid by his own hens, the agricultural poor lived in greater degradation than the poor in the cities. Yet poverty was rife in the cities. Social surveys proliferated in Edwardian Britain. Most of them demonstrated that, among the 77 per cent of the population who lived in urban areas, there were deep and wide pockets of real need.

Seebohm Rowntree judged that, in 1901, nearly 30 per cent of the population of York lived in poverty and he claimed that the social composition of that city's population was very similar, if not identical, to that of other towns and cities. The level of deprivation did not change with the years. Rowntree and Lasker, examining the history of 209 men who were unemployed in York during June 1910, found that a third of them lived below the poverty line. The rest were 'raised above it through earnings of other members of the family'. Every 'normal' sized 'working' family (defined as parents and three children) passed through poverty of some kind during its collective life. A dozen other surveys confirmed that pattern of life. As in England, so in Scotland. 'Lady Inspectors' visited 3029 Dundee families during 1905 to report on the *Housing and Industrial Conditions* in that city. Because of the nature of Dundee industry – dominated by jute processing – 769 of the 3029 families visited (25.4 per cent) were solely dependent on one (male) wage earner. Slightly fewer (684 or 22.6 per cent) depended on one female earner, 433 (14.3 per cent) on both a male and female earner, 656 (21.7 per cent) on two wages of other sorts (mainly parent and child) and 487 (16 per cent) on three earners. Half of the families which depended solely on one male wage had an income of less than £1 a week and were therefore well below the poverty line. Since women's wages were, throughout the period, invariably well below men's, at least four hundred of the families dependent on one female earner lived in similar deprivation. It is, therefore, reasonable to conclude that one third of all *working* families in Edwardian Dundee lived in primary poverty.[14]

Lady Florence Bell, the wife of a Middlesbrough ironmaster, published *At the Works*, a survey of poverty on Teesside based on 'voluntary visits' carried out during 1907. Since only ironworks' employees were visited, Lady Bell anticipated that few of the families in the study would be in 'absolute poverty'. But of the '900 houses carefully investigated, 125 were found to be absolutely poor' and 'never have enough to spend on clothes to be able to protect their bodies adequately, enough to spend on their houses to acquire a moderate level of comfort'. Another 175 houses were 'so near the poverty line that they are constantly passing over it'.[15] 'Lack of thrift' and lack of 'skilful management' were, in Lady Bell's opinion, an important contributory cause to the unhappy condition in which a third of her husband's employees found themselves.

Even they were well off as compared with the unemployed, particularly the elderly. The 1834 Poor Law Amendment Act required the parish to provide relief that was 'inferior to the standard of living that a labourer could obtain without assistance'.[16] Between 1906 and 1914 the wages of men on the lowest rates for unskilled labourers rose from 19s 6d to 21s a week.[17] In 1912, at the middle of that period, the Liberal Christian League found that Norwich old people received between 3s 6d and 4s 6d a week, married couples 6s to 7s a week with an extra 2s for each child.

Maud Pemberton Reeves, who worked in Lambeth to record the lives of working families for a survey called *Round About a Pound a Week*, rejected the notion that the poor had only themselves to blame. 'Married men in full-time work who keep their jobs on such a wage do not and cannot drink.'[18] She noted the annual volume of beer drunk had declined from an average of 34 gallons a head to 28 gallons over the last twenty-five years of the nineteenth century. The contributing factors in the descent into grinding poverty were neither incompetence nor incontinence but acts of God and nature – births, deaths and illness. Sometimes the very poor were too responsible for their own good.

> It is a common idea that there is no thrift among them. It would be better for the children if this were true. As a matter of fact, sums varying from 6d a week to 1/6d, 1/8d or even 2/- go out from incomes which are so small that these sums represent perhaps from 2½ to 10 per cent of the whole household allowance. The object of this thrift is, unfortunately, not of the slightest benefit to the families concerned.[19]

The savings were made to cover funeral expenses.

Reeves pointed out that, if the families had not invested in funeral insurance, social pressures would have forced them into other expedients for raising the funds that were necessary to finance 'a good send-off'. It could easily be argued that a near-pauper family, which neglected food and clothing in order to pay for one ham tea, might be described as incorrigibly irresponsible. The defence against that charge is more than the irresistible force of superstition and convention. Families which neglected to show proper respect at funerals would have fallen foul of the Edwardians' distinction between the deserving and undeserving poor. The phrase was immortalised in Bernard Shaw's *Pygmalion*, written in 1912. Alfred Doolittle, the dustman father of Eliza, happily accepted the accusation that he had no morals. 'Can't afford 'em.' He then went on to admit, 'Undeserving poverty is my line.'

Maude Davies found very few Alfred Doolittles in her English village. Her enquiry showed that what she described as 'deficient children', even when they had 'every advantage of good air and healthy surroundings', was a condition 'mainly due to malnutrition'. Only market gardeners, who enjoyed access to cheap fruit and vegetables, 'succeeded by some means in avoiding the deadly grip of poverty'. Unless we make the unreasonable assumption that market gardeners were more responsible parents than other employees in other trades, we have to accept that circumstances rather than character deficiencies were the cause of poverty and the malnutrition which followed.

In 1904, the Report of the Inter-Departmental Committee on Physical Deterioration concluded that a third of all schoolchildren 'went hungry', and Rowntree's examination, *Poverty* (which was published in the same year), judged that 'mothers and children habitually go short'. The principal working-class foods were bread, potatoes, milk, eggs, vegetables, sugar, jam and occasionally meat (usually beef). In Glasgow, labourers' families survived on the 'barest necessities of life'. The 'monotonous existence'[20] which such limited ingredients made unavoidable was rendered all the more tedious by the way in which food was prepared. It had to be easily and quickly prepared by women who had few cooking utensils and little time to spend on cooking. As a result bread was the staple diet.

It is cheap . . . It comes into the house ready cooked. It is always at hand and needs no plate or spoon. Spread with a scraping of butter, jam or margarine – according to the length of purse of the mother – [children] never tire of it as long as they are in their ordinary state of health. They receive it into their hands and can please themselves as to where and how they eat it.[21]

In London, out-of-work families sometimes spent as little as a penny per day per person on food and, as a result, 'the lives of the children of the poor [were] shortened and the bodies of the children of the poor starved and stunted'.[22] Surveys attributed rickets in Glasgow and tuberculosis in Birmingham directly to poor diet. Booth's *Life and Labour*, which analysed 1894 working-class family budgets, noted that, in London, something like 3 per cent of food expenditure (more than in any other part of the country, and more than was spent in London on sugar, potatoes, fish and vegetables) was devoted to meals out. That extravagance turned out to be fish and chips.

The most thrifty families struggled on with an existence which, though frugal, was thrown into crisis only by a sudden emergency that it was impossible to anticipate and for which no preparation was therefore possible – illness or unemployment. Lady Bell concluded her Middlesbrough survey with a reproof and a confession.

> We forget how terribly near the margin of disaster the man (even the thrifty man) walks, who has in ordinary normal conditions but just enough to keep himself on. The spectre of illness and disability is always confronting the working man, the possibility of being, from one day to the other, plunged into actual want is always confronting his family.[23]

Family members tried to help one another. 'Reciprocity between the generations, mutual support in times of need was as notable as the dependency of aged parents.'[24] But there were sudden emergencies which even generous siblings or willing children could not overcome. Then more desperate remedies were necessary. 'The curve of income and expenditure is, to some extent, smoothed by the help of the pawn broker, the money lender or both. In bad weeks, clothes and furniture are pledged and debt incurred. In good weeks the surplus is spent on getting straight again.'

Although low wages remained a feature of Edwardian Britain, and working families on each side of the poverty line suffered all the detriments of an inadequate diet, one section of the population saw the belated glimmerings of a better life. Women – by 1900 a majority of the population* – began to enjoy improved health as the direct result of a reduction in family size and birth rate. By 1900, the process had only just started, though couples married in that year had only half as many children as had been born to their parents. The trend

---

*The actual figures were: 1901 – males 17,752,000 females 18,934,000; 1911 – males 19,775,000, females 21,112,000.

continued. In the early Edwardian years, 'professional' families averaged 3.5 children while miners (the most fertile occupation) fathered, on average, 7.36 sons and daughters.[25] From 1900 onwards the birth rate fell. 'The headlong collapse of the birth rate of this country during the past twenty years – a fall greater than that in any other nation in Europe – is a phenomenon to which all the classes, save the very poorest, are probably contributors.'

Masterman – too much of a gentleman even to consider how the birth rate might have been affected by the increased availability of contraception – recognised that family limitation was a conscious decision by men and women who were dissatisfied with their standard of living. Unable to increase their wages, they attempted to improve their material well-being by making sure that they had fewer mouths to feed. Masterman called it 'climbing through the window when the door is closed'. That was not, in its context, the happiest of images. But the idea behind it – the relationship between a fall in the birth rate and the desire for a better material life – was undoubtedly correct.

The penalty which women paid for constant pregnancy was vividly illustrated in a collection of case studies published by the Women's Co-operative Guild.

> I was married at the age of 22 and by the time that I had reached my thirty second birthday was the mother of seven children and I am sure that you will pardon me if I take credit for bringing up such a family without loss of even one seeing that it entailed such a great amount of suffering to myself.
>
> During pregnancy I suffered much. When at the end of ten years I was almost a mental and physical wreck, I determined that this state of things should not go on any longer and if there was no natural means of prevention then of course artificial means must be employed . . .
>
> I often shudder to think what might have been the result if things had been allowed to go on as they were.
>
> Two days after childbirth I invariably sat up in bed knitting stockings and doing general repairs for my family.
>
> My husband at that time was earning 30/- per week and . . . claimed 6/6 in pocket money.[26]

That woman, with 23s 6d a week to spend, was appreciably better off than many Edwardian wives and mothers. And she was at least spared the burden of taking paid employment. The 1901 Census showed that 77 per cent of women between the ages of 15 and 34 did some sort of paid work. For the age group 35–47 the figure fell to 13 per cent. Almost 29 per cent of women (32 per cent of women over ten, then the statutory school leaving age) were in full employment. Most of the employed women were working class. Unlike their more prosperous contemporaries, they did not begin jobs when their children were grown up. They worked during the childbearing and rearing parts of their lives. That was the time when their families most needed the extra income. Many more were engaged in casual labour or took in home work – according to Howarth and Wilson, very often to 'meet some definite party of family expenditure, such as children's clothes and boots'.[27] Over 54 per cent of them were widowed or unmarried. In Birmingham, Cadbury discovered that 6 per cent of the working women were widows whose status 'made it compulsory for them to work'. Since they normally earned less than men in similar employment – even when the men took home subsistence-level wages – those working women and their children were living in dire poverty.

Most women worked in occupations which could accommodate the rival demands on their time that came with motherhood. The largest single group was in domestic service – 11.1 per cent of the entire adult female population of England and Wales. Some trades employed almost as many women as men. In Stoke, Burslem and Hanley, it was assumed that women like the eponymous heroines of *Anna of the Five Towns* and *Hilda Lessways* would work in the potteries. In Leicester, married women 'finished' stockings at home. In Scotland, but not in England, printing was women's work. And some Lancashire textile mills paid equal rates to both sexes, so the female weavers earned more than male farm labourers. But women had still to break into the professions. In 1901 there were 172,000 women teachers and 64,000 women nurses, but only six architects, three veterinary surgeons and two accountants. There were no solicitors or barristers because only men could practise law. But women had, at last, reached the status which is necessary for a slaves' revolt. They enjoyed enough freedom to make them demand more.

Although they were not allowed to vote in parliamentary elections, women ratepayers had been able to stand for election as Poor Law Guardians – the controlling committees of workhouses and providers of 'outdoor relief' – since 1834, but social pressures had, initially, proved as discriminating as the law. No female candidate was nominated until 1875. Female England awoke during the Edwardian era. By 1914, there were 1,546 women guardians. At the turn of the century, 270 women served on school boards, useful employment which even some men thought suitable to their gentle nature. When the boards were abolished in 1902, the government discovered that the female character had a sharper side. The school board members who were about to lose their seats complained so loudly that the government instructed every local education authority to co-opt two women. Although women remained reluctant to join the principal agent of social protest – they made up only 7.8 per cent of trade union membership in 1900 – they were regarded (in the minds of even the more progressive members of the Establishment) as in league with organised labour in the campaigns to change society. Masterman thought that the parties to that endeavour would help to change 'the Condition of England'.

'Has there been a row?' asked a journalist of a gathering at Westminster summoned by 'Suffragettes' and unemployed leaders. 'No,' was the cheerful reply, 'but we still 'ave 'opes.' It is a crowd which still ''ave 'opes' that forms the matrix or solid body of those agglomerations of humanity whose doings today excite some interest and some perplexity among observers of social change.

Masterman's view of the society around him was not always as patronising as that passage suggests. He was certainly apprehensive about how 'the crowd' would behave in the future. 'No one,' he wrote, 'can pretend that a condition of stable equilibrium exists' in a society in which, despite 'the removal of super natural sanctions and the promise of future redress, the working people find a political freedom accompanying an economic servitude'.

Masterman's analysis of England's condition is dangerously sentimental. When he quotes from *A Poor Man's House* – the account of life in a Devon fishing village written by Stephen Reynolds, an aspiring Edwardian novelist – he chooses the passage which illustrates the virtue of Old England. The fishermen regard haggling over the price of hiring a boat as an 'unpardonable offence', not because it reduces their income but because it reveals a lack of gentility in the holiday-makers from the towns. But Masterman does not mention 'nine year old Tommy [whose] working day was from 3.30 a.m. to 10.00 p.m.' or the prodigal son, whose brief return is marked by the purchase of so much beer for his old friends that he has to borrow the fare back to London.

One thing is clear from every page of *The Condition of England*. The whole nation was changing at a speed which sent a clear message to the politicians. The way in which Britain was governed had to change too. But a nation in transition was ready to redeem its failures and rectify its faults. In Masterman's words, Edwardian Britain was 'full of energy and promise'.

PART TWO

'Enough of this Tomfoolery'

Two sorts of men had dominated Queen Victoria's parliaments: aristocrats, and members of the great mercantile families who had achieved both wealth and status in the eighteenth and nineteenth centuries. They were men of great public spirit and undoubted patriotism. The Cavendishes, Cecils and Primroses (representing bloodline and birth) and the Peels, Chamberlains and Gladstones (representing industry and commerce) thought of Parliament as a calling. But they did not regard it as a job. Their only duty was to preserve the peace and secure the realm. The rival factions represented interests – town versus country, industry against agriculture – rather than ideologies and the notion of party government, together with the manifesto and the mandate, did not become a feature of the British political system until Gladstone won the General Election of 1867. Even then it was slow to take hold.

At the turn of the century, only one-third of adults had the vote, and the entirely hereditary House of Lords enjoyed equal status with the elected House of Commons. The notion that government was best left in the hands of inspired amateurs was demonstrated by the conduct of Members as well as the composition of the Parliament in which they served. Arthur Balfour, nephew of the Marquis of Salisbury, scholar and the most influential Tory in Edwardian England, personified the dedicated dilettante. Despite his great legislative achievements he behaved as if politics was a gentleman's pastime.

Balfour led the Conservative Party to defeat in the Liberal landslide of 1906. He lost his own seat and, after being returned to the House of Commons in a by-election, failed to notice that both the mood and the Membership had changed. Working men sat on the government benches. Fifty-three Members of Parliament called themselves 'Labour'. Parliament had become a place of work. When he tried to dazzle the House with verbal gymnastics and studied elegance, the new Prime Minister, Henry Campbell-Bannerman, dismissed him with a couple of sentences. 'Enough of this tomfoolery. It might have answered very well in the last Parliament, but it is altogether out of place in this . . .'

CHAPTER 5

Unfinished Business

The Boer War was part of the Victorian legacy to Edwardian Britain and the beginning of a global revolution which was not to be completed until the end of the century. For a hundred years, the white man's right to rule the 'lesser breeds without the law' had been taken for granted and enforced with the maxim gun. Many of the proconsuls who devoted their lives to the Empire believed, with absolute sincerity, that Britain had a moral duty to spread Christian civilisation amongst the savage races of the world. They found it hard to argue that the invasion of Matabeleland by Dr Leander Starr Jameson, the slaughter of three thousand natives and the pillage and burning which followed was carried out expressly in the interest of the indigenous population. But they consoled themselves with the thought that Lobengula, King of the Matabele, had risen up against lawful authority. Few of them had any doubts that God had ordered England to have dominion over the palms and pines of South Africa. Unfortunately a number of extremely pious Boers believed that Providence had provided them with exactly the same mandate.

Belief in Anglo-Saxon superiority had convinced the Victorians that Cape Colony, the British outpost in South Africa, would dominate the region for ever. That view was reinforced by the presence in the continent of Cecil John Rhodes. His initial interest in the Cape was gold. But he quickly developed a sense of destiny. 'I walked between earth and sky and when I looked down I said "This earth should be English" and when I looked up, I said "England should rule the earth"[1] His enthusiasm and uninhibited acceptance of the Europeans' right to govern – indeed to own – South Africa attracted even some Afrikaners. Jan Christian Smuts, destined to fight against Britain from start to finish of the long Boer War, was explicit about Rhodes's essentially racist attraction. 'The Dutch set aside all considerations of blood and nationality and loved him and trusted him and served him because we believed that he was the man to carry out the great idea of an internally sovereign and united South Africa in which the white man would be supreme.'[2]

Perhaps Smuts – always a moderate by the extreme standards of nineteenth-century South Africa – would have been content for the Cape Colony to remain the centre of a white man's paradise. But fate and geology decreed that the whole future of South Africa would be built around the predominantly Boer republic of the Transvaal, 'given away', much to the Prince of Wales's distress, by Mr Gladstone after the defeat of the British Army at Majuba Hill in 1881. Five years later gold was discovered at Witwatersrand, and Johannesburg, the capital of the Transvaal, became the economic capital of the whole region. Within ten years of the gold fields opening up, the annual income of the Transvaal rose from £196,000 to £4 million.[3]

The new prosperity eluded most Transvaal Boers. Cecil Rhodes, Prime Minister of Cape Colony after 1890, attributed their relative misfortune to the natural superiority of the English minority which they governed. Whatever the true reason, the consequences were plain for the Boer government to see. By 1896, Uitlanders – British immigrants – made up two-thirds of the Transvaal population. Half of them had entered the republic from Cape Colony and the rest had emigrated directly from Britain. Johannes Paulus Kruger, the Boer Prime Minister, could see his colony gradually being anglicised. And he objected to more than the prospect of immigrants dominating his country. Kruger lived according to the tenets of the Dutch Reformed Church. The presence of so many newcomers who did not subscribe to its exacting moral rules made Johannesburg 'hideous and detestable'. They encouraged 'luxury without order, sensual enjoyment without art, riches without refinement and display without dignity'.[4] Five years later, when Britain was at war with the Boer Republic, Lloyd George, a bitter opponent of the conflict, described the Uitlanders in very similar language. 'They prefer to lounge about in the hotels of Cape Town while English homes are being made desolate on their behalf.'

Kruger wanted the Uitlanders to stay in the Transvaal but planned to make them, if not a subject people, at least second-class citizens. His rejection of their demands for equal civil rights was accompanied by the brusque but entirely justified allegation, 'It is my country you want.' If the Uitlanders were given the vote they would, he knew, make the Transvaal an English colony. On the other hand, the British government knew that it had a patriotic duty to defend its sons and daughters from Boer tyranny and confirm its position as the predominant power in South Africa.

The years between the discovery of Witwatersrand gold and the outbreak of the Boer War were the high point of British emotional imperialism. It was the era in which the Royal Niger Company evolved into a Crown Colony, the Sudan was reconquered and the French expedition to Fashada – a handful of soldiers reconnoitring the White Nile – provoked the solemn warning of the consequences which would follow the 'unfriendly act' if relief or reinforcements were despatched to a part of Africa which Britain regarded as in its sphere of influence. The idea of empire achieved its most extreme expression in the raid which Dr Jameson, the victor of the Matabele campaign, led into the Transvaal in 1895. Its organisers – Rhodes among them – believed that, inspired by the courage of the reckless raiding party, the Uitlanders would rise up against their oppressors. Rhodes was wrong.

The Select Committee of the House of Commons which enquired into the origins of the raid acquitted Joseph Chamberlain (Colonial Secretary in Lord Salisbury's last government) of all complicity in the raid's preparation. Indeed it unanimously agreed that he did not even know that it was planned. The verdict was generally accepted because Harcourt and Campbell-Bannerman – competitors for leadership of the Liberal Party which Chamberlain had deserted – endorsed it. But doubts remained. The South Africa Company refused to release copies of telegrams which, it was rumoured, would have proved

Chamberlain's guilt, and the whole of the Committee's proceedings were called into question by its composition. Chamberlain, as well as being the subject of its investigation, was a member. The enquiry was conducted according to the mores of the Victorian gentleman's parliament. And that parliament was about to pass into history.

Whether or not Chamberlain knew about the Jameson Raid before it happened, he certainly approved of it in retrospect, and Lord Rosebery (the Liberal Leader) praised it as an 'Elizabethan adventure'.[5] With the nation in such a mood, war in South Africa was inevitable. But for months the talk of war rumbled on without either of the eventual protagonists being willing to fire the first shot. The Kaiser infuriated his uncle in Marlborough House by congratulating Kruger on the ignominious defeat of Dr Jameson's raiding party, and slight alarm was felt in the Colonial Office when the Transvaal and the Orange Free State signed a pact of mutual defence. But there were also moments of hope. Kruger twice met Sir Alfred Milner, the new British High Commissioner, and, at their second meeting, offered a complicated formula for the revision of the franchise which would, in time, give the Uitlanders full civil rights. In return, he demanded that Britain relinquish its claim to sovereignty over the Transvaal. If the interests of settlers had been Milner's only concern he would have accepted the compromise, but because the glory of empire was his chief preoccupation, he rejected it out of hand. Chamberlain's note endorsing Milner's action was written in even stronger language than that which the High Commissioner had used. Yet the peace was still preserved. Lord Salisbury believed that 'The country as well as the cabinet – excepting perhaps Mr Chamberlain – is against war.'[6] But the mood was to change – not least because of the partnership which was formed between Joseph Chamberlain and Alfred Milner.

Milner – half German but educated exclusively in England – began his working life as a journalist on the radical *Pall Mall Gazette*. He then joined the Civil Service and rose in 1870 to become Chairman of the Board of Inland Revenue at the age of thirty-six. Much of his early life was devoted to radical causes and it was his reforming influence which persuaded Sir William Harcourt to introduce death duties. Had he remained in London, he would, no doubt, have retained the progressive impulse which had inspired his ideas on

domestic policy. But he went to Africa and became the archetypal
Radical Imperialist. He did not want to fight the Boers. As late as
November 1899, Chamberlain told Hicks Beach (then Chancellor of
the Exchequer), 'Both Milner and the military authorities greatly
exaggerate the risks and the dangers of the campaign.'[7] But Milner
believed that war could only be averted, and British interests protected
to the full, if Her Majesty's Government maintained its belligerent
stance. Unfortunately the judgement to which he came after the
meetings with Kruger proved tragically wrong. His telegram to the
Colonial Office insisted that 'the Boers are still bluffing and will yield
if the pressure is kept up'.

Anxious though he was to avoid war, Milner was even more
determined that both the Uitlanders' and Britain's standing in the
world should be protected. Invited by Chamberlain to summarise
the situation in a despatch which could be published, he chose to
report home in language he knew represented the prejudice of
the Colonial Secretary: 'The spectacle of British subjects, kept
permanently in the position of Helots . . . does steadily undermine
the influence and respect for the British Government within the
Queen's Dominions.'[8]

No doubt Chamberlain's decision to present the Boers with an ultimatum – immediate full citizenship for the Uitlanders or war – was
intended to produce the pressure that would finally bring the capitulation which the High Commission had predicted, but Milner had
grievously underestimated the resolve of one of the world's most
stubborn races. On 9 November 1899 the Boers published an ultimatum of their own. No more British troops, they insisted, should be
landed in any part of South Africa. Three days later, the first shots
were fired.

The impertinence of the Boers' ultimatum, combined with the
memory of Milner's comparison of British subjects and Greek slaves,
turned the tide of public opinion. In October Asquith – already the
Liberal heir apparent – had denounced the 'irresponsible clamour,
which we heard from familiar quarters, for war'.[9] A month later, he
justified the robust response to the Boer ultimatum with the insistence
that Britain's bellicose reaction 'was neither intended nor desired . . .
it was forced upon us without adequate reason and against our will'.[10]

Campbell–Bannerman, the Leader of the Opposition, caught the national mood. The Boers, he told Parliament, had 'committed aggression which it was the plain duty of all of us to resist'.[11]

It was assumed that the British Army would swiftly dispose of the Boer irregulars who, the War Office disdainfully reported, were led by 'officers elected by the burghers they command'.[12] It was, as Lloyd George scornfully observed, like 'the British Army against Caernarvonshire'.[13] But for the first few months, Caernarvonshire had the upper hand. Reinforcements had set sail during November 1899, but Rudyard Kipling's 'gentlemen in khaki going south' were both badly led and inadequately equipped. L. S. Amery accompanied the 'forty thousand horse and foot going to Table Bay' on behalf of *The Times*. He described the experience as leaving in his mind 'an ineffable impression of the incapacity of many of our senior officers, of the uselessness of most of our army training . . . and the urgent need of a complete revolutionary reform of the Army from top to bottom'.[14]

The British Army was under the command of General Sir Redvers Buller who, according to Balfour, had drunk too much for ten years and 'allowed himself to go down hill'.[15] Fortunately, the Boers wasted time and resources by laying siege to three Transvaal towns – Ladysmith, Mafeking and Kimberley. It was the siege of Mafeking which caught the headlines, principally because the officer in command, Robert Baden-Powell, possessed a remarkable talent both for inventing ingenious ways of frustrating the enemy and for publicising his own achievements. Twelve hundred British soldiers (supplemented by a couple of hundred 'native' irregulars) faced six thousand Boers; though, when it became clear that the garrison did not intend to counterattack, the number was reduced. The Boers possessed a ninety-four-pound siege gun, so Baden-Powell 'dug in' and amused himself by employing 'ripping wheezes' to distract the enemy.

The siege lasted for two hundred and seventeen days, during which time the cavalry killed and ate their horses, drainpipes were disguised to look like field guns, postage stamps (with Baden-Powell's head on them) were printed and jolly messages were sent home via 'Kaffir runners' who crossed the enemy lines at night. Baden-Powell became a national hero. Then, inevitably, iconoclasm set in. It was claimed that the Black South Africans were left to starve, that the Boer troops were fewer than the despatches reported and that the British could and should have broken out. But while the euphoria lasted, the rejoicing represented a view of the world which was essentially Victorian. The Edwardians came to see life differently.

Despite the diversion of the pointless sieges, the Boers managed to overcome the forces of the Crown three times in one 'Black Week' in 1899. There were British defeats at Magersfontein, Stromberg and Colenso, and, by the time of the relief of Kimberley in 1900, they had won a pyrrhic victory at Ladysmith which, although much celebrated at the time, guaranteed that they would lose the war. The Boers attacked the town with such ferocity that Buller recommended its surrender. He was relieved of his overall command and replaced by Lord Roberts.

Roberts was sixty-eight when he was appointed, but he assured the Secretary of State for War that he was still young enough to do the job. 'I've avoided evening parties. I go to bed early. I think I ride to hounds as well as I did ten or eleven years ago. You see, I've always felt the country might need me some day.'[16] But the new C-in-C was a veteran of the Crimean War in which he had won a Victoria Cross. In the Afghan Campaign of 1879, from which he took his title (Roberts of Kandaha), he had pacified the country after a forced march from Kabul to Kandaha. The army which King Edward was to inherit, despite having changed, to the King's distress, 'from royal red to dreadful khaki' was old fashioned in attitude, equipment, strategy and leadership. However, the appointment of Roberts was, in itself, a boost to morale. On 7 February 1900, Victor Cavendish predicted 'We ought to have some big news soon . . . Roberts has started for the front.'

According to folklore, 'The Relief of Mafeking' was one of the great moments in imperial history. But it was the siege of Kimberley which illustrated what the colonies – the old empire which never quite recovered from the Boer War – were really about. Cecil Rhodes, Prime Minister of the Cape, was caught in the town when it was surrounded and he believed that he possessed the right to impose his will on the commanding officers. He argued about troop levels (sometimes too few and sometimes too many), had a bigger and better field gun made in the De Beers workshops (which normally constructed mining machinery), issued orders about personal safety to the civilian population and, in the fourteenth week of the siege, grew bored with what for him was relative inactivity. So he sent an ultimatum to the British government. Either Kimberley was relieved or he would surrender the town to the Boers. The High Command capitulated. Troops were diverted from other essential tasks and Kimberley was relieved on 14 February 1900. Rhodes then put the whole campaign in perspective with a speech to the De Beers shareholders. 'When we look back at the troubles we have gone through and especially all that has been suffered by the women and children, we have this satisfaction. We have done our best to preserve that which is the best commercial asset in the world, the protection of Her Majesty's flag.'[17]

It was a highly commercial Empire which King Edward inherited and led into the twentieth century. But, at the time, the lifting of the Kimberley siege was greeted as a classic victory for British aims and proof that Roberts would turn the tide of war. Victor Cavendish was ecstatic. 'Very good news . . . Roberts telegraphed that French has relieved Kimberley . . . A few more telegraphs during the day. All point to big successes. Mainly due, as far as we can see, to Lord Roberts and French.'

Roberts's tactics were indeed an immediate success. He used almost his entire force as mounted infantry and pursued the elusive guerrillas who were his opponents across the veld. It was necessary to hide from the British press and public the penalty which had to be paid for victory – the death of thousands of horses, killed by heat, exhaustion and starvation. But the success of the new plan made Roberts a national hero. In late February 1900, he defeated a force of 4,000 Boers outside Bloemfontein and, when Kruger left the Transvaal, it seemed that the war was won. In November of that year, the Boer Republic was officially annexed by the British Empire and Field Marshal Lord Roberts was able to return home to become Commander-in-Chief of the whole British Army, just in time to ride at the head of Queen Victoria's funeral procession in February 1901. His popularity was so great that the crowds of mourners burst into spontaneous applause as he passed. His response was a stern gesture of disapproval. The Edwardian Army was under the command of an officer from the old world of chivalry.

The war, which made Lord Roberts a national hero, made David Lloyd George the champion of radical Britain. From the start, the Liberal Party had been hopelessly ambivalent about the government's response to the Transvaal's treatment of the Uitlanders. At its worst moments, it was deeply and obviously divided. Lloyd George himself did not steer a steady course. He insisted that he was a 'radical imperialist' who wanted at least to keep the Transvaal within the bounds of the Empire, but he felt a visceral sympathy for the tiny nation in conflict with a major power, and he openly rejoiced that, during the early phase of the war, 'a small nation, with the size of an ordinary German principality, has been able to defy the power of Great Britain'.[18] He believed in something he called 'Home Rule All Round' – maximum autonomy for colonies big enough to be independently viable within the Empire. He regarded war of any sort as a calamity. The Boer War was particularly abhorrent to him because he believed that it was more motivated by the demands of trade than by the noble hope of spreading *pax Britannica*. And he was right. He clearly had Joe Chamberlain in mind when he complained that 'Some people talk as if they have the British Empire in their own back yard. They put up a notice. No Admittance Except on Business.'[19]

Lloyd George could never keep secret his contempt for the Uitlanders. 'The people we are fighting for,' he told a meeting in Caernarvon, 'are German Jews'[20] – a description which was as inaccurate as it was offensively anti-Semitic. He was not alone in feeling, and expressing, that particular prejudice, though he was almost certainly responsible for promoting it within Parliament. John Burns, soon to become the first 'working man' to reach the Cabinet, described the British Army in South Africa as 'the janissary of the Jews' and he combined with Keir Hardie to promote a resolution in the House of Commons which attributed the war 'largely to Jews and foreigners'. Even John Morley forgot the lessons he had learned at John Stuart Mill's knee and claimed that 'a ring of financiers . . . mostly Jewish, are really responsible for the war'.[21]

The campaign against the war was fought with all the weapons at the disposal of the government's enemies. When Lloyd George addressed the Palmerston Club at Balliol, he assumed the mantle of 'natives' friend' – a new role for a man who had often derisively referred to Indians, as well as Africans, as 'niggers'. 'There might be something magnanimous in a great Empire like ours imperilling its prestige and squandering its resources to defend the poor helpless black. Unhappily, here again is a fiction. The Kaffir workers of the Rand are better treated and have better wages and have more freedom under the dominion of the "tyrant" Kruger than they enjoy in Kimberley or Matabeleland.'[22]

The leader of the 'war party', Colonial Secretary Joseph Chamberlain, was even more unscrupulous in his attacks on people he called 'pro-Boer'. In the summer of 1900, he announced his discovery that Members of Parliament had been in direct communication with Boer leaders including President Styne of the Orange River Free State. It would, he said, be wrong to publicise the names of the men who had been in treacherous touch with the enemy, but he clearly anticipated everyone would take it for granted that Lloyd George was among them. Notwithstanding Chamberlain's conspicuous reticence, the letters were published in full at the end of August. Nothing in them was even remotely disloyal and none of them had been written or signed by the still Honourable Member for Caernarvon Boroughs. Vindication did not encourage magnanimity. The attack on Chamberlain for using the letters to smear an innocent MP was accompanied by personal allegations against the Colonial Secretary himself. Asked how he proposed to conduct his campaign against the Boer War, Lloyd George replied, 'Go for Joe.'

Initially he went for Joe's brother. Arthur Chamberlain was chairman of Kynochs, an engineering company which, according to Lloyd George, had been 'virtually made by the government' after being commissioned to work for the Admiralty despite 'offering the highest tender for the contract'. The Colonial Secretary reacted with appropriate outrage. 'It is a gross abuse to attack a public man through his relatives for whom he is not responsible.' Perhaps. But it made Lloyd George the rising star of an increasingly demoralised party.

The Liberals were so divided over the South African war that in June 1900 Asquith was able, with characteristic detachment, to write: 'I follow with languid interest the triumph of our arms and the dissolution of party.'[23] Worse was to follow. During the autumn of that year, Sir William Lawson moved a 'pro-Boer' amendment to a government motion endorsing the conduct of the war. It was supported by John Morley, Henry Labouchere, Lloyd George and twenty-seven other Liberal Opposition MPs. Edward Grey, the Liberals' authority on foreign affairs, endorsed both the government's resolution and its policy. So did Asquith and thirty-eight other Opposition MPs. Henry Campbell-Bannerman, the party leader, abstained together with thirty-four of his followers and explained that he was 'anti-Joe, not pro-Kruger'. The public demonstration of so deep a division presented the government with an irresistible temptation. Parliament was dissolved. The 'khaki election' followed in October 1900.

Joe Chamberlain, who had wanted an even earlier election, became the star of the Unionist campaign. He fought on the slogan, 'A seat lost to the Government is a seat won by the Boers', and he concentrated his fire on the 'pro-war' Liberals, many of whom had explicitly supported government policy. James Garvin, later editor of the *Observer* and Chamberlain's official biographer, wrote that the campaign's 'main object was to break the Liberal imperialists' in the hope of destroying the party as an effective political force. That aspiration was not gratified. The Unionist majority was increased, but only by four seats, and the popular vote split in the government's favour by only 2,400,000 to 2,100,000. Writing to Lord Rosebery, Winston Churchill suggested that the result demonstrated 'the strength not the weakness of the Liberals'.[24]

The campaign had certainly demonstrated who was the Liberals' coming man. Lloyd George's opponents issued a leaflet which asked rhetorically why the Caernarvon Boroughs should vote for their Conservative candidate. The Tory answer was, 'Because his opponent has been on the enemy's side throughout the war and he insults the generals and the soldiers of the Queen.' Lloyd George replied in even more evocative language. 'The man who tries to make the flag the object of a single party is as great a traitor as the man who fires at it.'[25] When his majority increased by a hundred votes (2,412 to his opponent's 2,116), he was so moved by his success that the Manchester-born Welshman made unsupportable claims about the virtue displayed by the country of his adoption: 'I am more proud of my countrymen tonight than ever before. While England and

Scotland are drunk with blood, Wales is marching with steely step on
the road to liberty and progress.'

In fact, Wales marched in step with the rest of Great Britain. The
'anti-war' Liberals – Labouchere, Burns and Campbell-Bannerman
himself among them – were all returned to the House of Commons
with comfortable majorities which they attributed to their highly
principled stance. It was the 'pro-war' Liberals who began to worry
about their standing within the party. Their response was the creation
of the Liberal Imperial Council and the divisive announcement, 'The
time has come when it is necessary to clearly and permanently distinguish Liberals in whose policies in regard to Imperial questions
patriotic voters may justly repose confidence from those whose opinions naturally disqualify them from controlling the actions of an
Imperial Parliament.'[26] Campbell-Bannerman was offended by more
than the syntax. His denunciation of the Council at a meeting in
Dundee was made more aggressive than he intended by a slip of the
tongue. He did not intend to imply that his critics were on the point
of joining Lord Salisbury's government, but he referred to the 'Liberal
Unionists' rather than the 'Liberal Imperialists'.

At the opening of the new session of Parliament, the Liberals briefly
closed ranks in support of various assaults on the record and reputation
of Joseph Chamberlain. Most spectacular among them was David Lloyd
George's amendment to the Loyal Address, the device by which the
House of Commons debates the government's programme at the opening of the parliamentary year. Ministers of the Crown, the amendment
declared, should have no 'interest, direct or indirect, in any form or
company which contracts with the Crown' unless they 'have taken
precautions effectively to prevent suspicion'. Everybody who was anybody knew which Ministers of the Crown Lloyd George had in mind.
But, to remove all doubt, he let it be known that the Chamberlain
family – Arthur, Joseph and Austen – held shares in Hoskins and Sons
Limited and Tubes Limited, in addition to those in Kynocks, about
which he had complained during the general election campaign.

It was by such self-promotion that Lloyd George achieved national
fame, or at least notoriety. By the time of King Edward's accession he
had achieved the status of potential national leader. His new status was
demonstrated by the ease with which he broke the monopoly of

popular newspapers in support of the South African war. The *Daily Chronicle* – one of London's 'penny papers' – had initially been solidly against government policy. But its proprietors demanded that it change its mind. H. W. Massingham, the editor, resigned and joined the *Manchester Guardian*. The *Daily News*, the *Chronicle*'s direct competitor, had always been 'Milnerite' in all its attitudes towards imperial questions. Faced with the possibility that there would be no popular newspaper supporting his cause, Lloyd George organised an 'anti-war' syndicate to take over the *Chronicle*. George Cadbury (a Birmingham Quaker who, like so many of his faith, made chocolate) donated £20,000, giving the enterprise the name of the 'cocoa press'. But there were other equally significant, if less newsworthy, benefactors. Among them was J. P. Thompson, a textile manufacturer from Bolton. He made the new company an interest-free loan of the same size as the Cadbury donation.

Lloyd George had become influential with Liberals all over the country, especially those of a Nonconformist persuasion. He was, he still insisted, a Liberal Imperialist. But he was a different sort of Liberal Imperialist from Asquith and Grey. The nuances of Liberal foreign policy became increasingly important during the early months of Edward's reign when the government made a distressing discovery. The Boers were fighting on. The war was not over.

When Lord Roberts returned to England as Commander-in-Chief in early 1901, it was reasonable to assume that the few Afrikaners who had chosen to battle on rather than to surrender would soon be defeated by a policy which had been especially devised to defeat the elusive Boer commandos. The guerrillas were to be deprived of the refuge into which they disappeared when the raiding parties had done their work. The hinterland at their disposal was made up of farmhouses. So the farmhouses would have to be burned down. At first the policy was applied with some discretion. But it still attracted the wrath of radical Liberals and their newspapers: 'Lord Roberts has written to General Botha to say that when a railway line near a Boer farmhouse is damaged, the farmhouse will be destroyed and the cattle and sheep will be removed . . . Is it civilised warfare to starve women and children? The remedy is to abandon the call for absolute surrender.'[27]

Gradually the policy was extended. After his victory at Bloemfontein in February 1900, Lord Roberts had issued instructions that farms which were harbouring men 'still in league with the enemy' should also be destroyed. He had attempted to justify the new tactic with the revelation that Boers had attacked British soldiers under the cover of a white flag. No doubt they did. Like all guerrilla campaigns, the final stages of the Boer War were fought with unrestrained savagery. It was not only the English who burned farmsteads: Botha destroyed the homes and livelihoods of any of his followers who surrendered to the enemy, requiring Lord Roberts's soldiers to defend and care for Boer women and children. Convenience, or so it was claimed, obliged the refugees to be housed – 'concentrated' was the neutral word then commonly in use – in camps at Bloemfontein and Pretoria. The gratitude expressed by Boers whose families were saved from execution by their erstwhile comrades is not recorded. But British intelligence did report that separation from their families, after being taken into either punitive or protective custody, undermined the commandos' morale. So a new policy was born and mercilessly pursued by General Horatio Herbert Kitchener, promoted from Chief-of-Staff to Commander-in-Chief on the departure from South Africa of Lord Roberts. The veld would be cleared of Boers, square mile by square mile.

In part, the decision to depopulate large areas of the veld was the product of desperation. The Boers were beaten, but they would not give up. Their tactic was to hit and then run and Kitchener concluded that there was only one way in which to deal with such ungentlemanly behaviour: barbed wire would divide the open country like a chess board and a concrete blockhouse would be built at the corners of the fenced squares. Each area was then systematically cleansed of insurgents. Men, women and children were taken to the 'concentration camps' and their farms burned. The Boers, driven to desperation, attempted a doomed invasion of Cape Colony. Not even the Cape Dutch supported them.

Yet the Boers would still accept peace only on their own terms. During the last week of February 1901, a little more than a month after Edward VII succeeded to the throne, Kitchener and Botha met at Middleburg. Kitchener suggested that, in the right circumstances, he would agree to an amnesty for all 'Afrikaner rebels'. Milner – claiming, as High Commissioner, to speak with the authority of the British government – said that the Commander-in-Chief exceeded his authority. Botha then returned to his ancient demands for independence. So Kitchener renewed his 'blockhouse and wire' strategy with increased severity.

In June 1901, there were 60,000 men, women and children in the camps. By August the number had almost doubled and the adult mortality rate had increased to 117 per thousand. Among children it was 50 per cent. The British Army, short of medical supplies for its own troops, was incapable of containing the outbreaks of typhoid, diphtheria and enteric fever. In the thirteen months between January 1901 and February 1902, 20,000 internees died. Most of the 'pro-war' Liberals remained convinced that their cause was respectable if not quite righteous. But the moral outrage of the 'pro-Boers' was uncontrollable. Sir Henry Campbell-Bannerman, speaking at a meeting of the National Reform Union in the Holborn Restaurant, broke one of the abiding rules of Westminster politics. He attacked the conduct of British troops under fire. 'The phrase often used is "war is war", but when one comes to ask about it, one is told no war is going on, that it is not war – when is a war not a war? When it is carried on by methods of barbarism in South Africa.'

The Liberal Party was divided over South Africa by genuine and passionate differences of opinion, as it was divided over every other great issue of the day. But Rosebery, still highly resentful about the disloyalty which had first crippled and then killed off his premiership, added a more personal bitterness to the conflict. During the summer of 1901 he exploited the differences over the Boer War as a justification for speaking out. However, he did not confine his criticisms to one area of policy. He was against Home Rule, against Gladstone's Newcastle Programme (with its promise of manhood suffrage and disestablishment) and against the policies which Gladstone had set out during the Midlothian Campaign. He was against everything that the Grand Old Man, once his mentor, had stood for. South Africa was the occasion, not the cause, of Rosebery's assault on his successor.

No one was sure if the opening salvo in Rosebery's sustained barrage was fired off in a moment of sudden emotion or if it was the result of careful calculation. For the speech was delivered, apparently impromptu, to a lunch at which Rosebery had refused to make a formal address. It began with the demand that the Liberal Party 'start again with a clear slate as regards those cumbersome programmes with which [it was] overloaded in the past'. He moved on to a maudlin passage about his own future. 'I must plough my furrow alone. That is my fate, agreeable or the reverse.' Then he ended on what sounded almost like a threat. 'But before I get to the end of that furrow, it is possible that I shall find myself not alone.'[28] The Liberal Establishment grew anxious. Did Rosebery hope to regain a place in the Liberal leadership or was he merely, and characteristically, making trouble?

Their fears were increased by a letter which Rosebery published in *The Times*. It described attempts to restore Liberal Party unity as 'an organised conspiracy'. The remarkable events of December 1901 heightened the crisis. On 16 December Rosebery spoke in Chesterfield. The speech, which lasted for two hours, was a frontal assault on the government. Anxious Liberals studied it in the hope of finding confirmation that it was made in a spasm of jealousy rather than as the beginning of a long campaign. But it was by no means certain that abdication was the intention which Rosebery meant to convey. The substance of his speech was summed up in a single, obscure image. The time had come to abandon 'fly-blown phylacteries' – a strange metaphor built around the leather wallets, containing Hebrew texts, which Orthodox Jews wear as evidence of their obedience to the law. Rosebery certainly meant to dissociate himself from every aspect of Gladstonian orthodoxy. But he struck where he thought his blows could do most damage. The war in South Africa had moved on. So he was emphatic that he 'could have nothing further to do with Mr Gladstone's party' in its pursuit of Home Rule.

Campbell–Bannerman, hoping that reconciliation was still possible, met with Rosebery to discuss the views they held in common. Rosebery was irreconcilable. Indeed he was on the point of issuing a public repudiation of the party leadership. For a time it seemed that Campbell–Bannerman was doomed. Asquith, his natural heir, made a less than heroic speech which, while not wholly antagonising the peace wing of the party, made clear that he did not share his leader's conciliatory views. For the war to end, the Boers had to be convinced 'of the finality of the result and the hopelessness of ever renewing the struggle'. At the end of January 1902 he abstained on the Opposition's official amendment to the Loyal Address, even though he had helped to draft what was meant to be a form of words which would unite all strands of Liberal opinion.

The rival forces began to regroup. The Liberal Imperial Council was disbanded and replaced by a slightly more moderate but, in terms of membership, far more powerful Liberal League. Rosebery was President, Asquith and Grey were his deputies. Some of its wilder members talked of purging the party of men who were not fit to govern the Empire. No one suggested that the dissidents should be disciplined, but Rosebery, in a choice of words which might have been carefully calculated to excite passions and increase anxieties, promised 'to prevent [his] friends from being drummed out of the party'. Although Asquith said that he would 'have nothing to do with any attempts to weaken or destroy the organisation of the party', there were real fears (and, among some imperialists, some hopes) that the Liberals would split in two. It even seemed possible that the imperialists would make a rapprochement with the Liberal Unionists who had deserted Mr Gladstone during the Home Rule debate. The disagreements were so great that it seemed the Liberal Party might never be elected to office again.

Throughout the months of controversy, one young Liberal managed to keep independent of both the factions but, at the same time, remain irresistibly in the public eye by employing the simple expedient of attacking his opponents rather than his friends. On 18 December 1901, two days after Rosebery had told the Chesterfield Liberals that 'the slate must be wiped clean', Lloyd George addressed an anti-war meeting in the Birmingham Town Hall – an imitation of the Temple of Castor and Pollux which was built (or at least started) as a celebration of the 1832 Reform Bill. The police warned him that his safety could not be guaranteed. Lloyd George was still going for Joe, and Birmingham was Joe Chamberlain's own country.

When he accepted the Birmingham invitation, Lloyd George made clear that he was an unrepentant 'imperialist' and asked for the meeting to be chaired by a local Liberal with similar views. Neither of those concessions to Joe Chamberlain's supporters did much to assuage the animosity which he had, apparently intentionally, attracted during the previous few months. In Pontypridd, as well as describing Campbell-Bannerman as a leader with 'cool head and stout heart', he had told a group of suffragettes in the audience that if women had been allowed to vote 'there would not have been all this bloodshed'. In Wrexham he had counted the cost of the war to the borough – 'One hundred and twenty thousand pounds and *per contra* six little graves in Africa.' Perhaps most inflammatory of all, during what was billed as a scholarly lecture on empire, he had announced, 'We will never govern India as it ought to be governed until we have given it freedom.'[29] It is not surprising that the jingoistic Birmingham *Daily Mail* and *Daily Post* regularly described the unwelcome visitor as 'the most virulently anti-British' Member of Parliament.

Two days before the meeting was due to be held, the Chief Constable recommended that it should be cancelled, and the 'imperialist' chairman found that he must attend another pressing engagement. Despite the obvious risks to his safety, Lloyd George insisted on going ahead. Three hundred and fifty policemen surrounded the Town Hall, facing more than 30,000 demonstrators. When the mob rushed the door, valiant attempts were made to hold them back. Two people, including a policeman, were killed and forty sufficiently badly injured to be taken to hospital. The meeting was abandoned without a word being spoken from the platform and Lloyd George was smuggled out of the artistes' entrance disguised as a policeman. It is hard to imagine the diminutive, long-haired Welshman making a convincing constable, though easy to understand how he felt on the long journey home. 'Going for Joe' had made him famous. But the Liberals, as well as the Boers, had lost the war.

The Boers fought on into 1902. By the end, British losses were 5,774 killed, 22,829 wounded and 16,000 dead from disease. The Boer losses were unknown. The cost to the British Exchequer was £222 million. The price, in terms of lives as well as treasure, may well account for the subdued language with which Victor Cavendish recorded the moment of victory. 'Nice day. Great excitement over peace. Great stir in H of C . . . The Ministers were well cheered.' In

Bradford, Rowland Evans spread the news, in half-inch letters, over a whole page. 'Sunday June 1st 1902. Boer War Ended. Peace Proclaimed. This Memorable Day Has Come at Last.' That was a prelude to a cartoon published in the local paper by arrangement with the *Westminster Gazette* and carefully glued into the diary as an illustration of young Rowland's view on the conduct of the war. The cartoon showed the angel of peace shaking hands with Lord Kitchener. It was captioned, 'Thank you. I knew you would be a good friend to me.' The young diarist added, 'What a great blessing it will be to the parents of the soldiers who are fighting in South Africa.'

CHAPTER 6

A Preference for Empire

The end of 'Joe's War' was marked by peace terms – embodied in the Treaty of Vereeniging in May 1902 – which, by the standards of the time, were remarkably magnanimous. The Dutch and English languages were to be afforded equal legal status in the new South Africa. Both languages were to be used and taught in schools. The Boer commandos, who held out to the end, were (with the exception of those who were said to have ignored the articles of civilised war) granted honourable pardons and, like the other farmers of the veld, allowed to license and keep their sporting rifles. The British Treasury provided £3 million towards rebuilding and restocking the farms which the British Army had devastated. The promise of self-government in 1906 was kept.

Despite that, all the Boer generals were dissatisfied with the offer and some of them refused to accept it. Campbell-Bannerman's assurance that the terms were just and fair helped to convince Botha that the English would keep their word. The more moderate Boers remembered that the Liberal Leader had spoken out against 'methods of barbarism'. But Botha could not be finally reconciled to the terms until he had visited London and been personally convinced that there would be no better offer. Kruger outraged British opinion by touring continental Europe appealing for both financial and political support. The Kaiser implied his sympathy, to the fury of his English cousin who recalled that he had sent a message of congratulations to Commandant Conje after the Jameson raiders had been repelled at Doornkop. In an attempt to win favour at Windsor, Wilhelm II then proclaimed his affection for Britain in a way which caused Edward VII even more offence: in an interview with the *Daily Telegraph*, he claimed that he was the author of the 'wire and blockhouse' strategy which had won the war for Britain.

For a moment it seemed that South Africa slept and the Empire was secure. But the debts incurred during the war – and the cost of the voluntary reparations, had still to be met. Joe Chamberlain – who had several solutions to every problem – proposed that the tariff imposed on corn imports as a wartime expedient should be made permanent, but that exports from the colonies should be granted a 'preferential reduction'. In November 1902, the Cabinet approved the scheme despite the reservations of Charles Ritchie, the Chancellor. At first he reluctantly accepted his colleagues' decision. As he worked on his budget, Ritchie grew increasingly opposed to Chamberlain's scheme and more and more resentful that it had been forced upon him.

Believing that the plan for 'imperial preference' was set in the stone of government policy, Chamberlain set out on a celebratory tour of South Africa. The clash of wills which followed destroyed the apparently invincible government and condemned the Tory Party to almost twenty years in the political wilderness. Joe Chamberlain was to become the only politician in British history to split two parties and destroy two governments of which he was a member. But the real blame lay in the shifting sands of history. The Mother Country was not quite sure how to hold fast colonies which were no longer her obedient children.

Chamberlain returned to England in March 1903 and was greeted by the government as a hero. The Earl of Selbourne joined his liner at sea and the Prime Minister, accompanied by his sister, was waiting on the platform at Waterloo. The warmth of the reunion did nothing to reconcile Chamberlain to a swathe of policies which the Cabinet had adopted in his absence. He was opposed to the Irish Land Purchase Bill because it gave government money to old landlords and created new ones (two classes of men which he despised), and he objected to the Education Bill because its central proposition, the

abolition of school boards, meant that church schools would be subsidised from public funds.[*][1] Chamberlain's mind was as capricious as
it was fertile. At a time when the government was putting aside its differences with Germany in the interests of a joint demand that the
Venezuelan navy should cease to harass Anglo-German shipping, he
changed his opinion about the balance of power in Europe. France, he
decided, was Britain's natural ally and Germany the inevitable enemy.
Chamberlain was looking for trouble. He found it in the argument
over free trade which had been renewed in his absence by the United
States imposing increased tariffs on British imports.

He was not alone in feeling aggrieved about the increasing exclusion of British goods from American markets. A Cabinet minute
recorded the government's reaction to an invitation for Britain to
participate in the St Louis International Exhibition. It reflected the
resentment which was felt by the whole Cabinet. Ministers had been
asked to urge private companies to take part, but they found 'no
small absurdity in asking them to show their best products in a country which absolutely excludes them from its markets'.[2] Canada,
although the first dominion in the worldwide commonwealth, had
followed the American pattern of trade and imposed import duties on
British exports. However, at the turn of the century, the government
in Ottawa had cut tariffs by 25 per cent in favour of British goods.
Germany, which enjoyed no such concession, retaliated by imposing
import duties of its own. Chamberlain was determined that – by
retaining import duties on corn, with special remission for Canada –
the British would repay the Dominion's imperial loyalty. But his
scheme had a wider and greater purpose. He wanted to bind the
whole Empire together by creating a federation of colonial nations
which offered trade concessions to the members of the insoluble
union but denied them to foreigners. Ritchie destroyed Chamberlain's
dream. With the budget statement which he was to present only days
away, he announced that, despite his earlier concession, the government must make a choice. If the corn tariff was not removed
completely, he would resign.

---

[*]For details of the Education Bill see Chapter 12, 'Useful Members of the
Community'.

Balfour, who in 1902 had succeeded Salisbury as Prime Minister, was not an enthusiast for free trade. As a young man, he had attacked Richard Cobden's self-righteous view that protectionists sacrificed the general good in order to guarantee their own prosperity. 'It is absurd to ascribe corrupt motives to large bodies of men, merely because the economic theories they adopt are in accordance with their own interests.'[3] Holding that view it was his duty as Prime Minister to override Ritchie and accept his resignation from the Cabinet, but that was not Balfour's way. 'In his early years he seemed rather cynical and intolerant of stupidity, but in later life he put up with almost anything and anybody . . .'[4] He did, however, work in devious ways. Ritchie's threat to resign before the budget, made in a private conversation with Balfour, was reported to Austen Chamberlain who, as the Prime Minister expected, arranged for his father to receive news of the ultimatum before he arrived back from South Africa. The letter, warning him that his scheme for 'imperial preference' might well be rejected, reached him when his ship docked in Madeira. He had several days to plan how he would react before he arrived to a tumultuous welcome in London.

At the three successive Cabinet meetings held during the last two weeks in March 1903, Chamberlain argued for a retention of the corn tariff with 'preference' for Canada. A majority of the Cabinet supported him. But they also supported Balfour's insistence that the government could not afford to lose the Chancellor of the Exchequer on the eve of the budget, and Ritchie was adamant that he and import duties were incompatible. Ottawa had claimed that there were special reasons for Britain to discriminate in favour of Canadian exports. Pretoria, through the intervention of Lord Milner, claimed identical help for South Africa. That confirmed the Chancellor of the Exchequer in his belief that there should be no preference for anyone. If the Cabinet believed otherwise, he would go. The Prime Minister would not risk losing him.

Chamberlain – who believed, but did not say, that an extension of 'colonial preference' to South Africa was Britain's imperial duty – fought back against his free trade colleagues by mounting guerrilla warfare against their policies. He demanded that 30,000 troops be stationed in South Africa rather than the 15,000 that the War Office proposed, and encouraged the anti-German press (the *Spectator*, the *Morning Post* and *The Times*) to campaign so strongly against British investment in the extension of the Baghdad Railway to the Persian Gulf that Lord Lansdowne, the Foreign Secretary, abandoned the idea. Unabashed, Ritchie presented his budget statement on 23 April. It proposed a total abolition of corn duty.

The protectionists struck back. Two of their leaders, the Duke of Rutland and Henry Chaplin (President of the Local Government Board in Lord Salisbury's last government), demanded to see the Prime Minister. A meeting was arranged for 15 May. Balfour had thought it wise to prepare for the meeting by discussing the whole tariff question with his Cabinet. He reported to the King that there had been agreement on 'the possibility of reviving the tax if it were associated with some great change in our fiscal system'. This hypothesis was too general to bear much meaning, but the Prime Minister's letter suggested two 'eventualities' which might justify the change: 'the necessity of retaliation on foreign countries or the expediency of a closer union with our colonies'.[5] All this had been agreed unanimously by the Cabinet, including Ritchie, and the unanimity had allowed Chamberlain to give notice of his intention to make a speech in Birmingham three days later. He explained that 'he proposed to say . . . much the same thing as [the Prime Minister] proposed to say to the deputation, only in a less definite manner'.[6]

Chamberlain kept just within the boundaries of collective responsibility. He undoubtedly made out his case for 'imperial preference'. But his concluded with the qualification that is always the refuge of ministers who want to hover on the brink of rebellion without rebelling. His only wish was to begin a serious debate on a matter of undoubted public importance. 'I leave the matter in your hands. I desire that a discussion on this subject should now be opened. The time has not yet come to settle it . . .'

No one in the hall accepted the speech as merely a contribution to the study of a yet undecided question of fiscal policy. The fervour with which the questions were asked left little doubt about what the answers should be. Chamberlain's peroration removed what doubt remained: 'Do you think it better to cultivate trade with your own people or to let that go in order that you may keep the trade of those

who are your competitors? . . . I believe in a British Empire . . . and
I do not believe in a Little England which shall be separated from all
those to whom it would, in the natural course, look for support and
affection.'

Leo Amery – perhaps a little carried away by his devotion to
Chamberlain – described it as 'a challenge to free trade as direct and
provocative as that which Luther nailed to the church door in
Wittenburg.' The *Annual Register* for 1903 judged that 'No political
event in recent years has provided so startling an effect as the pro-
nouncement on fiscal policy made by Mr Chamberlain.'[7]

According to the Duke of Devonshire, 'Chamberlain had not given
the least sustained thought to the consequences of his theories.'[8]
However, the expression of his inadequately examined ideas marked
a turning point in British history. The force of the speech lay in the
tone of its delivery, rather than the language in which it was composed. But the rhetorical passion would not have set Britain alight had
it not reflected an equal passion in a substantial proportion of the
British people. Manufacture was in decline. The Industrial Revolution had, in reality, ended more than half a century earlier. The
consequences of failure to innovate and invest were just working their
way through into the economy. Declining industries longed to be
protected by a tariff. The hysterical support which Chamberlain's
Birmingham speech attracted was not an expression of enthusiasm for
an import duty on corn, qualified by an exception for Canada. It was
the assertion that protection was right in itself and that in the twentieth century the British Empire must stand together against the world.

True to his nature, Arthur Balfour faced the uproar with an insouciance which bewildered his friends and infuriated his enemies. His
strength and his weakness was the contempt he always felt for both
extremes of any argument. He wanted a measure of protection to
moderate absolute free trade. It was in that spirit that he opened the
debate in the House of Commons on 28 May. 'I always regret the
manner in which political economy is treated in this House or on
public platforms. It is not treated as a science or as a subject which
people approach impartially with a view to discovering what is the
truth. They find some formula in a book of authority and throw it at
their opponent's head.'[9]

Balfour went on to demonstrate his determination to consider the
real economic issues. He first paid tribute to Chamberlain's examination of the particular dilemma created by German discrimination
against Canadian exports. Then he discussed the propriety and necessity of retaliatory tariffs – as if Canada had needed to retaliate against
Germany rather than that Germany had thought it necessary to retaliate against Canada. He was not sure if the British people would
accept a tax on food or if the Colonies would be prepared to modify
their network of import duties, and he echoed Chamberlain's call for
an enquiry. 'Remember – this question is not a question that this
House will have to decide this session or next session or the session
after. It is not a question that *this* House will have to decide at all.'

The clear implication was that the decision between free trade and
protection would be taken after the next general election. That guaranteed that the debate on the subject would be the central issue of the
campaign. Chamberlain agreed, but he could not resist immediately
going on to argue the tariff case. An increase in food prices would be
unavoidable and the working classes would pay at least three-quarters
of what amounted to a tax on food. But the 'very large revenue' could
and should be used for policies like the introduction of a universal
old-age pension. The tariff was no longer a necessary expedient for
financing already incurred debts, nor even a form of self-protection.
It had become an end in itself which, almost incidentally, raised additional revenues that could be used for desirable purposes. A tariff
with 'preference' for the colonies would be the hoop of steel which
bound the Empire together.

Chamberlain's agreement that the decision on imperial preference
had yet to be taken was enough to satisfy Balfour that the Colonial
Secretary accepted sufficient collective responsibility to allow his continued membership of the Cabinet. It did not convince the diehard
free traders in the government that Chamberlain – who possessed an
almost unique talent for attracting personal animosity – was a trustworthy colleague. They were sure that he should go. Their leaders
and spokesmen – Ritchie, Lord George Hamilton and Lord Balfour of
Burleigh – were neither as devious nor as tolerant as Arthur Balfour.

Esher wrote in his diary for 10 June 1903 that, on the previous day,
'AJB saw the King and did not seem very hopeful about keeping his

team together.' Esher himself was even more gloomy. 'They will break up this year. There is little doubt of it.'[10] Balfour's reports from Parliament to the King explained how the division over 'tariff reform' had immobilised the process of government: 'The whole time of the Cabinet was occupied by a discussion of the present position created by . . . recent utterances on the subject of retaliation and Colonial preference. On this subject, as Your Majesty knows, the Cabinet is not agreed. The divisions amongst us greatly weaken our position and give the opposition a new and unexpected advantage in the parliamentary game.'[11]

On 11 September, the Cabinet discussed a Blue Paper on the subject of 'retaliatory tariffs' – a policy which it was at least possible to argue was not 'protectionism' but the unavoidable response to discrimination against British goods. That, in a sense, was its weakness. It did not attract – or at least it did not enthuse – Joe Chamberlain, who wanted to make the Empire a worldwide customs union which was held together by bonds of trade as well as the ties of history. But it did antagonise the out-and-out free traders, the Liberal Unionists who had learned their politics at Gladstone's knee and still agreed with everything which he had taught them save for the necessity of Irish Home Rule.

The Prime Minister should have known – and possibly did know and rejoiced – that 'the Cobdenites' within his Cabinet would not accept what he regarded as a modest proposal. The free traders decided they had a duty to make a stand. Ritchie and Balfour of Burleigh sent a memorandum of their own to every Cabinet minister which contradicted many of the Blue Paper's conclusions. That might have been acceptable, but it also dismissed (in trenchant language) *Economic Notes on Insular Free Trade*, the Prime Minister's own writing on the subject. That was a declaration of war too overt and gratuitous to be overlooked. At the Cabinet meeting of 14 September, Balfour made clear – more by attitude than words – that the two critics of his paper would have to go. Lord George Hamilton, also regarded by the Prime Minister as, in the slightly dismissive phrase, 'a Cobdenite', took it for granted, as a matter of honour, that he would go with them. Letters of resignation – the obligations of honour – were sent but never published nor formally accepted. Balfour was scheming to save his government.

The next day the Prime Minister sent the usual letter to the King reporting on the day's Cabinet meeting. It suggested that the free traders were right to suspect that Balfour had become sympathetic to the principle of colonial preference. He saw 'retaliation' as the first step towards much more general 'tariff reform'.

> The root principle for which Mr Balfour pleads is liberty of fiscal negotiation . . . There are, however, two quite different shapes in which this freedom to negotiate might be employed – one against Foreign Governments, the other in favour of our own Colonies . . . It is hard to see how any bargain could be contrived which the colonies would accept and which would not involve taxation on food . . . There are ways in which such taxation could be imposed which would add in no degree to the cost of living of the working class.[12]

The scheme which the Prime Minister described to the King was virtually identical to Joseph Chamberlain's plan for subsidising a state pension with the income raised from customs duties. It would not have been difficult to recruit the Colonial Secretary's services in its implementation, but the co-operation of Chamberlain caused more problems than it solved. The Duke of Devonshire had for some time hinted that he found it difficult to serve in the same Cabinet as Chamberlain – ostensibly because of the Colonial Secretary's protectionist views but equally because of a personal antipathy which amounted to hatred. Without Devonshire the Unionist coalition would collapse. Yet Balfour had no doubt that the Duke would feel an obligation to resign if he learned that three 'free trade ministers' had left the Cabinet because of their irreconcilable opposition to 'Chamberlainite' policies. The Prime Minister needed time to manoeuvre. Fate and royal protocol provided an opportunity. Balfour of Burleigh was 'minister in attendance' on the King at Balmoral. The announcement of the resignations could be plausibly delayed until his return.

It was not difficult to convince Devonshire that there was no need for him to leave the government. Gambling on the Duke's less than complete mastery of tariff reform's arcane details, the Prime Minister began by arguing that a final decision had still to be taken. He promised that a speech he was to make in Sheffield to the National Union of Conservative Associations would make clear that he remained personally agnostic. He might have added that, on 9 September, Joseph Chamberlain had written to him with what can best be described as a post-dated resignation saying that he wanted the freedom to campaign for protection. But Balfour chose to tell Devonshire only half the truth. After the Cabinet meeting of 14 September, Devonshire was asked to stay behind for a private word. He described the conversation which followed when later, belatedly, he too resigned: 'I had an interview with the Prime Minister in which he again referred to the possibility of the resignation of Mr Chamberlain. But even at that time it was not presented to me in such a manner as to lead me to understand that a definite tender of resignation had been made, still less that it was likely to be accepted.'[13]

There can be little doubt that, although Chamberlain did not propose to go at once, he certainly had every intention of going sooner or later. In an extraordinary compact with the Prime Minister, it was agreed that, when he ceased to be Colonial Secretary, a promotion would be offered to his son, Austen – thus preserving the family's connection with the Cabinet. The news of Chamberlain's imminent departure would certainly have kept Devonshire in the Cabinet – necessary in the Prime Minister's view, to avoid the collapse of the coalition. But it might also have made Hamilton, Ritchie and Balfour of Burleigh offer to withdraw their resignations. The Prime Minister wanted them out, not so much for opposing his policy of retaliation but because of what they might do in the future when the issue of tariff reform came to a head. But he did not want to provoke a rank and file revolt by apparently turning on (and turning out) the 'Cobdenite' Cabinet ministers or risk the future of the coalition by alienating Devonshire. One obvious, though apparently undetected, aspect of Balfour's sleight of hand was his habit of talking of the free traders' resignation in public and their dismissal in private.

Balfour knew that the Duke's sense of honour far exceeded his intelligence. So it was necessary to explain how he could remain in the government with a clear conscience. Ritchie and Balfour of Burleigh had, he insisted, behaved in a way which Devonshire would not even contemplate. Their resignations would be accepted, not because they held views which the Duke shared, but because they had expressed them in a disloyal way. John Dunville, the Duke's private secretary, made a note of what at least one party to the Downing Street conversation believed had been said. 'Mr Balfour's remarks led you to believe that Lord Balfour and Ritchie were dismissed on account of the memorandum on the fiscal question which they had recently circulated . . . He hinted that Chamberlain might resign.'[14]

The next day, at least according to the Duke's diary note, Balfour went a little further. Once again news of Chamberlain's intention was linked to an explanation of why the free traders had to go. Their insubordination had not been confined to one incident. Indeed the Memorandum was the least of their offences. Devonshire showed no sign of noticing that the explanation had changed. 'You saw Mr Balfour at 7 pm. He informed you that Chamberlain was almost certain to resign. Asked you not to mention it to anyone. He further informed you that Ritchie and B of B were not dismissed on account of the Memorandum which they circulated but on account of the attitude that they had assumed towards the fiscal question through all its stages.'[15]

Balfour must have believed that his object had been achieved. But the Duke of Devonshire had qualms about breaking ranks with his free-trade comrades. The qualms were not sufficient to make him resign on the spot, and his wife was determined that he should not sacrifice what was left of his career. According to one acerbic observer, she had 'not yet surrendered the ambition that he should be Prime Minister'*[16] and found it easy to convince her husband that it was his public duty both to survive in government and to make sure that Chamberlain did not. So he took advantage of Balfour's calculated ambiguities to claim that he feared that Chamberlain would remain – a situation which he would find intolerable. On 15 September, the day after the 'confidential' conversation, Devonshire sent the Prime Minister a formal letter of resignation. It virtually invited Balfour not to accept it. Once again he provided his own record of events with a

---

*The Duke had married, late in life, the Dowager Duchess of Manchester. As a result she became known as the Double Duchess.

note dictated to his secretary. 'After leaving Mr Balfour you decided to send on your letter of resignation with a covering note saying that if you had written under any misapprehension of the position, it would be for Mr Balfour to correct you if he wished to do so.'

The letter itself was intended to meet the demands of honour by appearing to assert his solidarity with his free-trade colleagues. What at first sounded like an assertion of loyalty was really preparation for abandoning his friends. 'If I am acting under any misapprehension it was shared by others who after consultation with me have taken more prompt action than I did . . . I could not honourably reconsider my position in any way without further communication with them.'[17] The Duke was desperate to find grounds for reconsideration – or to have the Prime Minister find them for him. Balfour decided that another meeting was necessary if his objectives were to be achieved.

Before his success could be confirmed he had work to do. Lord George Hamilton, Ritchie and Balfour of Burleigh were notified that their resignations had been accepted. Chamberlain decided, or agreed, to make his resignation public at the same time and to make equally plain that he remained in general support of the government. Balfour drafted a telegram to the King to tell His Majesty that he had lost his Chancellor of the Exchequer, Secretary of State for India, Secretary of State for Scotland and Colonial Secretary on the same afternoon. He thought it prudent to add that he was 'uncertain about the attitude of the Duke of Devonshire'.[18] On the next day he called on the Duke at Devonshire House (itself a sign of the wish to conciliate) and told him that Chamberlain had definitely gone. Devonshire, in a fine show of loyalty, replied that if he was asked to reconsider his position, 'the natural course would be to ask [the Prime Minister] to extend a similar invitation to the other ministers'. That the Prime Minister declined to do. The Duke, having made his token gesture, then 'consented to withdraw [his] resignation'.[19] Victor Cavendish recorded his amazement and anxiety. 'Uncle Cav induced to stay in at last moment. It all came as a great surprise. Impossible fully to judge what the result will be. Probably there will be an election soon.'[20]

The Duke of Devonshire's letter of explanation to Charles Ritchie was a model of self-justification. 'I have . . . seen Balfour and am able now to tell you of what I think you will agree with me is a fundamental alteration . . . To my astonishment he informed me last night of the probability, and has today assured me of the certainty, of Chamberlain's resignation. This wholly unexpected result has led me to reconsider the decision which I formed.' Not surprisingly, Ritchie was outraged. Lord George Hamilton and Balfour of Burleigh reacted with more aristocratic detachment and declared that they had no cause for complaint. But Lord James of Hereford (Leader of the Liberal Unionists and outside the Cabinet) wrote to tell the Duke, 'Your agreement to become a supporter of Balfour's Protectionist Views has caused me as much sadness as surprise.'[21]

Ritchie himself waited twenty-four hours before he wrote his reply.

> Goschen and Beach★ came to see me . . . to ask how it happened that I sent in my resignation when you remained, it having been impressed upon me, as I think I told you, that it was most essential that we should act together. I am, of course, obliged to tell them what took place, namely that we separated on the Tuesday with the understanding that all our resignations were to go in that night with the proviso (on your part) that Balfour wished to see you before you took your final step. You, however, said that there was no chance of his altering your determination.[22]

The Duke of Devonshire replied that he had no recollection of 'any understanding that we should all act together',[23] but Lord George Hamilton endorsed Ritchie's view. 'I clearly understood that we were all acting together and that, in recognition of this co-operation, the Duke (on behalf of us four) conveyed our resignation to the Prime Minister.'[24]

Even as the bitter correspondence continued, Balfour must have believed that he had achieved his objective. G. E. Buckle, the editor of *The Times*, was an ardent supporter of the government, but, even allowing for the prejudices of a partisan, his editorial seemed to do more than set out the details of the Prime Minister's devious triumph. 'While Mr Balfour is backed by the Duke of Devonshire and

★Both Liberal Unionists who had served as Chancellor of the Exchequer.

the rest of the Ministry, except the Cobdenite seceders, and while he has Mr Chamberlain's loyal and independent support, the reconstruction of the Cabinet need not be expected to involve very serious difficulties.'[25] Buckle was wrong.

The King had asked to be consulted before the resignations were announced and the Prime Minister had replied to the request with an apology which was expanded by a barely credible explanation. News of the royal request had not reached Downing Street until after the announcement had been made. Anxious not to offend His Majesty a second time, Balfour asked 'permission to approach Lord Milner for the Colonial Office'. The King gave his enthusiastic agreement. Milner, still in his post as the High Commissioner for South Africa, was a hero of imperialistic England. To the consternation of both the King and the Prime Minister, he declined. The King, deeply offended by Milner's rejection of what he regarded as a royal command, told Balfour, 'When a public servant of the Crown is asked by the Prime Minister to undertake a duty which the latter considers him well qualified to fill, it is in the King's opinion decidedly wrong of him to decline it'. He added, in a note of intentional (though meaningless) menace, 'The King will not forget now or in the future.'[26] No doubt Balfour faced the prospect of Milner's future punishment with his usual equanimity, but he must have been at least irritated by the King's consequent determination to interfere in what was left of the reshuffle. Alfred Lyttelton was accepted, after some argument, as the new Colonial Secretary, but the suggestion that Arnold Foster should become Secretary of State for India the King rejected outright. Edward VII, irked by Balfour's failure to consult him about the resignations, was determined to exercise his full constitutional rights before endorsing the replacements. The tedious business of filling the gaps and placating the King had not been completed by the time that the National Union of Conservative Associations assembled for its annual meeting.

Almost two weeks had passed since the resignation of the free traders and the recriminations which had followed the Duke of Devonshire's decision to remain, when, on 1 October 1903, the National Union met in Sheffield. It was clear from the start that supporters of Chamberlain and 'imperial preference' made up a majority

of the audience. Perhaps that is why Balfour took as the theme of the
eve of congress address his *Economic Notes on Insular Free Trade*. The
Duke of Devonshire listened to the speech with mounting anxiety.
Two days earlier, he had shown Lord Derby the letter which he had
received from Ritchie and complained, 'To think that I have gone
through all my life and then at the end of it to have those sort of allegations thrown at my head.'[27] He was looking for an excuse to clear
his conscience and redeem his good name. The speech was slightly
more enthusiastic about a retaliatory tariff than Balfour's address to the
Cabinet of 14 September had been. The pretext had been provided.
Devonshire resigned from the government, and a ministerial career,
which had begun forty years before, was over.

It is impossible not to feel some sympathy for the old man, but
there is little doubt that he deserved to take a share of the blame for
the fiasco which followed. The chief culprit was Balfour. His apolo-
gists, led by Winston Churchill, insisted that he had written to the
Duke of Devonshire as soon as he knew of Chamberlain's definite
intention to resign and that the Duke, out at dinner without the key
to the red Cabinet box in which the letter was sent, had only himself
to blame for being overtaken by events. Balfour himself never made
such a claim. Indeed, in his letter of reconciliation to Devonshire
(written years later) he got very near to admitting that he had chosen
to divide the free traders in order to rule a protectionist Cabinet: 'I
regarded them [Ritchie and Hamilton] . . . as having practically sev-
ered their connection with the Fiscal Reform Cabinet. I regarded you
as still potentially a member of it and I was therefore quite prepared to
discuss with you what I should certainly have never discussed with
them.'[28]

In what he must have prided himself was an admirable understatement of Balfour's guilt, the Duke of Devonshire admitted that he
'shared the feeling that the Prime Minister's ingenuity is open to criticism'.[29] But the Prime Minister was only able to achieve his objective
because Devonshire was so willing to be tricked – if, as a result, he
could retain both the leadership of the House of Lords and the undi-
minished respect of his colleagues.

After the failure of his strategies, Balfour's contempt for the Duke
of Devonshire was boundless. On receiving the resignation letter

which he had done so much to avoid, he dictated an angry reply – as he explained, to emphasise his fury – 'before [he] had even had his bath'.[30] The report he made to the King suggests that his mood did not change during the rest of the day. 'The Duke of Devonshire's conduct has been pitiable. Nor is it possible to excuse, or even understand, his vacillations without remembering that he has, without doubt, put himself somehow in the power of Mr Ritchie and his friends. He is forced to behave badly to me, lest he should be publicly taxed with behaving badly to them.'[31] Nor did his opinion alter with the years, though by 1910 he chose to diminish the Duke's reputation with mock sympathy, not open assault. 'Dear Devonshire! . . . It was all a muddle. He got himself into such a position that he had to behave badly to someone – and there it was! But it never made the slightest difference to my love for him.'[32]

It seems unlikely that the Prime Minister exhibited even mock sympathy for the old Duke in the immediate aftermath of his protracted resignation. Devonshire had left the government in a shambles. Austen Chamberlain became Chancellor of the Exchequer – a far more senior office than any ministry his father had ever occupied – and Hugh Arnold Forster (despite the King's reservations) went to the War Office. But the Unionists were still deeply divided over tariff reform and the resignations had, as always, added personal bitterness to profoundly held conviction. Naturally enough, the Liberal Party set out to exploit the divisions.

The 1904 Parliament opened on 8 January. The Opposition proposed an amendment to 'the Loyal Address' which explicitly condemned 'food taxes'. Arthur Balfour was in bed with 'a feverish cold'. That accounted for only one of the absentees from the government lobby. The Unionists' nominal majority in the House of Commons was one hundred and thirty-four. On the food tax vote it fell to fifty-one. The government was on the point of collapse and Balfour was advised by John Sandars, his long-standing private secretary and indispensable confidant, that the road to survival led from South Yorkshire. The government might be rallied round 'the Sheffield Policy' of applying tariffs to those countries which discriminated against British exports. By adding that the taxes should not be imposed on food imports – and emphasising that he accepted that other Conservatives felt differently –

Balfour was able to limp through most of the next year. His prospects of survival were much increased by the robust support of Joseph Chamberlain, who wrote to his son, 'In no case am I going to fight against Balfour's government. I would much rather go out of politics.'[33] And he added – with the bellicosity that was sometimes a stronger feature of his politics than sound judgement – that the tariff reformers in the Tory Party had nowhere else to go. He was proved wrong almost immediately. Eleven Unionist free traders, including Winston Churchill, crossed the floor of the House of Commons.

The government needed Joe Chamberlain, and he continued to support Balfour because he hoped that, sooner or later, he would be able to elbow the Prime Minister into accepting across-the-board tariff reform. He knew that the unequivocal rejection of free trade which he planned could only result in the Unionists losing their House of Commons majority and that, in the general election which followed, Balfour would be defeated. But, when the election was over, the Unionist parliamentary party, that would make up the Opposition, would contain a protectionist majority. And who could predict what the consequences of that would be? A new leader would certainly replace Balfour.

The Prime Minister had quite different – indeed diametrically opposed – objectives. When Austen Chamberlain suggested a colonial trade conference to buy him more time, Balfour seized on the idea at once and announced, during a speech in Edinburgh on 2 October 1904, that he intended to call the Empire together. He then added, without the knowledge of Joseph Chamberlain, that the conclusion of the conference might form the basis of tariff reform which a Unionist government would implement after the proposal had been endorsed in two general elections.

Although Joseph Chamberlain was reluctant to wait so long, he was still inclined to support Balfour as the best hope of tariff reform on offer. To him it was 'inconceivable . . . that the Prime Minister can contemplate a conference with the colonies without being prepared to give immediate effect to any policy agreed to . . .'[34] But to make sure that he had not overestimated Balfour's respect for the Empire, Chamberlain determined to tie the Prime Minister's hands by committing first the Council and then the full Conference of the

National Union of Conservative Associations to tariff reform. His agent, Henry Chaplin, achieved both objectives and succeeded in defeating a free trade resolution.

The Prime Minister's public humiliation, which Chamberlain must have intended, was avoided by the diversion of the general public's attention towards a tragic, but undeniably bizarre, incident on the Dogger Bank. The Russian Baltic fleet, steaming to the Far East to pursue the war against Japan, mistook a group of Hull trawlers for the Japanese navy steaming in the opposite direction. The Russians opened fire and killed or wounded ten Hull fishermen. For a moment, all of Britain was consumed with fury. Russia offered an immediate apology and massive compensation. But it was some weeks before Balfour was able to return to the toils of free trade and the stream of House of Commons motions which demanded that the government abandon all thought of tariff reform. Many of them appeared on the order paper above the name of Winston Churchill.

A more cunning motion than anything which the impetuous young turncoat proposed moved that 'a proposition laid down by Mr Chamberlain in 1903 in Glasgow to the effect that on average ten per cent all round [tariff] on manufactured goods shall be opposed . . .'[35] It was not only the passionate 'Cobdenites' who wanted to see the resolution carried; in the House of Commons Chamberlain attracted a good deal of personal animosity. Austen Chamberlain's proposal that opposition to his father's policy should be made a matter of confidence – 'put on all the pressure we can and dare our men to turn us out' – was therefore far too dangerous for Balfour's taste. The Prime Minister knew that the free traders would be reinforced by MPs like Iwan Muller who told him, 'I would far sooner risk defeat . . . than carry on with Highbury patronage.'[36] (Highbury was Chamberlain's Birmingham home.)

The Prime Minister believed that, by prevarication, he could hold his party together. He refused to have the resolution dismissed by a technical device which avoided a vote. Instead, with a fine lack of consistency, he agreed that the government should ignore the vote completely. 'Courteous to the last, he remained to hear the vigorous speech delivered across the table. Then with smiling countenance, languorous grace and lingering step, he fared forth out of the chamber.'[37]

Unfortunately two government back-benchers were not so quick-witted or fleet-footed. The resolution was carried by two hundred and fifty-four votes to two. Chamberlain was not amused. The government, he decided, was doomed. The longer it hung on, the greater its eventual defeat would be.

Problems always multiply for broken-backed governments. So it was with Balfour's administration. The Empire was experiencing growing pains. Curzon – infuriated by the Cabinet's decision to give Lord Kitchener, Commander-in-Chief, sole and supreme command of the Indian Army – resigned the high office of Viceroy. Although he had leaked his criticisms of the government to newspapers through the device of making a 'policy speech' to the Indian Legislative Council, the Cabinet accepted the resignation with courteous regret. Curzon responded with a statement which made clear that he disagreed with more government policy than its view on the proper chain of military command. Then, worse still, the recruitment of Chinese 'indentured labour' to work in the gold mines of South Africa was, perhaps unreasonably, judged to be the government's responsibility.

The mine owners of the Transvaal constantly needed additional workers. The obvious source of new labour was China. 'Coolies' were anxious to volunteer, but the racial prejudices of the Boers did not allow them to enter the country as free men. Ten thousand Chinese labourers were imported into South Africa, all of them indentured to live and work like slaves. They were confined in compounds which they were only allowed to leave, for the whole period of their indenture, during their daily shifts in the mines. Disease was rife, punishment for misdemeanours brutal and, since no women were allowed in the compounds, homosexual rape was common. The High Commissioner, Milner, saw the whole issue as no more than a question of labour economics and therefore well outside the jurisdiction of the imperial Parliament, but a coalition of moralists and radicals thought differently. It was not a situation with which Balfour was ideally equipped to deal. His insouciance looked like indifference. Support for the government was haemorrhaging away. Joe Chamberlain smelt blood.

The tariff reformers grew increasingly restless. On 15 April 1905,

Chamberlain presided over a meeting of potential supporters. As is the way with putative parliamentary revolts, the gathering began with the counting of heads. It concluded that three hundred and forty-three of the three hundred and seventy-four Unionist MPs demanded some sort of tariff reform. In common with parliamentary revolts down the ages, fewer than half of the dissidents signed the petition which Chamberlain presented to Balfour. The Prime Minister still searched for a stratagem rather than a policy, and since nobody doubted his ingenuity, few people were surprised when he suggested an amendment to his own plan. There was no need to hold a general election until 1907. The Colonial Conference, which had been adjourned in 1902, was due to reconvene in 1906. The Prime Minister proposed that the House of Commons consider 'colonial preference' at the conference and go to the country committed to whatever was there agreed when the Parliament completed its full term. He had bought himself two years. Or so he believed.

Joe Chamberlain had become impatient. Two years was a long time to wait and he had always been in a hurry. He wanted Balfour to be more positive, perhaps even enthusiastic, in his acceptance of tariff reform, but enthusiasm was not Balfour's style. Chamberlain began to show displeasure by finding fault with the government which he was pledged to support. Balfour addressed the party faithful in the Albert Hall but Chamberlain complained that it did not give enough emphasis to the fiscal issue. When the Conservative Central Office – 'the spring of all abomination' in Chamberlain's opinion – issued a leaflet based on the Albert Hall speech, he complained that it had not dealt with colonial preference at all.

Balfour's style did not suit a government under siege. On 22 May, pressed in the House to set out his own position on the question which obsessed the House of Commons, he remained 'lolling with studied negligence on the Treasury Bench'. After forty minutes of uproar, he rose in his place. 'It is not consistent with usage or ideas of justice that the criminal in the dock – and that is the situation which I am supposed to occupy – should offer his defence before he has heard the whole of the accusation.' Forty more minutes of mayhem followed. Then the Deputy Speaker adjourned the House. Nobody believed that the government could last much longer. On 20 July 1905 it was actually defeated in the House of Commons on the motion to accept the Irish Estimates. Sir Michael Hicks Beach, Unionist Chancellor of the Exchequer only three years earlier, rushed into the Prime Minister's outside office and, in a passion which resulted both from his opposition to tariff reform and from respect for parliamentary propriety, announced, 'The Prime Minister must accept defeat and resign.'[38]

The King, on the other hand, 'insisted that every effort be made by Mr Balfour to maintain himself in office'.[39] The Prime Minister gladly accepted his sovereign's advice. Indeed, hanging on – motivated far less by personal ambition than the conviction that only his party could preserve the interests of the country – had become an obsession. 'Surveying a suddenly riven party, he set himself the task of preventing any widening of the fissure . . . He had answered at question time, made speeches in successive debates and never committed himself by an embarrassing admission. That may not be the highest form of statesmanship. As an intellectual feat it is unparalleled.'[40]

On 10 August 1905 the Unionist leadership considered the arguments for an immediate election. Once again, like governments down the ages, it found the case for staying more persuasive than the alternative. Outrage over the Chinese indentured labour was subsiding. The Liberals were running out of money to maintain their organisation in the country. Given time, the party might rally round its leadership. That view was not confirmed when, three months later, the Duke of Devonshire declined, with appropriate aristocratic hauteur, to announce his reconciliation with the Prime Minister.

Then, in November, it seemed that the Unionists' luck had at last changed. Lord Rosebery, speaking in Bodmin, denounced the Liberal Party's traditional commitment to Irish Home Rule in the clear belief that he represented a substantial number of Liberals who opposed the party's policy but lacked the courage to speak out against the Ark of Gladstone's Covenant. In fact Asquith – who had openly expressed his own doubts about Home Rule – had come to an accommodation with Campbell-Bannerman. Indeed the Liberal Leader's announcement of step-by-step devolution represented a compromise which had been successfully designed to unite two extremes. Lord Esher, who was with the Prime Minister when the decision to call an election was taken, claimed that, shortly after he had convinced the Cabinet that the time to dissolve Parliament had come, Balfour met Asquith and only then discovered that the Liberals would fight the election campaign united. 'He seemed a little moved, which was not strange on relinquishing his great office, but his spirits revived almost immediately.'[41]

His despondency was justified. The Liberal Party – the beneficiary of circumstances as much as of wisdom and foresight – had pulled itself together. There was still dissatisfaction with Campbell-Bannerman. A clear majority of the parliamentary party would have preferred Asquith as leader. But, thanks to the prospect of office, open revolt was replaced by silent dissatisfaction. The 'Compact of Regulas' – a name taken from the place in which the plot was hatched had aimed at persuading Campbell-Bannerman to take a peerage while Lord Spencer became party leader and putative prime minister and prepared the way for the party's real choice. Hopes of success were encouraged by Campbell-Bannerman's still deteriorating health and his growing concern for his wife's even greater sickness. They were at first reinforced in their determination by the King who, in the early months of his reign, had taken such a dislike to the Liberal Leader that he was reluctant to dine at the same table. The dissidents then began to worry that Campbell-Bannerman's radical supporters would accuse them of intriguing at Court against their lawful leaders. That problem was solved by Edward VII, who met the object of his dislike while on holiday in Marienbad and decided, after all, that he was not a bad fellow.

The plot to remove him was finally frustrated by Campbell-Bannerman himself who – when the Tory tariff war seemed likely to topple the government – proceeded to prepare for office as if his right to the Downing Street tenancy was unquestioned and unquestionable. On 13 November 1905, Mrs Asquith, who was having her hair washed in her bedroom, was interrupted by her excited but not altogether contented husband. He gave her a verbatim account of a meeting with Campbell-Bannerman. 'Suddenly he said that he thought things looked like coming to a head politically and that any day after parliament met, we might expect a general election. He gathered that he would probably be the man the King would send for . . . What would you like? The Exchequer I suppose?'[42]

Balfour resigned office on 4 December 1905. There was some disagreement within the Opposition leadership as to whether the
Liberals should take office or force an immediate general election,
and the sort of horse-trading which invariably accompanied the
allocation of the senior portfolios when a new government was
formed. The Compact of Regulas, still in the minds of Asquith and
his friends, made them hope that the retirement which they could not
impose might be accepted voluntarily. And there was a moment when
they thought that Campbell-Bannerman might step aside. But the
prospect of office encouraged renewed loyalty. Asquith – so involved
with the composition of the government that he left a fancy-dress
party at Hatfield House and drove to Belgravia to impress his opinions
on the putative prime minister – became universally acknowledged
heir apparent. Parliament met only for the dissolution.

Campbell-Bannerman, anxious to preserve unity in his party,
promised no Home Rule until after a second general election and
Rosebery, misjudging the mood of the moment, tried so hard to
alienate the Liberal high command from their leader that he only succeeded in alienating it from him. Ireland was barely an issue. Polling
began on 13 January 1906. The Unionists won 157 seats in the House
of Commons, Labour 53 and the Irish Nationalists 83. The Liberals,
with 377 Members, had a majority of 132 over all other parties and
could assume that, in most divisions, it would be supported by the
Labour MPs, some of whom called themselves 'Lib-Labs'. The apparently invincible Unionists had been defeated and the Liberals (once
thought to be destroyed by Home Rule) began a full decade of government. They had still to reconcile deep division over Ireland and
conscience and conviction had begun to turn Parliament's mind to
Ireland once again. But conscience and conviction were not enough
to encourage the new Liberal government to expose its divisions.
The defeated Unionists' one consolation was that Campbell-
Bannerman did not need the support of the Irish Nationalist
Members of Parliament. The best for which Irish nationalists could
hope was Home Rule by stealth and by instalments.

CHAPTER 7

Uniting the Nation

For most of the nineteenth century, men of goodwill and sound judgement had believed, despite the empirical evidence all around them, that the problem of poverty could be solved only by the poor themselves. The belief in self-help had, largely thanks to Jeremy Bentham, become the social doctrine of radicals as well as reactionaries. For a hundred years, politicians of all persuasions accepted that the encouragement to industry and thrift should be matched by disincentives to irresponsibility and sloth. In 1900, the Poor Law Amendment Act of 1834 still restricted paupers' access to 'outdoor relief' and offered them the daunting alternative of the workhouse, which Edwin Chadwick, the inspiration of the legislation, described as 'uninviting places of wholesome restraint'. The notion that poverty was usually self-induced and could be reduced by imposing fearful penalties on the poor survived the death of Queen Victoria, but at the beginning of King Edward's reign influential voices had begun to advance a different social theory. Perhaps the starving multitudes should be helped rather than punished.

In 1890, William Booth, the founder of the Salvation Army (and no relation to Charles, his namesake, the social statistician), had published *In Darkest England*, a gloriously impractical plan for the elimination of unemployment. He proposed the creation of 'Overseas Colonies' to which willing workers would go after learning a craft in the 'City Colonies'. In 1904, an Interdepartmental Committee on Physical Deterioration proposed a variation on the same idea. The 'waste element in society' should be transported.

Like so many early Edwardian policy-makers, the Committee members drew a sharp distinction between the needs of the deserving and the undeserving poor. Only four years earlier that distinction had been given official recognition. The House of Commons Select Committee on the Aged and Deserving Poor had recommended that ancient worthies should not be left to the mercy of the Boards of Guardians and the Poor Law Commissioners. They had proposed that £7 million be made available for distribution to anyone over seventy who was destitute and could be proven to have done all in his or her power to avoid becoming a pauper – including becoming dependent on the Poor Law. Its provisions were overtaken by a genuine, if not hugely generous, national insurance act.

However, even in the harshest days of what Alfred Doolittle called 'middle-class morality', the government understood that, while some adult citizens might be beyond redemption, most children were capable of salvation and that healthy minds were most likely to mature in healthy bodies. So the 1904 Committee's recommendations included medical inspection in all schools and the provision of free school meals. It was not the beginning of the state's acceptance of its obligations towards the very young. A year earlier, the Royal Commission on Physical Training in Scotland had proposed the introduction of school meals. But the 1904 report amounted to official sanction for a whole swathe of ideas which had gained ground in Parliament ever since the new Labour Members had come together to form a coherent group.

It had been a Labour MP who had moved, from the back benches, a bill which the government adopted and passed into law as the Education (Provision of School Meals) Act, 1906. That legislation empowered local education authorities to provide meals for the 'necessitous poor'. In the same year, the Education (Administrative Provisions) Bill instituted the system of medical inspection which the Committee on Physical Deterioration had proposed two years before. An amendment to add the creation of a schools medical service, which would have allowed diagnosis to be followed by treatment, was defeated, but the notion of child welfare had become clearly established in the official mind. In 1907 'borstals' were established for young offenders. The regimes were rigorous, but minors were no longer to serve their sentences in adult gaols. The Children's Act of 1908 made neglect a criminal offence for the first time. The decision, taken in 1902, to require the registration of midwives was of equal benefit to mothers and babies. Registration was only available to women with rudimentary nursing knowledge and skills. Mrs Gamp's day had passed.

Improvements in welfare have always resulted from a combination of altruism and political expedience. In 1905, Balfour – oppressed by divisions within his party over tariff reform and harassed by the Labour Party – was anxious to make a gesture of friendship towards organised labour. He was not prepared to meet the unions' demand for legislation which reversed the Taff Vale Judgement – the High Court ruling that made them liable for damage caused by their members to the interests and property of employers.* But he was willing to take action against unemployment. He regarded providing work for the willing as right and necessary on its own merits. Balfour was amongst the first Conservatives to realise that Britain would only maintain its position in the world if the health and education of the labour force were improved. Rowntree, Cadbury and Charles Booth had made clear that health depended on standard of living and that standard of living depended on remunerative and regular employment.

Balfour therefore introduced an Unemployed Workers Bill which he hoped would meet the nation's needs and the trade unions' demands at a minimal cost. An even cheaper palliative was the Aliens Bill which fulfilled the promise of the 1900 election to restrict the number of immigrants who entered the country. Cabinet fears that imposing restrictions on entry would be 'full of difficulties' had been confirmed when, in 1904, the first bill failed to gain a parliamentary majority. It was redrafted so as to require immigrants to prove that they could support themselves rather than to prohibit categories of immigration and was passed in 1905.

---

*For a full account of the Taff Vale Judgement, its reversal and consequences, see Chapter 11, 'United We Stand'.

The Unemployed Workmen's Act, which did little more than monitor local levels of unemployment, was approached with great caution, under the supervision of Gerald Balfour, the Prime Minister's brother, who had succeeded Walter Long – essentially a country squire despite his years in government – at the Local Government Board. The acceptance that the government should take even indirect action to alleviate unemployment amounted to a huge shift in both the political philosophy and the economic judgement of the Conservative Party. Indeed, even Gladstonian Liberals believed that Parliament's only duty was to protect the nation from invasion and its citizens from crime. Balfour had, therefore, made a great ideological leap. His letter to the King of 28 February 1905 demonstrated how anxious he was not to appear to be hurtling headlong into uncharted territory. In London, a local employment committee supervised by the Board of Guardians and the borough councils had already initiated schemes which matched unemployed workers to jobs. If such a scheme were implemented with 'severe but kindly conscientiousness . . . much good would be done and many persons who would otherwise sink into pauperism and become a charge on the rates might be able to tide over the season of commercial depression and wait for better times.' However, there were dangers. It was particularly important to make sure that the funds made available by the Bill were not squandered on schemes which debilitated rather than redeemed.

> It would be a social calamity if these labour committees were to make such a use of the penny rate as to create a new class of semi-paupers . . . i.e. labourers who got employment in the ordinary way during the summer months and each recurring winter claimed from the local authority to be provided with work out of public funds. Those persons would have the privileges of pauperism while retaining the full rights of citizenship.[1]

To prevent such a calamity, the President of the Local Government Board examined the draft bill 'to see if anything could be done to guard against abuse'. The objective was achieved by changes which 'cut out everything which involved the payment of wages out of rates'.[2] The result was what Balfour called 'a machinery bill'. It gave the Local Government Board power to set up local employment committees on its own initiative. Local rates could be used to keep a register of the unemployed, establish labour exchanges, assist emigration and acquire land for farm colonies – another adaptation of the ideas laid down by William Booth in the much derided *In Darkest England*. They could not, however, be used for direct payment to the unemployed and the immediate relief of distress. A public appeal for funds, led by Queen Alexandra, raised £125,000 to supplement the committees' activities. But it was not the extension of the privilege of pauperism that caused Balfour most concern. He knew that the machinery which the Unemployed Workmen's Act set up to fit men to jobs did little to reduce unemployment. Realising that more was needed, but uncertain about how to proceed, he took refuge in the expedient employed by uncertain prime ministers down the ages. He set up a Royal Commission on the Poor Law. It was almost his last act before leaving office.

Lord George Hamilton, a free-trade rebel, was the surprise choice for chairman. Balfour's motives were altruistic, but his instinct was political. He had therefore hoped to embarrass the Opposition by asking Lord Rosebery to take on the job. But colleagues had convinced him that the former Liberal Prime Minister would grow bored with the continual meetings and abandon the work half done. Balfour's first approach was made instead to the Duke of Devonshire in the expectation – justified as it turned out – that he would be flattered, but would decline. Hamilton was appointed, partly because Balfour thought that he should earn the 'first class pension' which he had received after resigning from the India Office over the issue of free trade and the Cabinet in 1903. It was an unpropitious beginning to what turned out to be a crucial step along the road to the new view of the government's responsibilities: the condition of the poor was becoming the government's concern.

The selection of the Royal Commission's members, discussed at the Cabinet on 23 June 1905, was 'the subject of most anxious deliberations'.[3] The result was the appointment of genuine experts in the subject but, with three exceptions, experts who held the view that the principal object of organised charity should be the moral improvement of those who received it. C. S. Lock, Helen Bosanquet and

Octavia Hill were all prominent in the Charity Organisation Society which formally espoused that philosophy. The minority was led by Beatrice Webb. She conducted what at first was a single-handed campaign against the Local Government Board's attempt to persuade the Commission that it should 'recommend reversion to the principles of 1834 . . . [in order] to stem the tide of philanthropic impulse that was sweeping away the old embankment of deterrent tests for the receipt of relief'.[4] Eighteen thirty-four was the year of the Poor Law Act. The evidence given to the Commission by J. S. Davy, the head of the Poor Law division of the Local Government Board, confirmed the Establishment's determination to retain the principles of punitive relief. Asked whether the deterrent tests, laid down by the Poor Law Amendment Act, were suitable to a pauper who had lost his job because of a trade depression, he replied in a paraphrase of the 1834 report: 'A man must stand by his accidents. He must suffer for the general good of the body politic.'[5]

That view was wholly consistent with the philosophy on which the Poor Law had been based. To be eligible for 'relief', a pauper must suffer 'first the loss of personal reputation (which is understood by the stigma of pauperism itself), second the loss of personal freedom (which is secured by detention in a workhouse) and third the loss of political freedom (which is secured by disenfranchisement)'.[6]

The success with which the workhouses had pursued those aims was confirmed by evidence to the Women's Local Government Society* in 1909.

Women nosed around (often literally so) those sanitary facilities and 'parts of the hospitals and workhouses which the gentlemen very rarely visit' . . . Mrs Evans suspected that the ophthalmia and ringworm she noted spread because fifty-six girls bathed in one tub of water, shared half a dozen towels, five dirty brushes and two and a half broken combs between them. Another workhouse, they found, had two small hand basins for 120 and

---

*The WLGS encouraged women's involvement in the institutions to which they could be elected in the years before they obtained the parliamentary franchise.

WCs without paper which were locked at night . . . Dunmore in
1904 swarmed with rats . . . Billericay sick, in 1905, were still
sleeping on the floor. Louisa Twining found euphemistically
described 'dust heaps' and stained and dirty linen lying around
the wards.[7]

By the time that the Royal Commission reported in 1909, the
great Liberal landslide had swept away the Unionist government and
put in its place an administration more likely to be sympathetic to the
inevitable outcome of Beatrice Webb's disagreements with the
bureaucrats of the Local Government Board – a minority report. The
majority report, signed by the chairman and fourteen other members,
wanted, in effect, a more compassionate Poor Law. Some of the
stigma should be removed, it argued, by a change of name as well as
a change in attitude towards the types of social need which did not,
under the 1834 Act, qualify for relief. The minority report – signed by
Beatrice Webb, George Lansbury and Francis Chancellor, a future
bishop of Birmingham – wanted to replace the old Poor Law with a
completely new system of 'assistance'. The underlying principle of its
recommendations was that poverty was more likely to be the result of
the way in which the economy was organised than of the moral failings of the unemployed. There is no doubt that the three Fabian
Socialists wanted 'better people'. But they believed that improvement
was more likely to come about by changes in society than by individual exhortations and intimidation.

Both the minority and majority reports proposed what amounted
to the creation of new institutions for the distribution of 'assistance'.
The elected boards of guardians – which defined destitution in a
variety of different ways and judged 'need' against criteria which
varied only in degrees of severity – should be abolished. Their duties
ought to be assumed by local authorities which distributed help –
no longer to be thought of as 'relief' – according to nationally determined standards. The minority report also recommended a more
radical organisation. Separate departments within the national government should accept responsibility for supervising the assault on the
different causes of social distress – ill health, old age and fluctuations
in the labour market. The notion that able-bodied men should, during

periods of economic depression, receive government help in the search for jobs was near to revolutionary. The minority report went further. It advocated a Ministry of Labour which, as well as supervising labour exchanges and organising retraining programmes, actually invested in public works. Four million pounds should be provided each year to spend as necessary to see the economy through periods of slump.

It is not surprising that the minority report – anticipating both Keynesian theories of cyclical management and what amounted to some of the administrative structure of the mid-century welfare state – should have been unacceptable to the Edwardian Liberal Party and the government which it formed in 1906. But the rejection of the majority report – or at least its neglect – needs some explanation. It is provided by the character and career of John Burns, President of the Local Government Board and the first working man to become a Cabinet Minister.

John Burns was by trade an engineer and, by early conviction, a Marxist Socialist. In 1884 he had joined the Social Democratic Federation, but four years later formed the Independent Battersea Labour League and, as its nominee, became a member of the London County Council. Eight years later, he became Battersea's Member of Parliament but refused either to be called 'Labour' or to be associated with the trade union group in the House of Commons. When Campbell-Bannerman formed his government in 1905, he offered Burns the Presidency of the Local Government Board. Burns replied, 'Well done, Sir 'Enry. That's the most popular thing you've done yet.'[8] Lord George Hamilton, the chairman of the Royal Commission, believed that, had the Board of Local Government been led by any other Liberal of the day, the majority report (certainly) and the minority report (possibly) would have been implemented.

Two years before he joined the Cabinet, Burns had set out his personal social philosophy. It might have been designed to prepare the way for the Royal Commission's minority report. 'Individual effort is almost relatively impossible to cope with the big problem of poverty as we see it. I want the municipality to be a helping hand to the man with a desire of sympathy, to help the fallen when it is not in their power to help themselves. I believe the proper business of the

Municipality is to do for the individual, merged in the mass, what the individual cannot do so well alone.'[9]

The syntactical inadequacy of that declaration cannot obscure its progressive message. But office changed Burns's view of life. He became absolutely certain that the institutions of the state should not 'supersede the mother and they should not, by over-attention, sterilise her initiative and capacity to do what every mother should be able to do for herself'. The practical result of his conversion was an enthusiasm for the workhouse in preference to outdoor relief. Beatrice Webb had no doubt about its cause. 'Burns is a monstrosity, an enormous personal vanity feeding on the deference of flattery yielded to patronage and power. He talks incessantly and never listens to anyone except the officials to whom he must listen in order to accomplish the routine work of his office. Hence he is completely in their hands and is becoming the most hidebound of departmental chiefs.'[10]

Fortunately, other members of the Cabinet were of a more independent turn of mind. Prominent among them was Winston Churchill – aristocratic by origin and Conservative by initial political conviction but, by nature, an active rather than a passive minister. In the early years of the century, as he adjusted his personal philosophy to accommodate the Liberal Party which he had joined, he defined himself as 'both a collectivist and an individualist . . . The existing organisation of society is driven by one mainspring – competitive selection . . . I do not want to see impaired the vigour of competition, but we can do much to mitigate the consequences of failure . . . We want to have free competition upwards. We decline to allow free competition to run downwards.'[11]

In 1908, Winston Churchill had been promoted from Under-Secretary of State for the Colonies to President of the Board of Trade. A year earlier he had shown an interest in domestic issues by his support for the Eight Hour Bill. That proposal to limit the coalminers' working day was welcomed as much by the small colliery owners – who wanted to restrict the big pits' output of coal – as it was by the miners. But Churchill chose to represent it as a triumph of the working man:

> The general march of industrial democracy is not towards inad-
> equate hours of work but towards sufficient hours of leisure . . .
> Working people, all over the country, are not content that their
> lives should remain an alternative between bed and the factory.
> They demand time to look around them, time to see their
> homes by daylight, time to see their children, time to think and
> read and water their gardens – time, in short, to live.[12]

That speech, improbably enough made to a miners' gala in the
Rhondda Valley, set the tone of his two years at the Board of Trade.
Inclination and necessity coincided. Because of adverse movements in
the terms of trade, exports, and therefore employment, were in
decline. The Tory solution was a tariff to protect domestic industry.
Labour talked windily about 'the right to work'. The Liberals needed
a more practical alternative.

The progressive fashion of the time was to examine and benefit
from the experience of Imperial Germany. Thirty years earlier, the
Foster Education Act had been profoundly influenced by the German
example, and Balfour's attempts to create a national network of secondary schools (which culminated in the 1902 Act★) was prompted by
the knowledge that Berlin promoted training with an enthusiasm
which London would have dismissed as dangerously collectivist. As
the Royal Commission on the Poor Law trudged through its weary
weeks of evidence, social scientists naturally looked to Germany to see
if it offered yet another example of how progressive governments
behaved.

In many ways, Germany was so far ahead that its example disheartened rather than encouraged emulation. Germany protected
twelve million of its citizens against the perils of sickness disability and
old age through schemes in which the potential beneficiary contributed towards the cost. The majority report of the Royal
Commission was agnostic about financing social policy through the
insurance principle, and the minority report was strongly antipathetic.

★For a detailed description of the 1902 Education Act, see Chapter 12, 'Useful
Members of the Community'.

But insurance was not the only policy with which Germany combated unemployment. The Germans believed in labour exchanges matching supply to demand. William Beveridge, an Oxford social scientist and *Morning Post* journalist, went to Germany to find out what Britain had to learn. He was confirmed in his view that periods of unemployment reduced the quality of the labour force. National efficiency required the government to improve the working of the labour markets. Germany also taught him another lesson. What he saw there made him a complete convert to the idea of national insurance as protection against every social emergency. It was the principle on which he built the report which, forty years later, became the foundation of the welfare state.

During the autumn of 1907, Beveridge had related the German example to British experience by analysing the unemployment statistics which were collected under the provisions of the 1905 Unemployed Workmen's Act. The results made new converts in the Board of Trade. On 6 April 1908, officials of that department gave evidence to the Royal Commission 'in favour of a voluntary system of labour exchanges combined with experimental schemes of compulsory unemployment insurance'.[13] It took the new President three months to make up his mind that he shared the view which Beveridge had made irresistible to his officials. In July 1908 Churchill told Hubert Llewellyn Smith, his permanent secretary, that he proposed to promote a network of voluntary labour exchanges – in advance of the Royal Commission's report. Beveridge wrote an explanatory memorandum which was circulated to the Cabinet over Churchill's name. The President of the Board of Trade was not altogether motivated by ideological and intellectual conviction. The recently formed Labour Party had introduced an Unemployed Workers Bill in 1907 which the government had opposed and defeated. Churchill wanted the trade unions to be on the side of the Liberal Party.

In December 1909 a second memorandum, again the work of Beveridge, set out the outline of a bill which would simultaneously encourage the creation of labour exchanges and introduce unemployment insurance. Churchill had become convinced that the two policies must go hand in hand.

The establishment of Labour Exchanges is necessary for the efficient working of the insurance scheme. For all foreign
experiments have shown that a fund for insurance against unemployment needs to be protected against unnecessary or
fraudulent claims by the power of notifying situations to men on
benefit as soon as those situations become vacant.[14]

On the other hand:

Labour exchanges will always be most seriously hampered in
their work as long as they have any apparent association with the
direct relief of distress. As instruments of industrial organisation,
they need industrial management. The central supervising
authority should be the Board of Trade.[15]

Churchill, as well as proposing a revolutionary new social strategy,
was suggesting that he assume powers which were naturally the preserve of the Local Government Board. And he was also trespassing on
territory which Lloyd George, at the Treasury, intended to occupy.
But the two men, despite the disparity in their origins and temperaments, were, in effect, to become the partnership that provided the
emotional energy that drove on the social revolution.

Lloyd George set out his principles in the clearest possible terms. 'I
should like to see the state embark on various novel and adventurous
experiments . . . I look forward to the establishment of minimum
standards of life and labour. I do not think that Liberalism can cut itself
off from this fertile field of social effort.'[16]

Churchill was clearly the junior member of the partnership. After
discussion with the Chancellor of the Exchequer, he beat an uncharacteristic but strategic retreat. Unemployment insurance would be left
for inclusion in Lloyd George's general scheme of comprehensive
social insurance. But that did not prevent Churchill from bombarding
Mr Asquith, the Prime Minister, with his ideas.

The need is urgent and the moment ripe. Germany, with a
harder climate and less accumulated wealth, has managed to
establish tolerable conditions for her people. She is organised not

only for war but peace. We are organised for nothing except party politics. The Minister who will apply to this country the successful experience of Germany in social organisation may or may not be supported at the polls, but he will at least have a memorial which time will not deface.[17]

He went on to set out 'the series of measures' which he regarded as bipartisan. Since they included 'railway amalgamation with state control and guarantee' it is unlikely that his 'big slice of Bismarckianism' would have received the bipartisan welcome for which he hoped. Indeed – since their result, whatever their object, would have been an increase in the power of the state – there is no reason to believe that they were welcomed by Asquith. For the time being, the Prime Minister was content for the President of the Board of Trade to promote the creation of labour exchanges. Indeed he probably realised that resistance was not within his power. Winston Churchill, with all the impetuosity of youth – he was thirty-four – had written to Lloyd George: 'If we stand together we ought to be strong enough either to impart a progressive character to policy or, by our withdrawal, to terminate an administration which has failed in its purpose.'[18] We do not know how the Chancellor of the Exchequer reacted to the notion that he should be ready to resign and bring the government down. Fortunately such extreme action was not necessary. The social revolt drove on.

Churchill encouraged the bipartisan acceptance of that part of his grand design by describing it in one way to the employers and another to the trade unions. The employers feared that labour exchanges would give their workers an undesirable degree of independence by demonstrating that if they lost one job they could quickly obtain another. They were assured that men who were discharged because of misconduct would not receive sympathetic treatment. The trade unions suspected that the state would become an agency for recruiting blackleg labour to replace striking workers. They were placated by an amendment to the bill which guaranteed that no worker would be penalised by a labour exchange for refusing to accept a vacancy created by a trade dispute or for rejecting an offer of employment at lower rates than those which had been negotiated by the appropriate trade union. The technique of giving 'answers to the employers which were directly contrary to those given to the unions' worked.[19] When the time came for Churchill to announce his proposals to Parliament, the House of Commons was bitterly divided over Lloyd George's budget and the general scheme for social insurance which it contained. But F. E. Smith, one of the most rebarbative members of the Conservative front bench, welcomed Churchill's scheme and promised an easy passage to the bill, which gave it legislative effect. The first labour exchanges were opened on 31 January 1910.

Winston Churchill, with all the enthusiasm of a recent convert, had become not only a Liberal but a 'new Liberal'. The phase did not last for long. But for his two years at the Board of Trade and at least part of his time at the Home Office after his second promotion, he was the main exponent of the 'constructive radicalism' which Gladstone – ten years after his death, still a major influence on Liberal thinking – so deplored. Churchill's enthusiasm for active intervention in the economy was confirmed by his determination to improve wage levels in what was called 'sweated industries' – an initiative concurrent with the proposals to encourage the creation of labour exchanges and one which, although less prominent in the Churchill biographies, was more important in terms of the government's acceptance of social responsibilities.

The demand to take action against starvation wages had built up in the years before Churchill arrived at the Board of Trade. Sir Charles Dilke – a rising star of the Liberal Party before a lurid divorce case led to his disgrace – introduced private member's bills in six consecutive years which proposed the creation of government machinery to regulate wages. The *Daily Mail* ran a campaign which called for the government to take immediate action, and the trades unions – although viscerally opposed to government interference in wage determination – were instinctively on the side of the poor. Tories, who argued for tariff reform, regarded the imposition of higher wages in the sweated trades as providing a sort of protection from the importation of goods made by cheap labour. Women's groups of every sort – some concerned with morals and others with welfare – supported Dilke's bills. On 21 February 1908, when the House of Commons debated the idea of regulating the sweated trades, 'the principle was approved by the whole House without distinction of party or class'.[20]

The need for legislation had been emphasised by a select committee of the House of Commons. The most moving evidence that it received was given by a Mr Holmes, who described himself as 'a police court missionary' working in London.

> I was drawn to the home workers first about ten years ago. I met two or three widows at the police court charged with attempted suicide and I naturally took interest in them. I visited their homes and became aware of the conditions in which they lived. The prices paid for their work, the hours generally worked and the amount of rent they paid and the kind of food they ate and everything of that description.

Mr Holmes's view that the attempted suicides were directly attributable to the deprivation of 'sweated' home workers was confirmed by what he discovered about three other widows, similarly employed, who had also attempted to kill themselves. 'The story of their lives, their manner, their appearance and their broken spirit was a revelation.' One of the widows 'had done nothing else than work at these little things [the matchboxes which she assembled] at her own house in Bethnal Green for forty years and her payment for that work is practically the same as it was at the beginning'.[21]

Churchill's assault on the sweated trades was so uncharacteristic of his class that it is hardly surprising that his motivation was dismissed as *grand seigneurial*. 'He desired in Britain a state of things where a benign upper class dispensed benefits to a *bien peasant* and grateful working class.'[22] But, during his Liberal hour, he advanced policies which were far more progressive than the proposals made, or even contemplated, by any other member of the party. It was his nature to proceed, urgent step by urgent step. At the Board of Trade he developed a 'grand plan' with six unquestionably radical elements – 'Labour Exchanges and Unemployment Assurancy, National Infirmity Assurancy, State Industries (Afforestation and Rock Quarrying), a Modernised Poor Law, Railway Amalgamation and Nationalisation, and Education, compulsory until 17.'[23]

On 28 April 1909, Winston Churchill wrote to his new wife, Clementine, that 'the Trades Board Bill has been beautifully received and will be passed without a division . . .'.[24] The next day he was able to write, in triumph, that the debate had gone as predicted. 'Such amiable speeches from Mr A. Balfour and A. Lyttelton . . .'[25] The letter included the domestic details which always dominated the correspondence between the Churchills. 'I hope you communicated with the scrubbing people in Victoria Street and commanded them to scrub forthwith.' We have no information about the wages of the scrubbing people.

The bill was, in fact, a modest affair. It applied to only four trades – ready-made tailoring, paper box-making, machine lace-making (an industry which the police court missionary had chosen for particular censure) and chain-making. It covered only 200,000 workers, 150,000 of them females. Committees, made up of employers, employees and independents, were empowered to fix hourly and piece rates. The legislation's title – Trades Board rather than Wages Board Bill – was meant to emphasise the benefits that decent pay would provide to both sides of industry. And, in case the coded signals of moderation were not deciphered, Churchill emphasised his enduring belief in private enterprise: 'The methods of regulating wages by law are only defensible as exceptional measures to deal with diseased or parasitic trades. A gulf must be fixed between trades subject to such control and ordinary economic industry.'[26]

He also emphasised the need for the boards to respect the realities of the market which they replaced. 'The screw up of home wages without a proportionate movement of factory wages might only improve the home worker into extinction.' But that did not prevent him from arguing that the government should intervene in areas of particularly high unemployment. Because of a slump in shipbuilding, 'the distress on the Tyne and on the Clyde [could not] fail to be exceptionally acute' and was likely to 'produce a grave unrest among the artisan class.'[27] It was therefore only sensible, he argued, to bring naval contracts forward and create jobs. In addition, he proposed that 'certain recognised industries of a useful, but uncompetitive, character like, we will say, afforestation' should be 'managed by public departments' 'since they are capable of being expanded or contracted according to the needs of the labour market'.[28]

Churchill's radicalism was more the result of a temperamental need to promote and participate in feverish activity than an ideological conviction that the nature of society should be altered. But the result – combined with, or despite, his open desire to rise to the pinnacle of parliamentary politics – made his promotion from the Board no more than a matter of time. After the general election of 1910 – with the government weakened both by a reduced majority and the impending constitutional conflict with the House of Lords* – Churchill was offered the Irish Office. He declined with a recklessly frank explanation of his reasons: 'Except for the express purpose of preparing and passing a Home Rule Bill, I do not wish to become responsible for Irish administration.'[29] The Prime Minister had spent much of the previous decade trying to edge the Liberals away from the Home Rule policies which had split the party in 1886; but Churchill, who had the knack of getting away with lese majesty of every sort, was made another, more acceptable, offer. He became Home Secretary. It provided him with the opportunity to implement the theory of active government which was consistent with his character if not his political philosophy. Churchill believed in more than the government 'holding the ring'. In much the same way that employment opportunities had to be created for men who wanted work, the criminal justice system had to do more than punish wrongdoing. It had actively to promote lawful behaviour. Churchill believed in the government getting involved in the daily life of the nation.

The Edwardians took crime and punishment seriously. Between 1900 and 1910, as the population rose from 35.7 to 39.2 million, convictions in superior courts increased from just over 8,000 to almost 12,000. But it was not just the disproportionate rise in the number of proven offences (30 per cent as compared with a 10 per cent population growth) that troubled respectable opinion. The problem was the number of crimes which did not lead to conviction. In 1901, 29,079 indictable offences had been committed in England and Wales. Less than 20 per cent were 'cleared up'.

In the early years of the century, the Metropolitan Police were

---

*See Chapter 8, 'Who Shall Rule?'

2,000 constables under strength and neither the hard-pressed London officers nor the better staffed provincial forces commanded the confidence of the general public. It was widely believed that incompetence was matched by corruption. In a press which specialised in sensation, every alleged misdemeanour was described in lurid detail. The most famous cause célèbre was the prosecution of George Edalyi, the son of a Parsee Church of England rector. Edalyi was convicted and imprisoned for horse maiming. Conan Doyle – whose Sherlock Holmes stories had convinced popular opinion that every crime was capable of solution by the inductive method of detection – initially suspected no more than that Edalyi's race had induced the judge to sentence him to a savage seven years of hard labour. His investigations led him to believe that the Parsee – a short-sighted solicitor's clerk who had written the standard text on railway law – was innocent. Conan Doyle's claims that Edalyi was the victim of racial prejudice were published in a series of *Daily Telegraph* articles and the conviction declared 'unsafe'.

The sensationalisation of murder trials made the dramatis personae national celebrities. Sir Bernard Spilsbury, forensic pathologist, and Sir Edward Marshall Hall, King's Counsel, commanded as many inches of newsprint as the stars of the music hall. They were not, however, as newsworthy as the defendants – particularly if they were murderers. During 1910 Hawley Harvey Crippen was the most talked-about man in Europe. Frederick Seddon, a poisoner, was a classic villain and Ruxton provided added excitement by being black and called 'Buck' by even his closest friends. Crippen had the remarkable distinction of figuring in the first pursuit and capture of the new scientific age. After he killed his wife, he fled to Canada with his mistress, Ethel le Neve, who was disguised as a boy. He was recognised by the captain of the liner on which they travelled. A message was sent to the owner 'by wireless telegraph' and Inspector Drew of Scotland Yard pursued the couple in a faster vessel and effected the arrest at sea.

Science was coming to the police's aid. In 1902 the technique of fingerprinting was introduced, if not perfected. On Derby day, fifty-two men were arrested at Epsom for pickpocketing. They were fingerprinted and, although the results were not accepted in evidence, twenty-nine of them were identified as possessing previous convictions. The identity of a burglar who mutilated his own hand in a Clerkenwell warehouse gate was proved on the evidence of the amputated finger rather than the print. But, on 14 September 1902, a burglar who had broken into a house in Denmark Hill was convicted on the evidence of fingerprints alone.

Unfortunately, the police were slow to take advantage of other scientific developments. The *Police Gazette*, which circulated details of wanted men, illustrated the descriptions with woodcuts long after photographs could have been used to improve the prospects of identification. Until about the time of Churchill's arrival at the Home Office, the telegraph was preferred to the telephone because of the fear that operators might overhear the conversations, and the Criminal Records Office did not co-ordinate the details of modus operandi, convictions and sentences until 1914.

The police and the processes of criminal justice were ripe for reform, and Churchill thought of himself as a reforming Home Secretary. But improvements in administration and efficiency were not the sorts of improvements which attracted him. His great concern was prison and prison policy. Before he could follow his natural inclination, he had to deal with a more immediate cause of concern. In 1910 two mining disasters reminded the nation that a collier who completed his whole working life in the pits had survived a one-in-twenty chance of being killed. Most years, a thousand coalminers were killed by roof falls, flooding and explosions. Generally they died in small numbers, which attracted little attention, but in 1910, 132 miners died in an underground explosion in Cumberland and 320 lives were lost when a roof collapsed in a Bolton pit. Churchill's Mines Bill – not passed into law until late 1911 when he had moved on to the Admiralty – increased the minimum age for employment in the pits from thirteen to fourteen, improved the training of mines inspectors and stipulated minimum standards for safety and haulage machinery. Having prepared a Coal Miners Bill for enactment by his successor, Churchill then completed the passage of the Shops Bill – limiting hours of employment to sixty hours a week – which had been prepared by Herbert Gladstone before he left the Home Office to become Governor General of South Africa.

Gladstone's valedictory letter to his successor had concluded, 'as regards prisons, it won't be a bad thing to give a harassed department a rest'.[30] It was not advice that the new Home Secretary was inclined to accept. Wilfred Scawen Blunt – poet, libertine, Tory supporter of Home Rule and friend of Lord Randolph Churchill – had served two months in Kilmainham gaol. Churchill, after hearing a harrowing account of Blunt's experiences, announced, 'I am dead against the present system and, if I am ever made Home Secretary, I will make a clean sweep of it.' Six months later, when he got the job, he began to make good his promise.

Although Churchill was against prison, he was absolutely opposed to the relaxation of other punishments. He arranged for the defeat of a private member's bill that aimed to abolish flogging and he attempted to introduce a new punishment into the criminal lexicon which he called 'defaulters drill . . . Swedish gymnastics with or without dumbbells . . . The boys should not be exhausted but training should be severe and rigorous discipline preserved.'[31] Despite the strong objections from the Chief Constable of Birmingham – 'punishment which is not improving to individuals . . . is not good to any person and breaks a man's spirit'[32] – the proposal was included in a Cabinet paper. Only the legislative logjam, created by the government's conflict with the House of Lords, prevented the plan becoming law. Churchill had already chosen a title for the Bill: the Abatement of Imprisonment.

Throughout his political life, Churchill's policy decisions were built upon sudden impulses that his admirers called inspiration. Great pronouncements, which owed more to instinct than careful study, set out the boundaries of his philosophy of government. The principle on which he based his Home Office reforms was to guide all of his most enlightened successors. 'The mood and temper of the public with regard to the treatment of crime and criminals is the one unfailing test of the civilisation of any country.'[33] Within a week of becoming Home Secretary, he attended the first night of John Galsworthy's *Justice* in the company of Evelyn Ruggles-Brise, the chairman of the Prisons Commission. The play convinced the new minister that 'separate confinement', imposed on all prisoners for the first nine months of their sentence, was inhumane. Herbert Gladstone had already planned to reduce the regime to three months. Churchill reduced it to one month for all but recidivists. The play changed the language as well as the policy. Prisoners and prison reformers began to talk of 'solitary confinement'.

Prison reform was not, however, as important to Churchill as effecting a reduction in the prison population. He told the House of Commons on 10 July 1910, 'The first real principle which should guide anyone trying to establish a good system of prisons would be to prevent as many people as possible getting there at all.' He expanded that view with a comment on the imprisonment of sixteen- to twenty-one-year-olds which sounded like propaganda in the class war: 'It is an evil which falls only on the sons of the working classes. The sons of other classes may commit many of the same kind of offences and in boisterous and exuberant moments, whether at Oxford or anywhere else, many do things for which the working classes are committed to prison, although injury may not be inflicted on anyone.'[34]

The number of juveniles in custody was reduced by the introduction of secondary legislation which cut the number of offences that carried a prison sentence. Churchill was even more successful in minimising the number of men in prison for debt and fine default. In the ten years which followed his appointment to the Home Office, the number of prisoners serving sentences for fine default fell from almost 100,000 to 20,000.

There were other marginal reforms. Some gaols created libraries and others offered rudimentary training to discharged prisoners. But it was the reduction in the prison population which, together with the trade boards and the labour exchanges, was Churchill's great contribution to the emancipation of the working classes. In his brief 'new Liberal' phase, Churchill spoke for men who, during the rest of his political career, regarded him as a natural enemy.

Churchill's profound antipathy to trade unions (as demonstrated during the General Strike of 1926 and exaggerated after his intervention in the riots at Tonypandy*) confirmed the spirit in which he embarked on all his Home Office reforms. His anxiety to help the

---

*See Chapter 11, 'United We Stand'.

poor was moderated by a resentment of their presumption in trying to organise help for themselves. And in Edwardian Britain, as throughout the rest of his political life, his policies were suddenly changed by the impulses of unrestrained emotion. After visiting Dartmoor Prison and meeting David Davies, a recidivist shepherd who had been sentenced to three years' penal servitude and ten years' preventative detention for stealing two shillings from a church offertory box, he circulated the courts instructing that only the most dangerous offenders should be imprisoned to protect society from anticipated crimes rather than as punishment for past offences. When he heard that Charles Bulbeck, a twelve-year-old boy, had been sentenced to birching and six years in a reformatory for the offence of stealing four penny-worth of cod, he instantly intervened. He was too late to stop the birching, but the boy was discharged to the custody of his parents. Sir Edward Troup, the permanent secretary at the Home Office, both suffered from and admired the characteristic which Churchill's friends called mercurial and his enemies described as capricious. 'Once a week or oftener, Mr Churchill came into the Office bringing with him some adventurous or impossible projects but after half an hour's discussion something was evolved which was still adventurous but possible.'[35]

Perhaps the real Winston Churchill was revealed to the general public on 3 January 1911. Three weeks earlier, a group of men, thought to be Latvians, had been disturbed while attempting to tunnel into a jeweller's shop. They escaped, after killing two policemen, but were discovered to be hiding in a third-floor flat in Sidney Street, Stepney. Police surrounded the building and fire was exchanged. A detective sergeant was wounded. Reinforcements were called, including seven hundred and fifty police officers and a detachment of Scots Guards with a machine gun. There was talk of bringing up a field gun, sending for Royal Engineers to sap and mine or setting fire to the building. On the second day, the Home Secretary arrived at the scene wearing a top hat and a coat with an astrakhan collar. According to the rumour current at the time, he borrowed a rifle and took a pot shot at the desperadoes. Churchill found trouble irresistible. On the day before the Sidney Street siege he had written to the Prime Minister arguing that, if the reluctant Tory peers – determined to oppose

Lloyd George's budget and the introduction of national insurance –
refused to accept the supremacy of the House of Commons, the government should 'clink the coronets in their scabbards'. However
dubious the quality of the metaphor, Churchill was making clear that
he was ready to fight the Lords to the death.

CHAPTER 8

Who Shall Rule?

Henry Campbell-Bannerman resigned from the office of Prime Minister on 3 April 1908. The Cabinet, part impatient and part apprehensive, had realised since the New Year that the resignation could not be long delayed. So had the King. He had asked the sick incumbent to remain at his post at least until the royal holiday in Biarritz was over. Doctors advised otherwise and the seals of office were surrendered. However, the holiday had to be completed. So Herbert Asquith, the unchallenged successor, was required to travel to France to kiss hands and receive the King's commission to form a government. He left London on the overnight boat train alone with 'cap pulled well down over his eyes to preserve his anonymity'.[1] Initially the King proposed to summon all the new Cabinet to Paris where, according to his plan, he would hand them their seals of office in the Hôtel Crillon. Wiser counsel, in the urbane form of Lord Knollys, prevailed and the King returned to England two weeks later.

Asquith had been a cautious Chancellor of the Exchequer. Between 1906 and 1908 he had reduced the national debt by £45 million and kept the budget in permanent surplus. He was deeply reluctant to increase public expenditure. It may have been the fear that his successor would be less prudent which, at first, inclined him to fill the double role of Chancellor and Prime Minister. The King endorsed the idea after he had been assured that a precedent had been set by Mr

Gladstone in 1873. On reflection, Asquith decided that, in the intervening twenty-five years, government had grown too complex for the
two jobs to be successfully combined. David Lloyd George was promoted to the Treasury and was succeeded at the Board of Trade by
Winston Churchill – only thirty-three years of age and a Liberal since
he had crossed the floor of the House of Commons in 1904.

News of the promotions was published in the *Daily Chronicle* before
the official announcement was made. The culprit was assumed to be
Lloyd George. His letter of denial to the Prime Minister ended with
a reproof which revealed the class consciousness that was to inform
much of his policy. 'Men whose promotion is not sustained by birth
or other favouring conditions are always liable to be assailed with
unkind suspicions of this sort. I would ask it, therefore, as a favour that
you should not entertain them without satisfying yourself that they
had some basis in truth.'[2] The raw nerve which the allegation exposed
never quite healed over.

The budget of 1908 was, with Lloyd George's agreement, presented to the House of Commons by the Prime Minister, who had
prepared it before his elevation. Asquith therefore takes his place in
history as the true begetter of the old-age pension. For the previous
two years the radical wing of the Liberal Party had tried, without success, to persuade him to implement what they regarded as an essential
element of social policy. But he had refused to advance into what he
called, in his budget speech, 'the still unconquered territory of social
reform'. Where arguments of principle failed, political necessity succeeded. In 1907, the Liberal Party was beaten in two by-elections it
expected to win. The Labour candidate was returned in Jarrow, and
Victor Grayson, the romantic and mysterious independent socialist,
secured an even more unlikely victory in the Colne Valley. At the
TUC Annual Conference in Bath, a resolution demanding the introduction of the old-age pension was carried unanimously.

The government responded by announcing its intention to present
a pension bill to the House of Commons in time for the scheme to be
in operation by 1 January 1909 – the date which the TUC resolution
had identified as the essential starting point. The Bill's provisions
were, however, far more modest than the trade unions had demanded.
At Bath the proposal had been five shillings a week for every man

aged sixty or over. Asquith offered five shillings a week at seventy (seven and sixpence for a couple) with the proviso that it should be withheld from criminals, lunatics, vagrants and anyone with an income of more than ten shillings a week. The TUC, always happy to accept half a loaf, was delighted. Its pleasure was increased by the knowledge that Lloyd George would be the responsible minister. During his election campaign in 1895 he had argued in favour of establishing an old-age pension and proposed that it should be financed by increased death duties and land taxes. His heart, the trade unions knew, was in the right place. But it was Asquith's good fortune to make the announcement. He also made provision for financing the first three months of the scheme's implementation. Reasonably enough, he left the long-term financial arrangements to the budget of 1909.

Lloyd George, despite his enthusiasm for social legislation, was, in general, what he liked to call 'an economist' – not an expert on the works of Alfred Marshall but a chancellor who chose to economise. Winston Churchill held the same view. So the two great war leaders – each of whom was to become Prime Minister at a moment of national crisis and then lead the country to victory – were allies in a campaign to hold down military and naval spending. The argument about how much the nation could afford had survived Campbell-Bannerman. After much argument, Asquith's Cabinet agreed to an extended naval building programme with an estimated cost of £10 million in the fiscal year 1909-10. Added to the cost of financing a full year's old-age pension, that meant that Lloyd George had to finance £15 million of new expenditure.

The need to raise extra revenue did not quite amount to a financial crisis, but the behaviour of the Opposition did put the government's whole programme in jeopardy. The Tory Party, which had always regarded the two Houses of Parliament as separate entities, decided, after the 1906 defeat, to co-ordinate its strategy in the Lords and the Commons. The Conservative leadership suspected that radicals within the government longed for an opportunity to emasculate the Upper House. It was therefore agreed between Balfour (who after his defeat in Manchester had returned as Member for the City of London) and Lansdowne (the Tory Leader in the Lords) that, 'while tactics would have to be left flexible', the basic plan would be to 'fight all points of principle very stiffly in the Commons and make the House of Lords the theatre of compromise'.[3]

For a time, the scheme worked well. The (Nonconformist) Education Bill of 1906, which aimed to restrict denominational teaching of religious instruction in state schools, was amended by the Lords to a point at which the government, although unable to claim that it had been rejected, decided that it was no longer worth the expenditure of parliamentary time. On the other hand, the Trades Disputes Bill (which re-established Trade Union immunities and, in effect, negated the Taff Vale Judgement*) was regarded as too politically popular a measure to be rejected by an unelected House. Their Lordships were content to denounce it as offering one section of society 'privileges fraught with danger to the community as a whole'. They then allowed it to pass into law. But the back-bench Tory extremists, who never regarded any other party as capable of forming a legitimate government, grew impatient. In 1906 the Lords rejected outright the Plural Voting Bill. Five government bills were lost in 1907 and five more early in 1908. Then (at the insistence of the brewers and their tenants but against the advice of the Church of England bishops) the Lords defeated the Licensing Bill. Nonconformists were scandalised by the rejection of the notion that the number of licensed premises in any one area should, in part, be governed by the size of the community they served. Lloyd George threatened to retaliate by increasing excise duties, and there was much discussion about incorporating the lost legislation into the Finance Bill. According to the parliamentary convention, the Lords never defeated, and rarely obstructed, 'supply' – the raising of taxes.

Some historians have suggested – and there was a time when the Tories actually feared – that Asquith and Lloyd George planned to use a controversial budget as a means of first challenging and then breaking the Lords' authority. It is far more likely that the Liberal leadership never even considered the possibility of the Upper House emasculating the Finance Bill – although they undoubtedly enjoyed the prospect of the peers being humiliated by being forced grudgingly to endorse legislation with which they passionately disagreed. Balfour had argued strenuously against the Old Age Pensions Bill, largely on the slightly

---

*Details of that legislation are to be found in Chapter 11, 'United We Stand'.

tenuous grounds that it would be impossible to check the age of applicants. But he accepted that, because it was a money bill, the Lords would let it through. To the government, that seemed confirmation that they would do the same with the Finance Bill which followed.

Almost a century later, it is impossible to imagine that the Lords would ever have accepted the 1909 Finance Bill without a fight. It interfered with a part of the nation's life which the peers believed was theirs to have and to hold in perpetuity – the ownership of the land. That was only one of the radical ingredients in a budget which was so controversial that it took the Chancellor some time to convince his own colleagues of its wisdom. Roy Jenkins, in his biography of Asquith, suggests that 'he had some difficulty with the Treasury as well'.[4] Sir George Murray, the Permanent Secretary, notified the Prime Minister on 7 April 1909 (less than three weeks before Budget Day) that 'only two blots' remained in a fiscal package which was 'more or less shipshape'. The Cabinet, examining the budget item by item at a specially convened meeting, was not so sure.

When the package was finally completed, Lloyd George, resentful that he had been forced to endure such detailed scrutiny, told his half-brother, 'Asquith alone was helpful'.[5] Later he was more generous. 'I should say that I have Winston Churchill with me and above all the Prime Minister has backed me up through thick and thin with splendid loyalty.'[6] Other members of the Cabinet had been less supportive. Harcourt had been particularly difficult, 'obstructing [the proposals] while posing all the time as a Radical.'[7] Crewe and Runciman had demonstrated their reservations by studied silence.

The Cabinet met fourteen times during the six weeks before Budget Day. Asquith's letters to the King reported the Chancellor's defeats. 'Cabinet rejected a proposal . . . to tax the ground rent of lands built upon . . . and the provision for the additional taxation of land values was carefully revised.' Both changes were made to protect the sanctity of contracts.

That demonstration of respect for the unfettered rights of property was not altogether consistent with Gladstone's Second Irish Land Act, which had stipulated a limit on the requirements that landlords could legally impose on their tenants. But if, in that particular, the Cabinet was more conventionally respectable than its nineteenth–century Liberal predecessor, in other ways it broke new ideological ground. Asquith, said Lloyd George, 'had real sympathy for the ordinary and the poor'[8] – not a characteristic which is always associated with the Balliol Brahmin. It may well be that, as well as accepting 'the abandonment of the old limitations attaching to the raising of revenue', he positively welcomed what amounted to a revolution in the ways in which budgets were prepared. For the first time in British history a Chancellor of the Exchequer approached his task in the belief 'that taxation should be used for the purposes of social regeneration'.[9] Lloyd George held that view with an absolute sincerity born out of a combination of compassion and admiration for the virtues of the working class. His speech during the Second Reading debate on the Pensions Bill set out his philosophy exactly.

> The provision which has been made for the sick and the unemployed is grossly inadequate in this country, yet the working classes have done their best during fifty years to make provision without the aid of the state . . . These problems of the sick, of the infirm, of the men who cannot find the means of earning a livelihood . . . are problems with which it is the business of the state to deal.

Thus, in the words of historian John Grigg, 'Lloyd George utterly repudiated the Victorian view of poverty and the Gladstonian concept of government'.

In these cynical times, Lloyd George is often regarded as an opportunist who, in the words of his severest critic, 'did not mind in which direction the taxi was travelling as long as he was the driver'. But during his years at the Treasury he was a real believer in providing 'assistance' to the old, poor and sick. He was a supreme politician. So when he realised that the forces ranged against widows' and orphans' benefits were invincible, he retreated. But he advanced, often against great odds, wherever and whenever progress was possible. And he advanced for the right reasons. When he turned to medical insurance in 1911, he told his civil servants that 'most illnesses are due to the abuse of some prudent rule of nature', but homespun Welsh philosophy did not obscure his determination to apply his basic rule: help should be provided on the basis of need and need alone. The 1911 Insurance Act contained, on his explicit instruction, a clause which provided 'that medical treatment shall be given without regard to cause or nature of disease'.[10] Contributors to the scheme earned a universal entitlement. There was to be no distinction between the deserving and the undeserving poor.

Lloyd George's proposals for raising revenue in his 1909 budget were, by any standards, controversial. Income tax was increased from a shilling to one and twopence in the pound on unearned income and on incomes of more than three thousand pounds a year. A 'supertax' of sixpence in the pound was to be levied on the amount by which incomes of £50,000 or more exceeded £3,000. Petrol was taxed at threepence on the gallon and motor car ownership was taxed according to a sliding scale based on engine horsepower.* Excise duties on tobacco and spirits, stamp duty and estate duty were all increased. A general tax on liquor licences was accompanied by the reform of the licensing system which had been proposed in the lost bill. The one major relaxation was the exclusion of ten pounds a year from the income tax assessment of men with children.

But the most controversial proposals – in a budget which raised an additional thirteen and a half million pounds and met the rest of the increased expenditure by a transfer of three million pounds from the sinking fund – were the package of land taxes. A tax of 20 per cent was to be levied on the unearned increment of land values, payable when land changed hands by sale, gift or inheritance. There was also to be a capital tax of one halfpenny in the pound on the value of undeveloped land and minerals. A 10 per cent 'reversion duty' was to be charged on the financial recompense which came to a lessee at the end of a lease.

The land tax proposals were modified during the Committee Stage of the Finance Bill, but the changes did little to assuage the anger of the landowning classes. The Chancellor himself, predicting tax rises even before he made his budget statement, seemed more anxious to provoke than to placate his enemies. Lloyd George embodied all that the landowners feared and hated. Most of them took it for granted that his budget was motivated by malice and envy: for on questions concerning the land, Lloyd George had 'form'.

---

*The government promised to use the income from both those innovations to pay the cost of the highway improvements made necessary by the increasing popularity of the automobile. The road works were to be carried out by a Roads Board. Thus was the fiction of the road fund born.

The Agricultural Land Bill of 1897, which had proposed a 50 per cent reduction in the rating of farmland, had been based on the recommendations of a Royal Commission that had been set up by Gladstone. Implementing the report was probably essential to the economic welfare of British farming. But the young Lloyd George had regarded it as a gift to the Tory landlords and, by personalising its benefit to ministers, behaved in a way which was inconsistent with the gentlemanly traditions of the Victorian House of Commons. He had calculated that, thanks to the Bill, the Tory Cabinet as a whole would be better off by about £67,000. Salisbury, the Prime Minister, would pay £2,000 less in rates, Balfour (his nephew and political heir apparent) would have his rates reduced by £1,450. The Duke of Devonshire would be the greatest beneficiary of all. His annual payment to the numerous local authorities in whose areas he owned land would fall by £10,000. Men, and the descendants of men, who had been deeply offended by the suggestion that they were motivated by personal greed rather than by public spirit – and the implication that they could be corrupted by comparatively small sums of money – took it for granted that the Chancellor was still pursuing a vendetta. Vested interest combined with resentment at what they believed to be a policy which was both vindictive and punitive. When it was discovered that Philip Snowden – one day to become Chancellor of the Exchequer himself and to abandon the Labour Party to serve in Ramsay MacDonald's national government – had proposed a similar pattern of land taxes to the Independent Labour Party, they were convinced that Lloyd George was a not-very-secret socialist.

Lord Hardinge – about to become Viceroy of India and still, theoretically, a public servant rather than a politician – announced that the budget was 'cunningly devised as a vehicle for the socialist revolution' and that it contained 'all the doctrines of the extreme Socialist Party while it provides, at the same time, all the machinery that is necessary for carrying these doctrines into effect at any time hereafter'.[11] Rosebery – like most apostates, extreme in the denunciation of his old friends – spoke of 'ships crossing the Atlantic carrying stocks and bonds as ballast in order that they might be got away from the jurisdiction of His Majesty's Government'.[12] Lord Northcliffe – always looking for sensational reports – led the Tory newspapers' claim that the budget of 1909 was so alien to the spirit of England that it represented a sort of treason against all that the country stood for. The Conservative Party eagerly echoed the claim that the new taxes were treason. It was a tactic the Tory Party was to employ time and time again in an attempt to obstruct the work of elected governments. Lloyd George, the object of their fear and hatred, encouraged (and probably enjoyed) the Establishment's animosity. His explanation of the need to raise extra taxes to finance the old-age pension was calculated to excite apprehension. 'I have no nest eggs at all. I have got to rob somebody's hen roost next year. I am on the look-out for which will be the easiest to get and where I shall be least punished and where I shall get the most eggs and not only that, but where they can be most easily spared.'[13] The rhetoric with which the idea of a redistributive budget was supported and the reputation of its author combined with its contents to create what George Dangerfield in his 1935 book *The Strange Death of Liberal England* called 'a Budget crying out to be vetoed'.[14]

It is difficult to judge from Dangerfield's elaborate prose what he believed the government's motives to be. He described the budget as 'a wonderful trap to catch the House of Lords in', reminded his readers that many of the Cabinet were 'allied by birth and friendship with the rich whom it assaulted' and added that 'to humble the House of Lords was the devout vindictive wish of all good Liberals'.[15] To humble is not the same as to destroy. The budget, which Lloyd George proposed on its merits and Asquith supported out of conviction, was, as a by-product of its more contentious clauses, expected to convince the Lords that, in the modern world of the twentieth century, they could never frustrate the will of the elected House of Parliament, no matter how strong their objection to what the Commons proposed. Lloyd George believed in his budget and did not want to see it destroyed. He assumed that the House of Lords, obsessed with precedent and bound by convention, would accept its own constitutional limitations and not stand in the way of a money bill.

There were hotheads on both sides of the argument. Churchill – a recent convert to radicalism and spoiling for a fight on behalf of the government – announced over dinner, 'We shall send them up such a budget in June as shall terrify them. They have started a class war. They had better be careful.'[16] Joseph Chamberlain (who had crossed the floor of the House of Commons in the other direction from Churchill) was determined that the Unionists should use the occasion as an opportunity, no matter how slight, to bring the government down. Lloyd George, to Chamberlain's fury, had found a way of financing both a social and a naval building programme which did not rely for its finance on a general tariff moderated by 'imperial preference'. He knew that for him, at the age of seventy-three, time was fast running out. Both Balfour and Lansdowne – Leaders of the Opposition in the Commons and Lords – remained cautious. It was against both their instincts and their philosophy to precipitate what traditionalists regarded as a conflict with the constitution. But influential voices sounded a more reckless note. Lord Ridley, land-owner and chairman of the Tariff Reform League, offered timid Conservatives a justification for defying the Commons. To reject the budget of 1909 might well amount to the defence of, rather than an assault on, parliamentary democracy.

> He did not think that any member of the House of Lords ought to say what he thought the House of Lords would do with a measure which had not yet come before it. But he was clearly of the opinion that they had not only a perfect constitutional right to throw it out, but . . . a perfect constitutional right to amend it, and that circumstances might arise in which it would be desirable to assert that right.

He then moved on from unsubstantiated assertion to a mixture of dubious constitutional theory and undoubtedly genuine abuse. But the importance of his speech lay in neither the language nor the logic. Ridley was inventing a spurious justification for the Lords' veto.

> The mistaken impression of many people that the House of Lords could not touch finance was founded on a resolution of the House of Commons passed centuries ago. The Lords had hitherto acquiesced to decisions of the House of Commons because government had been conducted by sane men, but there was now a House of Commons controlled by madmen and they had to take a different view.[17]

The official Tory leadership quickly took up, and significantly extended, the theory that the House of Lords had a duty to frustrate policies which would lead to national ruination. At a dinner of the Liberal Union Club on 3 May, Lansdowne promised only that Balfour would fight Lloyd George's 'reckless financial policies'. But Bonar Law, a tough Scottish-Canadian who, in 1911, was to succeed Balfour as leader of the Tory Party, thought it possible to go a step further. He called the decision to ignore the judgement of the Lords 'a revolution in itself' and said that, if the government's will prevailed, the Upper House would 'simply exist as a debating chamber'.[18] It was not long before Rosebery – by then totally disenchanted with the party which he had once led, endorsed the notion that, were the Lords to defy the Commons and reject the budget, they would be defending the rule of law. The Finance Bill would, he said, 'be carried over the heads of the people . . . without the slightest attempt to ascertain the views of the people on the vast changes projected. The British citizen will have no more control over them than if they were Tartars or Lapps.' And, developing Bonar Law's theme, he gave the Lloyd George enemies a slogan which they were to repeat time after time and blazon across the platforms of their protest meetings. 'Not a budget, but a revolution.'[19]

The procedure by which 'supply' was examined in the Edwardian Parliament imposed a particularly heavy burden on Treasury ministers. In 1909 the budget resolutions were debated for thirteen days before the Finance Bill had its First Reading on 26 May. In June, the Second Reading debate occupied four days. The Committee Stage began on the twenty-first of that month and lasted for forty-two parliamentary days – half of them all-night sittings.[20] Lloyd George possessed both stamina and energy, but it is doubtful if even he could have stood the strain had he not resolved a personal crisis six weeks before Budget Day on 29 April. On 12 March the Chancellor of the Exchequer appeared in court and swore on oath that there was no truth to the allegation – made indirectly in the *People* newspaper – that he had avoided being cited as a co-respondent in a lurid divorce case only by paying the plaintiff £20,000 of 'hush money'.

The *People*'s implication of adultery was the second threat of scandal to face Lloyd George since his promotion to the Treasury. A year earlier, the *Bystander* had reported that the new Chancellor had 'been overloaded with flattery . . . especially from the fair sex which is always difficult for a "man of temperament" to resist". The result was the 'rumour of an embarrassment'. That case was settled out of court with an apology and a payment by the *Bystander* of £300 to the Caernarvon Cottage Hospital. The *People* case ended in a much greater flourish. Rufus Isaacs, Raymond Asquith and F. E. Smith represented Lloyd George. Sir Edward Carson acted for the newspaper. Both cases turned on letters – written by a Mrs Gardner in the *Bystander* case and a Mrs Griffiths as quoted in the *People*. They were undoubtedly affectionate, though not obviously amorous. The Chancellor of the Exchequer survived. As the House of Lords grew more aggressive, Lloyd George became increasingly determined that his budget should do the same.

The Cabinet rallied round. Naturally enough it was Churchill – always the enthusiast – who accepted the Presidency of the Budget League, an organisation founded to counteract the publicity cam-paign which had been mounted by Lloyd George's critics. The Chancellor addressed the inaugural lunch and cheerfully dismissed the assaults upon him as 'the same old drivel . . . Lord Rothschild . . . said that the Budget was socialism and collectivism. Now I wonder if he knows what socialism means . . . I suppose it would be too much to ask a financier, ruined by the Budget, to spend any money on politi-cal literature. Somebody should present him with a sixpenny handbook . . .'[21] Meanwhile Lord Onslow warned his workers that many of them could be sacked if the budget became law. Lord Selborne announced that he would have to reduce expenditure on the upkeep of his estate and Ben Tillett, the dockers' leader, complained that to call the budget socialist was a libel on socialism.[22]

Lansdowne (despite his intransigence, in many ways still more a diplomat than a politician) told the National Union of Conservative Associations, 'I do not think that you will find the House of Lords is at all likely to proclaim that it has no responsibility for the Bill and that, because it is mixed up with the nation's financial affairs, we are obliged to swallow it whole and without hesitation.'[23] Everybody assumed that he was signalling the peers' reluctance to reject the Bill outright – everybody except Winston Churchill. He could not resist replying with a threat. 'Unless Lord Lansdowne and his landlordly friends choose to eat their own mince again, Parliament will be

dissolved and we shall come to you in a moment of high consequence for every cause for which Liberalism had ever fought.'[24] The
reference to 'mince' was a tortuous extension of Lansdowne's analysis of the form of budget which he could 'swallow'.

At the Cabinet meeting of 21 July, Churchill was formally rebuked
for threatening a dissolution; but he continued, with the true zeal of a
convert, to make out the ideological case for a budget that took from
the rich and gave to the poor. J. A. Hobson described the speeches
which he made during 1909 as 'the clearest, the most eloquent and the
most convincing exposition of New Liberalism'.[25] The paradox of
Churchill's position was illustrated by Lloyd George's fear that, deep
inside, he was 'Blenheim minded'[26] and therefore, in his heart, on the
side of the landowners. But once Churchill had recognised his duty to
campaign for the Cabinet, he carried out the task with unrestrained
gusto. The result, whether he knew it or not, was speeches which
might have appeared in a manual on how to conduct the class war. At
Leicester in September he mounted a frontal assault on the idle rich.

> We do not only ask today 'How much have you got?' We also
> ask 'How did you get it?' Did you earn it yourself or has it just
> been left to you by others? Was it gained by processes which are
> themselves beneficial to the community in general or was it
> gained by processes which have done no good to anyone, only
> harm? . . . Was it gained by supplying the capital that industry
> needs, or by denying, except at an extortionate price, the land
> which industry requires?[27]

Having demolished, to his own satisfaction, the rentiers who would
pay 'supertax', he moved on. At Balls Mill, Abernethy, on 16 October
he attacked the generality of the budget's critics.

> While the working class have borne the extra taxation upon
> their tobacco and whisky in manly silence, rage and fury is
> poured upon the Government by the owners of this ever-
> increasing fund of wealth and we are denounced as Jacobins, as
> Anarchists and Communists and all the rest of the half-
> understood vocabulary of irritated ignorance.[28]

Later in the same day he told the Scottish Liberals that 'the security of property depends upon the wide definition among great numbers and all classes of the population'.[29]

The substance of Churchill's speeches was so close to an exposition of the socialism which the Tories feared that it now seems extraordinary that the Opposition made so little of them. Perhaps they were deflected from pursuit of the President of the Board of Trade by the irresistible temptation to chase a bigger quarry. On 30 July 1909, the Chancellor of the Exchequer had addressed a meeting of the Budget League in the Edinburgh Castle — a public house turned temperance hall — in the East End of London. 'The Limehouse Speech' made a head-on conflict between government and peers inevitable.

It began by comparing the public spirit of the classes. The national interest demanded that 'Dreadnoughts' be laid down to increase the fire-power of the British Navy. 'We wanted money to pay for the building. So we sent the hat round. We sent it round among work-men . . . They all dropped in their coppers. We went round Belgravia and there has been such a howl ever since that it has well nigh deafened us.' The budget's social aims were 'provision for the aging and deserving poor'. That required extra revenue. 'There are many in this country blessed by Providence with great wealth. If there are amongst them men who grudge out of their riches a fair contribution towards their less fortunate fellow countrymen, they are very shabby rich men.' Having caused deep offence by setting out the general principles, Lloyd George went on to provoke outrage by illustrating his argument with examples. Owners of what had been marshland in the Lea and Thames Valleys had, through no effort of their own, suddenly become landlords of a 'golden swamp'. Values had risen from three to three thousand pounds an acre because of increased trade in the Port of London. Why should the landlord be the sole beneficiary of the whole community's enterprise?

The general assault on the rights of property was, in itself, a heresy against the beliefs of the Edwardian Establishment. Lloyd George went on to particularise. The Duke of Northumberland had exploited a local council which needed 'a small plot of land as a site for a school to train children who, in due course, would labour upon his property'. The Duke of Westminster, on the discovery that Gorringe's

store had become a great commercial success, had increased the property's ground rent from 'a few hundred a year to four thousand
pounds'. Finally he turned on the coal owners, whose sins he recalled
when 'the other day' he 'sank down into a pit half a mile deep' and
met miners who daily risked 'mutilation and death'.

> When the Prime Minister and I knock on the door of these
> great landlords and say to them, 'Here, you know these poor fel-
> lows who have been digging up royalties at the risk of their
> lives, some of them are old, they have survived the perils of
> their trade, they are broken, they can earn no more, won't you
> give something towards keeping them out of the workhouse?'
> they scowl at us. We say, 'Only a halfpenny, just a copper.' They
> retort, 'You thieves!'

After the emotion there came what sounded remarkably like an ultimatum. 'If this is an indication of the view taken by these great
landlords, of their responsibility to the people who, at the risk of life,
create their wealth, then I say that the day of reckoning is at hand.'
    The Limehouse Speech was meant to stake out the battleground
which divided peers from people. So it was necessary to end with a
statement of how David would deal with Goliath. 'They have
threatened like this before. But in good time they have seen that it is
not in their interests to carry out their futile menaces.' That hardly
amounted to a declaration of war. The speech did, however, contain
a number of passages which were calculated to enrage the enemy. The
rhetorical question, 'Who ordained that a few should have the land of
Britain as a perquisite?' offended the idea of inalienable rights to
property and inheritance. But it was the insults, not the philosophy,
which drove their Lordships to fury. 'The question will be asked
whether five hundred men, ordinary men chosen accidentally from
the unemployed, should override the judgement – the deliberate
judgement – of millions of people who are engaged in the industry
which makes the wealth of this country.'
    That was an insult for which the Lords could not forgive him and
more provocation was to follow. At the Limehouse overflow meeting
held nearby, Lloyd George was carried away by the passion of his

convictions. After a brilliant impromptu aside which described 'bombastic commonplaces' as Lord Curzon's 'stock in trade', he reached his inflammatory peroration. 'I say to you, without you we can do nothing. With your help, we can brush the Lords like chaff before us.'

The Limehouse Speech produced 'a state of great agitation and annoyance' in the King.[30] For almost a year he had convinced himself that nothing would come of Asquith's determination 'to treat the veto of the House of Lords as the dominating issue in politics'. But when, in the summer of 1909, sovereign and subject met at Cowes, there were complaints about the Chancellor's 'inappropriate language'. Lloyd George wrote to the King excusing himself on the grounds that he had been subject to 'criticism, the virulence of which . . . is without parallel'. Edward was not placated, not least because he was surrounded by what Asquith called 'an atmosphere full of hostility to the [budget] proposals'.[31] However, the hostility was being overlaid (though not honestly moderated) by fear. Reports reaching the Opposition confirmed the budget's popularity. Lord Northcliffe, the proprietor of the *Observer, Times* and *Daily Mail*, began to wonder how long his editorials could remain in conflict with his readers' opinions. J. L. Garvin, the editor of the *Observer*, persuaded him to hold firm. Capitulation would encourage further excesses. The battle was on.

The Tories, although determined to fight, were at first undecided how the enemy should be engaged. By August, Balfour (and Acland Hood, the Opposition Chief Whip) were both firmly in favour of outright rejection. Lansdowne preferred, and argued for, a series of incapacitating amendments. By September the Tory leader in the Lords was persuaded that the veto, desirable or not, was unavoidable. However, the Cabinet, despite having no doubt about the Opposition's intentions, decided 'not to determine any definite cause of action'[32] until the Opposition declared its hand. So the manocuvring began.

The King – who, like everyone else of influence, knew what Balfour intended – attempted to persuade the Unionists not to put the constitution in jeopardy. He suggested to Asquith that the government should offer to hold a general election before the budget was implemented on the understanding that, after a victory which amounted to a clear mandate from the people, the Lords would not obstruct the Finance Bill. Asquith rejected what at Court was thought of as a compromise, but was recognised in Downing Street as the concession that the Lords could insist on a dissolution before accepting the will of the Commons. Asquith decided instead to draft a Finance (No. 2) Bill which, since it included only the uncontroversial taxes, was unlikely to be obstructed and would at least allow the collection of revenue while the budget battle raged on. The Clerk to the House of Commons persuaded him that the bill would be just another admission that the Lords were entitled to reject tax proposals. It was then that Asquith and his ministers formally accepted what they had long known to be true. On 19 November 1909, the Cabinet agreed that, if the Lords rejected the budget, there would be an immediate general election.

Although Asquith had told his Chancellor of the Exchequer that it was important to behave as if the Lords might still see sense – not least out of respect for the King, whose hopes of compromise withstood all the evidence that it was impossible – Lloyd George contrived to make inflammatory speeches. Rejecting the allegation that political uncertainty had undermined economic confidence, he returned to his favourite theme. 'Only one stock has gone down badly. There has been a great slump in dukes. They used to stand rather higher in the market, especially the Tory Market. But the Tory press has just discovered that they are of no real value.'[33]

The Finance Bill received its Third Reading in the Commons on 4 November – and was carried by 379 votes to 149. Its consideration by the House of Lords was scheduled to begin on 11 November. On the night before, the Unionists took the formal decision to reject the budget and Asquith addressed a Liberal Party rally in the Albert Hall.

> I tell you quite frankly, and I tell my fellow countrymen outside, that neither I nor any other Liberal Minister supported by a majority in the House of Commons is going to submit again to the rebuffs and humiliations of the last four years. We shall not assume office and we shall not hold office unless we can secure the safeguards which experience shows us to be necessary for the legislative utility and honour of the party of progress.[34]

On 30 November 1909, the House of Lords rejected the budget by 350 votes to 75. 'Liberty', said Lloyd George, 'owes as much to the foolhardiness of its foes as to the sapience and wisdom of its friends . . . At least the course between the Peers and the People has been set down for trial in the grand assize of the people. The verdict will come soon.'

It came in the form of the general election on 15 January 1910. The budget was just as popular as the government hoped and the Opposition feared. However, general elections are rarely fought on the issues of the parties' choice. The Unionist coalition won 273 seats to the Liberals' 275 – a net gain for Balfour of 116. Asquith remained in office thanks to the support of 82 Nationalist and 40 Labour MPs. Politics had returned to the normal pattern of party allegiance. The Liberal landslide of 1906 had been an aberration brought about by the civil war in the Unionist Party. The 'swing' had been less against the government than in favour of old loyalties. In fact the Liberals had hung on to a remarkably large number of the votes which had 'floated' their way four years earlier.

The relative success of the Liberal campaign did not reduce the problem which might have followed so close a result. Fortunately John Redmond, the Nationalist leader, was at least as determined to break the power of the Lords as the most radical Liberal, for he feared that in 1910, as in 1895, the Upper House would block Home Rule. That one policy was the object of Redmond's political existence so, despite his reluctance to return to the issue that had destroyed Gladstone, it was the price which the Prime Minister had to pay for the Nationalists' support. There was no doubt that the budget resolutions would be carried in the new Parliament. But what if the House of Lords rejected it again? How was Asquith to fulfil his pledge to 'secure the safeguards' essential to the working of a democratic government?

Asquith had no doubt that he had a mandate to curb the power of the peers. His Cabinet had not agreed on what form the changes should take, but Lloyd George was publicly explicit. The people had already voted for reform and the budget. There had been 'two questions on the same ballot paper' – the budget and the House of Lords. But the popular will would only prevail if the bill in which it was set out was supported by both Houses of Parliament. The solution was to create – or, better still, to succeed by threatening to create – enough new peers to change the composition, and therefore the character, of the hereditary chamber.

Peerages – although then as now usually the product of political patronage – are, according to constitutional theory, the gift of the sovereign. Asquith had therefore made discreet enquiries in early November 1909 about the King's likely reaction to a request for Liberal reinforcements. The reply from Lord Knollys, King Edward's private secretary, was diplomatic but categoric. 'To create 570 new peers, which I am told would be the number required . . . would practically be almost an impossibility, and if asked for would place the King in an awkward position.'*[35] Knollys later added that His Majesty might be prepared to create three hundred new peers after a second general election. Although he did not explain why that specific number gained royal favour, he did set out, in stark language, the King's reasons for demanding a second poll. 'The King regards the policy of the Government as tantamount to the destruction of the House of Lords and thinks that, before the creation of a large number of peers is embarked upon or threatened, the country should be acquainted with the particular project for accomplishing that destruction.'[36] The King did not believe that there were two questions on one ballot paper.

Asquith had therefore gone into the January 1910 general election knowing that, whatever its outcome, the constitutional crisis would drag on. When the campaign was over and the limited victory won, the Cabinet resumed its inconsequential discussions about how the Lords was to be reformed. Harcourt wanted to concentrate on limiting the power of veto. Churchill wanted general reorganisation. Pressed to set out his policy, Asquith told the Commons 'wait and see', a phrase which critics claimed revealed his whole philosophy of government. When it was discovered that the King would prefer a 'plan which followed the line of Campbell-Bannerman's resolution of 1907',[37] opinion hardened around a variation of that proposal: a bill

---

*It would also have been of doubtful value to Asquith. The House of Lords 'admits' peers at its own discretion – normally at the rate of two a day on three days each sitting week. It would have taken three years for 570 new peers to take their seats.

passed in three successive sessions of Parliament by the House of Commons should become law whether or not it was endorsed by the House of Lords.

Still unsure of the King's reaction, Asquith moved to ensure the support of the Irish Nationalists. Redmond inflated the price of his support. Increases in spirit duty damaged the Irish whiskey industry and must be dropped from the budget. Asquith reported to the King the government's unanimous view that 'to purchase the Irish vote by such a concession would be a discreditable transaction'.[38] No doubt the King was impressed, but Asquith knew that most of the Irish (with Home Rule in mind) would support the budget anyway. And so they did. On 27 April 1910 it was carried on the Third Reading by 324 votes to 231.

On the same day, the Archbishop of Canterbury convened a meeting at Lambeth Palace. Its ostensible purpose was to avoid embarrassment for the King by achieving a compromise which insulated him from controversy. But, since it was attended by the Leader of the Opposition, it was not altogether objective in its analysis of what needed to be done. By then it was agreed that the Lords would let the budget through and fight the government, not on the right of dukes to exploit the increased value of their development land, but on the need to protect the state from arbitrary government. The Lords passed all the stages of the Finance Bill on the following day without one division. Asquith, after dining with Lloyd George to celebrate the budget's eventual acceptance, drove with Margot, his wife, to Portsmouth. There they joined the Board of Admiralty Yacht *Enchantress* for a Mediterranean cruise.

On 6 May, shortly after the *Enchantress* left Gibraltar, the Prime Minister received a wireless message from Lord Knollys: the King was mortally ill. The *Enchantress* turned for home. On 7 May, a second message reached the Admiralty Board Yacht. It was signed on behalf of George V. King Edward VII was dead. Asquith, who had travelled to Biarritz to receive his seals of office because the old King was on holiday, received his commission from the new King while cruising off Lisbon. The circumstances in which Asquith's premiership began, and his service to Edward VII ended, contributed to the myth that Edwardian Britain always put pleasure before work.

The Boer War was the poisoned inheritance which Edward VII was bequeathed by his mother. The constitutional crisis, Peers versus People, was the rancid legacy which he passed on to his son. Asquith, conscious of his obligations to a grieving son and inexperienced sovereign, said he 'would endeavour to come to some sort of understanding with the Opposition to prevent a general election'.[39] In any event, the idea of a constitutional conference appealed to him. The alternative was a dreary repetition of the events leading up to the January election and, in the absence of new peers, another stalemate. The talks covered a remarkably wide terrain, including, at Lloyd George's suggestion, a grand coalition of the major parties to resolve all the outstanding issues from Home Rule to Lords' reform. But there was no real common ground. When the talks broke down, the Cabinet could only resume the 'old fight against the Lords'[40] with another dissolution and another general election.

To make sense of the repeat performance, Asquith needed assurances from the new King that the second general election having been held and won, new peers would be appointed. At first the King was strongly opposed – partly because of confusion in his mind about whether it was the guarantee of elevations or the elevations themselves for which the Prime Minister asked. Asquith made his request clear by saying that the guarantee need not be made public until it was redeemed in a future Parliament. The notion of what amounted to a secret compact greatly impressed Knollys, who advised the King to agree to the Prime Minister's request. It was clearly in the interests of the monarchy as well as the monarch for him to do so. If he refused, Asquith would feel it was necessary to resign, and the brief Balfour administration which followed would end with a general election in which the King's conduct would be the chief source of dispute between the parties.

Nevertheless, Sir Arthur Bigge, the private secretary who had been with the King since he was the Prince of Wales, argued against accepting the government's proposal. And Bigge – although junior to Knollys, closer to the King – might well have got his way had the senior adviser not deceived his sovereign. As a result of the Lambeth Palace meeting a message had been sent by the Archbishop of Canterbury to King Edward. It explained that Balfour had made clear that he would be prepared to form a government to 'avoid the King being put in the invidious position which would follow a demand for new peers'.[41] It never reached the new King. Instead Knollys predicted, perhaps even said, that he had been informed that Balfour would decline to form a minority (and necessarily brief) administration. The King's mind was made up. He had no choice but to accept his Prime Minister's request. The alternative was parliamentary anarchy. The King wrote in his diary, 'I agreed most reluctantly to give the Cabinet a secret undertaking that, in the event of the government being returned with a majority at the General Election, I should use my prerogative to make Peers if asked for. I did dislike doing this very much, but agreed that this was the only alternative to the whole Cabinet resigning.'[42]

That meant that Asquith had won. But before victory could be declared, there had to be a general election (in which the Unionists lost one seat and the Liberals three) and long, weary nights of discussion and division on a Parliament Bill which reduced the Lords' power of veto to the ability to delay. Between 28 June and 6 July the House of Lords emasculated the Bill. It returned to the Commons and, at the King's insistence, was sent back to the Lords, restored to its original form with a request for reconsideration. The Unionists in the Upper House, suspecting (or perhaps knowing) that Asquith would ask for new peers, were deeply divided about whether to fight a gallant rearguard action or retreat. Despite that, passions ran high in both Houses of Parliament. On 24 July 1911, Asquith was shouted down in the Commons in an unprecedented scene of verbal violence. He was called 'Traitor!' and subjected to the strange, rhetorical question 'Who killed the King?'[43] The Tories in the House of Commons maintained the *esprit de corps* of a public school. So the deeply divided Shadow Cabinet gave the two warring factions nicknames. Both were puns on agricultural occupations. The 'Hedgers' were ready to surrender. The 'Ditchers' wanted to fight on.★ The 'Ditchers' had a slight majority in the Shadow Cabinet. But Balfour wanted to hedge. So hedge became their recommendation. Asquith, who either did not

---

★The 'Hedgers' were Balfour, Bonar Law, Lansdowne, Curzon and Long. The 'Ditchers' were Chamberlain, Smith, Carson, Selborne, Salisbury and Halesbury.

know or did not believe that the Opposition would draw back, prepared for another rejection. A list of potential Liberal (or at least
reformist) peers was drawn up. It included Gilbert Murray, Thomas
Hardy and J. M. Barrie.

The King, although determined to keep his promise, began to lose
his nerve. It was, he said, essential that his reluctance to create new
peers was made clear. Then, anxious only for the drama to end, he
urged the Unionists to give way gracefully. Grace was beyond them,
but they did give way. On 10 August 1910 the Parliament Bill, in the
form sent up to the House of Lords for a second time, was carried by
131 votes to 114. The government's majority included thirteen bishops and thirty-seven Unionists who, under the influence of a suddenly
emollient Lord Curzon, had eventually accepted that the House of
Lords, like the rest of life, must change from time to time.

Of course it remained a basically Edwardian institution. It was
Edward who, realising the English love of pageant, tradition and ceremony, had revived the State Opening of Parliament with the Lords
in their ermine-edged scarlet robes in attendance on their sovereign.
He had brought *Iolanthe* to life, and the reforms which began in his
reign (and were completed with the confused co-operation of his son)
moved the Lords just far enough into the real world to guarantee its
survival. It was a strange combination of show and cynicism which, in
the end, produced progress. In that it was typically Edwardian.

PART THREE

'The Force Majeure which Activates and Arms'

By 1900 Britain had reached the point of general prosperity at which most working men and women possessed both enough to eat and sufficient self-confidence to ask for more. Often their demands were articulated on their behalf by the middle classes. But increasingly the calls for greater influence and an improved standard of living were supported by mass movements of their own, dedicated to achieving a radical change in society. The people's century had begun. A substantial section of the working class – Conservative voters included – was no longer willing to be ruled by its 'betters'. Rebellion began to replace deference. The rich man remained in his castle but the poor man at the gate wanted to play some part in the determination of his own destiny.

Trade unionists, women, Irish Nationalists all campaigned with renewed vigour for what they regarded as their natural rights. Even the Establishment came to believe that success – perhaps even survival as a Great Power – required a better educated working class and an extension of higher education beyond the boundaries of the ancient universities. The century of the common man, and woman, had begun.

The campaigning escalated from rhetoric to revolt. First the disadvantaged and dispossessed – ranging from Methodists who believed that the new schools system discriminated against their faith to Irish Republicans who demanded Home Rule – tried to work within the system. Then it became clear that the citadels would fall only to a direct attack.

The trade unions – always respectable – decided to travel to power by the parliamentary route. Women and the Irish attempted to follow but were rebuffed and decided on more dramatic protests. Militancy was encouraged by a comment made by the Home Secretary, Herbert Gladstone, during one of the many debates on women's suffrage. Success, he unwisely said, is achieved only by application of 'the force majeure which activates and arms'.

CHAPTER 9

Ourselves Alone

English politicians have never understood Ireland and the Irish. At the beginning of the twentieth century, it was still the view, in Westminster and Whitehall, that the fate of the nation and people would be determined by the Imperial Parliament. The Irish character dictated otherwise. The formal legislative decisions remained with the Houses of Commons and Lords. But after 1900 the pace at which Home Rule was approached, and the form which it eventually took, was imposed on hesitant and reluctant governments by pressure from the 'nationalists' on one hand and the 'loyalists' on the other. The rival factions both demonstrated their ruthless determination with an identical threat which they undoubtedly meant to make good. Each of them announced that, if the final settlement was not to their liking, they would set up their own provisional government and, if necessary, defend it by force of arms.

The Boer War had distracted English attention from the demand for Home Rule, but had served to confirm nationalist opinion about the ruthless brutality of imperialist government. Michael Davitt, an old Parnellite and Nationalist MP, went to South Africa as the war stuttered to its bitter end and wrote on his return:

England has killed Christian children, has imprisoned Christian women in barbed wire enclosures, has devastated Christian churches where there was less poverty and less vice than in any other Christian community in the world and has armed savages to help her in a war which has its origins in motives as base and as odious as ever prompted a Sultan of Turkey to burn an Armenian village . . . And yet Cardinal Vaughan,★ in the name of the Catholic Church in England . . . calls down God's blessing on the arms which are exterminating Christian nations.[1]

Younger and more militant republicans took up arms in defence of the Boers. Arthur Griffith – a founder of Sinn Fein and one day to become the President of the Irish Free State government – and John MacBride – pillar of the Celtic Literary Society and active member of the revolutionary Irish Republic Brotherhood – had gone together to the Transvaal to work in the Langlaagte gold mine.[2] MacBride remained in South Africa and organised an Irish Brigade to fight with the Boers against the British. Most of its members were Americans of Irish origin, but they fought under a gold-fringed green banner which was emblazoned with a harp and the motto 'Our Lord. Our People. Our Language'.

A second Irish Brigade, under the self-styled Colonel Lynch, South African correspondent of *Collier's Weekly*, was largely made up of Afrikaners and augmented by German and French mercenaries. Between them, the two battalions did not number five hundred men, whereas several thousand Irishmen – some in Irish regiments but most in 'English' infantry battalions – fought for the Empire. The London music hall audiences sang 'Brave, Dublin Fusiliers' and asked 'What Do You Think of the Irish Now?'.[3] But the *Inghinidhe na hEireann* (Daughters of Ireland) organised by Maud Gonne, the daughter of a Unionist colonel in the British Army, were doing all they could to undermine the morale of British soldiers stationed in Dublin. Young women who 'walked out with Redcoats' were harassed in the street. The Board of Guardians was persuaded to enquire into the number of illegitimate children in the Dublin

---

★Cardinal Vaughan's contribution to Edwardian life and thought is discussed in Chapter 17, 'Would You Believe It?'

workhouse, with the clear implication that the responsibility lay with the British garrison. Irish nationalism depended on a combustible combination of romanticism and violence. So, despite her success on the streets and Irish battalions' failure in South Africa, Maud Gonne believed that 'the band of Irishmen in the [Boer] Brigade had done more for Ireland's honour than all of us at home'.[4]

Maud Gonne's introduction to Irish politics had been conventional social work among the starving peasantry of the western counties. She was immortalised by W. B. Yeats – who loved her and lost her – in his poem *Easter 1916*:

> What voice more sweet than hers
> When young and beautiful . . .?

That unlikely description of a revolutionary was complemented by an even more surprising, but equally forlorn, encomium to two other women whose names are forever linked in the cause of Irish nationalism:

> The light of evening Lissadell
> Great windows open to the south,
> Two girls in silk kimonos, both
> Beautiful, one a gazelle.

Lissadell was the family home of Eva and Constance Gore-Booth. Like Maud Gonne, the Gore-Booth sisters were daughters of the Protestant ascendancy. In her youth Constance Gore-Booth had shared Maud Gonne's enthusiasm for hunting. The Master of the Sligo Hunt said that she rode as well as the best men in the field. She also, wrongly as it turned out, believed herself to possess artistic talent. At art school in London, she showed no interest in politics. After she married Count Markievicz, a minor Polish aristocrat, and returned to Ireland she patronised rather than practised the arts and helped to raise funds for the Abbey Theatre which Yeats and Lady Gregory had founded in Dublin. During amateur dramatics rehearsals, she found a copy of the magazine *Sinn Fein* lying about. She read it while waiting for her cue. It set out the argument for taking Irish nationalism out of

Westminster and on to the Dublin streets. She was instantly converted to Arthur Griffith's cause. Paradoxically, the Countess Markievicz was to become the first woman to win election to the Imperial Parliament – though she would not take her seat in the Commons. Yeats turned against her. But the nationalists forgave her for the upper-class accent which made her speak of her devotion to 'Ahland'. By the time she joined them, they were used to the habits of the Protestant ascendancy. When a nationalist prisoner was released, emotionally unstable, from Portland Gaol, she saved him from mental hospital by what she described as 'confining him to my old nurse in her peaceful little house'.[5]

During the blockhouse and wire phase of the South African war, Irish nationalists in Dublin constantly demonstrated in favour of the Boers or, to be more exact, against the British. They would have supported anyone who was fighting against the Empire, but there was, amongst Irish nationalists, a genuine sympathy for oppressed people of every sort. That attitude was typified by Roger Casement, scholar, diplomat and mystic. In 1904, he became a centre of world attention when his report on the Belgian colonial administration of the Congo exposed the 'atrocities' which were an established feature of the regime. A year later he wrote an account, for the *United Irishman*, of his father's campaigns with Louis Kossuth, the Hungarian patriot. Like many middle-class nationalists, he was eclectic to the point of eccentricity in his pursuit of the Irish ideal. While abroad on Consular Service, he had insisted that his address was the Consulate of Great Britain and Ireland, and he wanted a separate team to represent Ireland in the Olympic Games.[6] He held less than practical views on how the campaign for independence should proceed: Irish Nationalist MPs should desert Westminster and return to Dublin and form a National Executive to 'create a confident, reliant National mind in the country'.[7] Whatever the implausibility of his plans, he contributed to the emotional impetus that kept nationalism alive in early Edwardian Ireland when Westminster believed that the dream had died. Like Yeats, Maud Gonne and the Gore-Booth sisters, Casement thought of himself as a servant of Cathleen ni Houlihan, Ireland's mystic queen.

The social and cultural elite formed only a small part of the hinterland from which Nationalist politicians could draw strength.

Despite Gladstone's two Land Acts, Ireland remained 'the most dis-
tressful country'. Sixty-three per cent of Dublin's population – about
194,000 out of 304,000 people – were officially designated as 'working class'.[8] Half of the 'working class' lived in tenement houses.
Half of those families occupied only one room. Communal 'stand
pipes' provided water. Sometimes one tap served as many as ninety
individuals. The same number of families often shared two earth
closets. 'We cannot conceive', an official report concluded, 'how any
self-respecting male or female could be expected to use accommodation such as we have seen.' Throughout the early years of the
twentieth century, the standard of living in Ireland was appreciably
below that in mainland Britain. The cost of living rose more quickly
in Dublin than in London, but Dublin wages, always below London
levels, did not keep pace. Printers were paid about 90 per cent of the
London wage, skilled building workers 70 per cent and labourers 54
per cent. The time was ripe for intervention by the trade unions
which had been a feature of English industrial life, at least for skilled
craftsmen, for seventy years.

James Larkin, the son of a poor Irish immigrant, worked (like his
father) in the Liverpool docks. He became the General Organiser of
the National Union of Dock Labourers. In 1907 he extended his
work to Dublin and then moved on to Belfast. A year later, he
founded the Irish Transport and General Workers Union and became
its general secretary. Larkin was essentially a syndicalist, for whom
Home Rule took a poor third place to an increased hourly rate for
Irish industrial workers and the eventual dictatorship of the proletariat. Griffith, of *Sinn Fein*, thought of Larkin as a representative of
English trade unionism in a nation which wanted to put aside all
things English; but the preface to the Transport Union's handbook
held out hope that Larkin would one day be an effective ally. A series
of land acts had, in Larkin's Marxist judgement, transformed Ireland
from a feudal to a capitalist society. He wanted to free its people from
the 'soulless, sordid, money-grabbing propensities of the Irish capitalist class'. The land belonged to people who were 'entitled to the
fullness of the earth and the abundance thereof'.[9] Those views he
propagated, to the immense advantage of Irish nationalism, in *The
Irish Worker*, a newspaper with a circulation ten times as great as

Arthur Griffith's *Sinn Fein*, the official journal of the party which later took that name, ever achieved.

James Connolly was, like Larkin, the son of an Irish labourer who had emigrated to find work. Young James, with no better prospects than his father – carting refuse in Edinburgh when his son was born – enlisted in the British Army. He remained with the colours for almost seven years but – at least according to legend – deserted when he had only a few months left to serve.[10] He returned to Scotland, first to Perth and then to Dundee, where two branches of the Marxist Social Democratic Federation competed for his attention with the advocates of 'New Unionism', the industrial organisation of unskilled labourers. Connolly's militancy was the product of experience. His father, having suffered an accident at work, was demoted to lavatory attendant on a wage reduced from 19s 6d to 7s 6d a week.[11]

In 1895, Connolly was appointed full-time organiser of the Dublin Socialist Club and returned to Ireland. A year later, he became active in the Republican movement. Neither Connolly nor the cause prospered. In 1903 he emigrated to America where he lived with his cousins in up-state New York and was employed as agent for the Metropolitan Life Insurance Company.[12] His fellow workers were deeply unimpressed by his advocacy of the principles laid down in Marx's Erfurt Programme, and in 1910, disillusioned once more, he returned to Ireland to become the Belfast organiser of Larkin's Irish Transport and General Workers Union. He remained an unrepentant Marxist. 'If you remove the English army tomorrow and hoist the green flag over Dublin, unless you set about the organisation of a socialist republic, your efforts would be in vain . . . England would still rule you to your ruin, even while your lips offered hypocritical homage at the shrine of that freedom whose cause you betrayed.'[13]

Maud Gonne, who adopted Griffith's Sinn Fein policy 'because it taught self-reliance and called for the withdrawal of the Irish Members from Westminster and the setting up of the Irish Council responsible for the Irish nation', described herself as the 'link between Griffith and James Connolly on one side and between him and Yeats on the other'.[14] But about one subject they needed no intermediary to reconcile their views. Both men knew that independence alone would not solve the land's problems.

> Parnell came down the road, he said to a cheering man
> 'Ireland shall get her freedom and you still break stones.'

At the moment of 'terrible beauty' in 1916, James Connolly –
leading his Irish Citizens' Army from Liberty Hall, the headquarters
of his union – established his place in Republican folklore as a warrior
and he went on to achieve immortality as one of the martyrs of the
uprising. He stands, in the pantheon of Irish nationalism, alongside
Eamonn de Valera and Michael Collins, both late recruits to the
cause. De Valera, a mathematics teacher, did not become formally
associated with the nationalist movement until November 1913.
Connolly was essentially an organiser who was planning revolution in
Dublin when young Michael Collins was still making his way from
Clonakilly to the Post Office Savings Bank in London's West
Kensington, and then through Horne and Co. (Stockbrokers) to the
Board of Trade. In 1916 Collins and Connolly were shoulder to shoulder alongside Plunkett, MacDonagh, Pearse and MacDiarmad in the
Dublin General Post Office, while de Valera was directing fire on the
same English enemy from Boland's Mill. Connolly's claim to stand
apart from and above them rests on the years of methodical work he
put in for Irish nationalism and Ireland's poor which preceded the
declaration of the Republic in 1916.

In Westminster, despite the signs of burgeoning revolution which
Connolly, Larkin, Gonne and the Gore-Booth sisters typified, the
politicians continued to think of Home Rule as a matter to be
decided by the normal process of parliamentary and party business.
The Unionists reiterated that they were against it for ever and the
Liberals did business with John Redmond, the leader of the
Nationalist Party, according to their needs and his strengths. When
they could form a government without his support, Ireland was
forgotten.

In defence of the imperial Parliament, it has to be acknowledged
that it was difficult for English gentlemen to believe that politics
could be taken from the ballot box on to the streets with such effect
that the government of the greatest empire that the world had ever
known would be forced into a change of policy. They had been
warned. In the *United Irishman* Arthur Griffith set out the position

plainly enough. 'The era of constitutional possibilities for Irish nationality ended on the day that Charles Stewart Parnell died.'[15] But
Griffith, they believed, was whistling in the dark. Irish nationalism
had run its course. When Charles Dolan, the Nationalist Party
Member of Parliament for North Leitrim, resigned his seat and fought
the by-election as a Sinn Fein candidate he was beaten decisively. The
assumption in Whitehall was that 'Fenian outrages' were, like every
other aspect of Republicanism, part of Ireland's unhappy history.

In 1903 Arthur Griffith's *United Irishman* (a republican paper older
than his own *Sinn Fein*) interrupted the advocacy of route marching
and musket drill to call for a boycott of King Edward's visit to Ireland.
'To Irish Nationalists, the King is as foreign as the Akond of Swat, but,
unlike that potentate, he claims to be the sovereign of this country.'[16]
The King was welcomed with almost universal rapture. 'No sovereign',
wrote the *Cork Examiner*, 'visiting our shores ever met with anything
like the hearty good will, the honest unaffected welcome extended by
the people of all classes in every part of the county . . . This fortnight
has made history.'[17] The newspaper was, by implication, comparing
the King's reception with the hostility with which he had been greeted
when, as Prince of Wales, he had visited Ireland in 1885.

It seemed that the political tide was moving against Home Rule.
And Lord Rosebery's several attacks on Campbell-Bannerman, which
had begun when the new party leader was under threat because of his
outspoken views on the Boer War, had been increasingly focused on
the Liberal Party's continued commitment to Irish self-government. It
seemed that the opponents of what was still official party policy had
found the champion they needed. The Liberal Imperial Council,
founded at the turn of the century, was emboldened to issue a bla-
tantly divisive manifesto. 'The time has arrived when it is necessary to
clearly and permanently distinguish Liberals in whose policy with
regard to Imperial questions patriotic voters may justly repose confidence from those whose opinions naturally disqualify them from
controlling the actions of an imperial Parliament.'[18]

Opponents of Home Rule were waiting for a politician of standing
and stature to lead the fight. Rosebery was clearly the man. In
February 1902, he had published a letter in *The Times* which expressly
repudiated Campbell-Bannerman's leadership of the Liberal Party.

The letter was a reply to Campbell-Bannerman's who had asked rhetorically if Rosebery's criticisms of Liberal policy were made from the 'interior of our political tabernacles or from some vantage point outside?' Rosebery's answer was that he 'remained outside the tabernacle, but not . . . in solitude'. The threat was implied but obvious. Then Rosebery struck again with his 'fly-blown phylacteries' speech in Chesterfield and the rejection of 'Mr Gladstone's party' for as long as it supported Home Rule – a particularly damaging assertion since Campbell-Bannerman had just recommitted the party to support that policy.

Campbell-Bannerman, who was in no mood to temporise, denounced what amounted to a call for schism. In the passionate debate which followed, many of the speeches were made at lunches and after dinners. So it came to be called 'war to the knife and fork'. But there was very little that was congenial or gregarious about the spirit in which the demands and counter-demands were made. From time to time, Liberal politicians were distracted from their internecine warfare by Lloyd George's allegation that the Chamberlains were the beneficiaries of government contracts for Boer War military supplies. Beneath the surface of superficial unity in face of a common enemy, the disagreements rumbled on.

There was talk of attempts, by Liberal Home Rulers, to oust 'imperialists' and plots by 'imperialists' to unseat Home Rulers. Campbell-Bannerman – who had survived a vote of confidence in his leadership – told a party meeting, perhaps as the price of his survival, that he had no objection to the expression of differing views, only to the creation of organisations formed with the intention of 'perpetuating and accelerating' them. Asquith, whose manoeuvring on the subject was more astute than honourable, was, Campbell-Bannerman believed, in a strong position to calm the agitation. A request that he should not speak at one of the 'imperialist' banquets was rejected with the typically urbane explanation that he had already accepted the invitation and it would be discourteous not to fulfil his obligation.

The campaign against Campbell-Bannerman gained force. Opponents leap-frogged each other as they extended their criticism from South Africa to Ireland and from Ireland to the man who persisted in advocating Home Rule. Haldane exploited Asquith's

determination to maintain his position as 'Prime Minister in waiting'
by asking him to lead the demand for a change of direction with a
public repudiation of the Liberals' traditional commitment to Irish
self-government. Asquith responded with speculation about the possibility of a 'clean slate' promoting a reconciliation with the Liberal
Unionists. When he addressed his constituents he endorsed Rosebery's
view of Home Rule but was silent on the subject of Campbell-
Bannerman. Asquith used the high regard in which Gladstone was
held to justify the rejection of his most passionately held belief. Even
Gladstone's 'magnificent courage, unequalled authority and
unquenchable enthusiasm' had not convinced the British people of
the need for an Irish parliament.

> Is it to be part of the policy and programme of this party that, if
> returned to power, it will introduce into the House of
> Commons a bill for Irish Home Rule? The answer, in my judge-
> ment, is No. A reconciliation of Ireland to the Empire and the
> relief of the imperial parliament from unnecessary burdens can
> only be attained by methods which will carry with them . . . the
> sanction and sympathy of British opinion. To recognise facts
> like these is not apostasy, it is common sense.[19]

For a time, objections to Home Rule and reservations about
Campbell-Bannerman's leadership of the Liberal Party were both
obscured by the Unionist government's suicidal inclination to prove
that, despite its apparently unassailable majority in the House of
Commons, it was too divided to serve out the full Parliament. There
were damaging divisions in the Cabinet about the way in which the
Chancellor (Ritchie) had chosen to pay for the war, the Education
Bill which reorganised the management of elementary and secondary schools throughout England and Wales and, above all, tariff
reform – more accurately described as the introduction of protection
in place of free trade. One night in May 1903, after the Chancellor
had defied the protectionists by repealing the corn duty which had
been imposed during the war. Campbell-Bannerman announced
when he arrived home, 'Wonderful news today. It is only a matter of
time when we shall sweep them aside.'[20] His optimism was entirely

Queen Victoria's funeral cortège. 'Farewell to an era, the greatness of which we can scarcely judge.' *(Hulton Archive / Getty Images)*

Edward VII: 'Kind, debonair and not undignified, but too human.'
(*Ernest H. Mills/Getty Images*)

A country house weekend. 'The disposition of bedrooms . . . was tactful and discreet.'
(Camera Press)

Alice Keppel. Churchill
asked, 'Will she be
appointed First Lady of
the Bedchamber?'
(Camera Press)

A. J. Balfour. 'He saw a great deal of life from afar.' *(Topical Press Agency / Getty Images)*

Joseph Chamberlain 'talked as if he had the British Empire in his own back yard and put up a notice "No Admittance Except on Business"'. *(The National Archives)*

Asquith and his wife outside St Margaret's, Westminster. 'Neither I nor any other Liberal minister is going to submit again to the rebuffs and humiliations of the last four years.' *(Mirrorpix)*

David Lloyd George. 'Provision for the aged and deserving poor.' *(Hulton Archive/Getty Images)*

Winston Churchill. The House of Lords 'has started a class war. They had better be careful.' *(Ernest H. Mills/Getty Images)*

The Evans family. Rowland, the
diarist, stands next to his mother.
(Courtesy of Christine Glossop)

The diarist Kate Jarvis
at the time of her
marriage. *(Courtesy of
Gervald Frykman)*

Edward Elgar. 'I ask for no reward, only to live and hear my work.' *(Mirrorpix)*

W. B. Yeats. 'The most perfect expression of the vague enchanted beauty' of the Celtic twilight. *(Hulton Archive/Getty Images)*

justified, though few people would have shared his view at the time. A couple of months earlier he had almost been swept aside by his own party.

Asquith – motivated either by personal ambition or by public spirit – had first announced his considered judgement that the Liberal Party should never again take office if its House of Commons majority depended on the support of the Irish Nationalist Party. Then he accepted the vice presidency of the Liberal League – the Liberal Imperial Council by another name – under the presidency of Lord Rosebery. It was argued by Asquith's Liberal detractors that he was using his opposition to Home Rule to guarantee that he became leader. His supporters insisted that he already knew that the succession was his and that he was motivated only by a determination to prevent yet another Liberal government from being destroyed by its preoccupation with Ireland. Asquith's undoubted impatience to assume first the leadership of his party and eventually the premiership was accentuated by the always mischievous Lord Rosebery who – supported by Haldane and Grey – committed himself to doing all he could to replace Campbell-Bannerman.

In Ireland, nationalists were revising their history rather than realigning or revitalising their forces. Arthur Griffith had written a number of articles in the *United Irishman* which urged Irishmen to emulate the behaviour of those Hungarian patriots who, by emphasising their cultural differences with Vienna and boycotting the Imperial Parliament, had at least won the concession of equal status for their country within the double monarchy of the Austro-Hungarian empire. Nobody had been very impressed. In November 1905, just as Arthur Balfour was leaving office, the First National Convention of the Gaelic League met under the slogan 'Sinn Fein' – the title of the newspaper which was to become the name of a political party. It marked a new emphasis on self-reliance. Consistent with the policy of 'Ourselves Alone', the Convention resisted what it described as the insult of the Westminster government's offer to devolve some items of administration from London to Dublin.

The new Liberal government – conscious that its cautious attitude towards Home Rule had helped win the election – did nothing to convince the Nationalists that its Devolution Bill was worth having. The Council which it offered to create (a name normally associated with local government) was to have 106 members – 82 elected and the rest appointed by government. It was to have no law-making or tax-raising powers, and its duties were limited to performance of the administrative tasks previously discharged by eight of the forty-five departments within the Irish Office. But the way in which ministers spoke of the proposals did more to prejudice Irish opinion against them than the limited nature of the proposals themselves.

August Birrell, the Chief Secretary for Ireland, introduced the Bill with a speech that concentrated almost exclusively on its limited scope and boasted that it did not contain 'a touch or a trace, a hint or a suggestion of any new legislative power or authority'. At first Redmond and the parliamentary Nationalists welcomed the proposals as better than nothing. Popular opinion was so antagonistic that they retracted their support and announced their intention to vote against the Bill in the Commons. Devolution, as distinct from Home Rule, was dead. But the inadequacy of the government's proposals and the feebleness of the parliamentarians' response had reawakened old passions where the battle for Ireland was to be fought and won – on the streets.

The Irish Nationalist Members of Parliament had begun to recognise the danger that the battle for Home Rule would be taken out of their hands. They took it in turn to reassure each other that there was nothing to worry about. Dillon wrote to Redmond, 'This Sinn Fein business is a very serious matter, and it has been spreading pretty rapidly for the last year.' But then he added a cheerful postscript. 'If the [Irish National] party and the movement keep on the right lines, it will not become very formidable because it has no one with any brains to lead it.'[21] Perhaps he was right in 1906, but intellectual reinforcements were on their way. And the army which marched behind the green banner was already led with burning passion. Westminster and Whitehall were not equipped to understand MacBride, Gonne, Yeats, Gore-Booth, Casement and the other romantics who kept Irish hopes alive – with a little financial help from John Devoy's Clan-na-Gael in America – while Home Rule lay fallow in the imperial Parliament.

Help, when it came four years later, was in the unlikely form of the English electorate. When Campbell-Bannerman resigned because of his fast deteriorating health, he was replaced by Asquith, who had been Rosebery's first lieutenant on the Liberal Imperial Council. Asquith needed the Irish Nationalists. When, in 1909, the House of Lords had rejected Lloyd George's 'People's Budget', Asquith determined to secure the allegiance of the minor parties in Parliament. On 10 December 1909 he had promised a Liberal rally in the Albert Hall, 'a policy which, while explicitly safeguarding the supremacy and indefectible authority of the Imperial Parliament, will set up in Ireland a system of full self-government in regard to purely Irish affairs'. The two general elections of 1910 confirmed how wise that decision was. In the second – called to clarify the uncertainties which followed the first – the Liberals and Unionists each won two hundred and seventy-two seats. The balance of power was held by eighty-two Irish Nationalists and forty-two Labour Members.

Asquith kept his word but, once again, the crucial influence on Ireland's future was exerted by Ireland itself – not through the 'democratic process' of the Imperial Parliament but by the direct threat of force. The Prime Minister clearly believed that the future of the province would be decided by the Commons and Lords – as it had been decided in Gladstone's day. He had not made proper allowance for the Unionists, whose resistance to Irish autonomy was at least as fierce as the Nationalists' support for separation, but better organised and more adequately financed. And Unionist rebels, unlike their Nationalist adversaries, enjoyed the support of a large part of the English Establishment. When changing circumstances put them on the wrong side of the law, the treason of 'loyalists' was either ignored or excused.

The Home Rule Bill of 1912 was, in a very real sense, the Irish Nationalists' reward for supporting the government during the constitutional crisis which ended with the Parliament Bill and the reduction of the House of Lords' powers. But, since it took almost two years for gratitude to be translated into legislation, 'Loyalists' were able to prepare their resistance even before the details of the proposed settlement were announced. The 'Orange Lodges' – part social, part political and wholly bigoted in their view of Catholics and

Catholicism – were always at their strongest when Home Rule was on the agenda of the Imperial Parliament. Even in 1904 – when the worst they had had to fear was limited devolution – two Ulster Unionist MPs had announced that the prospect of even so modest a measure provided 'an opportune moment to revive on a war footing the active work of the various Ulster Defence Associations'.[22] The Ulster Unionist Council – established in 1905 and guaranteeing 'consistent and continuous action' – regarded the Home Rule promise that Asquith had made in the Albert Hall before the first 1910 election as sufficient justification for escalating its state of readiness. By the time that the election came, Walter Long, the leader of the Ulster Unionists, had abandoned his seat in Dublin South for a more convenient London constituency. The Unionists chose as his successor Sir Edward Carson, the Member of Parliament for Dublin University. Before the second 1910 election the Council had set up an armaments fund.[23]

Carson, although a liberal in matters of domestic policy, was a Unionist zealot. Robert Kee in *The Green Flag*, his monumental study of Irish history, quotes Carson's two statements of principle – 'It is only for Ireland that I am in politics' and 'It is only for the sake of the Union that I am in politics.' Kee suggests that Carson regarded the two explanations of his motives as self-evidently the same. From the very beginning of his leadership, he assumed that Home Rule must be resisted and could only be defeated by what amounted to rebellion. In January 1911, in London on parliamentary business, he told Lady Londonderry, 'I wish I could be in Ulster to know whether men are desperately in earnest and prepared to make great sacrifices.'[24] He wrote to James Craig, the Member of Parliament for East Down and whiskey millionaire who was to become his co-conspirator, in even more apocalyptic language. 'What I am very anxious about is to satisfy myself that people over there really mean to resist. I am not for a mere game of bluff and unless men are ready to make great sacrifices, which they clearly understand, the talk of resistance is no use.'[25]

Craig was equally intransigent in his opposition to the 1912 Home Rule Bill. But while Carson felt an obligation to Ireland as a whole, Craig's concern was for Ulster. Carson and Craig formed so formidable a partnership that, even before the Home Rule Bill was debated, the government had prepared the route of its retreat. Faced with the prospect of open rebellion, the Cabinet considered 'at great length and from a number of diverse points of view' how best to meet the threat. One possibility was partition. Asquith's report to the King does not suggest that the discussion on that subject had been easy or that ministers were in unanimous agreement with the eventual conclusion. The best that could be said of the meeting was 'at the end the Cabinet acquiesced' to what began with a bold reassertion of established policy. The Home Rule Bill 'should apply to the whole of Ireland'. But after that initial show of strength, ministers 'held themselves free to make such changes to the Bill as fresh evidence of facts or the pressure of British opinion may render expedient'.[26] Carson and Craig were not the men to miss such an obvious opportunity. If the Cabinet's mind could be changed, they would change it.

Craig organised the first great anti-Home Rule demonstration in his own house, Craigavon, on 23 September 1911. The Bill, which was still being drafted, was not to be debated in Parliament for another six months – but almost fifty thousand Orangemen, some of whom had marched to Craigavon in military formation, heard Carson's declaration of war.

I now enter into a compact with you and, with the help of God, you and I joined together will defeat the most nefarious conspiracy that has ever been hatched against a free people . . . We must be prepared, in the event of a Home Rule Bill passing, with such measures as will carry on for ourselves the government of those districts of which we have control . . . We must be prepared, . . . the moment [that] Home Rule passes, ourselves to become responsible for the Protestant Province of Ulster.[27]

During Easter week 1912, two days before the Home Rule Bill was introduced into the House of Commons, an even bigger demonstration was held on the agricultural showground in Balmoral, a prosperous Belfast suburb. One hundred thousand men and women assembled under the largest Union Flag ever made. Carson and Craig spoke with their confidence renewed. Andrew Bonar Law – the new Leader of His Majesty's Loyal Opposition – joined them on the platform to fulfil his promise that, when the Orangemen refused to accept the will of Parliament, 'they would not be wanting help from across the water'. All the Unionist rebels had another reason to rejoice. Field Marshal, the Earl Roberts of Kandahar, KG, VC, had visited the province a couple of weeks earlier and told Carson, 'I hope something will come of it.'[28] His good wishes had been taken to be more than a platitude. 'Bobs' would, they believed, speak up for them to the generals. Their hopes were reinforced during the debate on the Second Reading of the Home Rule Bill, when Sir J. B. Lonsdale (the Member of Parliament for mid-Armagh) cried out across the chamber, 'Try it. Call out the British Army to compel Ulster and see what happens.'

Even the Ulster Unionists had been slow to recognise that the British Army might be called upon to put down an armed rebellion which spread across all Ulster. At the Craigavon rally 'it had been noticed that a contingent of Craigmen from Tyrone . . . displayed a greater degree of smartness and precision, both in their marching and in their turn-out generally. Upon enquiry, it transpired that these men had, for some time, been learning the elements of military drill.'[29] Surprise in Belfast was matched by astonishment in London.

The men who opposed Home Rule believed, with a sincere passion, that the government's conduct justified what, in different circumstances, they would have called high treason. The constitution – always a concept so vague that it could be called in aid of every attempt to hold back change – had been violated. That section of society which did not believe that a democratic mandate should override its prejudices and vested interests claimed that the House of Commons had become what later generations called 'an elective dictatorship'. What was more, as Bonar Law told one of the Unionist rallies, the Liberals had 'sold themselves' to the Nationalist MPs in order to command the majority necessary to keep Mr Asquith in Downing Street. 'Under such circumstances . . . to try to force the circumstances upon you . . . would not be by government at all . . . It would be tyranny naked and unashamed and not the less because the tyrants have usurped their power not by force but by fraud.'

Bonar Law's description of the government's conduct legitimised his party's treason. In the fight against tyranny, every sort of weapon could be used with a clear conscience. Earl Roberts drafted a letter for publication (but never published because it was overtaken by events) which explained that the normal rules of military discipline do not apply during a civil war![30] Bonar Law's approach to the King was less bizarre but a constitutional outrage of even greater proportions. There was, the Leader of the Opposition said, no obligation for His Majesty to sign the Home Rule Bill into law because the Liberals' Parliament Bill had reduced the power of the House of Lords. 'They may say that your assent is a purely formal act and the prerogative of veto dead. That is true as long as there is a buffer between you and the House of Commons. But they have destroyed that buffer and it is no longer true.'[31]

The Unionists reinforced their consciences with the argument that Edwardian England had remedied almost all of Ireland's material grievances. The Irish Land Purchase Act of 1903, supported by Nationalists no less than by 'loyalists', 'did solid good to Ireland by speedily bringing about nearly everywhere . . . a system of out and out peasant proprietorship'.[32] In 1909 Cardinal Newman's dream of a 'Catholic Oxford on the banks of the Liffey' was at last recognised by the creation of Dublin University. But the Unionists were no more capable of understanding the Catholics' emotional need for the self-respect that comes with self-government than the Cabinet was of appreciating the strength of Protestant determination to maintain the Union.

John Redmond and the other parliamentary Nationalists were themselves out of touch with Irish opinion. That is the only explanation for their acceptance of a bill which was explicit in entrenching the supremacy of the imperial Parliament 'beyond the reach of challenge'. The Irish legislative – and the executive which was to be formed within it – was to receive powers which were limited to purely domestic government. Foreign affairs, defence and most taxes remained at Westminster, as did control of the Royal Ulster Constabulary. Sinn Fein announced its implacable opposition to the Bill on the day it was published, but the parallel antagonism of their natural enemies did nothing to placate the Orangemen who followed Carson and Craig. On 28 September 1912 the 'Solemn League and Covenant to Resist Home Rule' was inaugurated in Belfast Town Hall. Carson signed first, signifying his refusal, whatever Parliament might decide, to recognise Home Rule. Within a week, 218,206 other names had been added to the Covenant. Some were signed in blood. Only men were invited to reaffirm their loyalty to King and country, but 228,991 women signed a petition signifying support for the men who would fight to maintain the Union. And, just to prove that Protestant Ulster was in deadly earnest, the Belfast shipyards shut down for the day.

The Ulster men were not the 'asses' which the Liberals, by their derisive allusion to 'the brayings of civil war', had hoped them to be. Craig and Carson were adjusting their position. Realism required their forces to be concentrated on a battle they might win. Craig set out the new strategy in language which sounded almost emollient: 'We all know . . . the vast majority of our fellow countrymen in the South and West of Ireland will have Home Rule if the Bill becomes law and we shall have no power to stop it. All we propose to do is to prevent Home Rule becoming law in our part of the country.'

In the House of Commons on New Year's Day 1913 Edward Carson moved an amendment to the Home Rule Bill which would have allowed Ulster to remain within the Union. Asquith briefly sounded sympathetic, but the Nationalists would not have partition at any price. And the government, still sceptical about the size and strength of the Orange threat, came down, temporarily, on the side of the Ireland – undivided and in domestic policies free – that was at least a modified version of the Gaelic dream.

Ministers did not have to wait long for their lesson in Unionist determination. The opponents of Home Rule decided to raise a Volunteer Force – 100,000 men, between the ages of seventeen and sixty-five, who were to be organised around the Orange Lodges in county battalions. At first they drilled with dummy rifles, but gradually real weapons were smuggled into the country. Earl Roberts, by then the senior Field Marshal of the British Army, on the 'retired list' but still in possession of the King's Commission, recommended the appointment of General Sir George Richardson (late Indian Army) as the Volunteers' commanding officer, with Colonel Hacket Pain as his Chief of Staff. Yet the Nationalists continued to treat partition as a bad joke and no one in the government, apart from Winston Churchill, seemed even offended by the incipient mutiny. When Churchill told the Liberals of Bradford that the Ulster Voluntary Force (UVF) was 'a self-elected body composed of people who, to put it plainly, are engaged in a treasonable conspiracy',[33] his colleagues attributed his outburst to the desire to increase his popularity within the party. They were certainly not in favour of his view that 'the time has come to go forward and put these grave matters to the test'.

So the idea of partition was allowed to take root and grow. Carson wrote to Bonar Law as if it were already accepted in principle. 'A difficulty arises in defining Ulster. My view is that the whole of Ulster should be excluded, but the minimum would be the six plantation counties.'[34] The King – partly out of Protestant sympathy and partly because he feared a civil war – told Churchill and Bonar Law, while they were staying with him at Balmoral, that partition was the proper solution. Churchill, never the most consistent of politicians, made a speech which demanded that Ulster's special status be considered with respect and understanding.

John Redmond made his party's position clear. He was prepared to compromise on the extent of the Irish parliament's powers but not on Home Rule. 'Irish Nationalists [will never be] assenting parties to the mutilation of the Irish nation. Ireland is a unit.'[35] Nevertheless, Asquith began to consider several variations on the partition theme in the hope of finding an agreed solution. Ulster could be given administrative autonomy within the new Ireland. The Six Counties, or Ulster as a whole, might be exempted from Home Rule for three or six years. Redmond – realising that nothing better was on offer – agreed, with the greatest of reluctance, to six. As Asquith might have anticipated, the concession solved nothing. Carson rejected what he described as a 'sentence of death with stay of execution'.[36]

There was nothing left for Asquith to do except insist that the law, as passed by the imperial Parliament, would have to be obeyed. The Orange Lodges chose to describe the operation of democracy as 'The Coercion of Ulster' – a policy which, in their view, justified the creation of what amounted to a private army. One hundred thousand men – under the command of retired or half-pay officers, supported by their own medical, transport and intelligence corps and armed with machine guns as well as rifles – were ready to do battle with the British Army. However, there was some doubt whether or not the regiments stationed at the Curragh in County Kildare were prepared to do battle with them. When General Sir Arthur Paget, Commander-in-Chief in Ireland, visited the War Office in London to receive orders as to how he should respond to the anticipated emergency, he expressed some concern about the attitude of the men under his command. He was told that civil war was not expected imminently and there was certainly no plan to suppress expressions of dissent. Troops would, however, guard railway junctions and reservoirs. What, Paget asked, if the troops refused?

The response revealed some sympathy for Ulster's cause. Officers with families in Northern Ireland would be allowed, if trouble broke out, to disappear from their units in order to look after their wives and children. But the rest − it went without saying − would be expected to obey King's Regulations. Paget returned to Ireland and − probably as a result more of stupidity than malice − called his officers together and repeated what he had been told in terms so extreme that he conveyed very little of the War Office's true intention. Officers not resident in Ulster were offered the opportunity of either agreeing to implement government policy or being dismissed from the service. General Sir Hubert Gough, commanding the Curragh's Cavalry Brigade, immediately reported that he and fifty-nine of his officers chose dismissal. The Curragh had mutinied.

The rebellion was not limited to the cavalry. A majority of the infantry officers in Ireland decided that they too would leave the Army but were persuaded not to offer their resignations until they received news of the War Office's reaction to the crisis. General Douglas Haig, Commander-in-Chief of Aldershot District, told Sir Henry Wilson, Director of Military Operations at the War Office, that half of his officers would resign their commissions if Gough were to be disciplined. General Wilson reported the news to Lord French, the Chief of the Imperial General Staff, with undisguised pleasure. He had spent much of the previous years discussing with fellow Unionists within the Army how the government's policy and the will of Parliament could be frustrated.

The government panicked. Instead of condemning the 'mutiny' out of hand, it attempted to placate the mutineers by assuring them that the dispute had been the result of a 'misunderstanding'. French, with ministers' agreement, gave Gough a written statement which contained assurances that the Army would not be called upon to suppress dissent in Ulster. The paragraph which made that intention explicit went far further than the Cabinet intended. It was added to the document by Lord French and James Seeley, the Secretary of State for War, after ministers had seen what they believed to be the final draft. Troops, the late addition promised, 'would not be called upon to enforce the present Home Rule Bill on Ireland'. Gough returned in triumph to Ulster. Triumph at the Curragh was matched by outrage in Downing Street. When French and Seeley admitted that they had tampered with the Cabinet statement, both men were forced to resign. Asquith himself became Secretary of State for War in the hope that the appointment would make clear that the Constitution would be enforced. Whatever the future of Ireland, it would be decided by the lawful government.

The Ulster Volunteer Force continued to make preparations for secession. At Larne and Bangor, police and customs officers felt able only to watch as 24,000 rifles and 3,000,000 rounds of ammunition were landed to use in the fight to keep Ulster within the Union. Supporters of the Orange cause concentrated, with single-minded dedication, on the achievement of their objective. The Green battalions were, on the other hand, faced with a major distraction.

In 1911, Dublin employers had founded an association to 'meet combination with combination' and to seize the industrial initiative from Jim Larkin and his Irish Transport and General Workers Union. For two years the balance of power had remained in favour of the Trades Council. Then William Walter Murphy – whose many commercial interests included the Dublin Tramway Company and the *Independent* newspaper – took command of the employers' campaign. On Friday 15 August, 1913, he sacked forty workers from the *Independent*'s despatch department. The provocation had the result for which he hoped. Other workers struck in sympathy. In response, Murphy demanded that all his employees sign an understanding not to respond to an anticipated call for industrial action. The following week, tram drivers, apparently spontaneously, stopped work. All Murphy's workmen were 'locked out'. A protest meeting, called by Larkin and meant to assemble in O'Connell Street, was ruled to be illegal. Larkin, despite hiding in the house of Constance Markievicz and, for a time, wearing a false beard, was arrested. In London the *Daily Herald* asked, not unreasonably, why Carson had not been arrested for committing an identical offence.[37]

There followed days of trade union demonstrations, all of which were dispersed by unremitting police brutality. Outside the Metropole Hotel, 'There was a continual rapping of batons on people's heads . . . You could hear from the shrieks and cries that the same thing was happening opposite the Metropole and the Post Office.'[38] Although, back in 1908, Larkin had argued for the creation of an Irish Citizens' Army – partly to fight for Home Rule and partly to defend workers' rights – there were aspects of the Irish character which he never fully understood. At the height of the dispute with the Dublin Tramway Company he arranged for the starving children of strikers to be sent on holiday to England in the homes of sympathetic British trade unionists – but he could not guarantee that the benefactors would be Catholic. To his amazement the children were 'rescued' for the true faith by a band of marauding priests who intercepted the holiday-makers, first in the public wash-house, then on the road to Kingston dock, and eventually on the deck of the ferry which was carrying them to perdition.[39]

The events of August 1913 convinced sceptics of the need for a paramilitary organisation – a notion which was encouraged by Republicans with no real interest in the industrial struggle, but a single-minded determination to prepare for the political battle which lay ahead. The Irish Citizens' Army was formed with its headquarters at Liberty Hall, the home of the Irish Transport and General Workers Union, under the command of James Connolly, Larkin's deputy.

So the rival forces were assembled for a conflict that seemed only months away. The future of Ireland, as Arthur Griffith predicted, was to be decided not in Parliament but on the streets and in the hills of Ireland itself. But before the new boundaries could be defined, the Great War – which marked the end of Edwardian Britain – intervened. Gough, Wilson and French became household names. Millions of Irishmen fought for the Empire they longed to leave. After August 1914, in Dublin, no less than in London, nothing was ever the same again.

CHAPTER 10

Votes for Women!

The real campaign for women's suffrage, like so much else that has come to characterise Edwardian England, was born in the reign of Queen Victoria, but only made a major impact on history when her son was on the throne. Ever since the Greeks created a democracy of sorts in Athens there had been women who rebelled against the absurd injustice of second-class status. But it was always difficult – usually impossible – to defy the prevailing prejudices of male-dominated societies and put together an 'organisation' to further their cause. The Great Reform Bill of 1867 stimulated the idea that women might be included in the extended franchise. In 1887 the Victorian pioneers Lydia Becker and Millicent Fawcett became founding members and presidents of the National Union of Women's Suffrage Societies, but their political endeavours were probably less influential than the social and economic pressures towards greater equality. Chief amongst them was the Married Women's Property Act of 1883.

It was not the first step towards social emancipation. Girton College had opened in Hitchin in 1869 and moved to Cambridge in 1872. Six years later, Lady Margaret Hall had been founded in Oxford. London University had long admitted women undergraduates and the Victoria University, with colleges in the great provincial cities, had welcomed them from its start at the turn of the century. For years women were allowed to study in Oxford and Cambridge without being awarded Oxford and Cambridge degrees. But, when women came regularly at, or near to, the top of the examination list, it became increasingly difficult to deny them formal graduation – though Cambridge managed to resist for fifty years. So in Edwardian Britain it was already being gradually accepted that women were as clever as men. When it was also agreed that, once married, they remained able and entitled to own property and run a company (rather than hand over both their bank accounts and their businesses to their husbands), their right to vote became more difficult to dispute.

In 1884, a backbench Suffrage Bill, which offered the vote to single women who were also householders, was defeated in the House of Commons. A year later, when the County Finance Bill proposed to increase the electorate to between three and five million and introduce the principle of 'one vote, one value', a women's suffrage amendment was put down on the order paper. It was rumoured that Salisbury, the Prime Minister, and his two principal lieutenants, Northcote and Hicks Beach, were sympathetic.[1] And *The Times* called women's suffrage 'the trump card which Lord Beaconsfield kept in his hand'.[2] But Gladstone threatened to drop the whole bill if the new clause was added and the amendment was lost by 271 votes to 135. By 1886, the idea of 'votes for women' had become so popular amongst MPs that the Second Reading of a Suffrage Bill was actually carried after a brief private members' debate. In the same year, Mrs E. E. Dawson graduated from the Irish College of Surgeons and became the first woman legally entitled to perform operations.

Even without the vote, women were beginning to demand – and in some cases exercise – the freedom which men enjoyed. Lady Harberton founded the Rational Dress Society and offered a prize for the design of knickerbockers which were at once serviceable and seemly. It is an item of dress that most accounts of Edwardian 'style' omit to mention, though it is no less representative than the clothes which are often said to typify the age. The huge 'picture' hats, the bustles and the long dresses with the flowing trains were worn by an infinitesimal proportion of the female population.

In a sense, none of the alternative explanation for 'Edwardian women's dress' is of much consequence. The styles were less symbolic of an age than of a class. The 'wasp waists' were proclamations that women whose corsets constricted their breath and their digestion were not required to inconvenience themselves with physical effort. The high neck was less a sign of the era's modesty than a desire to copy Queen Alexandra who, according to rival rumours, hoped to hide the marks of syphilis, smallpox or old age. The hobble skirt – which forced even the most robust woman to mince – was either a wilful decision to make women walk like mechanical dolls or a recognition that, the muddy roads having been eliminated from the cities, it was no longer necessary to hitch up skirts to cross from side to side. The brassiere, introduced in 1912, was either a decision to emphasise sexuality (unlikely, since it helped to reduce the Victorians' extravagant levels of *décolletage*) or an aid to maternal health and hygiene.

The women about whom Charles Booth wrote in his survey of the London working class lived in another world – one which even the dedicated social scientist did not fully understand. 'There is a consensus of opinion . . . that while there is more drinking, there is less drunkenness than formerly and that the increase in drinking is to be laid mainly to the account of the female sex. This latter phase seems to be one of the unexpected results of the emancipation of women.'[3] He does not seem to have considered the possibility that women's increasing influence on men might have contributed to the reduction in drunkenness. But, despite male prejudices, women of every sort were on the march. All they needed to fuse their demands into a coherent movement was leadership. It was provided by a combination of fate and the Pankhurst family.

Richard Pankhurst was a barrister who moved from London to Manchester to practise more successfully on the Northern Circuit. He brought with him his wife, Emmeline, his daughters, Christabel, Sylvia and Adela, and his son, Harry. Emmeline, who had presided over a radical salon in London, had always possessed social pretensions. When she left the Lancashire and Cheshire Union of the Women's Liberal Federation and joined the Independent Labour Party at the end of the 1890s, she had complained that she was no longer invited to civic functions in Manchester Town Hall. But the gaps in her diary were soon filled by visiting socialist celebrities who stayed at her house during visits to the North-West. Keir Hardie, John and Katherine Bruce Glasier, Tom Mann and Robert Blatchford were among them.

Keir Hardie became a particular friend – attracted, it seems certain, by the prospect of the company of lively young women. Hardie's susceptibilities have not been included in the miasma of myth and legend which surround him as the first Labour Member of Parliament and first Leader of the Party, but from the mist of folklore, some certain facts can be extracted. He was a self-educated miner whose commitment to the moderate form of socialism which became the British model of that philosophy was absolute. Hardie was a brilliant orator, a poor tactician and he wore, not a cloth cap, but a deer stalker's hat. His historical importance was the determination he displayed to make 'Labour' an independent political organisation. His support for the Pankhursts adds a footnote to his paragraph in the history books.

In 1894, after failing to secure a seat on the Manchester School Board, Emmeline Pankhurst stood as an Independent Labour Party candidate for the Board of Guardians and won. By then, Richard Pankhurst had become so prominent in the party that he was nominated to contest Gorton on its behalf in the 1895 by-election. Although the Liberal candidate stood down in his favour, he lost. From then on Richard Pankhurst concentrated his energies on good (generally legal) works. He defended the ILP against the Manchester Council when the party was prosecuted for holding unauthorised public meetings on a piece of public land called Boggart Hole Clough, supported the engineers of Trafford Park in their campaign for an eight-hour day and represented (as honorary counsel) the Peak and District Preservation Committee in its campaign to secure a right of way over Kinder Scout. Despite a rapid deterioration in his health – which his family seemed not to notice or thought it best to ignore – he must have enjoyed considerable professional success. In 1898 his wife took her eldest daughter, Christabel, on holiday to Geneva. They got as far as Paris, where Emmeline intended to revive memories of time she had spent there as a girl. Then the telegram arrived. Her husband had collapsed with stomach pains.

Mother and daughter left at once for England. On the train from London to Manchester she read, in a fellow passenger's newspaper, that her husband was dead. His coffin was covered in red roses and carnations and the carriage on which it was borne to the cemetery was accompanied by an escort of socialist cyclists from the Clarion

Wheelers. The family moved to a less expensive Manchester suburb and rented a smaller house. They spent the next few months in recrimination and anxiety. Which of them deserved most blame for the failure to persuade Richard that his stomach ulcer needed treatment, and how were they going to survive in the years that lay ahead?

The second question was answered by Emmeline becoming Registrar of Births and Deaths for the Rusholme District of Manchester and re-establishing, as a serious source of income, Emmersons', the 'fancy goods' business which she had run in London when selling William Morris prints had been no more than a diverting pastime. But economies were still necessary. Adela was sent to a 'dirty board school'[4] where she acquired head lice. Harry, a chronic invalid, was denied the spectacles he obviously needed. Christabel, who had spent the summer of her father's death in Geneva, returned to England with neither ambition nor energy. She declared herself suitable for a job which began at ten in the morning and ended at four in the afternoon. Her mother set her to work in Emmersons'. The one ray of light in a dark year followed the visit of an art dealer who called on the Pankhursts to value pictures which they were forced to sell. He noticed some of Sylvia's sketches and suggested that she had enough talent to win a scholarship to Manchester School of Art. He proved to be a good judge and she took up her place the following September.[5]

Still depressed, Emmeline looked for a diversion from her sorrow and an outlet for her still boundless energy. She found it in the Independent Labour Party. In 1899 she was elected a member of the National Administrative Council and the following year won a place as an ILP nominee on the Manchester School Board. When the Education Act abolished the school board system, she was co-opted on to the Manchester Local Education Authority. In 1901 she attended the ILP's annual conference, held that year in Leicester. Sylvia and Christabel went with her.

The excitement of the event brought Christabel Pankhurst back to life. At Keir Hardie's suggestion (and undoubtedly with his help) she spoke against the organisation of passive resistance to the education reforms which Nonconformists claimed affronted their consciences by subsidising Church of England schools from public funds. But the call to rely on politics and Parliament, rather than direct action, did not mark her permanent re-awakening. That came about as a result of her meeting Esther Roper and Eva Gore-Booth – two crucial figures in · radical north-western politics. Eva Gore-Booth (sister of Constance, the Irish nationalist) came to Manchester to work in the University Settlement which Esther Roper had helped to found. Esther Roper was the daughter of a missionary. Her mother had died of anaemia, which was attributed to far too frequent pregnancies, and Eva had been brought up in the austerity of a Church of England home. She was one of the first women to obtain a degree from Manchester's Victoria University. Christabel, whose lack of interest in men in general and marriage in particular was a constant source of surprise (and often the occasion for concern) to her parents, no doubt felt at home in the company of two women who were sufficiently liberated to live in an irregular union. They came into Christabel's life shortly after Esther had become joint secretary of Salford Women's Trade Council, an organisation devoted to improving women's wages and conditions of work.

Christabel met her two mentors at the end of a Manchester University 'extension' lecture which she attended, with some reluctance, at her mother's suggestion. It was her nature – as she had demonstrated in Leicester at the ILP Conference – to participate rather than to observe. So, although she could have known very little about politics and poetry, she asked the lecturer a question. Esther Roper, who had chaired the occasion, was deeply impressed – or at least claimed to be. After the lecture was over, she took Christabel back to her house to meet Eva Gore-Booth. Christabel became part of their circle and they suggested that she should attend law lectures in the University. They then persuaded her to apply for membership of Lincoln's Inn. They knew, or should have known, that women were not allowed to practise either as solicitors or barristers. So her request 'to eat dinners' in preparation for joining the Bar was refused. Resentment combined with what almost amounted to infatuation. Christabel Pankhurst became a suffragist of a special stripe. Much of the movement at the turn of the century was essentially middle class. Esther Roper and Eva Gore-Booth worked amongst the factory girls of Lancashire. As a result, their instinct was for militancy rather than respectability.

In 1902, Christabel, Eva and Esther went on holiday together in Venice. That was the year in which Emmeline began to complain that her daughter was never at home but spent all her time either campaigning for women's suffrage or in a variety of intellectual pursuits with the two older women who had 'taken her up'. Emmeline had other causes for concern. Christabel spent hours massaging Eva's head and neck in an attempt to relieve her neuralgia, although 'she had never been willing to act as nurse to any other human being'.[6] The author of the joint biography of Eva Gore-Booth and Esther Roper concludes that neither woman had a lesbian relationship with Christabel,[7] and the biographer of the Pankhursts urges readers not to judge the friendship of the three women against the standards of modern Britain. In Edwardian England women often lived together in affectionate celibacy.[8] But if the triangular partnership was not physical, it was certainly highly emotional. Without the passion it engendered, Christabel would never have shaken off her adolescent torpor. With Eva and Esther as her inspiration she devoted thirteen years, between the ages of twenty and thirty-four, to the suffragist cause. That, she said, was why she never married. One thing is certain. A deeply complex woman was inspired by a profoundly complicated relationship to become a central figure in one of the most emotive as well as the most bizarre episodes in the history of Edwardian England.

The Edwardian suffrage movement moved gradually – and, in the case of some members, reluctantly – from politics to direct action. Emmeline Pankhurst, her faith in politics restored, played a major part in the parliamentary campaign with which the twentieth century began. At the Leicester ILP 1901 Conference she had been content to entertain the delegates on the piano while Christabel made the speech. At the Conference a year later she moved the crucial suffrage resolution: 'In order to improve the economic and social condition of women, it is necessary to take immediate steps to secure the granting of the suffrage to women on the same terms as it may be granted to men.'

The resolution was carried unanimously. So was a motion calling for complete adult suffrage and the enfranchisement of the millions of men who were still denied the vote because they did not fulfil the

property requirement. The second resolution was given priority over
the first. Keir Hardie was instructed to prepare an adult enfranchisement bill and introduce it in the House of Commons. ILP members
were engaged in the first battle in what was to become a long conflict
between the demands for gender and class equality. Philip Snowden –
national chairman of the ILP and, twenty years later, Chancellor of
the Exchequer in the first Labour government – explained that to
extend the franchise 'on the same terms' as applied to men, before
complete adult suffrage was achieved, would extend the voting power
of the upper and middle classes.⋆ His logic was impeccable but the
Pankhursts were infuriated. It was not their way to hide their feelings.
The bitterness of their complaints antagonised even close friends. John
Bruce Glasier (who had spoken at Richard Pankhurst's funeral) became
a particular target for their scorn. He had become chairman of the ILP
and was, in consequence, held responsible for the party's reluctance to
elevate women's suffrage above all other issues. Because of his annoyance at their habit of 'belabouring' him, he began to question both
their public commitment and their personal conduct. 'Really the pair
are not seeking democratic freedom but self-importance.'[9] What was
worse, 'Christabel paints her eyebrows grossly and looks selfish, lazy
and wilful'.[10] His damning conclusion was that 'they want to be ladies
not workers and lack the humility of real heroism'. Glasier grew
increasingly impatient with what he regarded as the Pankhursts' essentially bourgeois view of female suffrage and his criticisms were
extended from Christabel to Emmeline. 'Her idea is that women
should be relieved of all work and have rest and intellectual delights.
I told her that work was good and that, under socialism, she would
likely have to do more than she now does seeing she has other
people's daughters acting as her private servants.'[11]

For a few months more the Pankhursts remained members of the
Labour Party, very largely because of their close association with Keir
Hardie who was devoted to the whole family. But in the spring of
1903 Christabel resigned. In what must have been an act of calculated

---

⋆The 1884 Reform Bill had extended the vote only to adult male householders in
the counties as well as the towns and to '£10 male lodgers'. In 1918 all men over
twenty-one were enfranchised together with women over thirty.

bridge-burning she wrote to the *Labour Leader*, Keir Hardie's paper, with the complaint that the party was neglecting women's interests.[12] 'Never in the history of the world have the interests of those without power to defend themselves been properly defended by others.' It was the beginning of a strategy which was to characterise the rest of the suffragists' campaign. The attacks were directed not towards opponents but negligent supporters. There was 'nothing to choose between an enemy and a friend who does nothing'[13] – except, in the slightly cynical view of the Pankhursts, that an indolent friend was more likely to be bullied into providing active assistance.

During the summer of 1903, Sylvia Pankhurst completed the murals that had been commissioned to decorate the Manchester meeting hall which the ILP proposed to dedicate to her father. Emmeline, who visited the hall to watch her daughter at work, was distressed to discover that it was regularly used by a branch of the party that did not admit female members. When Bruce Glasier and Snowden arrived for the opening ceremony, Christabel refused to speak to them. Emmeline withdrew her contribution to the wage fund by which Labour Members of Parliament, including her friend Keir Hardie, were paid and began to talk about forming an independent women's movement.

Initially Emmeline intended to call her new organisation the Women's Labour Representation Committee – a reflection, which some loyalists found offensively reminiscent, of the conference that came together to form what became the Labour Party. Her second choice was the Women's Social and Political Union (WSPU), a grandiose title for what was a very small organisation. Its weekly meeting, initially held in the Pankhursts' house, rarely attracted two dozen members. One member – Tessa Billington, a school teacher who had approached Emmeline years before in the hope that the Manchester School Board would absolve her from the obligation to give religious instruction – was asked to write a constitution. The tedious business of administration did not appeal to the Pankhursts and their followers. They wanted action. An ideal opportunity arose in the early weeks of 1904.

Winston Churchill, Tory Member of Parliament for Oldham, until he had crossed the floor of the House of Commons in protest to the government's abandonment of free trade, had to find a new seat. In the hope of contesting Manchester North-West as a Liberal, he spoke at a meeting in the Free Trade Hall. Somehow Christabel obtained a ticket which entitled her to sit on the platform. Churchill had spoken for about ninety minutes and was proposing a rhetorical resolution supporting free trade when Christabel rose to her feet and moved that it be amended to include a declaration of support for women's suffrage. The chairman appealed to her sense of reason and order. Her proposition was, he said, contentious and the object of the meeting was to obtain a unanimous majority against the imposition of import duties. Christabel, to her own surprise, subsided. But she almost immediately regretted her moderation. She never made the mistake of being reasonable again.

Churchill was an ideal, as well as a convenient, target. He was young, controversial and therefore constantly in the news, clearly a rising star of whichever party he favoured at any one time and, perhaps most important of all, in support of women's suffrage. But he was not sufficiently devoted to the cause to escape the Pankhursts' classifying him as a friend who was no better than an enemy. By 1905 the Pankhursts were looking for ways of publicising the cause in the country. Parliament would, they were sure, betray them.

The Labour Representation Committee had failed them already. At the 1905 Conference John Husband of the Engineers had moved a resolution which supported votes for women 'believing it to be a step towards adult suffrage'. But Henry Quelch of the London Trades Council had proposed an amendment which the comrades and friends overwhelmingly accepted. 'Any women's franchise bill which seeks merely to abolish sex discrimination would increase the power of the propertied classes . . . Adult suffrage is the only reform which merits any support from Labour MPs.' Quelch was motivated by more than the electoral logic of his agreement. Like many trade unionists, he saw female suffrage as an essentially middle-class cause promoted by middle-class women – some of whom numbered among the worst employers in the country.[14]

Emmeline, perhaps in memory of her husband's ambition to enter Parliament, sustained hope that the democratic process might provide the answer. And when a private member's bill (which proposed a limited extension of the suffrage) was 'talked out', she actually approached Arthur Balfour with a request for the government to provide time for another bill to complete all its stages. The Prime Minister courteously refused to oblige. But the private member's bill was not moved in vain. On the day of its brief discussion, members of the Women's Co-operative Guild met outside the House of Commons. One of them, a grandmother of seventy-three, climbed on to the plinth of Richard the Lionheart's statue in the forecourt of the House of Lords. When the police intervened, Keir Hardie led the protesters to a nearby side street and addressed them from the pavement edge. The resulting publicity was, to Christabel, more evidence of the importance of making trouble.

Churchill provided constant opportunities for causing disruption. On 13 October 1905, Sir Edward Grey (soon to be Foreign Secretary) addressed a public meeting in Manchester's Free Trade Hall. Churchill was the supporting speaker. Christabel Pankhurst, in the audience, was supported by Annie Kenney, a factory worker from Oldham, who had been virtually adopted by the Pankhursts. As soon as Churchill rose to speak, Annie Kenney asked him if, once they came to power, the Liberals would 'make women's suffrage a Government measure'.[15] Churchill did not answer. Both women began to chant the question, sometimes in turn, sometimes in unison. The Chief Constable of Manchester, unaccountably in the audience, persuaded them to write out their request and he handed the scrap of paper to the platform. When there was still no answer, they began to chant again. The police then led them to an anteroom where Christabel gratuitously struck and spat at a constable. A senior officer urged the two women 'to behave like ladies'. Christabel spat in his face and hit, for a second time, the unfortunate constable who had been the victim of her first assault. The police were left with little option other than to charge both women with disorderly behaviour and assaulting a police officer. Christabel was fined ten shillings with the option of seven days' imprisonment, Annie Kenney five shillings with a three day option. To Emmeline's consternation, the two defendants chose prison. Churchill, asked to comment on Christabel's sentence, said that he 'hoped the quiet and seclusion may soothe her fevered brain'.[16] It had quite the opposite effect. Annie told Christabel, 'We got what

we wanted.' Christabel agreed. 'I wanted to assault a police officer.'[17]
The militant wing of the still infant movement regarded the whole
episode as a triumph. Wiser supporters, Emmeline among them, were
not so sure. The suffragist movement could only achieve its objective
when it was supported in Parliament by the sort of men its activists
alienated.

Churchill's advice to his agent illustrated the risks that the militant
suffragists ran. 'You should attempt to come to some understanding
with them and point out how damaging their action is to their own
cause. I am certainly not going to be henpecked into a position on
which my mind is not fully prepared, and if I am subject to any further annoyance I shall plainly say that I do not intend to vote for
female suffrage in the next parliament.'[18] Of course, the alternative
view – 'Twenty years of peaceful propaganda has not produced such
an effect'[19] – prevailed. Suffragists disrupted a Churchill election
meeting in January 1906. As a result, he announced 'Nothing would
induce me to vote for giving votes to women.'[20] The campaign continued. Yet, as late as 1910, Churchill was still claiming to be agnostic
but open to persuasion – 'still of the opinion that sex disqualification
[from voting] was not a true or logical disqualification . . . He was,
therefore, in favour of the principle of women being enfranchised
but declined utterly to pledge himself to any particular bill.'[21] At one
of his worst gadfly moments, he argued the merits of holding a
national referendum on whether or not women should be enfranchised. Only men would have been allowed to vote. The suffragists'
attempt to dislodge him from the fence took the form of a young
woman with a horsewhip who assaulted him on Temple Meads station
in Bristol.

For Christabel life was full of excitement. Sylvia, on the other
hand, was happy neither with the WSPU nor with her chosen career.
In 1904 she had won a second scholarship, but within weeks of arriv-
ing at the Royal College of Art in South Kensington, she became
convinced that the Principal discriminated against women in the distribution of internal awards. Outraged, she approached Keir Hardie
and asked him to put down a parliamentary question on the management of the Royal Colleges. It was a strange request, but Hardie
agreed. The great puritan had a weakness for young ladies.

Sylvia, far from home and lonely, began to visit Keir Hardie in his humble flat. At first it was the relationship of father and daughter. She cooked simple meals while he read aloud. Then they grew more adventurous and went regularly to the theatre together and occasionally even to restaurants. At some time during 1906 the twenty-one-year old student and the forty-seven-year-old married Labour MP became lovers.

Nineteen hundred and six was the year of Liberal triumph, but the Pankhursts placed no hope in the new government. Their pessimism was confirmed by the Government's failure even to mention women's suffrage in the King's Speech. They reacted first by requesting a meeting with the new Prime Minister, Henry Campbell-Bannerman, and then, when it was refused, by holding a protest meeting in Downing Street. Suffragists got inside both the official residence and the official motor car and were, in consequence, arrested. They were released on the specific instruction of Campbell-Bannerman. The women were, he said, 'seeking notoriety which would be successful if they appeared before a magistrate'.[22] He did, however, agree to meet a delegation of what, by then, had become 'suffragettes' rather than 'suffragists'.

The description 'suffragettes' – originally used by the *Daily Mail* as a term of abuse – was taken up by the *Daily Mirror* because it made the women sound young and irrepressible. The women themselves were delighted that the newspapers at last regarded them as sufficiently important to be called names, and the Prime Minister's agreement to meet them further confirmed that they had become a force to be reckoned with. To the suffragists' delight Campbell-Bannerman told the delegation, 'You have made before the country a conclusive and irresistible case.' But their joy was diminished by the explanation that he could not promise to translate their irrefutable arguments into legislation. The rallies and the protest meetings grew more menacing. The *Daily Mirror*, now finally on the suffragettes' side, wrote that 'parliament has never done anything without being bullied'[23] and the saintly Keir Hardie told a rally of 7,000 supporters in Trafalgar Square, 'patience, like many other virtues, can be carried to excess'. By the end of the year there were twenty-one suffragettes in prison. Most of them were middle class and had been awarded the status of 'first-class prisoners' which spared them the indignity of broad arrow uniforms.

Disturbance was not, however, the only strategy. The movement was attracting members with money. As a result it could afford to improve its organisation. Christabel moved to London, and the flat in which she lived with the Pethick-Lawrences (a perfect caricature of a Fabian marriage) became its headquarters. She became chief organiser (on a salary of two pounds a week) with three paid assistants to help her. 'Women's Parliaments' were held to coincide with great occasions in the House of Commons, in the belief that they would exhibit the power of female reason and logic. Demonstrations continued outside Parliament (and inside when the attention of the police and the custodians could be distracted), but they were aimed in a new direction. Christabel had begun to turn her attention away from the Liberal and Labour Parties towards the Tories. At first her change in allegiance amounted to no more than a refusal to support Liberal by-election candidates. Then she openly asked for the support of Arthur Balfour. Like every other political leader, he was vaguely sympathetic but unable to make any specific promise. His trustworthy lieutenants, Austen Chamberlain and Lord Curzon, adopted a more positive approach. They formed the League Opposing Women's Suffrage.

The annual Labour conference of 1907 rejected (by a majority of three to one) a motion calling for female suffrage. The vote was in part a reflection of the view that was strongly held by Arthur Henderson, who had succeeded Keir Hardie as leader of the party. The principle of votes for women was undoubtedly right, but some of the proponents were intolerable. Two of the people Henderson had in mind – Christabel and Emmeline Pankhurst – resigned their Labour Party membership.

Christabel grew increasingly autocratic, an attitude which Mrs Pethick-Lawrence tried to justify by describing the suffragist movement in familial terms. Christabel 'could not trust her mental offspring to politically untrained minds'.[24] The metaphorical mother did, however, seize the opportunity to increase her hold over the Women's Social and Political Union. A new committee, nominated by Christabel, took office without an election. Members were asked to sign a declaration promising not to support the candidates of any party which was not in formal agreement with the WSPU's aims.

Christabel's leadership – its style as well as the method of its assumption – was accepted without question by her mother, but other members were less tolerant than Emmeline. A breakaway organisation, the Women's Freedom League, was formed.

Christabel was supported and, when necessary, physically protected by a group of devoted followers who called themselves the Young Hot Bloods and gloried in the performance of dangerous duties – activities which, under Christabel's leadership, became an increasingly important part of the WSPU's work. Indeed she planned for illegal acts to become so extensive that the leadership of the movement was instructed not to take part in any demonstration which was likely to lead to prosecution, conviction and imprisonment. Only the volunteers should risk incarceration. The high command must remain free to plan more demonstrations of female determination.[25]

The peaceful work went on side by side with the civil disobedience and violence. The Pethick-Lawrences founded a weekly paper, *Votes for Women*. By May 1909, eighteen months after the first issue was published, it had a circulation of 22,000. There was a self-denial week, during which John Galsworthy and Laurence Housman sacrificed luxuries and contributed their cost to the WSPU. Then, in February 1908, there was another of the House of Commons votes on a private member's bill which proposed an extension to the franchise. It ended in the usual frustration – a majority of 273 to 94 in favour on the Second Reading but the knowledge that it would progress no further towards the statute book. The real significance of the debate was the Home Secretary's thoughtless speech. 'The predominance of argument alone . . . is not enough to win the political day. Men have learned this lesson and know the necessity for demonstrating the greatness of their movements and for establishing the *force majeure* which activates and arms a government for effective work.' To Christabel Pankhurst, that sounded like an admission that she would only win the day by sustained violence.

When, in April 1908, Asquith became Prime Minister, Winston Churchill was promoted to President of the Board of Trade. Before the First World War, a ministry was regarded as an 'Office of Profit Under the Crown' which automatically disqualified the holder from Membership of the House of Commons. Churchill was therefore required to fight a by-election in the Manchester seat which he had won a month earlier. He lost, but was returned to the House of Commons shortly afterwards as Member for Dundee. As a result he escaped the attentions of north-western suffragettes whose militancy was increased by the knowledge that the new Prime Minister was likely to be even less sympathetic to their cause than the old. Emmeline again suggested to Balfour that he might take up her cause, arguing that he could 'outflank' the Liberals. Once more he courteously declined. A huge rally and march was planned for Hyde Park to demonstrate the extent of popular support.

The objective was magnificently achieved on Sunday 21 May 1908. Thirty-six packed railway trains brought the provincial marchers to London. Together with their comrades from the capital, they formed up at seven different starting points. Thirty thousand men and women, bearing seven hundred banners, then set off to Hyde Park, passing on their way twenty platforms from which what would now be called 'celebrities' wished them well. H. G. Wells, Thomas Hardy, Bernard Shaw and Israel Zangwill were all en route to lend their support.[26] Estimates of the size of the crowd varied from 300,000 to 500,000. Christabel entranced them. 'Rising to speak' she became 'a different being . . . Her whole being lit up with fire.'[27]

Buoyed up by their triumph, the suffragettes again asked to meet the Prime Minister. Once again their request was refused. The WSPU was fast approaching the point at which even John Locke and Thomas Hobbes would have accepted that direct action was justified. They did not possess the political rights necessary to bring about democratic change. Indeed, it was those rights which they were demanding. Parliament constantly supported their claim, but the executive refused to implement the will of the legislature. Usually the Prime Minister refused even to meet their leaders. Asquith's refusal on 30 June so incensed Mary Leigh and Edith New that they took a taxi from the House of Commons to Downing Street and threw stones through the windows of Number 10. 'It will be bombs next time,' said Mrs Leigh. A new and more violent phase in the war for women's right to vote had begun.

The violence did not come from the suffragettes alone. When Emmeline Pankhurst spoke in the Newcastle by-election – on behalf of women's suffrage, not one of the candidates – her platform was overturned and she only escaped serious injury because of police protection from the violent mob. But the Pankhursts could always exceed the excesses of their enemies. In the autumn of 1908 they issued a pamphlet headed 'Help the Suffragettes to Rush the House of Commons on October 13'. Six thousand people crowded into Trafalgar Square on the previous Sunday to learn the plan of attack. Emmeline and Christabel were summonsed for behaviour likely to cause a breach of the peace. They gave themselves up too late in the day to be bailed. Their night in the cells was made slightly more acceptable by a Scottish Liberal called James Murray who sent them an evening meal from the Savoy Hotel.

Christabel – who had completed her LLB studies and been awarded a first-class honours degree – defended herself. When she discovered that Lloyd George (by then Chancellor of the Exchequer) and Herbert Gladstone (the Home Secretary) had been in Trafalgar Square on 11 October, she subpoenaed both ministers. Told by the presiding magistrate that she could not cross-examine her own witnesses, she first quoted precedent and then performed in a way which left Max Beerbohm, in the public gallery, marvelling at the 'contrast between the elation of the girl and the depression of the statesman'.[28]

CP You were not alone, I think.

LG No I had my little girl with me.

CP How old is she?

LG She is six.

CP Did you think it safe to bring her out?

LG Certainly. She was amused not frightened.

Despite Christabel's forensic triumph, she and her mother were both convicted. Emmeline was sent to gaol for three months and her daughter ten weeks. The public outcry against the severity of the sentence was increased by the decision that, as they were to be treated as common criminals, they would be subject to the rule which obliged the early weeks in prison to be passed in solitary confinement. The Home Secretary was unsympathetic. With some justification, he told C. P. Scott, the editor of the *Manchester Guardian*, that 'these ladies' do all they can to make sure that they are sent to prison and 'when they get there want to be relieved of its main inconvenience'.[29]

Naturally the suffragettes exploited their suffering. The 1909 Women's Exhibition at the Prince's Skating Rink in Knightsbridge included (as well as the first soda fountain to be seen in England) two replicas of the cells in which Emmeline and Christabel had served their sentences. Respectable opinion began to speak out in their favour. Lady Lytton, sister of the painter, poet and aesthete, appeared on suffragette platforms with Christabel for reasons which she explained without embarrassment. 'There is a social layer which will be drawn by my name who would not be drawn by hers.'[30] Big London stores began to advertise in *Votes for Women*. The annual WSPU income rose to £33,000.

Old habits persisted. Throughout 1909, attempts were made to meet the Prime Minister, protest meetings which began with rhetoric ended in violence, women were imprisoned. Marion Wallace Dunlop painted a message on the wall of St Stephen's Hall in the Palace of Westminster. She was sentenced to four weeks' imprisonment, but released in less than four days after she refused to eat prison food. Christabel told C. P. Scott, 'We feel that the new policy of hunger strikes has given us the means of entirely baffling the government. They cannot imprison us . . . unless, of course, they prefer that we should die in Holloway prison.'[31]

On 17 September Asquith spoke at a public meeting at Bingley Hall in Birmingham. Mary Leigh and Charlotte Marsh climbed on to the roof and bombarded, with tiles and slates, the police who were protecting the Prime Minister. On conviction for assault, they were sentenced to three and two months' prison respectively. In Winson Green prison, both women refused food. After four days of starvation, Mary Leigh was forcibly fed. Two doctors were assisted in the procedure by eight wardresses. 'While I was held down, a nasal tube was inserted. It is two yards long with a funnel at the end . . . Great pain is experienced during the process, both mental and physical . . . The tube is pushed down twenty inches . . . About a pint of milk, sometimes eggs and milk, is used . . . I was very sick on the first occasion after the tube was withdrawn.'[32]

Adela Pankhurst might have been the second victim of forced

feeding. Desperately unhappy because her brother's illness had been diagnosed as terminal, and driven to even greater despair by the fear that Annie Kenney was beginning to take her place in the affection of her mother and sister, she decided to play an independent part in the campaign and spoke at a WSPU meeting in Aberdeen. She was physically assaulted and her car damaged in sight of a police officer who chose not to intervene. She then heard that Winston Churchill, the family's old foe, was speaking nearby at Kinnaird. The road outside the meeting hall was closed, but Adela led half a dozen volunteers in a charge against the barricade. A week later she was sentenced to ten days in gaol. The prison doctor classified her physically and mentally frail, allowing the Secretary of State for Scotland to discharge her before the question of forced feeding arose. That became the Scottish pattern of crime and punishment – brought about equally by the judges' abomination of the way the women were treated in England and the fear that Scottish nurses would not perform an essentially unmedical task. In England, the Lord Chief Justice ruled that forced feeding was necessary to prevent the crime of suicide. In 1909, as thereafter, London and Edinburgh saw life very differently.

In the House of Commons, the Prime Minister, with a constitutional crisis to overcome, unwittingly gave the suffragettes hope. The House of Lords had rejected Lloyd George's 'People's Budget'. As part of the campaign of threat and counterthreat, Asquith had floated the idea of an Act of Parliament which would give the vote to disenfranchised men. Asked if it would be susceptible to an amendment that extended the suffrage to women, he could only reply that it would. His behaviour hardly amounted to a conversion, but it was enough to offend the King. The suffragettes did not occupy much of Edward's attention. His view on the role of women in society was quite different from theirs. But he did, from time to time, mention them in passing to other business. In March 1907 he had ended a letter congratulating Campbell-Bannerman on 'putting his foot down regarding the Channel Tunnel', on a note of regret. 'I only wish you could have done the same regarding Female Suffrage. The conduct of the so-called Suffragettes has really been outrageous and does their cause (for which I have no sympathy) much harm.'[33] A couple of years later Knollys, expressing royal regret that in a moment of impulse the King had made the German Kaiser an Admiral of the Fleet, ended with a terse postscript. 'The King deplores the attitude taken up by Mr Asquith on the Women's Suffrage Bill.'[34]

The suffragettes, who were by then picketing Parliament night and day, did not share the King's apparent view that Asquith was beginning to support their demands. One of Herbert Gladstone's last acts before leaving the Home Office was the transmission of a warning sent, through him, from the police to the Prime Minister. Women were practising pistol shooting in Tottenham Court Road.[35] Gladstone judged that 'there is now definite ground for fearing the possibility of the PM being fired at by one of the pickets at the entrance to the House'. The police were confident that they could restrain the would-be assassin before she 'damaged' the Prime Minister. But should the pickets be forcibly removed? Asquith said no.

The Pankhursts hoped that the 'Peers versus People' election of 1910 would result in a Liberal defeat. Their wish was very nearly granted. Asquith's majority was so reduced that he was forced to rely on Labour and Irish Nationalist MPs to secure the passage both of his budget and the House of Lords reform. As part of a whole series of penal reforms Churchill, the new Home Secretary, instructed that suffragettes be treated as 'political prisoners' – an innovation in English law. But the concessions did not bring peace. On 18 November 1910, 'Black Friday', heavy-handed police reaction to a Trafalgar Square demonstration provoked six hours of street fighting. There were two hundred arrests. On the orders of Churchill, most of the women in custody were released without charge. That, the suffragettes said, was clear evidence that the police dare not risk their brutality being exposed in court. When, four days later, a group of women invaded Downing Street, Churchill identified the ring leader and told the police, 'Take that woman away.' He was accused of personally directing the anti-suffragette brutality.[36]

Sympathy for the 'brutally treated' women took many forms. Wealthy supporters gave recently released suffragettes holidays in country houses so they could recover from the rigours of prison life. The composer Ethel Smyth threw her considerable weight behind the peaceful campaign which, after the eruption of Black Friday, seemed to offer hope of more dialogue and less damage. Smyth, large, aggressive and dressed in manly tweeds, was every reactionary's idea of a radical lesbian. Gay relationships were common among the suffragettes. Annie Kenney, after a number of brief associations, settled down first with Mary Bathurst (the daughter of a West Country philanthropist) and then with Grace Roe who had once hoped (almost certainly without success) to partner Christabel Pankhurst. Ethel Smyth had been more overt in her affections. Shortly after meeting Emmeline Pankhurst she had written, 'I knew that before long I should be her slave.'[37] The Pankhursts themselves, concerned only with serious business, examined proposals for a Conciliation Bill with a combination of hope and alarm.

The bill was the idea of a group of MPs (25 Liberal, 17 Conservative, 6 Labour and 6 Irish Nationalist) who hoped that politicians and protestors would compromise around giving the vote to women whose property had a rateable value of ten pounds or who were independent householders. Suffragettes were always split over offers of compromise. Some saw them as victories, others as defeats. It was then that Lloyd George and Churchill began to develop the same doubts as those which had prejudiced the Independent Labour Party and the TUC against an extension of the suffrage that simply gave women the same rights as men. A limited extension would increase the size of the Tory vote. Lloyd George made private enquiries about the scope of the bill being extended and was told that the 'long title' (which set out its general aims) made extension impossible. On 7 July 1910, the Second Reading of the bill was carried by 298 votes to 189, and it was then 'sent to a Committee of the whole House'. The decision to allow every Member to examine every clause meant that there was no hope of the full legislative process being completed by the end of the parliamentary session. The Conciliation Bill would be lost.

Christabel Pankhurst wrote to C. P. Scott asking, 'Can you and other Liberals wonder that we have come to the conclusion that we must take up again the weapons we laid down after the general election?'[38] But, although there was another great demonstration in Hyde Park (forty platforms and one hundred and fifty speakers) and the Prime Minister's motor car was damaged in Downing Street, the year petered out comparatively peacefully. A rally in the Albert Hall at the end of January 1911 was enlivened by the first performance of Ethel Smyth's *March of the Women*. Although the King's Speech for that year did not mention votes for women, a Liberal MP won first place in the private member's ballot and announced his intention of introducing the Conciliation Bill once more. Christabel Pankhurst promised her support. Both Asquith and Grey gave assurances that time would be made available to complete all its stages. Lloyd George again had doubts about 'a bill which would, on balance, add hundreds of thousands of voters to the strength of the Tory Party'.[39] The Liberal government should, he argued, decide whether it 'would put workmen's wives on the register as well as spinsters and widows or whether it will have no female franchise at all'.

So Asquith announced the government's intention at last to bring forward a bill to extend the male franchise and added that it could be amended to include votes for women. Christabel, firmly in charge of the WSPU, was outraged. She had agreed to compromise on conciliation. The offer of all-or-nothing had outflanked her and made her look both weak and foolish. Anger turned to rage when, at last, the Prime Minister agreed to meet a WSPU deputation. He told them that, personally, he was opposed to votes for women. Christabel made herself ridiculous by saying they would find a new Prime Minister.

Another deputation was organised, without any real hope of a meeting, for 21 November. The participants were told to bring a change of clothing – prison was not so much to be expected as sought and welcomed. As Mrs Pethick-Lawrence led her troops towards Westminster she boosted their morale with the reminder that Churchill's relaxed prison regulations still held good.

A second group of women had assembled at the Women's Press Shop. As well as a change of clothing, they brought hammers and stones. They spent the day vandalising government property. So began an accelerating campaign of moral intimidation and physical destruction. On 13 December, Emily Wilding Davison set fire to three pillar boxes at the beginning of a rampage across the country which included locking herself to the statue of Lord Falkland in the Palace of Westminster's St Stephen's Hall and only ended when she fell under the King's horse, halfway through the 1913 Derby. Emmeline, touring America, told her admiring audience, 'The argument of the broken

pane of glass is the most valuable in modern politics.' At home, suffragettes took her at her word. On 1 March, they smashed their way
down Regent Street, Bond Street, Oxford Street and the Strand.
Three days later, they rampaged along Knightsbridge and Kensington
High Street.

C. P. Scott judged: 'They are mad. Christabel has lost all sense of
proportion.' She had not, however, lost all instinct for self-preserva-
tion. True to her injunction that the WSPU leaders should avoid gaol,
she left London disguised as a nurse and took the Folkestone boat
train to Boulogne. Then she moved on to Paris. She stayed there until
August 1914. The suffragists had lost their leader and Christabel had
sacrificed much of the heroic reputation which she had once enjoyed.

There was talk of applying to the French government for
Christabel's extradition, but Reginald McKenna, who had succeeded
Churchill as Home Secretary, was content for her to remain in Paris.
Other suffragists served out their prison terms, but Emmeline and the
Pethick-Lawrences were granted bail as they awaited trial on the
greater charge of conspiracy. Emmeline foolishly chose to defend
herself. Her argument that she was motivated by politics, not innate
violence, could only have ended in conviction. Despite the jury's
recommendation of clemency, she was sentenced to nine months'
imprisonment. Martyrdom allowed her to claim the leadership of the
WSPU. She established her position by expelling the Pethick-
Lawrences (her only rivals) and telling an Albert Hall rally on 17
October 1912, 'Be militant in your own way. Those of you who can
break windows – break them.'[40]

Despite all the brave talk, the WSPU was degenerating into a
Pankhurst fiefdom and the unity of even that limited alliance was put
in jeopardy by Sylvia's sudden discovery of socialism and her decision
to support George Lansbury in a campaign for universal suffrage for
both sexes and all classes. But in January 1913 the Speaker of the
House of Commons ruled that the Franchise Bill dealt only with
voter registration. An amendment to extend the franchise would be
beyond its scope. Mr Asquith was genuinely surprised and therefore
should be absolved from all accusations of duplicity. 'This', he told the
King, 'is a totally new view of the matter . . . In Mr Asquith's opinion,
which is shared by some of the best authorities on procedure, the

Speaker's judgment is entirely wrong.'[41] But there is no doubt that he welcomed the decision. On 7 January he told Venetia Stanley, 'The Speaker's *coup d'état* has bowled over the women for this session. It is a great relief.'[42]

Speakers' judgements on such matters are rarely challenged with success, and it was the nature of the suffragettes to identify betrayal where it did not exist. The belief that they had been cheated was a great incentive to renewed activity. The inevitable result was more violence. Letters sent to the Chancellor of the Exchequer and the Prime Minister contained crude phosphorus bombs. No one was hurt. But on 3 April Emmeline stood trial for causing the explosion that damaged Lloyd George's house. She had no direct responsibility for the outrage, but she refused to plead. Her speech from the dock warned that, if sent to prison, she would immediately go on hunger strike – if necessary unto death. The judge was not impressed. The sentence was three years' penal servitude.

In prison, although Emmeline was offered food more appropriate to the dining room of a London hotel, she always refused to eat. She also refused to submit to medical examination. Eight days after her arrival in Holloway, the medical officer adjudged her too weak for forcible feeding. She was put in a hansom cab and sent home. Her official status was 'prisoner on licence'. The Home Secretary was operating the policy that he proposed to legitimise under the Prisoners' Temporary Discharge Bill which he was about to introduce into the House of Commons. Suffragettes on hunger strike to the point of death were to be released. They were to be rearrested and returned to prison for the completion of their sentence when in liberty they had recovered their strength.

Emmeline was back in prison on 26 May and released again on the 30th. Her licence expired on 7 June, but she failed to return and was arrested on the 14th. She was discharged on 16 June with licence to remain at large until the 23rd. The distasteful process of what came to be called 'The Cat and Mouse Act' dragged on throughout the summer. Philip Snowden, the Sea Green Incorruptible of the Labour Party, claimed to speak for the nation when he said with impeccable, if slightly callous, logic, 'She is punishing herself because she will not take the punishment which a court of law has imposed upon her for outrages which no community can allow anyone to perpetrate.'[43] He probably overstated the level of national antagonism to the women's behaviour. But the suffragettes themselves constantly undermined their own cause by behaviour which was simultaneously childlike and destructive. In May 1914, a police raid on a flat in Maida Vale resulted in the confiscation of half a ton of pebbles, three hammers and a hatchet. In July of that year the 'Rokeby Venus' in the National Gallery was slashed. The perpetrators were on the point of prosecution when the Great War broke out. Even the suffragettes had the sense to realise that while men fought and died in France the British people would have little patience with women who smashed shop windows. However, Christabel, with the insensitivity which so often characterises the champions of great causes, proclaimed: 'This great war . . . is God's vengeance upon people who held women in subjection.'[44]

The Great War both made votes for women irresistible and postponed a reform which justice and agitation had already ensured would come about. Lloyd George, who had never really wanted to resist, replaced Asquith as Prime Minister and, after four years in which women had done men's work, it was impossible to deny them men's rights. Emancipation came slowly. But it came – not in Edwardian Britain, but because of what had happened during the Edwardian era. Asquith, as was so often the case, typified the feelings which simultaneously promoted and retarded female emancipation.

> There are very few issues in politics upon which more exaggerated language is used both upon one side and upon the other. I am sometimes tempted to think, as one listens to supporters of women's suffrage, that there is nothing to be said for it. And I am sometimes tempted to think, when I listen to the opponents of women's suffrage, that there is nothing to be said against it.[45]

The suffragettes defied the spirit of Victorian England by preferring tumult to calm and passion to reason. They were the street fighters in the social revolution which was Edwardian Britain.

CHAPTER 11

United We Stand

The Taff – surprisingly not the origin of the nickname by which Welshmen are known worldwide – is not the sort of river along which history is supposed to flow. But, during the high summer of 1901, the behaviour of the little railway company which took its name from that thin line on the map changed the British political landscape. In the second week of a sweltering August, a signalman who had led the agitation for increased pay was sacked. His comrades, believing that his dismissal was unrelated either to conduct or competence, cried 'victimisation' and came out on strike. Their trade union, the Society of Railway Servants, declared the dispute 'official'.

Ammon Beasley, the Taff Vale Railway Company's general manager, was not the man to attempt immediate conciliation. Instead of arguing the justice of his cause or even waiting for his workers and their union to lose hope of victory, he called in William Collison, a former omnibus driver and one-time trade union activist, who had set up the National Free Labour Association to deal with exactly such situations. Collison supplied 'blackleg' labour to companies whose regular workers were on strike. The NFLA had helped to defeat the Amalgamated Society of Engineers when they had campaigned for an eight-hour day. The Railway Servants' executive were determined that their union should not be Collison's second victim. Richard Bell, the general secretary – and a man destined to play an equivocal role in the long march to parliamentary representation – urged caution. But he was overruled. The premises of the Taff Vale Railway Company were picketed and virtually closed down.

Beasley consulted the Employers' Parliamentary Council, an organisation which had been set up to co-ordinate the work of the many employers who sat in the House of Commons. Its main purpose was the organisation of lobbying on behalf of business interests, but it had also published *The Case Against Picketing* by W. J. Shaxby. The text suggested that, on the precedent of *Lyons* v. *Wilkins* (a dispute in 1896 between a leather goods manufacturer and the Amalgamated Trade Society of Fancy Leather Workers), the Taff Vale Railway Company was likely to obtain an injunction prohibiting the picketing of its premises and might even be awarded damages against the union. Shaxby proved a wise counsel. The courts both granted the injunction and agreed that the union must pay. Gratified by his legal victory, Beasley offered mediation which the union, chastened by its defeat, accepted. The dispute was settled within eleven days. But the legal processes went on and, to the delight of the union, the Court of Appeal reversed the original decision and absolved it from payment of damages. Then, in July 1901, the House of Lords reversed the decision again and added, crucially for the future of organised labour, that the funds of a trade union could be sequestrated to pay damages incurred by its individual members and officials.

Some of the more legalistically minded (and pathologically optimistic) general secretaries believed that there was some benefit to be gained from trade unions' recognition as legal entities. In theory, corporate existence paved the way for legally enforceable agreements between masters and men. But reality made most trade unionists accept that the Taff Vale Judgement imposed debilitating restrictions on their activities and posed a serious threat to their funds. It had cost the Society of Railway Servants £23,000 in damages and another £3,000 in costs. Combined with a second House of Lords Judgement – *Quinn* v. *Leathem* – which prohibited the promotion of boycotts, the precedent of Taff Vale could bankrupt any union which sought to defend its members' interests by direct action. It also threatened to impose financial penalties on union leaders. Offended companies could seize officials' savings or property as a contribution to the payment of the damages. John Hodge, Secretary of the Steel Smelters, announced – probably unnecessarily and certainly theatrically – that he had 'made over his little possessions to his wife by deed of gift'.[1] Protecting trade union funds by promoting legislation that reversed the House of Lords judgement – and therefore following the parliamentary route to power – gained hitherto unrecognised attractions. The idea of trade union representatives in the House of Commons – previously regarded as unacceptable 'political action' – began to gain ground.

The leaders of the older unions, most representing skilled crafts and ancient trades, remained dubious about the Trades Union Congress, which had co-ordinated union activity since 1868, playing any part in politics. The men who created 'New Unionism', mostly to organise the dockers and the gas workers, had less professional pretension and fewer inhibitions. Even so, in 1899, a TUC resolution – suggesting no more than that those unions which chose to do so should come together to consider political representation – had been carried, on a block vote, by only 546,000 to 434,000. Unions representing a third of the total voting strength had abstained.

Before the turn of the century, what politics the TUC allowed was carried on by its Parliamentary Committee. Ten years earlier, Sidney Webb had complained that 'the work annually accomplished by the Committee . . . has, in fact, been limited to a few deputations to the government, two or three circulars to the unions, a little consultation with friendly politicians and drafting an elaborate report to Congress.'[2] But until 1901 there were many general secretaries who gladly accepted its inactivity. When he was elected to lead the Shipwrights Union, Alexander Willie described himself as apolitical and argued that the shipwrights' aims should be achieved by industrial action. He was then persuaded that the Liberal Party best represented his members' interests. But, after Taff Vale, he became a 'Labour man', and when he stood for Parliament in Sunderland, it was only with the greatest reluctance that he accepted the description 'Lib-Lab' instead of 'Lab' alone.[3]

Initially the Boilermakers had expressed doubts about the wisdom of the Railway Servants picketing at Taff Vale. 'Many of us', wrote D. C. Cummings, the general secretary, 'no doubt believe that mistakes have been made and lack of tact displayed.' But the House of Lords' judgement convinced him that something must be done to 'ensure the safety of the funds we have for long years been building up for relief of sickness, old age and accident, death and want of work'.[4] He reinforced his argument with the demand for a Boiler Registration and Inspection Bill.

The executive of the Boilermakers went further and asked the members of their society to endorse a resolution which called for 'working-class opinion being represented in the House of Commons by men sympathetic with the aims and demands of the Labour movement'. It was carried by 26,478 votes to 8,905. The Executive Committee then considered the controversial question of remuneration and agreed that, if one of its members should be elected, he should receive an annual salary of £325. A more generous amendment proposing £350 was defeated. It was also agreed that, since the House of Commons sat for only half the year, a Boilermakers MP must also act as an (unpaid) union organiser.

Until Taff Vale, most trade unions regarded politics as peripheral to their real work. Miners in all of the coalfields which made up the several loosely allied federations were not sure that their traditional militancy needed the help of parliamentary representation. In Lancashire, where, unlike other mining counties, the colliers did not live in homogeneous pit villages but were minorities in textile towns, there had been a residual affection for the Conservative Party. The Tories had passed the Mines Act of 1860 and, because of John Bright's criticism of the bill – based on his extreme view of *laissez faire* – the Liberals in general were thought to be unsympathetic to the miners' cause. The Tories were also opposed to Irish immigration which, according to the miners, was the reason why their wages were constantly depressed. The most commonly held view in the Lancashire coalfield was that the miners should represent themselves. But they realised that even a collier was more likely to succeed if he was supported by sympathetic colleagues. In other coalfields, miners claiming greater self-confidence judged they could fight their own corner without parliamentary help. So alone among all the mining unions of Great Britain, the Lancashire Federation sent delegates to the inaugural conference of what came to be called the Labour Representation

Committee. One of them, Tom Greenall, topped the poll in the vote for trade union representation on the national committee and was appointed vice-chairman. Two months later, the Lancashire miners decided not to confirm their affiliation and he was forced to resign.

The inaugural conference of the Labour Representation Committee was held in the Memorial Hall in London's Farringdon Street on 27 February 1900. It was attended by delegates who spoke on behalf of less than half the TUC's total membership. Despite the presence of delegates from both the Independent Labour Party and the Social Democratic Federation (Marxist despite its name) it was certainly not a gathering of socialists – a doctrine which many of the trade union leaders dismissed as a continental affectation. The real problem, at the turn of the century, was that some trade unionists were equally sceptical about the need for parliamentary representation. Inevitably, the running was made by the full-time politicians, not the full-time trade unionists.

Keir Hardie and Ramsay MacDonald, acting on behalf of the Independent Labour Party, sent the Conference Standing Committee what they hoped would be the basis of the LRC's constitution. They realised that partisan origins would prejudice some of the unions against their draft. It was, however, a practical, not an ideological, document and they assumed that general secretaries, used to the formalities of organised debate, would welcome a statement around which the discussions could be built. The ILP paper made three basic proposals.

1. That candidates be run by Trade Unions, Socialist and other labour bodies and have no connection with either Liberal or Tory parties.
2. That each party (to the agreement) run its own candidates and find its own money.
3. That a joint committee of the organisations running candidates should co-ordinate the various campaigns.

The Steering Committee proposed that the Conference consider seven separate resolutions. The ILP proposals were included among them. But the full Parliamentary Committee insisted on debating a new resolution of their own composition. The idea of nominating and supporting 'labour' candidates was common to all the proposals. The differences arose over how the nominees should be chosen and who should finance their campaigns. Halfway through an afternoon of discursive debate, Keir Hardie moved the amendment which changed the nature of English politics by creating a party based on the social class of its supporters. He proposed the establishment of 'a distinct group in parliament who shall have their [sic] own whips and agree upon their policy which must embrace a readiness to co-operate with any party which, for the time being, may be engaged in promoting legislation in the direct interest of labour and be equally ready to associate themselves with any party in opposing measures having an opposite tendency'.[5] It was carried, despite the opposition of the Lancashire miners.

As an indication of the moderation which was to characterise British (as distinct from continental) trade unions and working-class politics, George Brown of the Engineers – a member of the ILP and once thought to be a follower of Tom Mann, a suspected syndicalist – moved a resolution which confirmed that the Representation Committee would not limit its patronage to working men. To confirm its permanence, the LRC appointed a general secretary. James Ramsay MacDonald was on his way.

MacDonald, the illegitimate son of a Lossiemouth domestic servant, had moved his way across politics from the Liberal Party, through the Scottish home rule movement and Marxist SDF, to the Independent Labour Party. His progress had been motivated more by intellectual curiosity than either ideological promiscuity or opportunism. He impressed his colleagues by both his confident manner and his imposing appearance, but his real attraction was not, as he would have wished in his early days, his philosophic originality but his natural aptitude for strategic thinking. He was a pragmatist and, perhaps because of him more than any other one individual, Labour became a pragmatic, rather than a doctrinaire, party.

The Labour Representation Committee got off to a slow start. In 1900, the year of its foundation, it claimed the affiliation of trade unions which represented 353,070 members. The affiliation fee was 'ten shillings per thousand members or part thereof'. In 1900, one-sixth of the total income of £180 was devoted to supporting general election candidates. The £30 did not prove a fruitful investment. Fifteen candidates were formally endorsed, eight of them after they had been nominated by the ILP. Will Thorne (the founding father of the gas workers' which became the Municipal and General Workers' Union) was the unsuccessful nominee in West Ham. Richard Bell of the Society of Railway Servants stood in the railway city of Derby and was elected. Keir Hardie, as was common at the time, stood in two constituencies. He lost in Preston but won in Merthyr Tydfil. They were the only two victories that the LRC could claim. Trade union candidates were never likely to prosper in a 'khaki election'.

There is no way of knowing if the unhappy electoral experience of 1900 would, without any other stimulus to action, have inspired the trade unions to greater political activity or driven them to the gloomy conclusion that the parliamentary route was not for them to tread. But the Taff Vale Judgement – and the menacing precedent it created – left most trade union leaders in no doubt that they must change the law through Parliament. In the two years which followed the Farringdon Street meeting, the LRC's affiliated membership rose only to 455,450. But the lesson of Taff Vale was being gradually learned. A new wave of support for parliamentary representation, led by the United Textile Factory Workers, was sweeping through the British trade unions. By 1903 membership had risen to 860,000. Perhaps more important, at least in terms of increased confidence, the big (and previously antagonistic) unions began to join the LRC. First the Engineers. Then the Lancashire Textile Workers. In 1901 the Labour Representation Committee spoke for forty-one unions. By 1903, the total had risen to one hundred and thirty.

Emboldened by its new strength, the Committee decided to extend its powers and clarify its constitution. In early Edwardian Britain, Members of Parliament needed a private income to survive. The LRC set up a fund, financed by a levy of one penny from every member of each affiliate, to make reality of its promise to pay its members. The figure on which the delegates eventually agreed was £200 a year. A national organisation needs a purpose as well as a bank account. The Glassworkers believed that the Committee should set out its ideological boundaries and defend them against infiltration.

That union therefore proposed that 'members should strictly abstain from identifying themselves with, or promoting the interests of, any section of the Liberal and Conservative parties'. It went on to assert, 'Labour representatives in and out of Parliament will have to shape their own policy and act upon it, irrespective of other sections of the political world.'[6] The resolution was carried by a large majority. The Labour Representation Committee had become a political party.

Trade unions depend for their success on solidarity and trade unionists are instinctively faithful to comrades and brothers. The creation of an institution which was made up of old friends but demanded new loyalties inevitably produced friction among men who had worked together for years. Activists within the Boilermakers Society tried, without success, to remove James Cranley from the list of potential candidates on the grounds that he was a Liberal. After some argument he retained his membership of both the party and the parliamentary panel.[7] And, in the summer of 1903, Ramsay MacDonald wrote to the Lancashire Miners to suggest that their nominee in Accrington stand down in favour of the Liberal nominee. The miners declined and their candidate opened his campaign with what must have been a painful justification of his conduct. He could not possibly be accused of splitting the anti-Tory vote. Most Lancashire miners always voted Conservative.[8]

The Taff Vale Judgement had established the trade unions' legal status (and in consequence their obligations and liabilities) under the law, but the public debate about their place in society continued. Clarence Darrow – the American labour lawyer who had defended Eugene Debbs, the socialist leader of the Pullman Carmen's strike, and achieved worldwide fame by representing the Tennessee school teacher who had been prosecuted for teaching the theory of evolution – wrote passionately about the need to avoid 'incorporation'. Once unions had a legal existence, strong and ruthless employers would impose their will on their workforce by action through the courts. The British unions, thanks to Taff Vale, were 'incorporated' already.

There then emerged a theory of British industry decline which was to be repeated, irrespective of the evidence, time after time during the following hundred years. *The Times* published a series of articles which argued that British companies were losing business to their American and German competitors because the unions were too strong. 'The Crisis in British Industry' claimed that both the low quality and high prices of British exports were due to the malign influence of restrictive practices. To the alarm of the TUC, the article went on to insist that the only hope of improvement lay in creating a contradiction. The labour market should be completely unregulated, but the powers of the unions should be circumscribed by law. The leaders of the TUC chose to comfort themselves with the belief that both the prognosis and the prescription were the work of William Collison, the founder of the National Free Labour Association and a man of such extreme views that he rarely represented influential opinion. In fact, the series was written by E. A. Pratt, the paper's regular industrial correspondent. Intellectual reinforcement for the trade unions was, however, at hand. Alfred Marshall, the great Cambridge economist, laid the blame for Britain's economic failure on masters, not men.★ Party politics were taking on a new dimension. Conflicting ideologies were taking the place of rival interests. The trade unions had become a force to be reckoned with. Capital and labour glowered at each other across the House of Commons and the two great parties – Liberal and Conservative – fought out their battles on the factory floor while a third waited, nascent, in the wings.

The unions expected help from the Liberals but could not wait for an election. So in 1903 they decided to promote a private member's bill in the Tory-dominated House of Commons. It aimed to legalise peaceful picketing, amend the law on conspiracy so as to absolve union officials from responsibility for the actions of their members, and protect union funds from claims for damages. The bill's Second Reading was defeated by the surprisingly small margin of 228 votes to 258. Asquith, Lloyd George and the enthusiastic new recruit to the Liberal Party's ranks, Winston Churchill, all voted in favour. The government responded by setting up a Royal Commission to examine Trade Disputes and Trade Combinations. Its members included

---

★After Balfour's defeat in 1906, the Liberal government chose to publish Marshall's essay as a White Paper.

Sidney Webb, already a distinguished political scientist as well as a founding member of the ILP, but there was no representative of what, in the jargon, was called 'organised labour'. So the TUC recommended that its members refuse to co-operate with the enquiry.

In the following year, the TUC tried again to change the law. A second bill was drafted in terms almost identical to the first. Balfour decided that it had to be taken seriously and wrote to the King with an explanation of the dilemmas which he faced. The letter began with a philosophical comment on the bill.

It has to be observed that peaceful picketing is, or may be, a most serious form of intimidation and as such can scarcely be permitted unless surrounded by precautions which the bill does not contain. As against trade union funds, it may be perfectly right that the portion of those funds which is devoted entirely to charitable purposes (pensions and so forth) should not be liable to seizure, but it can hardly be right that funds promoting strikes should possess privileges which *no other corporate funds in the United Kingdom* are allowed to enjoy.[9]

The merits of the bill were not, however, the Prime Minister's only concern. The Labour Representation Committee had still to establish an effective bridgehead in Parliament. Its members were, however, beginning to make their voices heard and their votes count. Balfour confessed to the King that 'although the bill ought not to pass . . . It seems impossible to defeat its second reading . . . Members are afraid of the trade union elements in their constituencies.' Cynical as ever, he went on to explain that, realising that shortage of time would prevent the bill from becoming law, MPs who deeply opposed it might feel entitled to placate trade union opinion by abstaining. He therefore 'did not propose to make the subject a government matter', though he would certainly speak (and probably vote) against it. Balfour's prediction proved correct. The Second Reading was carried by a majority of thirty-nine. Thirty-one Conservatives voted in favour. Like so many private member's bills it was then buried at the Committee Stage and forgotten.

The TUC, motivated by a combination of fear and fortitude, announced that it proposed to sponsor a third bill during the 1905

Parliament. On 11 November 1904, the Cabinet discussed 'certain demands for legislation made by the TUC' as if they had only just been made aware of the judgement which had concerned the nation's unions for four years. 'The fact is that the House of Lords, acting as Court of Appeal, has made one or two decisions which, though excellent law and excellent sense, are very distasteful to the trade unions.'[10] The causes of the TUC's concern and the remedies which they hoped to incorporate in legislation had been reported to the King in Balfour's letter on the day before the 1904 bill received its Second Reading in the House of Commons. Despite that Balfour thought it necessary to write again, explaining the government's objection to the TUC's proposals. The letter was written in the language of a child's guide to the Taff Vale Judgement. The Lords' decision, he explained, 'puts the Trades Unions in the same position as every other company or corporate body . . . and makes them subject to the ordinary law of the land. Mr Balfour has no doubt that this is substantively right and that the singular freedom of this country from unnecessary trade disputes is largely owing to it.'

The subsequent explanation of Unionist MPs' reluctance to vote against the bill differed from previous accounts of trade union power in one important particular. The Prime Minister admitted that he faced a personal dilemma. 'It will no doubt put those members of the Unionist Party who have a large trades union element within their constituencies (as Mr Balfour himself does) in considerable difficulty.' But the patriarch prevailed over the populist. 'The Cabinet was very clearly of the opinion that, in spite of the electoral considerations, it was our duty in the interests of the country at large to resist any demands which we conceive to be contrary to the interests of justice and sound policy.'[11] That pious statement of honourable intent hid the fact that the government thought it necessary to resist the bill by stealth.

In March 1905, the Second Reading of the third trade union bill was carried on a free vote. Once again the legislation was bogged down in the morass of the Committee Stage. Then damage was added to delay by the incorporation of emasculating amendments. After three months of discussion, the bill's sponsors decided that there was no point in wasting time on legislation which no longer met the TUC's needs. The bill was abandoned.

After the House of Commons rejected what the TUC called 'elementary justice' for the third time, the demand for the unions to be directly represented in the House of Commons was accepted by the whole trade union movement. Indeed the sudden enthusiasm for parliamentary power grew so fast that the General Federation of Trade Unions (a loose association which promised to support each other during strikes and lock-outs) announced that it would nominate parliamentary candidates without reference to the Labour Representation Committee.

Fearful that competition would reduce the impact of its advance into parliamentary politics, the TUC called a special conference for February 1905. The agreement not to nominate rival candidates which the delegates supported took its name from the place in which the conference was held. The Caxton Hall Concordat was not as important as its grandiose title suggests. Both parties agreed to support every candidate who was nominated by either the Labour Representation Committee or the Parliamentary Committee of the TUC. But, unbeknown to the General Council, back in 1903 Ramsay MacDonald (the Secretary of the ILP) had made a compact with Herbert Gladstone, the Liberal Chief Whip. Whatever candidates were nominated by trade unions, the ILP would always support 'Lib-Lab' nominees.

When the general election came in January 1906, organisations affiliated to the LRC nominated fifty candidates. The ILP sponsored ten of them and the unions which had chosen to go it alone ten more – most of them members of one of the regional miners' federations. Together with an assortment of independents who claimed trade union support and boasted socialist sympathies, they made up the first effective working-class assault on parliamentary power – and began a transformation of British politics for which only the visionaries among them could have hoped. Halfway through the long Edwardian afternoon, the working classes awoke.

The Tories had resigned office in December 1905 and, as an affronted *Times* chose to describe the consequence, 'Sir Henry Campbell-Bannerman succeeded in forming a ministry.' Balfour's worst fears, described in his letter to the King, proved justified – he lost his seat in Manchester. The Irish Nationalists enjoyed a pyrrhic victory, winning seats but losing influence. Mr Asquith did not need them to sustain his judgement, so the prospects for Home Rule could not be improved by threatening to bring the government down. In 1906 it was the success of Labour candidates which showed the world had changed. The paradox that the new party provided did not become clear for another ten years. Because of its emergence – 29 Labour MPs supported by 24 'Lib-Labs' – the great Liberal victory of 1906 also marked the beginning of the Liberals' terminal decline. The Labour Representation Committee, which changed its name to the Labour Party, was to brush it aside.

Labour had become a national party with influence that spread far beyond the twenty-nine constituencies which it won. John Sandars, Balfour's secretary and confidant, wrote to the defeated Prime Minister with his own analysis of the disaster. Chief amongst the reasons for so heavy a defeat was his theory that the pendulum (a predictable feature of nineteenth-century elections) which had been arrested in 1900, had only swung back harder in 1906. The organisation of the labour and socialist vote[12] had influenced the results in constituency after constituency. All over the country working men had been urged to vote anything but Conservative. The working-class vote had begun to count.

The new Labour Members, euphoric as new Members always are, anticipated the early publication of a bill designed to set the Taff Vale Judgement aside. Their optimism was not entirely justified. Asquith, a lawyer as well as the real force in Campbell-Bannerman's Cabinet, was opposed to a return to the *status quo ante Taff Vale*. He wanted to restrict the law of agency, offering some protection to trade union funds without discriminating explicitly in their favour.[13] The case against complete reversion was increased by the report of the Royal Commission which had been published during the general election. It proposed the statutory recognition of trade unions as legal entities, an obligation (placed on union executives) to separate benefit, strike and general funds (allowing money raised for welfare and pensions to be protected against claims for damages) and the restoration of the right of picketing. The government accepted the report as a basis for action and drew up a bill to implement its principles.

The Cabinet cannot have been surprised that what by then was called the Parliamentary Labour Party was outraged. One of its members, Walter Hudson, introduced a private member's bill which set out the reforms that the PLP had assumed would be implemented by the government. Campbell-Bannerman was so impressed by the argument which Hudson employed that, after a meeting with Labour MPs, he accepted (without consulting his colleagues) the case for absolute exemption from actions for damages and offered to amend the government's bill so as to meet the TUC demand. Asquith, by then Chancellor of the Exchequer, took the unusual step of making a personal statement during the consideration of the Bill in a Committee of the Whole House. He was, he said, still dubious about offering the unions complete immunity, but, since the government's proposals benefited associations of masters as well as men, he would reluctantly accept it. The House of Lords, believed to be in a mood to frustrate the new government at every turn, let the Bill pass into law. The Tory Party was still apprehensive about losing what, for the first time, was called 'the trade union vote'.

The task which had given life and vitality to the Labour Representation Committee had been accomplished. Why, asked the Liberals within the TUC leadership, do we still need a Labour Party? That question was given added force in 1908 when the Liberal government introduced legislation to limit the working day in the pits to eight hours. The miners, with a political perversity which has often characterised their position, thanked the Liberals – and affiliated themselves to the Labour Party. The acceptance of the Labour whip by their Members of Parliament virtually destroyed the 'Lib-Lab' group within the Commons. The Labour Party remained inextricably intertwined with the trade unions, but it was no longer a TUC pressure group. It was a political party with a clear philosophy and work to do.

Labour's emergence as a political force was the work of two Scotsmen – both illegitimate, both self-educated and both by turns worshipped and vilified. Keir Hardie was 'the most abused politician of his time. No speaker had more meetings broken up on more continents than he . . .'[14] Ramsay MacDonald, who slightly inaccurately described Hardie as Moses, was the man who eventually led Labour into the promised land of government. But, after he formed the

National Government in 1931, he became the symbol of betrayal which haunted the party he helped to found – and prejudiced the rank and file's relations with its leaders for the next fifty years.

Keir Hardie had entered the House of Commons in 1892. By then he had already made his name with an attack on the Liberal leadership of the TUC. A year later, he played a crucial part in the foundation of the Independent Labour Party. Defeated in the 1900 election, he failed to persuade the Ayrshire Miners (for whom he had been Secretary) to attend the inaugural conference of the Labour Representation Committee. Back in the House of Commons in 1906 he became, not least on the rule of seniority so beloved by the TUC, the Leader of the Labour Party in Parliament. His contempt for economics made him a limited spokesman for a party which believed in a radical change in the pattern of ownership, and his complicated private life – occasional flirtations with spiritualism and a regular liaison with the young Sylvia Pankhurst – might easily have destroyed his reputation as an incorruptible Christian Socialist. But he felt an instinctive passion for the Labour Party's great causes – the battle against unemployment, colonial freedom, women's suffrage and world peace. He was in many ways the least practical of politicians. One of his policies for alleviating poverty was the creation of a 'workers' colony' on Hackney Marshes – an idea which he borrowed from William Booth's *In Darkest England*. But he was a great House of Commons performer and that, together with the strength of his simple convictions, made him Labour's undisputed leader. Without him, the party might never have been established.

Because of his apostasy in 1931 Ramsay MacDonald has become the authentic villain of Labour history. But the informal partnership he set up with Liberal radicals (before he became the Member of Parliament for Leicester in 1906) was crucial in securing the Labour Party's early aims and establishing it in the House of Commons. Without the knowledge of the party, he maintained regular contact with the Liberal whips – first when they were in opposition and then during the years of Liberal government. The result was Labour support for the Insurance Act of 1911 – even though it was financed by what amounted to a poll tax. But his most important achievement, in those early days, was to provide a theoretical basis for a party which, then as now, despised political theory. He was not much of a philosopher and nothing of an original thinker – *Socialism and Society*, *Socialism and Government* and *The Socialist Movement* are books which boast little intellectual distinction. They did however offer the new radical party an alternative theory to the Marxism of the SDF. The man who pioneered the 'Progressive Alliance' with the Liberals and insisted that 'Socialism retains everything of value in Liberalism'[15] created the intellectual foundations for the party which, because it was more interested in practice than theory, pushed the Liberal Party aside.

The alienation of organised labour from the Liberal Party can, at least in part, be attributed to myths that surrounded the behaviour of Winston Churchill, Home Secretary and the rising star of that Liberal government. The notion that Churchill was, at heart, always an enemy of the unions was encouraged by his conduct during the General Strike in 1926, when he behaved in such a bellicose fashion that Viscount Davidson, the Prime Minister's closest confidant, warned Stanley Baldwin that 'the Chancellor of the Exchequer thinks he is Napoleon'.[16] He began (perhaps unfairly) to acquire that reputation as a result of his reaction to disturbances in Tonypandy in 1909.

The Eight Hours Act came into force during July 1909 and the miners, flushed with victory, decided to attempt a further advance into enemy territory. Their next objective was a minimum wage. At the same time as the unions were demanding an hourly increase, the mine owners were planning a reduction to compensate for the loss of working hours. The inevitable strike which followed went on for months despite government attempts at conciliation. By 1 November it had closed down all the collieries in the Rhondda Valley.

Six days later, what came to be known as 'flying pickets' toured all the pits owned by the Cumbrian Combine, what are always called 'violent clashes' occurred between police and strikers at the Llwynpia Colliery, a quarter of a mile from Tonypandy.[17] The Chief Constable of Glamorgan was probably right to fear that, without assistance, his officers would be overwhelmed. The extent of the help which he requested was, however, undoubtedly excessive. Two companies of infantrymen and two hundred cavalry were a big enough contingent to put down a small revolution. The request was made directly to brigade headquarters of the local command. The Home Office, at which Churchill presided, was informed on the following day.

Churchill's reaction was described at the time as oversympathetic to the miners. He instructed the Chief Constable to halt the cavalry's advance at Cardiff and hold the infantry at Swindon. Officers of the Metropolitan Police, rather than soldiers, would reinforce the hard-pressed Glamorgan constables. His telegraph to the rioting miners was astonishingly emollient. It was read out to a mass meeting on 8 November. 'Their best friends here are greatly distressed at the trouble which has broken out and will do their best to help them get fair treatment . . . But rioting must cease at once so that the enquiry shall not be prejudiced and to prevent the credit of the Rhondda Valley being impaired.'[18]

The rioting continued despite the sympathetic tone of the basically meaningless message. Indeed it spread from outside the Glamorgan Colliery to the main square of Tonypandy. A skull was fractured and the injured man died. Shops were looted. Churchill countermanded his own orders and the troops were allowed to move into the town. Next day, Lancashire Fusiliers defended the colliery at Llwynpia.

For the next sixty years Churchill was regarded in trade union folklore as 'the man who sent troops to subdue the Tonypandy miners'. But the government in which he served, perhaps out of necessity rather than conviction, was, in essence, the trade unions' friend. Cynics will argue that Lloyd George and Churchill worked hard to accommodate the unions purely out of self-interest. After the general election of 1910 – when 275 Liberal Members faced 273 Conservatives across the House of Commons – the government needed the 40 Labour MPs to help keep its hold on power without being totally reliant on the always demanding Irish Nationalists. And, even in the earlier years of landslide glory, the two men had been shrewd enough to know that the circumstances which brought the triumph of 1906 could never be repeated. One day the Labour Party's support would be essential to maintain Liberal government. But they were motivated by more than self-interest.

Policies for which Churchill himself and Lloyd George were responsible – at first thought by the unions to be inimical to their interests – turned out to be immensely beneficial. The Parliamentary Committee of the TUC accepted the idea of the government's agencies setting minimum wages only after much persuasion, and they remained reluctant to accept Lloyd George's scheme. Their resistance was motivated by a determination to protect the boundaries of the trade union empire. Many of the trade unions provided insurance schemes for their members and they were not prepared to stand aside in favour of state benefit schemes. Lloyd George agreed to compromise – though his critics called it capitulation. The unions were afforded the status of 'approved societies' and invited to administer the national scheme on behalf of their members. The result, possibly foreseen, but not intended, was a giant leap in trade union membership. In 1911, unions affiliated to the TUC represented 1,661,000 men and women. By 1913 the total had risen to 2,682,000.[19]

The government was firmly on the trade unions' side. The courts were not. In December 1909 another House of Lords judgement – the second in a generation – sapped the trade unions' strength. Taff Vale had virtually destroyed their industrial power. Osborne did the same for their political influence. And once again it was the Railwaymen against whom the initial action was taken.

W. V. Osborne, a member of the Society of Railway Servants' Walthamstow branch, was an enthusiastic Liberal. In the spring of 1908 he applied to the High Court for an injunction to prevent the union from using part of its income – and by implication a proportion of his subscription – to finance the Labour Party. Political expenditure was, he argued, *ultra vires* for trade unions which existed for quite different purposes. The High Court refused his application but the decision was reversed on appeal in the High Court, and the appeal was upheld by the House of Lords. Three of the Law Lords ruled that the union's lawful operation was confined to rights and obligations laid down by the Trade Union Acts of 1871 and 1876. They were explicit in their condemnation of the trade unions' relationship with the Labour Party. The obligation of trade union-financed MPs to obey a party whip was 'subversive of . . . their freedom'. Once again the TUC demanded a change in the law. The resolution calling upon the government to legislate for 'union freedom' was carried by the Trades Union Congress by 1,717,000 to 13,000.[20]

The Liberal Party was sympathetic. The Irish, on whom the government was dependent, insisted that a Home Rule Bill was the first necessity and made clear that, without it, they would not support a National Insurance Bill or the legislation which might be necessary to reduce the powers of the House of Lords and guarantee its passage. The reversal of the Osborne Judgement had to wait. The Labour Party was offered, by way of compensation for its disappointment, a bill which authorised the payment of MPs. The House of Commons would no longer be an occupation for gentlemen.

It was not until 1913, five years after the Osborne Judgement, that Parliament legalised trade union funds being used to finance the Labour Party. Even then, the Trades Union Act did not provide the unfettered rights for which the union leaders hoped. The freedom to take part in political activities – not stipulated in earlier Acts – was recognised, but before payments could be made to a political party, a ballot of the whole membership had to approve the creation of a distinct political fund. The right to 'contract out' of political payments – paying a reduced subscription which did not include the political levy – was established in law.

The agreement that trade unions should take part in the democratic process became a moderating force in late Edwardian politics. The years between the reversal of the Taff Vale Judgement and the annulment of the Osborne Judgement marked a period of unusual militancy. One cause of the numerous disputes was an increase in the cost of living, which rose twice as quickly between 1909 and 1912 than it had risen between 1902 and 1908.[21] The militancy was also, in part, the direct result of the unions' inability to fight their battles through politics and Parliament. Civil liberties aside, the Osborne Judgement, which aimed to separate the unions from the Labour Party, had deeply damaging consequences for the British economy. Industrial action was, the trade unions believed, the only weapon at their disposal.

In 1908, the Engineers in the north-east refused to accept a proposed wage cut and the Durham Miners rejected three-shift 'continuous working'. Year by year the number of days lost, often in regional and unofficial disputes, increased and 1911 was a year of widespread strikes. The *Olympic*, a new liner, was prevented from sailing by stevedores demanding a wage increase. There was a brief general strike in the Port of London and a nationwide railway stoppage. Largely thanks to the solidarity of other unions – which threatened action against recalcitrant companies – the Shipping Federation was forced to recognise the Sailors' Union. The Miners' Federation called out its members in support of their demand for a national minimum wage of five shillings an hour for men and two shillings an hour for boys. As a result, thousands of other workers lost their jobs when factories were closed down for want of coal. The London docks dispute dragged on into a second year, and Ben Tillett, the dockers' leader, became notorious because of his prayer for the future of the Chairman of the London Port Authority. 'Oh God, strike Lord Devonport dead!'[22]

The period of militancy coincided with – or perhaps was directly related to – the growth of syndicalism throughout Europe and America. In 1905 the Industrial Workers of the World was founded in Chicago and adopted the slogan 'the working class and the employing class have nothing in common'. In England, Tom Mann, the Marxist ex-engineer who led the Dockers' Union, returned from organising the industrial workers of Australia and, after taking advice from Georges Sorel, the French syndicalist, began to spread the gospel in the London docks and beyond. His publication, the *Industrial Syndicalist*, and his organisations, the Industrial Syndicalist League and the Plebs League, made some converts.

The Committee of the South Wales Miners' Federation published a pamphlet which called for the 'elimination of the employer'. That aspiration was wholly consistent with the syndicalist aim. Their first objective was to make sure that the workers were thoroughly organised and therefore ready to achieve the main purpose of a union's existence – 'to gain control of and then administer [the mining] industry'. Although syndicalism briefly dominated the politics of the South Wales coalfield, it was not an idea to fire the imagination of the staid, and essentially constitutional, leadership of the TUC. One of Mann's ideas did, however, commend itself to some of the unions. Amalgamations were, he said, the first step towards the goal of the 'real democracy' of workers' total control. The Railwaymen liked the first step, though they had no wish to move further forward. The

Amalgamated Society of Railway Servants, the General Workers Union and the United Pointsmen and Signalmen's Society joined together to become the National Union of Railwaymen.[23]

There was wild talk of amalgamating the Miners, the Railwaymen and the Transport Workers – a proposition which was rejected as much because of the power which some union leaders would undoubtedly lose as because of a resistance to the extreme continental ideology which motivated it. But when Robert Smillie, the President of the Miners' Federation, proposed co-operation rather than amalgamation, the practical leaders of the other unions accepted the idea immediately. Everybody kept their existing jobs and the joint power of three mighty unions could be employed in a 'Triple Alliance'. But nothing happened in the TUC without negotiation and negotiations moved slowly. The movement towards a common contract date – designed to enable each of the three unions to confront the employers simultaneously – was almost completed, but before the documents could be signed the world was at war.

The trade unions played their patriotic part. No one should have been surprised. A year before the war began, the TUC had been offered a real opportunity to contribute to a syndicalist victory. In Dublin, members of the Irish Transport and General Workers Union, under the leadership of Jim Larkin, were in dispute with the Dublin Municipal Tramways. Strike followed lock-out. After almost eight months, Larkin asked the British TUC for help – specifying that his greatest need was 'sympathy strikes', the syndicalist prescription for overcoming the power of the capitalist classes. Larkin was not the sort of man with whom the TUC did business. He was a friend of James Connolly and Maud Gonne and he believed in his own sort of Irish Home Rule – a workers' republic. The TUC donated £60,000, not to finance the strike, but to the fund which had been set up to alleviate hardship among the strikers' families. Not least because of the wisdom of the Liberal government, the British trade unions and the Labour Party which they created had become implacably moderate.

CHAPTER 12

Useful Members of the Community

The Education Act of 1870 – although extolled in history as the great achievement of Mr Gladstone's first administration – had left the English schools system in general confusion and, in some areas, actual chaos. It certainly increased the number of children in primary education – though not to the extent that was suggested by W. E. Forster, the author of the Act, who both overestimated the size of the improvement which it brought about and the number of children who had received no education before it passed into law.[1] The Forster Act was accepted as proposing a feasible change to the pattern of English education because, even before it was passed, a majority of children were already spending four or five years in the local state school. It failed in its aim to give every child the same start in life – with five or six years of primary education – because it spread the governance and management of schools too wide.

Legislation based on the experience of another country should always take into account the difference in national circumstances. The 1870 Education Act was inspired by the success – both military and economic – of Prussia. The English Establishment retained the belief that Waterloo had been won on the playing fields of Eton. The needs of that sort of school had been met with the Public Schools' Act of 1868 and the Endowed Schools Act of 1869. But the Austro-Prussian War of 1866 had been won in Bismarck's elementary schools, and the Franco–Prussian War of 1870 made it impossible for even the most myopic British observer not to recognise the strength which comes from a universally educated people.

As a result, England followed Germany's example in 1870 and Scotland did the same in 1872. But both nations had to overcome obstacles which Bismarck did not face: the churches – which ever since the Middle Ages had provided what education there was – were not prepared to abandon their ancient authority, and all the government dared to do was provide state 'maintained' schools where religious 'voluntary' schools did not exist.

The churches had been less provident than they claimed. The distribution of schools – and their very existence in some parts of England – depended on the strength of Anglican, Nonconformist or Catholic presence in an area. Even then, the quality of the provision varied with the enthusiasm of the local rector, minister or priest. The government provided minimal aid. Grants depended on matching funds being raised locally, levels of attendance and attainment, and the number of qualified teachers on the staff. As a result, only half the parishes of England had government-aided schools[2] and the provision in Scotland was even worse. In the Western Isles only 15 per cent of schools qualified for grants.[3] The charitable organisations chose (and often had no choice but) to send the children of the poor to private schools. In 1851, 700 teachers in private schools could not fill in the census because they could not sign their names.

The Act of 1870, intended to fill the gaps that the churches had left, certainly spawned dozens of new schools. It also provided further management in a form which appeared to have been designed to maximise complications and minimise efficiency. The 2,500 school boards which were created were wildly different in size. In remote rural areas the responsibility might be for no more than two schools. The London School Board managed 1,500 and employed 13,500 teachers. The voluntary schools in England and Wales often resented (and sometimes felt threatened by) the secular alternative. In Leeds, Manchester, Salford and Sheffield, representatives of the churches took over the boards, kept the maintained schools short of funds and used government grants 'for the education of indigent children' to subsidise their own voluntary alternative.[4] In other parts of the country, secularists blocked attempts by the churches to do more and better. Although some boards were indisputably excellent, creating 'special', residential, 'truant' and 'higher grade' schools, the results of the 1870 Act were simultaneously a triumph and a disappointment.

After 1870, whenever 'efficiency managed' voluntary schools did not meet the needs of a whole parish, locally elected school boards were empowered to set up 'maintained' schools in which religious instruction was required by law to be non-denominational. The boards could compel attendance and, by 1873, 40 per cent of the population lived in a school board area where it was compulsory. In some rural areas landowners, who dominated the boards, were not convinced that farm labourers needed even elementary education. In 1876, compulsion was extended but, as the years wore on, no serious educationalist thought that the 1870 Act provided a system which would meet the needs of the twentieth century.

Ironically, dissatisfaction with the way in which the 1870 Act worked came to a head as a result of attempts to improve it. By 1889 the pressure for English and Welsh maintained schools to provide free education – intensified by the Scottish Local Government Act which enabled local authorities north of the border to make grants which replaced school fees – had become irresistible. The voluntary (church) schools immediately complained that their natural pool of pupils was being diverted into the secular, or at least the non-denominational, sector. Maintained schools, they complained, would be able to finance a better quality of education free of charge.

In 1891 the Prime Minister, Lord Salisbury, addressing Tory MPs in the Carlton Club, persuaded his followers that government grants should be paid to all schools – even though that would inevitably involve some government influence on the quality of the teaching as well as the buildings. His argument was part political, part principle. If the Liberal Party 'should obtain a majority in a future parliament they would deal with the issue [of free education] in such a manner that voluntary schools would be swept away'.[5] The 1891 Act abolished fees in all elementary schools, but the voluntary schools remained at a disadvantage. Maintained schools could invest far more in their buildings and staff than the churches could afford to finance. The fear was that the standard of voluntary school teaching would become so obviously inferior that many of them would be forced to close.

There were, in 1900, 14,359 voluntary schools in England and Wales, with 2,486,597 pupils on their rolls. Within that total, 11,777 were Anglican (with 1,885,802 pupils) and 1,045 Roman Catholic (with 255,030 pupils). The ties between the Established Church and the Tory Party were close and constant. In 1895, Arthur Balfour – even then the heir presumptive to the Conservative Leadership – had promised that, if he was elected to government, he would do his best to protect the interests and guarantee the continued existence of church schools.

The great reorganisation that he accomplished – and which set the pattern of school administration for the next hundred years – has become, according to the conventional histories, one of the fortuitous products of party politics – government responding to the demands of its traditional supporters. Certainly the political imperative provided the stimulus to quick action. But there were ministers – and professional educationalists – who knew that the education system in England and Wales was, irrespective of the demands of the Established Church, in urgent need of overhaul. Fortunately Arthur Balfour was among them.

In 1895, a Royal Commission under the Chairmanship of Sir James Bryce – scholar, lawyer and Liberal MP – had reported on the state of secondary education. It had concluded that development of schools policy had been 'neither continuous nor coherent'[6] and that, in consequence, the 'first problems to be solved' must be 'those of organisation'. The first need was 'greater unity of control'. That could only be achieved by a 'local authority'. Since some central direction would be necessary, there 'should also be a central authority'.[7] The Commission therefore recommended the creation of a distinct and autonomous education ministry under the control of a Cabinet minister. 'Local authorities' – county councils, county boroughs and other boroughs with more than 50,000 inhabitants – should set up Local Education Authorities which would be responsible for all matters of administration in every state school in its area of jurisdiction. Inevitably this call for a new system of education administration covered the management of all schools – elementary and technical as well as secondary.

Passionate voices were raised in opposition. The Bishop of London feared that the tighter organisation of schools policy would 'politicise' education. He conceded: 'There are some advantages, no doubt', but went on to say, 'The disadvantages are obvious enough, namely that you let in upon education (which ought to be a steady thing) all the fluctuations of party politics. The advantage of not having education under Parliament is, of course, that it ought to be independent of all those fluctuations of opinion.'[8]

A unified Education Ministry was set up in 1900 by the amalgamation of the old Education and Science and Art Departments of the Privy Council with the division of the Charity Commission which supervised endowed schools. It was to take responsibility for the elementary schools (1870 Act), Technical Schools (1889 Act), Voluntary Schools (1897 Act) and whatever development of secondary schools followed the Bryce Commission's Report. There – in a state of complacent chaos – it might have remained had it not been for the vision of Arthur Balfour and the determination of one Robert Morant, a dedicated, indeed some would say obsessive, civil servant. The two men's endeavours were assisted by a happy chance which enabled them to seize the moment and revolutionise the organisation of schools in England and Wales.

The new Education Department was briefly headed by the Duke of Devonshire who – as Lord President of the Council – had previously been responsible for all those aspects of government which were not supervised by a specific ministry. The Vice President, John Gorst, MP, was soon to take over – though his reign was cut short by the eventual acceptance that his abrasive personality was not suited to the delicate work of reconciling diametrically conflicting interests. But the real tension within the department – unusually creative, as it turned out – was between full-time officials.

The permanent secretary was Sir George Kekewich, a gentle civil servant who – although he had fought hard and successfully to replace the 'payment-by-result system' with an agreed teachers' salary – was not tough enough to stand up to Gorst. In consequence he was blamed for all failures of policy, including the abortive bill of 1896 which was supposed to resolve the dispute between 'maintained' and 'voluntary' schools but proved unacceptable to each strand of religious opinion represented in the House of Commons. The effective deputy secretary was Michael Ernest Sadler, whose official title was Director of Special Enquiries and Reports – the Education Department's research branch. Sadler spent a great deal of his time visiting other countries to see what he could learn from their schools. He persuaded Kekewich that the research department needed a deputy director. R. L. Morant, educated at Winchester and New College, Oxford – and sometime tutor to the Crown Prince of Siam – was appointed to the new post.

Morant became convinced, from evidence acquired in his research into English schools, that the School Boards were a major obstacle to educational advance. In his view, the development of 'higher grade schools' offering more than basic instruction was at best complicated and at worst actually prevented by the form in which the 1870 Education Act had chosen to administer education. And higher grade schools – indeed all forms of education which were 'higher' than elementary – were essential to national prosperity. Some board schools provided what they called 'higher tops' – more advanced instruction for pupils who were thought likely to benefit from the extra tuition. A few school boards trespassed on previously religious territory by organising higher grade schools to which children of especial talent could be sent when their elementary education was completed. The churches – particularly the Church of England – argued that the provision of 'an education, the curriculum of which cannot possibly be defined as elementary'[9] was *ultra vires*. In London, opposition within the school boards themselves prevented the creation of higher grade schools until 1890. The opposition did not come just from within the boards or from the churches. The ancient grammar schools – particularly those with generous scholarships and bursaries – objected to the pool of working-class talent being drained by a rival which was subsidised by the state. Often the school boards yielded to their pressure. Morant's determination to see them replaced in a general reorganisation in line with the Bryce Commission's recommendations became a near obsession. His research remained eclectic. Adult education schemes were encouraged, and the Macmillan sisters supported in their pioneer work in the development of nursery schools. But the school boards were always on his mind. His article on Swiss education which appeared in volume three of *Reports*

on Educational Subjects confirmed, apparently casually, that it was illegal
to spend money earmarked for elementary education on the higher
grade or technical schools.

It was then that fate intervened. Morant was acting as temporary
private secretary to John Gorst, the minister, just as a dispute between
the London School Board and the London Technical Education Board
came to a head. The School Board had, the Technical Education
Board claimed, acted *ultra vires* by subsidising 'higher grade' education.
A complaint was made to the minister on the Technical Education
Board's behalf by the Camden School of Art. Gorst – relying on
Morant's advice and happy to humiliate Kekewich – found for the
Camden School of Art and referred the whole case to T. B. Crockerton,
the Government Auditor.

Balfour now realised that the ambition which he had cherished for
years could be achieved. He had attributed the Tories' unexpectedly
good result in the 1895 election at least in part to his promise to save
the voluntary schools, and he had tried several times without success
to be as good as his word. The problem which had stood in his way
was not any lack of enthusiasm amongst his honourable friends for
saving the church schools. The insurmountable opposition arose
when he tried to use the crisis in religious education as a vehicle on
which to carry forward education reforms in which he had believed
since he had read the Bryce Commission report. The wrangles inside
the Cabinet and fears of obstruction by the Opposition had forced
him to lower his sights.

> The general objections to state aid are familiar to the Cabinet as
> also is the single strong argument in its favour – the argument
> that, without state aid, it would be difficult, perhaps impossible,
> in the face of the growing appetite of parents, for educational
> luxuries and the growing expenditure of School Boards to meet
> (and very often to anticipate) that appetite, for Voluntary Schools
> in large towns to hold their own now or to avoid extinction in
> the near future.[10]

There, but for the intervention of the Camden School of Art, the
reorganisation might have rested, with the Church of England

satisfied, the Nonconformists disgruntled at the ever closer relationship which was developing between Church and state, and the government doing no more than meeting the basic demands of its Church of England back-benchers. But Gorst referred Camden's complaint to Crockerton and the Auditor found against the London School Board.

Crockerton ruled that neither instruction in science nor fine art could legitimately be described as 'elementary education', the only activity for which the Board was entitled to spend public money. The London School Board appealed and the case moved slowly through the courts until it reached the Master of the Rolls. In 1901 he found for Camden. Unless the law was changed, board schools all over the country would be required to abandon the provision of anything like secondary education.

The strong view about the inadequacy of the English school board system – held in the Department by Morant and the Cabinet by Balfour – was confirmed. Balfour decided that he must at least attempt to reorganise the whole provision of education in England and Wales. The churches were outraged both by the delay in Balfour's rescue operation and by the prospect that the new legislation might result in the board schools still providing better education than the religious schools could offer. But Balfour was not a man to draw back, particularly when he had a plausible justification for doing, at last, what he had wanted to do for years. The result was the great Education Act of 1902, a major reorganisation of school management and the guarantee of eternal life to denominational schools of every sort.

There is no doubt that Balfour saw the need for a new Education Act as more than his party's obligation to protect Church of England denominational education. Asked at a public meeting in Manchester to justify 'disturbing the public peace' by introducing a bill to which the Nonconformist churches objected, he replied, 'The answer is this. The existing educational system of this country is chaotic, ineffectual, is utterly behind the age and makes us the laughing stock of every advanced nation in Europe and America.'[11]

The need for a major overhaul of the education system was, much to the surprise of the whole Cabinet, heartily endorsed by the Duke of Devonshire who, as a Whig aristocrat, was not in the habit of either mastering the details of public administration or supporting government intrusion into the lives of the people. The day-to-day responsibility for the Bill was, however, left in the hands of Sir John Gorst – to whom the acceptance of new responsibility did not bring caution or wisdom. Gorst, who had once been a member of 'The Fourth Party' and co-operated with Balfour and Lord Randolph Churchill in harrying his own front bench, never quite adjusted to the demands of government. He openly described the Duke of Devonshire as a 'living wet blanket' and rejoiced when his public criticism of Conservative policy 'made Balfour squirm'. In July 1901[12] his indiscretions returned to haunt him. A radical MP reminded him of a long-forgotten speech in which he had explained why Tory governments neglected education.

> The members of the government were selected from a class which was not entirely convinced of the necessity or the desir-ability of higher education for the people. They held the opinion which is sometimes expressed by great professors of the univer-sities in their speeches that there were certain functions which had to be performed in the modern life of civilised communities which were best performed by people ignorant and brutish.

A combination of what Balfour called 'a degree of opposition which seems to be wholly irrational' and Gorst's unconventional way of defending government policy made it impossible to proceed with the general reform for which Balfour hoped. But a short bill which legitimised expenditure outside the 1896 Act was passed into law. During the Second Reading debate, Balfour made clear that he intended to return to the subject for reasons which went far beyond the need to protect the interests of the Church of England. 'You tell us that we are falling behind the Germans in industrial matters because we do not educate our people.' It was therefore 'incumbent on the House, as soon as may be, to establish that secondary author-ity which shall deal with secondary education for all classes of the country'.[13]

Balfour argued successfully for the preparation of another bill. The Cabinet agreed, but 'insisted on his conducting it through the

Commons. They would not have Gorst at any price.' Balfour's style encouraged one of his friends to complain, 'the worst of it was that he did not believe in education'.[14] It was a pose. He accepted the burden of his new responsibility and wrote to the Duke of Devonshire, not to complain (which would have been against his nature) but to explain (as was essential to his style) that he was not seeking to extend his empire. 'I have as you know been dragged (much against my will) into questions connected with education.'[15] What would now be called a 'mixed committee' – both ministers and civil servants – was appointed to work out the details. It was dominated by Robert Morant.

Balfour set about the task of both preserving and improving secondary education throughout the country 'in the lowest possible spirits about the whole question', for it seemed that his hopes of securing a general improvement in education might well be frustrated by an alliance in the House of Commons between Anglicans, who thought that the Church of England was receiving too little help, and Nonconformists, who thought that it was receiving too much. Morant's paper on the contents of the new bill supported Balfour's determination to make revolutionary, as well as comprehensive, changes in the whole organisation of education, but it also revealed how many conflicting objections had to be overcome before that was achieved.

> If we are tempted to include Elementary Education in the Bill in order to save the Denominational Schools [which will otherwise] be swept away by the next radical government and to raise enthusiasm for the Bill, we must necessarily face the question of removing the existing denominational restrictions upon all aid, of losing the cumulative vote, of raising denominational struggles . . . in the election of local bodies, and above all of deciding on a proper relation between the County and its component areas and on the proper organisation of Local Authorities, each with clearly defined functions for various types of school.[16]

Balfour, determined that the governance of elementary schools should be included in his bill, was willing to face all those hazards. So

he examined a number of alternative solutions to the problems which
Morant set out. It might be possible to allow the new authorities he
intended to create a choice between assuming a responsibility for elementary as well as secondary education or simply supervising the
new secondary schools which the government intended to encourage.
His first instinct was to determine the nature of religious education in
state elementary schools by what was called 'the Clause 27 Rule' – the
provision in the 1896 Act which allowed denominational instruction
if that was the clear preference of a majority of parents. Nonconformists had fought bitterly against that change to the principle,
laid down by the 1870 Act, that religious teaching in board schools
should have no denominational bias. Nonconformity was far stronger
in the Parliament of 1901 than it had been in the Parliament of 1896.
Balfour's contempt for religious bigots was undisguised: 'I do not
approach the topic in the least as a Member of one particular denomi
nation. Indeed the division among Protestants has in my judgement
done such incalculable harm to Christianity that I should be reluctant
indeed to embitter them.'[17]

But the most intractable problem facing Balfour was the apparently
irreconcilable conflict between preserving the independence of the
church (voluntary) schools and, at the same time, providing them
with the funds necessary to guarantee a quality of education which
was comparable with that available in the secular alternative.

> As I understand the present situation, those interested in the
> maintenance of these [church] schools desire to have all their
> current expenses, connected with secular education, paid out of
> the rates, they (in exchange) to hand over their existing build-
> ings, to keep them up and where necessary add to them . . . But
> I take it that, in a very large number of cases, the buildings are
> inferior to the Board Schools and that, if Voluntary School
> Managers were required to bring them up to that standard, their
> financial position would hardly be improved by the change.[18]

Despite Balfour's initial pessimism, a combination of his political
strength and Morant's intellectual agility made sure that the conflicting needs – improved standards and continued church participation –

were as nearly reconciled as possible. The basis of the new bill was the complete abolition of the School Boards and the assumption of the responsibility for education by committees of county and county borough councils. Each of the councils – including the larger non-county boroughs which were brought within the scope of the bill during its committee stage – was to create a committee which included co-opted members with special interest in education. Most often, they turned out to be leaders of the local religious communities. The Local Education Authorities (as the committees became) were empowered to provide both elementary and secondary education. Their task was to encourage the general provision of a curriculum that was already available in the most progressive local authorities which used to the full their powers under the 1889 Technical Education Act. In Bradford, Rowland Evans, about to become an engineering apprentice, described in his diary life in the 'top section of the 2nd year' in the senior department of a board school. His working day under the supervision of 'Mr Pendlebury . . . a very strict teacher' was certainly not 'elementary' education. 'The first lesson was scripture and he was talking about parables and their meaning. Then we had French and mathematics. In the afternoon we had Latin and were reading Shakespeare.'[19] The object of the 1902 Bill was the provision, throughout the country, of what was already available in places like Bradford.

The Church of England's needs were met by the government accepting (in slightly more generous terms) the bargain – premises in exchange for the promise of running costs – which Balfour had earlier rejected. The churches were to appoint their own teachers, but their schools were to be subject to government inspection. The Catholic Church, after years of doubt about an educational partnership with the state, changed its mind and rejoiced that 'the general effect of the new law is to make Christian and Catholic Education a part of the law and constitution of England'. Cardinal Vaughan believed the 1902 Act to be 'a large and important advance'.[20] His views were a triumph for realism. 'Our hope for the future lies in our schools and our schools can never be self-supporting. The idea that we in England could ever hope to throw off state aid and maintain effective schools (such as the government would recognise as efficient) out of our own private means is a pure chimera.'[21] The Non-conformist churches had few schools of their own, but the defence of those which existed was fierce and unremitting. They feared that the Act would 'ensure permanent subsidisation of the Established and Roman Catholic Church'.[22] The Baptists were particularly critical of proposals which the Reverend Doctor Clifford called 'Rome on the Rates'.

The Nonconformist objections grew stronger with the discovery that Cardinal Vaughan had asked Irish Members of Parliament to stay in London throughout the summer and guarantee the successful passage of the Bill. Nonconformists on the Opposition benches had hoped that the Church of England schools would wither and die. The Bill would reprieve them. Very often they were the only schools in travelling distance of whole communities. In consequence there was the permanent prospect of Nonconformist children being educated in Church of England schools – rather than attending the board schools (called 'provided schools' after the Bill was passed) and receiving their religious education at home and on Sundays. The Nonconformists had a second concern. They knew that Balfour was in favour of allowing the 'provided schools' to offer whichever sort of religious instruction the parents wanted. That, they feared, would always be Church of England. The notion of parental preference was abandoned, but the Nonconformists were not reconciled. They decided that the non-denominational education which was an obligatory part of the board schools curriculum would be indistinguishable from the teaching of the Established Church.

The Nonconformists had an ally in the Cabinet. Joseph Chamberlain was a Unitarian by birth and a troublemaker by nature. Fortunately for the future of the Bill, the Duke of Devonshire 'surprised all his colleagues by displaying a complete mastery of the issues involved. He unfolded his views with great cogency, not allowing himself to be disturbed by the interventions of Mr Chamberlain.'[23] However, the Cabinet did agree – worn down by constant argument and Chamberlain's implicit threat of resignation – to include a clause which gave each county or borough council the 'local option' of not implementing the Bill.

Chamberlain was mollified but not content. Victor Cavendish

noticed that the Duke of Devonshire 'seemed very worried about the Education Bill. Afraid there may be trouble. May break up the party.'[24] It took fifty-seven sessions in all for the Bill to pass into law. One of them should have given the government particular satisfaction. Had the local 'opt-out' clause been allowed to stand in its original form the Bill's basic purpose would have been frustrated. But an amendment to delete it – insofar as it applied to elementary schools – was moved while Joe Chamberlain was away from the House recovering from a hansom cab accident. Emboldened by his absence, the government asked its supporters to vote in favour of the amendment and it was carried.

Outside the House of Commons the battle over denominational instruction raged. Radicals combined with Nonconformists to campaign for the removal of religious instruction from the school syllabus. More than three years after the Bill became an Act, the Reverend Evans (young Rowland's father) went from Bradford 'up to London . . . to meeting in connection with Secular education. The meeting was called to form a national league. Father on committee. The name of the league is the Secular Education League.'[25] By then, Nonconformist hatred of the Education Bill had contributed to Unionist defeat in the general election of 1906. But the bill had changed the quality of English and Welsh education.

The changes came about slowly, for although Balfour knew that the fundamental reorganisation of the education system was essential to the well-being of the country, his political philosophy prevented him from imposing the reforms on unwilling county and borough councils. The key to progress was the creation of Local Education Authorities with the power to set up and supervise schools of every sort. Balfour told the House of Commons that the government 'had been most careful not to bind this authority instantly to produce a great scheme of secondary education in their areas'.[26] The final clause of the bill prompted but did not compel: 'The local authority shall consider the needs and take such steps as seem to them desirable, after consultation with the Board of Education, to supply or aid the supply of education, other than elementary, including the training of teachers and the general co-ordination of all forms of education.'

By the time that the Local Education Authorities were set up and had begun to plan improvement and expansion, the Board of Education (with whom they were required to liaise) was under the command of a new permanent secretary. Kekewich had been pushed aside and Morant had taken his place, determined to create new secondary schools in the image of his own education. Winchester and New College, Oxford, had left their mark. Despite all the talk about the need for technical education, the new schools would teach a syllabus which was a reflection of the public-school curriculum. The bias, although damaging to Britain's industrial future, had honourable origins. 'Extending opportunity to the working class meant [offering them] a right to share a liberal education in its highest form.'[27]

The elementary schools were expected to develop a syllabus which combined the improvement of practical skills with the acquisition of knowledge. In 1904, a Code for Public Elementary Education – the only outline of education's purpose to be drawn up in almost a hundred years – was published by the new ministry. It stands up very well to the test of time – with the exception of its use of the word 'children'. Over the years they became first 'pupils' and then 'students'.

> The purpose of the Public Elementary School is to form and strengthen the character and to develop the intelligence of the children entrusted to it . . . With this purpose in view it will be the aim of the School to train the children carefully in the habits of observation and clear reasoning so that they may gain an intelligent acquaintance with some of the facts and laws of nature . . .

Children must be taught in a way which was likely

> . . . to arouse in them a living interest in the ideals and achievements of mankind, to bring them to some familiarity with the literature and history of their own country and to give them some power over language as an instrument of thought and expression.

The formal education of school days should only be a beginning. So

> while making them conscious of the limitations of their knowl-
> edge, to develop in them such a taste for good reading and
> thoughtful study as will enable them to increase that knowledge
> in after years by their own efforts . . .
>
>   The School must at the same time encourage to the utmost
> the children's natural activities of hand and eye by suitable forms
> of practical work and manual instruction and afford them every
> opportunity for the healthy development of their bodies, not
> only by training them in appropriate physical exercises and
> encouraging them in organised games, but also by instructing
> them in the working of some of the simpler laws of health.

The Code included an admirable expression of the need to balance
the interests of the individual against the needs of the whole community.

> It will be an important though subsidiary object of the School to
> discover individual children who show promise of exceptional
> capacity, and to develop their special gifts (as far as this can be
> done without sacrificing the interests of the majority of the chil-
> dren) so that they may be qualified to pass at the proper age into
> Secondary Schools.

The secondary schools were clearly not intended to complete the
education of all the children. But all parents were to be involved

> in a united effort to enable children not merely to reach their full
> development as individuals but also to become upright and
> useful members of the community.[28]

Few children of the working classes passed at the appropriate age
into secondary schools. Indeed the working class barely benefited at all
from the implementation of the Bryce Commission's proposals. 'The
chances of the children of labouring parents obtaining secondary
schooling were not immediately enhanced.'[29] For the new schools
charged fees. Some free places were available immediately after it

became lawful to provide them in 1905, but even after 1906 – when the Liberal government required a quarter of the entrants to be elementary school pupils who had won scholarships – the middle class still dominated the rolls. By 1911, 60 per cent of all secondary school pupils (82,000 or more) had begun their education in maintained elementary schools, but most of them were the sons and daughters of clerks, artisans and shopkeepers. However, thanks to the perseverance of Balfour and Morant, by 1914 60 per cent of children in England and Wales stayed at school until they were at least fourteen.[30]

In Scotland the reorganisation of schools took a slightly different course – as was to be expected in a country where the commitment to education was traditionally far greater than it was in England. In 1496 the law had required barons and wealthy 'free holders' to send their children (of both sexes) to school for three years, and John Knox's *First Book of Discipline*, published in 1560, had prescribed universal education as essential to the creation of a God-fearing nation. 'Most of the progress in Scottish Education since Knox's day had consisted of advancing towards his ideals.'[31] A Scottish (or 'Scotch' as it was surprisingly called) Education Department – distinct from other ministries – had been created to co-ordinate school policy in 1885, fifteen years before the same rationalisation was thought necessary in England and Wales. State funds were made available for secondary and technical education during the 1890s and many elementary schools created 'higher grade classes' from among their pupils. The examination for the Scottish Leaving Certificate (inaugurated in 1888) was opened to all board school pupils in 1892. So by 1902, when the Scottish Education Act was passed, there were four hundred schools in Scotland that were already providing some sort of secondary education. And, crucial to the development of an educated nation, the profession of teaching was treated with a respect which it did not enjoy south of the border.

The status of teachers in England is illustrated in the case studies which brilliantly enliven Pamela Silver's *The Education of the Poor*. In 1905, Mr H. Sprigge was appointed head of Saint Mark's, Kennington Oval, National School. It seems that he discharged his duties creditably for seven years and worked amicably with his committee of management. Then, in 1912, a disagreement arose and he discovered his proper place in society. 'Vicar called: discussed service for Ascension Day. Instructed the headmaster to inform the staff that a special communion service for teachers would be held after the children's service. He stated that staff were expected to attend. Headmaster replied that he could exercise no power over staff in this respect. The vicar said, "Do not argue, you must remember that you are here to obey me."'[32]

Mr Sprigge had studied for two years at Cheltenham Training College and obtained his teaching certificate in the second division, and was therefore one of the better qualified members of a 'profession' which still contained many products of the 'pupil-teacher' system – beneficiaries of an apprenticeship which no craftsman in industry would have regarded as adequate. By and large, Morant's Oxford-educated administrators regarded teachers in general with undisguised contempt. In 1905, Edmund Holmes, the Chief Inspector of Schools, was sufficiently unwise to express his opinion in writing. Describing to Morant the difficulties faced by the inspectorate, he began his litany of problems by stating, 'Apart from the fact that elementary school teachers are, as a rule, uncultured and imperfectly educated and that many, if not most, of them are creatures of tradition and routine . . .' His memorandum became public as a result of one of those errors which almost seem intentional. It was sent, by mistake, to one of the department's political critics. The National Union of Teachers, already offended by Morant's *de haut en bas* attitude, joined forces with the Tory Party to force the Chief Inspector to resign. Morant felt that honour required him to do the same. So ended one of the careers which helped make Edwardian England a time of positive change.

Of course, the change was greater for boys than for girls, men rather than women. By 1914 there were more than four thousand secondary schools in England and Wales. Only 586 of them admitted girls – 349 exclusively and 237 alongside boys. But the ancient universities were beginning to accept the idea of women as undergraduates – slightly improbably under the influence of George Nathaniel Curzon, Chancellor of the University of Oxford.★ The colleges of the new

---

★For details of women and the professions see Chapter 10, 'Votes for Women!'.

Victoria University in the northern provinces were co-educational from the start.

The Universities of Manchester, Liverpool, Leeds and Sheffield had all begun as part of Victoria University, a federation of existing colleges that came together gradually during the 1890s. Manchester University began as Owens College, Leeds University as the Yorkshire College of Science, Sheffield as Firth College and Liverpool as a new institution of learning created by the Municipal Corporation in 1881. All were helped by the existing medical schools in the cities' great hospitals and advised by the 'external delegacies' of the ancient universities. The Victoria University – then incorporating only Liverpool but intended to embrace other colleges – received its Royal Charter in 1880. Its pioneers believed that it might exist in its federated form for ever, but religion intervened. Manchester wanted to create a Faculty of Theology. Leeds and Liverpool objected. The solution was separation. So each of the northern universities was an Edwardian creation – Manchester and Liverpool in 1903, Leeds in 1904 and Sheffield in 1905. Birmingham can claim seniority over all four. The Mason College and Queens College in that city had amalgamated in preparation for applying to join the Victoria University. But, inspired by Joe Chamberlain and the civic pride which he embodied, its governors decided that they should be independent from the start. Supported by a gift of £5,000 from Andrew Carnegie, they applied for, and received, a charter in 1900. The first Chancellor was, of course, the Right Honourable Joseph Chamberlain.

Ruskin College, Oxford, was founded – materially to provide young men and women with 'a training in subjects which are essential for working-class leadership and which are not a direct avenue to anything beyond'. The founders – Mr and Mrs Vrooman and Professor Beal – were American idealists who (although they spoke of teaching 'men who have merely been condemning our institutions . . . to transform those institutions . . . so that they will begin methodically and scientifically to possess the world'[33]) at heart believed in a liberal education. Many of their early students did not. They wanted to learn about the Marxist dialectic and how the victory of the proletariat (which, although certain, nevertheless had to be brought about by a popular revolution) could be hastened. After a long and bitter dispute about aims and objectives, the Marxists on the staff, who had formed themselves into the Plebs League, resigned in order to encourage 'independent working-class education on Marxian lines'. The result, in 1909, was the Central Labour College in London which, despite the support of the South Wales Miners and the Society of Railway Servants, never prospered. It dwindled into the National Council of Labour Colleges which provided tutors for trade unions but, because of its overt political commitment, never enjoyed the success which government support and public money would have guaranteed.

The failure of the Central Labour College was an unhappy exception in an age when adult education prospered and adult colleges multiplied. The Mechanics Institutes (founded by Lord Brougham during the first half of the nineteenth century) had been taken over by the emergent middle classes. Cambridge University pioneered what it called a 'University Extension Movement'. It attracted only a small percentage of the potential army of eager working-class students. It was too formal and therefore too forbidding. The Adult School Movement, pioneered by the Society of Friends, made some progress among men and women who were hungry for learning, but there was still a need for a dynamic movement which promoted and provided liberal adult education. It was met by what became the Workers' Educational Association.

The WEA was the creation of three organisations and one man, Albert Mansbridge – a junior civil servant who became a clerk with the Co-operative Wholesale Society – who brought together the trade unions, the Co-operative movement and the universities which sponsored 'extension' courses. They formed the Association to promote the Higher Education of Working Men, with Mansbridge as honorary secretary. The first branch was established in Reading in 1904, the second in Rochdale. In 1905 Mansbridge successfully argued for a change of name. By 1908 the Workers' Educational Association had fifty branches and two influential recruits. William Temple (soon to become Bishop of Manchester and eventually Archbishop of Canterbury) became the WEA's President, and Robert Morant persuaded New College, Oxford, to make the organisation an annual grant on the understanding that it adopted Oxford ways. So the tutorial system infiltrated adult evening classes – reinforced by the stern regulation that financial support would be available only to groups of thirty or more. The need to learn came together with the urge to teach. For a year R. H. Tawney taught at Longston, in Staffordshire, on Friday evenings and Rochdale, in Lancashire, on Saturday afternoons.

The urge to improve was not confined to adults too old to benefit from the new secondary schools. At the turn of the century the mood of the whole nation – whether the product of hope or fear – was to prepare for the future. Indeed, one of the strangest organisations of self-improvement – devoted entirely to the moral and physical development of young people – was built on the injunction 'Be Prepared'. The Boy Scouts were not the first benign military youth movement in Britain. Indeed their inspiration was provided by the Twenty-First Birthday Parade of the Boys' Brigade. The inspecting officer was General Robert Baden-Powell, the hero of Mafeking who had – or so he claimed – been considering ways of occupying aimless youths since he had recruited boys for various duties during the siege. The Boys' Brigade seemed to him concerned with the wrong sort of military training – parade ground drill rather than the encouragement of the initiative and resourcefulness which had been so valuable on the veld. What he achieved has often, unfairly, been the subject of derision and sometimes questions about the passions which drove 'BP' on. But Baden-Powell is one of the few men who, in their own lifetime, created a worldwide movement.

It all began with an 'experimental camp' on Brownsea Island, off the Dorset coast, in 1907. Boys of every social class lived for a week under canvas and received instruction in the subjects which Baden-Powell believed produced 'manliness' – physical fitness, personal hygiene, field-craft (most of it based on what he had learned with the Army in India and South Africa), patriotism, good manners and the Christian faith. Pursuit of these harmless objectives might not have spawned an international movement had 'BP' not been taken up by Arthur Pearson, the newspaper tycoon, who published the movement's textbook, *Scouting for Boys*, and its magazine, *The Scout*. Pearson was motivated by real enthusiasm for an idea which he found both morally inspiring and good business. Northcliffe, his great (and in many ways more successful) rival had been a competitor for the sponsorship of the new organisation. *The Scout* sold 100,000 copies a week.

In 1910, the Boy Scouts colonised America, taking over, at its foundation, the Sons of Daniel Boone and the Woodcraft Indians. Theodore Roosevelt became the Scouts' vice-president. Membership rose to 300,000 in three years. Soon there were to be Scout 'troops' all over the world. All of them propagated the ideals of the Edwardian Empire.

It is easy enough to laugh at the bare knees and the classes in knot-tying, the camp fire 'yarns' and the habit of teaching boys from the East End of London how to survive on the plains of Matabeleland. And there were other aspects of early 'Scouting' – philistinism chief amongst them – which were unequivocally deplorable. But in its bizarre way it was an attempt to make things better. Like the new universities and the secondary schools, the Boy Scouts were a proclamation of the belief in progress. The optimism which characterised their view of life was typical of the Age of Improvement in which they were created.

PART FOUR

'Everybody Got Down off their Stilts'

The Edwardians took their pleasures seriously. For all their supposed frivolity, the years before 1914 heralded a cerebral, if not sober, century.

The poetry of the age was generally trivial and jingoistic. Only Yeats could stand comparison with the great Victorians. But every year between 1900 and 1914 at least one great novel was published. They were the stories of real people living in a real country. That country was England and much of Edwardian fiction was written in its praise.

The stage became serious in a different way. The turn-of-the-century drawing-room dramas were gradually superseded by the theatre of ideas. Vesta Tilley and the Gaiety Theatre caught the public imagination, but Shaw, Galsworthy and Granville Barker were all making the playgoing public think. At the same time they were challenging the Lord Chamberlain's right to prevent them stimulating thought about the subject that Victorians had believed should never be mentioned in public – sex. It was an age of robust realism. In Yeats's words, 'Everybody got down off their stilts'.

The great institutions of national sport (with the exception of cricket, an essentially eighteenth-century foundation) had been created in Victoria's reign. In the years immediately after her death, games reached out to the people in a new way. Edwardians, with more leisure than previous generations, became paying spectators. A hundred thousand football fans watched the 1901 Cup Final at Crystal Palace. Some games were becoming a trade as well as a pastime.

In the countryside, traditional 'sport' prospered as never before. It was the age of the 'shooting party' and the long country-house weekend. Racing became literally 'the sport of kings' – at least for the one King whose horses won the Derby and the St Leger. Everybody who was anybody played croquet and tennis. People who were nobody hiked. The whole country found time for pleasure.

CHAPTER 13

Ideas Enter the Drawing Room

Some drama is for an age, not for all time, so it is not altogether surprising that *The Heart of Achilles* (the story of how the Russian plan to annex India was foiled by a playboy turned patriot) and *A Queen for a Wife* (in which the future of a backward Balkan state is determined by the amorous adventures of a central European princeling) should have been immensely popular in Edwardian Britain and then forgotten after the world turned upside down in 1914. And, during the early years of the twentieth century, the British stage reflected more of national life than the politicians' preoccupation with 'the great game' and 'the eastern question'. Edward's reign was a time of great social change. Britain — particularly England — was struggling to come to terms with a new class structure and altered class relationships. The stage reflected the growing doubts about deference and the increasing enthusiasm for radicalism and reform by abandoning its preoccupation with 'drawing-room drama' and replacing it with 'the theatre of ideas'.

The old values died hard. In 1904 J. T. Grein, regarded in his time as a serious critic, expressed strong doubts about the merits of J. M. Barrie's *The Admirable Crichton*. 'Was it necessary', he asked, 'to contrast a very lowly type of kitchen maid with refined society?' Grein was at least consistent. In 1910, when ideas were in vogue, he acknowledged that *Smith* was 'in many ways the best of Somerset Maugham's plays', though he had one reservation about its construction. 'The fact that his central figure is a servant somewhat lowers the standard of the comedy.'[1]

At the beginning of the century the working classes were usually allowed on stage only as members of the full supporting cast – butlers, policemen and rude mechanicals. Bernard Shaw, who had satirised the Balkan obsession in *Arms and the Man*, explained (we must assume ironically) in his preface to *You Never Can Tell* that he felt a sudden obligation to gratify the playgoing public's appetite for watching 'eating and drinking by people with an expensive air attended by an impossible comic waiter'.[2] He was contributing to a well-established tradition. The stage directions for *The Liars* by Henry Arthur Jones specify 'Lady Rosamund's drawing room, Cadogan Gardens, a very elegant apartment, furnished in good taste.' *The Return of the Prodigal* by St-John Hawkin is set in 'The Jacksons' drawing room at Chedleigh'. Hubert Henry Dawes's *Lady Epping's Lawsuit* begins in 'The drawing room at Epping House' and much of the action in his *Captain Drew on Leave* takes place in Mrs Moxon's drawing room. It was not only the now forgotten playwrights who leant heavily on that device. The cast of Arthur Wing Pinero's *Mid-Channel* were marooned in 'A drawing room decorated and furnished in the French style' and Maugham's *Smith* (despite, according to Grein, reflecting the author's inclination to vulgarity) at least allowed the actors to perform in 'Mrs Dallas-Bower's drawing room at Crediton Court, Kensington' where the furniture 'is in excellent taste'. Drawing–room drama deserved its name.

The stage drawing room had a purpose. It facilitated the movement which both the comedy and the melodrama of the time required. In Rudolf Besier's *Don* the stage directions were precise and specific: the drawing room in the Oldwick Rectory had 'a door at the middle of the back' and 'on the right, windows looking out onto a short drive' – a convention which, when real life began to force its way across the Edwardian footlights, was derided as the defining characteristic of formula drama. For while it facilitated the standard progression of betrayal, revelation, confession and repentance, it certainly inhibited (and probably prevented) innovation and experiment. All those limitations are to be found in the work of the now largely forgotten Henry Arthur Jones, co-author of *The Silver King*, perhaps the most popular melodrama in Victorian England. His last success was *Mrs Dane's Defence* in 1900. Twenty-three years later, he was still complaining about the emergence of plays which were written 'for a clique or coterie of superior persons'.[3]

Established playwrights defended the convention of plays for plebs about patricians. Pinero, who had made his name in Victorian England with *The Second Mrs Tanqueray* and *Trelawney of the Wells*, believed it essential to write about people who 'lived at the rate of five thousand pounds a year . . . Wealth and leisure are more productive of dramatic complication than poverty and hard work.' That judgement was based less on the demands of the stage than on the perceived inadequacies of the lower orders. 'You must take into account the inarticulateness, the inexpressiveness of the English lower and lower-middle classes – their reluctance to analyse, to generalise, to give vivid utterance to their thoughts and their emotions.'[4]

That view of the theatre and of life was shared by most early-Edwardian playgoers. It certainly represented the dramatic judgement of the King himself. Edward preferred dining with actors to watching them perform on stage. His most celebrated theatrical excursion was a visit to the Haymarket Theatre to support Lillie Langtry on the occasion of her 'acting debut with a professional company'. He found her performance in Squire Bancroft's production of *She Stoops to Conquer* 'a great success' and confided in a letter to his young brother, 'She is so very fond of acting that she has decided to go on the stage.'[5] But he almost certainly took less pleasure from the play than the players. He most enjoyed 'modern society pieces containing plenty of caustic and subtle psychology'.[6]

By the end of his reign, ideas – some of them, by his standards, subversive – were not regarded as inconsistent with entertainment. The old school was represented by the design of its sets. So the new wave, when it began to wash against the theatrical shore, defined its more cerebral attitude by critical reference to the old conventions. John Galsworthy – whose commitment to social realism was proclaimed in the titles of his plays – prided himself on 'putting his characters on the stage simply and straightforwardly'. The author of *Strife, Justice* and *The Mob* did not 'think it necessary to have three doors and a French window in every scene . . . on the grounds that stage rooms are like that'.[7]

The traditional conventions and the old habits might have disappeared more quickly had it not been for the survival of the Victorian actor-manager. Writing in 1901, the theatre critic Joseph Knight asked, rhetorically, if 'any serious menace exists to the dramatic art?' He replied that, 'although no lover of art would dream of dispensing with it', the 'system of actor management leads at times to such over elaboration of style in a principal part as destroys the firm balance on which the highest efforts rest'.[8] In short, when one man played both parts, the manager always made sure his role occupied centre-stage. The result was the cult of the great dramatic personalities and a theatre which, both in London and the provinces, depended for its commercial success more on the reputation of the actor than the quality of the play.

It produced a gallery of star actresses – all of them beautiful but not always possessing equally obvious dramatic talent. When Mrs Langtry played to capacity audiences in New York, *Punch* produced a cartoon of her opening performance illuminated by a spotlight which cast the shadow of King Edward across the stage. Some of the female actors were regarded with such reverence that they were always billed and addressed with appropriate respect. Madge Kendal was always Mrs Kendal until she became Dame Madge. She retained her star billing – and played with Ellen Terry in *The Merry Wives of Windsor* – even when she had become known as 'the Matron of British Drama'.

When Dame Madge retired from the theatre in 1908, the first pretender to her throne was Mrs Patrick Campbell, who had made her name in *The Second Mrs Tanqueray* and gone on to play Juliet and Lady Teazle with equal acclaim. Bernard Shaw was in love with her. 'It is impossible not to feel that those haunting eyes are brooding on a momentous past and the parted lips anticipating a thrilling imminent future.'[9] He wrote *Caesar and Cleopatra* for her (although his Queen of Old Nile was a girl) and hoped she would be his Eliza Doolittle ('your pretty slut' Mrs Campbell called her) in *Pygmalion*. Mrs Campbell is now chiefly remembered as the object of Shaw's infatuation. She deserves better. By general consent, she was both the best Hedda Gabler of her time and the most turbulent actress in Edwardian England. 'She preferred temperament to talent and threw away a career as a great actor so that she might provide slight people with conversation.'[10]

Some of the women were made famous by more light-hearted productions. Julia Mielson (wife of actor-manager Fred Terry) hoped for an operatic career but, on the no doubt unwelcome advice of W. S. Gilbert, gave up her initial ambition and (in partnership with her husband) triumphed on the stage in *Sweet Nell of Old Drury* and *The Scarlet Pimpernel*. Eva Moore starred as the innkeeper's daughter in *Old Heidelberg* – a play which became a musical comedy with the title of *The Student Prince*. But in the unequal days of Edwardian Empire, while actresses were objects of admiration and desire, it was the more orotund charms of the male leads that attracted the audiences. And the abiding hero of the English stage was Sir Henry Irving.

Irving had been the star of the Victorian stage. *The Bells* by Leopold Lewis (in which he had first played during 1871) made him famous. He was still playing it in 1905, the year in which he died. By that time he had become the acknowledged leader of his profession, a knight and, after he took over the Lyceum in 1878, the most famous of the Victorian actor-managers. 'He was essentially a character actor rather than a tragedian [for] he lacked the physical power necessary to anyone who would scale the heights of tragedy.'[11] And he knew it. According to Ellen Terry's memoirs, he realised his limitations – and rejoiced in the way they had been overcome. 'My legs, my voice – everything has been against me. For an actor who can't walk, can't talk and has no face to speak of, I've done pretty well.'[12]

Part of his appeal was the essentially theatrical character that made him the model on which a dozen fictional Victorian thespians were based. And his posthumous reputation was reinforced by the manner of his death. On 1 January 1904 he announced that he proposed to retire after fifty years on the stage and that it would take him two years to say farewell. There would be two London seasons, three twelve-week provincial tours and return visits to America and Canada. The long goodbye began in Cardiff in September 1904. Four months later he began his second provincial tour in Portsmouth. In March he was taken ill in Wolverhampton. The rest of the tour was abandoned and the America visit postponed. But the show must go on. After a brief recuperation in Torquay, he was back on the Drury Lane boards in a performance of Tennyson's *Beckett*. Reinvigorated by his rapturous reception he set off again. On 2 October he played in Sheffield. It was another triumph, but before he moved on it was agreed that *The Bells* was too demanding to remain in his repertoire. So it was only *Beckett* in Bradford.

On 13 October 1905 the curtain came down on Henry Irving for the last time. The final words of the play and his final words in the theatre were 'Into Thy hands, O Lord! Into Thy hands'. He died, late that night, in the Bradford Midland Hotel. When his funeral took place on 20 October, only one floral tribute was placed on his coffin for the journey from church to crematorium. It was a cross which had been sent by Queen Alexandra. The message, which the Queen had written in her own hand, was 'Into Thy hands, O Lord! Into Thy hands.'

Death in Bradford ended what might well not have been the last of Irving's several 'farewell seasons'. In 1901 he had 'said goodbye' with a performance of *Coriolanus* (with Ellen Terry as his mother, Volumnia) at the London Lyceum, which puzzled at least one critic. 'It is difficult to see why Sir Henry should have selected a Shakespearean tragedy such as this which, though it lends itself well to scenic magnificence, affords leading parts entirely unsuited to either his own or Miss Ellen Terry's personalities.'[13] The answer lay in the question. Scenic magnificence was one of the secrets of Irving's success. When retirement was temporarily abandoned, he appeared at Drury Lane in an adaptation of Dante's *Inferno* which, *The Times* believed, qualified the translators for a place on Hell's innermost circle of ice. 'But', it added, 'there is always the scenery, the stupendous mechanical effects, the triumph of stage management.'[14]

After Irving died, Herbert Tree (eventually transmogrified into Herbert Beerbohm Tree) became both the undisputed leader of the English stage and its greatest exponent of the spectacular production. When Edward VII came to the throne, Tree was forty-eight and had already made his name as Svengali in *Trilby*. The fantastical always appealed to him. The sets for the plays he produced, and in which he performed, reflected that enthusiasm. Lady Tree, after his death, recalled his passion for the spectacular. 'How he loved to try to bring woods and streams and fountains and mountains on to the stage. And pillared palaces and long aisles, stately castles, grim battlefields, pine forests, beech woods, fields jewelled with daisies, and yellow sands.'[15]

Tree did not allow Shakespeare to stand in the way of his scenic imagination. His *Much Ado About Nothing* in 1905 included an 'intermezzo' in Leonato's garden. During the passing of the night, birds of every description took it in turn to awake and serenade the audience. The *Illustrated London News* was scandalised. 'No manager can be blamed for making Shakespeare thoroughly entertaining, but the question remains whether Mr Tree, in his laudable anxiety to do his best for his author, has not sometimes on the smallest authority over-elaborated his illustrations.'[16] The *Daily Chronicle* disagreed. It reminded its readers of 'how great an extent our present stage has to be grateful to Mr Tree for driving Shakespeare home to the hearts of the greater public by every means at his disposal'.[17]

Between 1910 and 1914 there were 150 productions of Shakespeare's plays on the London stage – many of them at Beerbohm Tree's Lyceum. In his *A Midsummer Night's Dream* the woods were inhabited by rabbits as well as fairies. The witches in his *Macbeth* flew. His ingenuity was not unique. Oscar Asche's *Merry Wives of Windsor* presented Falstaff (with some slight textual justification) in thick snow. When the play got in the way of the scenery, Edwardian actor-managers changed the play.

Sometimes the text was altered because the actor-managers thought that they knew better than Shakespeare. Beerbohm Tree's *Antony and Cleopatra* opened with the fourth scene of the first act and swiftly moved on to Alexandria in order to facilitate the early entrance of the lovers. At the Lyric Theatre in 1902, John Forbes Robertson's *Othello* was purged of 'passages and scenes . . . of a character which might prove distasteful to a modern audience'[18] – Desdemona was called a 'wanton', not a 'whore'. At least the rewrite men could not be accused of attempting to popularise Shakespeare by culling the obscurities and emphasising the well-loved lines. When William Poel produced *Troilus and Cressida*, Ulysses' speech, 'Time hath, my lord, a wallet at his back', was omitted.

Poel, although an eccentric, normally displayed the reverence which is Shakespeare's due. Indeed, directors of the Beerbohm Tree school described him as the 'Father of the Puritan Revolution'[19] because he eschewed exotic effects and extravagant scenery in favour of a visual austerity which did not distract attention from what he called 'the tuned tongue'. Harley Granville-Barker (who had acted for Poel in his time) hoped, as a director, to strike some sort of balance between sight and sound. The woods in his 1913 *A Midsummer Night's Dream* were enchanted by every stage effect he could employ, but the palace was a model of classical simplicity. Toys – electrical and mechanical – which had been so novel at the beginning of the century were becoming commonplace. From then on, the Royal Academy of Dramatic Art, which Sir Herbert Beerbohm Tree had founded, was less influenced by the extravagance of his early productions than by the discipline of his maturity.

Writing about his production of *A Midsummer Night's Dream*, Granville-Barker described the cast as 'a company inspired by such scholarly ideals as Benson could give'.[20] That was a generous tribute to a man whose reverence for Shakespeare allowed none of the improvisation by which Barker made his name. Frank Benson directed the festival at Stratford-upon-Avon before the creation of a resident company extended the Shakespeare season into three-quarters of the year. He also performed each year in London at the Comedy and the Lyceum theatres but, because his productions were brief and scholarly, the capital thought him a poor relation of Irving and Beerbohm Tree. His real forte was touring. Sometimes two or three 'Frank Benson Companies' were playing simultaneously in different towns. Edwardian England provided plenty of opportunity for the expression of his peripatetic talent. In 1901, there were 260 provincial theatres in Great Britain – eight in Liverpool, seven in both Manchester and Glasgow, six in Newcastle and five in Birmingham and Edinburgh. It was to them that, over the years, Benson took almost the whole canon. 'Poor players or begging friars we go up and down the land [so] that the people may never go without an opportunity of seeing Shakespeare played by a company dedicated to his service.'[21] One of the paradoxes of life in Edwardian England – a time at which the lights of London were thought to be irresistibly enticing – was that perhaps the best, and certainly the purest, Shakespeare was to be seen in the provinces.

At the turn of the century, provincial playgoers were paying two shillings for a seat in the stalls and fourpence for a place on one of the wooden benches in the gallery. On Saturday nights a ticket for 'the

gods' went up to sixpence and patrons had to endure 'packers' lean-
ing on the unfortunate who sat next to the aisle until the row was
sufficiently compressed to make room for latecomers. In London,
where attendance at the theatre was, for a certain class of person, a
social obligation rather than a pleasure or aesthetic experience, a seat
in the stalls might cost as much as half a guinea. But, since even the
greatest stars went regularly on tour, the provincial and metropolitan
repertoires were much the same.

People went to the theatre in much the same way as people went
to the cinema in the 1950s. In January 1902, Victor Cavendish saw
two plays in three days – '*Sherlock Holmes* (very good)'[22] and '*The
Mummy and the Mocking Bird* (quite good).'[23] *Ben Hur* the following
April[24] did not merit a classification. Rowland Evans, a patron of the
provincial stage after he moved to Leicester to complete his engineering apprenticeship, chose more serious drama – Pinero's *His
House in Order*[25] and Sullivan's *The Prodigal Son*.[26] In May of the
same year, he celebrated his birthday by going 'to the Palace to see
Vesta Tilley'.[27] Even Kate Jarvis, the nursemaid whose regular recre-
ation was walking in cemeteries, patronised the stage – *The Duchess of
Bayswater*[28] and *Diana of Dobsons*.[29] The forgotten plays of the
Edwardian theatre do credit to the era's enthusiasm if not to its critical judgement.

Dozens of new plays were written and produced throughout the
country each year. Most of them had little merit. When the London
theatres reopened after the week of mourning which followed Queen
Victoria's death, the plays on view make up a roll-call of the forgotten second-rate – *The Awakening, A Message from Mars, The Noble Lord,
Mr and Mrs Daventry* and *A Cigarette Maker's Romance*. It was thirteen
years since the first night of Oscar Wilde's *Lady Windermere's Fan* and
almost six years since the explosive opening of *The Importance of Being
Earnest*. In 1898 *Plays Pleasant* was published in advance of the production of some of the plays which it contained. They included *Arms
and the Man, You Never Can Tell* and *Mrs Warren's Profession*. George
Bernard Shaw had arrived on the scene. The theatre of ideas was
about to challenge drawing-room drama, whimsicality and the sentimentality of lovers' betrayals and lives ruined by the incompatibility of
the classes.

To think of Edwardian theatre as the forum for a conflict between frivolity and philosophy is to ignore the pure and simple entertainment which, in many ways, epitomised the period. Twenty years before Edward VII came to the throne, Victorian England had made the theatre more secure and respectable. The law which required a safety curtain to separate stage from auditorium had changed the character of neither the plays nor the playgoers, but the obligation to confine both the sale and consumption of alcohol to specifically licensed bars behind the stalls and circle had closed down many of the small music halls. In their place had risen up theatres which prided themselves on providing 'family entertainment'. The sexual innuendo of Victorian Variety was replaced by the escapism of musical comedy. The male impersonators, led by Vesta Tilley, became daring rather than salacious. More and more shows were 'produced' by a new phenomenon – the theatrical impresario who regarded the stage, like any other commodity, as a vehicle for making money.

Chief amongst them was Oswald Stoll, an Australian who, on the death of his father, came to England with his widowed mother. Mrs Stoll's second marriage, to the owner of the Parthenon Music Hall in Liverpool, ended equally prematurely. So, in 1880, at the age of fourteen, young Oswald was assisting in the management of a provincial theatre. Success encouraged expansion, first to Cardiff and then, at the turn of the century, to London itself. Stoll acquired the Coliseum. He went on to own and manage the Empires at Hackney, Holloway, New Cross, Stratford-atte-Bow and Shepherd's Bush, and Empires or Coliseums in virtually every large town.

Stoll's principal rival was Edward Moss, who owned the London Hippodrome and a chain of provincial theatres. Like Stoll he boasted that he provided family entertainment. His productions were usually brief dramatic interludes interspersed with romantic songs and clean jokes. Sarah Bernhardt and Ellen Terry both appeared at the Coliseum in one-act plays which occupied half of the bill. Tamara Karsavina (one of Diaghilev's prima ballerinas) danced as part of the Coliseum's programme and Pavlova appeared at the Palace Theatre.[30]

The demand for respectable lowbrow entertainment reflected the emergence of a new upper-working class and lower-middle class. It was eventually gratified by the gradual emergence of the musical comedy.

The process had begun three years before Queen Victoria's death with Edna May in *The Belle of New York*, but it only really flowered after the opening of the Gaiety Theatre in 1903 – in the presence of King Edward and Queen Alexandra. Part of the theatre's attraction was its chorus, the Gaiety Girls, three of whom went on to be respectively Baroness Charston, Countess Powlett and the Countess of Drogheda. By the time of their elevation, musical comedy had become the fashion and Frank Curzon, a tailor by trade who owned the Piccadilly Hotel, turned his attention to the popular theatre. He rebuilt the Strand and obtained controlling interests in the Avenue, the Camden Coronet, the Prince of Wales, the Comedy and the Criterion. The musical and the operetta had several homes from which to choose.

At the top end of the cultural scale there were the works of Edward German – *Merrie England* and *Tom Jones*. They could not compete, at least in terms of popular appeal, with the romantic escapism of *The Arcadians* and *The Quaker Girl*, but their sentimental patriotism had an appeal which made the impresarios believe that English operetta was always good box office. Unfortunately, in 1907 no new English operetta was available, so the gap was temporarily filled with Franz Lehár's *The Merry Widow*. It ran for more than two years and established the Austrian (or perhaps Ruritanian) style of musical comedy as a feature of the English stage. Neither *The Count of Luxembourg* nor *Gypsy Love* achieved the commercial success of *The Merry Widow*, but Lehár's first operetta was a unique popular success. The King saw it four times. And those of his loyal subjects who could not obtain or afford a ticket made the composer's fortune by buying the sheet music. The waltz alone sold almost a quarter of a million copies.

As always, some commentators confused commercial success with intrinsic merit and claimed that the arrival of the musical comedy amounted to the emergence of a new popular culture. G. K. Chesterton, in his *Illustrated London News* column, dismissed the claims in his usual trenchant language. 'The fact is, that we have reached so high and rarefied a level of humbug that the most serious thing we have left is popular songs.'[31] He ought to have known better, for he was spending happily pedantic days touring the country in order to debate the great issues of life, death and religion with the principal proponent of the theatre of ideas, George Bernard Shaw.

In the now forgotten *Lady Epping's Lawsuit*, the playwright who is the hero complains, 'Nobody seems to think a play serious unless it is about unpleasant people.' The young man was mistaken. Certainly some dramatists made their names by creating conventionally disreputable characters. Somerset Maugham's early fare depended on the louche habits of the *dramatis personae*. The stage directions for Act 3 of *Lady Frederick* typified the whole play. 'The eponymous heroine comes through the curtain. She wears a kimono. Her hair is dishevelled, hanging about her head in a tangled mop. She is not made up, and looks haggard, yellow and lined.' Bernard Shaw would not have wasted time on such triviality. Whether or not Shaw's people were unpleasant depends on personal taste. But he certainly peddled what polite society regarded as unpleasant notions. That brought him into constant conflict with the Lord Chamberlain's office, which believed that it existed to prevent the dissemination of ideas which were either subversive or degenerate.

Shaw's long-running battle with S. A. Redford, the Lord Chamberlain's 'examiner of plays', had begun on 11 March 1898 when the manager of the Victoria Hall Bijou Theatre was informed that he would not receive a licence for the public performance of *Mrs Warren's Profession*, a morality play which revolved around a successful young woman's discovery that her education had been financed by her mother's earnings from prostitution. Without a licence Shaw could still put on his plays, but he had no protection against prosecution under the obscenity laws – a technicality the author thought amusing. He wrote to the 'examiner' – a one-time bank manager whose qualification for his public position was his enthusiastic participation in amateur dramatics – in language which was calculated to score debating points rather than obtain a reversal of the decision. 'I quite recognise the impossibility of anyone sharing with me the responsibility for such a play.'[32] Naturally Redford's reply confirmed the previous ruling and quoted Shaw's admission of sole responsibility as an acceptance that no reasonable man could have anticipated that a licence would be issued.

In July, nine years later, B. Iden Payne, an actor-manager closely associated with Anne Horniman, the manager and benefactor of the Midland and Gaiety theatres in Manchester, sought to have the 1898 ruling overturned. 'The play has become part of the repertory of the ordinary reputable German and Austrian theatres. The question of its morality has been definitively raised in America and decided in the author's favour in the United States Courts.' Mr Payne in his righteous anger reminded Redford that plays by Tolstoy and Dumas had been refused licences and then, to the embarrassment of the Lord Chamberlain, subsequently approved for performance. Reference to his fallibility did nothing to change the examiner's mind. The licence was again refused.[33]

Redford subsequently refused to license *Press Cuttings*, a one-act sketch about votes for women which was written to be performed at two charity matinees in aid of the London Society for Women's Suffrage. *The Shewing-Up of Blanco Posnet*, a version of *Don Quixote* which Shaw wrote at the suggestion of Beerbohm Tree, received the same treatment.[34] The piece was composed in five weeks and sub-titled 'Sermon in Crude Melodrama'. Shaw meant the adjective to apply to the speed of the play's construction. Beerbohm Tree, who lost his nerve, thought it an appropriate description for the reference to God – 'a sly one . . . a mean one' – which the play contained. The allegation that one female character had experienced 'immoral rela-tions with every man in this town' confirmed Beerbohm Tree's judgement and prompted the suggestion that some of the more con-tentious passages should be removed. Shaw refused to censor his own play and the Lord Chamberlain's certificate was withheld.

Shaw was not alone in his resentment of censorship. By the summer of 1909 the campaign to end a system which allowed the per-formance of vulgar (and often sexually charged) farce but prohibited the performance of plays that examined serious social questions had attracted the sort of support which guarantees publicity. Seventy-two theatrical and literary celebrities wrote a barrage of letters to the national newspapers. Shaw boasted that he had 'sent a tremendous series of letters to *The Times*'[35] and increased the examiner's embar-rassment by arranging for *Blanco Posnet* to be staged at the Abbey Theatre, Dublin, beyond the Lord Chamberlain's jurisdiction. Faced with a campaign led by Algernon Swinburne, H. G. Wells, Thomas Hardy, George Meredith and James Barrie (as well as Shaw), Henry Campbell-Bannerman, the Prime Minister, agreed to meet a deputation to discuss 'a procedure' which the protesters claimed was 'opposed to the spirit of the Constitution, contrary to common justice and to common sense'. The deputation was persuasive. Campbell-Bannerman (always dangerously susceptible to rational argument) agreed to set up a Joint Committee of Both Houses 'to inquire into the censorship of stage plays, as constituted by the Theatres Act of 1843 . . . and to report any alterations of the law and practice which may appear desirable'. Its chairman was to be Herbert Samuel, and among its members was A. E. W. Mason, Liberal MP, former actor, future secret service agent and eventually famous as author of *The Four Feathers*.

Bernard Shaw composed, and published at his own expense, 11,000 words entitled *Evidence in Chief of Bernard Shaw before Joint Committee on Stage Plays*.[36] In a letter to Gilbert Murray he compared it – those who did not know him thought jocularly – to Milton's *Areopagitica*. It was much concerned with the fear that the irresistible assault on the Lord Chamberlain and his 'examiner' would result in local authorities being given the right to prohibit productions within their boundaries. He was adamant that writers must 'fight censorship in every form'. The point was made time after time during his oral evidence to the Committee. That was essential to Shaw's determination to leave a permanent mark on the debate. The Committee would not agree to the modern *Areopagitica* being treated as an official document and published in the record of proceedings.

The Committee held its first meeting on 29 July 1909. During the weeks which followed, it heard evidence from Shaw, James Barrie, Beerbohm Tree, Arthur Wing Pinero, W. S. Gilbert, Harley Granville-Barker and Squire Bancroft – the last of the actor-manager knights. *The Times*, reporting the proceedings, judged that 'many of the witnesses were at once interesting and amusing and some even brilliant . . . The atmosphere of the footlights seemed to have found its way into the Committee Room.'[37] Much of the evidence revealed less about the witnesses' views on Edwardian theatre than their beliefs about Edwardian society. Like the members of the Committee, they were obsessed with questions of class.

Shaw could not resist overstatement. 'A very large percentage of the plays which take place at present on the English stage under the censorship licence have as their objective the stimulation of sexual desire . . . If you prosecute for incitement to sexual vice, you immediately make it possible to prosecute a manager because the principal actress has put on a pretty hat or is a pretty woman.' Other celebrities felt it equally necessary to act in character. G. K. Chesterton, giving evidence 'on behalf of the average man', was in favour of censorship but against the censor. 'I would trust twelve ordinary men but I cannot trust one ordinary man.' Israel Zangwill, the archetypal absent-minded professor, announced that he would 'suppress half our plays for their indecency and the other half for their fatuity'. But the participants on both sides of the table who were more interested in the future of the stage than in their own immediate performances returned time after time to the character of the typical audience.

W. S. Gilbert, a supporter of censorship, did not regard the stage as a 'proper platform upon which to discuss questions of adultery and free love before mixed audiences, composed of persons of all ages and both sexes, of all ways of thinking, of all conditions of life and varying degrees of education'. W. L. Courtney, the drama critic of the *Daily Telegraph*, thought that the 'stalls and boxes have always favoured the lighter comedies and that they do not care much about the deeper laws of life or of morality'. However, in 'the last row of the stalls and the first two rows of the pit' were people who 'do not go [to the theatre] for amusement but because they are interested in drama'. The notion that a serious play was incompatible with a good night out was endorsed by several witnesses. George Edwards, the musical comedy impresario, described the theatre as existing 'to provide harmless entertainment' and admitted, 'I do not care about any higher function'. Under cross-examination he agreed that the Hull Town Council had tried to ban *The Merry Widow* which the local newspaper had described as 'the most improper and immoral play ever produced'.

The serious playwrights of the period – Shaw, Galsworthy, Granville-Barker and Pinero (who believed censorship 'degrades the dramatist by placing him under a summary jurisdiction otherwise unknown to English law) – spoke up for artistic freedom. The politicians believed that the public – particularly the public in the gallery and the gods – had to be protected from corrupting ideas. The rival views were encapsulated in a rhetorical question from Colonel

Lockwood, 'a plain blunt Member of Parliament' and the reply he received from Granville-Barker.

> 'Do you think that it is a wholesome thing for the drama that your advanced views should be put straight in front of the public without any further question?'

> 'Yes. There is nothing to be gained by treating the public as children.'

Nobody could possibly suggest that Granville-Barker did not practise in the theatre what he preached in the Committee Room. His three great plays – as good as anything that was written in Edwardian England and better than most of what Shaw wrote during his whole career – dealt with essentially 'adult' issues. *The Voysey Inheritance* tells the story of a successful solicitor who discovers that his law firm has built its reputation (and in consequence his wealth) on a fraud. *The Madras House* (with a cast of twenty-five actors, seventeen of them female) dealt with women's subservient place in early twentieth-century society. It was not quite *A Doll's House*, but it did speak for the unemancipated half of the population who, led by the theatre-going classes, were about to rise up and demand the vote. *Waste* was the tragedy of a rising politician whose career was ruined by the exposure of an extra-marital affair. Because it included dialogue about abortion – one of the possible escape routes for the doomed anti-hero – the Lord Chamberlain refused to give it a certificate. The 'banning of *Waste*' did more than any other single act of censorship to promote the 1909 demand for a change in the law. The esteem in which Granville-Barker was held by intellectual society was illustrated by its 'walk-through' reading in 1908 – a formality necessary to guarantee the play's copyright. The readers included Laurence Housman, Bernard Shaw, Gilbert Murray, Mr and Mrs H. G. Wells and Mrs John Galsworthy.[38]

The Select Committee Inquiry endorsed the status quo as Select Committee Inquiries often do. Its report reaffirmed that 'the public interest required theatrical performances to be regulated by special laws' and that the Lord Chamberlain should remain 'The Licenser of

Plays'. It pointed out that there was no legal obligation to submit a play for licence before it was performed in public, but it recommended that, if an unlicensed play was 'open to objection on the grounds of indecency', the Director of Public Prosecutions should remain empowered to take action against both the playwright and the manager of the theatre in which it was performed. Of course, the decision as to whether or not the play was 'open to objection' was, by implication, taken by the Examiner of Plays when he considered whether or not to issue a certificate. So the Establishment, as represented by Sir Squire Bancroft, an actor-manager of the old school who wanted the Examiner's powers strengthened, triumphed, and the avant-garde, as typified by John Galsworthy, who thought that censorship 'deters men of letters from writing for the stage', was confounded. But the theatre of ideas had expressed its collective voice and would never again be regarded as the minority interest of a self-styled intellectual elite.

The transition was gradual and often unconscious. Pinero, who in 1880 had produced the paradigm line of drawing-room drama – 'It is embarrassing to break a bust in the house of a comparative stranger' – wrote *Mid-Channel* in the year of the Select Committee's Inquiry. That play attempted (with mixed success) to explore the complications of marriage by analogies with the hollow joys of sporting victory. Shaw was never convinced that Pinero was capable of much more than frippery. After paying a curious compliment to Granville-Barker – '*Ann Leete* [is] by far the finest bit of literature since Stevenson's *Prince Otto*' – he argued that anyone who thought otherwise 'ought to be condemned to sit out a Pinero Festival'.[39] He was, in a back-handed, Shavian sort of way, much more complimentary about J. M. Barrie. He told August Strindberg that Barrie 'wrote a sort of fairy play called *Peter Pan* . . . ostensibly as a holiday entertainment for children, but really as a play for grown-up people'.[40] *Peter Pan* is both weird and whimsical. The complicated sexuality of its characters and the strange representation of vice and virtue were made all the more strange by a line added for the first revival. 'To die', says Peter, 'will be an awfully big adventure.' *What Every Woman Knows* was a genuine commentary on the role which able women filled, gladly or reluctantly, in Edwardian England. When it speaks of charm, it is obeying the rules of drawing-room drama – 'It is a sort of bloom on a woman. If you have it you don't need to have anything else' – but it also contains lines which belong to a more astringent theatrical tradition. 'There are few more impressive sights in the world than a Scotsman on the make.'

John Galsworthy spoke unequivocally for the new world of ideas and idealism or, as his critics would have said, a social sentimentality which was inconsistent with the stern and undemonstrative British character. 'The writer is himself an entire Humane Society. He sides with the fox against the man in pink, the hen-coop against the marauding fox, the chickweed against the chicken and whatever it is that the chickweed preys on against the ferocious plant.'[41] Galsworthy's plays concerned real people in the real world – tin-plate workers on strike in *Strife* and a clerk who was convicted of forgery in *Justice*. The tin-plate workers were in conflict with a management that held beliefs as strong as those which inspired the men they employed. It was not a simplistic story of the battle of good against evil but an attempt to make an adult audience understand the inherent conflicts of industrial life.

Audiences who hoped for less complicated expositions of the triumph of virtue over vice waited for the arrival of a Wilson Barrett touring company. The highlight of its repertoire was *The Sign of the Cross*, a drama of ancient Rome in which the heroine chose martyrdom (and presumably the eternal life which it guarantees) rather than a life of pagan luxury. Nobody could complain that the Edwardian theatre failed to cater for every taste. While Wilson Barrett's Christians were preparing for death behind provincial footlights, London stages were illuminating an entertainment which met the taste of 'mashers'. 'They were also known as the crutch and toothpick brigade because it was the fashion to carry smart walking sticks with crutch handles and chew toothpicks. They frequented the Gaiety Theatre for the sake not only of the very pretty music but also the charm and grace of that most beautiful and graceful of dancers, Kate Vaughan.'[42]

Although both the sacred and the profane appeared on stage in almost every interpretation of good and evil, Thomas Hardy – who had written more sternly of moral retribution than any of the Edwardian playwrights – temporarily forsook the fate of mortal men and the justice of the gods to write a long verse play about Napoleon Bonaparte. *The Dynasts* was not originally intended for theatrical production – even the most extended company finds it hard to stage the Battle of Austerlitz on six evenings a week and two matinees. But produced it was. Hardy was not the only literary figure of the time to forsake his usual trade for the stage. John Masefield, who we now think of only as a poet, wrote two plays – *The Tragedy of Nan* and *The Tragedy of Pompey the Great* – in prose. *Nan* – staged, as was the Edwardian habit with plays of dubious popularity, only at matinees – had a strangely Hardyesque theme: the heroine was an orphan whose father had been hanged for sheep stealing. But nothing could compare for Grand Guignol with J. M. Synge's *The Playboy of the Western World*.

In *Riders to the Sea*, Synge had already expressed black Irish gloom in a tragedy. It ended with a speech which was not designed to send the audience home happy.

> Bartle will have a fine coffin out of white boards and a deep grave surely. What more can we want than that. No man at all can be living for ever and we must be satisfied.

Riders to the Sea was first produced at Dublin's Abbey Theatre, the home of the Irish National Theatre Society.* Its natural repertoire was the mystical Celtic plays which Lady Gregory wrote in collaboration with W. B. Yeats. But the Ireland of *Cathleen ni Houlihan* and *The Unicorn and the Stars* was not the country that *The Playboy of the Western World* inhabited. In his preface to the play, Synge paid tribute to the 'rich and living' Irish cultural tradition; but the Abbey audience on the opening night did not think that the spirit of Ireland was ideally represented by a young man who becomes a hero by pretending that he has murdered his father, splitting him 'down the chine' with a single blow from a spade. When the first-night audience attempted to storm the stage at the end of the third act, a member of

---

*The Irish Literary Theatre (founded by W. B. Yeats and Lady Gregory in 1899) became the Irish National Theatre Society in 1903. It moved into the new Abbey Theatre in 1904.

the company held them off with an axe from the property department. According to Lady Gregory, the animosity was caused more by the language than the plot. Particular exception was taken, she claimed, to a description of 'all the girls in Mayo standing in their Shifts'. Whatever the reason for those first-night troubles, the Abbey Theatre attracted an audience with particular perceptions. They were part of the Irish awakening – the reassertion of a cultural identity that produced drama which was essentially Irish and dramatists who did not make their names in London. *The Playboy of the Western World* was a comic aberration. But it was part of the awakening too.

Wisely, *John Bull's Other Island* – written by Bernard Shaw at Yeats's request as 'a patriotic contribution to the repertory of the Irish Literary Theatre' – was put on by the Court Theatre in London, the scene of many Bernard Shaw first nights. Had it started life in Dublin it would have provoked riots which made the *Playboy* disturbances seem trivial. The audience would have enjoyed the satire on the traditional English attitude to Ireland. Much to his credit, King Edward, at a royal command performance, laughed so much at the caricature of his subjects that he broke his chair. But the play was intended to be 'uncongenial to the whole spirit of the neo-Gaelic movement'. No doubt the visionary priest who sees heaven as 'a godhead in which all life is human and all humanity divine' would have caused deep offence amongst the pious Catholics in the auditorium. But it would have been the judgement on Irish Nationalists that brought the house down – in the wrong sort of way. 'If you want to interest an Irishman in Ireland, you've got to call the unfortunate island Kathleen ni Hoolihan and pretend she's a little old woman. It saves thinking.'[43] The audience would not have realised that – out of either ignorance or malice – Shaw had misspelt the name of Ireland's mystical queen.

George Bernard Shaw was an English playwright who happened to have been born in Ireland – a quality he shared with Oscar Wilde. In other respects they could hardly have been more dissimilar. Shaw was, by nature, an activist. He was present at the inaugural conference of the Independent Labour Party, editor of the *Fabian Essays on Socialism* and he campaigned for causes which ranged from votes for women through vegetarianism to a new English alphabet. He was an unsuccessful novelist and occasional journalist until he wrote, for the

Saturday Review, a series of articles on what he regarded as the inadequacies of the late Victorian stage. But, paradoxically, it was a political event which defined his view of the theatre. A Fabian Society lecture series – portentously entitled Socialism in Contemporary Literature – included a paper by Shaw on the work of Henrik Ibsen. It was expanded and published as *The Quintessence of Ibsenism*. Its title renounced all claim to literary criticism but claimed to examine Ibsen's contribution to a civilised education. It was also a plea for iconoclasm. Realism – 'the unflinching recognition of facts and the abandonment of the conspiracy to ignore such of them as do not bolster up our ideas' – was only the beginning. It was essential 'to get away from idolatry and get to the truth'. Shaw had set out the quintessence of his theory of drama.

The application of that theory to the real stage often resulted in hard pounding for the audience. Fortunately he found a theatre that was prepared to produce new plays which it was reasonable to expect would become critical triumphs but commercial disasters. Harley Granville-Barker – who had played Marchbanks in the 1900 production of *Candida* and received Shaw's commendation for his comedy *The Marrying of Ann Leete* – was hired by J. H. Leigh, a wealthy businessman and amateur actor, to produce a series of new plays at the Royal Court Theatre in Sloane Square. Granville-Barker 'believed in taking risks'. He practised what he preached in 1904 when he opened his first season with six performances of Gilbert Murray's translation of Euripides' *Hippolytus*. The risk he took most regularly was George Bernard Shaw.

Granville-Barker believed that long runs were 'bad for plays and bad for acting'[44] – an unusual view amongst producers. But Shaw's *Man and Superman*, performed at the Royal Court in 1903 without its third act, ran for 176 performances. It might well not have enjoyed such longevity if the 'Don Juan in Hell scene', in which the hero dreams, amongst other things, that he is the captive of Sierra Nevada brigands, had been allowed to add another thirty minutes of philosophical discussion to the end of the play. Had a part of the Edwardian public not been scandalised by the heroine's brazen pursuit of the man she hoped to make her lover, the run might have lasted even longer. Four years later, the Royal Court staged the 'Don Juan in Hell' scene as a play – or at least a moral discussion – in its own right. It shared the bill with *Man of Destiny*, Shaw's 'trifle' about the life of the young Napoleon Bonaparte.

There followed, in 1905, *Major Barbara* in which the hero, Adolphus Cusins (nicknamed Euripides to emphasise his intellect), was based on Gilbert Murray. Next year the Royal Court was home to fifty performances of *The Doctor's Dilemma*. Shaw never wrote to order, but he always rose to a challenge. *Man and Superman* was his response to a suggestion made by Arthur Bingham Walkley of *The Times* that he would find it difficult to write a play about Don Juan. *The Doctor's Dilemma* was the result of the demand from William Archer (a leading theatrical critic and close friend) that Shaw try his hand at a full-length death scene. It became an argument about the sanctity of life. Shaw, with some justification, believed himself to be a philosopher as well as a playwright.

Max Beerbohm believed that the works of George Bernard Shaw were better 'on the page than on the stage'. That was the form in which thousands of intellectuals first became acquainted with them, for very often they were printed and published years before production. How many Shavian devotees worked their way through the prefaces or read *The Revolutionists' Handbook and Pocket Companion*, which accompanied *Man and Superman*, it is difficult to say, but there is no doubt that Shaw had brought ideas on to the Edwardian stage. Indeed he had encouraged their exposure in both the Hapsburg and Hohenzollern theatre. At the end of the Edwardian era, *Androcles and the Lion* was published in Berlin and performed in Hamburg, and *Pygmalion*, a play entirely concerned with the English preoccupation with the symbols of status and the incompatibility of the classes, was staged in Berlin.

At the beginning of the century, Scotland, still reacting against Walter Scott's notion that it was North Britain, was determined to assert its own cultural identity. The Scottish Repertory Theatre opened in Glasgow in April 1909 with the stated purpose of guaranteeing 'Scotland's own theatre, financed by Scottish money, managed by Scotsmen and established to make Scotland independent of London for its dramatic supplies'. What became the Citizens' Theatre lacked a national playwright – writing for Scotland – of the status of Synge or Lady Gregory in Ireland, but it enjoyed the distinction of presenting Chekhov's *Seagull* for the first time in Britain.

Light comedy and the drawing-room drama did not disappear from the English stage. Indeed it continues still. But Edwardian England began a real debate about the fundamental purpose of the theatre. By 1912 London audiences were prepared to accept Stanley Houghton's *Hindle Wakes*, a play about a marriage between the classes. But, because the heroine declined to be made 'an honest woman' until her own good time, it was not the sort of play that London had come to expect. Masefield satirised in three lines the progress of the normal way in which a 'fallen woman' was expected to behave.

> Curtain rises and discovers housemaid scrubbing floor
> She speaks
> O the misery of a double life!

Stanley Houghton's heroine was made of sterner stuff.

> I'm a Lancashire lass and so long as there's weaving sheds in Lancashire I shall earn enough brass to keep me going. I wouldn't live at home again after this, not anyhow . . . I'm going to be on my own in future . . .

Working women of independence – and working men of character – had established their place in English drama. Their position at the centre of the stage was to be confirmed, when the era had passed, by the new theatrical phenomenon which was to close the provincial theatres and make playgoing an occasional occupation rather than a regular form of entertainment.

In America in 1893, Thomas Edison had made a two-minute film which depicted the execution of Mary, Queen of Scots. In the following year the Broadway kinescope opened to show 'moving pictures'. Five years later, the French made a film called *The Trial of Dreyfus*. Britain lagged behind in production, but the demand created by a popular enthusiasm for the new entertainment was met by foreign film-makers. In 1902, Georges Méliès' *A Trip to the Moon* (made in Paris) ran in London for nine months. In 1908 the growing interest was illustrated by a tragic example of the excitement the cinema caused. In Barnsley, four hundred children attended a 'moving picture show' in a church hall specially hired for the purpose. A crowded staircase made some of them fear that they would not get a seat. They began to push. Others panicked. Sixteen children were crushed to death. In the following year local authorities were required to issue 'safety licences' before films were shown.

Although Britain was the first country to put safety regulations in place, the Edwardians were dilatory in pushing forward with film production. A young man called Charlie Chaplin, who had played the wolf in the first performance of *Peter Pan* on stage, took his comic genius to America and made thirty-five films for Mack Sennett in 1914. In the year that the world changed, popular entertainment began to change too. But the 'theatre of ideas', resurrected, if not born, in Edwardian Britain, endured, and remains.

CHAPTER 14

Literature Comes Home

Most historians agree about who the Edwardians were and how long the Edwardian era lasted. Usually they extend the actual period of the reign from the turn of the century to the outbreak of the First World War, so that they can work within distinct boundaries. They can agree that Balfour, Lloyd George and Asquith were the dominant political figures, that Churchill was on his way up, Joe Chamberlain was on his way out, that female suffrage, Irish Home Rule and trade union rights stirred genuine passions and that the world was never quite the same again after August 1914.

But a life in literature often lasts longer than a career in politics, so there are arguments about whether writers who did the best of their work in Edwardian England can properly be called 'Edwardian' if most of their poetry or prose was published in another reign. And there are more fundamental questions to be answered. Did literature, during the early years of the twentieth century, have a defining characteristic? Is Edwardian fiction simply identified by a publication date, or does it denote a spirit, a style and a view of life? And is Edwardian poetry in some way a reflection of its time and place?

In one paradoxical particular, it is possible to draw a poetic boundary line. The 'Georgian Poets', whose work was published 'in the belief that English poetry is now putting on a new strength and beauty', were Edwardians. G. K. Chesterton, Ronald Ross and Sturge

Moore were included in the first *Georgian Anthology*[1] but omitted
from the second with a gracious apology. 'They belong to an earlier
poetic generation and their inclusion must be admitted to be an
anachronism.' Wilfred Owen, W. B. Yeats, T. S. Eliot and Ezra Pound
were not included in the original collection, but Housman was
offered a place. He declined with the message, 'I do not belong to
you.' *A Shropshire Lad* had been written in 1896. Housman did not
believe that he belonged to anybody. 'To include me in a book of the
nineties would', he wrote with a strange choice of image, 'be just as
technically correct and just as essentially inappropriate as to include
Lot in a book on Sodomites.'[2]

The search for a common theme in Edwardian literature is complicated by the diverse reactions to the new age that Edwardian
writers recorded. W. B. Yeats thought that he noticed a change in attitude on or about New Year's Day 1900. From then on 'everybody got
down off their stilts. Henceforward, nobody drank absinthe with their
coffee. Nobody went mad. Nobody committed suicide. And nobody
joined the Catholic Church.'[3] He was celebrating the eclipse of
the 'aesthetic movement' in all its extravagantly romantic forms – a
welcome event which he associated with the death, at the end of the
nineteenth century, of Oscar Wilde and Aubrey Beardsley.

H. G. Wells rejoiced at what he believed to be a new liberalism
which he hoped would sweep through England after Queen Victoria's
death. He thought of the Old Queen as a paperweight that held the
country down. Without her looming presence, there was less inhibi-
tion and restraint, 'So things blew about all over the place.'[4] Thomas
Hardy was less optimistic about the chances of change and improvement. His fiction had always won the acclaim of at least part of the
intellectual Establishment, but the general public, encouraged by a
popular press which was both prudish and prurient, regarded his
novels as immoral. That is to say they dealt with commonplace, but
irregular, sexual unions. *Tess of the D'Urbervilles* (1891) and *Jude the
Obscure* (1895) had been the subject of particular vilification. Hardy
feared that he would fare little better at the mercy of Edwardian
hypocrisy than he had in the hands of Victorian propriety. So he gave
up fiction and the risks of writing about forbidden love. He lived until
1928. But, in Edwardian England, he lived as a poet.

Rudyard Kipling sensed a new spirit and set off in a new direction. He had anticipated the national mood of doubt and disillusion which was to follow Queen Victoria's Golden Jubilee and written 'Recessional', 'lest we forget'. The Boer War, which he witnessed at first hand, changed, at least for a while, his whole poetic style. The poet of Empire and the Army which had 'salted it down with its bones' had become famous for

It's 'Tommy this an' Tommy that, an' 'Tommy go away!'
But it's 'Thank you Mister Atkins, when the band begins to play.

Back home he wanted to write about a quieter England:

They shut the road through the woods
Seventy years ago

With 'the gentlemen in khaki' once again 'fighting penny wars at Aldershotit' he gave up martial verse. The First World War reignited his patriotic fervour, and his son's death in battle revived his emotional attachment to what he had once called 'a thin red line of 'eroes'. But in Edwardian England there were no poems about South Africa's new relationship with the Mother Country or the imperial duty (pace Joe Chamberlain) to impose import duties on 'foreign goods' and so give 'preference' to trade with the colonies. He wrote about England.

One poet, throughout the whole period of 1900 to 1914, spoke – loud and clear – for the significant section of Edwardian England who remained true to the simple patriotism that Kipling had represented. Sir Henry Newbolt never wrote about the exacting innovations of the new century. Votes for women, the motor car, wireless telegraphy, the creation of a self-governing Commonwealth all passed him by. He represented that strong and vocal section of society, with members in all the classes, who gloried in Britain's illustrious past and believed that the example of historic heroism could inspire a new generation to build a more mighty nation. For twenty years he received 'almost daily enquiries from editors who wanted poems from him'.[5] And he wrote what came to be the most satirised poem in the English language.

Newbolt's critics have concentrated most of their time on the first two lines.

> There's a breathless hush in the Close tonight –
> Ten to make and a match to win

But what they disliked about 'Vitaï Lampada' – 'an especially nasty kind of imperialistic jingoism'[6] which 'exalted public school verities' – is better represented in the second stanza.

> The Gatling's jammed and the Colonel dead,
> And the regiment blind with dust and smoke,
> The river of death has brimmed his banks,
> And England's far, and Honour a name,
> But the voice of a schoolboy rallies the ranks:
>   'Play up! Play up! and play the game!'

The banality of 'Vitaï Lampada' is beyond dispute, and the whole poem is littered with examples of imperial hypocrisy. The 'sodden red' desert sand which that last verse would bring to most readers' minds was undoubtedly a stretch of open ground outside Omdurman – the scene of the last cavalry charge in British military history. The battle (which took place in 1898) ended with fewer than three hundred British casualties and (since most of the Gatling guns had not jammed) twenty thousand Dervishes dead or wounded. In the circumstances, 'Play up! and play the game!' seems an inadequate description of the way in which the engagement was conducted.

'Vitaï Lampada' is one of the few examples, in the whole of Newbolt's canon, of a poem about contemporary, or near contemporary, heroism. Newbolt normally inspired his patriotic listeners with stories of ancient valour. The titles of almost all the poems which made him famous were evocations of English (not British) history – 'Drake's Drum', 'Admirals All', 'The Fighting Temeraire'. There were exceptions. Some poems exalted the public school virtues. But they were all related to imperial greatness.

Clifton College (where Newbolt 'thought the thoughts of youth') made him. His contemporaries at the school included Douglas Haig

and Francis Younghusband. Haig, after meritorious service in South
Africa and India, commanded the British forces in the Battle of the
Somme. Younghusband just failed to climb Everest, discovered the
secret kingdom of Tibet and then negotiated a Treaty of Friendship
between the Dalai Lama and King Edward. Like them, Newbolt
served the King and Empire.

The part of England for which Newbolt spoke should have been
represented in verse by Alfred Austin who, until 1913, was Poet
Laureate, but he did not possess the talent to express either adequately
or frequently the imperial echo. His appointment owed more to his
politics than to the quality of his verse. Before he was called into Queen
Victoria's poetic service, he was a journalist of Conservative persuasion.
On appointment, he immediately performed the task which was
expected of him by composing an ode in praise of the Jameson Raid.
There was almost universal agreement, even among the 'jingoists' of the
period, that his job should have gone to Rudyard Kipling, said to have
been denied the laurel wreath because of a poem which was entitled
'The Widow of Windsor'. Kipling had a talent for capturing the spirit
of Empire, but after the death of 'Mrs Victoria' (as the offending poem
called the Queen) he chose not to do so. Only Newbolt was left to
write of England's glory. He did so in lines of imperishable triviality.

> Admirals all for England's sake
> Honour be yours, and fame!
> And honour, as long as waves shall break,
> To Nelson's peerless name.

Kipling, in contrast, was a grown-up patriot, who despised both
'muddied oafs' and 'flannelled fools'. It is impossible to imagine him
describing an Englishman awaiting death at the hands of rebellious
native tribesmen and thinking, as the day of execution dawned, of his
school sports day.

> He saw the School Close, sunny and green,
> The runner beside him, the stand by the parapet wall,
> The distant tape, and the crowd roaring between,
>   His own name over all.

Newbolt wrote of England in the language of a man who was untroubled by doubt – an essentially Victorian attitude to life. Admirers of Newbolt described his defining characteristic (with some justification) as love of country. And it may well be that affection for England, in all its different forms, is the quality which binds Edwardian poets together – that and the constant presence in all their drawing rooms of Ford Maddox Heuffer, a minor but ubiquitous novelist, and J. B. Pinker, a literary agent and entrepreneur.

The idealised view of England, wistfully observed from exile, is generally thought to be best represented by Rupert Brooke's 'The Old Vicarage, Grantchester'. There is, however, at least a possibility that Brooke – a man with radical inclinations as well as a tendency to write bad love poetry – wrote about the Cambridge village as a satire on the romantic view of Edwardian England. 'Grantchester' may be a utopia in which time is suspended.[7] 'Stands the Church clock at ten to three?' If it is satire, 'Grantchester' is very good satire indeed. It makes the Cambridgeshire village part of a rural idyll.

> And after, ere the night is born
> Do hares come out about the corn?
> Oh, is the water sweet and cool
> Gentle and brown above the pool?
> And laughs the immortal river still
> Under the mill, under the mill?

The enquiry about honey with which the poem ends is probably intended as an attack on sentiment as distinct from romance. But it was possible to write about the sights and sounds of England without indulging in either excess, as Robert Bridges demonstrated.

> When men were all asleep the snow came flying
> In large white flakes, falling on the city brown,
> Stealthily and perpetually settling and loosely lying,
> Hushing the latest traffic of the drowsy town.

Bridges, to prove his affection for all things English, also wrote about football, but it is unlikely that his poem on that subject was crucial in securing him the Laureate's crown when Austin died in 1913.

> Thus in our English sport, the spectacular game
> Where tens of thousands flock, throttling the entrance gates.

Bridges' first collection of poems was published in 1873, his last in 1929. A. E. Housman's poetic career lasted almost as long. *A Shropshire Lad* was published, at his own expense, in 1896, his last anthology in 1936. But, unlike Bridges, he offered the public nothing new at all during the whole Edwardian period. He was busy writing poetry and translating (usually bawdy verse) from the classics throughout his years of silence. Between 1896 and the publication of the first extract from what he called his 'notebook' in 1922, nothing appeared in print. He is best thought of as a Victorian.

So is G. K. Chesterton – at least as a serious poet. He spent much of the twentieth century's first decade writing light essays, literary criticism and religious polemics. His poems of the period were conspicuously a celebration of England's Englishness and a defence of the values he thought to be embodied in beer and beef. 'The Rolling English Road' is a tribute to English eccentricity and it is impossible to pretend that what that rumbustious poem has to say has much in common with Walter de la Mare's 'England'.

> The clouds – how often have I
> Watched their bright towers of silence steal
> Into infinity

John Masefield's Edwardian affection for England is often thought to be confined to the seas around Britain's coast. His reputation largely rests on *Salt Water Ballads* – and one poem in that collection, 'Sea Fever', expresses perfectly the urge to sail which typifies much of his work. But he too had a landlubber's affection for the English landscape.

> The dawn comes cold: the haystack smokes
> The green twigs crackle in the fire

The dew is dripping from the oaks
The sleeping men bear milking yokes
Slowly towards the cattle byre.

By the time that the second (not entirely maritime) Masefield anthology was published in 1910, Thomas Hardy, who knew more about dripping oaks and smoking haystacks than any man alive, had forsaken Wessex for Napoleonic France. *The Dynasts*, part pageant and part verse play, had two conflicting characteristics. Hardy was obsessed by the need for accurate detail. But, because he wanted his drama of destiny and death to be performed on stage, he sacrificed truth for dramatic effect. So Nelson soliloquised on the eve of Trafalgar about his impending death and the pangs of guilt which are the reward of adultery.

Some contemporary critics judged that *The Dynasts* was the high-water mark of Edwardian poetry. Lascelles Abercrombie wrote that it had 'attained something that the age of Tennyson and Browning quite failed to effect'. He built that dubious proposition on what he believed to be the Zeitgeist. Napoleon, the doomed titan, illustrated the Edwardians' loss of faith in heroes and men of destiny. If that was so, nobody had told Sir Henry Newbolt.

To describe Hardy (or any Englishman) as the best poet to live, write or publish in the reign of King Edward VII is to forget that Ireland, in its entirety, was then part of the United Kingdom. For in Dublin in 1900 William Butler Yeats – a poet of uncontested and incontestable genius – published *The Shadowy Waters*. Yeats (born in Ireland but partly educated in England) intended, in youth, to become an artist, but turned instead to literature. There was always something of the mystic in him. It is revealed by his study, long before he could call himself a professional writer, of William Blake. His interest in unseen forces naturally turned towards Irish mythology. The result was *The Wanderings of Oisin and Other Poems* and *Fairy and Folk Tales of the Irish Peasantry*. The music of Blake's mysticism echoes through his earlier poems and his regret that he does not possess 'heaven's embroidered cloths, enwrought with golden and silver light'. That poem ends with one of the most famous, as well as the most evocative, lines in the English language. 'Tread softly because you tread on my dreams.'

Yeats's enthusiasm for mysticism, in its lowest form, encouraged involvement in a number of probably disreputable and certainly risible secret societies. He became Chief Instructor in Mystical Philosophy to the Hermetic Order of the Golden Dawn. He was a Freemason and a Rosicrucian. At a higher level of romantic perception, he thought of himself as a literary Pre-Raphaelite, committed to the noble values of a less materialistic age and determined to reveal its beauty in language as clear and colourful as the paintings of William Morris. T. S. Eliot was elegantly offensive about the combination of Pre-Raphaelite values, mystical inclination and Irish folklore. 'The Shadowy Waters seems to me one of the most perfect expressions of the vague, enchanted beauty of that school. Yet it strikes me . . . as the western seas descried through the back window of a house in Kensington, Irish myth for the Kelmscott Press.'[8]

Yeats moved on from Irish mythology to the creation of the institutions of Irish culture – the New Irish Library, Irish literary societies in London and Dublin, and the Irish Literary Theatre, which became (with the help of Anne Horniman, a regular benefactor of Irish causes) first the New Irish and then the Abbey Theatre. In 1902, the theatre produced Yeats's play Cathleen ni Houlihan. The part of the mythological queen was played by Maud Gonne. It marked the end of Yeats's celebration of the 'Celtic Twilight' – a phrase he invented to express, not the decline that it has come to represent, but an age of Irish greatness which was shrouded in the mists of antiquity.

Yeats met Maud Gonne in 1889.* He described the meeting as 'the moment when the troubles of my life began'. From then on his obsessive love – unrequited and unreciprocated – dominated his whole existence. Much of his most moving poetry was either dedicated to Maud Gonne or provoked by her inability to love him as he loved her. In November 1902, he described himself as in 'the best good spirits' and wrote of a happy day spent with Maud.

> We sat together at one summer's end
> That beautiful mild woman your close friend
> And you and I talked of poetry.

---

*Maud Gonne believed that she had seen Yeats in his father's studio in 1885. Yeats disagreed.

It was not one of his best poems. Perhaps he was only inspired by sadness. If so, he did not have to wait long for the muse to return. A month later, Maud Gonne – who could never have loved him and never pretended otherwise – left for Paris to meet John MacBride, a member of the Irish Republican Brotherhood, who had become a hero of Irish nationalism by fighting with the Boers against the British in South Africa.

Yeats had first proposed to Maud Gonne ten years earlier and she had refused him for reasons which she refused to explain. She had become convinced – part of the dark side of her mysticism – that her dead child (about whom Yeats knew nothing) would be reincarnated if she conceived again, with the same father, on holy ground. At least the bizarre episode produced Yeats's greatest love poem.[9]

> When you are old and grey and full of sleep
> And nodding by the fire, take down this book
> And slowly read, and dream of the soft look
> Your eyes had once, and of their shadows deep

The 'reincarnation' of Maud Gonne's son had taken place in 1890. Unfortunately the new baby was not the same gender as the dead sibling. Despite the arrival of the mystical child, Yeats remained anxious to marry Maud. But she was still unwilling to marry him. Her marriage to MacBride – probably precipitated by the desertion of the father of her two illegitimate children – left Yeats with a permanent feeling of betrayal. But anger never diminished his love. It was because of her that his cultural nationalism turned into support for violent revolution. And it was for her that he wrote the most moving of his early poems. 'No Second Troy' balanced resentment against gratitude. 'The Folly of Being Comforted' laments with love 'the little shadows come about her eyes'. Yeats was to write better poems as the century moved on. But Maud Gonne was part of most of them.

Although it was blessed with Yeats, the Edwardian era was not notable for its poets and poetry. That shortcoming has been attributed to the philistinism of the age, which is too often remembered only for its sybaritic King. But, if there was a cultural malaise in the century's early years, it did not depress the quality of the period's fiction. At least one classic novel was published in almost every year – Samuel Butler's *The Way of All Flesh* was posthumously published in 1900, Galsworthy's *The Man of Property* in 1906, Conrad's *The Secret Agent* in 1907, Bennett's *The Old Wives' Tale* in 1908, Wells's *Tono-Bungay* in 1909, Forster's *Howards End* in 1910, Wells's *The New Machiavelli* in 1911 and Lawrence's *Sons and Lovers* in 1913. And the reign began with three novels from the greatest novelist of his time, Henry James. *The Wings of the Dove* was published in 1902, *The Ambassadors* in 1903 and *The Golden Bowl* in 1904.

James celebrated the new century by shaving off his whiskers, moustache and beard. He thought that changing the way he looked was symbolic of the different way in which he looked at the world. The United States, which he had left, had invaded Cuba and become an imperialistic power. Britain, which he had made his home, had behaved with equal vulgarity by fighting the Boers. His natural paci-fism was in brutal conflict with his instinctive patriotism. Half hoping for a quick victory and half fearing a slow defeat, he was in a constant state of turmoil. The result was an increase in the detachment which he felt from both his origins and the country of his adoption.

The beginning of the century was marked, like every other time in James's life, with an incessant social round. But he still managed to draw up an outline of a new novel. It was to be called *The Ambassadors*. It took longer to complete than he anticipated and he then had to wait for what he called 'the vulgar Harper serialisation'.[10] James then contracted a debilitating bowel infection which, together with his extensive social life, held up publication for even longer. As a result, his three greatest novels – each of them substantial as well as inspired – were published in three successive years.

The Ambassadors embodied, more completely than anything else he wrote, James's own view of literature and life. Lewis Lambert Strether, its main character – it would be wrong to call him a hero – leaves America for England in order to discover why a young friend has refused to return from the old world to the new. There is a suspicion that the voluntary exile has become involved with an undesirable older woman. Strether, like James himself, finds that his ideas change in his new environment. Pragmatism becomes more important than principle, and compassion takes precedence over formal morality. Like James, Strether (who is about the same age as his creator) has the ambivalent (and convoluted) satisfaction of being an observer observing himself making observations, not a participant. He embodied James's heightened sense of 'looking over his shoulder at where he had come from and where he is now'.[11] It was an ideal position from which to view the beginning of the twentieth century.

The capacity to give the impression of looking forward as well as back made Henry James, in one sense, personify the first years of the new century. But his conduct and character were essentially Victorian. His homosexuality was hidden, not always successfully, behind an apparent preoccupation with grace and good manners; but when he met Rupert Brooke, he felt 'rather like an unnatural intellectual Pasha visiting a Circassian Harem',[12] and he fell openly, as well as hopelessly, in love with a young Norwegian sculptor. He lived an extravagant social life of fancy-dress balls and formal dinners in London, Florence, Paris and Rome. It was not unusual in Edwardian England for even the most serious of men to regard such things as an essential part of their existence. Mr Asquith left a ball at Hatfield House to discuss with Campbell-Bannerman the role he would play in a soon-to-be elected government. He returned, after midnight, to continue the enjoyment. Henry James was simply a follower of the same theory of living life to excess. Intellect and frivolity were not incompatible.

James clearly believed that entertainment and education were indistinguishable. In Rome he visited Sargent and Burne-Jones. In Paris he entertained Whistler and Turgenev. In Florence he met Fenimore Cooper. At home, at Lamb House in Rye, he saw G. K. Chesterton (who was a neighbour), H. G. Wells and Rudyard Kipling, whenever Kipling could be persuaded to send his car to carry James along the coast to Rottingdean. The alternative was to travel up to London by train and down again, by an almost parallel line, to the south coast. And that was not James's style. He was the writer as grandee and that set him apart from other Edwardian novelists. For fiction, in the early years of the century, came home to the middle classes, the suburbs, the shops and factories and the industrial poor. Edwardian fiction portrayed both a changing world and the anxieties which those changes brought about. In *The Napoleon of Notting Hill*, Chesterton wrote of 'This strange indifference . . . the strange loneliness of millions in a crowd.' It was not a new idea.

> How often in the overflowing streets
> Have I gone forward with the crowd and said
> Unto myself, the face of everyone
> That passes by me is a mystery.

The Edwardians who felt 'alone in the city' were, unlike William Wordsworth, experiencing the effects of a society that they found new and intimidating. In *The Author's Craft*, Arnold Bennett wrote of walking through the capital 'with the intention of perceiving London as if it was a foreign city'.[13] But most Edwardian novelists described, not their own detachment, but the alienation of a less fortunate class. E. M. Forster, tucked comfortably away in Cambridge, had very little in common with Leonard Bast, the serial victim in *Howard's End*.

Four of Forster's five great novels were written in Edwardian England – *Where Angels Fear to Tread* (1905), *The Longest Journey* (1907), *A Room with a View* (1908) and *Howards End* (1910). All of them are autobiographical in their depiction of places if not people. The pension in which Forster and his mother stayed in 1901, with its room affording a view over the Arno, is easily identified. Howards End (the house) is virtually identical to Rooksnest, Forster's Hertfordshire home for ten boyhood years. The London house of the formidable Schlegel sisters, Margaret and Helen, was 'suggested' to Forster by the layout and decoration (though not the architecture) of the house in All Souls' Place, London, at which he visited one of his Cambridge teachers, Goldsworthy Lowe Dickinson. Houses – representing an idea, a prejudice, an age or an attitude – play a great part in Edwardian literature. But Howards End has a mystical importance. Margaret Schlegel tells her sister, 'It is sad to suppose that places may be even more important than people.' But she comes to realise that the house makes deeper personal relationships possible.[14]

Members of the Freudian school of literary criticism have seen Forster's view of houses as somehow related to his homosexuality. There is no doubt that, because (at least in part) of the prejudices of the time, he remained emotionally unfulfilled until middle age. He was part of, though only at the edge of, 'Bloomsbury'* – to misquote R. H. Tawney 'not the pleasant London district, but the silly sect' – and *Howards End* reflects the best and the worst of that movement. It is, at least for the time, immensely broad-minded about sex. Helen – the younger of the Schlegel sisters – has an affair with the unfortunate Leonard Bast, bears his child almost as an act of pity, but has no residual Victorian shame about her state and her condition. Her sister marries the rich Henry Wilcox, who brushes aside the revelation that he has had a long relationship with a prostitute (wife of Leonard Bast, on whose head every misfortune is heaped) with the explanation, 'I am a man and I have a man's vices.'

Wilcox's wife finds it easier to forgive his sexual indiscretions than to condone either his callous attitude to his employees (Leonard Bast again) or his generally philistine view of life. She is George Moore's *Principia Ethica* made flesh, for she relates virtue to artistic appreciation, as well as to a gentle disposition.† Forster's Wilcox reveals his lack of either culture or compassion in speech after speech. 'By all means subscribe to charity – subscribe to them largely. But don't get carried away by absurd schemes for social reform. I see a good deal behind the scenes and you can take it from me that there is no social question – except for a few journalists who try to get a living out of the phrase. There are just rich and poor. There always have been and there always will be.'

Wilcox possesses a motor car. To Forster, the internal combustion engine represented all that he feared and hated about the fast-changing world. He described the traffic on the roads of 1908 as 'pestilential'. Science 'instead of freeing man' had 'enslaved him to machinery'.[15] Wilcox, who regarded the demolition of an attractive street as a sign of progress and prosperity, was the prophet of a new age

---

*It is worth noting that 'Bloomsbury' provided little work of importance until the First World War. Virginia Woolf's first novel, *The Voyage Out*, was published in 1915, Lytton Strachey's *Eminent Victorians* in 1918. They were about in Edwardian England, but reviewing other people's books for the *Spectator,* the *Nation* and the *Edinburgh Review*.
†See Chapter 17, 'Would You Believe It?'

in which 'the fields will stink of petrol and air ships shatter the stars'.[16] The argument about the state of England encapsulates a common feature of Edwardian fiction. Like the poets of the period, in one way and another, the novelists 'came home'. Their concern was England.

There are times when the reader of *Howards End* wonders why the cultivated and independent Miss Schlegel ever even contemplated becoming Mrs Wilcox – apart, that is, from her mystical desire to own Howards End. She was what Edwardians called 'a New Woman'*. Together with her sister she had 'walked over the Apennines with [her] luggage on her back'. New Women were strong and prepared to act, and sometimes live, without the support and approval of men. Margaret Wilcox (née Schlegel) in part observes those rules by becoming the rock on which her husband finds refuge in times of trouble. The same dominant characteristic is displayed by the 'heroines' of Forster's other novels. In *A Room with a View*, Lucy Honeychurch abandons convention and (with a little help from the Fabian, Mr Emerson) acquires the courage to marry the man she loves. In *Where Angels Fear to Tread* and *The Longest Journey*, less admirable women assume control of male destinies. They become the harbingers of doom and destruction.

Forster wrote in the age of female emancipation. The foundation, in 1903, of the Women's Social and Political Union was the political manifestation, amongst a small minority of women, of the determination to acquire equal status which many more women felt. Women had begun to take employment, in large numbers, as clerks, schoolteachers and shop assistants. The age of women solely as wives and domestic servants had passed. Marriage was no longer the sole female ambition. The change in attitude was reflected in 'women's literature' – much of it written by women. There were no Edwardian Brontës or Austens, but Maria Corelli, Baroness Orczy, Ethel M. Dell and Elinor Glyn all had huge popular success, while Frances Hodgson Burnett (*The Secret Garden*), E. Nesbit (*The Railway Children*) and Beatrix Potter (*The Tale of Peter Rabbit*) wrote with great success for a

---

*The description first appeared in the *North American Review* of 1894. It was applied to campaigners for female suffrage who based their views on John Stuart Mill's *The Subjection of Women*.

younger generation. The course of women's emancipation did not run smooth. D. H. Lawrence – the sickly son of a coal miner and part-time schoolteacher – described the head-on collision between women of the old and new order. He also wrote of love and loss, broken dreams and passionate jealousy. The characters in *Sons and Lovers* are set firmly in the Edwardian East Midland coalfield. Lawrence wrote of his time and place but revealed the conflicts of eternity.

Eastwood, where D. H. Lawrence was born, was notable, before it became a place of literary pilgrimage, as the town in which the Midland Railway Company was created. Apart from that single moment of glory, everything of note that happened there was, in some way, associated with coal and coal miners. Boys assumed that, when they left elementary school, they would work in the pit. But Lawrence was different. Under his mother's influence, he won scholarships first to Nottingham High School and then to Nottingham University College. Armed with a 'teacher's certificate', he began work at Davidson Road School in Croydon. It was there, where he remained until 1912, that he completed his education by reading the books which the University College had not thought essential to teacher training, Tolstoy and Hardy amongst them. One of his earliest published works was *A Study of Thomas Hardy*.

Poems sent to the *English Review* gained him the friendship and patronage of the ubiquitous Ford Maddox Heuffer, and in 1911, while he was still a teacher, he published his first novel, *The White Peacock*. In its original form it was the story of a woman who becomes pregnant by one man and marries another. The pregnancy was not included in the published version, but the agony of choice remained. Laetitia Beardsall (another 'New Woman') was forced by fate to choose between a refined, but timid, mine-owner's son and a physically attractive, but lumpen farmer. There was a supplementary plot constructed around the relationship of Cyril (Laetitia's brother) and a fallen clergyman-turned-gamekeeper. Every aspect of the story concerns disappointment and gloom. The strong become weak and the beautiful grow ugly.

It was not until 1913 and the publication of *Sons and Lovers* that Lawrence began to develop the theme which became the trademark

of his fiction – sacred and profane love. By the time the book was finished, he had experienced both. He had eloped with Frieda von
Richtoven, the wife of the Professor of French at Nottingham
University College. They travelled together in Europe and Australia
and married in 1914. There is no doubt that their overt involvement
in what was regarded as a scandalous liaison contributed to the belief
that Lawrence wrote scandalous novels. *Sons and Lovers*, published
between their elopement and marriage, was excoriated for what was
described as sexual frankness. It contained none of the explicit
descriptions which became commonplace at the end of the twentieth
century, but it dealt openly with sexual attitudes, inhibitions and
appetites. The scandal was intensified by Lawrence's choice of characters. The people about whom Lawrence wrote were not aristocrats
from a distant age whose indiscretions were part of a fantasy world
with which the reader could not identify. They were the sort of
people who lived next door. So their foibles and failings seemed real
and, therefore, all the more shocking.

Paul Morel, the central figure in *Sons and Lovers*, was D. H.
Lawrence in all but name. Each dreamed of a more elegant life. Both
had ambitions which were fuelled by their mothers, about whom they
had not altogether healthy obsessions. As an exposition of the ambivalent relationship between the brutal miner and his neglected wife, the
story of Paul Morel's parents is not as successful as the near-perfect
Widowing of Mrs Holroyd and *The Odour of Chrysanthemums* – a play
and a short story on identical themes – but *Sons and Lovers'* importance lies in what it has to say about Paul Morel's feelings for two
women: Clara Dawes, married and possessing progressive ideas, and
Miriam Leiver, whose love for him has more to do with sacrifice than
satisfaction. Mrs Morel's elevated feelings about her son merely com-
plicate his attempts to resolve the emotional conflict. In the end, he
abandons both women and considers joining his mother 'in the darkness' to which she goes, hastened by an overdose of morphine which he
administers to end a long and painful illness. It is one of the few unreali-
stic moments in an otherwise naturalistic novel. Lawrence demonstrated
in his fiction the truth on which 'realism' is built. Ordinary people live
extraordinary lives.

The stories of 'ordinary people' – when told by writers of genius –

can contain all the drama which lesser novelists regard as the sole preserve of the rich and glamorous. English Realism, as Raymond
Williams called it, was not invented by the Edwardians. George Eliot's
Middlemarch (published in 1891–2) certainly deserves that description.
But Edwardian novelists, responding to the social changes of their
time, extended the genre to embrace the working classes of industrial
Britain and made the mundane irresistible. Few places can be more
prosaic than the Victorian potteries, six towns on the Staffordshire
map which Arnold Bennett chose to call 'The Five Towns' because he
liked the sound of the smaller number. *Anna of the Five Towns* was
published in 1902. *The Old Wives' Tale*, published six years later,
begins in a draper's shop in the Market Square in Victorian Bursley.
But it is not just about one shop in one town in one county. It is
about life.

Bennett, the son of a solicitor, originally intended to follow his
father into the law. Like many ambitious young men, he assumed that
success was only to be found in London, so he moved to the capital.
There journalism, rather than jurisprudence, captured his imagination. He began modestly. His first job was writing for *Woman*
magazine. His first novel, *A Man from the North*, was published in 1898.
The 'Five Towns' novels followed – *Anna of the Five Towns* (1902), *The
Old Wives' Tale*, *Clayhanger* (1908) and *Hilda Lessways* (1911). The cycle
was completed by *These Twain* and *The Roll Call*, published during the
First World War.

Anna of the Five Towns conforms exactly to the definition of English
Realism set down by Sir Paul Harvey in the first edition of the *Oxford
Companion to English Literature*: 'Realism is the representation of real
life – especially if it is gloomy.' It is difficult to imagine a more gloomy
novel than *Anna* or a more desperate heroine than Anna herself, a
young woman who, despite (or perhaps because of) her Wesleyan
upbringing, finds life a vale of tears. Bennett, a Methodist by origin,
wrote the novel as his father was dying. As a result, it portrays a jealous God who expects His followers to accept, without complaint, the
misery which is their fate.

Anna Tellwright is tyrannised by her miserly father to the point at
which he insists on effectively managing the property that she was
left in her mother's will. She meets, and is enormously impressed by,

Henry Mynors, a Methodist local preacher and successful businessman. Confusing love and admiration, she agrees to marry him but becomes involved, first out of sympathy and then emotionally, with Willie Price, the son of one of her father's tenants. Despite Anna's attempts to save their livelihood and reputation, the Prices slide into bankruptcy. The father commits suicide and the son emigrates. Anna, although in love with Willie, marries Henry Mynors.

There are few more bleak novels in the history of fiction. But Bennett was also author of *The Card* (1911), the story of Edward Henry Machin, the solicitor's clerk who became Mayor of Bursley and described his role in life as 'the great mission of cheering us all up'. The contrast between the two books illustrates the eclectic extent of Bennett's work. The range of style and subject he covered, combined with his phenomenal energy, enabled him to produce work at such a rate that it was suggested (not entirely complimentarily) that he hang a notice outside his door, 'Articles written while you wait'.

> By the end of 1901, Bennett was doing more work of more sorts than seemed credible. He was editor (until September) of one journal and the mainstay of two others. He was reviewing books at the rate of more than one a day and also writing criticism of a very high order. He counted the number of articles he wrote during the year as 196. He also wrote six short stories, one one-act play, two full length plays . . . *The Grand Babylon Hotel* and most of the first draft of *Anna of the Five Towns*.

But we must assume that he was not satisfied with the quality of his work. He went to France where he hoped that the atmosphere would be conducive to the composition of a work of genius. Ironically, the only weak chapter in *The Old Wives' Tale* is set in Paris. The rest concerns the draper's shop in Bursley.

Bennett consciously wrote this novel in what he thought of as the continental tradition of realism as pioneered by Zola and Maupassant – and, true to the genre, struggled to achieve an 'artistic, shapely presentation of the truth'. It is easy enough to believe that Constance and Sophia Baines (daughters of the draper with a shop in the main square of Bursley) really existed, for Sophia's rejection of her mother's advice against marrying the unreliable Gerald Scales and Constance's contrasting acceptance of humdrum security were, in themselves, everyday events. They are made more real by the detail with which Bennett describes the background to their lives – the arrangement of their mother's kitchen, the bull-terrier that wandered into the shop, the doors 'bordered with felt to stop ventilation'. But Bennett makes their lives a story.★ *The Old Wives' Tale* is about irresistible nonentities, three of whom are strong women. It is Edwardian in context, not just because of its date of publication.

Although H. G. Wells was fascinated by London rather than the provinces, he too was inspired by a suburban muse. His early life was spent as a shop assistant in Bromley, an experience reflected in both *The History of Mr Polly* and *Kipps*. *Love and Mr Lewisham* owes its title to the adjacent London borough and in *The New Machiavelli* Richard Remington explains what must have been Wells's own fascination with the capital: 'London is the most interesting, beautiful and wonderful city in the world to me, delicate in its incidental and multitudinous littleness and stupendous in its pregnant totality.'[17]

When Virginia Woolf read the novels which were inspired by the new sprawling cities, she complained that '. . . in all this vast conglomerate of printed pages, in all this congeries of streets and houses, there is not a single man or woman whom we know'. That only confirms that Mrs Woolf spent her life among strange people. The shop assistants of our acquaintance may not, like Mr Polly, burn down the premises in which they spend their unhappy working lives, but many of them have similar immortal longings. And we read most weeks of someone who, like Arthur Kipps, has found that the acquisition of a fortune brings more problems than pleasures.

H. G. Wells 'came home' to the reality of lower-middle-class life. He arrived at his new destination straight from space. *The Time Machine*, *The Invisible Man* and *The War of the Worlds* were written in

---

★The most bizarre event in *The Old Wives' Tale* is the escape of an enraged circus elephant and its death at the hands of the local militia. Anyone who doubts that such events disturbed Victorian tranquillity should visit the Eyre Arms in Hassop, Derbyshire. It displays a picture of an elephant shot by the Bakewell Volunteers in 1890.

and for Victorian England, while Wells, the holder of a first-class
honours degree in zoology – won after acquiring a place at London
University through the hard discipline of night school – still turned his
mind to science. When he also became a Fabian and a radical, he
wrote *Ann Veronica*, in which the eponymous heroine proves she is a
New Woman by running away with the man she loves. In *Tono-
Bungay* – the name of a patent medicine which is 'nothing coated in
advertisements' – Wells exposed what he believed to be the corrupt
techniques of new-century commerce.

Like all the best novels, *Ann Veronica* and *Tono-Bungay* are both
essentially autobiographical, but they are biographical in an unusual
way. H. G. Wells was a notorious philanderer, a weakness which he
tried to justify by the espousal of 'free love' as a liberating way of life.
It is claimed, though Wells denied it, that he was once pursued to
Paddington Station by an angry father with a horsewhip.[18] His most
famous love affair was with Rebecca West, and his most cruel with
Amber Reeves, a young woman who thought it her duty to sacrifice
herself to his genius. 'As you will my lover. But for me it doesn't
matter. Nothing is wrong that you do. I am clear about this. I know
exactly what I am doing. I give myself to you.' It was Ann Veronica
speaking, but the sentiment is Amber Reeves's.

In *Tono-Bungay*, Wells replicates a more admirable aspect of his
life – his determination, during his years as a shop assistant, to educate
himself. George Ponderovo, bewildered by London as young Wells
was in life, also kept his sanity by self-education. 'Sitting under a
dormer window on a shelf above great stores of tea, I became familiar with much of Hogarth – I read and understood the good sound
rhetoric of Tom Paine's *Rights of Man* and his *Common Sense*, excellent
books once praised by bishops and since sedulously lied about.'

Neither sexual freedom (which Wells applauded) nor commercial
licence (which he loathed) now attract the astonished horror which
they were afforded in Wells's day, and the self-educated working-
man-made-good is an endangered species. So *Ann Veronica* and
Tono-Bungay, both heralded as classics in their day, have become
museum pieces. John Galsworthy's *The Man of Property*, written before
either of Wells's consciously modern novels, has survived because it
deals with timeless human weaknesses, even though Galsworthy

presented them in an essentially Edwardian context: Soames Forsyte regarded his wife as one of his possessions.

Galsworthy had good reason to believe that women should be free to follow their own star. The wife of his cousin left her husband, while he was fighting in South Africa for Queen and country, to live with him. Life with Ada Galsworthy changed him. The Harrow and Oxford-educated barrister turned against the conventions of the upper-middle classes. His rebellion was first reflected in unsuccessful novels and short stories written behind the protection of a pseudo-nym. *The Island of Pharisees*, fiction, but a polemic against poverty and false respectability, won critical approval. In 1906 *The Man of Property* transformed his fortune and his reputation.

Soames Forsyte and his extended family faced all the moral dilem-mas and social embarrassments that it is possible for middle classes, in any reign, to endure. Young Jolyon ends his loveless marriage and sets up home with his children's governess. As a result, he is disowned by his father. Soames, married to the penniless Irene, who is less in love than desperate to escape from her recently acquired step-father, pro-poses to build a house at Robin Hill in the hope that the pleasure of its possession will increase her wifely affection. But Irene falls in love with the architect, Philip Bosinney. When Soames discovers his wife's infidelity, he rapes her – or, in the language of the day, 'exercises his rights'. Bosinney, overcome with horror at the outrage for which he feels, in part, responsible, is killed by a hansom cab as he stumbles home in a London fog. The plot of *The Man of Property* is unques-tionably melodramatic. But it is balanced by the austere character of Soames and the materialism of the Forsyte family. The result is the revelation of all the vices which hid under the smooth surface of turn-of-the-century England.

Even among the Edwardian middle classes, who showed little sign of recognising the revolution within which they lived, one novelist anticipated the great upheaval which was to change the world in 1914. In 1903, when half the Cabinet and distinguished members of both the Board of Admiralty and the general staff were agreed that France was the real enemy, Erskine Childers wrote *The Riddle of the Sands*. It foreshadowed imperial Germany's ambition to dominate Europe. Childers, English by birth but Irish by adoption, was regarded at the time as a figure of impeccable respectability whose background and education had qualified him to become a Clerk in the House of Commons. He was later to become so embroiled in the violent agitation for a united and independent Ireland that he was executed by the Army of the Free State for bearing arms against the Dublin government which ruled after partition in 1922. Perhaps his novel, in which two amateur yachtsmen discover the Germans' secret naval build-up in the Baltic, reveals something of his split personality. The two sailors are men of startlingly different character. One is a natural renegade and the other shares the values of the Establishment. That made *The Riddle of the Sands* more than a thriller. The two yachtsmen represent respectability and revolt. The novel explores the rival merits of those qualities.

The same can hardly be said about John Buchan's *The Thirty-nine Steps*, another novel anticipating the Great War which was written (but not published) before it began. *Prester John* anticipated by a greater margin the rise of militant African nationalism. Buchan's books about Richard Hannay, the South African mining engineer who became the hero of *Greenmantle* as well as *The Thirty-nine Steps*, all had racist as well as anti-Semitic overtones: in *Prester John* the Reverend John Laputa, who claimed to be the reincarnation of Prester John, is a far more attractive character than Henriques, the corrupt Portuguese-Jewish trader who supports the African revolt because he is interested in profit not principle. The Empire and the world are saved by David Crawfurd, a clean-cut Englishman, who discovers 'the meaning of the white man's duty. He has to take all the risks, reckoning nothing of his life or his fortune and well content to find his reward in the fulfilment of his tasks. That is the difference between white and black, the gift of responsibility, the power of being in a little way a king.'

The war in South Africa and the battle for colonial preferences were both fought by men who shared Crawfurd's view of the imperial obligation and the duty of leadership which was inherited by the British race. That idea was so strong that it captivated Teodor Josef Konrad Nalecz Korzeniowski, a Polish seaman, self-taught literary critic and undisputed literary talent. *Lord Jim*, his first successful novel, is a classic story of a man who, having failed in his duty, redeems himself through service and the sacrifice of his life rather than the loss of his honour. The book was so well received that the author described himself as 'the spoilt child of the critics'. He was better known as Joseph Conrad.

Conrad's greatest novel, the work which elevated him into the highest rank of the English literary pantheon, had an equally dashing plot. In *The Secret Agent*, a Russian spy, the recipient of St Petersburg gold who has failed to justify his salary, is instructed to earn his keep and foment immediate insurrection by blowing up Greenwich Observatory. The spy's incompetence makes *The Secret Agent* a black comedy. But although most of the action is described through the eyes of a Russian anarchist, the attention to detail makes it part of the realist tradition. Even Verloc, the spy with a humdrum home life, has 'come home' to South London.

There were, of course, Edwardian authors who stood out against the spirit of the age. Arthur Conan Doyle who, in Victorian England, had written of the essentially English Sherlock Holmes and the quintessentially English Doctor Watson, turned to the Monmouth Rebellion and the Napoleonic Wars for inspiration. But Britain at the turn of the twentieth century was beginning to come to terms with the new world of working women, self-educated men and a middle class which challenged the aristocracy's right to run the country. That new Britain was all represented in Edwardian literature.

CHAPTER 15

The End of Innocence

Although there was widespread poverty in Edwardian Britain, rea wages of skilled and semi-skilled workers had increased by 30 per cent during the last quarter of the nineteenth century. Most women remained tied to oven and sink. But many of the men who had additional money to spend had more leisure time in which to spend it. That was particularly true of the north of England where engineers had finished work at twelve o'clock on Saturdays since 1890 and textile workers, whose hours of work were regulated by Parliament, had worked a five-and-a-half-day week since 1901. A new race of sports enthusiasts was born. Its members were called 'spectators'.

The influence of northern working men, able for the first time to watch as well as play games, was particularly pronounced in the development of association football. Spectators paid at the gate. So players could be paid. The game which, in Victorian England, had been the preserve of public-school old boys, fashionable regiments and London gentlemen's clubs was taken over by professionals from the north and the Midlands. Between 1900 and 1914 only three southern teams – Southampton, Tottenham Hotspur and Bristol City – played in the FA Cup Final. Only Tottenham won. The south had to wait even longer for success in the Football League. The first southern champion was Arsenal at the beginning of its long inter-war supremacy in the 1931–32 season.

Football became the people's game. Nearly 112,000 spectators

watched Tottenham Hotspur beat Sheffield United in the 1901 Cup
Final – almost ten times as many as saw Blackburn Rovers play
Scotland's Queen's Park amateurs in the final fourteen years earlier.
Ibrox Park in Glasgow was the first ground in Britain to experience
the horrors of a sporting crowd disaster. So many supporters – of both
teams – crushed into the main stand for the 1902 England versus
Scotland international that it collapsed. Twenty-six men were killed
and five hundred injured.

In England, cricket came a respectable second to football as the
national spectator sport. On a sunny Saturday, Yorkshire could attract
a crowd of 30,000 for the first day of a three-day county championship match against another major county. Athletics appealed more
to doers than to watchers. But when, in 1908, the Olympic Games
were held in London, 90,000 people packed the White City for the
finals of the track events – still the biggest crowd ever to watch athletics in Britain. Boxing moved from public house yards to the small
halls, where it proved popular enough to attract the attention of 'promoters' who put up the 'purses' and collected the gate money.
Despite the rival attractions of the Northern Union, soon to be called
Rugby League, Rugby Union could attract crowds of 20–25,000 for
the early rounds of the Yorkshire Cup. The All England Club determined the popularity of tennis by the amount of gate money which
they collected at the Wimbledon Championship. In 1902 it was
£3,408. Two years later it was over twice as much.

The new and more confident working class wanted to play as well
as watch. By 1914, 750,000 men and boys were registered players with
the 12,000 football clubs which competed in the myriad professional
and amateur leagues. In 1907, the London County Council provided
442 'reserved' cricket pitches in its parks and on its recreation grounds.
They were used by established clubs with a total of 10,000 playing
members and combined fixture lists of 3,000 matches each summer.
Hundreds of other rougher pitches accommodated casual games and
scratch teams. Eighteen years after its foundation in 1897, the Amateur
Athletics Federation had 200 affiliated clubs. By 1914 the number had
risen to 502. Rugby Union suffered from the great schism of 1895 and
the number of clubs in England and Wales fell from 481 in that year to
244 in 1903. But for the rest of the decade, the two 'codes' combined

shared an interest in watching and playing rugby which grew at about the same speed as the increase in enjoyment of other games.

Golf, which had prospered in Scotland for more than a century, became so popular south of the border that, by the time King Edward came to the throne, more than half of the 'club professionals' in England were home grown. It was not a pastime for ordinary people. The average price of club membership was £18 a year – about two months' wages for a clerk, the lowest rung on the social ladder from which it was acceptable to swing a mashie or a niblick. By 1914, golf ball sales were worth £200,000 a year and new clubs were looking for open spaces on which to build eighteen-hole courses. Thanks to the increase in life expectancy, the London Necropolis and Mausoleum Company had more land than it needed for burials. What might have been a cemetery became the Woking Golf Club.

Working men had been employed as professional pugilists and cricketers since sport had become a preoccupation of the Regency aristocracy, but they had been essentially rich men's servants. In late Victorian England the professional became a craftsman, working alongside his amateur social betters. In cricket (which took the distinction between professionals and amateurs so seriously that it employed its own language to emphasise the difference) the increasing number of 'players' competing with 'gentlemen' for places in the county sides caused the ruling Marylebone Cricket Club continual concern. Part of the problem was the growing tendency for 'gentlemen' to expect to be paid as much, or more, than players – albeit in a more surreptitious form. The most flagrant sham-amateur of them all was W. G. Grace, a 'gentleman' who received £9,073 from a testimonial fund – four times more than the largest 'benefit' a professional had ever collected. But W. G. was above reproach.

In any event, it was not sham-amateurism which most concerned the Bourbons of the MCC. It was the influence that the influx of real professionals was having on the character of cricket. C. B. Fry – as well as a Test Match batsman, the world long jump record holder, English football international and amateur member of the Southampton team which lost to Sheffield United in the 1902 Cup Final – wrote with real passion about how the intense competition of league football ruined the winter game. Fry believed in spectators, not supporters.

He was fearful that the same partisan spirit would infect the summer. 'A magnificently fought-out game, ending in a goalless draw, will leave the crowd sullen and morose. They wend their way home from the ground with black looks, cursing the bad luck of the home side. An undeserved victory for the home team will leave no regrets. There is no sportsmanship in a football crowd . . . Partisanship has dulled the idea of sport and warped its moral sense.'[1]

Professionalism, in every sense of the word, spread fast in football after the formation of 'the league' in 1888. The payment of players had been accepted by the Football Association since 1885, but the creation of a competitive league – with all its original members in the north of England or the Midlands and its headquarters in Preston – changed the character of the clubs as well as their relationship with the men who turned out for them on Saturday afternoons. After the creation of a 'second division' in 1892, football became so popular that, by 1911, there were only four towns in England with populations of more than 10,000 that did not have a professional club – Birkenhead, Gateshead, Halifax and South Shields.[2]

The new clubs were overtly commercial – limited liability companies which usually included in their articles of association a clause that limited the distributed dividend to 5 per cent. In every case, the self-denying ordinance was unnecessary. Football clubs in Edwardian England rarely made money. When they did, it was ploughed back into the team. The men who ran football – usually the commercial middle classes – hoped for prestige, not profit. Edward Henry Machin, the solicitor's clerk turned businessman and hero of Arnold Bennett's *The Card*, was typical. He made himself sufficiently popular to become mayor by buying a centre forward for Bursley AFC.

By 1914 there were 158 professional football clubs in England and Wales and thirty more in Scotland, where a league had been formed in 1894. Many of them were subsidised, to some degree, by their directors, but all of them relied for most of their income on money taken at the turnstiles. Football had become a strange variation of big business. The average Edwardian attendance at a First Division League Match was over 15,000 and the 'gates' were even bigger at Cup Ties. The partisanship which C. B. Fry so deplored combined with the size of the crowd at the 1909 Scottish Cup Final to create the first football riot. The game was drawn at full time and spectators, angry that there was to be a replay rather than the hope of a result in 'extra time', refused to go home.

Big crowds brought big money into football and its use had to be regulated to give less wealthy clubs a sporting chance. In 1901, the English league introduced the 'maximum wage', which it set for that year at £4 a week. Players were bought and sold like commodities and usually received a 'signing-on fee' when they joined a new club, providing an easy opportunity for the richer members of the league to attract the best players by a large initial lump-sum payment. The 'signing-on fee' was, therefore, limited to £10. The attempt to limit the size of the transfer fees – prompted, in 1905, by the first £1,000 signing – failed because the rich clubs wanted to exploit their wealth. The rule that no more than £500 could change hands when a player moved teams was rejected by the clubs whose spending power it was meant to neutralise. The domination of football by the big clubs had begun.

Football's popularity was both acknowledged and encouraged by its inclusion in the 1906 official elementary school curriculum. Three years later it became an explicit part of the Board of Education's physical education syllabus. But football's capacity to create healthy minds within healthy bodies was only a minor reason for the huge increase in its popularity: Britain, ignoring Italy's claim that football began in the piazza in Siena, regarded the game as its gift to the world. And, throughout the Edwardian era, England demonstrated that it was a game at which the Anglo–Saxon race excelled. Football was an extension of an imperialist foreign policy. Southampton travelled to South America in 1904. The Corinthians (a team of gentlemen whose goalkeeper never even attempted to save a penalty if the captain thought that their opponents deserved a goal) toured Europe and Africa and visited Brazil three times during the first decade of the new century. The English visitors beat the local champions in every match. England was once more demonstrating its superiority over the lesser breeds without the law. An England XI, selected from both amateur and professional players, beat Austria and Bohemia and Hungary in the first international matches ever played and in both 1908 and 1912 England won the football tournament in the Olympic Games. 'And when they say, "we've always won" . . .' The achievements of

Victoria's Soldiers of the Queen were replicated in Edward's Footballers of the King.

Professional footballers became 'personalities'. Although they never became rich, they did become famous. Their names were mentioned in music hall jokes and their triumphs recorded in popular songs. Steve Bloomer of Derby County and Middlesbrough scored twenty-eight goals in twenty-four appearances for England, and Billy Meredith, who competed with Lloyd George for the title of Welsh Wizard, played 1,568 games for Manchester City and Manchester United. Bob Crompton of Blackburn Rovers earned the distinction of being the first professional footballer to captain England. His fans were astonished to discover that he owned a motor car. He was the first, and for some considerable time, the only, professional footballer to do so. The celebrity footballer had arrived.

The irresistible attraction of 'the personality' infected even the Olympic Games, a field of sporting endeavour which proclaimed that participation was more important than success. The most famous participant in the 1908 London Games could rightfully claim that he upheld the Olympic ideal when he became a hero not by winning, but by taking part. Durando Pietri, an Italian competitor in the Marathon walk who shielded his head from the sun with a knotted handkerchief worn in a manner common on the Blackpool beach in summer, was within yards of the finishing line with none of his rivals in sight, when he collapsed from heat exhaustion. The White City stewards picked him up and helped him over the finishing line. He was, of course, disqualified. The British love a gallant loser and Pietri became the favourite of the Games and the recipient of a special gold cup, presented to him by Queen Alexandra.

The 1908 Olympic Games were opened by the King, who no doubt took pride in the discovery that, of the 1,001 athletes who marched past him on the opening day, 226 were British.[3] All the participating countries apart from America and the three dominions of Canada, Australia and South Africa were European. The United States topped the unofficial championship table.[4] The Games ended on a controversial note when C. B. Fry, regarded as an authority on all things athletic, suggested that, in future, Olympiads should be limited to contestants from the Empire and the United States of America. He feared that the

Europeans did not understand the true spirit of the noble event. His reservations encompassed Greece where the Games began.

Fry was in a constant state of agitation about what he regarded as the deteriorating standards in sports of every kind. His views reflected the prejudices (which they called principles) of the Marylebone Cricket Club, cricket's governing body and the home of its establishment. The increasing importance of 'players' and the consequent reduction of both the number of 'gentlemen' taking part in the game and their influence upon it filled the MCC with dread. Paradoxically, while football was sweeping the country as a result of the working class enjoying more leisure, *The Times* attributed cricket's problems to the 'fact that people have to work more than they did forty years ago'. The apparent conflict can be reconciled. 'The people' whom *The Times* wanted to run cricket were, by and large, significantly different from 'the people' who played and watched football.

Cricket's old guard was typified by Lord Hawke who, despite possessing very little talent for the game, captained Yorkshire for twenty-seven years. He told the *Manchester Guardian*, 'I am no advocate of wholly professional sides . . . Amateurs are, to my mind, the moral backbone of the county sides. Once you do away with them, you will inevitably create an eleven which will only play for the gate.'[5] However, 'gentlemen' with a private income which allowed them to spend the whole summer in the field and enough talent at least to compete with the growing army of 'players' were becoming increasingly hard to find. The county played amateurs whenever they could, for reasons of cost as well as of attitude. The great Sydney Barnes was on the point of leaving home to join the Warwickshire team when he received a telegram, 'Do not come, amateur playing.'[6] But the problem was complicated by the 'gentlemen's' ungentlemanly habit of demanding surreptitious payment. The Honourable R. H. Lyttelton – poet, politician and right-hand bat – turned King's Evidence in an article which was published in a sporting anthology called *County Life*. 'The winning of matches being the golden key to financial prosperity, the Committee have been driven to adopt a system of paying the amateurs money and what, thirty years ago, was done in one or two instances is now a matter of universal practice.'[7]

Lyttelton was in favour of payment but against deceit. 'The calling of a profession is, in every way, an honourable and good one. What puzzles many of us is, this being the case, so many should opt for the profession but deny the name.'[8] But Lord Hawke understood why men of birth and independent means did not want to be confused with the journeymen who batted and bowled for money. In 1909 he devised a formula by which they could be paid, but remain 'gentlemen'. He explained it to *The Times*: 'The real distinction is not whether A receives £5 or £2 for playing in a match, nor whether B receives £200 and his expenses of £50 and his expenses for representing England on tour, but does he make his living out of playing the game?'

To be fair to Lord Hawke and his like, it must be explained that his interest in preserving amateurism – even sham amateurism – was motivated by more than a desire to keep the classes apart. He believed the professional would change the nature of the game, a view that was widely shared by other genuine cricket lovers. P. C. Standing, in *Cricket Today and Yesterday*, expressed the widely held fear that cricket would follow football and become a business: 'The sordid side of what should simply be a splendid sport is to be deprecated by everyone having the interests of the game at heart. We cannot rest satisfied if it is to degenerate into a mere gate money affair.'

The undesirable option of gate money was not a necessity for most cricket clubs. Yorkshire, Middlesex (spared the expenses of their own ground), Lancashire and Nottingham could survive without the patronage of wealthy supporters. So could Surrey. Though, when the size of the crowd made it impossible to host the Cup Final at the Oval without risking terminal damage to the outfield turf, the County Club lost a substantial part of its income. Most counties survived on a combination of patronage and ticket sales, both of which depended on a combination of exciting play and constant success. The real dilemma of Edwardian cricket was how to reconcile those two often conflicting objectives. Nobody was sure how it could be done. Everybody was certain that the problem had been caused by cricket becoming too competitive. The *Manchester Guardian* expressed regret that a league – with the elevated title of the County Championship – had put such a premium on winning. The newspaper accepted that 'it is too late to accept that originally cricket was a game and that the element of grim toil is a little out of place. The obvious reply is that the championship is here to stay.' But, it then piously added, 'We shall never, we hope, forget that the game is more than the championship.'[9]

Variations on the theme that some sportsmen took winning more seriously than gentlemen should were a feature of Edwardian sporting journalism. Philip Noel Baker (destined to become one of the founders of the League of Nations, a Member of Parliament and a Minister of the Crown) was, in 1912, no more than an Oxford middle-distance runner. His description of United States training methods, written in *Granta,* was wistfully envious.

> The American athlete specialises in one or two events: before any race of great importance he devotes most of his energics and time to training: he has a coach – often a professional – who likewise devotes his entire time and energy to coaching: he has an organisation behind him which is managed by paid organis-ers. The system depends on organising ability and intelligence supported by a reasonable amount of money.[10]

The men who ran county cricket felt no such envy. When P. C. Standing wrote 'Professionalism, pure and simple, nobody has a right to shy at, but it is essential to regulate the relations between those who pay to play and those who are paid to play', he meant something more than that it was necessary for the professionals to be kept in their place. He meant that it was essential to prevent professionals acquiring so much influence that the game abandoned its nobility in favour of the wish (perhaps even the need) to win. The distinction which such men believed divided the amateur and professional approach to cricket is illustrated by the progress of play in the final Test Match – England versus Australia – in 1902. It was the classic game of what is still called 'the golden age of cricket'.

On the final day, with the Ashes already won by Australia and only self-respect at stake, England needed 263 to win. With the score at 48 for 5 all seemed lost, but in came Gilbert Jessop, a gentleman batsman who had proved his amateur status by playing cricket for Cambridge during four consecutive seasons but failing to take the examinations which might have resulted in his graduation. He scored 104 in seventy-five minutes off seventy-five balls. The two dropped catches, which might have ended his innings, were forgotten. Gentlemen like Jessop gave the game dash and daring.

When Jessop was out, after the thunder and lightning of the fastest hundred in Test Match cricket, England still needed 76 to win. In the end, it was the partnership of two Yorkshire professionals, George Hirst and Wilfred Rhodes, which completed the victory. The way in which they scored the winning runs has also become part of cricket folklore, though the character of the fable is quite different from the legend of Jessop's century. Rhodes, the last man in, was supposed to have said to Hirst, 'We'll get 'em in singles.' The story is apocryphal. But it demonstrates the attitude towards the game which Edwardians believed was typical of professionals. Perhaps they were not far wrong. The professionals' livelihood depended on winning. It was Rhodes who, irritated by the slackness in the field of a young colleague, cried out to him, 'We don't play for fun you know.'

The Edwardian Establishment wanted to play in pursuit of an Olympian ideal. It was typified by C. B. Fry whose record of runs – two thousand in a season six times, a thousand in twelve, ninety-four centuries, a first-class average of over fifty and the undefeated captaincy of England during the triangular tournament of 1902 – qualifies him for a place in the pantheon of great cricketers. But his defining characteristic was his apparently effortless superiority. At Wadham College, Oxford – where of course he graduated with first-class honours – he was regarded as the intellectual equal of F. E. Smith, his exact contemporary. His choice of career was an anti-climax. He financed his cricket, and his numerous other sporting activities, by journalism. He edited the *Champion* (a boys' weekly paper) and *C. B. Fry's Cricket Magazine* as well as writing regularly for the *Daily Express*. Fry was absolutely open about how he earned his living. That was a great improvement on the behaviour of many of his colleagues. Many 'gentlemen' – including Sir Pelham ('Plum') Warner, a crucial figure in the government of cricket for over fifty years – reported matches in which they took part, but wrote under the cover of a pen name or the anonymity which Edwardian newspaper editors preferred to by-lines. They completed the deception by describing their own exploits in the third person. In 1904 *Punch* published a cartoon of a cricket match in which the fielders were all writing in shorthand notebooks.[11]

Despite the extent of their achievements and the elegance of their style, it was neither Fry nor Jessop who came to personify the glory of the golden age. That distinction belonged to A. C. MacLaren, captain of Lancashire and England. MacLaren scored a century on his first class debut, a month after leaving Harrow. Five years later, he made 474 in 470 minutes. He treated the professionals who played under him in much the same way that he treated his under-gardeners, and took an almost equally *de haut en bas* view of his relationship with the governing committee of the MCC. In 1901, the authorities at Lord's declined to organise a tour to Australia – according to R. H. Lyttelton because they could not or would not pay the 'amateurs' the fees and expenses they demanded for a winter in the Antipodes. MacLaren took over and selected his own 'England team'. The MCC did not respond to MacLaren's initiative with good grace. Lord Hawke decreed that, since Rhodes and Hirst were paid winter wages, they were Yorkshire property all the year round and could not join the touring party. The tour was a sporting failure, but a great financial success.

Edwardian cricket accepted professionals like Hirst and Rhodes as great exponents of the game. Their record allowed nothing less. Rhodes was the only bowler in the history of the game to take 4,000 first-class wickets and he worked his way up the batting order from number eleven to number one. Hirst took 2,800 wickets and scored more than a thousand runs each season during nineteen consecutive summers. Yet there was a fear throughout cricket that if too many men with similar motivation came into the county game it would acquire the character which was typified by S. F. Barnes of Staffordshire, Warwickshire, Lancashire and several Lancashire league clubs. Barnes was almost certainly the greatest bowler of his age and perhaps the greatest bowler of all time. In three of the first four Australian innings during the MCC tour of 1901–2 he took 6 wickets for 45 runs, 6 for 42 and 7 for 121 – but he found it hard to treat 'gentlemen' with appropriate respect and constantly worried about long-term security and pay rates. The MCC would have been willing, if not happy, for a handful of such men to play in the county game. There was a fear that the profession would take cricket over.

Talented amateurs left cricket to pursue sterner (and more remunerative) occupations. Gilbert Jessop said that he could not afford to play in the 'expenses only' tour of Australia in 1903–4 and chose, instead, to report on the matches for the *Daily Mail*. Both C. B. Fry and (later) Sir F. S. Jackson turned down the leadership of MCC tours to Australia. Sir Pelham Warner, who stood in when C. B. Fry pulled out in 1911, took the world role of the Marylebone Cricket Club very seriously. He asked, without the slightest irony, 'whither should the Empire turn for guidance but to the club which has grown up with the game?'[12] But although the MCC regarded itself as the paradigm of imperial glory, in the real world too many of its replica proconsuls preferred the real thing to the reflection. Sir F. S. Jackson gave up the game to become a Member of Parliament, junior minister and Governor of Bengal.

Romantics made a concerted attempt to revive the spirit of chivalry. E. V. Lucas, writing in *The Times*, knew that something must be done, but was not quite sure what it was. 'Any step that can bring sentiment again into first-class cricket' was to be welcomed.[13] 'Hard utilitarianism and commercialism have for too long controlled it.' The alternative approach was represented by Alfred Lyttelton, brother of the rashly frank R. H., who suggested that the Laws of the Game (or the rules that clarified them) should be changed in a way which made watching cricket a more attractive pastime. He proposed that the lbw law should be changed to prevent the batsman from ever defending his wickets with his pads, wherever the ball pitched or the batsman stood. He justified the revolutionary suggestion with the intolerable allegation that 'at present cricket is somewhat dull'.[14] It was dull, in critics' opinion, because of the supremacy of bat over ball. Part of the problem was the improving quality of wickets. Whatever the reasons, the number of drawn matches had increased by 20 per cent in a century.

Neither Lyttelton's proposal nor the suggestion by the Lancashire County Club (accepted a hundred years later) that the Championship should be divided into two divisions with promotion and relegation, was acceptable to the MCC. Sir Pelham Warner spoke for the men who rejected any form of change: 'I assure you I have the best interests of the game at heart. I have played it all over the world and I think I am entitled to an opinion. This has been the finest game in the world to many generations. So I ask you to beware how you tamper with the present laws.'[15]

Cricket had made one change in the rules of the County Championship in 1900. A team which on the second day had bowled out its opponents for 150 runs less than its own first innings score was allowed to require them to 'follow on' – bat again immediately. But the instinct of both the county committees and the governing MCC was otherwise to leave things as they were. Indeed, there were dreams of returning to a cricketing Camelot in which the rules were never broken, amateurs were never paid and the governing classes were allowed to govern. The fact that it had never existed made it all the more attractive. At least Lord Hawke attempted to make the dream come true in one respect. When he eventually resigned as Yorkshire captain he secured the succession, first for Sir Everard Ratcliffe and then Sir Archibald White. Neither of them was a player of first-class quality. Both could be relied upon to resist revolution.

The extraordinary paradox about Edwardian cricket was the way in which – despite all the huffing and puffing and authorities that were wholly unrepresentative of the paying public – it remained a truly national game. The era which began with the retirement of W. G. Grace and ended with the emergence of J. B. Hobbs embraced all the classes. Victor Cavendish's diary for June 1902 records with rejoicing the end of the Boer War. Rowland Evans's diary does the same. But it was not the only cause for celebration which both the aristocrat and apprentice engineer noted with equal delight. On 3 June Cavendish wrote, 'Education Bill. Majorities good but progress not very fast. Yorkshire beat Australians by five wickets. Got them out for 23.' Young Rowland, writing about the same day, was more expansive. 'In the morning we had Solid Geometry. In the afternoon we had art. I drew a Marsh Marigold and painted it. Father went on his bicycle to Leeds to watch Yorkshire versus the Australians. Yorkshire were all out for 107 and then the Australians went in and came out for 23. One of the lowest totals ever. There was a very big crowd.'

Rugby Union, like cricket but for different reasons, saw no reason to change its ways. The 1870s had been its decade of rules' revision and, after the introduction of the points system in 1886, the game seemed to have become what both players and supporters wanted it to be. The great schism of 1895 was brought about by an argument about pay – 'compensation for bona fide loss of time' – not how the game was played. Rugby League – the Northern Union as was and the product of that rebellion – changed its rules to please the crowds in 1906. The size of teams was reduced from fifteen to thirteen to encourage more open play, and the loose rucks and mauls were replaced by the 'play the ball rule', which required a player in possession when he was brought down to pass the ball behind him with a back-heel between his legs. So, instead of a tackle being followed by a heap of writhing bodies, the running and passing game was resumed at once. Rugby Union saw no need to find additional ways of pleasing the crowds. Its crowds were already both substantial and enthusiastic.

They were not, however, as large and enthusiastic as the crowds for Rugby Union in Wales. Swansea in the early years of the century regularly attracted crowds of 20,000, and a visit from Cardiff swelled the home gate of their opponents. In Bristol in 1903 the usual 5,000 increased to 8,000 and in 1905, when only 12,000 spectators watched Ireland play England, 40,000 saw Ireland play Swansea. Wales confirmed its domination of the game by defeating the previously invincible New Zealand All Blacks in 1905.

Edwardian Rugby Union, like all Edwardian amateur games, grew anxious about the increasing domination of professionals. Many small Welsh towns built their whole social life round the rugby club, and there was general agreement that a sovereign, dropped into a player's boot while it was awaiting his arrival in the changing room, was a price well worth paying to keep the team's local character. The Scots took exactly the opposite position. They thought that sham amateurism would inevitably lead on to the open employment of mercenaries and were so rigid in their opposition to all forms of reward and remuneration that they refused Pontypridd permission to make a presentation to D. M. McGregor, a Scottish international. When the French champions, Stade Bordelais, advertised for a half-back – offering the incentive of a well-paid local job – the Scottish Rugby Union insisted that the club be expelled from the French League.

The high moral tone of Rugby Union, the romantic nostalgia of cricket and even the prosaic populism of association football were all notably absent from Edwardian boxing, Britain's oldest nationwide spectator sport. In 1910 its popularity was boosted by a less than

George Bernard Shaw. 'Get away from idolatry and get to the truth.' *(George Eastman House/Getty Images)*

Henry James celebrated the beginning of the new reign with an expression of contempt for 'Edward the Caresser'. *(Hulton Archive/Getty Images)*

Keir Hardie. 'No speaker had more meetings broken up than he.' *(Hulton Archive/Getty Images)*

The suffragettes 'do all they can to get sent to prison and when they get there want to be relieved of its main inconvenience'. *(Hulton Archive/Getty Images)*

Archie MacLaren's England team. The 'gentlemen' (Fry, Jackson, MacLaren, Ranji and Jessop) sit. The professionals (including Hirst and Rhodes), being 'players', stand. *(Empics)*

The Edwardian England football team. 'Partisanship has dulled the idea of sport and warped moral sense.' *(Empics)*

Durando Pietri was disqualified from the marathon race in the 1908 Olympics. The gallant loser received a gold cup from Queen Alexandra. *(Empics)*

Ernest Rutherford 're-identified the properties and therefore the very nature of matter'. *(Hulton Archive/Getty Images)*

Claude Grahame-White. 'No one cared whether the aviator who approached was a Frenchman or an Englishman.' *(Topical Press Agency/Getty Images)*

The Honorable Charles Rolls. 'Our legislators refused to allow motor cars to run on English roads.' *(Camera Press)*

Lord Northcliffe. 'The old lady of Printing House Square gathered up her skirts and shrieked at the sight of a man under her bed.' *(Mirrorpix)*

Sir Edward Carson. 'Desperately in earnest and prepared to make great sacrifices.'
(Hulton Archive/Getty Images)

Ernest Shackleton ends the Edwardian era with a voyage of epic endurance.
(Spencer Arnold / Getty Images)

'Had we but lived'. Scott wanted to prove that men could challenge the gods.
(Time Life Pictures / Getty Images)

The Kaiser on manoeuvres. 'The Emperor continues to trump up imaginary grievances against the King.' *(Mirrorpix)*

elevated enterprise – the search for a 'great white hope' to defeat Jack
Johnson, the black, and therefore disputed, heavyweight champion of
the world. Johnson had been denied a fight with his predecessor,
Tommy Burns, partly because Burns's backers had thought the title
would change hands and partly because they feared that a riot would
follow a black victory. Hugh McIntosh, realising the attraction such a
fight would have, promoted the long-awaited bout in Australia.
Johnson won easily. Finding a white man to beat him was the path to
a fortune.

In 1910 McIntosh heard of a soldier who had become the heavyweight champion of India during the previous year. The winner of
what amounted to the British Army championships was William
Wells, a twenty-two-year-old bombardier in the 6th Mountain
Battery of the Royal Artillery. McIntosh bought him out of the Army
and matched him, in an £8 bout, with an opponent of no great distinction. The soldier proved popular with the crowd. Bombardier
Billy Wells had become, with remarkably little effort, a contender for
the heavyweight championship of the world.

McIntosh paid Wells £100 for three fights – an immense amount by
the standards of the time. For the third match, with Gunner Moir, the
posters advertised 'The Search for a White Champion'. The fight was
held in January 1911 and, according to the *Referee* magazine, 'Every seat
was occupied. I heard that all sorts of prices were offered for admission
by latecomers, but there was no room . . . Boxing at Olympia was
going to be a great success.'[16] It was not such a success for Wells. At the
end of the first round, betting (always an essential feature of boxing) was
20 to 1 on the bombardier. Halfway through round three, Moir
knocked him out. The bombardier had what was called a 'glass jaw'.
But Wells, handsome and patriotic, drew crowds. McIntosh announced
that the bombardier was still the chief contender and the match against
Johnson was set to take place at the Empress Hall, Earls Court on 11
October 1911. Johnson was to receive £6,000, Wells £2,000.

Johnson, theoretically in London to train, became the star of a
vaudeville show at the Walthamstow Palace. The *District Times*
reported that again 'every seat is occupied at every performance' and
'large numbers have been quite content, if they have standing
room . . . The huge black's exhibition bouts . . . have been rapturously

applauded and his genial way of making a speech or singing a song . . .
considerably enhances the popularity of the smiling giant.'[17]

However, everyone knew that once Johnson was in the ring the
smile disappeared. The Free Churches objected to the fight on principle. Lord Lonsdale – whose father had given his name to the famous
belt which champions were awarded – denounced the bout as a mismatch because Wells had no chance. The London County Council
threatened to revoke the Empress Hall's entertainment licence and the
Metropolitan Railway, the Earls Court freeholder, applied for a court
injunction to prevent the misuse of its property. The fight was cancelled.

Wells boxed on. He lost twice to Georges Carpentier of France and
made history when he was knocked out by Joe Beckett in the Holborn
Stadium. Until then the British Boxing Board of Control, a lineal
descendant of the National Sporting Club, had decreed that all title
fights must take place on its premises. Bombardier Billy Wells, flat out
on the ring floor but still the British heavyweight champion – because
the venue of the bout did not allow the title to change hands – put an
end to that restrictive practice. But his personal popularity endured. He
became the man who struck the gong before the credits of Rank
Films appeared on the screen. Prize-fighting had evolved into a matter
of personality and appearance as well as straight lefts and right jabs.

In racing the personalities were the horses. Minora won the 1909
Derby for the King and was then sold to Russia. Witch of the Air,
another of Edward's horses, won at Kempton Park on the day of the
sovereign's death. That victory was said to be the subject of the last
message passed to Edward VII before he was left to spend his final
moments alone with Mrs Keppel. The King had enjoyed extraordinary
success as an owner when he was Prince of Wales. Persimmon, his Derby
winner of 1896, sired Sceptre. The mare won thirteen races in 1902,
including the St Leger, the Oaks, the Two Thousand Guineas and the
One Thousand Guineas. The Sport of Kings had become more regal
than ever before. The seal was set on his success in 1900 when both the
Derby and the Grand National were won by the Prince of Wales's horses.

Accession changed Edward's luck. During his first six years on the
throne, his horses performed so badly that Colonel Hall Walker, an
Irish gentleman steeplechaser who claimed that he had persuaded the
Aga Khan to race in Europe, leased his yearling colts to the King. The

owner had more success than the horses he gave away. The King's results remained mediocre. But Hall Walker, after giving his blood-stock as the foundation of the National Stud, became Lord Wavertree. The one winner which Hall Walker provided for the King was Minora, a horse which, it was universally agreed, would not have won the Derby if the favourite, Bayardo, had been fit.

Three great families – the ancient Derbys and Primroses and the recently arrived, if not nouveau riche, Astors – extended their influ-ence over both racing and breeding, while the Duke of Westminster sold his stable in 1900. None of the dominant owners was, by nature, an innovator. They bought and bred horses and won as many races as they could, confident in the knowledge that they could employ the best trainers and hire the best jockeys. Steve Donohue had not yet made his name and Fred Archer was dead, killed by his own hand. The most important jockey of the period, and perhaps the most tal-ented, was an American called Tod Sloan.

Sloan had visited England in 1897 and won twenty races out of fifty-three rides using what was called 'the forward seat'. It had been employed ten years earlier, without success, by another visiting American who was more notorious because of his colour than for the revolutionary posture he adopted in the saddle. Black jockeys were not welcome on English race courses. Sloan took up an even more exaggerated posture – weight taken by the stirrups, posterior well clear of the saddle and body hunched over the horse's neck. He 'won races on bad horses which no English jockey would have won'.[18] The following year he rode for the Pierre Lorilland and Lord William Beresford partnership. Some of the more aristocratic owners were scandalised: 'Monkeyship has replaced jockeyship' wrote one racing journalist.[19] But as American jockeys came to Britain and won more and more races in the American style, the more upright posture was gradu-ally abandoned. By 1914, elegance had totally given way to efficiency.

It was not the only American import to affect racing. George Lamport, part of the wave of imports who followed Sloan, openly admitted that he 'doped' his horses before a race with cocaine. Why not? In Victorian England, administering stimulants had been a per-fectly legal activity. It was forbidden by the Jockey Club in 1906.

That was also a year of legal regulation. Fearful that gambling was undermining the character, as well as the finances, of the working class, the government reacted in a fashion which typified the spirit of Edwardian Britain. The Street Betting Act did not reduce either the number of bets made or the amount of money laid; it simply hid gambling from public view. Lord Durham complained that the government was 'turning what is only a human instinct into a crime' by 'interfering with the amusements of the working class'. In fact, all it did was inconvenience small gamblers. The Edwardians knew that racing depended on gambling and, in consequence, would never have taken any action which cut its lifeline. The Edwardian Jockey Club wanted to encourage and extend the sport, to improve the health of horses and enhance their performance. The United States' example proved especially beneficial. They kept their horses cool, without blankets, in stables in which the doors and windows were open in all but the coldest weather. Their training methods were radically differ-ent from those employed in England. They favoured sharper work over shorter distances and they had perfected a lighter shoe ('plate' in racing parlance) which, because of the way they trimmed hooves, fitted the hoof more closely. All those innovations were incorporated into English stables,[20] and the changes were accompanied by a near invasion of American horses. Over a hundred mares and yearlings bred in the United States were sold at Newmarket in 1908. The Jockey Club was not altogether sure that all the American imports were gen-uine thoroughbreds. So Lord Jersey was asked to provide a new definition. He ruled that a horse could only be called a thorough-bred 'if it could be traced without flaw on both sire's and dam's side of its pedigree'. The invasion of horses was halted. But the intrusion of the new ideas was irresistible. Some of them were more important than the posture of a jockey and the size of a horseshoe – for in Edwardian Britain women were beginning to argue that they had a part to play in national sport. It was a symptom of the fast-burgeoning feeling that women should be free to take their place in every part of society.

Golf and tennis led the way. In 1900 women's competitions in both sports were included in the Olympic Games, and Charlotte Cooper of Great Britain became the first woman Olympic gold medallist when she won the tennis singles championship. Six years later, women golfers from Britain and America met in international competition; Britain won by six matches to one. In 1908, Mrs Gordon Robertson replaced a man as a professional at Prince's Ladies' Golf Club. But there were strong voices which argued that even a limited achievement in sport was likely to have damaging consequences. 'Doctors and schoolmasters observe that the excessive devotion to athletics and gymnastics tends to produce what might be called the newer type of girl.'[21]

The 'newer type of girl' was not regarded by the old type of male as the sort of woman he would want his son to marry. And it was not only prejudice which held women athletes back. Tennis and golf, the two most 'ladylike' sports, were expensive pastimes, the necessary clothes as costly as the essential equipment. Most female sport remained an essentially middle-class activity. However, the dam had been breached. Women were seen in energetic physical activity, engaged in serious competition and showing the emotions of gracious winners and bad losers. Their appearance on the golf course and tennis courts meant that they had taken at least one step down from the pedestal which was also their prison.

Male sport became more and more the preserve of the working classes and was welcomed by politicians as a convenient way of keeping the proletariat out of trouble. F. E. Smith – perhaps prejudiced against games by losing the academic competition at Wadham to C. B. Fry – became an unlikely football supporter.

> What would the devotees of athletics do if their present amusements were abolished? The policeman, the police magistrate, the social worker and the minister of religion, the public schoolmaster . . . would each, in the sphere of his own duties, contemplate such a prospect with dismay . . . The poorer classes in this country have not got the tastes which superior people or a Royal Commission would choose for them. Were cricket and football abolished, it would bring upon them nothing but misery, depression, sloth, indiscipline and disorder.[22]

Those sentiments demonstrate how deeply Edwardian Britain was divided by class. The social distinctions, although rigorous and rigid,

were also complicated and confused. Hunting, then as now, was said
to unite the gentry in their top hats and the tenant farmers in their
brown bowlers. In *Memoirs of a Fox-Hunting Man*, Siegfried Sassoon
described the top-hatted gentry riding out with bowler-hatted tenants
and tradesmen. The novel, which is in truth a memoir, is full of nos-
talgic charm and describes village cricket with the same boyish
enthusiasm as it sets out the joys and terrors of hunting. It also contains lines which illustrate how the myth of the long Edwardian
afternoon came about. 'Aunt Evelyn always enjoyed a game of croquet with him at a garden party.'

The 'him' in question was Squire Maundle, a man who, as befitted
his status, took dogs seriously. 'House dogs bury in the shrubbery,
shooting dogs bury in the park . . .' Sassoon left stories of shooting to
the rather better sequel, *Memoirs of an Infantry Officer*. But the normal
habit of Edwardian country gentlemen was to begin shooting a month
before cubbing began in September. Victor Cavendish shot at
Chatsworth and at Bolton Abbey in North Yorkshire, the traditional
home of the Devonshire heir apparent or presumptive. On Saturday
24 August 1901 he 'got to Bolton about 3.30'. His diary for his week's
visit confirms that the passion of the Edwardian upper class for shooting turned the sport into an industry. They could not possibly have
eaten all those birds themselves.

Saturday August 24
Very hot . . . So far they had got just under 4000 birds. They say
there are a lot left.

Tuesday August 27
Fine but very windy . . . Good day. About 200 brace. Did not
shoot very well.

Wednesday August 28
Got 128 brace.

Thursday August 29
Shot fairly well.

Saturday August 31

Mild morning . . . I shot badly at what might have been a very
good drive for me. We got just under 200 brace. Total bag is
9000 birds (about 180 more than the claim). If the weather had
been as fine all this week as today, we should have killed 1500
brace.

The Bolton Abbey 'bags' were not exceptional. Indeed, by comparison with the most assiduous shots, they were modest. Lord Ripon,
who was the champion shot of his day, killed 556,813 head of game
between 1873 and 1923.

A couple of months later Victor Cavendish was out with the
Quorn, though his diaries give the impression that he hunted more
out of duty than enthusiasm. Siegfried Sassoon, on the other hand,
experienced the joy of a chase even when it did not end in a kill. He
writes of Edwardians hunting in the manner of a recent convert.

On one of my expeditions, after a stormy night at the end of
March, the hounds drew all day without finding a fox. This was
my first experience of a 'blank day'. But I was not as upset about
it as I ought to have been, for the sun was shining and the prim-
rose bunches were brightening in the woods. Not many people
spoke to me. So I was able to enjoy hacking from one covert to
another and acquiring an appetite for tea at the Blue Anchor.
And after that it was pleasant to be riding home in the latering
twilight, to hear the 'chink–chink' of the blackbirds against the
looming leafless woods and the afterglow of sunset and to know
that winter was at an end.[23]

Sassoon hunted, in unfashionable company, during the sport's last
patrician period. In other parts of the country, proceedings were less
relaxed. When the Earl of Lonsdale, Master of the Quorn, suspected –
wrongly as it turned out – that some riders had committed a never-to-
be-forgiven breach of etiquette by overtaking the hounds, he called off
hunting for the day. He was gratified to receive a telegram which read,
'Entirely approve of your action. Wilhelm I.'[24] Gradually the nouveaux
riches moved in. By the time of Edward's accession, Gilbert Greenall, a

rich brewer, had taken over from the Duke of Rutland as Master of the
Belvoir. As a result of the infiltration of the middle classes, manners de-
teriorated in general. In 1908, Lord Rothschild found it necessary to
write to followers of the family staghounds in the Vale of Aylesbury. 'We
beg them that they will in every way conform to the wishes of the Field
Master and, further, we should take it as a compliment if the etiquette of
hunting dress were more correctly observed.'[25]

The vulgarity of the middle class was said to have encouraged the
breeding of hounds which 'ignored their hunting qualities. What was
gained in looks was lost in stamina and drive.'[27] In an article written
for the *Field* by Charles McNeill, the Master of the Grafton, Greenall
was accused of such unforgivable mismanagement as failing to ensure
that bitches sent to the Belvoir were properly serviced. The assault was
so personal and bitter that the Duke of Rutland thought it necessary
to resign. But by 1906 *Balys* magazine announced that in racing 'the
feudal system is as dead as the dodo'. Farmers increasingly agreed. In
1912 Buckinghamshire farmers banded together to demand a pound
from every horseman (who neither owned nor rented property in the
county) who crossed their land.

Part of the problem was that hunting costs rose as agricultural
incomes fell. But the real change was in the composition of society. In
the north, coal owners had taken over the Tynedale and the Braes of
Derwent. Merthy Guest, the son of an ironmaster, had been Master of
the Blackmoor Vale. He could afford to keep eighty grey horses for
himself and his hunt servants. The new middle classes introduced
practices which the old aristocracy would not have tolerated. Foxes
were imported from Germany and vixens with litters were killed and
their cubs reared in captivity.[27] No doubt the old-style Masters and
their huntsmen believed – rather as the Bourbons of the MCC
believed – that their sport was being corrupted by the irresistible rise
of trade and commerce.

It was no coincidence that foxhunters led the campaign to defend
the House of Lords against the Liberal reforms of 1911. Willoughby de
Broke told his noble friends, 'I have been brought up in the midst of
stock breeding of all kinds all my life and I am prepared to defend the
hereditary principle whether it is applied to Peers or whether it is
applied to foxhounds'. His leadership of 'the diehards' attracted the

accusation that he lacked loyalty to Lord Lansdowne, the Unionist leader in the Upper House who had agreed to 'hedge'. His defence was, 'As a Master of the Hounds, I don't like killing a fox without my huntsmen, but it is better than losing my hounds.'

The new middle-class hunters usually wanted to conform. Sassoon was anxious at least to look right. 'A few minutes later I was sitting on a hard, shiny saddle and being ciphered all over with a lump of chalk. The sallow little man who fitted my breeches remarked that buff Bedford cord which I had selected was "a very popular one". As he put the finishing touches with his chalk, he asked me to stand up in the stirrups. Whereupon he gazed upon his handiwork and found it good.'[28] Sassoon's Master was one of the new breed – 'a middle-aged man who hunted to hounds himself' rather than employ a huntsman 'and did everything as cheaply as possible. He bought the most awful old screws from Tattersalls and made his stablemen ride them all the way down from London to save the expense of a horse box.'[29]

The middle-aged man so despised for his parsimony by Sassoon displayed another aspect of the way in which sport of every sort was changed during the brief reign of Edward VII. Old money was moving out and new money was moving in. Some of it was the recently earned millions of manufacturers. Most was the gate money paid by the working and middle classes. In the people's games, Corinthian innocence had passed and was being increasingly replaced by a sterner sort of competition. In more patrician sports, the commercial classes wanted to behave according to their own standards, not the mores of a fading aristocracy. But, however it was financed and organised, sport – whether passively or actively enjoyed – had become an essential feature of the nation's way of life, a pleasure which could be purchased for a few coppers at football and cricket grounds, athletics tracks and race meetings, all year round.

CHAPTER 16

Gerontius Awakes

In 1901 the Mall was redesigned from end to end. Nothing more typifies the spirit of Edwardian Britain. The layout was to be grand as well as modern, both imperious and suitable to a monarchy which wanted to move closer to the sovereign's subjects.

The work was given to Sir Aston Webb, commercially the most successful architect of the day. Sir Aston had maintained his supremacy by combining his undoubted talent with an uncanny knack of representing, in brick and stone, the spirit of the age. He had, as a result, become the great exponent of Edwardian baroque. The Mall made slow progress from the Victoria Monument, sculptured by Sir Thomas Brock in 1901, to Admiralty Arch, which was not built until 1911. The new east front to Buckingham Palace came two years later when Webb began to sense a change in mood. The façade is *beaux arts* classical and the whole scheme is, like the Edwardians themselves, a strange mixture of confidence and uncertainty, the solid and the superficial. For a full decade, Edwardian architects were searching, with mixed success, for a style that represented the age and culture within which they lived.

Artists were equally confused. The Royal Academy, having come late to appreciate the genius of the Pre-Raphaelites, could not believe that anything could replace them. More daring spirits offered a variety of suggestions about the way forward. Walter Sickert had no doubt. His stern injunction mirrored the changing mood of the time. 'The more our art is serious, the more it will tend to avoid the drawing room and stick to the kitchen. The plastic arts are gross arts, dealing joyously with gross material facts.'[1] That was not the spirit in which Sargent and Lavery painted their society portraits. But then, the attitude of Edwardian painters is typified by John Singer Sargent's artistic ambivalence. The friend of Claude Monet and disciple of Edouard Manet made his reputation and fortune as the Joshua Reynolds of high society.

Edwardian musicians were less anxious to sound a new note. Perhaps, by their nature, they were more instinctive and less intellectual. But they too, consciously or not, produced work that, despite possessing merit which transcended time and place, clearly had its roots in Edwardian England. England, not Britain. The artistic glory of the age was a man who looked, and in many ways was, the archetypal Edwardian country gentleman.

Edward Elgar had the appearance, including the magnificent moustache, of a major-general. Nothing gave him greater personal pleasure than lunch at his local Conservative Club and an afternoon at a county cricket match. And he possessed one of the temperamental weaknesses of the English middle classes. He wanted to obscure his humble origins.

Sir Arnold Bax – who succeeded Elgar as Master of the King's Musick – complained of his predecessor's unnatural reserve and contrived hauteur. He attributed both mannerisms to Elgar's desire to prove that, although he was the son of a music shop owner who had begun his working life as a church organist and jobbing violin teacher, he had become a gentleman. It was a quality which made him the occasional victim of a martial muse and inordinately proud when he received a message of commendation from the Court. His desperate desire to do the right thing sometimes led him into error. On the morning that he was made a freeman of the City of Worcester, he arrived at the ceremony wearing the robes which had been presented to him at Yale when he became Doctor of Music (*honoris causa*). Elgar's natural instinct was to side with the Establishment. It was an unusual attribute for an artistic genius. But, in one particular, he remained triumphantly and victoriously an outsider. Edward Elgar was a Roman Catholic.

In the dying days of Victoria's reign he had begun to make his name for the composition of music which possessed an unusual combination of characteristics – being essentially English and of undoubted high quality. The *Enigma Variations* (first performed in St James's Hall, London, in June 1899) had been a huge success. The *Musical Times* called them 'effortlessly original' and J. R. Buckley, Elgar's contemporary and near-official biographer, wrote that they 'set the seal' on his reputation. *Sea Pictures* (first performed for the Norwich Festival in the same year) had almost as much popular appeal. The poems which Elgar set to music were undoubtedly second-rate. One of them 'blessed the land where corals lie'. But the music was the sound of the Severn flowing gently into the Bristol Channel, not the blue waters of the Pacific lapping on reef and atoll.

Perhaps it was the confidence that comes from success that made Elgar move on to something more spiritually rewarding. Or it may have been a long-held ambition to use his talent in an expression of his deep Catholic conviction. Whatever the cause, the result was *The Dream of Gerontius* – the greatest English oratorio since Handel's *Messiah*. The work was conceived during the first week of 1900, finished in June of that year and performed in October at the Birmingham Music Festival.

The early twentieth century was the age of music festivals. In the space of six years Elgar wrote commissioned work for Worcester, Norwich, Leeds, Morecambe, Blackpool, Hereford, Sheffield and New Brighton. Birmingham and *Gerontius* went naturally together. The oratorio set to music John Henry Newman's poem of redemption. Newman, after he left the Church of England, had accepted voluntary exile from London in Birmingham and founded the community known as the Oratory. *Gerontius* was inspired not far from the Lickey Hills in which Newman is buried.

At home in Worcester, Elgar encouraged musically inclined friends to help him with the trivial tasks associated with composition. R. P. Arnold (son of Matthew) read proofs. Miss Capel Smith sang parts of unfinished work. Father Bellasis gave general encouragement and relaxed companionship. Elgar's diary for 14 September 1899 records 'E walked with Father Bellasis'.[2] The result was *The Dream of Gerontius*. Father Bellasis was the son of one of Cardinal Newman's closest friends. The work which Newman inspired was a lay miracle – an oratorio which, despite its Catholic mysticism, was acceptable to Protestant audiences assembled in concert halls for entertainment rather than worship.

The complex inspiration of *The Dream* contributed to the ecumenical spirit of the music. For years Elgar had wanted to write a tribute to General Gordon who had died defending Khartoum in 1865. Gordon – although he had encompassed his own death by ignoring Mr Gladstone's instructions to withdraw from the Sudan – was regarded as both saint and martyr by Christian imperialists. Gordon, under siege by the Mahdi's dervishes, had kept a copy of Newman's poem by his bedside and marked the passages which he found a particular inspiration and comfort. Reproductions of Gordon's copy of *The Dream* were made for the admiration of pious and literary Catholics. When Elgar saw one in the Birmingham Oratory he realised that two ambitions could be realised simultaneously. His walk with Father Bellasis confirmed that a great oratorio should be written in praise of God and General Gordon.

Elgar's original intention was to prepare the work for the Gloucester, Worcester and Hereford 'Three Choirs Festival', but the *Enigma Variations* intervened. As a result, and appropriately enough, *The Dream of Gerontius* went to Birmingham. On 1 January 1900 'Mr & Mrs G. H. Johnson came to church and arranged for E's work, Birm. Fest. Deo Gratias.'[3] The terms were accepted by telegram the next day and the work was finished in five months.

Newman's poem is not great literature. It describes the passage of the soul from the body at the point of death and its journey, accompanied by attendant angels and less well-disposed demons, to heaven. It included twenty-nine verses, which repeated, every sixth stanza, 'Praise to the Holiest in the Height'. The last six verses, sung to Elgar's music, became a popular hymn. But before the first performance, there were great doubts – in everyone's mind except Elgar's – about popular acceptance of the whole piece. The result, an oratorio which was both secular and reverential, astonished even his friends.

August Jaeger, Elgar's editor at Novello's publishing house and 'Nimrod' of the *Enigma Variations*, wrote with obvious astonishment of how little it resembled sacred music as generally understood.

Indeed, 'There is nothing to show that the composer considers Gerontius either priest or saint. On the contrary, he seems to look upon him as an ordinary man and sinner who, after leading a worldly man's life, is near to death and repenting. The music is individual, a personal reflex of the composer's feelings and filled with full-blooded romantic fervour.'[4]

The first performance in the Birmingham Town Hall was not a resounding success. The choir master died during the rehearsals and his replacement, although distinguished, was too old to stand the rigours of the necessarily intense preparations. There were some good notices. The *Morning Leader* wrote of 'an ingenuity besides which the attempts of other Englishmen seem but clumsy imitations of this or that dead master'. The music 'had a tone of its own'. But that did not compensate for the poor performance of a piece which Elgar hoped would confirm that *Sea Pictures* and the *Enigma Variations*, were, for all their charm, the lighter work of a profoundly serious composer.

Even the critics who were usually well disposed to Elgar found *The Dream* difficult. The *Manchester Guardian*'s music critic described it as 'Dantesque' and then went on to say, 'I am more than unusually troubled by the sense of utter inadequacy in these notes and can only hope that I may have some opportunity of doing better justice to a deeply impressive work.'[5] Elgar was near to inconsolable and wrote to Jaeger, 'As far as I am concerned, music in England is dead . . . I have worked for forty years and, at the last, Providence denies me a decent hearing of my work. Anything obscene or trivial is blessed in this world and has a reward. I ask for no reward, only to live and hear my work.'[6]

However, worldly recognition – as represented by offers of visiting professorships and the award of honorary degrees – multiplied with the years. But the acclaim was not for *The Dream of Gerontius*. It was for the *Enigma Variations*, *Sea Pictures* and the great body of 'patriotic' work which had begun with *The Banner of Saint George*. Events, as much as Elgar's choice of themes, conspired to make him the muse of imperial glory. In the autumn of 1901 he began to write a series of marches which were eventually to acquire the title 'Pomp and Circumstance'. He certainly did not create the imperial mood of the time. It is not even clear that he consciously responded to it. But, either by coincidence or design, he became Master of All the Nation's Musick.

Pomp and Circumstance No. 1, a March in D, was an instant success. Its first performance in Liverpool, on 19 October 1901, was followed by its inclusion in a concert at Queen's Hall, London, three days later. The reception was so ecstatic that the conductor, Henry Wood, who had just begun to achieve fame as the originator of the Promenade Concerts, thought it necessary to make a note of the evening's events. 'I shall never forget the scene . . . The people simply rose and yelled. I had to play it again with the same result. In fact they refused to allow me to get on with the programme.'[7]

Sir Walter Parratt, the Master of the King's Musick, had already invited Elgar to set some verse by A. C. Benson to what he called a Coronation Ode. The invitation was initially refused on the grounds that the composer had more serious work to do. Then Elgar heard of the royal proposal for setting Benson's words to the Pomp and Circumstance March in D. The regal origins of the proposed match were confirmed in a letter to Dame Clara Butt. 'King Edward was the first to suggest that the air from Pomp and Circumstance should be sung and eventually the song as we now know [it] was evolved via the Coronation Ode.'[8] Elgar was not a man to refuse a royal request. The song, thus born, was 'Land of Hope and Glory'.

Jaeger was dubious about the words fitting the music. But a suitable arrangement was made in time for Dame Clara to sing the Ode at the Coronation Gala at Covent Garden on 1 April 1902. The Gala never took place. Like the Coronation itself, it was abandoned because of the King's appendicitis. So the Ode was sold in sheet music before it was performed. It was a runaway success. Elgar was, however, pre-occupied with more serious matters – *Caractacus* at Liverpool, *Lux Christi* in Worcester and a minuet to be written for New Brighton.

Despite his 'popular' success, Elgar continued his extraordinary output of entirely serious music. Alongside the Concert Allegro, the one sizeable piano work in his whole canon, there was the Cockaigne Overture, a tribute to London and Londoners written after a visit to the Guildhall, when he had 'seemed to hear, far away in the dim roof, a theme, an echo of some noble melody'.[9] It was just one item in a body of work which was as extensive as it was eclectic. The Concerto for Violin and Orchestra (opus 61) was a work of undisputed genius. 'Great is the Lord' (opus 67) was unapologetically reverential. The

Serenade for Strings (opus 20) was described by Elgar himself as 'little tunes' and aimed at the wider public. The Imperial March (opus 32) was Elgar in his high patriotic mood. The breadth of Elgar's genius made him a revered figure in Edwardian England – all the more loved and admired because of his talent for composing music which, although it transcended national boundaries, remained essentially 'English'.

Elgar's status as the spirit of English music was enhanced and extended by the character and conduct of his contemporaries. All the composers with ability which might compare to his had blurred national identities. The most wilfully contrary – though hardly in Elgar's class as a composer – was Edward German, whose real name was Jones. He assumed the Teutonic sobriquet before writing operettas about Queen Elizabeth and the Earl of Essex. Percy Grainger was almost equally perverse. The composer of 'Shepherd's Hey', 'Mock Morris' and 'Country Garden' was an Australian who was persuaded to collect English folk songs by Edvard Grieg and only turned to serious music – new structural forms and adaptations of medieval music – when he settled in America in 1914.

At least Percy Grainger's name seemed appropriate to the horticultural Elysium about which he wrote. Frederick Delius, the Bradford-born composer of the essentially English 'Brigg Fair' and 'On Hearing the First Cuckoo in Spring', failed (like Edward German) to proclaim his origins in his name. His father was an immigrant to Britain who could not afford a public-school education for his children. So Frederick was sent to Bradford Grammar School. He began his working life as a travelling salesman for his father's woollen mill. Neither wool nor the West Riding appealed to him, so he left England, first for Florida (where he became an orange planter) and then for Leipzig where he lived off his American savings while he studied composition. Much of his early music – *Fennimore and Gerda*, *Appalachia* and *Paris; the Song of a Great City* – was better known and more appreciated in the Berlin of Kaiser Wilhelm II than the London of King Edward VII. But his work was promoted in England by Thomas Beecham, founder of the New Symphony Orchestra, conductor of Chaliapin's London concerts, associate of Diaghilev and the Russian Ballet and therefore, himself, something of a figure in

Edwardian society. But Delius never returned to Britain and remained, in the public mind, a foreigner.

Gustav Holst was, like Delius, the son of an immigrant to Britain. His life and upbringing were as conventional as was to be expected of a Cheltenham child and a Royal College of Music graduate. During his years as a student his only deviation from the normal was the choice of trombone as his specialist instrument. At first, he accepted the humdrum life of a member of the Carl Rosa Opera Company Orchestra, but in 1905, determined to better himself, he became a music master at St Paul's Girls' School, an appointment he celebrated with the *St Paul's Suite* for strings. Almost alone amongst the composers of his day he resisted involvement in the folk-song revival and all other manifestations of 'Englishness'. The London schoolmaster – Morley College after St Paul's – remained stubbornly continental in interests and attitude. He was the very antithesis of Ralph Vaughan Williams (Charterhouse, Cambridge and the First World War), whose early work included *Norfolk Rhapsodies* and a folk-song anthology most notable for 'Linden Lea'.

Samuel Coleridge-Taylor (born into a very different sort of family in Croydon) made his name in folk music, but it was the folk music of the southern states of America. That, combined with his most famous work – the trilogy *Hiawatha's Wedding Feast, The Death of Minnehaha* and *Hiawatha's Departure* – convinced even some of his most ardent admirers that he was a citizen of the United States, an error encouraged by the fact that he was black. His West African father, prevented by prejudice from becoming a doctor, deserted his wife and son when young Samuel was five. The local Presbyterian church paid for his musical education. It is, perhaps, not surprising that he felt no compulsion to sing the praises of his native land.

So the field was left open for Edward Elgar. Perhaps his contemporary Hubert Parry, who set William Blake's 'Jerusalem' to music, can claim to have composed the one song which is most associated in the public mind with this green and pleasant land. But it was Elgar who, because of the nature as well as the quality of his work, became England's Orpheus. Although his music was essentially English, all Britain benefited from his genius. Before Elgar the whole nation had been dismissed in Europe as a musical wilderness, a country which, since Handel and Purcell, had produced no composer whose work

was good enough for continental halls. Elgar changed all that with
music which spoke of his time and place.

Three men – Giles Gilbert Scott, Edwin Lutyens and Charles
Rennie Mackintosh – are popularly supposed to have set the standards
and determined the style of Edwardian architecture. Their individual
and distinctive genius is not in dispute, but their influence on the
design of buildings which we now regard as typical of the early twentieth century was nothing like as great as the pressure exerted by the
largely forgotten Alfred Waterhouse. Arnold Bennett, writing about
E. A. Rickards – his friend and architect of Westminster Central Hall –
explained why Waterhouse, who died in 1905, had such a posthumous
importance: 'R . . . explained to me how one man – Waterhouse
RA – came to influence the character of nearly all modern building.
As most of these are put up for competition among architects and
Waterhouse is usually chosen as assessor, the creative men who have
made a speciality of such competitions have learned Waterhouse's preferences and prejudices and are careful to study and stoop to them.'[10]

Bennett was overstating the cynicism with which Edwardian architects competed for the commissions which could make their fortunes
and reputations. Most of the competitors shared the same basic notion
about the style that represented their generation. Rickards described
his designs as 'touched with French and Austrian exuberance'.
Waterhouse thought of Wren and Vanbrugh as his architectural
antecedents and spoke of the English 'grand manner'. Both of them
described their style as 'baroque'.

The differences in their designs were less important than the characteristics which they all had in common. They shared the capacity to
represent in stone the pride and prosperity of a great empire, and they
represented an aesthetic and intellectual reaction to the indiscipline of
what the Victorians called 'free style' – three converging, some critics would say conflicting, notions of nineteenth-century modernity.
Devotees of the Queen Anne style argued that it was red brick at its
restrained best. The Aesthetic and the Arts and Crafts Movements
represented strongly held views about the unity of architecture, painting, sculpture and furniture design.

Each new architectural style owes something to its established predecessor. So, to a degree, Arts and Crafts became baroque when John

Belcher, a member of the Art Workers Guild, returned from Genoa, infatuated with the buildings he had seen there. The result was a winning design in the competition for the new building which had been commissioned by the Institute of Chartered Accountants – Arts and Crafts with baroque adornments.

One attraction of baroque architecture was its undoubtedly indigenous origins, whatever its variations. The national mood was strongly in favour of public buildings which were distinctively British. English baroque was matched, in Scotland, with an even more indisputably native 'baronial style'. Paradoxically both schools of design, although deeply buried in history, were particularly receptive to developments in building technology. Baroque might have been invented with the idea of hanging a light stone skin on the steel frames which were beginning to revolutionise the building industry.

Baroque developed in several distinct different forms – defined by critics as grand, capricious and Arts and Crafts. The capricious style produced some buildings of undisputed magnificence. Arthur Davis, influenced by the Parisian *Beaux Arts* movement – designed the Ritz Hotel, the largest steel frame building in London, and the Royal Automobile Club in Pall Mall. Aston Webb, although he called himself a Baroque devotee, designed for Birmingham University a complex of buildings that included a great hall which was undeniably Byzantine and a tower, named after Joseph Chamberlain, which would have looked at home attached to a mosque.

Baroque became – in its most exuberant form – the Grand Manner. All that was needed to qualify for the description was the impression of power and wealth. Those two attributes were most eloquently expressed by John Belcher and his partner, J. J. Joass. Their Royal London House in Finsbury Square was a celebration of commerce, and the Royal Medical Society in Henrietta Street was a tribute to Edwardian scientific progress. The apotheosis of the movement was John Belcher's Ashton Memorial in Lancaster, which had no other purpose than homage to the success of power and wealth in their own right.

Although Edwardian baroque dominated the design of public buildings and represented the optimism which prosperous Edwardians felt, more humble buildings continued to be constructed according to more traditional styles. The most successful of the survivors was

Edwin Lutyens, architect of the Cenotaph in Whitehall and the government buildings in New Delhi. The design for the apogee of
imperial glory owed nothing to Indian influence. The Viceregal Lodge
was described as the 'Oriental apotheosis of the Grand Manner'.
Advised to prepare for his task by visiting three Mogul cities, Lutyens
thought that the authorities had gone 'clean mad on Indo-Saracenic'
and asked, rhetorically, 'what on earth can an Indian Rajah know
about architecture and its ethics'.[11] He was more accommodating
about indigenous British influences.

The Arts and Crafts Movement was most vividly exemplified by
Munstead Wood, a house in Goldalming which was designed by
Edwin Lutyens and decorated by Gertrude Jekyll, for whom it was
built. It was the beginning of a partnership which resulted in dozens
of south of England 'farmhouses' – most of them unconnected to
farms and farming. Lutyens demonstrated his adaptability and the
eclectic nature of Edwardian architecture by designing Deanery
Gardens in Berkshire (Arts and Crafts) for the owner of Country Life
in 1901, and the Country Life offices in Covent Garden (the Grand
Manner) in 1902. Then followed the great Lutyens monuments to
rural grandeur in which the marks of Arts and Crafts were just visible
on baronial splendour – Heathcote, near Ilkley, and Castle Drogo on
Dartmoor. When he agreed to design St Jude's in Hampstead, he
became unavoidably involved in the essentially theological argument
about what sort of church represented the true faith.

In every generation a movement arises in the Christian church
which calls for a return to the purity of the Early Fathers. The
Evangelical Movement in Edwardian England argued that church
design, no less than liturgy, should reclaim its ancient purity. In
1907, Sir Charles Nicholson read a paper on the subject to the
Royal Institute of British Architects.[12] Its title was 'Modern Church
Design' but it advocated the adoption of ancient values. It represented the view of the Alcuin Club, a society dedicated to study of
the Book of Common Prayer. Sir Charles reminded the architects of
the rubric, describing acceptable church design, which the Prayer
Book contained. 'Church ornament' should be no different from
what it was in 1549, the Second Year of the Reign of Edward VI.
Altars should be lower and candles fewer than had become the

common practice. The reredos screen should not tower above the east window.

Naturally the Anglo-Catholics fought valiantly for the rubric to be respected. The Church of England Establishment fought valiantly against the influence of Rome. But Rome was not always confounded. So St Cyprian's, Clarence Gate, in St Marylebone (consecrated in 1903) was designed as a virtual reproduction of St Peter Mancroft in Norwich, built in the fifteenth century. Its architect, J. N. Comper, explained that his design 'neither sought nor avoided originality'. His only wish was to 'fulfil the ideal of the English Parish Church . . . and to do so in the last manner of English architecture'.[13] The implication was clear. There had been no original church design in England in five hundred years. Nor, during the same period, had a new cathedral (as distinct from a redesignated parish church) been consecrated in England.

The Edwardians changed all that. The building of three cathedrals was started, or at least commissioned, during the brief reign. Because of the long gestation period of all things episcopal, their construction was finished – or left still incomplete – in the Britain of George V. Edwin Lutyens designed a new Catholic cathedral for Liverpool, but only the foundations were laid in the years before the First World War, and a new architect was appointed thirty years later. Giles Gilbert Scott was a twenty-two-year-old prodigy when he won the competition to build the city's Anglican cathedral. That was in 1902. It was consecrated over twenty years later. Charles Rennie Mackintosh, an unsuccessful contender, must have been runner-up to Scott, for his design is strangely similar to the winning entry. Mackintosh was already the architect of Hill House in Helensburgh (a 'sixteenth-century Scottish tower house' with distinctive Mackintosh wardrobes in the bedrooms) and of the Willow Tea Rooms in Glasgow. Had he won the Liverpool competition he might be remembered as a monumental architect rather than a furniture designer of genius. As it turned out, he was more admired in Berlin than in London or Edinburgh.

John F. Bentley, the architect of Westminster Cathedral – where the first mass was celebrated in May 1902 – is remembered for a design imposed on him by Cardinal Vaughan. Bentley wanted gothic, neoclassical or perpendicular. Vaughan – determined to avoid comparison with Westminster Abbey down the road – insisted on 'a Roman Basilica with the constructive improvements introduced by the Byzantines'. Two hundred miles north, Scott was allowed by the Anglicans of Liverpool to choose neo-Gothic. Cathedrals were spared the agony of arguments about returning to the purity of 1549. In Hampstead Garden Suburb, Lutyens simply ignored the Prayer Book rubric and called St Jude's 'free gothic'. He was no more prepared to take advice from Christians than from Hindus or Muslims.

In 1907 Lutyens became adviser to the Hampstead Garden Trust which had just bought 243 acres of land from Eton College with the stated intention of building a 'garden suburb'. It was not the first attempt to remedy a disease which Lord Rosebery attributed to London becoming 'a tumour, an elephantitis, sucking into its gorged system half the life and blood and the bone of the rural districts'.[14] At the turn of the century, Ebenezer Howard had argued that the best way to combat the flood of humanity into London was to organise at least a trickle out into the suburban countryside.

The textbook of the movement was Howard's *Tomorrow, a Perfect Path to Real Reform*. The Garden City Association was formed at the turn of the century, and established its first site at Letchworth in Hertfordshire. The Garden City Limited was founded in 1903. Its board of directors included a Cadbury, a Rowntree and a Lever.[15] Its stated object was the realisation of John Ruskin's dream – houses which are 'strongly beautiful and in groups of limited extent, walled round so that there need be no festering and wretched suburbs anywhere, but clean and busy streets within and the open country without, with a belt of beautiful garden and orchard round the walls, so that from any part of the city, perfectly fresh air and grass and sight of the far horizon might be reachable in a few minutes' walk.'[16]

The second edition of Howard's book, *Garden Cities of Tomorrow*, stimulated what amounted to a national movement. A Cheap Cities Exhibition was held at the Garden City in 1905, and the Great Northern Railway organised cheap day-excursions for prospective tenants, owner-occupiers and pioneers of the new movement. The exhibition had three categories of cottage on display – the £150 cottage, the five-room semi-detached cottages at £300 a pair and larger houses costing no more to buy than £35 a room. The Concrete

Machinery Company exhibited houses made entirely from prefabricated blocks, and the New Expanded Metal Company promised, but did not deliver, a cottage made entirely of iron and steel.

Raymond Unwin, one of the Letchworth architects, became the advocate for the whole garden suburb movement. When the Reverend Samuel and Mrs Henrietta Barnett determined to repeat the Letchworth experiment at Hampstead, he persuaded Lutyens to act as consultant for the entire scheme as well as to design both the Established and Free Church. Lutyens's plan aimed at creating a rural community on the edge of London. Its aim was to build closes and cul-de-sacs with alternate houses set back from and built close to the road. Every house was thus given a view from both front and back windows as well as easy access to a 'village green'. The cost varied from £435 to £3,500, a range of prices which the Hampstead Trust believed would attract all classes of resident.

The Trust was wrong. The prices made a mixture of the classes impossible. Hampstead met only the needs of the progressive Edwardian professionals. The great houses built for the very rich by Lutyens and C. F. A. Voysey (Cragside in Northumberland and the Orchard in Chorley Wood) may well, as Nikolas Pevsner says, have been 'imitated by speculative builders all along the arterial roads and all over the suburbs' of early twentieth-century Britain. But it was Hampstead which radiated the respectability of the Edwardian middle classes.

In *Everywoman's Encyclopaedia for 1912*, W. S. Rogers (a civil engineer) offered middle-class families advice about choosing a house.

When, owing to the smallness of the household or slenderness of means, one has to seek a house of moderate rental, a difficulty will be found in regard to the class of people who may be one's neighbours. In towns and suburban districts, the street takes its character from the majority of its occupants, and persons of refined tastes would find it impossible to live up to their usual standards of comfort in a district inspired by a different set of ideals.

He went on to list the horrors of choosing the wrong district – 'the presence of noisy children in the roadway, street music in generous abundance, hawkers of sturdy voice and disturbances from early risers and late home-comers'. Hampstead could offer the Edwardian middle classes a refuge from all of those Edwardian manifestations of the lower orders.

The lower orders were not, however, ignored. Indeed work on their behalf helped to keep alive and vigorous the other two elements in the Free Style Movement which Edwardian Baroque was able to overwhelm but not eliminate. The Housing of the Working Classes Act (1884) had given local authorities the power to build. The County Council Act of 1888 had extended those powers, and the Education Act of 1902 had given the larger authorities responsibility for schools and therefore school building. Each extension of municipal responsibility had led aldermen and councillors to believe that they must create edifices worthy of their status. 'Queen Anne style' – a reflection, its exponents insisted, not a pastiche of a golden period in British domestic architecture – flourished in the creation of London board schools. Arts and Crafts thrived in the work of the London County Council's Architects' Department and the Millbank Housing Estate, built over six years between the Tate Gallery and Victoria Station, is still occupied in the twenty-first century.

The third element in Free Style, the Aesthetic Movement, neither expected nor received local authority commissions. Its greatest exponent was Edward Godwin, friend of Oscar Wilde, who, as a young man, had shocked respectable society by conducting a long and public affair with Ellen Terry, the actress wife of George Frederick Watts, the portrait painter. The movement which he led shared with Arts and Crafts the belief in artistic unity. But its members took the idea a stage further. Music, literature and art should all be as one. They survived the ridicule of Gilbert and Sullivan's *Patience* and became, in their way, the advance guard of Bloomsbury.

Despite the insistence on their own distinction from the uncouth world around them, they shared with Edwardian Baroque, Queen Anne style and even the medieval purists of church architecture one common characteristic. They were looking for something which was both new and native to Great Britain. Architecture, no less than music, wanted to come home.

Fine art, on the other hand, reacted to the new world in a dramatically different way. It looked abroad for inspiration.

The Bloomsbury Group – intellectuals who hovered precariously between the aesthetic and the decadent – developed a habit of identifying moments when the earth stood still. J. M. Keynes felt transported to a 'new heaven and a new earth' when, in 1903, he first read G. E. Moore's *Principia Ethica*, and Virginia Woolf claimed that the world had changed out of all recognition as a result of an exhibition which opened at the Grafton Gallery in 1910. Perhaps she meant not that the world changed but that she, and people like her, began to look at it in a different way. The Post-Impressionists, as the artists on show came to be called, were thought, by their fiercest critics as well as their most devoted supporters, to offer a new view of life as well as a new school of painting.

They were not, however, the first Edwardian painters to disturb the tranquil surface of the Victorian artistic legacy. The artistic Establishment continued its belated love affair with the Pre-Raphaelites, the aristocracy commissioned portraits which were larger (and more beautiful) than life, and the middle classes maintained their affection for scenes of village life which painted a moral. But new and revolutionary ideas were already abroad – they were to be found in Camden Town.

The Camden Town Group was not officially launched until 1911, by which time its devotees had already superseded the members of the New English Art Club as the principal radical painting group in Britain. Seven years earlier, Walter Sickert, the Camden Town Group's founder and continual inspiration – had returned to England from France. He had immediately begun to exhibit what William Rothenstein, a more conventional artist, called his 'genius for discovering the dreariest houses in which to work'.[17] His Fitzroy Street Group, named after his studio, had attempted to bring British painting down to earth a whole decade before the more famous Camden Group was created.

The move to Camden Town was both literal and symbolic. Sickert chose to live and paint amongst the working people of North London as a demonstration of his theory of aesthetics. The smoke and grime of Camden Town enabled Sickert both to imbibe and to express the spirit of working-class, industrial Britain. *La Hollandaise* – a large, partly clothed woman sitting inelegantly in an old chair, painted in

1906 – came to epitomise the 'iron bedstead' movement. Then, in 1907, fate provided Sickert with the ideal subject for his work. Emily 'Phyllis' Dimmock, a Camden Town resident, was found dead. Her throat was cut from 'ear to ear'. For the next two years Sickert constantly returned to the theme. In his pictures the woman was always naked and the man clothed, adding to the squalor of the painting. By 1911 Spencer Gore, Gilman, Ginner and Lucien Pissarro (son of Camille) were following in the same tradition. Romance had given way to reality.

In a different sense it had arrived, at least in Chipping Camden, at the turn of the century. In 1902, Charles Ashbee, a craftsman as well as an architect and town planner, had set up a company to finance the Guild of Arts and Handicrafts which he had established in the unsuspecting Gloucestershire town. It produced goods of every sort, united only by a high level of design and quality. In his testament, *Craftsmanship in Competitive Industry*, he set out what he hoped to achieve. The Arts and Crafts movement was not . . .

> . . . what the public has thought it to be or is seeking to make it: a nursery for luxuries, a hothouse for the production of mere trivialities and useless things for the rich. It is a movement for the stamping out of such things by sound production on one hand and the inevitable regulation of machinery and cheap labour production on the other . . . The Arts and Crafts movement then, if it means anything, means Standard whether of work or life.[18]

The Arts and Crafts Movement had no doubt that artistic decline would follow mass production – it was visionary as well as revolutionary. It anticipated, and hoped at least to alleviate, the mistakes of the new age.

The Chipping Camden experiment collapsed through lack of capital in 1907. Neither the general public not the artistic Establishment had realised by then that times were changing. Initially they rejected Chipping Camden, and they were slow to recognise Camden Town. Their rejection of fine art's most significant development was just as negative and far more violent.

During the winter of 1904–5, Durand-Ruel, the French art dealer, brought an exhibition of Monets, Renoirs and Seurats to London. Frank Rutter, the art critic of the *Sunday Times*, opened a subscription list in his newspaper with the object of buying some of the Impressionists for the nation. The National Gallery announced that Boudin (1824–98) was the most modern artist whose work it would accept. 'The ironic consequence of this insular resistance is that Impressionism was old-fashioned before it was fashionable in England.'[19]

Slow as Britain undoubtedly was to accept the importance of Impressionism, the notion of Post-Impressionism was born in London. Roger Fry, one day to become Slade Professor of Fine Art in the University of Cambridge, supplemented his Edwardian earnings by advising galleries on what was available for exhibitions and what would sell. 'Learning that the Grafton Galleries had no show between their usual London Season and the New Year, [he] proceeded to convince them that they might do worse than hold a stop-gap exhibition of foreign artists.'[20] It was almost a casual suggestion, for he had been preoccupied with other business. He had just returned from Poland where he had made a purchase on behalf of Frick, the American industrialist whose private collection now makes up New York's most sumptuous gallery.

Fry lost enthusiasm for the venture before it began. He wrote to his mother, 'I've perhaps foolishly been the instigator of an Exhibition of modern French art at the Grafton Gallery this winter and, although I am not responsible and have no post in regard to it, I'm bound to do a great deal of advertising and supervising.' He decided to recruit help. Desmond MacCarthy, literary and dramatic critic, was made exhibition secretary. The gallery director offered MacCarthy a fee of £100 and 'added – and here he threw in a pitying smile – that if there were any profits, Desmond would receive half of them. His attitude implied that few people were likely to be interested in such art, let alone want to buy it . . . MacCarthy walked off with his share of the profits – £400 – a lump sum larger than any other he ever earned.'[21]

The exhibition was a commercial success because it caused what Duncan Grant – painter, critic and Bloomsbury friend of the organisers – called an 'art-quake'. Almost a century on, Manet, Gauguin, Cézanne and Matisse are universally accepted as artists of undisputed genius. In 1910, their names were known only to experts and their painting was thought to be alien to the spirit of the time. The novelty of their work is illustrated by the organisers' difficulty in finding a name for the exhibition that explained the style of their work. Discussing this problem with MacCarthy and the gallery owners, Fry lost patience. 'Oh', he is reported as saying, 'let's call them post-impressionists', a term which he went on to point out was at the very least chronologically accurate.[22]

Press day was 5 November. MacCarthy had realised that some newspapers would go to the exhibition looking for – and, if necessary, would be prepared to create – a sensation. Nudity, which might be described as erotic, was excluded. A few minutes before the doors opened two pictures were removed from view. Roger Fry's introduction to the catalogue explained that the artists whose work was on display aimed to reveal 'the emotional significance which lives in things'. The critics did not accept his interpretation of pictures which they regarded as the crude work of brash amateurs. They also looked for, and therefore thought that they detected, gross impropriety. The result was a basically cynical press, hiding its prurience behind the pretence of outrage. Desmond MacCarthy described the scene: 'Soon after ten the Press began to arrive. Now anything new in art is apt to provoke the same kind of indignation as immoral conduct, and vice is detected in perfectly innocent pictures . . . Anyhow, as I walked about among the tittering newspaper critics busily taking notes . . . I kept overhearing such remarks as "Pure pornography", "Admirably indecent". Not a word of truth in this of course . . .'[23]

The Times led the assault. It anticipated, and attempted to refute, the favourable judgements which it suspected that Bloomsbury and its followers would publish.

It is to be feared that when Roger Fry lends his authority to an exhibition of this kind, and gives it to be understood that he regards the work of Gauguin and Matisse as the last word in art, other writers of lesser sincerity will follow suit and try to persuade people that Post-Impressionists are fine fellows and that their art is a thing to be admired. They will even declare all who do not agree with them to be reactionaries of the worst type.

It is lawful to anticipate these critics and declare our belief that this art is itself a flagrant example of reaction. It professes to simplify, and to gain simplicity it throws away all that the long-developed skill of past artists has acquired and perpetuated.[24]

Robert Ross, art critic and faithful friend of Oscar Wilde to the last, expressed 'a certain feeling of sadness that distinguished critics . . . should be found to welcome pretension and imposture'.[25] T. P. Hyslop, a qualified medical practitioner, delivered a learned paper which argued that the Post-Impressionists were clinically insane.[26]

Wilfred Scawen Blunt, writing in his diary, was barely less dismissive. '15 November. To the Grafton Gallery to look at what are called the Post-Impressionist pictures sent over from Paris. The exhibition is either an extremely bad joke or a swindle. I am inclined to think the latter, for there is no trace of humour in it.' He expressed the strongly held view of most of those patrons of the arts who claimed no partic-ular expertise or knowledge but could recognise 'a good picture' when they saw one. There were resignations from the Grafton Gallery's committee. Scribbles claiming to be superior works of art were sent through the post. Eric Gill wrote to William Rothenstein in India to tell him that he was 'missing an awful excitement'. Gill, insisting that he was neither part of the movement which the Post-Impressionists hoped to supersede nor the new style which they hoped to establish, claimed 'the right to feel superior to Matisse'. Rothenstein replied that he had seen a Matisse sculpture and 'was not impressed'.[27]

Post-Impressionism was more than a vulgar sensation. It was the subject of discussion in the most elevated society. A feature of the Edwardian upper class – or at least the intellectuals within it – was an interest in ideas which transcend political differences. Roger Fry himself carried the message of Post-Impressionism to house parties with guests from a wide variety of political positions. 'A. J. Balfour and Lord Morley are both here', he wrote to his mother from Lady Curzon's country house in December 1912, 'so we have some delightful discussions. As I hoped, Balfour tumbled to my idea about Post-Impressionism tho' he has not liked the pictures hitherto . . . but he sees how logical the theory is. Lord C denounces it as pure humbug. So we have very heated discussions.'[28]

Thanks to the 'heated discussion' among the opinion-forming classes and what Desmond MacCarthy called 'press notices . . . calculated to rouse curiosity . . . the public flocked in and the big rooms echoed with explosions of laughter and indignation'. Four hundred visitors attended the exhibition every day. Most of them were offended, outraged or merely contemptuous. Fry watched from the Palladian heights of understanding, knowing that he was right and his assailants were wrong.

At least, they were wrong in their artistic judgement. They were right to judge – or subconsciously feel – that the Post-Impressionists were somehow connected with changes in society which the sort of people who patronised private galleries both hated and feared: 'threats and anxieties were accumulating that made for an underlying nervousness. Industrial unrest had erupted in the Welsh coal miners' strike, which was broken up that month by troops. The Irish were demanding Home Rule and the Suffragettes were gaining strength. Only a few days after the show opened at the Grafton Gallery, the Suffragettes marched on the House of Commons.'[29] It was not only the nervous middle classes who saw a connection between an artistic and social upheaval. Frank Rutter published a pamphlet in support of the Post-Impressionists. It was called *Revolution in Art* and it called for support from 'Rebels of either sex all the world over who are in any way fighting for freedom of any kind.' Quentin Bell judged that the Grafton Galleries had 'destroyed the whole tissue of comfortable deceit on which that age based its views of beauty, propriety and decorum'.[30] The philistines were right to be anxious.

Much to its credit, the Grafton Galleries, undeterred by the furore of 1910, mounted a second Post-Impressionist exhibition two years later. British artists – Clive and Vanessa Bell, Duncan Grant and Roger Fry himself – joined Cézanne, Matisse and Picasso. 'The Red Studio' by Matisse, described by Fry as possessing 'a purity and force which has rarely been seen equalled in European art' was the sensation of the collection. Fifty thousand visitors seemed to confirm that Post-Impressionism was no longer rejected and derided by the informed public – even if the artistic Establishment was slow to learn. Sargent, who had refused to endorse the 1910 exhibition, remained unreconciled. Fry described him as 'as gentle a man as he was striking and undistinguished as an illustrator and non-existent as an artist'.[31]

Fry went on to set out the principle which, he believed, more than vindicated his two Post-Impressionist exhibitions – his theory of aesthetics which united artistic time and space and firmly established the criteria by which all future schools and styles should be judged. The Edwardian world was moving on.

> What quality is shared by all objects that provoke our aesthetic emotions? What quality is common to San Sophia and the windows at Chartres, Mexican sculpture, a Persian bowl, Chinese carpets, Giotto's frescoes at Padua and the masterpieces of Poussin, Piero della Francesca and Cézanne? Only one answer seems possible – significant form. In each, lines and colours combined in a particular way, certain forms and relations of form stir aesthetic emotions.[32]

Although the Post-Impressionists dominated the 1912 headlines, another exhibition in that year pointed a more revolutionary path to the future. While the Whistler Retrospective at the Tate reflected established values, the Sackville Gallery exhibited the work of the Italian Futurists. The meaning of Futurism had been set out – not to everybody's satisfaction – in an article published by Filippo Marinetti (an Italian poet and novelist) in *Le Figaro* during 1909. It demanded the renunciation of traditional aesthetic criteria and cultural values and the replacement of 'old art' with painting, sculpture and poetry which depicted the machinery and violence, the manifestations of the modern world. The second Futurist manifesto, published in 1910, illustrated the ideas of the movement by using a cubist style to represent motion. It took two years for their ideas to gain enough support in Britain to produce a London exhibition. It might have stimulated more interest had the newspapers discovered that, in the same year, the Russian Futurists had defined their movement as 'A Slap in the Face for Public Taste'.

Futurism could be associated with whichever extreme ideology its individual adherents chose. The Russian Futurists supported the Revolution of 1916 but were subsequently suppressed by the Soviet government because of their innate fascism. The Vorticist group – an entirely British art movement, which followed the Futurists in both time and their preoccupation with technology and the accelerating pace of modern life – was essentially associated with the philosophy of the far right.

The Vorticists were led by Wyndham Lewis, an American by birth who was brought up in England and studied under Augustus John at the Slade. John, the great romantic who later lived in a caravan on Dartmoor with his wife, his mistress and the children of the ménage, was more inspired by the Celtic Twilight than by a rejection of the so-called failures of liberal civilisation. That was the constant theme of *Blast*, the magazine of the Vorticist group which Wyndham Lewis edited. The magazine took its name from the lists of the 'blasted' and the 'blessed' which it published from time to time. The Bloomsbury Group was blasted more often and with greater venom than any of the other objects of scorn and hatred. Its crime, according to Wyndham Lewis, was decadence – the sin held against every sort of opponent by the British Fascist Party which he came to support.

Yet, in their different ways, Futurists, Vorticists and Post-Impressionists (for whose emergence Bloomsbury must be given much credit) occupied common ground. They were all dissatisfied with a view of art that believed painting and sculpture to be the exclusive preserve of a complacent elite. And in that they represented the restless energy of the new century.

The Vorticists and Futurists were impatient with the old artistic order in a way which had little in common with Bloomsbury's criticism of the Establishment. Not for *Blast* the benign notion that an innate sense of aesthetics existed in every human being. Its readers held a harder view of art and believed that it ought to represent the ruthless march of unsentimental progress. But every school of painting shared one common view. The Edwardian age was not the end of an old era but the beginning of a new. That was perhaps best illustrated by the artistic progress of the man who personified Victorian painting, John Singer Sargent. During the two decades which preceded Queen Victoria's death, he painted as many as twenty-five life-size portraits each year. The undertones of impressionism had always been there. So had the interest in a wider view of life and art. Then came 1914. His painting, 'Gassed', hangs in the Imperial War Museum.

PART FIVE

'Full of Energy and Purpose'

The uncertainty with which the Edwardian era began did not last for long. The louche sections of society buried their insecurity in pleasure. The self-confident cultural elite saw how the world was changing around them and decided that, during the new century, man would become the undisputed master of the universe.

The Churches witnessed the beginning of the new enlightenment with a mixture of excitement and apprehension. Because of science, men would learn to live like gods. But the 'higher man' would only be led to God himself through science, not faith. In the age of modern miracles, the mysteries of the Church were becoming hard to accept.

Thanks to the wireless, telephone and telegraph, good news was travelling faster than ever before. So were men, on sea and land and in the air. The timeless dream of flight came true. Turbine-powered ships crossed every ocean in record time. The motor car evolved from a curiosity into a commonplace. An increasingly educated people, fascinated by the wonders of the modern world, bought and believed newspapers which spoke their language.

The old certainties were challenged, one by one. The discovery that the atom was not a single, indivisible entity combined with a new definition of energy to revolutionise understanding of the nature of matter itself. Philosophers proposed new ways of thinking as well as new directions in which thoughts about morality ought to be guided.

Everything seemed to be changing – except man's contained capacity to strive for greatness. The 'higher man' struggled to chart what was left of the unknown world. And even when he failed to reach his goal and complete his task, he proved – by his determination and endurance – that nothing was beyond him. Even Charles Masterman, the apprehensive author of *The Condition of England*, had no doubt that Britain faced the new century 'full of energy and purpose'.

CHAPTER 17

Would You Believe It?

On 7 October 1903 John Maynard Keynes, a twenty-year-old scholar of King's College, Cambridge, wrote to his 'best friend' Bernard Swithinbank at Balliol College, Oxford, in unusually effusive language. 'I have just been reading Moore's *Principia Ethica* which has been out for a few days – a stupendous and entrancing work, the *greatest* on the subject.'[1] Most professional philosophers were at least as impressed with Moore's *Refutation of Idealism*, a paper which had been published in *Mind* a few months earlier. All in all, 1903 was a good year for epistemology. It ended with the publication of Bertrand Russell's *Principles of Mathematics*.

If Keynes's immediate reaction was totally uncritical, a year's reflection made his enthusiasm more selective. In 1904, still an undergraduate, he read a paper to the 'Apostles' – that Cambridge collection of intellectual exquisites – which attacked Moore's view on the management of uncertainty. The theory which he then laid down was to develop into his *Treatise on Probability* – published in 1913 but written years earlier – and it formed much of the philosophical underpinning of his later work. But, despite that area of disagreement, Keynes acknowledged his debt to Moore throughout his life. Indeed he believed that because of *Principia Ethica* the world – or his view of the world – changed out of all recognition. Indeed, during the decade before the First World War he got very near to sharing Lytton

Strachey's gushing view that Moore had 'shattered all writers on Ethics from Aristotle and Christ to Herbert Spencer ... Truth', Strachey added, 'is really now on the march. I date from October 1903 the beginning of the Age of Reason.'[2] To Strachey, and people like him, 'reason' was defined as morality without superstition. 'They wanted metaphysics without God. Platonism was an alternative to Christianity.'[3] Moore helped to meet a long-felt want.

Bertrand Russell's work – in particular *Principia Mathematica*, the development, in 1912, of the idea that 'logic is the youth of mathematics and mathematics is the manhood of logic' – is, these days, regarded as far more important than anything which Moore produced. But the intense intellectuals of Edwardian Britain – particularly 'Bloomsbury', to whom he became resident philosopher – believed that Moore had found the secret of the universe and, at the same time, mounted a challenge to orthodox religion which maintained the atheists' position on the high ground of both aesthetics and morality.

Moore's ideas were enhanced by his literary style. Keynes believed that he had 'carried the use of ordinary speech as far as it could ever be able to carry it in conveying meaning'.[4] But his real claim to attention was his success in establishing a framework of ethical principles which were in tune, if not with Edwardian Britain as a whole, at least with those men and women who believed themselves to represent the ideas and spirit of the new age. Moore's importance lay not so much in his analysis of what the best ethical system might be as in his description of how an ethical system should be determined. To his contemporary enthusiasts, his great attraction was that he wrote – with the authority of Cambridge philosophy – what they wanted to read.

Moore refuted philosophic 'idealism' – the doctrine that the external world is created, as well as perceived, by our senses – in all its forms. His rejection was accompanied by an impatience with idealists, from Kant to Bishop Berkeley, who wanted to argue about the existence of material things. He wrote 'in defence of common sense' and was 'more sure that he had two hands than he could be sure of any argument to the contrary'.[5] His critics claimed that he had once illustrated the point by waving towards the far end of the lecture room with the words, 'We know that to be a window.' It was, in fact, *trompe l'oeil*.

Although his first contention sounded like a plain man's philosophy – not at all the sort of thing to appeal to Keynes and Lytton Strachey – his second proposition both reflected a more complicated view of existence and demanded a higher level of understanding. Moore believed that many ethical systems were built on a fundamental error – the notion that 'goodness', the central object of ethical energy, could be best defined by listing the 'natural' properties with which it was associated. The so-called 'naturalistic fallacy' confused 'identification' with 'attribution'. There is a fundamental difference between the two statements, 'water is wet' and 'water is H_2O'. The mistake which Moore claimed to identify confused attributes of 'goodness' with the nature of 'goodness' itself.

The result, he argued, was a philosophic tautology. The utilitarians argued that 'goodness' was achieved by the pursuit of happiness. If that were true, it would make no sense to ask, 'Is this good as well as pleasant?' Yet that question is essential to the philosophic argument about morality. Moore concluded that 'good', unlike pleasure, was not 'natural' to the human species. In consequence, the definition of good must be influenced by the mores of the time. That doctrine was irresistible to intellectuals and aesthetes far beyond Bloomsbury, for it contained the clear implication that superior people are likely to have superior intuition and are therefore entitled to lay down the ethical standards of their age. It was less attractive to Christians whose faith was based on received truth which, in turn, laid down immutable standards of ethical behaviour – standards which remain constant over time and space because they are divinely inspired.★

Bertrand Russell, whose most original philosophic work was completed before the outbreak of the First World War, broke brilliant new ground in the application of mathematical reasoning to the examination of ethical questions. The three volumes of *Principia Mathematica* – written in co-operation with Alfred Whitehead – were filled with proposals for improved analyses which simultaneously enhanced the prospects of understanding. It also contained formulations which fascinated the intellectually ingenious – even to the point of employing,

---

★It is worth noting that D. H. Lawrence was a vigorous critic of Moore's philosophy. He believed in moral values that did not change through time.

to illustrate one of his more complex formulations, the 'liar paradox' of Epimenides the Cretan. The statement 'I am a liar' is only true if it is false.

The 'liar paradox', turned into 'Russell's paradox' in 1903, was meant to exemplify the 'theory of classes' in 'set theory'. Some sets (collections or classes) are members of themselves. A set of horses is not a member of itself because it is a set not a horse. On the other hand, a set of non-horses is a member of itself. Russell asked if a set of all sets which are not members of themselves is a member of itself? If it is, it is not. If it is not, it is. The conclusion which Russell drew from this analysis was that 'sets' and 'classes' should be determined by their composition rather than by their characteristics. Views of such complexity, although appealing to a certain sort of mind, were less immediately influential than the parallel view on religion which was either inherent or explicit in Russell's work.

The existence of God and the possibility of personal immortality were, Russell asserted, logical possibilities at best. Indeed no evidence to support the belief can be found in the experience of the human race. But, without making an irrefutable logical connection, Russell went further. Religion was positively harmful, intellectually, socially and morally. Despite the difference in discipline and methodology, Moore and Russell combined as eloquent opponents of the Christian beliefs which had held Victorian society together. And the philosophers' assault on simple faith was reinforced, perhaps inadvertently, by the advance of science.

The sure and certain world of the nineteenth century had been rocked by the publication of Charles Darwin's *Origin of Species* and the passionate advocacy of his theory of evolution by his fearsome 'bulldog', Thomas Huxley. Twenty years later, the campaign against religion seemed to turn into a conspiracy in which philosophy combined with every sort of science to promote the notion that no thinking man or woman could possibly accept the teaching, either moral or spiritual, of any church. For the intelligent believers wracked by doubt, there was very little consolation to be gained from the discovery that anthropologists could trace the path of error into which British Christians, like every other religious community, had fallen.

Back in 1890, James Frazer had described the process by which modern man had reached the religious phase in the progress towards genuine and complete civilisation. *The Golden Bough* told enchanting stories of ritual killings, dying gods and the eternally mysterious fisher king. It was the tales of romance which made it an Edwardian best-seller – reprinted in three extended volumes in 1900 and twelve volumes between 1911 and 1915. The explanation that all societies evolve first through magic to religion and that the West had pro-gressed to the final scientific stage of civilisation's development, did more than identify religion's place in the ascent of man. It diminished the notion of an *eternal* father who was strong to save. And it reduced the island race to the level of other tribes who were travelling the same route, albeit at different rates of progress. It was offensive to think of Britain as merely a development of, say, Fiji where 'the chief of the Namosi always ate a man as a precaution before he had his hair cut', in order to ensure that he lost none of his mystic power.[6] But it was science, not anthropology, that stood the Edwardian idea of the world on its head. Ernest Rutherford reidentified the properties, and therefore the very nature, of matter.

Rutherford was a New Zealander who, in 1894, won an '1850 Exhibition' Scholarship to Cambridge. There he immediately demonstrated his ability as an inventor as well as a theoretical physicist by constructing apparatus for the detection of electromagnetic waves. He also worked on the properties of ions – electrically charged atoms or groups of atoms which are formed when they attract or repel elec-trons – and identified alpha and beta rays in uranium radiation. After four years in England he was appointed Professor of Physics at McGill University in Montreal, and his real life's work began.

In Montreal – working with Frederick Snoddy, an Oxford physicist who had followed him there – Rutherford developed the 'disintegration theory'. Radioactivity, the two men argued, was an atomic, not a molecular or chemical process. Until then, the molecule was thought to be the simplest unit of a chemical compound that can exist, made up of two or more atoms held together by chemical bonds. The atom was thought to be indivisible. Indeed its name, taken from the Greek, is a statement of its indivisibility.

Victorian physicists convinced themselves that their science had progressed as far as it could go – that there was nothing to learn about the physical world that had not been learned already. Rutherford and Snoddy broke new ground by demonstrating that atoms could change their nature and structure. Radioactivity, they claimed, was a process in which atoms of one element spontaneously disintegrated into atoms of an entirely different element. Rutherford summarised the findings in *Radioactivity*, which he published in 1904. The 'force' that he defined was unaffected by changes in temperature, generated more heat than a normal chemical reaction and produced new types of matter.

In 1907 Rutherford returned to Britain and became Longworthy Professor of Physics in the University of Manchester. Then he worked with Hans Geiger to find a method of counting the number of alpha particles emitted from radium samples. It was a mark of his distinction as a scientist of unlimited scope and vision that in 1908 he was awarded the Nobel Prize, for chemistry – though he believed that science, apart from physics, was 'just stamp collecting', and chemistry 'no more than stinks'. However, his great achievement was still three years ahead.

In Montreal, Rutherford's work on the scattering of alpha rays had led him to speculate on the composition of the atom. In Manchester during 1910 he demonstrated that the pattern of that scattering resulted from the composition of the atom's inner core. The intense electric field that caused and accompanied the scattering was, he concluded, the consequence of all the positive charge, and therefore almost all the mass of the atom, being concentrated in a nucleus 10,000 times smaller in diameter than the atom itself. Three years later he examined the atom's inner structure and labelled elements with 'atomic numbers', which identified their properties.★

Rutherford described his work as 'turning out the facts of nature' – by which he meant that he had revealed simple facts of life that were available to any scientist who conscientiously searched for them. By searching and finding – and introducing the concepts of the 'nucleus'

★In 1919 Rutherford became Cavendish Professor of Physics in the University of Cambridge. His work led Chadwick to discover the neutron in 1932. Cockcroft and Walton split the atom in the same year. Rutherford died in 1937.

and 'radioactivity' to a far wider public than the community of academic physicists – Rutherford added another element of uncertainty to the thinking Edwardians' picture of a steady world. There is no reason to believe that he was intentionally or even consciously eroding confidence in religion. Nor did his work directly and necessarily have that result. But he demonstrated that the world was more complicated than the Victorians had realised. And religion depends on faith in simple explanations.

It was not only the steady pressure of new philosophic argument and scientific discovery that undermined Edwardian religion. All the churches felt the effect of the secularism that is the companion of progress. Some men and women, more prosperous than ever before, no longer needed the consolation of a better life to come. Because economic progress was modest and patchy, rather more found new material wonders – flight, wireless, telegraph, radio – to replace the magic and mysteries on which religion depended. The Labour Party – although in part almost indistinguishable from the Nonconformist Church – offered to some men and women a new view of moral and social improvement. Instead of attempting to build a new world through conversion to Christ of sinful men and women, more and more of the disadvantaged and dispossessed began to believe that it was society itself, not its members, which must be changed.

The Church of England, always anxious to encompass a broad spectrum of Christian belief, saw its task in Edwardian England as embracing and accommodating the new age. And because of its historic association with the scholarship of the ancient universities – the very places from which the intellectual heresies came – it felt a particular obligation to combat the philosophies of doubt. It did not face them head-on but attempted to argue for God in the language which Moore and Russell had used to argue against Him. Sir Oliver Lodge – the personification of advanced Edwardian thinking, Professor of Physics in Liverpool and first principal of Birmingham University – defined the moral make-up of what came to be called 'the higher man' – educated doubters whose certainty the Church had to restore: 'The higher man of today is not worrying about sin at all. As for Original or Birth Sin, or any other notion of that kind, that sits lightly on him. As a matter of fact it is non-existent and no one but a monk could have invented it.'

Lodge was doing no more than describing in lurid terms the loss of faith which many serious theologians predicted would inevitably follow the advance of education and prosperity. A society which exhibited 'the vigour of early manhood, possessing contentment still charged with ambition' – the characteristics of a 'race in England and Europe which was full of energy and purpose' – enjoyed more material prosperity than ever before.[7] As a result, the nation was 'losing its old religion'. C. F. G. Masterman, in *The Condition of England*, announced that 'the whole apparatus of worship seems archaic and unreal to those who have never felt the shaking of the solid ground beneath their feet or the wonder and terror of elemental fire'.[8] He was writing of the earthquake which follows moral uncertainty. The solid ground of natural science was shaken by Ernest Rutherford in a way which provoked impatience with archaic worship. In *Man and Superman*, George Bernard Shaw, the most famous iconoclast and atheist of his age, scoffed at the idea of a superior being. Within the Church of England, influential voices argued that a new Christianity was needed for the new age of the higher man. It was the Churches which saw the need to change – Roman Catholicism at one end of the spectrum and the Salvation Army at the other – which successfully survived Edwardian scepticism.

The argument that the Church of England must change or die was not supported by the figures of church attendance. On Easter Day 1901, 1,945,000 men and women (9.4 per cent of the adult population) took Holy Communion. By 1914, the total had risen to 2,226,000, though the percentage had fractionally fallen. However, 9.2 per cent was a considerable improvement on the second half of the nineteenth century, when the figure hovered around 8 per cent.[9] Membership of the Roman Catholic Church in England was inflated by Irish immigration. In 1891 there were 1,357,000 Catholics in Great Britain. By 1913 there were 1,793,000. Over the same period the number of churches grew from 1,387 to 1,845.[10] The Methodists, on the other hand, experienced a slightly greater decline than that which the Church of England suffered. Between 1901 and 1914 the several branches of that faith – Wesleyan, New Connexion, Primitive

Methodists, Bible Christians and the United Free Church –
accounted for 3.6 per cent of the population. By 1914 the figure had
fallen to 3.2 per cent.[11] Methodists insisted they were not in retreat;
Catholics were equally sure their advance was irresistible. In both
cases the complacency was misplaced.

In 1904, the Church of England began work on the new Liverpool
Cathedral. A year earlier, the Roman Catholic Church, after several
false starts and reluctant postponements, had at last felt sufficient confidence to confirm that it would build the symbol of its permanent
place in British life which had been the hierarchy's dream ever since
it had been re-established in 1856. In 1865, Cardinal Manning had
declared that 'The See of Westminster needed a cathedral proportionate to the chief diocese of the Catholic Church of the British
Empire.'[12] In anticipation of that achievement he had bought land
(including the old Middlesex County Prison) in Tothill Fields, close
to Victoria Station. The new basilica would, he announced, be dedicated to Cardinal Wiseman. But his priorities changed. There were
Catholic foundlings in Protestant workhouses and he 'could not leave
twenty thousand children without education and drain funds and
neglect my flock for piles of stone and brick'.[13] It needed Herbert
Vaughan, the son of a landowner from Ross-on-Wye (whose father
intended him for the Army, not the Church), to make the great leap
forward.

Vaughan was a gentleman and an 'ultramontane' who believed in
the absolute authority of Rome. Long before he became Cardinal
Archbishop of Westminster he bought control of the *Tablet* to ensure
that it maintained its unswerving support for the doctrine of papal
infallibility. He opposed Irish Home Rule (an extraordinary position
to be taken up by the head of the Catholic Church in England) and
complained bitterly about what he called 'the Canonisation of Charles
Stewart Parnell'. He had been passionately opposed to Cardinal
Manning's intervention in the London Dock Strike of 1889 and
accepted (as did his biographer) that he was deeply unpopular with
part of his flock. It needed a man of his disposition to insist that a
mighty cathedral must be built to proclaim the glory of God and
emphasise the importance of the London archdiocese and its cardinal.
On 12 March 1892, Herbert Vaughan was chosen as Archbishop of

Westminster. He immediately announced that building would begin that year. The foundation stone was laid in June 1895.

Then Vaughan had dreamed of Benedictine monks supervising the liturgy of the new cathedral which would become a shrine that held and honoured the relics of St Edmund. Those plans, like the promise to complete the building in eight years, were not fulfilled. The building is not finished yet. It was seven years before any part of the new cathedral could be opened for prayer or to the public.

On 7 May 1902, the first Mass was celebrated in the Chapter House. On Lady Day 1903, what was to become the Lady Chapel was made the temporary home of the local parish mission, and in early June that year, Elgar's *The Dream of Gerontius* (music by Edward Elgar and words by John Henry Newman) was performed in the still incomplete nave. The audience was not to know that what was to become the formal consecration was only weeks away: Herbert Vaughan died on 19 June 1903. 'Into the vast space of that still unfinished church, his body was taken . . . for the solemn requiem which, unforeseen, was to become the opening ceremony.'[14] What critics called 'Vaughan's Railway Station' or 'The Roman Candle' became the symbol of Roman Catholicism's permanent place in the life of England.

In the year that Cardinal Vaughan died – confident about the unity and strength of the Church which he led – Randall Davidson was enthroned Archbishop of Canterbury and began his twenty-five-year leadership of a Church which was divided and uncertain. It faced two immediate crises which, although distinct and separate, were both the result of a reluctance to face the reality of the twentieth century. One was doctrinal – the need to establish the Church's reaction to the new scepticism and to determine its willingness, as a broad Church, to accept the ritualism of the Anglo-Catholics. The other was the strange inability of either Canterbury or York to recognise the human needs of either priest or people.

At the beginning of the new century there was a sharp division of opinion about the quality of applicants for ordination. One view was that the best Oxford and Cambridge graduates no longer chose to enter the Church. The other was that applicants from the new universities – Manchester and Liverpool (established in 1903), Leeds (in 1904), Sheffield (in 1905) and Bristol (in 1909) – provided valuable new clerical blood. In most early years of the century there were two hundred curates looking for incumbencies. It was therefore hardly surprising that the number of candidates for ordination began to fall, both in absolute terms and as a percentage of the growing population. Many of the unemployed curates could not afford to take jobs in the new city parishes. The vicissitudes of the humble parson were described in an anonymous pamphlet published, at the turn of the century, in the parish of St Pancras. In common with the habit of the time, St Pancras had just been divided into thirty smaller parishes. The new incumbents earned between £700 and £173 a year. The average was £355 – a sum from which very considerable parish expenses had to be met. But they were the favoured and fortunate sons of the church. The St Pancras pamphlet described the lot of unattached clergy.

> Nothing could be more discreditable to the Church of England than the way she treats unbeneficed clergy. At present the almost universal qualification for a benefice is private means. Hundreds of appointments are made on this sole recommendation. The unfortunate curate who does not possess any private means cannot accept a benefice. His lot in any church but ours would be a happy and honourable one. But it is notorious that with us his career is practically over at forty years of age. The church which has impressed on him her indelible orders has no further use for him.[15]

It was not only the disenchantment of the urban priesthood which conspired to detach the Church of England from the people of the growing cities. The Church Schools, which established the bond between religious and secular town life were, at the beginning of the new century, under threat. So they remained until the Education Act of 1906 provided them with support from public funds. Although the Nonconformists were outraged, the Anglican Communion – always happy to see the bonds between Church and state strengthened – concentrated its attention on its theological problems in the belief that its essential place in the social life of the nation had been made secure. Its principal duty was to fight the new heresies. The duty to lead the crusade fell to Randall Davidson – sometime dean of Windsor and confidant of Queen Victoria and, as Bishop of Winchester, attendant bishop at her death.

Davidson was appointed Archbishop of Canterbury in 1903, the year of *Principia Ethica* and the *Principle of Mathematics*, and twelve months before the publication of *Radioactivity*. But his real challenge lay inside, not outside, the Established Church. His immediate and urgent task was to hold the Church of England together in some sort of theological unity. That meant dealing, in one way or another, with the theological radicals who, like Oliver Lodge, believed that changes had to be made to accommodate the 'higher man' of Edwardian Britain. At the time he took up residence in Lambeth Palace, not everyone was convinced that the new Archbishop's urbane talents were suited to preventing controversy from turning into crisis. Henry Scott Holland, Canon of Christ Church and Regius Professor of Divinity in the University of Oxford, was told that the new Archbishop was too anxious to please the King. He refuted the charge in a way which cannot have given the Primate much pleasure: 'Bishop Davidson's point of danger is not the Court. He has survived its perils with singular simplicity. Rather is it to be found in the Athenaeum. There swell the sirens who are apt to beguile and bewitch him . . . The Athenaeum is not a shrine to infallibility. Its elderly common-sense has no prophetic afflatus.'[16]

It was a harsh judgement which Holland repented with the years. But there is no doubt that Davidson believed himself to have three overwhelming obligations – to preserve the formal connection between Church and state, to avoid a schism within the worldwide Anglican Communion and to remind the Church he led that it had social as well as spiritual obligations. Holland welcomed Davidson's emphasis on the third imperative. But he believed that the Church, and its loyal sons, had a duty which transcended all other obligations – a task which, were it not properly discharged, might result in the slow death of religion itself. Faith and Reason had to be reconciled.

Holland saw, all around him, 'higher men' of the sort identified by

Oliver Lodge. They were suffused by 'an intellectual panic which is felt creeping over them like a contagion, as a plague breath that chills and unnerves and paralyses and sickens. Testimony, evidence, proof, witness – for these they anxiously, feverishly ask.'[17] Holland did not believe that the sovereign remedy for all those maladies was hard to find. The infection was caused by the belief that science challenged (and perhaps even vitiated) faith. He denied that reason and revelation were in conflict with each other. Indeed, he went further. The demands of a new and more intellectual world should be met. Scientific proof should be provided for what had previously been accepted as matters of faith. Science and religion must become allies not enemies. He was not alone.

Charles Gore, bishop first of Worcester, then of the new diocese of Birmingham and eventually of Oxford, wrote of the urgent need 'to conciliate the claims of reason and revelation, so as to interpret the ancient catholic faith so as not to lay intolerable strain on the free intellect.'[18] Gore had made his own contribution to the process back in 1891 with the essay which he had published in *Lux Mundi: A Series of Studies in the Religion of Incarnation*, that Holland had edited. The studies were intended 'to remove unacceptable dogma in order to strengthen the faith of a scientifically minded generation'. Gore's essay 'The Holy Spirit and Inspiration' had examined the veracity of the Bible. It had concluded that the New Testament was 'final and catholic' but that the Old was 'fallible and imperfect'. He did not, for example, accept the Genesis account of creation. But that required him to explain why Christ quoted the Old Testament with approval. So Gore was obliged to decide whether the Saviour of the World was dishonest or deluded. He concluded that Christ lived on earth 'through and under conditions of true human nature. Thus he used human nature, its relations to God, its conditions and experiences, its growth in knowledge and its limitations of knowledge. He shows no signs of transcending the science of his age.' In short, Jesus – having acquired human form – accepted human limitations and was simply wrong about the Old Testament. Gore was surprised that his conclusion outraged the Church.

The reconciliation of faith and reason came to be called – sometimes pejoratively, sometimes as a mark of approval – 'modernism'.

And 'modernists' began to appear in the most unlikely places. William Sandy, Regius Professor of Philosophy at Oxford, insisted that 'the Saviour of Mankind extends his arms towards the cultivated modern man, just as he does towards the simple believer'.[19] That was an entirely acceptable view since it amounted to no more than that the Lord's arms were opened wide. But Sandy had begun to lose traditional faith. He told friends that he could no longer accept the Bible's account of the miracles. Nor did he believe in either the Virgin Birth or the Resurrection.

'Modernism' began to take root. It propagated its views through its magazine, the *Modern Churchman*, and Ripon Hall – a theological college founded in 1897 by the essentially orthodox Bishop Boyd-Carpenter – became modernism's breeding ground. The new theology was supported (in one form of another) by theologians, philosophers, historians and (perhaps most damaging of all) biblical scholars whose studies of the texts convinced them that all the messages of the gospels were to be found in the religious teachings of earlier faiths. All the sceptics claimed to be devout Christians who insisted that their approach to the gospels and creeds was essential if Christianity was to survive. Lowes Dickinson spoke for them all. 'Religious truth is attainable, if at all, only by the methods of science.'[20]

That was not obvious to the simple believer. Kate Jarvis (who left the Wesleyan Elementary School when she was fourteen and became nurse to the children of the wealthy) never missed a Sunday service. She recorded in her diary each chapel she attended – Englefield Green Wesleyan Chapel with Lady Southampton's maid, Lochpilghead Chapel, the Wesleyan Chapel at Cowes and the Marlborough Road Chapel harvest festival.[21] To her and people like her, much of what 'modernism' stood for was pure blasphemy. Canon T. K. Cheyne, Oriel Professor of Exegesis at Oxford, may have expressed himself in scholarly language, but to Kate Jarvis and her kind, his views were only heresy.

> As the critical enquiry stands at present one may reasonably hold that one extraordinary teacher and healer called Jesus incurred the displeasure of the Roman authorities and suffered the

extreme penalty as a rebellious and unrecognised 'King of the Jews'. But is it not possible that the statements of the Messianic claims of Jesus, and consequently also the intervention of the procurator, may be imaginary?[22]

One challenge to both the authority of the Bible and the divinity of Christ followed another. Three months later Cheyne wrote

It is to me much more than merely possible that Jesus of Nazareth was not betrayed by, or surrendered to, the Jewish authorities, whether by Judas or by anyone else. The Twelve Apostles are to me (and I should think to many critics) as unhistoric as the Seventy Disciples.[23]

The Church of England could tolerate the questioning of its basic beliefs as long as the questions were asked by scholars. But once the same doubts were expressed by the humble clergy – men who supposedly earned their pittance by proclaiming the Word of God which the modernists challenged – punitive action was unavoidable. The Reverend C. E. Beeby, Vicar of Yardley Wood, Birmingham, gave his greatest service to the Church by offering himself as a candidate for ritual sacrifice. Mr Beeby claimed publicly that he was both morally and legally entitled to proclaim his scepticism about the Virgin Birth and the miracles, yet still retain his living.

Perhaps Beeby thought he would enjoy the support of his bishop, Charles Gore. If so, Beeby was badly mistaken. The Bishop of Worcester, as Gore then had become, had been ranked among the Modernists who doubted the divine inspiration of the Old Testament and suggested that Jesus had endorsed its more dubious claims because of human fallibility. But Gore had begun to believe that Modernism led to secularism and that secularism was only one step away from atheism. The bishop agonised about how he should deal with his turbulent priest.

The article was not the first example of Mr Beeby's apostasy. He had written and published a whole book to support the view that revelation did not require the support of miracles. That, ecclesiastical lawyers told Bishop Gore, provided much clearer grounds for action than the article. But the book had been written before Gore became bishop. Gore therefore felt himself excluded from action on the evidence of its contents. So began a long and desperate correspondence between Beeby and his bishop. It was followed by a painful interview. It left Gore still uncertain how to proceed. Fortunately Beeby, being a gentleman, decided to end his bishop's torment and resigned.

Bishop Gore was not satisfied with a local victory. He wrote to Randall Davidson, the Archbishop of Canterbury, with all the zeal of a convert from Modernism. 'Can we not in Convocation do something to reassure a great number of people that the Bishops would not connive at men being ordained who did not believe in the Articles of the Creed, particularly the Virgin Birth?' Davidson was doubtful. His worldly instincts told him that such a declaration would do more harm than good. But Convocation was with Gore and insisted that, as an absolute minimum, the two archbishops should write a pastoral letter setting out the inviolability of the Scriptures. Randall Davidson prevaricated and procrastinated. Before the letter was drafted, Armitage Robinson, the Dean of Westminster, published a scholarly examination of incarnation which made it impossible for the statement of traditional theology to be issued, since it would have been seen as a reproof to one of the Church of England's most distinguished priests. Robinson's preface insisted that 'to say that the historical fact of the Virgin Birth is a cardinal doctrine of faith is to use language which no Synod of Bishops, so far as I am aware, has ever ventured to use. It is to confuse the incarnation with a special mode of incarnation in a way for which Christian theology offers no precedent.'[24]

It was not only in England that Modernism was on the march. In Alsace, Albert Schweitzer published *The Quest of the Historical Jesus*. Its opening chapter warned, 'We must be prepared to find that the historical knowledge of the personality and life of Jesus will not be a help, but perhaps even an offence to religion.' The book was, at first, sentimentally described as emphasising the humanity of Jesus. In fact it made him out to be a fanatic who misunderstood his mission and his destiny. Modernism was spreading to all the denominations of the Christian Church. At the London City Temple, R. J. Campbell was preaching what he called the 'New Theology', defined by a critic as 'adapting the Christian message to the minds of the generation which had elected the Parliament of 1906–10'.[25] Only the Roman Catholic Church chose to act rather than attempt to accommodate. The Papal Encyclical *Pascendi* required all priests to swear an oath that they forswore Modernism in all its forms.

In the Protestant churches the argument went on. In fact, it is going on still. But, as the century progressed, it became more and more about what was right and true and less and less about what was necessary to keep the faith alive. In the 1907 Braunton Lecture, Canon H. J. F. Piele admitted defeat: 'The hope and purpose of Liberal Theology have been, and are more than ever today, to make Christianity a possible religion for the thinking man of the world. But in its further purpose of facilitating the wider acceptance of Christianity, it has largely and unexpectedly failed.'

A year later the Church of England performed what it hoped was the last rites over the still twitching corpse of the Modernism controversy. The ceremony was typically low-key. The Lambeth Conference reaffirmed the 'central importance of both the Apostles' and Nicene Creeds'. The implications of that commitment were not discussed.

To the Edwardian Catholics, the failure of Modernism to reinvigorate the Anglican Communion was not at all unexpected. They believed that compromise was death. G. K. Chesterton sought to gain recruits for Rome by exciting wonderment at the external mysteries which they thought essential to faith. In *Orthodoxy*, Chesterton argued for the whole-hogging sort of Christianity which became his trademark, with images that were more vivid than apt.

It is true that the historic Church has at once emphasised celibacy and emphasised the family, has at once (if I may put it so) been fiercely for having children and for not having children. It has kept them side by side like two strong colours, red and white like the red and white on the shield of Saint George. It has always had a healthy hatred of pink. It hates the combination of two colours which is the feeble expedient of philosophers.[26]

The Anglo-Catholics took a similar (if more cerebral) view of the Church of England's need to eschew theological compromise if it

hoped to prosper. The antagonism of the Modernisers was only to be
expected. But the Anglo-Catholics were unpopular throughout the
broad Church because of what was regarded as their pagan enthusiasm
for ritual. High Churchmen believed implicitly in weekly (and in
some cases daily) Communion, facing eastward while conducting services and decorating their altars with candles and crucifixes. Reserved
Sacrament in their churches proclaimed 'The Real Presence' of the
living Christ. Most offensive of all, they sought to 'enrich' the prayer
book with additions from the Catholic mass. The Protestant objection
to Anglo-Catholicism is often summed up in the single word 'vestments'. But the complaints against Anglo-Catholics were much more
comprehensive and fundamental than dislike of the green and gold
chasuble which their priests wore during the Eucharist. In 1904,
Percy Dearmer and W. H. Frere published the *English Liturgy*, an
attempt to demonstrate that the 'enrichment' was not an affront to the
Anglican Communion. The book was not accepted by devotees of
the Thirty-Nine Articles as proof that Catholics and Protestants could
share a common form of worship.

It was the duty of the Church of England bishops to protect their
flocks from Popish practices. But there was widespread feeling
amongst the more robust Protestants that, either out of sloth or a feeling of personal sympathy, the bishops were failing in their episcopal
duty. So they took matters into their own hands. The Church
Association began legal action in the Civil and Consistory Courts.
The Manchester Protestant Thousand, and other bands of hooligans,
broke up services which they believed to be conducted by clergymen
of High Church disposition. John Kensit and his Wycliffe Preachers
visited churches in which they believed 'illegality and idolatry were
practised . . . entered a protest' and, after being careful to 'leave the
building before Holy Communion', wrote to the appropriate bishop
to demand that he 'stopped all Romanising practices' in his diocese.[27]

Within days of his enthronement, Randall Davidson had received
urgent pleas to take immediate action against the rise of secularism in
the Church. Before he had had time to decide how to react, he was
presented with the demand that he protect the Prayer Book by stamp-
ing out ritualism. The concern about 'Popish practices' had spread to
the House of Commons, whose Members could claim to be the legal

guardians of the *Book of Common Prayer*. To prove that the whole nation felt alarmed about Papal effrontery, *Punch* began to lampoon both sides in the dispute, and a number of second-rate novelists wrote satires on the subject.★ The crisis had escalated because the Anglo-Catholics had reacted as men and women under threat often do. They had grown more militant. The English Church Union had been formed and the *Church Times* founded to propagate their cause. And they gloried in their apostasy. 'In going beyond what the prayer book allows, we get the results the prayer book intended.'[28]

Davidson's first public meeting after he became Archbishop in 1903 was with a hundred enraged Unionist MPs.[29] He procrastinated again, hoping that time would heal the House of Commons' pride, wounded by the two years' argument about the Prayer Book being conducted without their involvement. Quite the opposite happened. In early 1904, the Reverend Mr Bowden wrote a violently anti-Anglo-Catholic pamphlet and sent a copy to every Member of Parliament. The result was an almost immediate demand for a Select Committee to examine the degree to which the Church of England was failing to observe the form of service set out in the Prayer Book.

Davidson, all urbanity put aside, simply refused to accept a parliamentary enquiry. Because of the religious affiliations of MPs, a Committee of the House of Commons could come to only one conclusion – an outright condemnation of Anglo-Catholics and their High Church habits. That, he feared, might well lead to the schism which all Archbishops of Canterbury believe they have an overriding duty to avoid. Lord Halifax, the most patrician of High Churchmen, regarded the proposal as a 'gross impertinence'.[30] Anglicans of every sort, including some who were active in their opposition to 'vestments', were so offended by the proposal that Davidson thought it right to warn the government that, were a Select Committee Inquiry imposed upon the Church, the result might be immediate and irresistible demands for disestablishment. He suggested a Royal Commission as an alternative. Balfour, at first, could not agree. Indeed he was so

---

★Chief amongst them were Shawn Leslie, *The Anglo Catholic*, and E. P. McKenzie, *The Altar Steps*.

irritated by the suggestion that he reacted with uncharacteristic emotion. 'It is now clear to me that all the clergy, of whatever school, are equally stupid. I had thought the range of stupidity more limited. I cannot appoint a Royal Commission. It would not satisfy the House of Commons. They would vote against me if I urged it.'[31]

Davidson would not budge. The House of Commons, whatever its formal powers, could not sit in judgement on the Church of England. So Balfour, unwilling to challenge the Church and unable to brush the Protestant complaints aside, followed the stupid course and set up a Royal Commission on Ecclesiastical Discipline under the chairmanship of Michael Hicks Beach. The House of Commons complained, but did not rebel.

The Royal Commission met 118 times. Most of the sessions were taken up with representations from the two extremes. The Protestants (prompted by Mr Bowden of leaflet fame) produced witnesses who reported churches where incense was burned and priests wore vestments. The High Churchmen, led with great dignity by Lord Halifax, brought examples of services during which the Athanasian Creed had not been said and clergymen who did not dress appropriately for Communion. They added that were they, or any of their kind, censured for their conduct, they would refuse to appear before the Judicial Committee of the Privy Council whose jurisdiction over the Church they did not accept. The Royal Commission effectively endorsed their rebellion. 'A court dealing with matters of conscience and religion must above all others rest on the moral authority if its judgements are to be effective. As thousands of clergy with strong lay support refuse to recognise the jurisdiction of the Judicial Committee, its judgements cannot practically be enforced.'

The Commission did, however, believe that some liturgical practices might be unacceptable even in a broad Church. They should be dealt with by ecclesiastical courts rather than secular authorities. It also suggested the procedures by which the Prayer Book should be revised if revision was thought necessary. The Upper House of Convocation responded to the report by setting up a sub-committee which in 1908 produced a Historic Report on Ornaments. The whole process stimulated much discussion but no change in practice.

But on one subject the whole Church of England displayed

something approaching unity. 'There were very few Church leaders who did not adopt attitudes critical of industrial organisation and social order.'[32] That critical spirit was encouraged by the Christian Social Union, founded by the early (and eventually reluctant) Modernists Henry Scott Holland and Charles Gore, and the Church Socialist League, which was formed in 1906, the year of the general election which returned fifty-three Labour Members of Parliament to the House of Commons. Critics of the (often High Church) clergy who held radical views argued that they failed to attract working-class support and that they represented essentially Fabian, middle-class values.[33]

But 'it was unusual, after 1900, to find a bishop who did not regard the declaration of social principle as a primary duty'.[34] The emphasis on social policy had an inevitable influence on both dogma and Church membership. Despite the support of some Anglo-Catholics, 'The drift . . . towards a non-dogmatic affirmation of general kindness and good fellowship, with an emphasis rather on service of men than the fulfilment of the will of God'[35] had its effect on the arguments about faith which had disturbed the Church of England at the beginning of the century. It affected men on both sides of the dispute. No social con-science was more developed than that of Charles Gore – critic of the Boer War, supporter of female emancipation, advocate of equality and friend of T. H. Green, the only genuine philosopher English social democracy has ever possessed – but he was also the man who was accused of 'worrying' the Reverend Beeby out of his living. The man who made that accusation was Hastings Rashid, effectively the leader of the 'modernisers', supporter of all the social causes which Gore endorsed and member of the Christian Social Union which Gore had founded. The Church of England builds its unity on contradictions.*

The Nonconformists had emphasised the Christian duty to the poor throughout the nineteenth century; in Edwardian England, the nature of their commitment became more overtly political. At the

---

*A further example of the paradoxes on which the Church of England thrives was the part that Gore played in founding the Community of the Resurrection at Mirfield. The 'moderniser' was the first monk to become an Anglican bishop since the Reformation.

London Temple, J. R. Campbell told his Baptist flock, 'Go with Keir Hardie to the House of Commons and listen to him pleading for justice ... and you see the Atonement.'[36] The Methodists had always believed that 'whole Christians', who lived like Christ, performed 'good works', but their definition of that duty changed. Because they attracted most of their support from the working class, they developed close connections with the Independent Labour Party and the 'new trade unionism' of unskilled men. As a result they began to emphasise the importance of campaigning against social evils rather than performing works of individual charity. Instead of appealing for personal improvement, they argued for legislation which prohibited or limited practices of which they disapproved – drinking, gambling, prostitution and profaning the Sabbath.[37] The campaigns 'secularised' the chapels. Instead of praying for the Holy Spirit to purify and save, they called on Parliament to impose the rules which Christians should obey.

Methodists, who believed that only faith saved, regarded good works as the result of redemption rather than a guarantee of its achievement. The Salvation Army, the stepchild of Methodism, had little time to spend on theological speculation. But, at the turn of the century, William Booth, its nineteenth-century founder, began to wonder if his campaigns against poverty and prostitution had become ends in themselves rather than a reflection of the love of God. So in 1904 he set out on an evangelical tour of Britain, travelling in a white, open-topped motor with distinctive red wheels. By then General Booth, if not the great movement he led, had become almost respectable. In June 1904 he was given audience by Edward VII, to whom he reacted with surprising sycophancy: 'I had come to expect a selfish, sensuous personage, popular because of lending himself to recreations etc. – showy functions – unwilling to pose as treading in the shoes of Albert the Good. All at once the embodiment of a simple genial English gentleman was sprung upon me.'[38]

After a wrangle with the Earl Marshal, and the postponement which followed the King's appendicectomy, Bramwell Booth (the General's son) was allowed to attend the Coronation in his Salvation Army uniform. Bramwell was so impressed by the ceremony that he wondered if 'the Church of England had taken some lessons from the Salvation Army while hesitating to acknowledge it'. Perhaps he was unreasonably influenced by the creation of the Church Army twenty years earlier – undoubtedly a belated imitation of General Booth's righteous regiments. By the time of the Coronation the Church Army had decided to concentrate on gaols and beaches. Twenty-four of the forty-six British prisons had Church Army 'labour homes' close by to welcome released men back into society. And in the summer, there were few holiday resorts which did not echo to the Church Army's hymns.

The streets still belonged to the Salvation Army. The hopes of *In Darkest England* were dashed in Edwardian England. That plan for ending unemployment had required the creation of 'work colonies' in the dominions and – despite a meeting with Cecil Rhodes (persuaded by Booth to kneel in prayer in a railway carriage) and long conversations with David Lloyd George (the Chancellor of the Exchequer) and A. J. Balfour (the leader of the Opposition) – the South Africa Company could not find the requested £150,000 and the government would only pay a 'matching amount' of the investment which came from private sources. The Bible was vindicated on its insistence that the 'poor are always with us' and the Salvation Army, despite its General's newly found pretensions, showed a devotion to them which could not be matched by any other Christian denomination. When General William Booth died on 12 October 1912, the people remembered not the pomp of his final years but the life of service which had preceded them. Sixty-five thousand mourners, many of them the poor whose lives the Army had sought to improve, filed by the coffin to pay their respects. Five thousand Salvationists marched behind the hearse which bore the General's body to the cemetery. There were rumours, in the East End of London, that Queen Alexandra, hidden behind a widow's veil, had marched with them. It was not true. But the myth illustrated why Modernism failed to capture the Edwardian Churches. The people still wanted romance, not reason.

CHAPTER 18

Hardihood, Endurance and Courage

In the early years of the twentieth century, national admiration for 'hardihood, endurance and courage' – the qualities which Captain Scott attributed to the men who died with him in Antarctica in 1912 – was as great as at any time in British history. But another dimension was added to the popular definition of glory. The last line of Lord Tennyson's *Ulysses*, chosen as the epitaph on the cross which marks Scott's icy grave, celebrated the heroism of failure: 'To strive, to seek, to find, and not to yield.'

The two authentic heroes of Edwardian England both failed – Scott to be first at the Pole and Shackleton to reach it at all. Other explorers reached their destinations and achieved their goals. But it was Robert Falcon Scott and Ernest Shackleton who caught the public imagination and inspired a generation of schoolboys to struggle on against adversity. Both of them became quintessentially British heroes – even though their heroism was not displayed in those parts of the world which Britain had previously regarded as the proper field for gallantry and daring.

Africa had been the Victorian's continent. Britain had led 'the scramble' for that dark continent and taken both flag and Bible into its very heart. Burton, Speke and Livingstone had found the true source of the Nile. Further south, Rhodes had exploited the gold and diamond mines and dreamed of a continent, British 'from the Cape to

Cairo'. Other European countries had intruded in areas which Britain had thought not worth colonisation. But Africa was essentially 'ours'. And by 1900 there was nothing much left to explore.

Britain was late in realising the potential of the Pole. When in March 1901 the *Sphere*, an illustrated London weekly, wrote, with evident surprise, 'There is a perfect run on Antarctica', it was the Scandinavians – Nansen and Amundsen – who led the field. Allowing them to win an uncontested race would have been out of keeping with the British character. In those days it was thought that there would be very little to gain, in terms of trade or strategic influence, from planting the Union Flag in the ice and snow, but suddenly prestige was at stake. The South Pole provided another opportunity to demonstrate the indomitability that had made Britain win so many races after giving other nations a head start. In order to raise the essential funds it was necessary to present an expedition as a scientific exploration. But its real objective – and the motivation which caught the imagination of press and people – was to be first at the South Pole.

Although the British public did not know it – or knew and thought it barely worth their notice – there was a British explorer of equal resolution and greater achievement on whom their adoration could have been lavished. Marc Auriel Stein had published his *Chronicles of the Kings of Kashmir* at the turn of the century. He was taking part in his first expedition to Chinese Turkestan when Edward was crowned and had, during his travels, already both excavated the sites of those ancient civilisations and surveyed the head waters of the Khotan River as part of the Indian Trigonometrical Survey. Neither archaeology nor topography excited the British imagination, and Stein was a Jew who had been born in Budapest. So his achievements were not thought of as 'quite British'. His expedition along the 'Silk Road' (in 1904) was two years of assiduous scholarship conducted in conditions which tested both stamina and courage, but it attracted little attention except from the Trustees of the British Museum who were the beneficiaries of his unremitting dedication to the mysteries of Buddhist civilisation.

The Edwardians had no need for complicated heroes like Stein. For in Scott and Shackleton Britain had two perfect examples of the 'right stuff'. Their appearance was as appropriate to their role as their character. They were not only brave, bold and resolute but also possessed a stubborn streak which hovered attractively between independence and insubordination. Most important of all, they had no doubt about the task to which fate had called them. And they proceeded to fulfil it in a particularly British way. Both possessed a tender affection for animals. Stein's place in the pantheon of popular appeal might have been far different had it been known at the time of his exploration that he took his fox terrier with him into Central Asia. Stein was not the material of which legends were made, Scott was.

Sir Clements Markham, for twenty years the secretary of the Royal Geographical Society, had always hoped that, were he to become president, 'the equipment and despatch of an Antarctic expedition should be the chief feature of his term of office'.[1] When that happy day arrived, he claimed that the man whom he invited to lead it had been in his mind as the ideal choice for ten years or more. The young midshipman – whose captaincy of the winning crew in a West Indian boat race had so impressed Markham – was Robert Falcon Scott.

That story is inconsistent with Scott's own account of a chance meeting in Buckingham Palace Road during June 1899. 'It was on that afternoon that I learned for the first time that there was such a thing as a prospective Antarctic Expedition. Two days later, I wrote applying to command it.'[2] We know that in 1900 Scott was not Markham's first choice for the job. The President of the Royal Geographical Society wanted George Egerton, captain of HMS *Majestic*, the flagship of the Channel Squadron. Egerton was fifty-six and, on reflection, regarded himself as too old to stand the Antarctic winter. So, at least by Markham's account of what followed, he asked Egerton's opinion of Scott, the *Majestic*'s torpedo officer. The response was not so much a reference as an encomium. 'He is just the fellow for it, strong, steady, gentle, scientific, a very good head on his shoulders, a very good naval officer.'[3]

Whichever version of Markham's headhunting is correct, Scott was very lucky to receive the appointment. The government refused to fund the Royal Geographical Society's scheme, and business (doubting if the expedition would produce many commercial opportunities) was equally unhelpful. The Royal Society was asked to add the prestige of its ancient name to the project and a joint steering committee was set up to promote and manage the whole enterprise on the strict understanding that the purpose of the expedition should be purely scientific. Once that was agreed, the Royal Society argued that the leader should be a scientist, not a sailor. A resolution to that effect was narrowly defeated at a meeting of the steering committee only because Royal Society members were absent.

Scott did not receive an official letter of appointment until June 1900, twelve months after the supposed meeting in Buckingham Palace Road. During the intervening year, another attempt had been made to put a scientist in overall command. Scott, who had, no doubt, been told by Markham about the continuing controversy, replied to the eventual offer with what amounted to six stipulations. His letter began, 'I must have complete command of the ship and shore parties. There cannot be two heads.'[4]

Markham, who had probably drafted Scott's demands, accepted them in every detail and preparations for the great adventure began. The two men visited Dundee where the keel to the expedition ship, the *Discovery*, was being laid. The hull had been designed to withstand the pressure of the Antarctic pack ice, but because of the intended research into the Pole's magnetic field, it was to be made almost entirely of wood. That specification confirmed Markham's promise that the expedition's purpose was not 'to make a dash for the South Pole' but to complete a 'systematic exploration of the whole region'. On 31 July 1901, the *Discovery* left Dundee. On its way south it called at Cowes, where King Edward interrupted his duties at the Royal Regatta to present Scott with the Royal Victorian Order (Second Class).

The journey to the Antarctic Circle typified, in microcosm, the pattern of each of the four Edwardian polar expeditions. The men's behaviour exceeded the call of duty, but the success of the operation was imperilled by mistakes which could have been avoided. The *Discovery* leaked so badly that the sailors talked of 'Dundee hull', a criticism of the design, the workmanship and the reliance on wood. Seawater was taken in from a different point every day, ruining stores and equipment. The constant need to man the pumps was accepted with fortitude by a crew in which the mixture of Royal Navy and merchant service worked with greater harmony than the pessimists had expected. The high spirits of the third lieutenant responsible for 'holds, stores, provisions and deep water analysis' made a special

contribution to the maintenance of high morale. His name was Ernest
Shackleton. Shackleton's formal application to join the expedition,
made while he was serving with the Union Castle Line, had been
rejected, but he had met the son of one of Markham's few commercial sponsors and persuaded him to intercede with the *Discovery*'s First
Lieutenant. His boundless enthusiasm won him a place on board.

So the two great polar explorers of Edwardian Britain set sail together
on the first of the four Edwardian Antarctic Expeditions. The two men
were similar in temperament – determined, self-confident and resourceful – but came from widely different circumstances. Scott, although a
proud Royal Navy officer, was humiliatingly poor. Shackleton, despite
serving in the merchant marine, was the son of an Irish landowner who
could afford, in early middle age, to move to London and study medicine and, at the same time, send his son to Dulwich College.* Both
men were dedicated to ships and the sea, though Shackleton exhibited
a more ebullient affection than the reticent Scott would allow himself to
reveal. Shackleton convinced his biographer that 'he went off one fine
day and shipped on a sailing vessel at a shilling a month'.[6] Scott was
temperamentally incapable of such braggadocio. Yet, both extravert
and introvert possessed what are commonly regarded as the essential features of leadership – including an unshakeable belief in duty and
destiny – qualities more suited to a 'dash to the south pole' than to 'a
general exploration of the whole region'.

The *Discovery* crossed the Antarctic Circle on 3 January 1902, sailed
south along the eastern shore of Victoria Land and, after a brief landing at Cape Crozier, arrived at McMurdo Sound where Scott had
decided – without either consulting or telling his officers – to spend
the summer and test both his men and their equipment. The exercises
were planned to end with four officers – including Shackleton and
Edward Wilson, the second medical officer – and eight men taking
four sledges on to the great ice Barrier† under the supervision of

---

*Shackleton's pride took a different form. After his first expedition he applied for
a Royal Naval Commission but was turned down. An offer to promote him to
lieutenant in the reserve was contingent on his passing a drill examination. He
declined, without thanks, but continued to call himself Lieutenant.[5]
†Now called the Ross Ice Shelf.

Scott himself. The captain injured his leg in a skiing accident and Charles Royds, First Lieutenant of the *Discovery*, took command. On 4 March 1902 they set out for what was to be a characteristic Antarctic disaster.

Everything went wrong. The dogs fought each other and then went lame. The stores had been badly packed and burst open, and therefore strange mixtures of food had to be heated and eaten together. A typical meal was a conglomeration of tinned peas, chocolate and cheese. On the second day, wading through snow which was far thicker than they had anticipated, they advanced only five miles. On the fourth, Royds, realising that a rapid advance was beyond some of his companions' capabilities, sent most of the party back to the ship while he, with the two strongest men, pressed on. After another five days, they reached the edge of the Barrier, then, with only five days' rations left, turned for home to retrace the steps of a journey which had taken them nine days to complete.

Their miscalculation was to be repeated by every British Antarctic expedition. The absolute necessity of limiting the weight of their loads required them to carry just enough food to see them through their estimated journey time. Then, because the going was more difficult than they had anticipated, they fell behind their own schedule. As a result, they were left to choose between turning back or facing the Antarctic terrain (and summer temperatures of fifty degrees of frost) on half the rations which had been judged essential to their survival. They usually battled on. Not surprisingly, they did not always survive.

Royds was lucky. He completed the return journey to the ship without accident or injury. The men who (for their own safety) had returned earlier did not fare so well. They were within four miles of safety when visibility suddenly sank to zero. Instead of waiting for the snow cloud to pass, they decided – not least because they could make neither hot food nor drink – to press on. Although they did not know it, they were on a ledge halfway up a steep, ice-covered slope, yards away from a cliff edge, high above the half frozen sea. Three men lost their footing and plunged down the slope but were miraculously caught in patches of soft snow. Two stumbled over the cliff edge. The survivors struggled back to the ship.

The search then began for the two lost men. Shackleton was sent in the *Discovery*'s whaler to the bottom of the cliff – 'the worst part of it', according to Edward Wilson. 'There was a rough sea and the drift was racing down the slopes and burying the boats in frozen spray.'[7] Wilson himself took a sledge party north. Neither of the missing men was found. Almost four days later, one of them walked into camp. He had been trapped in a snowdrift and had slept, for most of the time, in the torpor that snow makes irresistible.

The expedition settled in the ship for the winter, amusing its members with entertainments which ranged from amateur theatricals to the publication of the *South Polar Times*, edited on board by Ernest Shackleton. Then, on 2 November 1902, Scott, Wilson and Shackleton set out south. There was no doubt about their intention. Wilson recorded in his diary, 'Our object is to get as far south in a straight line on the Barrier as we can, reach the Pole if possible, or find some new land.'[8] As part of his preparations for the 'walk into the absolute unknown'[9] he wrote a farewell letter to his fiancée, beginning (as such letters always do) with the hope that she would never read it.

On 25 November the three men reached the 80th parallel – beyond which there were no maps. Once again, because they had advanced more slowly than they had anticipated, the food began to run out. The weaker dogs were shot and fed to the stronger animals. Wilson was struck down with snow blindness which he attempted, unsuccessfully, to conceal. At latitude 82° 17' south and still 480 miles from the Pole, they turned back. They had travelled 300 miles further south than any other explorer and retained enough energy to make occasional diversions from the homeward route to collect geological samples. The dogs died, or were shot, one by one. The few that survived were allowed to follow the sledges while the men pulled. 'No more clearing of tangled traces, no more dismal stoppages, and no more whip', wrote Scott.[10] Then Shackleton became short of breath and began to spit blood – certain symptoms of scurvy. All unnecessary equipment was jettisoned and Scott and Wilson pulled the last sledge home with Shackleton stumbling by their side. 'As near spent as three persons can be',[11] on 3 February 1903 they were reunited with their comrades. They had covered 900 miles in ninety-three days and completed the first glorious failure of Edwardian exploration.

The *Morning*, an old Scandinavian whaler which Markham had bought to act as relief ship, had arrived in McMurdo Sound a week earlier. Scott still had work to do before he could return, but Shackleton was adjudged too sick to remain in the Antarctic. Much against his will, he returned to Britain on board the relief ship. Seven ratings from the *Discovery*, who had chosen not to sign on for the homeward journey, travelled with him. Typically, Scott insisted that he had always intended to dismiss them. According to rumour, he had intended to do the same with Shackleton but had offered him the choice of sailing north 'sick or in disgrace'.[12]

There were two conflicting explanations of Scott's dissatisfaction with his third lieutenant. One was a childish argument in which both men called each other bloody fools.[13] The other was Scott's belief – apparently confirmed by implication during a lecture Scott gave in London – that Shackleton had behaved less than heroically during the return journey in 1903. Scott wrote to the *Daily Mail* to correct what he claimed to be a false impression. 'Mr Shackleton . . . displayed the most extraordinary pluck and endurance.'[14] But the damage had been done. The two men's undoubted rivalry in the race for the Pole was assumed to be inflamed by personal antagonism.

There is no doubt that Scott came to resent Shackleton's intrusion into what he regarded as his own territory. During his last, fatal expedition he made constant denigratory references to Shackleton's account of his polar journeys, *The Heart of Antarctic*.[15] Shackleton, for his part, saw his rivalry with Scott in such bitter terms that when he got home he was prepared to encourage a young Norwegian to make a dash which might have beaten both of them to the Pole. Better anyone than Scott.[16]

It was not only the rumour of dissent which added the excitement of controversy to Scott's polar ambitions. He took so long to prepare for his journey north and home that the *Discovery* was iced in before he was ready to set sail. So, despite attempts to blast a way out of McMurdo Sound, he was forced to remain in Antarctica another full winter. The sponsor suspected that he had planned his entrapment because he wanted to remain south for longer than his contract allowed and accused him of disobeying orders. Thereafter Captain Scott was known as a 'difficult officer'.

Colonel Sir Francis Younghusband was a *Boys' Own Paper* hero. Although a scholar, he was also a man of action. When his friend George Nathaniel Curzon (then the Viceroy of India) asked him to lead an expedition to the Forbidden City of Lhasa, he saw his mission as part of 'the Great Game' of keeping Russia and Russian influence out of India. His formal task was to persuade the Dalai Lama to respect the commercial treaty which united India and Tibet. And at first he did no more than carry out his orders. Accompanied by an escort of Sikh riflemen he advanced across the border which divided India from Tibet, in the northern summer of 1903, camped at Khamba Jong and made clear that unless the Dalai Lama fulfilled the obligations of his treaty with Queen Victoria, he would advance on the Forbidden City of Lhasa.

The treaty in question had been signed by China and the government of India but – then, as now – Tibet was under Chinese rule and it was the Imperial Parliament which had promoted the initiative which it hoped would make the Dalai Lama look to Britain rather than to Russia. Lord Curzon's letters expressing disquiet that the Treaty was being flouted had been returned from Lhasa unopened – convincing the always suspicious Viceroy that the Dalai Lama was in league with the Czar. The Russians assured the British Foreign Secretary that they had no territorial ambitions or acquisitive intentions, but Younghusband's expedition continued on its way to Khamba Jong in the belief that at least it would induce the Tibetans to prove their good intentions by increasing trade on terms favourable to India. The Dalai Lama procrastinated and equivocated. London, anxious to avoid a confrontation, persuaded Curzon to recall Younghusband to India.

The new Secretary of State for India, St John Brodrick, was opposed to 'permanent entanglements' in Tibet, but Curzon was determined to settle the issue in India's favour once and for all. When trade did not improve as the Treaty required and the Dalai Lama had promised, he persuaded London to approve the despatch of a second and overtly punitive expedition. 'The advance', Brodrick told Curzon, 'should be made for the sole purpose of obtaining satisfaction and as soon as reparations are obtained, a withdrawal should be effected.'[17] Neither the Viceroy nor Younghusband accepted

Brodrick's view. Nor did they agree with each other. Curzon wanted guarantees of improved trade and the assurances that future Russian overtures would be rejected. Younghusband hoped to free the Tibetans – 'slaves in the power of ignorant and selfish monks'.[18]

Younghusband was by nature a man of independent action. Twice in the 1880s he had crossed Central Asia, travelling from Peking to India through the unexplored Mustagh Pass and, in the process, proving that the Karakoram Mountains were the watershed between India and Turkestan. At the end of the century he had explored and charted the Pamir mountain range. He was not the ideal leader of a trade delegation – even one which proposed to do business by force of arms.

In December 1904, Younghusband – accompanied by 2,000 troops, mostly Gurkhas under the command of Brigadier MacDonald – marched north, intending to make their first camp at Gyantse. They were slowed down by the bitter winter temperatures and disconcerted by the large number of Tibetans who followed them, apparently out of curiosity rather than any hope of halting or delaying the column's progress. At one point, Younghusband became so frustrated by their silent presence that he rode out alone to confront the monks who were in command of the accompanying Tibetans. They would only discuss dates for the expedition's withdrawal.

In March the expedition met passive resistance. The huge mob of Tibetans who blocked Younghusband's path showed no sign of flight, but MacDonald thought that they should be disarmed. In the scuffles which followed, a Sikh was shot. It was then that the Gurkhas opened fire. Hundreds of Tibetans were slaughtered.

Younghusband reached Gyantse in April. That was as far as his orders took him, but he believed that the situation had changed and, in the absence of new instructions, decided to press on to Lhasa. By 3 August 1905, it was a city forbidden to Westerners no more. Assurances about future trade and friendship with Britain were offered and accepted. It sounded like a triumph for active imperialism, but the Westminster government – having, by then, heard about the Tibetan deaths – lost its nerve and Brodrick publicly expressed his disapproval. The King persisted in regarding Younghusband as a hero and insisted that he become a Knight Commander of the Indian Empire.

When, in the winter of 1903, it became clear that Younghusband would lead a second expedition to Tibet, Marc Auriel Stein – who was waiting to take up his appointment as both Inspector General of Education and Superintendent of Archaeology in Baluchistan and the North West Frontier Province of India – decided that he must become a part of it. He had no interest in trade or the 'Great Game'. He simply wanted to see the Forbidden City. It remained forbidden to him. When he asked that his future employers should suggest his name to the Viceroy, his request was rejected out of hand. 'It would obviously be inconsistent and illogical for Colonel Dean (the Chief Commissioner for the two provinces) to recommend an officer, whose services he has so recently approved, to be sent away indefinitely to work away outside the Province before that officer had even joined his appointment in the Province.'[19] Stein took up his appointment in early 1904. It did not satisfy him for long. In October 1905, he left for Kashmir to prepare for a second expedition to Chinese Turkestan.

Stein's plan was to travel through the Hindu Kush along what was called the Wakham Corridor, but the British agent for the area insisted that that part of the route – the Lowerai Pass – was too dangerous to travel until the summer. When rebuffed, Stein always applied for help to higher authority. Permission was readily granted and he set out on 19 April 1906.

Snow still covered the Lowerai. All that was possible had to be done to prevent weight and vibration causing the snow to slip away beneath their feet. No carrier was allowed a load of more than forty pounds, and fifteen-minute intervals separated the twelve detachments into which the expedition was divided. The pass was negotiated without incident and Stein believed that he would achieve the object of his early start – a guarantee that neither the Germans nor the French would make the first surveys of Chinese Turkestan. The Congress of Orientalists had divided the region between the Great Powers' archaeologists, but the boundaries had not been drawn with any great precision and Stein knew that he was in a race. The first expedition to cross the Lop Desert would win the treasure and the glory.

The journey took seven days. Stein made his first finds at Lou Lan – wooden tablets which confirmed the survival of the Indian Kharotshi language long after the Chinese sixth-century invasion, and a scrap of paper which was inscribed with the first example of the lost Sogdian language that a Westerner had ever seen. At Miran he discovered mounds which were the earth-covered remains of Buddhist shrines that predated the Tibetan invasion. Excavations revealed the remains of painted frescoes. Stein carefully detached them from what was left of the shrines, packed them on his camels and moved on. On 12 March 1907 he reached the Tun-huang oasis. Twelve miles southeast lay the Cave of a Thousand Buddhas.

The annual pilgrimage to the shrines began two days after Stein's arrival and, anxious not to offend local opinion, the expedition held back until the rituals had been completed. It proved to be a shrewd tactic, for it enabled Stein to strike up a friendship with Wang, the shrine's guardian. Wang was persuaded by a combination of flattery and bribery first to show the expedition a selection of ancient manuscripts and then to allow Stein to enter the inner sanctum. It was filled with Chinese Buddhist manuscripts of the fifth century.

Stein gave Wang enough Chinese silver ingots to renovate the disintegrating shrine – 'a sum which would make our friends at the British Museum chuckle'.[20] In return the custodian agreed to the removal of the manuscript rolls as long as their illegal sale was kept secret until Stein's expedition had left Chinese territory. The rolls filled seven packing cases. Another five cases were packed with paintings and embroidery. Stein felt no need to justify the looting of Chinese national treasures. His justification was that they had been 'locked in a dismal prison' until he had liberated them.

Neither Stein nor his treasure arrived back in Kashmir until October 1908. During the return journey, he crossed the Taklamakan Desert from north to south, surveyed the Nan Shan Mountains and traced the Khotan River to its source. The price he paid for his achievement was frostbite and the amputation of his left foot. The reward, received almost four years after the booty had been classified and deposited in the British Museum, was a knighthood. But the real prize was already won. In 1904 Marc Stein had become a subject of King Edward VII by naturalisation.

It took Ernest Shackleton almost four months to travel from the *Discovery* in McMurdo Sound to England and far longer to find suitable employment. In December 1903 he was appointed Secretary/Treasurer of the Scottish Geographical Society. He interrupted his work to get married, to greet the arrival of Scott and the *Discovery* in London – a reunion of such warmth that the stories of dissent briefly seemed unlikely – and to be adopted as prospective Liberal Unionist parliamentary candidate for Dundee. When the election came in 1906, he resigned from the Society, but his defeat concentrated his mind on what he had always known to be his destiny. On 12 February 1907 he announced to a dinner of the Royal Geographical Society's Kosmos Dining Club that he proposed to return to the Antarctic. A subsequently forgotten Belgian called Arctowski announced that he too planned a polar expedition – and that he had the money with which to finance it.

William Beardmore, a Clydeside shipbuilder for whom Shackleton had briefly worked, guaranteed an overdraft. Shackleton expressed his gratitude by naming a glacier after his benefactor. The plan was to repay the overdraft by writing an account of the expedition. It was a perilous notion since the £10,000 Heinemann promised for the book was contingent on the expedition reaching the South Pole. His 'desire to wipe out *terra nova*'[21] – the passion attributed to him by his first biographer – was great enough for him to take the financial as well as the physical risk. His passion for the unknown was uncontainable. He told his sister, 'You can't think what it's like to walk over places where no man has ever been before.'[22]

Shackleton began to draw up a plan to use as a prospectus to attract backers. To complete it he needed to announce the names of the expedition's officers. When he approached George Mulock, who had replaced him in the 1903 expedition, he was told '. . . I have volunteered to go with Scott'.[23] It was the first time that Shackleton had heard of his old chief's new enterprise. The news that Scott was planning a second expedition meant that he could not use the base at McMurdo Sound. Indeed, in the estimation of Edward Wilson, it meant that he could not go at all in case he was thought to be competing with his old chief. Shackleton was not the man to allow such a consideration to hold him back.

It was unreasonable for Scott to treat the Pole as private property, but he had already written to the Secretary of the Royal Geographical

Society to request backing for a new expedition and therefore felt, with some justification, that Shackleton had stolen a march. The resentment that he must have felt was revealed by the letter which followed Arctowskis announcement: 'It will soon be on record that I want to go and only need funds . . . it won't look well for the Society if an inexperienced foreigner cuts in and does the whole thing while we are wasting time.'[24]

The tone of the message – demand rather than request – was typical of Scott's style. Shackleton's announcement, made two weeks later, was typical of his determination to let nothing stand in his way. Whether or not its timing was meant to pre-empt Scott or to balk Arctowski, the 'inexperienced foreigner', it looked like an unfriendly act. Scott certainly saw it as one. However, on 17 May 1907, Scott and Shackleton met in London and drew up a compact which, they hoped, would prevent the two expeditions that they planned to lead crossing each other's paths.

The agreement was not kept. On 7 March 1908, Scott read in his *Daily Mail*, 'A MESSAGE FROM THE ANTARCTIC. Lieutenant Shackleton is camped near the foot of Mount Erebus, the most southerly of the volcanoes.'[25] The promise to keep out of McMurdo Sound had been broken. Scott could not disguise either his distress or his rage.

Shackleton, on the bridge of the *Nimrod*, had left England for the Antarctic on 30 July 1907. He had reached the Antarctic Circle on 14 January 1908. After a winter of training and exercises – on the model of Scott six years earlier – he had set out for the Pole on 29 October, accompanied by Lieutenant Jameson Boyd Adams, Doctor Eric Marshall (the expedition's senior surgeon) and Frank Wild (an able-seaman who had been with Scott in 1902). It was 'a glorious day for a start . . . Everything that could conduce [to an] auspicious beginning.'[26]

The euphoria did not last for long. After only three days' march, Shackleton concluded that the rations, which had been intended to last for ninety days, would have to provide the expedition's food for one hundred and ten – a figure quickly revised to one hundred and twenty. There were new mistakes as well as the repetition of old. Some of the horses, thought to be superior to dogs, had to be shot. Acts of God added to the depression. Adams developed severe toothache. It took Marshall four attempts before he was able to remove the tooth.

Spirits were much improved on 26 November when Shackleton announced that they had passed the point at which Scott had turned back. They made camp two miles further south at latitude 82° 18½' south and celebrated with a bottle of orange curaçao which Mrs Shackleton had given her husband for use on such an occasion. The high spirits were dampened by the discovery that immediately ahead lay a mountain covered with snow and ice. Shackleton decided that, since it could not be circumnavigated, it would have to be climbed. What they saw when they reached the summit 'was well worth the double labour'.[27] In their elation they called the peak Mount Hope. 'To the South, a great glacier extended as far as the eye could reach, flanked on either side by rugged ice-covered mountains, until lost sight of sixty miles distant . . . The glacier flowed from the distant plateau, which we now realised guarded the secrets of the Pole itself.'[28]

Four days later, Socks, the one remaining horse, suddenly disappeared down a crevasse. From then on the sledges had to be manhandled in relays – one taken a short distance forward before the men returned for another. It took nine hours (double-hauling all day) to travel three miles. Food became so short that maize, intended for the horses, was ground between two stones and used like flour. Worst of all, as they pushed on across the glacier, the ground continued to rise steeply. They lived on the hope that tomorrow, or the day after, the glacier would flatten out and they would be on the plateau.

They marched on for four weeks. On Christmas Day they indulged themselves on cocoa, cigars and a spoonful each of crème de menthe. Then they decided to cut the rations again – spreading over ten days food they had decided, after two previous adjustments, was essential for seven. They also agreed to leave behind everything which was not absolutely necessary to the completion of their journey. 'It is the only thing to do for we must get to the Pole, come what may.'[29]

Spirits, Shackleton wrote in his diary, were kept high by the 'cheerfulness and regardlessness of self' displayed by his three companions. In temperatures of fifty degrees below zero (and with body temperatures below 94 degrees) they set out on a series of forced marches over ice which was covered in a ten-inch layer of soft snow. On 5 January they covered thirteen miles and reached latitude 88° 5′. Shackleton wrote in his diary, 'Tomorrow we march south with the flag.'[30] The unusually grandiloquent language was meant to boost his own morale. He knew the flag would not be planted at the Pole. The best he could hope for was a near miss of a hundred miles.

The hope that the last dash could begin on 6 January was not fulfilled. A sudden blizzard kept them in their snow-covered tent for two days. It abated on 9 January. Then they moved off, 'as hard as we could pelt over the snow'. But the adventure was over and the diary entry made no attempt to hide the anguish.[31]

> The last day out. We have shot our bolt . . . The wind eased down at 1am. At 2am we were up and had breakfast and shortly after 4am started south with the Union Jacks . . . At 9am hard quick marching. We were at 88.23 and there hoisted HM's flag. Took possession of the plateau in the name of HM and called it KE Plat. Rushed back over a surface hardened somewhat by the recent wind and had lunch. Took photo of camp Furthest South and then got away. Marching till 5pm. Dead tired. Camped. Lovely night. Homeward Bound. Whatever regrets may be we have done our best. Beaten the South Record by 366 miles, the North by 77 miles. Amen.★

Shackleton's view of leadership required him – and him alone – to take the decision to turn back, but he discussed the possibility of pressing on with his three companions. They still had a real chance of getting to the Pole. But there would be no hope of completing the return journey. Survival was given preference over a unique place in polar history. Safely back in England, Shackleton told his wife, 'I thought you'd rather have a live donkey than a dead lion.' He did not add that, lion or donkey, he meant to return to the Antarctic one day.

Shackleton returned a hero. Eight hundred guests, including the Prince of Wales, attended a banquet in his honour. He was awarded

---

★In the circumstances Shackleton can be forgiven for omitting several necessary full stops. I have taken the liberty of inserting them.

the Gold Medal of the Royal Geographical Society and knighted, and the government discharged the £20,000 debt which the expedition had incurred but could not meet. But one man, with some justification, felt less than joyful admiration. Scott had gone back to sea and become the Captain of HMS *Albion*. He was then retired on half-pay, brought back to the service (at a lower rank) and made captain of HMS *Essex*. On Shackleton's return, he made a generous speech at a Savage Club Dinner. It ended, 'Personally, I am prepared, and have been for the last two years, to go forth in search of that object. And before other countries can step in and take the credit of the result of these great works by Mr Shackleton, this country should come to the fore and organise another expedition.'[32]

Scott was right to fear the strength of international competition. On 6 April 1909, Commander Robert Peary of the United States Navy reached the North Pole at his sixth attempt. That goal having been achieved, attention turned south again. All pretence of scientific study was put aside. The newspapers wanted Britain to be the first at the South Pole, but potential backers did not share Fleet Street's patriotic ardour. Scott, determined that he should lead the next British expedition, was reduced to making fund-raising tours. Honour as well as pride was sacrificed. He had invited Lieutenant Reginald Skelton (a Royal Navy engineering officer) to become his second-in-command. When he discovered that another naval officer, Lieutenant Teddy Evans, was planning an expedition of his own and had already raised a considerable amount of money, he suggested an amalgamation. Evans would only accept the suggestion if he took Skelton's place. Scott agreed and Skelton was dropped.

As the money trickled in, the expedition's members were recruited – Edward Wilson, this time senior doctor and scientific director, Sub Lieutenant Henry Bowers of the Royal Indian Marine, Petty Officer 'Taff' Evans, who had been with Scott on the *Discovery*, and Captain L. E. G. Oates of the 6th Inniskilling Dragoons, a sportsman who had taken his own pack of hounds to India when his regiment was sent to reinforce the garrison at Mhow. Oates was recruited to take charge of the horses; for Scott was determined to set sail with every possible means of transport – dogs, horses and mechanised sledges. Dogs were bought in Siberia, but Scott retained a deep antipathy to using them. He agreed that, in practical terms, their advantages outweighed the problems they caused, but the advantages could only be exploited if they were treated with continual cruelty. Scott could not subject his animals to the treatment which Amundsen accepted as normal as well as necessary. When Major, his leading dog on the final expedition, disappeared, Amundsen wrote in his diary 'presumably he has gone away to die'.[33] Scott would have agonised for days.

Tender heart aside, Scott had another reason for wanting to leave the dogs behind before the last march to the Pole. He had a Promethean obsession with proving that man alone could beat the elements. 'In my mind no journey ever made with dogs can approach the height of that fine conception which is realised when a party of men go forth to face hardships, dangers and difficulties with their own unaided efforts, and by days and weeks of hard physical labour succeed in solving some problem of the great unknown. Surely in this case the conquest is more nobly and splendidly won.'[34]

Scott had wanted – because of the ship's suitability rather than his own sentimentality – to sail south in the *Discovery*, but the ship was chartered to the Hudson Bay Company who would not release her. So he bought the *Terra Nova* (the second relief ship on his first expedition) for a down-payment of £5,000 and an outstanding debt of £1,500. Because Scott was elected a member of the Royal Yacht Squadron, ships under his command were exempt from Board of Trade regulations. The Plimsoll line was painted out and on 1 June 1910 the *Terra Nova*, low in the water because of the weight of stores, set out for Cape Town. Scott stayed behind in England to raise more money. He sailed south on 16 July, waved off by (amongst others) Ernest Shackleton. The last £8,000 of his target would, he hoped, be raised in the Southern Hemisphere. So, after South Africa, the *Terra Nova* made for Australia. At Melbourne there was a telegram awaiting his arrival. 'Beg leave inform you proceeding Antarctica. Amundsen.'[35]

Amundsen (and ninety-seven Greenland dogs) left Christiana on 9 August in the *Fram*, a ship he had borrowed from Fridtjof Nansen. Its crew were not told where they were bound, and the telegram to Scott was not sent until the ship left Madeira. It was the last port of call before the Antarctic – a feat made possible by Amundsen's seamanship and the *Fram*'s diesel engines. Amundsen meant to be the first man at the Pole.

After a difficult journey south, and an unsuccessful attempt to land at Cape Crozier in rough seas, Scott tied up the *Terra Nova* in the McMurdo Sound on 4 July 1911. The first task was to establish depots along the early stages of the ultimate journey. To Scott's disgust, Hut Point – which he had built for the 1902 expedition – was not ready for his immediate occupation. When Shackleton left in 1909 he had failed to close the windows. Snow had blown in, melted, and then frozen into a block of solid ice which filled the entire hut.

Worse news was to follow. Scott and his colleagues had convinced themselves, with very little justification, that the Norwegian was several weeks behind them and that he would approach the Pole along a quite different route from theirs. On 3 February the *Fram* was sighted in the Bay of Whales. Amundsen had landed at a point which was sixty miles nearer the Pole than Scott's base camp and sent home an explicit message. 'We must, at all costs, get there first. Everything must be staked on that.'[36]

Hut Point was made habitable, but the forward depot-laying exercise met with almost every sort of disaster. Horses had to be slaughtered en route, with increasing brutality and mounting anguish. Lieutenant Bowers was almost lost on an ice floe. There was much talk about fate and providence – pious when their luck held, less so when it did not. Moments of barely credible recklessness imperilled the whole expedition. Edward Wilson took off a party to look for penguin eggs in the hope of discovering, through the examination of the embryos inside them, that scales evolve into feathers. After thirty-three days, during which the pus inside their frostbite blisters froze – they got back to base with three frozen eggs. Wilson's theory was found to be fanciful.

The hardship increased the *esprit de corps*. On 31 October 1911 – the day before the expedition set out on its last journey – Bowers wrote to his mother, 'I am Captain Scott's man and shall stick to him right through. God knows what the result will be, but we will do all a man can do and leave the rest in His keeping.'[37] In that spirit, the party hoped to cover 1,766 statute miles to the Pole and back. The morale held to the end – despite the failure of the motor sledges, the death (often in horrific circumstances) of the horses and the blizzard that kept them imprisoned at the foot of the Beardmore Glacier. As always, delays meant a cut in rations, which in turn weakened their resistance and slowed them down even more. Even so, on 3 January 1912, when Scott chose the five men to make the final journey, those who were to be sent back to the depot felt only regret.

For those who went on there were moments of great elation. On 6 January, they crossed the line of latitude at which Shackleton had turned back and believed that they had reached further south than any other human being. On 13 January, they marched fourteen and a half miles in one day. Two days later they saw something on the horizon which looked like a snow-covered cairn or tent. They all agreed it must be a trick of the light or a heap of snow thrown up by the swirling wind. Then they noticed that above the heap of snow a flag flew from a broken sledge-iron. Amundsen had beaten them to the Pole. The paw prints explained part of the reason for his success. He had relied on dogs, not human indomitability.

The knowledge of failure made it more difficult to ignore adversity. Oates, Evans and Bowers all developed severe frostbite. Gangrene infected a cut which Evans had sustained the previous day. They put on a half-smile for the photographs and noted with satisfaction that Amundsen had left a letter, confirming his success, for them to send to King Haakon. He, at least, had never doubted that they would reach the Pole. Then they set off back, '800 miles of solid dragging – and goodbye to the daydreams!'[38]

They covered less ground every day. Evans was the first to die, delirious from the infection in his hand. Scott's diary got very near to admitting that it was a blessed relief – not for Evans himself but for his companions, who could bear the burden of a sick and raging man no longer. A comparison of miles and rations led to an inescapable conclusion. 'I doubt if we can possibly do it.'[39]

Oates, half dead from frostbite and scurvy which opened the scar on his Boer War wound, had to be pulled on a sledge. He speculated about the morality of suicide and decided that, although it was a sick man's duty to relieve his friends of the liability, it was wrong to take his own life. So, on 17 March, having decided that he could go no further, and after being denied his request to be left in his sleeping bag in the snow, he walked out into the night. On the same day, Scott realised that his frostbite was so bad that, even if they got home, he would lose his right foot.

They did not get home. But somehow, Wilson, Bowers and the crippled Scott struggled on for twelve more days. They proposed to die like heroes. 'We shall march for the depot and die in our tracks.'[40] But that last dignity was denied them. The end came as the three last survivors lay in their snow-covered tent, too weak to move. It seems that Scott was the last to die. For his letters to the relatives of his comrades were written as if his companions were already dead. His message to the public was intended as a vindication. The expedition had been frustrated by bad luck and bad weather. In truth, that was only half the story. It had also been confounded by bad planning and poor preparation. Oates had written, even before the expedition had left Britain, that 'it would not be difficult getting to the Pole provided you have the proper transport, but with the rubbish we have it will be jolly difficult . . .'[41] He had identified 'narrow chested and knock-kneed horses', but thought it was not proper for him to question his commanding officer's judgement. British indomitability had been confounded by British respect for rank.

Amundsen was first to the Pole because he had relied on dogs and took the shortest route. But Scott had achieved one of his aims. '. . . for my own sake I do not regret this journey which has shown that Englishmen can endure hardships, help one another and meet death with as great a fortitude as ever in the past . . . Had we lived, I should have had a tale to tell of the hardihood, endurance and courage of my companions which would have stirred the heart of every Englishman.' The Promethean dream had come true. Men had lived and died with the courage of the gods.

Scott was not the last Edwardian to feel the irresistible attraction of Antarctic exploration. The Pole itself had lost its fascination, but in the autumn of 1913, Ernest Shackleton boldly announced his intention to cross the South Polar Continent – from the Weddell to the Ross Sea. It was, he said, 'the last great Polar journey that can be made' and he added, as an afterthought for potential backers, 'the complete continental nature of the Antarctic can be absolutely solved by such a journey'. The expedition, like Scott's before it, was a heroic failure. Shackleton's ship, the *Endurance*, was caught in the pack ice and crushed. The crew, stranded on an ice floe, seemed doomed, but after a forced march across the frozen sea found temporary refuge on Elephant Island. Then Shackleton, in one of the epic journeys of British history, navigated an open boat through the Antarctic Ocean before crossing the snow-covered mountains of South Georgia. None of the marooned men doubted he would return. It was another exhibition of the courage, hardiness and endurance which Scott valued so highly, and it marked the end of the Edwardian hopes of romantic glory. Shackleton's second expedition had sailed south from Plymouth on 8 August 1914.

CHAPTER 19

Halfpenny Dreadful

Alfred Charles William Harmsworth, First Viscount Northcliffe, although inclined to moments of maudlin sentimentality, did not heap on others praise which he thought was rightly due to him. But an obituary which he wrote for *The Times* in 1910 modestly renounced all claims to be regarded as the father of twentieth-century journalism. The leader of the Fleet Street revolution was, he insisted, George Newnes. 'Most of [his] earlier publications were new ideas hitherto untried in English journalism and their distinguishing mark was a striking unusual success. Mr Newnes had found a market which had been created by the spread of popular education and he proceeded to extend still further the operations of his publishing houses.'[1]

By identifying Newnes as the true begetter of what was called 'New Journalism' – a description which Matthew Arnold had first employed to distinguish the popular press from the more serious writing which bore his by-line – Harmsworth was uncharacteristically overgenerous. Newspapers had begun to change long before Newnes founded *Tit-Bits* in 1881. The press 'campaign', usually associated with a sensational cause, had been a feature of W. T. Stead's leadership of the *Pall Mall Gazette*, first as deputy and then as editor in the 1880s. His demands had included 'Send General Gordon to the Sudan' and 'Strengthen the Navy Now'. And what he had called 'The Maiden Tribute Modern Babylon' – the true story of a girl sold into prostitution – had aroused such passions that Stead was sent to prison after he demonstrated the ease with which a child could be procured by purchase.

The idea of campaigns, as a way of increasing circulation as well as changing the world, was taken up by T. P. O'Connor, a radical and Irish Nationalist MP. O'Connor founded the *Star* (an evening paper) in 1886 and the *Morning Leader* (its daily counterpart) in 1892. The *Star* claimed a world record by selling 142,000 copies on the first day of its publication. Each one of the papers subscribed to the 'New Journalism' as laid down by O'Connor himself. 'Lifeless' reports were condemned. Stories which described 'the habits, the clothes or the home and social life' of any famous person were exalted. According to O'Connor, the great Lord Macaulay was the pioneer of New Journalism. He 'did not neglect . . . the smallest detail – the kind of wig his hero wore, the food he loved, the way he tied his shoe . . . Apart from the value of personal journalism to historical material, I hold that the desire for personal details with regards to public men is healthy, rational and should be yielded to.'[2]

George Newnes, writing to W. T. Stead, defended his school of journalism in language which was less pretentious and therefore more convincing.

> There is one kind of journalism that directs the affairs of nations and makes and unmakes cabinets. It upsets governments, builds up great names and does many other great things. This is your journalism. There is another sort which has no such great ambitions. It is content to plod on, year after year, giving wholesome and harmless entertainment to crowds of hard-working people craving for a little fun and amusement. It is quite humble and unpretentious. That is my journalism.[3]

There were, in fact, two sorts of New Journalism. Both were intended for the consumption of the wider readership which, it was supposed, had been created by the 1870 Education Act. One hoped to present serious news more palatably. The other intended to entertain with items which were so inconsequential that they amounted to little more than trivia. Both realised that layouts had to be modernised in a way which matched the paper's content. When, in 1895, the *Morning Post* adopted 'cross heads' to split up long paragraphs, W. T. Stead believed it 'wonderful that such an innovation should be adopted by so conservative a journal'. *The Times*'s report of Goschen's 1888 budget speech had covered eight columns without break. What, Stead wondered, 'would have been thought of a publisher who should [*sic*] bring out a book without the relief of so much as a paragraph from start to finish?'[4] Yet the habit persisted. As late as 1913 Lord Rosebery asked the London Press Club, 'Did any leader of the last twenty years ever read the speeches which were reported? I have no doubt that those whose duty it is to criticise, laud or rebuke them in the Public press felt it their painful duty to read the speeches. But did anyone else? . . . I can conscientiously say, having been a speaker myself, that I could never find anybody who read my speeches.'[5]

Newnes felt no great obligation to report Lord Rosebery's speeches in a way which guaranteed their wider dissemination and understanding. According to folklore, while working as a fancy goods salesman he had noticed a particularly arresting paragraph in a newspaper and said to his wife, 'Now that's what I call a tit-bit. Why doesn't someone bring out a paper containing tit-bits like this?'[6] A year later, that is exactly what he did.

Tit-Bits – or to give it the full title which appeared on its first masthead, *Tit-Bits from all the Most Interesting Books, Periodicals and Newspapers of the World* – was an instant success. Six months after it was launched, a publisher who had refused to give Newnes credit before publication day offered to buy the title for £16,000. The offer was refused. Circulation was increased by the innovation of special offers and competitions. Readers were given £100 free insurance against railway accidents. A series of clues, published in successive issues, led the way to 'hidden treasure' of five hundred sovereigns. Within a year, circulation had increased to 700,000. Newnes was ready to expand.

The *Review of Reviews*, a digest of other newspapers which was launched by Newnes in conjunction with Stead, was not his style. He sold his interest to his partner. But a vast market awaited the launch of the sort of periodical which appealed to his populist nature. The end of the nineteenth century was the age of new publications. Between 1866 (when the Companies Act eased the rules of limited liability) and the beginning of the First World War, 4,000 newspaper companies were formed in London and the provinces. Newnes pioneered and published (as well as *Tit-Bits*) *The Strand Magazine*, the *Westminster Gazette*, the *Daily Courier*, the *Million*, *Picture Politics*, *Woman's Life*, *Navy and Army Illustrated*, *Country Life*, *Ladies' Field*, *World Wide Magazine*, the *Captain* and *C. B. Fry's Magazine*. During the years of his great expansion, he recruited and trained dozens of young journalists. Among them were C. Arthur Pearson, who went on to be the second most powerful newspaper tycoon of Edwardian Britain, and Alfred Harmsworth, the dominant figure in Edwardian journalism.

It was *Tit-Bits* that convinced Harmsworth that 'the Board schools are turning out hundreds of thousands of boys and girls annually who are anxious to read. They do not care for the ordinary newspapers. They have no interest in society but they will read anything which is simple and sufficiently interesting. The man who started *Tit-Bits* has got hold of a bigger thing than he imagines . . . [I] could start one of those newspapers for a couple of thousand pounds. At any rate I am going to make an attempt.'[7]

He did not launch the new enterprise at once. By the time that he was twenty he had edited both *Youth* and *Bicycling News*, a publication with its headquarters in Coventry. Harmsworth lasted in the West Midlands for just over a year. Then, with £100 of savings, he decided that the time had come to move on. He was ready both for marriage and editing his own magazine.

The two initiatives went naturally together. Molly Harmsworth was required to perform the drudgery of publication while her husband wrote the copy. The first issue of the new venture, *Answers to Correspondents*, was published on 16 June 1888. Its masthead claimed that it was 'number three'. For the idea of answers to readers' queries to be plausible, it was necessary to invent a time during which the questions might have been asked. In fact, most of them were written by Harmsworth himself.

The format proved hugely popular. Circulation rose so fast that the Harmsworths found capital easy to raise. When Harold – Alfred's brother, who was supervising the business side of the enterprise –

found difficulty in working with the family which had provided the initial loan, the early investors were paid off and bought out with an annuity of £2,400 a year. Newnes met the competition by increasing circulation. *Tit-Bits* would increase its sales not by improving its journalism but by 'promotions'.

A game – silver-plated ball bearings rolled into holes in the bottom of a two-inch-square glass-covered matchwood box – was available to *Tit-Bits*' readers at the concessionary price of twopence. Its name, Pigs in Clover, helped to increase sales to 2,500,000. Over 700,000 subscribers entered a competition to guess the amount of gold held by the Treasury on a nominated day. The impact of the stunt was increased by requiring every entry to be validated by five other *Tit-Bits* readers. The prize, a pound a week for life, was financed by the investment of £1,100. *Tit-Bit*'s annual net profit rose to £30,000.

Money, and the confidence it bred, led naturally to new enterprises. Harmsworth retaliated against his rivals with new titles. First came *Comic Cuts*, 'Amusing without Being Vulgar'. Then *Illustrated Chips* was launched, followed by *Boys' Home Journal, Pluck, Marvel, Boy's Friend, Home Sweet Home, Forget-Me-Not* and *Home Chat*, 'The Daintiest Little Magazine in the World'. But he still lacked a daily newspaper to give him the power and prestige that he craved.

Although he was one of nature's predators, Alfred Harmsworth did not prowl the newspaper jungle looking for carrion to bear away. The *Evening News* had been in deep financial trouble for years when two enterprising young men, Louis Tracy and Kennedy Jones, approached the Harmsworth brothers with the suggestion that it could make a fortune for an owner who dragged it into the age of New Journalism. Harold Harmsworth, always cautious, advised that it should be bought only 'if it could be picked up for a song'.[8] Alfred embarked on a more thorough investigation. 'After a hard day's work in editing, managing and writing our periodicals, my brother and I met Mr Jones night after night . . . in an endeavour to find out what was wrong with the *Evening News* and why that newspaper was such a failure.'[9]

The enquiry concluded that the paper lacked both 'continuity of policy' and 'management control'. The Harmsworth brothers sup-

plied both. They also changed the typeface from reticent to bold,
reduced the coverage of politics and Parliament and, in a stroke of
genius, introduced football pools. 'Talking Points' dealt with such
varied subjects as 'How Timetables are Made' and 'Should We Smoke
in Cemeteries?' The distribution system was reorganised, a system for
verifying sales figures was introduced to justify increased advertising
rates, and newsprint costs were cut almost in half.

Ownership of the most successful evening paper in London did not
satisfy Alfred Harmsworth. Nothing ever did. The next step forward
had to be a national daily. Planning began in 1894. Before the first
issue went on sale, £40,000 was spent printing five dummy runs. It
took two years to make sure that the new paper met the needs of an
increasingly demanding public. On 5 May 1896, what had originally
been called the *Arrow* went on sale under the name of the *Daily Mail*.
It cost one halfpenny.

The first issue was heralded by a unique advertisement. 'Four leading articles, a page of Parliament and columns of speeches will not be
found in the *Daily Mail*.'[10] It did, however, include 'a story about the
increasing cycle of crime' (which contained not one new fact) and an
article extolling the virtues of motor travel. The longest and the most
serious piece in the whole paper explained why it could be produced
and sold so cheaply. 'Our type is set by machinery and we can produce thousands of papers per hour – cut, folded and, if necessary, with
the pages pasted together. It is the use of these new inventions on a
scale unprecedented in any English newspaper office that enables the
Daily Mail to effect savings of 30% or 50%.' Estimates of the exact
speed at which the new machinery worked varied. Harmsworth himself claimed 96,000 copies per hour[11] but Kennedy Jones, retained in
the brothers' service after the acquisition of the *Evening News*, put the
figure at over 200,000.[12]

Lord Salisbury, the Prime Minister, sent Harmsworth a telegram
congratulating him on the *Daily Mail*'s success. In private, he called it
a paper 'produced by office boys for office boys'. His attitude was no
more ambivalent, some would say hypocritical, than the paper's own
attitude towards editorial policy. The Harmsworths spoke of, and
sometimes actually believed in, their papers' mission to educate. 'One
of the greatest forces, almost untapped, at the disposal of the press [is]

the depth of public interest in imperial questions.' The *Daily Mail* became 'the champion of the greatness, the superiority of the British Empire . . . The embodiment and the mouthpiece of the imperial idea . . . If Rudyard Kipling can be called the voice of Empire in English Literature, we may fairly claim to be the voice of Empire in London journalism.'[13]

An espousal of the high imperial ideal is not inconsistent with the pursuit of profit; but sometimes the Harmsworth papers made money in a way which was less noble than the defence of Britain's colonial greatness. The *Evening News*, in the early months of Harmsworth ownership, increased its circulation from 187,000 to 390,000 in seven days. That remarkable growth was achieved as the result of the way it covered the execution of James C. Read. 'The man who is executed in Chelmsford is pinioned in his cell, is walked quickly from there to a strange little room with gaudy dark paint and unpleasantly clean whitewash and is sunk into eternity in less than sixty seconds.'

By the time that Edward VII came to the throne, the success of New Journalism was so obvious and extensive that the Harmsworths' particular brand of populism was bound to attract competition which rivalled his *Daily Mail* and *Evening News* for sensationalism and triviality. It was provided by Arthur Pearson, another Newnes protégé. Like Harmsworth, Pearson had made his fortune from promotions – most notably a 'missing word competition' which offered a prize of £20,000, the whole sum received in entrance fees, to the first reader correctly to complete a specially commissioned poem. More ingeniously still, Pearson responded to an influenza epidemic by spraying his magazine with eucalyptus – a sovereign cure, he claimed, for the ailment. And like Harmsworth, Pearson used his profits to launch a newspaper. It was called the *Daily Express* and, in one particular, it launched a revolution. The front page was devoted to news, not to advertisements – the source of £1,400 in income to each issue of the *Daily Mail*. Pearson gambled on his readers' interest in the world around them – and won.

The Boer War enabled Alfred Harmsworth to establish, beyond popular doubt, his reputation as the spokesman for patriotic Britain. His attempts to represent respectable society while at the same time appealing to its more prurient instincts were temporarily damaged by his decision to follow the *Daily Telegraph*'s example and publish the *Daily Mail* on every day of the week. An expert on double standards should have known better. At the turn of the century a *Sunday Telegraph* was acceptable to middle-class opinion. A *Sunday Mail* was not. The seven-days-a-week paper was abandoned after six Sunday editions and Harmsworth returned to a safer way of increasing the number of copies sold – jingoism.

The idea that the *Daily Mail* and Rudyard Kipling worshipped the same gods had stuck in his mind, so the Poet of Empire was recruited to compose verses which would tug at every loyal heartstring. Kipling did better than rouse patriotic spirits. His poem was also a financial appeal. What posterity remembers is,

> Duke's son – cook's son – son of a hundred Kings –
> Fifty thousand horse and foot going to Table Bay

But what gained most credit for the *Daily Mail*, in which 'The Absent-Minded Beggar' was published, was the last couplet:

> Pass the hat for your credit's sake and
> Pay, pay, pay!

At its outset the war went badly for Britain, and the *Daily Mail* naturally responded with attacks on the government in general and the War Office in particular. The conduct of a military campaign had not been assaulted with such vehemence since *The Times* had exposed the incompetence of the campaign in the Crimea. Attacking the way in which a war is fought is always a dangerous business. For it is open to the criticism that it damages the morale of troops under fire. The *Daily Mail* was careful to make clear that it was the champion of the private soldier. 'Both Krupp and Canet turn out guns which . . . are able to fire projectiles of equal weight more accurately and at greater range. For want of these guns, the Ordnance Department (in order to save its own skin) is prepared to greatly prolong our campaign in South Africa, to risk the lives of men and the morale of the Army.'[14]

When the War Office announced a plan to improve the quality of British artillery, the *Daily Mail* wasted only a moment in celebration of what it called the victory for its 'Guns! More Guns! Better Guns!' campaign. Prolonged satisfaction would not have met its needs. The rearmament programme would be 'marred by the same military authorities who have bungled the question of our field guns'. And, what was more, the British Lee-Metford rifle was inferior to the Boers' Mauser. Accusations that Harmsworth had betrayed our boys at the front were met by what the *Daily Mail* hoped was irrefutable proof that its complaint was against the government, not the Army. A personal attack was launched on the competence of ministers: 'The birthday book of our War Cabinet shows that nearly all its important members are past the prime of life. At an age when, in every other kind of enterprise, men are laying down their work, a number of men, approaching or past three score years and ten, are embarking upon one of the largest military and political operations in history.'[15]

Even that did not fully exonerate Harmsworth from the charge of undermining the confidence of the Army, so, for a while, the *Daily Mail* concentrated on lurid despatches from the front. They included graphic, if slightly laconic, accounts of life in Mafeking during the siege, sent to London by Lady Sarah Wilson, sixth daughter of the Duke of Marlborough and wife of the ADC to Colonel Robert Baden-Powell, the officer commanding the garrison. But Harmsworth needed a more spectacular story to maintain his leadership in the market of mindless chauvinism. It was provided towards the end of the war by Emily Hobhouse, an English Quaker and social worker.

General Kitchener, the new commander-in-chief, was gradually clearing the veld of Boer commandos and the civilians who supported them by 'concentrating' the farmers' wives and families in overcrowded detention camps. By the time the war ended, 20,000 women and children had died of enteric fever, pneumonia and the attendant diseases of bad sanitation and poor food. Emily Hobhouse, reading reports of the conditions, travelled to South Africa with the explicit purpose of investigating the camps. What she discovered resulted in the formation of 'ladies' committees' by the English churches and expressions of outrage by that substantial section of opinion which had always assumed that the British fought its wars in a more gentlemanly fashion.

The feeling of outrage was not shared by Alfred Harmsworth. His righteous anger was reserved for Emily Hobhouse herself. She was 'not impartial' and had 'no balance in her judgements' and did not 'know anything about the war and its history'.[16] According to J. A. Spender, the editor of the *Westminster Gazette*, Harmsworth, when challenged about his excoriation of the gentle Quaker social worker, sent for the circulation ledger and, pointing to the improvement in sales figures, said (without a hint of embarrassment), 'You see, we were right.'

Sensationalism carries with it the inherent danger of going too far, and Alfred Harmsworth was not the man to resist that temptation. In the summer of 1901 Edgar Wallace, formerly a Royal Army Medical Corps orderly, was sent to South Africa to report on the war. *Daily Mail* correspondents never need to be told what is expected of them. So Wallace must have anticipated how enthusiastically Harmsworth would welcome the despatch which claimed that the Boers were shooting wounded British prisoners. The story was published in late June and immediately denied by St John Brodrick, the Secretary of State for War, who told the House of Commons that Kitchener himself had said that there was no foundation whatever for the allegations. The *Daily Mail*, under Edgar Wallace's by-line, repeated the accusations.

To everyone's astonishment, Kitchener then recanted. Reports of executions had been made to his officers and he had received letters from men who had witnessed them. Nevertheless, the government continued to repudiate the story. *Daily Mail* correspondents were obliged to leave South Africa because, according to the War Office, they had offered junior civil servants money in exchange for classified information. Harmsworth made the usual demand that the accusation be made outside the House of Commons. His bluster was based on a well-known trick. The libel against which he threatened to proceed was the claim that 'the *Daily Mail* has purloined public documents'. That was not Brodrick's charge. The House of Commons added more confusion to an already confused situation. Alfred Harmsworth's threats against the Secretary of State for War were adjudged to be a breach of privilege, but he was spared the usual punishments and humiliations.

Harmsworth, forced to rely on agency reports of the war, struck back. Wallace, sometime editor of the *Rand Daily Mail*, returned to South Africa without the handicap of official accreditation from the *Daily Mail*. His technique for collecting information was based on exactly the method about which Brodrick had complained. He bribed soldiers. One of the sentries on guard at the peace treaty negotiations sent him signals about the progress of the talks – red for stalemate, blue for a measure of agreement and white for complete success. As a result, the *Daily Mail* was first with the news that the war was over.

Not surprisingly, Wallace became Harmsworth's star reporter, sent out to cover the sensational stories on which circulation depended. When they turned out to be not sensational enough, Wallace could be relied upon to supply the missing ingredient. In the case of the soap-cartel, he remedied the deficiency with an enthusiasm which cost the *Daily Mail* record damages of £50,000.

On 18 October 1906, a letter from Alfred Harmsworth to William Lever, MP, announced that the *Daily Mail* intended to campaign against the 'soap-trust' which, the paper was right to conclude, was keeping prices unreasonably high. Harmsworth also thought it necessary to promise the 'strictest impartiality' between the various companies in the presentation of the story – although it must have been clear that Lever, the only well-known soap manufacturer, would receive more publicity than any of its rivals. A number of flamboyant headlines followed. 'Trust Soap Already Dearer' was followed by 'How Fifteen Ounces Make a Pound', a reference to Lever Brothers' decision not to increase the price of a bar of soap but to reduce the weight. Then Wallace was brought in to write a 'human interest story'. It concerned a widowed washerwoman in Liverpool and carried the headline 'Cruel Blow to the Poor'.

The widow supported her children by taking in washing – the family's only means of support. According to Wallace, by reducing the size of his soap bar and persuading other members of the trust to do the same, Lever had cost the widow an extra one and sixpence a week. As a result, her children no longer had butter on their bread. Lever sued on the advice of F. E. Smith, who stated, 'There is no answer to this action for libel, the damages must be enormous.'[17] By the time that the case came to court, the trust had collapsed and the *Daily Mail*, without any justification, claimed the credit for its demise. But that did little to soften the blow of the humiliation which followed. Acting for Lever Brothers, Sir Edward Carson read the operative sentence from Edgar Wallace's story. The widow 'lost one and sixpence a week through the increase in the price of soap'. That, he added, could only be true if she used ninety-six pounds of soap a week. The damages were set at £50,000.

By the turn of the century, many of the men and women who had benefited from the 1870 Education Act were approaching middle age and, it was assumed, likely to want both the information and the entertainment that only newspapers could supply. The consequence, motivated sometimes by greed and sometimes by a genuine hope of increasing understanding, was a glut of new titles and the constant amalgamation and relaunch of old. Between 1900 and 1914, ten evening papers were at one time or another available in London. The *Evening Times* lasted for barely a year. The *Evening Standard* is on sale today. The *Star*, the *Evening News* and the *Pall Mall Gazette* had periods of real prosperity and genuine influence. The *St James's Gazette*, the *Westminster Gazette*, the *Globe*, the *Sun* and the *Echo* are forgotten.

Morning papers, many of them created for the specific purpose of supporting a political party, proliferated as freely and died with the same depressing frequency. The *Tribune* (high-mindedly liberal) failed, according to Philip Gibbs, one of its feature writers, because it was 'too good and there was too much of its goodness'. Stead's *Daily Paper* failed for much the same reason. The *Majority*, 'The Organ of all who work for Wages or Salary', was doomed from the start. So was the *Picture Paper* (produced in Sheffield), the *Daily Citizen* and the *Daily Call*. The *Daily Sketch*, which amalgamated with the *Daily Graphic* and the *Daily Herald*, lasted for half a century. But even Harmsworth, with his unscrupulous eye for scandal and sensation, made a major error in the foundation of the *Daily Mirror* – a penny paper for women.

The *Daily Mirror*, with an 'all woman staff for an all woman readership', was led by the unusual innovation of a woman editor, Mary Howath, who was transferred from the features desk of the *Daily Mail* to produce a paper which promised to advise about 'flowers on the dinner table [and] the disposition of forces in the Far East'. In fact it specialised in the worst sort of *Daily Mail* stories. 'Mother's Tragic Fate' and 'Baby in the Dustbin' were juxtaposed with 'Beauty in the Bath' and 'Dainty Frocks for Children'. The first issue sold 276,000 copies. After six months the circulation had fallen to 24,000 and the net losses exceeded £100,000. A new editor (male) was appointed and the 'first daily newspaper for gentlewomen' (price one penny) was sold for a halfpenny and became London's first experiment in tabloid journalism.

In 1904, Harmsworth bought the Manchester *Courier* and told his friends that the object of the purchase was not so much commercial as personal. He had acquired an unreciprocated affection for A. J. Balfour and hoped, by providing him with local support, to guarantee his re-election. The Tory Party lost the election on a landslide and Balfour lost his seat, but Harmsworth, at the age of forty, was made a peer in the Dissolution Honours List. His elevation signified both hope of future favours and gratitude for past help. The newspapers owned by the new Viscount Northcliffe had taken a lively, if equivocal, interest in the issue which had brought the government down – tariff reform.

Although the *Daily Mail* and *Evening News* were regularly accused of imposing the proprietor's principles on an unthinking readership, there were times when their policy slavishly followed, rather than sought to determine, public opinion. In 1903 'spies and ferrets' were sent out into the provinces to gauge the national mood.[18] The reports from the 'Walking Enquirers', as they were officially called, appeared in the *Daily Mail* on 29 August 1903. Twenty per cent of the people interviewed had never heard of tariff reform. The rest were solidly against it. The editorial announced that the paper was 'not against food taxes *per se* but against food taxes which would raise the cost of living – in other words against stomach taxes'. The ambiguity was emphasised by the publication of extracts from both Joe Chamberlain's most recent protectionist speeches and his ancient advocacy of free trade. Throughout the summer the *Daily Mail* faced both ways at once.

During the autumn it defined its position more precisely. 'Any Unionist Member of Parliament who has been among his constituents recently must know that, almost to a man, they are in favour of putting a tax on manufactured imports.' A week later, when Arthur Balfour published his *Economic Notes on Insular Free Trade*, the *Daily Mail* declared a victory. 'Light at Last' it triumphed. 'Mr Chamberlain . . . unfortunately confined himself to exactly that form of tariff which it is madness to attempt. The taxation of foodstuffs was . . . one on which we have ever spoken in no doubtful language . . . We are a manufacturing country and must buy our bread in the cheapest market.'[19]

The *Daily Mail* announced that it would be 'polling the public . . . for the purpose of testing public opinion on the great fiscal question of the hour'. The initiative, like all Northcliffe's schemes, was more concerned with circulation than with democracy. Voting papers were issued with the paper and on 7 October the proprietor made his position clear. 'The taxation of foreign manufacture should precede . . . not the taxation on food.' Not surprisingly, the 'general election in advance' ended in a landslide victory for the opponents of 'stomach taxes'.

Chamberlain, whose principal object was binding the Empire together, made a subtle change to his policy. A tariff was necessary to protect home-grown food. 'Agriculture', he said on 7 October, 'has been practically destroyed.' The new emphasis allowed Northcliffe to edge closer to Chamberlain's position while claiming that Chamberlain was accepting the arguments of the *Daily Mail*. When the tariff reform position was again adjusted, with the announcement that import duties would cut rather than increase the cost of living, Northcliffe again declared a victory. 'Dealing with food taxes Mr Chamberlain proved that he has advanced further in the direction which the *Daily Mail* has demonstrated to be necessary.' Always anxious to avoid understatement, Northcliffe concluded the editorial, 'He has set out to accomplish the work which Cavour fulfilled for Italy and Bismarck for Germany.'[20]

Northcliffe's conversion to tariff reform was inevitable because it was espoused by Joseph Chamberlain, and Chamberlain had all the characteristics of a 'man of destiny' – qualities which Northcliffe later found irresistible in Hitler and Mussolini. On 31 December 1903 the *Daily Mail* announced, 'In politics and the whole realm of national affairs it has been Mr Chamberlain's year.' In the first month of the New Year Northcliffe described, in the stilted prose which was his trademark, how the hero of 1903 was going to achieve another triumph in 1904 by promoting the Commission set up by the Tariff Reform League. 'Under a drooping palm tree, symbolical of the Colonial Empire and in a blaze of electric light typical of the modern industry of Old England, Mr Chamberlain yesterday opened the Commission which has been charged to draw up a scientific tariff for Greater Britain.'

Northcliffe never became a thoroughgoing member of the Establishment. Both his background and his temperament made that impossible. But his alliance with Joe Chamberlain – or at least with Chamberlain's imperial ambitions – awoke interest in more than income and circulation. Respectability called. Despite his lurid personal life – several illegitimate children and the acceptance that his neglected wife would find solace elsewhere – the appearance of propriety was essential to Northcliffe's peace of mind. When the *Daily Mirror* ran a summer-long feature on Mary Kellerman, a Channel swimmer, he issued firm instructions that she was to be photographed either fully clothed or up to her neck in water.

In 1905, Associated Newspapers Limited was formed as the parent company to own and manage the *Daily Mail*, the *Evening News* and the various provincial papers which he had picked up along the way. A month after the incorporation Northcliffe bought the *Observer* (the oldest newspaper in Britain) for £5,000. He immediately invited J. L. Garvin – the editor of *Outlook*, an intellectual journal and an advocate of tariff reform – to join the paper. In 1908, Garvin was made editor and given a one-third interest in the paper. Northcliffe believed, correctly, that he had acquired the services of the most brilliant journalist in London.

Northcliffe was notoriously indulgent with those he favoured. Rightly believing that his new recruit could improve the *Daily Mail*, he suggested that Garvin should attend its afternoon news conferences. The suggestion was rejected in language that Northcliffe would have found intolerable from any other subordinate: 'I will be responsible for nothing but what I direct.'[21] Garvin was quoting from the Earl of Chatham – lese majesty in itself. Instead of sacking him,

Northcliffe asked him to accept, in addition to the *Observer*, responsibility for the political pages of the *World*, and agreed that he should also write regularly for the *Daily Telegraph*.

For three years the relationship flourished. Then, on 5 February 1911, the *Observer* attacked the *Daily Mail* for what Garvin called 'a campaign against Imperial preference'.[22] Once again Northcliffe drew back from the punishment which would have been imposed on any other employee. Instead of instant dismissal, Garvin was offered the chance to acquire full ownership of the *Observer* and given time to find a backer who would put up the two-thirds of the paper's equity that Northcliffe still held. Waldorf Astor bought the *Observer* outright, insisting (as a matter of principle) on complete, rather than partial ownership. But although Garvin was obliged to sell his shares, he was given – and received for thirty-six years – absolute control over the paper's editorial policy.

Northcliffe's generosity towards Garvin was not the result of any decline in his appetite for acquiring new titles. *The Times* was a natural target: it was a legend, a challenge and, because of its managerial incompetence, an affront to modern journalism. William Randolph Hearst, resenting Northcliffe's challenge to his title as the undisputed champion newspaper mogul of the world, got very close to understanding the urge to occupy Printing House Square as well as illustrating his contempt for the *Daily Mail* and *Evening News*. 'Harmsworth is trying to buy the London *Times*. He wants to own "a great paper; the greatest paper". Therefore he knows that he owns no such paper now. May he get the *Times* and, when he does, may he show the real Harmsworth, editing a real newspaper.'[23]

Northcliffe did not need the added incentive of Hearst's mockery to convince him that *The Times* must be his. He saw the most prestigious of all British newspapers as both a potential symbol of his status and as an asset which others had wasted and he could exploit. The suspicion that it needed new management was confirmed by the discovery that the editor, the legendary G. E. Buckle, opened his own letters. The inefficiency was compounded by a failure to recognise a good story when it found one. 'Did you know that there was a sub-editor at *The Times* who spiked an elephant? An elephant escaped from a circus in South London and went careering about the streets.

When the sub-editor received an account of the incident, he stuck it in the waste file with other rejected copy.'[24]

The Times's financial position was as precarious as its journalists were unimaginative. Acquisition of the rights of the *Encyclopaedia Britannica*, and the publication of a new edition, had only postponed the inevitable. Both ownership and management had to change hands. In December 1906, a wrangle over the legal definition of the paper was resolved and *The Times* was declared a limited liability company. The proprietor, Arthur Walter, realised that he could not raise the capital necessary for its successful survival, but he was determined to keep it out of the hands of Northcliffe. Rumours that it might be taken over by such a vulgar parvenu were dismissed as 'so absurd in themselves, and so utterly baseless in point of fact, that it might seem unnecessary to pay any attention to them'.[25]

At first, Moberly Bell, the general manager of *The Times*, agreed that the paper which was also a national institution ought 'never to be trampled in the dirt by men of the *Tit-Bits* school'.[26] Since Newnes showed no interest in such an expensive acquisition, it was clear that Bell was setting out his opposition to both Northcliffe and C. Arthur Pearson, whose career – *Evening Standard*, *Daily Express* and *Pearson's Weekly* – almost exactly mirrored Northcliffe's *Standard*, *Daily Mail* and *Answers*.

It is by no means certain from which direction Arthur Walter hoped the help would come – though it was rumoured that hard necessity had reconciled him to doing a deal with Pearson. Bell, who, like G. E. Buckle, the editor, had not been consulted about Walter's plans, became convinced that he had been kept out of the discussion because the new owner did not intend to employ him. He decided that if Pearson was the favoured suitor, he would do all in his power to ensure that the match was not made.

Northcliffe saw and grasped the opportunity and embarked on a remarkably audacious campaign of black propaganda. On 5 January 1908, the *Observer* announced that *The Times* was about to acquire a new proprietor. The immediate assumption was that it was Northcliffe himself. Two weeks later the *Observer*, at Northcliffe's suggestion, published the 'news' that Pearson had made an offer for *The Times* which Walter had accepted. It concluded that 'Mr Pearson is to be warmly congratulated upon acquiring *The Times* at a point comparatively early in his career.' Northcliffe added his 'best wishes' for Arthur Pearson's 'Newest and greatest enterprise'.

Pearson was touched. 'A thousand thanks for your best wishes, which I am glad to have.'[27] His message crossed with a letter to Bell from Lord Northcliffe. 'I am going to buy *The Times*. With your help if you will give it to me. In spite of you if you don't.'[28] To the general manager the message seemed to offer at least a chance of prolonged employment. It took him six weeks to convince Walter that he had found a more suitable buyer than Pearson. Then the proprietor agreed that *The Times* should go to a mysterious 'Mr X' for £320,000. Northcliffe became the proprietor on 16 March 1905.

Technically Bell remained in full control. Northcliffe had shown his faith in his new ally's probity by depositing £320,000 in Bell's bank account and leaving him to complete the transaction with Walter, but no such risk could be taken with *The Times*'s reputation. The man who had made his fortune from peddling tittle-tattle insisted on a unique clause being entered in the articles of association. 'It shall be a fundamental principle of the company that the efficiency, reputation and character of *The Times* shall as far as possible be maintained at the present high standard, and that on all existing political questions the independent attitude of the paper shall be maintained as heretofore.'[29]

The hope of acquiring *The Times* had been the apogee of Pearson's ambition. By nature a businessman rather than a newspaper tycoon, he nevertheless held strong political views which he hoped to propagate through the *Evening Standard* and the *Daily Express*. His support for tariff reform was so extreme that many Conservatives welcomed *The Times* becoming the property of a man who had the grace to equivocate on the issue.

Pearson had become an acolyte of Joseph Chamberlain and an active participant in the political campaign for 'tariff reform' – a role revealed to the Duke of Portland when Chamberlain asked for his help to carry the battle for imperial preference into Nottinghamshire. 'He asked me to allow a meeting to be held at Welbeck in order that he might explain the scheme to a large number of farmers and others interested in agriculture in the Midlands counties. I agreed to his request but stipulated that he should send some experienced person to help with the organisation of the meeting. "Certainly" said Mr Chamberlain "I will send you the finest hustler I know."[30]

The description stuck. Pearson became a knight, principally in recognition of his work in helping to found St Dunstan's Hospital for the Blind. But he remained, in public esteem, the 'finest hustler' in Great Britain. His hustling was not always successful. Attempts to promote his imperialist ideal (and to advertise colonial products) in a new daily paper, the *Standard of Empire*, failed. And the collapse of that newspaper, combined with the gradual deterioration of his sight, made him lose enthusiasm for, if not interest in, the newspaper business. He began to sell his shares, tranche by tranche. By 1911 Max Aitken was a major shareholder in the *Daily Express* and poised to become its proprietor.

On the day in 1905 when Northcliffe acquired *The Times*, its circulation was 35,000. He immediately set to work to increase sales by improving news coverage. *The Times* was reluctant to change, and he realised that the changes could not be made at the expense of the paper's distinguished reputation. His enemies accused him of attempting to create an 'edition de luxe of the *Daily Mail*'. In fact, he resisted the more extreme suggestions for reform with the complaint that too much 'popularisation would be like putting on a Punch and Judy show in Westminster Abbey'.[31] Instead of changing the paper, he attempted to change the habits of its staff – mastering *The Times* 'by mastering its principal members'.[32] The stratagem failed. Three years after the acquisition, the circulation had still only risen to 47,000.

He was, therefore, left with the last desperate expedient. In March 1914, he lowered the cover price to one penny. The circulation rose within days to 165,000. Geoffrey Dawson, who by then had become editor, did not receive the message of congratulation which he might have expected. Instead Northcliffe wrote, 'I hear that the old lady of Printing House Square gathered up her skirts and shrieked at the sight of a man under her bed in the face of a real increase in demand for *The Times* for the first time since her middle age.'[33] Northcliffe naturally took the credit, though the increase in sales was only partly the result of his policy. The prospect of war had stimulated interest in hard news. And Northcliffe anticipated the

'German menace' with a vehemence that none of his competitors could (or chose to) match.

Northcliffe was a weathervane who pointed in a different direction every time the wind blew. His instinct – as a Tory, a would-be gentleman and a peer – was to oppose the Asquith government's plan to limit the power of the House of Lords.★ He changed his mind shortly after Lloyd George's Limehouse Speech – the most controversial episode in the whole constitutional campaign – for reasons that the Chancellor of the Exchequer set out in a letter to his brother: 'Lord Northcliffe came to see me last night. He told me that the Budget has completely destroyed the Tariff Reform propaganda in this country. He said that they had all miscalculated the popularity of the Land Clauses. He wants to trim.'[34]

It was, surprisingly, their first meeting – though Northcliffe had turned down a previous invitation to 11 Downing Street on the slightly spurious grounds that 'journalists should be read and not seen'.[35] The two men got on so well that the Chancellor described the details of the Development of Roads Bill to his guest, even though they had not been reported to Parliament. The friendship did not last long. Garvin, having caught wind of Northcliffe's volte-face, wrote him an impassioned letter.

> . . . my sixth sense tells me that a Unionist Surrender upon the Budget is much more probable . . . The Government is, of course, less popular than last year. If they pass the Budget as it stands, they will have scored a parliamentary triumph as brilliant as any in our recollection. That alone will impress democracy, always more attracted by pugilistic force than by anything else . . . Men like Lloyd George and Winston Churchill will do anything to win. Upon the lines of the Budget they will keep winning if we submit now . . . Our Dukes should be warned to keep off the grass . . . In short the Budget ought to be rejected. That was not formerly my opinion. But now [we should] not encourage, by indirect means, . . . thoughts of surrender.[36]

★See Chapter 8, 'Who Shall Rule?'.

The strictures were accepted in remarkably good part, and Northcliffe returned to the party of true Unionism. His papers denounced both Lloyd George's budget and attempts to prevent the House of Lords from frustrating the will of the Commons. But opposing the instincts and inclinations of his readers always disturbed him. He was at his happiest, if not his best, reinforcing prejudices which he shared with the readers of the popular press. It was his capacity for rousing existing but dormant fears which made his enemies accuse him of the most cynical circulation stunt in newspaper history – starting the First World War.

As early as 1900, when the Kaiser was still pledging his undying fealty to his grandmother, Northcliffe had no doubt that Queen Victoria's Hohenzollern grandson was up to no good: 'This is our hour of preparation, tomorrow may be the day of world conflict . . . Germany will go slowly and surely; she is not in a hurry; her preparations are quietly and systematically made; it is no part of her object to cause general alarm which might be fatal to her designs.'[37]

Northcliffe's apprehension grew with the years and the German battleship programme, and in 1909 he commissioned Robert Blatchford, the socialist author of *Merrie England* and editor of the *Clarion*, to visit Germany and prepare a series of articles on 'the secret and insidious enemy'. Blatchford, as is the habit of journalists recruited for such enterprises, found that his sponsor's suspicions were totally justified. Attacked for working for the Northcliffe empire, he justified writing for the *Daily Mail* with the explanation that he wrote not for reward but because he believed 'that Germany is deliberately preparing to destroy the British Empire and because [I know] that we are not able or ready to defend ourselves'.[38] He went on to explain, irrelevantly, 'I am ready to sacrifice socialism for the sake of England, but never to sacrifice England for the sake of socialism.'[39]

By 1912, even the most complacent members of the Liberal government were beginning to worry about Germany's naval building programme. Northcliffe, with newspaper correspondents in Hamburg and Stettin, reported to the Cabinet that all German merchantmen were built under the supervision of the Admiralty in Berlin. 'It is necessary to build gun platforms into a ship while it is under construction, and I am assured that all the fast German liners have these platforms – invisible to the ordinary ocean passenger's view but capable of being uncovered and having guns mounted immediately the emergency arises.'[40]

Northcliffe, true to his nature, not only knew that the war was coming. He knew how it could be won. Perhaps the greatest of his Edwardian campaigns – transcending the urgent call for telephones to be installed in police boxes, the demand to abandon investment in electric tramcars when the petrol-driven omnibus was available and pleas to accept the importance of providing the London fire brigade with longer ladders – was his espousal of what he called 'the motor car of the air'. One day, he predicted, the 'sky would be darkened by flights of aeroplanes'. And in the very near future, he had no doubt, 'aerial power will be an even more important thing than sea power'.[41] Aeroplanes could become Britain's protection against Germany.

In 1906, when Alberto Santos-Dumont got his premature plane off the ground and flew it for two hundred yards, Northcliffe found it hard to believe that the *Daily Mail*, unimpressed by a flight of two hundred yards, buried the story at the foot of an inside page. 'It does not matter how far he has flown', Northcliffe raged. 'He has shown what can be done.'[42] Thereafter, showing what can be done became an obsession. The *Daily Mail* offered a prize of £1,000 for the first cross-channel flight, Calais to Dover, and £10,000 for the first flight from London to Manchester. Northcliffe wrote of roads being scrapped when everybody moved from place to place in 'a voyage through space'. But his immediate concern was air defence.*

The *Daily Mail* staff took up the theme. W. F. Bullock, cabling from America on the Wright brothers' early flights, thought 'AEROPLANE PRIMARILY INTENDED WAR MACHINE STOP . . . SHOULD HAVE NO DIFFICULTY DROPPING BOMB GREATEST NICETY ON ANY OBJECT ATTACK STOP'.[43] Agonised by what he thought to be the government's indolence, Northcliffe complained, after making a private visit to the Wrights' exhibition site, 'I notice that the Germans and French have military representatives here.' He then gave the War Office unsolicited and unwelcome advice:

---

*For a fuller account of the development of the aeroplane, see Chapter 20, 'The Shape of Things to Come'.

As I am constantly being chaffed by these foreign gentlemen with regard to the British army aeroplane, which they have nicknamed 'the steamroller', it occurs to me that, if it is worth the while of France and Germany to be on the spot, one of your young men might be sent down here to find out why it is that this aeroplane gets off the ground, and can fly for ten minutes or ten hours, if it chooses, and your Aldershot aeroplane . . . is unable to leave the ground.[44]

Richard Haldane, the Secretary of State for War, was both profoundly unimpressed and mightily annoyed at the impertinence. Northcliffe was easy to dislike. Indeed his behaviour often alienated people from the causes which he supported. He was right about air power, but his campaign failed. It sold newspapers but it did not change policy. The great populist and supreme judge of the national mood did not really understand the British attitude to newspapers and politics. His readers enjoyed angry editorials and fearless exposures. But journalists rarely changed the public's minds. The halfpenny dreadfuls made money by following public opinion. They rarely made policy by influencing it.

CHAPTER 20

The Shape of Things to Come

British motorists, believing themselves to be the harbingers of the brave new mechanical world, were determined to celebrate the arrival of the twentieth century in appropriate style. They were also anxious to convince doubters – almost certainly a majority of the population – that, despite the dust and fumes which it created, the automobile was the safe and reliable transport of the future. So the Automobile Club of Britain was persuaded to organise what, today, would be called a rally. In an unconscious concession to the doubters, they called it a 'trial'. And trial it turned out to be. In April 1900, sixty-five vehicles left Hyde Park Corner on a 1,010-mile journey which would take them to every major town and city in England and Scotland. To the organisers' relief – and the astonishment of the general public – all sixty-five completed the course.

There were many alarms along the way. Halfway to the summit of the Cumbrian Hills, the Ariel tricycle's clutch failed and it began to roll backwards – accelerating as it descended towards the valley floor. It was then that the driver discovered, to his surprise, that the brakes only worked when the vehicle was going forwards. He managed to steer successfully to safety with his left hand while turned in his seat to watch the road over his right shoulder. Unfortunately that required him to push his passenger out on to the road. Some accidents were more prosaic. The Simms Motor's wheels skidded on the tramlines in Bristol and overturned.

Mundane mechanical failures required heroic rectification. When the steering system on the Wolseley three and a half horsepower three-wheeler broke down, the driver completed the last fifty-two miles of the trial standing on the offside running board and kicking the front wheels in the direction he wanted the car to turn. The constant need for running repairs contributed to the competitors' sense of adventure and increased the excitement of the spectators, particularly when the work was accomplished with an exhibition of the competitors' insouciant ingenuity. The Marshall Dogcart broke its water pump just as it was about to begin the speed trials in the grounds of Welbeck Abbey. The engineer, the essential companion of every prudent driver, mended it with the aid of a champagne cork and two penny pieces. One competitor reported, 'Even if you broke down on a remote road, while you were doing repairs, crowds of people would appear apparently from nowhere and gather round you so closely that you could not get on with the job.'[1] There was, among the British population, a substantial minority of motor enthusiasts who were waiting impatiently for the general acceptance of what they knew to be the way in which the whole world would soon move from place to place.

Their impatience was understandable. The nation which had pioneered the canal and the railway engine had left the third stage of the transport revolution to countries which British patriots expected to follow the lead of Scottish engineers and English entrepreneurs, not point the way. Two Italians, Bassanti and Matteucci, had attempted to develop a gas-driven vehicle as early as 1853. It had not proved practical, but in 1859, Jean-Joseph Ellenoir, an engineer working for Gautier of Paris, adapted the idea so successfully that his company made and sold five hundred gas-driven automobiles in five years. Two Germans, Nickolas August Otton and Eugen Langen, saw the gas car and thought that they could develop a genuine internal combustion engine. They engaged a young engineer called Gottlieb Daimler, and by 1875 were selling over six hundred engines a year for installation in custom-built chassis. Karl Benz, comparing the success of the Daimler enterprise with the relative failure of his own metalworking business, decided that his hopes of prosperity lay in mechanical locomotion.

While continental Europe experimented, Great Britain slept. John Henry Knight of Farnham in Surrey built a steam car as early as the mid 1860s. Then, disheartened by the lack of public interest, he turned to the production of stationary engines in his Reliance Motor Works. In 1895 he built a three-wheeled car. But again his pioneering spirit was dampened by what he believed to be a bias against the automobile. The antagonism survived well into the twentieth century. 'It is this prejudice which has allowed Britain to be flooded with French and German motor cars and the sum of money which has crossed the channel for the purchase of these cars must have been very considerable. Money lost to this country because our legislators refuse to allow motorcars to run on English roads.'[2]

In fact, in 1896 Lord Salisbury had relaxed the Locomotives and Highways Act – a statute which had been designed to regulate the conduct of traction engines and steam-driven agricultural machinery but which was applied to passenger motor vehicles. By the turn of the century, it was no longer necessary for a driver on the public highway to be preceded by a man with a red flag. According to Knight the change of heart came too late.

> Had it not been for these restrictions we might have taken the lead in self-propelled carriages instead of leaving it to the Germans and the French. A lost trade is seldom, if ever, recovered. French-made cars are now to be found in most foreign countries and in our colonies and we may be sure that their makers will do all that they can to keep the trade they have obtained – partly through want of foresight on the part of the House of Commons.[3]

Motor manufacturers and traders are notorious for blaming the consequences of their own failures on circumstances beyond their control, but there is no doubt that before Liberation Day in 1896 – still celebrated with the London to Brighton vintage car run – the Establishment either disapproved or doubted the viability of motor locomotion.

The real cause of Britain's failure was the sudden disappearance of innovative mechanical engineers. During the half-century which preceded the First World War, what was once the workshop of the world had produced only two original inventions – the Parson's Turbine, which became the major source of electrical generation, and the Dunlop pneumatic tyre. The inflatable tyre had a particularly British genesis. It was developed by a cyclist with little scientific training to make pedalling over cobblestones less uncomfortable. By 1900, the age of casual inspiration had passed. Progress was promoted by ruthless investment and imagination, which the Victorians concentrated on the colonies. So, thanks to Siemens and Edison, there were electric tramcars in Berlin and New Jersey during the 1850s. It was another fifty years before they appeared on the streets of Britain.

Between 1850 and 1913, the number of towns and cities in Britain with a population in excess of 100,000 rose from twelve to fifty, a process encouraged by industrial development, the railways' increased ability to take food from farmers to shops and the reduced cost of domestic building. In Victorian Britain, horse-drawn trams carried workmen and their wives across Manchester, Leeds and Birmingham. Electrification – Kingston-upon-Hull led the way in 1899 – made the tramcar an essential part of Edwardian working life and leisure.

Britain had been slow to realise the electric tramcar's potential – as was it slow to recognise so many essential innovations. In 1902, over half of Europe's total tramway mileage ran through always-progressive Germany. British electrical manufacturing capacity expanded, when it expanded at all, equally slowly. Mather and Platt and the Electric Construction Company took root but bore little fruit. The United States – in the form of Siemens Brothers, Anglo-American, General Electric and Westinghouse – filled the gaps and provided vehicles to supply what – after a delayed start – amounted to municipal tramway mania. Between 1900 and 1914, 161 new electric systems were created in Great Britain. In 1905, the Royal Commission on 'Means of Transport and Locomotion in London' recommended a large extension of electric tramways in the capital – at a flat-rate fare. For amongst electric traction's many advantages was its minimal cost.

In Liverpool, the cost of travelling on a horse-drawn tram had averaged out at a penny for two-thirds of a mile. After electrification in 1903, the 'penny ride' was extended to two miles and a half. Ten years later, Birmingham had a 'halfpenny fare stage' of up to one mile and a half, as well as a 'workman's fare' of one penny for anything up to four miles. In both cities, over 80 per cent of journeys were made at, or below, the penny rate. The low fares liberated the urban poor. In 1901, the citizens of Manchester averaged fifty-six horse-drawn tramway journeys each year. When the system was electrified, the average number of journeys increased almost threefold, to 158.

Tramways became so popular that, for one brief moment, they were fashionable. At the official inauguration of the London County Council's Electric Tramway in 1903, the Prince of Wales was photographed with his hand lying lightly on the driver's handle – though there was no suggestion that he should actually drive a tram. On inauguration day a 'royal ticket' was issued to all travellers. It bore the Prince of Wales's feathers and the proud boast, 'The first ticket was sold to His Royal Highness for one halfpenny.' The *Tatler* entered into the spirit of the occasion with its idea of a joke. 'New responsibilities will be added to Royalty if hardworking Kings and Princes, in addition to laying foundation stones and planting trees, are to be called upon to drive tramcars.' At least the magazine had realised that the capacity, cost, speed and reliability had made the electric tramcar irresistible to the growing towns and cities of Edwardian Britain.

The motor car was welcomed with more caution. Even the *Automobile Journal*, which might have been expected to rejoice at the triumph of internal combustion, was apprehensive about the enthusiasm with which horseless carriages were being promoted. Its report of the Great Trial of 1900 was typical. Instead of rejoicing at the success which had been achieved in popularising the motor car, its editorial complained about the way in which salesmen had exploited the event: 'The public will be induced by misleading assertions to purchase vehicles which will disgust them, once and for all, with automobilism. The natural argument will be that if this is the sort of car which is able to be "first anywhere", a day spent in assisting an itinerant knife grinder now and again by way of relaxation would be equally exhilarating and less expensive.'

Lack of faith, as much as a shortage of capital, resulted in most Edwardian motorists being forced to rely for their vehicles on imports from Britain's more adventurous neighbours. In 1895 F. R. Sims had founded the Daimler Motor Syndicate to import German engines. A year later, his company was taken over by Harvey J. Lawson who – on the strength of having sponsored the Great Trial – believed himself to be the 'Father of the British Motor Industry'. He claimed further paternity to several 'ghost companies' – most of which never built or sold a car – before he was convicted of fraud and sentenced to twelve months' penal servitude. Edwardian England was in desperate need of an engineer of genius and a true entrepreneur to set the motor industry on its feet.

There was no shortage of volunteers for that role. Between 1900 and 1913, 198 new makes of motor car were offered to the British public. One hundred and three of them failed to establish a place in the market and were abandoned by the companies which made, or planned to make, them.[4] The most successful new models were developed by companies which enjoyed the advantage of experience in vaguely related fields. Star and Sunbeam (in Wolverhampton), and Swift, Rover and Singer (in Coventry) were bicycle makers. Wolseley (in Birmingham) made sheep-shearing machinery. It was men with dirt under their fingernails, not gentlemen enthusiasts in goggles and gauntlets, who began to build an industry.

Wolseley survived despite the resignation of Henry Austin, one of its more imaginative engineers. Austin's aspiration to found a motor company of his own was initially based on his attempt to build a motor car which could be sold for £150. By increasing the size of his engine he gradually increased the size of his business to the point at which the suffragettes thought his buildings were big enough to be worth burning down. William Morris, an Oxford cycle dealer, first diversified into motor sales and then began to assemble a two-seater with a distinctive brass 'bull-nose' from parts bought from other vehicle manufacturers. Morris and Austin were to become the motor giants of interwar Britain. They achieved that status by overcoming formidable opposition. Between 1903 and 1906, the annual value of motor imports into Great Britain rose from £800,000 to £1,448,000. Then, in 1908, Henry Ford began to export his American Model-T to Europe. Three years later he established a factory in Manchester for the assembly of motor parts imported from the United States.

Although the popular enthusiasm for motor cars was beginning to grow, the Establishment remained basically antagonistic. In 1905, the

Marquis of Queensberry – admittedly an eccentric – explained on his application for a gun licence that he needed something with which to shoot motorists who drove along the roads on his estate. In the same year a Mr E. A. Macdonald was prosecuted for causing a public nuisance in so much as 'he did use on the Highway, to wit Regent Street, a locomotive . . . which did not consume, as far as practicable, its own smoke'.[5] Popular disapproval matched, or perhaps even caused, a general reluctance to invest in vehicle manufacture. In November 1906, the *Motor Trader* offered its explanation of why France and Germany were keeping ahead of Britain: 'For the most part of ten years the British motor industry has been swimming on an ebb tide. It is generally agreed that one of the chief factors in the prolonged period of suspense and trial has been the disinclination of the British capitalist or inventor to put money into the industry.'[6] Fortunately, the men who established the reputation – if not the volume sales – of the industry were at hand. A few weeks after that editorial was published, Rolls-Royce announced its first public share issue.

Henry Royce was a polytechnic-educated electrical engineer. In 1884 he left the Electric Light and Power Company to make electrical components in his own factory. Initially he concentrated on the small end of the trade – electric bells, lamp-holders, switches and fuses. Then he expanded into the production of dynamos and switchboards. Within a couple of years he was building electric cranes, a remarkable advance for a company which was founded on capital of £75. His companion in all the new ventures was Ernest Claremont, a colleague from his earlier employment. Their partnership proved what, in Edwardian Britain, could be achieved by a steady hand guiding an innovator of genius.

In 1902 Henry Royce bought a DeDion 'Quad' – a four-wheeled motor-powered vehicle with such eccentric habits that Royce built a rockery at the end of his drive to act as a buffer when it ran out of control. He graduated to a DeVille which, although more reliable, did not meet his exacting engineering standards. Then he decided that the only car with which he would be completely satisfied was a vehicle of his own construction. So he began to build a two-cylinder ten-horsepower 'Royce' which, he hoped, would combine the values of silence, durability and reliability. The car made its first appearance on the public highway on 1 April 1904. It was such a success that one of the directors in the still expanding electrical company sent photographs to Charles Rolls, a gentleman car salesman and enthusiast who had driven the most powerful – that is to say twelve-horsepower – car in the 1900 Great Trial.

The Honourable Charles Rolls (Eton and Trinity) dealt in luxurious Panhards. Because of his aristocratic associations, he attracted a better class of customer. In 1903 Lord Rosebery bought a ten-horsepower two-seater as a coming-of-age present for his son, and the Crown Prince of Romania bought the same model a month later.[7] But there was a liquidity problem. Rolls sold his cars one by one, but Panhard delivered them in batches of four. For a while his father, Lord Llangattock, bridged the financial gap, but Rolls was anxious to find a manufacturer who was more understanding – and ideally British, not French.

It was a shareholder in Henry Royce's electrical crane company – Henry Edmunds, a founder member of the Automobile Club – who suggested that the Royce car ought to be produced for sale. Rolls was the ideal man to provide advice on the state of the market. At first Royce was reluctant to meet him, but Edmunds was persuasive. Neither man seemed enthusiastic about combining forces. On 26 March 1904, the matchmaker was still finding both parties difficult. 'I saw Mr Rolls yesterday after telephoning you and he said it would be much more convenient if you could see him in London, as he is so much occupied and further that several other houses are now in negotiation with him, wishing to do the whole part of his work.'[8]

Royce refused to go south, so Rolls and Edmunds travelled north – by train. The meeting, which took place in Manchester's Midland Hotel on 14 May 1904, got off to a bad start. Rolls thought that the 'Royce' which he had passed on his way from the station was a Deauville. But the afternoon ended with the agreement that Royce should make motor cars for sale to the general public and that Rolls should be his sole agent.

Once persuaded that his car would sell, Royce's ambition was boundless. The agreement between the two men required him to design and build four distinct chassis★ with different sized engines and to have at least one model ready for the Paris motor show of 1905. The ten- and twenty-horsepower models were exhibited complete, along with a fifteen-horsepower chassis and a thirty-horsepower engine. The ten-horsepower model was never put on the market. Royce realised that his strength was the ability to produce a car which met the needs of a more exclusive clientele. Its great virtue would be smooth running and silence. Indeed it was for those qualities that in December 1904 *Autocar* commended the ten-horsepower 'Tonneau'. It called the car a 'Rolls-Royce'.

From the start, Rolls had no doubt about the success of the venture. He was that kind of man. He moved his showrooms from unfashionable Fulham to Mayfair and cancelled first his Minerva and Orleans franchises and then his contract with Panhard. So great was the confidence of both partners that when, in 1906, it was decided to wind up the Rolls distribution company and amalgamate it with the motor car division of Rolls Limited, the *Motor Trader* believed that Rolls-Royce had overreached itself. 'We cannot help thinking the promoters have made a very weak appeal to the investing public. The price is steep for a name only a few years old.'[9]

The shares were offered in the hope that 'personal confidence in the personalities which appear in the directorate' would see them through. And so it did, with a little assistance from more tangible proof of the firm's visibility. In 1906 Rolls-Royce won the Manx Grand Prix and, with already substantial confidence further boosted, the company designed the forty-horsepower Silver Ghost – a car which established the company's reputation and remained in production for twenty-seven years. Then came victory in the 15,000-Mile Trial. It seemed that by any standard Rolls-Royce had fulfilled the boast of an early advertisement. 'Not one of the Best – the Best in the World.'[10]

Perhaps the venture would not have fared so well had it not been for Ernest Claremont, the third partner in the enterprise who, because

---

★The bodies were built by Barker, a coach-building company, which worked with Rolls-Royce for half a century.

his name did not appear on the radiator grill of the motor cars, is largely forgotten. He kept the dreamers' feet on the ground. As they grew more enthusiastic about producing the perfect motor car, he continually reminded them that there would be no perfection without commercial viability. His policy was set out to an annual shareholders' meeting. The Rolls-Royce Company was determined 'not to attract attention by the payment of large dividends, but to build up a solid business and effect the complete security of the capital invested in it'.[11]

Despite Claremont's prudence, there were some difficult days before the decade closed. Once or twice the banks had to come to the rescue. And there was a moment when it seemed that Rolls-Royce would be taken over by a Canadian adventurer called Max Aitken. But for most of the time things went well – perhaps too well. Charles Rolls liked an adventurous life and with the business running almost as smoothly as Henry Royce's engines, he increasingly turned to aviation, a passion which he financed by his work in the motor trade.

Rolls's aerial ambitions had originally been built around balloons. During a flight above South London in 1901 he had the idea of 'getting up a balloon club'.[12] By 1906, the Gas Light and Coke Company had laid a pipeline to the Hurlingham Club so that the exclusive gathering of enthusiasts could make an ascent each Saturday. To avoid the monotony of marvelling at the same panoramic view each week, Rolls had a balloon tender fitted to his Silver Ghost and rose above whichever part of the county took his fancy. As soon as aeroplanes were a practical prospect, balloons lost their charm. For Rolls, powered flight had two irresistible attractions. It was dangerous and it was being pioneered by the arrangement of competitions.

The first manned flight passed almost unnoticed in Britain. On 19 December 1903 the *Daily Mail* recorded, towards the bottom of an inside page, what it quaintly called the achievement of a 'Balloonless Airship'.

Messrs Wilbur and Orville Wright of Ohio, yesterday successfully experimented with a flying machine in Kittyhawk, North Carolina. The machine had no balloon attachment and derives

its force from propellers worked by a small engine. In the face of
a wind blowing twenty-one miles an hour, the machine flew
three miles at the rate of eight miles an hour and descended to a
point selected in advance.[13]

Three years later, Alberto Santos-Dumont flew two hundred yards
in twenty-one seconds. It amounted to very little when compared
with the Wright brothers' achievement, but it benefited from the fact
that Lord Northcliffe noticed. His excitement was attributable to his
apparent ignorance of what had happened at Kittyhawk back in 1903.
That was one of the reasons why he upbraided his journalists. 'It
does not matter how far he has flown. He has shown what can be
done. In a year's time, mark my words, that fellow will be flying over
here from France. Britain is no longer an island. Nothing so important has happened for a very long time. We must get hold of this thing
and make it our own.'[14]

Northcliffe was always prepared to make news in order that his
newspapers could report it, but he was genuinely excited by the idea
of flight. Personal enthusiasm combined with instinct for a good story
to produce a determination to take sole command and control of the
flying business in Britain. His method of achieving that end was, like
all his schemes, based on the assumption that money opens all doors.
So he announced that he would award aviation prizes – £1,000 for
the first flight across the English Channel from Calais to Dover and
£10,000 for a complete flight from London to Manchester. *Punch*
offered the same amount for a flight to Mars. The scepticism proved
misplaced.

For two years Charles Rolls resisted the temptation to abandon
everything else in favour of flying. As late as 1908 he gave up his place
in an international balloon race because duty called him to the Road
Congress in Paris[15] where he spoke of the Effect of Road Surfaces on
Motor Vehicles. But it was his last public involvement with motors
and motoring. Too much was happening in the air for him to remain
content with four wheels on the ground – much of it under the
supervision of Lord Northcliffe.

The *Daily Mail* decided to lionise the Wright brothers – who,
despite being American, it set up as clear-cut Anglo-Saxon rivals to

Santos-Dumont. They visited Northcliffe in France, reinforced by President Theodore Roosevelt's declaration that the *Daily Mail*'s prizes had increased interest in flying on both sides of the Atlantic. Interest in Britain was heightened to the point at which King Edward VII made a detour in order to meet the brothers at Northcliffe's French retreat. When they made a second visit in 1909, A. J. Balfour, Tory leader and until 1906 Prime Minister, was there to greet them. Another guest on that occasion reported that Wilbur Wright 'soars up with evident ease'.[16]

Many aviation prizes were established in the years before the Great War. They ranged from *Autocar*'s £500 for a British aero engine, to *Le Matin*'s £4,000 for the first flight from Paris to London. Northcliffe was merely following a trend. But he had a popular newspaper with which to publicise his patronage in Britain. It contained the first exclusive interview with Orville Wright, in which the sensation of flying was described as 'infinitely more exhilarating than motoring, easier and smoother'.[17] At a dinner given in honour of the Wrights, Rolls described flying's attractions differently. 'No dust, police traps or taxes.'[18] But when at last he was taken up by Wilbur Wright, his reaction was less prosaic. 'Once clear of the ground the feeling of security was perfect.' He was part of 'a new world conquered by man'.[19]

At the Wrights dinner Rolls mentioned, perhaps inappropriately, the military potential of flight. The *Daily Mail* reporter who had telegraphed London with the news of the earlier Kittyhawk flights had been sufficiently prescient to add, 'Aeroplane a war machine . . . .'[20] Northcliffe had ignored the prophecy until Balfour's visit to his house in France, when one of the party had again raised the military potential of the Wright brothers' achievement. He then telegraphed the Secretary of State for War urging immediate action, adding that, as a result of Britain's failure in the field, he was 'constantly being chaffed by foreign gentlemen'.[21] No doubt his embarrassment was increased when foreign gentlemen won both the aviation prizes which bore his name. On 25 July 1909, Louis Blériot landed his biplane on wooded ground between Dover Castle and the sea. Northcliffe, putting the promotion of his papers above his natural chauvinism, arranged (at barely twenty-four hours' notice) a lunch at the Savoy. The *Daily Mail* reported that it was attended by 'all the important people in the country'.[22]

Blériot's aeroplane, in need of only minimal repair, was brought up from Dover and put on display in Selfridge's department store. Amongst the thousands of visitors who filed past was Claude Graham-White – like Rolls and Blériot, himself a motor car salesman. He was entranced. Next month he attended the Rheims Aviation Meeting and met Blériot, from whom he bought an as yet unbuilt aeroplane. Graham-White spent six weeks at Blériot's factory helping with the construction of his purchase. When it was finished, he taxied it out of the hangar and, without any instruction, took off and flew successfully for twenty minutes. He then made a perfect landing.

Graham-White hoped to open an aviation school in Britain, a project which he thought was more likely to prosper if it could be announced in the blaze of publicity which would surround his receipt of the London to Manchester Aviation Prize. Money seems to have been no object. When he decided that his Blériot XII was not powerful enough to stay the course, he bought a bigger plane from Henri Farman, another pioneer aviator and aircraft builder. At 5.19 a.m. on the morning of Saturday 10 April, 1910, he took off from Park Royal in North London and, after circling a gas-holder near Wormwood Scrubs for the benefit of the Royal Aero Club referee, made for the London and North-Western railway line which he proposed to follow to Rugby, the first stop on the journey to Manchester which no aeroplane could complete in a single flight.

He landed smoothly, but the undercarriage stuck on a hillock. While his plane was being repaired, Graham-White talked to reporters. His highest altitude had been 1,100 feet and his average speed had been between thirty and forty miles an hour. 'It was wretchedly cold all the way and I was cold at the start. My eyes suffered towards the end and my fingers were quite numbed.' Ladies in his admiring audience, led by Lady Denbigh, lent him their fur wraps.

On the second leg of the flight, the north wind blew so hard that it twice blew Graham-White's aircraft round so that it pointed back towards London. But he struggled on until the engine stalled. Although it started again after a 100-feet glide it was impossible to go on that night with an unreliable engine. So there was another landing in another field and another wait while his supporting team found him. Graham-White went to bed in a nearby farmhouse. His mechanics rectified the fault but forgot to tie his plane down. It was blown over in the gale and its upper wing half torn off. The first attempt to win the prize was over. Graham-White returned to Park Royal certain that on his second attempt he would succeed.

When he arrived back in London he was given the bad news. Louis Paulhan, a Frenchman, meant to make it a competition. When he had heard that Graham-White had begun, but not completed, the flight to Manchester, he had abandoned the exhibition of German dirigibles in Cologne and left at once for London. Paulhan also possessed a Farman-designed aeroplane. He broke it down into its constituent parts so that it could be transported on the boat train. It arrived on 27 April and was immediately reassembled. On the same day, Graham-White confirmed with his mechanics that his plane was fit to fly. After an early afternoon test flight, he went to bed. He would need all his strength for the race which began next morning.

The race began that evening. At half-past five, Louis Paulhan – without waiting to test his plane's airworthiness in a trial flight – took off and headed for Hampstead Cemetery where, standing on a grave, the Royal Aero Club Referee waved him on his way. Twenty-seven minutes later, Graham-White was wakened and told that Paulhan was in the air. He was 'greatly vexed' by the Frenchman's unsporting behaviour but confident that he could catch and overtake him. He took off at half-past six, cheered on his way by hundreds of supporters who, having read the evening paper, had hurried to Park Royal to see the man whom they expected would, next day, become Britain's champion in a contest to decide which country ruled the air. The London to Manchester Aviation Prize had become a race for national glory.

Graham-White covered almost sixty miles before dark. Then he landed at Roade in Northamptonshire with the intention of continuing his flight at first light on the following day. His plane was almost immediately surrounded by a crowd, mostly made up of people who had looked for two aeroplanes approaching from the south. Unfortunately for the patriots among them, one plane had passed overhead almost an hour before the other. Paulhan was almost sixty miles ahead. There was only one way in which Graham-White could hope to win. After pausing only to sign autographs by the light of bicycle lamps, he set out on the first night flight in aviation history.

Friends in motor cars drove along the road to Manchester, hoping that he would follow their headlights to victory. He made good progress as far as Nuneaton. Then his engine failed again and he was forced to land at Polesworth. It was just after four o'clock on a cold spring morning, but three thousand people had gathered round the plane by the time that he left, an hour later, on what he hoped would be the final leg of the race. The high wind in the Trent Valley confounded him again. When he landed at Whittington he was told that Paulhan was already in Manchester. Gallantly he announced the bad news to the crowd which had hoped to cheer him on his way and, like a true Englishman, offered his sincere congratulations to the man who had beaten him.

Paulhan had tried to fly above the wind, but his hopes of 'finding a calmer patch' were not realised. He minimised neither the difficulties nor the dangers which he faced. 'I was almost torn from my seat. I had to hold on to the controls with all my strength.' However, both his engine and his nerve had held out, and the mechanics who travelled north on a special LNER train were not needed. Paradoxically, by using the railway to provide his support, Paulhan was able to gain most of the publicity as well as win the prize. Journalists who had travelled with his entourage had telegraphed news of his progress from every station.

Overnight the race became a sensation. In New York, the *Evening Post* described the gladiatorial contest as 'not the greatest of all the century but the greatest of all time'. *The Times* employed deep purple prose to describe how Manchester reacted to the whisper that a signalman had telephoned Piccadilly Station with the news that an aeroplane was five miles down the line.

> Every eye was directed to the sky-line of houses and trees to the south. The eastern horizon was crimson with the light of threatening sunrise. Overhead the sky was dull and grey and a light cold drizzle was driving along a south westerly wind . . .

Suddenly there was a scattered volley of breathless exclamations. 'Here he is. Paulhan is coming!' Over the tops of the trees appeared, small and faint at first, but rapidly increasing in size, the now familiar outline of an aeroplane. From the crowd arose cheer after cheer. No one cared then whether the aviator who approached was a Frenchman or Englishman. It was enough that he was a hero of the air.[23]

As with Blériot so with Paulhan. The *Daily Mail* organised an immediate celebration lunch at the Savoy. It was attended by such notables as H. G. Wells and Hiram Maxim, the eponymous inventor of the latest model in machine guns. Graham-White was presented with a '100 Guinea Cup' by way of consolation and (because the British love a gallant loser) became in the folklore, one of the pioneers of aviation. It was generally agreed to have been a good day for powered flight and flying. Before the lunch was over it was to become an even better one as the result of a near-catastrophe in Germany, about which the guests were to read on the following morning.

A *Daily Mail* reporter, influenced by Northcliffe's earlier passion for balloons, had been a passenger on the maiden flight of the massive Deutschland Zeppelin VII. He had enjoyed the trip so much that he had flown with the dirigible on its second outing. It crashed after 'the swerving, diving, rain-beaten airship fought inch by inch'[24] to stay in the air. No lives were lost, but the combination of Paulhan's triumph and Count Zeppelin's near tragedy confirmed Northcliffe's belief that the future lay with aeroplanes – and that he should play a major part in their development. At the end of the London-to-Manchester lunch he announced his sponsorship of a new £10,000 prize. The 'Great Cross-Country Race' would convince the general public that the future belonged to the aeroplane and the *Daily Mail*.

There were disasters and death in every form of early flying. Charles Rolls, who became a national hero after completing a ninety-minute non-stop flight to France and back, was killed in a crash-landing at Bournemouth while giving a flying display as part of the resort's Centenary Celebration. A few months earlier, he had asked to be relieved of his duties at Rolls-Royce, which he found 'irksome'. The company agreed, although it was already facing the strain of temporarily losing the services of Henry Royce. The Board of Directors had required him to take a holiday because of the fear that overwork was jeopardising his future and, therefore, the company's long-term prospects. The two different reasons for the men's absence from the motor industry reveal a great deal about their partnership. The reaction to Charles Rolls's death was equally indicative of public attitudes towards flying. He had made a glorious sacrifice in a noble cause. The cause was Britain's future leadership of the world's most exciting innovation – and the increased circulation of the *Daily Mail*.

Northcliffe did all he could to build interest in 'the first great cross-country contest between the champions of various nations'. His papers exalted the character of the pilots as much as they praised the quality of the planes. Both 'freak machines' and 'inexperienced airmen' were excluded from the contest. 'Personality', *Mail* readers were told, 'is the secret of success in an aerial contest.' It was proud to be associated with all the 'merry, careless, cigarette-smoking airmen'.

It took the Royal Aero Club a year to devise the rules and work out the stopping places on each leg of the race – Hendon, Harrogate, Newcastle, Edinburgh and almost every other large town in Great Britain. Nobody called it an imitation of the Century Road Race which had been contested over the same distance. The *Daily Mail* published biographies of the twenty-four accepted competitors and a race card not unlike one which might be obtained at Ascot or Newmarket.

The general public was invited to attend the staggered take-off at Hendon on 22 July 1911. A ticket to the enclosure cost two and six-pence for an individual and five shillings for a car. If the *Daily Mail* is to be believed, the crowd was 'vast beyond reckoning'. The enthusiasm was just as great at each of the places at which the pilots landed after the completion of each leg of the race. On the last day of the race the enthusiasm at Hendon was irrepressible at finishing-post as well as starting-line.

Gathered before midnight, an army of sightseers passed through the black night and grey dawn. Within a mile of the aerodrome, men and women slept by the roadside, heedless of the throng which passed onwards chanting choruses. There were native

French too. From one group encamped there arose the cry, Vive la France, whenever the click of tools from a shed punctuated the oft-repeated singing of the Marseillaise.[25]

The French were right to celebrate. André Beaumont, the favourite from the start, had won. Britain, said the flying fraternity, echoing Northcliffe ten years earlier, was no longer an island. It was, however, still a great maritime nation, which earned its living and safeguarded its borders because of the special relationship it enjoyed with ships and the sea.

Although Britain took second place to France in the air, traditional transport industries fared better − largely because Edwardian innovators and entrepreneurs found it easier to develop and expand existing companies rather than create new ones. The railways − the glory of Victorian Britain − were a particular beneficiary of the continued enthusiasm for investment in visible assets. And they prospered accordingly. In 1904 the combined market value of the twenty-two largest railway companies was over 70 per cent of the quoted worth of the fifty largest British companies.[26] That was the direct result of continued investment in rolling stock which produced a capital to labour ratio of £1,500 per employee. The comparable figure for Vickers Sons and Maxims, Armstrong Whitworth, John Brown and Camel Laird was something less than £600.

Yet the shipbuilding companies of Tyne and Wear, the Clyde, Barrow-in-Furness and Merseyside were amongst the most successful enterprises of the era. The early years of the century were the age of the big battleship. Between 1904 and 1910 the eight main maritime nations spent a total of £1,340 million on warships.[27] The Royal Navy generally relied on the Royal Dockyard where the Lords of the Admiralty had no doubt the work was done in the least time, up to the highest standards and at the lowest cost. Foreign fleets had to rely on private companies − two in America, Germany and Britain and one in Italy. Vickers, in the north-east, could compete with any shipbuilder in the world, but Armstrong, in the north-west, 'was the most successful exporter of warships in the world and held that position by the quality of its production and sales organisation'.[28] At the end of the nineteenth century, the company employed 2,500 men. In

1905 the value of their work was demonstrated when the Armstrong-built battleships of the imperial Japanese navy defeated the Russian fleet in the North Atlantic.

The warship boom swept through South America. In 1902, Chile (engaged in one of the more active phases of its perpetual border dispute with Argentina) heightened the tension by ordering two battleships. Vickers won the contract for the *Constitution*. In 1904 Brazil announced its intention of adding to its warship fleet. The *Minas Gerces* was to be built by Armstrong, and Vickers were to build the *São Paolo*. A third battleship was commissioned from Krupp of Germany, but Armstrong's chief salesman – Sir Eustace d'Agincourt, RN (Retired) – convinced the Brazilian minister of defence that the 'biggest battleship in the world' could be constructed on the Tyne for a good deal less than it would cost in Bremer-haven, so it was ordered from Britain at an estimated cost of £1,821,000. Each country – Chile, Argentina and Brazil – eventually decided that the ships cost more than they could afford. The three South American fleets were sold second-hand at knock-down prices to other navies, but that was of no account to either Vickers or Armstrong. They did the work, took the money and accepted no responsibility for the direction in which the twelve-inch guns were pointed.

Shipbuilding – civilian as well as naval – was thriving on a diet of cut-throat salesmanship. In the pursuit of foreign orders, nothing was sacrosanct. But there were some occasions on which officers and gentlemen expected to be kept free of commercialism. Fortunately for the future of Edwardian shipbuilding, one energetic entrepreneur broke the rules and produced, in consequence, one of the era's greatest industrial success stories.

In June 1897, 164 warships were assembled – in four lines, each five miles long – for inspection by the Prince of Wales. The Spithead Review was the Royal Navy's contribution to the celebration of Queen Victoria's Diamond Jubilee. *The Times* described it in suitably portentous terms. 'It possesses a significance which is directly and intimately connected with the welfare and prosperity of the Empire and may be regarded as an inspection or stock-taking of Britain's sea guard.'[29] It also turned into a sales promotion demonstration. As soon as the formal inspection was completed, a tiny ship – one hundred feet from bow to stern – rode up and down the line of warships at over thirty knots. It was called the *Turbina* and its owner, the Honourable Charles Algernon Parsons, broke the rules of seamanship and the laws of gentlemanly conduct to demonstrate the qualities of invention.

In fact the turbine engine, which gave his boat its name, was not new, but Parsons had devised a way of making it a practical means of propulsion. And the demonstration of her potential was so compelling that the *Turbina*'s owner and captain was forgiven his considerable indiscretions – which included twice overtaking the Royal Yacht, *Victoria and Albert*. The Admiralty began studies of turbine power within a month of Parson's exhibition. In December 1897 an order was placed for a turbine-propelled destroyer.

Two turbine destroyers, the *Cobra* and *Viper*, were in service by the beginning of the new century, but in August 1901 *Viper* fouled a tug off Alderney and *Cobra* unaccountably broke in two while anchored off the Lincolnshire coast. The Court Martial – which always follows the loss of a Royal Navy ship – exonerated the *Cobra*'s captain on the grounds that the design produced a result 'weaker than other destroyers' and added to its judgement a gratuitous codicil: the Tribunal 'regretted that such a ship was purchased into Her Majesty's Service'. The Board of Admiralty, still anxious to exploit the speed which turbines could provide, disagreed. A Committee of Enquiry was set up 'to examine the future construction of torpedo boat destroyers'. It gave a clean bill of health to turbine propulsion – perhaps not unexpectedly since Parsons was included in its membership. As a result, the character of shipbuilding changed.

The *King Edward*, the first turbine-propelled passenger ship in the world, was ferrying passengers along the River Clyde before the Admiralty took its decision to change engine type. In 1902, an almost identical ship, the *Queen Alexandra*, joined it in Port Glasgow. Then the cross-Channel turbine-driven package steamers the *Queen* and the *Brighton* came into service. In 1903, the steam yacht *Emerald* crossed the Atlantic under turbine power. The Allan Line chose turbine engines for the 13,000-ton *Virginia* and *Victoria* and the Cunard Company did the same for the 30,000-ton *Carmania*. Turbines had been accepted as safe and suitable for passenger liners. And they offered an opportunity to restore some of the maritime prestige which at the end of the nineteenth century had been unexpectedly diminished by Germany.

While the *Turbina* was showing its paces to the assembled fleet off Spithead, Norddeutscher Lloyd were planning an even more spectacular feat of speed. The company, supported and subsidised by the Berlin government, built the *Kaiser Wilhelm der Grosse* which, within months of its launching, won the Blue Riband of the Atlantic. The Kaiser was not satisfied. The Hamburg-America Line was encouraged to enter the competition. The *Deutschland*, launched in July 1900, broke the *Kaiser Wilhelm der Grosse*'s record. It was a pyrrhic victory. At high speed the ship vibrated so violently that its luxury (which was its main attraction for first-class passengers) was diminished to a point which deterred bookings. The *Deutschland* slowed down. But in 1902, the *Kronprinz Wilhelm* regained the title for Norddeutscher Lloyd. The *Deutschland*, regardless of its passengers' comfort, then broke the record for a second time and kept the Blue Riband for five years.

The response of the British government was dilatory but eventually decisive. The Cunard Shipping Company was lent £2.6 million at 2¾ per cent interest and promised an annual subsidy of £150,000 on condition that it built two turbine-driven liners which were capable of sustaining 25 knots – two more than the speed at which the Germans had challenged and beaten each other. The Cunarders were to be designed in a way which enabled their conversion to battleships in time of war. It took almost three years for the company, the government and Swan Hunter – the initially favoured shipbuilder – to agree the plans. But in late 1904 the deal was done. The result was the *Mauritania* and the *Lusitania*.*

Originally, the *Lusitania* was to be built in Barrow. But trials – with a forty-seven-foot replica in a tank which simulated Atlantic conditions – suggested that a broader ship would need less power to achieve

---

*The *Lusitania* was torpedoed by German U-boats off the coast of Ireland on 7 May 1915. 1,195 passengers and crew were drowned, 128 of them American. The Germans claimed that the possibility of conversion into a battleship justified their action. America disagreed. The antagonism which the sinking aroused contributed to the United States' decision to enter the war.

the stipulated speed. A beam of eighty-eight feet would make possible a top speed of 26.7 knots but it would also make the ship too big for construction in Vickers' yard. John Brown were more resourceful. They widened and deepened the Clyde. The keel was laid in May 1905 and the *Lusitania* was launched in June 1906. She went out on her maiden voyage from Liverpool to New York on 9 September 1907.

For some reason, it was the *Mauritania*, the *Lusitania*'s sister ship – built by Swan Hunter and Wigham Richardson on the Tyne, and launched in September 1906 – which had the popular appeal. Reason demands that the *Lusitania* should enjoy the accolades of history. It was the first four-propeller-driven liner and, at 40,000 tons, the biggest ship afloat. The Liverpool Landing Stage had to be extended to allow her to dock and in October 1907, a month after her maiden voyage, she won the Blue Riband for both the eastwards and westwards crossing. But two months later, the *Mauritania* made her first Atlantic crossing – and immediately broke the *Lusitania*'s record. The editor of the *Shipbuilder*, who was a passenger on that journey, regarded the ship as 'a floating palace'. Lack of originality did nothing to lessen the image's impact. The description which followed illustrated why journalists had been invited on the maiden voyage: 'The great entrance and staircase are treated in the fifteenth-century Italian manner. The woodwork is French walnut, the panels being veneered with some of the finest wood one could wish to see . . . The first-class lounge or music room is a noble apartment treated in the style which obtained in France in the last quarter of the eighteenth century.'[30]

That luxury was all available in a ship which possessed the speed that allowed it to cross the Atlantic in barely five days and, because of that, held the Blue Riband of the Atlantic for twenty-two years. And the record speeds could be sustained without unacceptable vibration because of the way in which Britain – in particular the Honourable Sir Charles Parsons and his Marine Steam Turbine Company – had developed a new nautical engine. British shipbuilding was again on top of the world.

British ships were not, however, always turbine-powered. The Oceanic Navigation Company, known, because of its flags, as the

White Star Line, did not power its liners with turbine engines. It chose luxury in place of speed for no better reason than the technical limitations of the yard which built the ships. The two liners which they commissioned to rival the *Mauritania* and the *Lusitania* were commissioned from Harland and Woolf, a firm which neither possessed nor professed much experience of turbines. But the Northern Ireland company could claim both enthusiasm and initiative. The Oceanic Navigation Company wanted both new ships to be built simultaneously. So Sir William Arroll – famous for the construction of the Forth Bridge – was employed to erect a new gantry in the Belfast dockyard. It was 840 feet long and 240 feet wide – enabling the two keels to be laid side by side. One was for a ship to be called the *Olympic*. The other was for the *Titanic*.

Thomas Andrews, managing director and chief designer of Harland and Woolf, believed that the two new liners surpassed in splendour anything that Cunard could offer. He was equally sure that, because it had a double-bottomed hull and was divided into sixteen watertight sections, his new ships were unsinkable. It was for that reason that he provided enough lifeboats to accommodate only 1,178 of the 2,222 passengers and crew who set out on the maiden voyage from Southampton to New York in April 1912. Six hundred miles south of Newfoundland, during the night of the 14th to 15th, the *Titanic* struck an iceberg. Five of the watertight compartments flooded and the ship sank, drowning 1,515 men, women and children. Among them was W. T. Stead, editor of the *Pall Mall Gazette* and prophet of the 'new journalism'.

Stead had, for several years, been fascinated by the supernatural – particularly 'automatic writing', which he either believed or hoped might enable him to have conversations with 'the other side'. He had made a pact with Julia Amos – a journalist on the *Union Signal* of Chicago, with whom he conducted a long and learned correspondence about the Oberammergau passion plays – that whichever of them died first would send a message from 'the other side'. Julia's first message was received in 1893. Then, in the following year, Stead's son, William, died. For the rest of his life the bereaved father was obsessed with 'keeping in touch' with his son. Spiritualism came to dominate his life – to the great detriment of his reputation and his career. Sometimes his premonitions were published in his paper.

Even before spiritualism became an obsession Stead made prophesies – based, he said, on intuition – about 'the shape of things to come'. In 1886, the *Pall Mall Gazette* had published an account of a mighty liner sinking in the Atlantic with immense loss of life. It ended with the warning, 'This is exactly what might take place and what will take place if liners set sail short of boats.' In the account of the *Titanic* sinking, the *Review of Reviews*, not altogether reasonably, blamed officialdom for not heeding Stead's warning. 'After twenty-six years of progress, the Board of Trade is responsible for the loss of 1600 lives . . . because there were not enough lifeboats.'

Amongst the tributes which followed Stead's death was one from a Sir E. T. Cole who revealed that, shortly before he left for America, Stead had told a friend 'when my work is done, I shall die a violent death. I have had a vision and I know it is true as surely as I am talking to you.' Survivors of the sinking said that he made no attempt to save himself 'but stood with the women and children, putting them into lifeboats' as if he knew that his time had come. Admiral Lord Fisher (with whom he had plotted to promote the idea that the British Navy was scandalously short of battleships) called him 'Cromwell and Martin Luther rolled into one' and imagined him encouraging the ship's band 'to play a cheerful tune'.[31] Praise for Stead's courage – and speculation about it being the result of a fatalist belief that it was time to meet his maker – punctuated the agonised search for culprits.

Most of the recriminations concerned neither the design of the ship nor the capacity of the lifeboats. The Leyland Lines' *California* was said to be barely twenty miles away but, because its wireless operator was not on duty, it did not receive the *Titanic*'s distress signals. The *Carpathia*, a Cunard liner, did pick up the SOS and, steaming at full speed, reached the site of the disaster eighty minutes after the *Titanic* went down. Seven hundred passengers were saved by the operation of a new miracle – wireless telegraphy.

When the *Carpathia* docked in New York, Guglielmo Marconi was waiting on the Cunard pier. During the subsequent inquiry into the disaster, it was alleged that he had insisted that the messages from the stricken ship must remain the exclusive property of his company. The *New York Times* – which sent a reporter with Marconi to the pier and may, therefore, have had a vested interest in his monopoly of the news – described his compassionate conversation with the survivors. He was planning a ten-million-dollar share issue with which to finance the purchase of the United Wireless Telegraph Company. These were heady days for Marconi and the system which he had perfected. It was taken for granted by Wall Street and the City of London that anyone who had been wise enough to invest in either his American or his British enterprises would make a fortune.

That view was clearly held by Sir Rufus Isaacs, the Attorney General in the Asquith government. In April 1912, a few days after the *Titanic* set sail, he bought 10,000 shares in the American Marconi Company from his brother, who in turn bought them from a third Isaacs brother who was managing director of the company. He immediately sold a thousand to Lloyd George (the Chancellor of the Exchequer) and another thousand to the Master of Elibank (the government chief whip) with the friendly intention of allowing them to share in the expected capital gain. In those more innocent days, Ministers of the Crown were allowed to own shares without depositing them in a 'blind trust' and could continue to speculate on the stock market. The three Members of Parliament were not, therefore, guilty of an impropriety; but their position was complicated by the fact that, a month earlier, Herbert Samuel, the Post-master General, had accepted – subject to parliamentary approval – the tender submitted by the Marconi Company of Britain for the construction of the Imperial Wireless Chain which the Sixth Imperial Conference, meeting in 1911, had decided was essential to the security of the Empire.

In fact, the ministers' conduct was no worse than unwise. The two companies – British and American – were entirely separate and the purchase of the American shares was not the result of any special knowledge which could be described as 'insider trading'. Equally important, Marconi of America did not hold shares in its sister company. So the value of Isaacs's purchase was not (directly at least) increased by the government contract. But rumours of impropriety began to circulate at Westminster. They were taken up by the anti-Semite clique led by Hilaire Belloc. Cecil Chesterton, brother to G. K., published the allegation in *Eye Witness*, the Catholic polemical journal which he owned and edited. Isaacs and Lloyd George wanted to sue. Asquith dissuaded them: 'I suspect that it has a very meagre circulation. I notice only one page of advertisements and that is occupied by books by Belloc's publisher. Prosecution would secure it notoriety, which might yield subscribers. We have broken weather and, but for Winston, there would be nothing in the papers.'[32]

The Marconi contract should have been ratified by the House of Commons in August. Technical questions about some clauses meant that Parliament's approval could not be sought before October. By then the rumours of impropriety made an easy passage of the proposal impossible. Herbert Samuel moved a resolution to set up a House of Commons Select Committee to enquire into every aspect of the contract. In the debate which followed, Isaacs and Lloyd George made categorical personal statements. They had bought no shares in 'the Marconi Company'. They later justified their conduct by arguing that they referred to the British Marconi Company which was the subject of the debate. The House of Commons accepted their assurances and the contract was endorsed.

It was then that, in Paris, *Le Matin* repeated 'libel' against Isaacs and added, for good measure, that Samuel had chosen Marconi to build the radio link as a favour to the Attorney General's brother. It was no longer possible to avoid the publicity of a prosecution. Winston Churchill, who was himself to become briefly and wrongly implicated, persuaded F. E. Smith to represent Samuel.[33] In consequence, the case achieved a status at the Bar which encouraged Edward Carson, the leader of the Ulster Unionists, to act for Isaacs. The hope that the involvement of two such prominent members of the Opposition would encourage the integrity of two Liberal ministers to be examined 'outside party politics' was not realised. And the proceedings, though unavoidable, did great damage to both plaintiffs' reputations. *Le Matin* withdrew its allegation unreservedly, apologised and paid all the costs, but Isaacs was forced to admit that he had bought shares in the Marconi Company of America. Although he had not lied to the House of Commons, he had been less than fully frank. If he was innocent of all impropriety, why had he hidden what he later insisted was an entirely respectable transaction?

Suspicions were heightened by the discovery that the Master of

Elibank (recently retired as government chief whip) had acquired some of the shares on behalf of the Liberal Party and then sailed, for an undisclosed purpose and period, for Bogotà. The mood of the House of Commons and, in consequence, the attitude of the Select Committee changed. Anticipating weeks of consideration and determined to concentrate on the questions of ministerial conduct, it delegated discussion on the technical aspect of the contract to an advisory committee, under the chairmanship of Lord Parker of Waddington, a patent judge. He quickly removed all doubt about Samuel's decision. 'The Marconi system is at present the only system of which it can be said with any certainty that it is capable of filling the requirements of the Imperial Chain.'

The question of propriety was not resolved so easily.

Select Committees of the House of Commons usually contain one or two Members whose enthusiasm outruns their discretion. So it was with the Marconi Inquiry. Other names were added to the list of possible miscreants. They included Winston Churchill, who was called to give personal testimony.

> Am I to understand that every person, Minister or Member of Parliament whose name is mentioned by current rumour . . . is to be summoned before you and asked to give a categorical denial to charges which, as I have pointed out, have become grossly insulting . . . I am grieved beyond words that fellow Members of the House of Commons should have thought it right to lend their sanction to putting such a question.[34]

Having complained so bitterly about the nature of the question, he went on to answer it in terms so categoric that his denial took up six lines of the Official Report. He then, typically, demonstrated his solidarity with the other accused ministers by ordering the Admiralty Board yacht to the Caernarvon coast and taking the Lloyd George family for a sailing holiday. Such things were acceptable in Edwardian Britain. The yacht was treated as private property by all senior ministers with the slightest connection with the Navy or naval policy.

Lloyd George and Isaacs offered their resignations to the Prime Minister in the clear expectation that he would refuse them – as, indeed, he did. But in private he described their conduct as both 'lamentable' and 'difficult to defend'.[35] That did not prevent him from defending them in public. Asquith told the House of Commons, 'Their honour, both their private honour and their public honour, is, at this moment, absolutely unstained.'

The Select Committee was not so sure. Inevitably, it divided on party lines. The Liberal majority concluded that 'the ministers concerned, when entering into the purchases, were all bona fide convinced that the American company had no interest in the agreement'. The Unionist minority claimed that an interest existed and that it was 'material, although indirect'. As a result, buying the shares was a grave 'impropriety'. More important, it aimed to censure both Lloyd George and Isaacs for 'wanting in frankness and in respect for the House of Commons' by failing to admit their involvement with the American company during the October debate.

Reports of Select Committees are usually debated in the House of Commons on a simple motion to accept their findings. Two amendments were moved to the Marconi report. One, in the name of a sympathetic Liberal back-bencher, spoke in unequivocal terms of the honour and rectitude of Lloyd George and Isaacs. The other, moved on behalf of the official Opposition by Andrew Bonar Law himself, asked only for the House to express its regret. Had it been carried, both men would have had to go.

Of course the Liberal amendment prevailed and the two careers continued uninterrupted apart from the occasional disturbance that promotion brings. Lloyd George became Prime Minister and Rufus Isaacs the Lord Chief Justice of England, in those days a natural progression for the Attorney General. There were rumours that Asquith had known about the American shares before the first debate and failed to insist on their existence being revealed; but his reputation was secure. Lloyd George was known to be devious and his reputation was confirmed. He was part of the new world of the twentieth century. And his progress was not to be halted, or indeed significantly impaired, by such a trivial matter as the concealment of dubious financial dealings.

The world had moved on for Marconi too. He had come a long way since the day in December 1901 when he had waited in Nova

Scotia to receive, from Cornwall, the first transatlantic wireless message. Short-wave radio had become international big business and Marconi, with the 1909 Nobel Prize to his credit, was the beneficiary. Two years after the *Titanic* sank, Sir Oliver Lodge wrote, without rancour, of how the miracle had been achieved. 'My friend Alexander Muirhead conceived the telegraphic application which ultimately led to the foundation of the Lodge–Muirhead Syndicate now bought up by the Marconi Co . . . Two years later, Marconi came over with the same thing in a secret box . . .'[36]

The *Titanic* disaster marked a moment in world history when the true potential of wireless telegraphy was recognised. It was one of the wonders which made the Edwardian world shrink at a speed that history has not acknowledged.

The Summer Ends in August

Queen Victoria died in the arms of her grandson, Kaiser Wilhelm II of Germany. Her son, who became Edward VII at that instant, moved forward and closed her eyes. Then he collapsed in uninhibited grief. The end had been anticipated. The family, led by the Queen's daughter Princess Louise, had already said their last farewells, and the Bishop of Winchester had completed the Aaronic blessing with the words 'give thee peace'. The ever faithful Doctor Reid assumed command and supervised the removal of the body in preparation for the complicated procedures – many of them stipulated by the Queen herself – which had to precede the burial.

Looking back, it seems that the Kaiser's intimate presence at that last moment was an augury of things to come. At the time, the King and Court thought of him as no more than an irritant. He had abandoned Berlin and his imperial duties as soon as he heard that his grandmother's illness was terminal and, despite telegrams from Osborne which were intended to dissuade him from intruding into British grief, he had travelled by royal train and imperial yacht to his dying grandmother's bedside.

His presence was particularly unwelcome to his uncle, the new King. The Kaiser had been openly sympathetic to the Boers, but there were also personal reasons for the animosity. Wilhelm was twenty-nine when he succeeded his father in 1888. In the early days of his reign, his policy – in so far as Bismarck allowed him one – had been the product of arrogance complicated by insecurity. Immediately on his accession he had imposed martial law on Berlin and confined his mother, King Edward's sister, to her quarters 'to prevent state or secret documents being conveyed to England'.[1] The gross offence against his mother's integrity and Britain's honour had been compounded by his subsequent harsh treatment of the woman who was Queen Victoria's daughter. What was worse, he was rarely civil to Queen Victoria's son.

Wilhelm had become Kaiser in 1888 and, during the thirteen years which followed, he regarded his Uncle Edward – no more than an Heir Apparent – as his obvious inferior. At his best, he was deeply conscious of the majesty of his imperial person, and he was rarely at his best in Britain. All sorts of obeisances were expected. Edward found it difficult to oblige and the Kaiser, as a result, believed the Prince of Wales and future king to be 'a peacock'. Although he despised his uncle, Wilhelm loved and admired his grandmother. Nothing could have kept him from her funeral. Throughout, he behaved in a way which illustrated why the King and Court did not want him there.

The Kaiser sent two battleships and two cruisers to augment the Royal Navy ships which formed a guard of honour across the Solent between Cowes and Portsmouth when the Queen's mortal remains set out on their last journey from Osborne to Windsor. The coffin was carried on the *Alberta*, the first of the three royal yachts in the convoy. Then came the *Osborne*. The *Victoria and Albert* followed – accompanied by the *Hohenzollern*, the Kaiser's own yacht.

Before the coffin was carried from royal ship to royal train, another complicated ceremony had to be performed. The captains of all the escort vessels boarded the *Alberta* and said their individual farewells. Then they waited while their sovereign arrived to lead the mourners in a short naval service. At the moment when the King paid his homage in front of the coffin, a steam launch set out from the *Hohenzollern*. The Kaiser was both captain and crew. One admiral muttered, more in hope than anxiety, 'He doesn't know the tide or the currents.' The *Schadenfreude* was misconceived. The Kaiser brought his boat alongside the *Alberta* and stepped on board with easy elegance.[2] It was the first of his many insensitive intrusions. When, next day, the great funeral procession got under way in London, the King rode immediately behind the royal standard. On his immediate right, the Kaiser was mounted on a milk-white charger – one of six he had brought over to make sure that he respected his grandmother's wishes. Queen Victoria wanted a white funeral.

For the rest of King Edward's reign, Wilhelm II was the source of continual embarrassment and anxiety to both the monarch and his ministers. Personal animosity mingled with political ambition to create a smouldering tension which burst into flame every other year. In 1904, anxious to demonstrate that the Entente with France was not a threat to Germany, Edward suggested that he visit Berlin. His nephew suggested Kiel. Although he knew that the alternative venue had been chosen so that the Kaiser could display his increasing naval might, the King agreed. The visit was a great success until the Kaiser suggested that Japan's victory over Russia would result in the 'Yellow Peril' menacing all Europe. Edward laughed out loud. Because of the King's undisguised amusement at his nephew's naiveté, the two monarchs were not on speaking terms for more than a year. It is hard to decide who was more foolish, the King or the Kaiser.

On 15 August 1905 the King received a letter from Count Gotz von Seckendorff, an old friend who had been Marshal to Edward's sister, the Empress Frederick. It begged the King to visit Hamburg to effect a reconciliation with Wilhelm. Inevitably, Edward dismissed the suggestion as impertinent. Knollys was instructed to reply that 'in no circumstances would he consent to run after the Emperor . . . it would be undignified for him to play such a part'.[3] The letter concluded with a passage which, whether or not it was intended to be emollient, had quite the opposite effect. 'His Majesty . . . directs me to tell you that he does not know whether the Emperor retains any affection for him but, from one or two things which he has heard recently, he should say *not* so that it would do no good were he to pay a dozen visits a year. To show however that he has no animosity against either the Emperor or Germany, the King has invited the Crown Prince of Germany to visit Windsor in November next.'[4]

The Kaiser was outraged. He had never been invited to Windsor and he told the British Ambassador to convey his wishes to London.

He wished to be the King's guest. Knollys replied to the Berlin foreign office, 'Perhaps *next* year unless the Emperor continues to trump up imaginary grievances against the King and intrigues, whenever he has the opportunity, against this country . . .'[5] The intrigue to which he referred was a draft treaty, drawn up at the Czar's invitation by the Kaiser himself, to commit Russia and Germany to protect each other against 'English and Japanese arrogance and insolence.'[6]

President Theodore Roosevelt, with whom Edward VII carried on a stilted correspondence, hoped that he could avert the danger of a Russian-German alliance by brokering a peace treaty between Russia and Japan. But uncle and nephew found new grievances over which to fight. On 7 June 1905, Norway dissolved its union with Sweden. A new king was needed. Wilhelm wanted the throne for one of his younger sons. Edward wanted it for his son-in-law. The King won. Prince Charles of Denmark became King Haakon VII of Norway. He was still on the throne when Germany invaded Norway in 1940.

In 1907, it seemed as if a lasting peace was about to break out. The Kaiser was to make a state visit to London, beginning on 11 November. On 31 October, the King – racing at Newmarket – received a message from his ambassador in Berlin. The Kaiser was feeling weak from a recent attack of influenza and felt unable to face the journey. No one in London accepted the explanation – the real reason was either pique or embarrassment. One of Wilhelm's friends was on the point of standing trial for offences under Germany's penal code. He was accused of sodomy. Sir Edward Grey, the Foreign Secretary, suggested another reason for the sudden change of plans. The Royal Navy had expressed great reluctance to accommodate the accompanying German battleships in Portsmouth and the Kaiser thought that dignity required him to be escorted into harbour by a substantial proportion of his fleet.

Both the German and British foreign offices were terrified by the prospect of the contretemps which cancellation would create. The Emperor was shown details of the arrangements which had been personally made by the King. He was convinced – by the splendour of his proposed reception, rather than by the chaos his absence would cause – that the state visit should go ahead.

According to Lord Esher, the state visit was an unqualified success –

at least in the estimation of the guests. 'The banquet last night was said, by the Germans, to be finer than any spectacular display of the kings they had ever seen.'[7] The hosts were not so sure. The King sensibly left the discussion of political matters to his ministers. The Kaiser, on the other hand, conducted his own diplomacy, often without showing complete mastery of his subject. He also made constant attacks on Jews and Jewish influence – not a popular prejudice at the Court of Edward VII. But it seemed that, even though the thaw had not set in, some ice had been melted. Then the Kaiser announced that he proposed to stay on in London for a month's 'private visit'.

The Kaiser rented Highcliffe Castle on the Sussex coast and Colonel Edward Montagu Stuart Wortley, its owner, was asked to remain in residence as a guest. On 28 October the *Daily Telegraph* published what it described as an interview with the Kaiser. There is no doubt that Wilhelm saw it before publication and gave his approval, but the work had been done by Montagu Stuart Wortley. It included a claim that the Kaiser had often made in private company – that he had drawn up the 'blockhouse and wire' plan which gradually cleared the veld of Boer commandos, yet had received no thanks or credit from the King, whose military honour he had saved.

London society was more amused than infuriated, but in Germany, where support for the Boers remained strong, the Kaiser's claim was greeted with fury. Seeking to ingratiate himself with domestic opinion, Wilhelm gave another press interview. He told W. B. Hale of the *New York World* that Edward VII was personally corrupt, that his Court was decadent and that war between Britain and Germany was inevitable. The King complained, the newspaper apologised and the Kaiser repudiated all the opinions which he had expressed to Hale. But the damage was done. Wilhelm was never forgiven.

The Foreign Office, on the other hand, saw Anglo-German relations more pragmatically. With great reluctance the King agreed to make a return state visit to Berlin in 1909. He collapsed in the Berlin Rathaus – almost strangled by the tight collar of his Prussian military uniform – but, apart from that, little of note took place. The royal party went on to Biarritz, mirroring the private holiday with which the Kaiser had followed his state visit to London. From there the King wrote, 'It is sad to see the difficulties we have to contend with . . . It is strange that, ever since my visit to Berlin, the German Government has done *nothing* but thwart and annoy us in every way.'[8]

German conduct appeared all the more sad and strange because of the peculiar place Germany itself occupied in the minds of Edwardian politicians. They were fascinated – indeed, almost hypnotised – by its economic success. German industry was pursuing, overtaking and surging ahead of its British competitors, and thinking ministers attributed this to the social policies of the government in Berlin. When in 1902 A. J. Balfour faced criticism of his Education Bill, he admonished his opponents by reminding them, 'You tell us we are falling behind the Germans in industrial matters because we do not educate our people.' He wanted 'an authority which shall deal with secondary education for all classes of the people' on the German model. Six years and a change of administration later (when Winston Churchill, at the Board of Trade, wanted to persuade the Prime Minister to move more quickly towards a system of social insurance), he too had no doubt about the strongest argument at his disposal. 'Germany, with a harder climate and less accumulated wealth, has managed to establish tolerable conditions for her people . . . the Minister who applies to this country the successful experience of Germans in social organisation may or may not be supported at the polls, but he will at least have a memorial which time will not deface.' He went on to advocate a 'big slice of Bismarckianism'.

Churchill based his argument on more than an intrinsic admiration for the 'Iron Chancellor'. William Beveridge, an Oxford academic and *Morning Post* journalist, had produced a report on German public policy. Twelve million German citizens were protected against sickness, disability and the poverty which comes with old age through schemes which were financed by the beneficiaries' contributions. And the labour market was made to work more efficiently through 'exchanges' in which supply was matched to demand. Britain would benefit from the adoption of German attitudes and methods.

It was not only the great swathes of German national policy which impressed and worried Britain. Germany and things German increasingly pervaded British life – usually in the form of an invention or improvement which Britain adopted. Mercedes and Benz developed reliable motor cars long before Rolls met Royce. Lister's work – the

'antiseptic revolution' – was overtaken by Robert Koch who identified bacteria as the principal agent of infection. Northcliffe wrote to
the government with the complaint that the High Command in
Berlin, unlike the War Office in London, realised the military potential of the aeroplane. A German liner won the 'Blue Riband of the
Atlantic', stimulating Britain's only direct response to the growing
challenge. Specific German industries pushed their way into traditional British markets. Sheffield was particularly worried about cutlery
from Soligen and Birmingham complained bitterly about the low
quality of the metalwork which came out of German factories.
Paradoxically, the Berlin Patent Office added strength to their concerns. Many German exports were stamped DRGM – 'Deutsches
Reichs Gebrauchs Muster', the mark of the lower grade patent, suitable for the 'German Utility Model'. As anti-German feeling built
up – incited by Northcliffe's propaganda in the *Daily Mail* – little boys
saw DRGM and translated it as 'Dirty Rotten German Muck'.

So Edwardian Britain thought of Germany as many things – shining example, dangerous competitor, admirable innovator and
imminent military threat. That ambivalence was encouraged by the
inability of the Kaiser and his government to steer a steady course.
Contemporary observers thought Germany's foreign policy was as
capricious as it was aggressive. The violent swings in attitude towards
Britain were attributed to the personal influence of the unpredictable
Kaiser, but in part they were a conscious element in Berlin's strategy.
Every opportunity had to be exploited in pursuit of Germany's greater
glory and influence. Sometimes Britain was treated like an enemy and
sometimes like an ally. In the absence of a steady foreign policy,
Germans found it hard to maintain permanent friendships.

In June 1900, ships of the British Navy had intercepted and
boarded the *Bundesrath*, a German mail steamer, in the belief that it
was carrying contraband (probably arms) to the Boers. The cry of
'piracy on the high seas' had been met by the Admiralty with an
abject apology. Count von Bülow, the German Chancellor, supported
by Admiral Alfred von Tirpitz, the minister of marine, seized the
moment. He told the Bundestag that the threat posed by British aggression – as witness the *Bundesrath*'s boarding, justified an immediate
increase in the naval estimates. It was agreed that the Kaiser's fleet should

expand to twice the size that had been thought necessary two years earlier. The size of the rival fleets – Britain and Germany – was to be a contentious issue in the British parliament throughout Edward's reign.

Later that year, German and British forces fought side by side, though the Kaiser's troops made a belated arrival at the field of battle. Members of a Chinese secret society opposed to foreigners living and working in their country had murdered the German minister in Peking and besieged the diplomats of every Western power in their legations. Japan, Russia, France and Britain, with forces in the region, formed a multination force to put down what came to be called the Boxer Rebellion. Germany, with troops no nearer than Europe, contributed to what amounted to a brief occupation after the revolt had been extinguished – and only then by courtesy of the British Navy's coaling stations along the way. The Kaiser's troops compensated for the humiliation by suppressing the few remaining Boxers with exemplary brutality.

Germany, having thus established the right to hold a view on future relations between China and Europe, combined with Great Britain in the Anglo-German Convention to maintain an 'open door policy' for trade with the Far East. The month after it was concluded, President Kruger toured Europe in the hope of winning support for the Boers during the second stage of the war. The Kaiser refused to receive him, but President Loubet of France honoured him with an official national welcome – and convinced Joseph Chamberlain that he was right to argue that Britain's real friends were in Berlin, not Paris.

It was not until his overtures were rebuffed for a third time that Chamberlain abandoned his hopes of negotiating an Anglo-German convention. His attempts to promote an alliance between Berlin and London illustrate what a strange position he occupied within both Salisbury's and Balfour's governments. Chamberlain was Colonial Secretary and foreign treaties were none of his business. Yet he was allowed to work away at arranging an Anglo-German alliance while Lansdowne, the Foreign Secretary, looked on and the Prime Minister wrote notes to other members of the Cabinet drawing their attention to the weakness of Chamberlain's plan.

There was a good deal of rejoicing – between enemies of Chamberlain as well as friends of France – when his final attempt at

a convention ended in the Colonial Secretary's personal embarrassment. In an attempt to reconcile German opinion to the war in
South Africa – and in particular to the tactics which Kitchener had
employed to beat the Boers – he made what he thought was a flat-
tering comparison of the British and German armies. He meant to say
that British troops had behaved with the same gallantry and courage
that the German soldiers had displayed in the Franco-Prussian War of
1870, but German newspapers accused him of saying that Germany
had treated the French as brutally as Britain had treated the Boers.
Von Bülow denounced him in the Bundestag.

While Chamberlain hoped in vain for friendship with Germany,
Lansdowne forged closer links with France by settling differences
about the two countries' rival interests in Egypt. During the King's
visit to Kiel in 1904, the Kaiser made clear – much to the relief of
British diplomats – that he had no territorial interests in North Africa.
But in March 1905 Wilhelm visited Tangiers and announced that all
the powers had 'equal rights' in an 'absolutely free' country and his
presence in the capital signified Germany's intention of exerting its
'great and growing interest in Morocco'.

The purpose of the declaration was to test the strength of the
agreement in the hope that Britain would be exposed as an unreliable
ally. There was a difference of opinion about how the German
démarche should be treated. France, unlike Britain, accepted the
demand for an international conference to determine which of the
powers could regard the Magreb as within the sphere of its influence.
Delegates assembled at Algeciras in January 1906. Grey, the new
Liberal Foreign Secretary, stood firm behind France and the result
was humiliation for the Kaiser. Only the Austro-Hungarian Empire
supported Germany's claims to 'equal rights' in Morocco. Italy, Spain,
Russia and Great Britain (with support from the United States) were
all determined to keep Germany out of the Mediterranean. Morocco
remained under the influence of France and Spain.

The Kaiser's mischief was not, however, quite finished. In May
1911, he visited London for the unveiling of Queen Victoria's memorial in the Mall. Within weeks of his return to Berlin, the Kaiser
announced his interest in North Africa. Moroccan tribesmen had
risen up against the Sultan, and French troops had occupied Tangiers

'to protect life and property'. That, Germany said, amounted to full annexation, for which she must be compensated. A gunboat was sent to Agadir and German troops landed. The Berlin newspapers demanded that the Kaiser announce the annexation of at least part of Morocco, and the German Ambassador in London, pressed to explain his government's intentions, replied that he had no instructions on the subject. Fearful that Germany was about to achieve its long-desired foothold in the Mediterranean, Lloyd George, the Chancellor of the Exchequer, changed the text of his Mansion House speech.

> I would make great sacrifices to preserve peace . . . But if a situation were to be forced upon us, in which peace could only be preserved by the surrender of the great and benevolent position Britain has won by centuries of heroism and achievement, by allowing Britain to be treated, where her interests were vitally affected as if she were of no account in the Cabinet of Nations then I say emphatically that peace at that price would be a humiliation intolerable for a great country like ours to endure.[9]

Germany, realising that Britain had, in effect, issued an ultimatum, withdrew. But the policy which most perturbed the British government continued. Germany was expanding its navy to a size which would enable it to challenge Britannia's rule of the waves. Britain began to worry about her martial strength.

The early defeats of the Boer War – and the obvious inadequacies in the British Army which it revealed – made military reform inevitable. St John Brodrick, the Unionist Secretary of State for War, had proposed the reorganisation of the Army into six corps, three in fighting readiness at full strength, the others in the form of cadres which could be expanded into complete units on mobilisation. The plan was never implemented. Brodrick's time was taken up with two other inquiries – one into the Boer War itself (which amounted to very little), the other into the Army medical service.

A second enquiry did make radical recommendations. In 1903, Hugh Arnold Forster – the orphan son of Matthew Arnold's sister who had been adopted by W. E. Forster, the pioneer of the 1870 Education Act – became the Secretary of State for War. He appointed a three-man committee – Esher, Sir John Fisher (the First Sea Lord) and Colonel Sir George Clarke, included because of the controversy surrounding other names – to examine the Army's command structures. It recommended the abolition of the post of Commander-in-Chief, and the creation of an Army Council on the lines of the Board of Admiralty – one beneficial consequence of the decision (extraordinary by the standards of the time) to invite an admiral to judge the efficiency of the Army. Unfortunately it ignored the most pressing need – the creation of a general staff.

In early 1905, Earl Cawdor, the Chairman of the Great Western Railway, became First Lord of the Admiralty. He remained in post for only nine months, but during that time his partnership with 'Jacky' Fisher reorganised and revitalised the Navy. Fisher had a record of reform. As Second Sea Lord he had revolutionised officer training by replacing the *Britannia* training ship with the naval college at Dartmouth. When he was promoted to the head of his profession, his first recommendation to Cawdor was the redeployment of the whole fleet – a proposal which, when made by a new First Sea Lord, was irresistible.

The smaller stations were reduced to token size and the best of their ships concentrated in three European commands. The Mediterranean Fleet was to be based in Malta, the Atlantic Fleet in Gibraltar and the Channel Fleet in the home ports. Fisher, the man who had suggested 'Copenhagening' the German navy, had no doubt about the nature of the threat or the nationality of the enemy.

Much of the existing fleet was, in Fisher's opinion, antiquated. He had no doubt how he should deal with them. 'The first duty of the navy is to be instantly ready to strike the enemy and this can only be accomplished by concentrating our strength into ships of undoubted fighting value, ruthlessly discarding those that have become obsolete.'[10] More than 150 ships were condemned as unfit for active service. Ninety of them were offered for sale to various minor powers. The rest were laid up – without guns or crew.

Fisher was determined that the obsolete ships' replacements should embody both the essential ingredients of modern naval warfare – maximum firepower and maximum speed. Many of the traditional precepts were abandoned. Heavy plate was rejected. 'Hitting the thing, not armour' was what Fisher had in mind. 'The most power-fully arranged armaments have been the first consideration', he told the Prime Minister. 'Absolutely nothing has been allowed to stand in the way of the power and scope of the guns . . . Being a battleship she will have to fight other battleships. Having speed, she can choose the range at which she will fight.'[11] Fisher was creating a whole new class of warship. It took its name from the prototype and paradigm – the *Dreadnought*.

History has given Fisher personal credit for the Dreadnought rev-olution, but there is no doubt that the idea originated with Vittorio Cumberti, an Italian designer who, having had his plans for a 'big battleship' rejected by Rome, described the virtues of size and speed in the 1903 annual edition of *Jane's Fighting Ships*. Fisher, by force of personality, ensured that Drake's precept was respected. The true glory lay not in setting out on an adventure, but in its completion. Fisher made sure that the *Dreadnought* was built to his exacting specifications.

Fisher wanted the *Dreadnought* to be capable of twenty-one knots, a third as fast again as the standard British warship could steam for any substantial period. That could only be provided by turbine engines – still, according to the conservative standards of the Admiralty, too unreliable for the largest fighting ships. Powerful voices argued in favour of the tried and tested, but Phillip Watts, Director of Naval Construction, was adamant. Without turbine engines 'these ships will be out of date within five years'.[12]

The Royal Naval Dockyard at Portsmouth had built a battleship in thirty-one months – the shortest construction time on record. Fisher wanted the *Dreadnought* in a year. Sea trials were completed on 11 December 1906, three weeks ahead of schedule. During the annual naval review in 1907, the King, Queen Alexandra and the Prince of Wales (accompanied by carefully selected journalists) were invited on board both to experience the smooth speed generated by the turbines and to marvel at the quality of the gunnery which the stability made possible. The Queen was so impressed by the *Dreadnought's* marks-manship that she commanded that the targets be towed in and hung – perforated with direct hits – from the ship's fantail. One rival captain described the gesture as 'cheap swagger'. His description was undeniably accurate, but the boasting was very near to being justified. British–built ships were the best in the world.

The *Dreadnought* embodied Fisher's concept of the ideal battle-ship – a floating gun platform with maximum firepower and maximum range. Her main armament was the twelve-inch guns, each one capable of firing 850-pound shells. A *Dreadnought* broadside fired a barrage of 6,800 pounds of high explosive. The standard battleship, before the *Dreadnought* was designed, carried four twelve-inch guns and a variety of smaller guns.[13] As well as possessing heavier firepower, the *Dreadnought* had longer range. It could therefore avoid, or at least reduce, the danger from the latest innovation in naval warfare – the torpedo.

Traditional naval warfare – as well as depending on the luck, courage and judgement of sailors – is, like a motor race, profoundly influenced by the quality of the competing equipment. So the com-pletion of *Dreadnought* – at the huge size of 17,900 tons and with its unique firepower – required that the rival navies of the world built comparable battleships. At least that was necessary if they intended to compete with Britain, either in the battle for prestige or in a real naval war. Nobody doubted that Germany would rise to the challenge. But Germany had a problem. A battleship the size of *Dreadnought* could not pass through the Kiel Canal into the North Sea. On the day that the *Dreadnought* was launched, work began on deepening and widening it.

Dreadnoughts are expensive and Liberal administrations, by their nature, prefer peace negotiations to rearmament programmes. It was the misfortune of the new Campbell-Bannerman government to be confronted not simply by the apparent need to increase the naval budget but also by an imminent obligation to come to the aid of France. On 10 January 1906, the French ambassador to London told Edward Grey, the Foreign Secretary, that French intelligence con-firmed that Count Schlieffen, the German Chief of Staff, had urged the Kaiser to embark on 'the fundamental clearing up of relations with France by a prompt war'.[14] Grey would not promise that, in the event of invasion, Britain would come to France's aid, but he did agree to representatives of the two armies holding secret talks about how they might co-operate in the face of German aggression. Eight years later, when Germany invaded Belgium as the opening move in the Schlieffen Plan, Britain and France at least understood each other's military capability.

With the tension at its height in 1906, the Germans accepted the judgement of the Algeciras Conference. Better still from the point of view of Campbell-Bannerman and the new Liberal government, German ministers agreed to attend a conference in The Hague at which the powers discussed détente and disarmament. It was at least possible that France had misunderstood Germany's intention. The sudden switch from fear to hope encouraged the Liberals to believe that they could revise the Dreadnought programme. A second battleship, of the same class, was dropped from the 1906 naval estimates.

That was not the only economy in the détente budget. Haldane cut three million pounds from the Army estimates and, at the same time, created a more efficient military capability. The idea of two complementary forces was resuscitated, but in a different form. The regular Army would be made up of 160,000 men organised in six divisions. Four divisions of part-time soldiers – called Territorials because they were not committed to serve outside the territory of the United Kingdom – were to act as a permanent reserve. By comparison with Haldane's savings, the reduction made in the estimates by postponing the building of a second Dreadnought was small beer. Fisher had kept the price of his floating gun platform to an absolute minimum in order to reduce parliamentary criticism – the total cost was established at £1,850,000,[15] only about £181,000 more than would be spent on a Lord Nelson- or Agamemnon-class battleship.[16] But postponing the building of a Dreadnought was a positive sign of peaceful intentions. Campbell-Bannerman was pleased to make it.

The Hague Conference laid down the 'laws of war' (which were constantly ignored between 1914 and 1918) but failed to do much more. Von Bülow announced that Germany would veto both proposals for and discussion of disarmament proposals. It was a sad blow to Campbell-Bannerman's hopes of a more peaceful world, but he remained radical to the last. Addressing a London meeting of the Inter-Parliamentary Union a few days after the Csar's cossacks had suppressed the Russian parliament in 1907 he began his speech, '*La Douma est morte. Vive la Douma!*' The romantic incident was overshadowed by the news that Germany was rearming again. It was a dangerous moment, for the two senior admirals of the British Navy were in public and bitter disagreement.

Admiral Lord Charles Beresford and Admiral Sir John 'Jacky' Fisher had never got on. Part of the problem was temperamental. There was also an element of jealousy – Beresford thought he should be First Sea Lord – and a genuine difference of opinion about how the Royal Navy should be run. Lord Charles, supported by the Navy League, wanted a general inquiry into Admiralty policy. Fisher, not unreasonably, refused outright. On 25 January 1908 he told the Cabinet, 'the Admiralty fear no inquiry, but it would be simply impossible for Members of the Board to retain office if such a blow to the authority of the Admiralty as an investigation into its fighting policy by its subordinates were to be sanctioned.'[17] The Navy League and Lord Charles Beresford's supporters launched a press campaign for Fisher's removal.

A few weeks before Asquith became Prime Minister, the argument about the Navy's state of readiness descended to the level of farce. Lord Esher, attempting to defend Admiral 'Jacky' Fisher, the First Sea Lord, against calls for his resignation, wrote a reckless letter to *The Times*.[18] 'There is not a man in Germany,' it ended, 'from the Emperor downwards, who would not welcome the fall of Sir John Fisher.' The Kaiser – offended by Esher's implication of hostility – told his uncle, Edward VII, that he proposed to complain personally to the First Lord of the Admiralty. The King, meaning to patronise his nephew, agreed to 'the new departure' and nine pages of imperial rebuke duly arrived at Admiralty House. Lord Tweedsmuir, the First Lord, was so impressed by the direct approach that he demonstrated his goodwill by sending the following year's naval estimates to Berlin – before they had been presented to the House of Commons. When Asquith formed his government, Tweedsmuir was replaced by Reginald McKenna.

The mood, as well as the Prime Minister, changed. Germany was building battleships at a speed which Britain had not attempted to match. McKenna, using the authority of recent appointment, proposed that the potential discrepancy between German and British sea power should be forestalled by the simple but expensive expedient of 'laying down' eighteen Dreadnoughts during the next three years. Churchill and Lloyd George – 'the economists' – resisted the proposal with such vigour that Asquith confessed 'there are moments when I am disposed summarily to cashier them both'.[19] Several compromises were proposed. None of them suited both the extremes. Admiral Alfred von Tirpitz, the German minister of marine, then told the Reichstag that the shipyards of Hamburg and Stettin were ready and anxious to accelerate their shipbuilding programme. The naval lobby began to press for eight new Dreadnoughts to be laid down at once. The popular clamour – encouraged by the yellow press and Balfour's expression of 'profound anxiety'[20] – was encapsulated in the slogan, 'We want eight and we won't wait'.

Cabinet agreement was eventually secured around an amendment to Lloyd George's original solution – a flexible building programme which could be varied according to circumstances. Four Dreadnoughts were to be laid down immediately and plans were made for another four to be commissioned if the need arose. Fisher had won his most important naval battle.

The British government, however, remained anxious to promote peace and in 1911 suggested, as a friendly gesture, that it would reduce its reliance on battleships if Germany would do the same. It seemed that the offer was welcomed in Berlin. Sir Ernest Cassel, Edward's old friend, was told that the German government would welcome a visit from a British minister. Haldane, the Secretary of State for War, who, according to King Edward, was a 'German professor', was chosen for the task. He discovered that the Germans hoped that the meeting would end with an agreement that Britain would remain neutral if war was forced upon Germany or, in other words, would not go to France's assistance in the event of a German invasion. No such assurance was possible. Britain and France were not partners in a formal alliance, but the Entente carried undeniable implications. The German *démarche* acted as an early warning. France and Britain began to work more closely together.

Events on the very edge of Europe took over from diplomacy in determining the prospects for peace. The Christian states of the Balkans formed a secret alliance. In September 1914 they mobilised on the pretext of protecting their co-religionists within the chronically turbulent Ottoman Empire. Fearful that the balance of power would be disturbed, Germany and Austria announced that they would not tolerate a change in the status quo. The Christian states nevertheless invaded and defeated the Turks – to the universal acclaim of European liberal opinion.

Russia – as always wanting to secure a warm water port – would have welcomed a weak Turkey. That, matched by her own domination of the Slav Peninsula, would, she believed, guarantee access to the Bosporus and the Dardanelles. The Austro-Hungarian Empire wanted the Slav States to stay small, weak and divided so that they would not rise up against her. The victory of the Balkan Christians over the Turks gave a clear advantage to Russia – the one Great Power which had been made party to their secret compact. It also set off a chain reaction which, every statesman knew, could ignite an explosion across Europe. Germany could not look passively on while Austria's interests were diminished by an extension of Russian influence. If war came, France would be obliged, under the terms of its Dual Alliance with Russia, to come to the assistance of its ally. Even if Britain remained neutral, the Channel ports would be at risk.

In London, a conference of ambassadors aimed at keeping the peace by finding a mutually acceptable role for Turkey. In the chair, Sir Edward Grey astonished participants by showing an obvious sympathy for the Austro-German axis. He believed that both Berlin and Vienna feared encirclement by unfriendly states and he wanted to reassure them that he understood their concern. His attempt at emollience was not a success. The Germans and Austrians were not in a mood to be comforted, and the Balkan Christians, who hoped to divide up the European territories which they had captured from the Turks, refused to abandon the spoils of war. Romania then attacked Bulgaria.

In the reallocation of territory which eventually resulted, Serbia was the one real winner. The gains were about to be ratified in the Treaty of Bucharest when Austria suggested to Germany and Italy that they should make a direct assault on Belgrade. Italy declined and thus postponed the Great War by a full year. Few politicians in continental Europe – and no one in Germany – doubted that war was coming. The Reichstag was asked to legislate for a conflict which the Kaiser clearly regarded as desirable as well as unavoidable. There was to be no exemption from military service. All fit men would be conscripted, increasing the number of annual recruits from 280,000 to 343,000. A capital levy of 1,000 million marks was to be raised to cover the added expenditure. Germany was not, as Grey had believed, concerned about being surrounded. It was determined to expand.

The likelihood is that Germany had decided to go to war in August 1914 more than a full year before its advance into Belgium began. August was the month in which its army was at full strength and at the height of readiness. The Schlieffen Plan allowed six weeks for the defeat and occupation of France. If the German army was at the Channel by mid-September, there would still be time to turn east against Russia before the winter set in. And by the first week in August the widening of the Kiel Canal would be complete. The Grand Fleet would then have an easy passage from the Baltic to the North Sea again.

Britain, in the unlikely form of Winston Churchill, by their First Lord of the Admiralty, retained its faith in negotiation. Germany planned to lay down two capital ships during 1913 and Britain four. Twice during the year, Churchill suggested a 'naval holiday' in which neither navy expanded. Twice the Germans refused the offer. The rebuff did not encourage Britain to increase its preparations for war. Three major naval bases – Rosyth, Cromarty and Scapa Flow – were known to be vulnerable to attack. Nothing was done to improve their defences. Instead, ministers (who wanted to believe that there would be no war) told each other that Prince Lichowsky, the German Ambassador, was a gentleman whose goodwill to Britain was not in doubt and that he expressed the true position of the government which he represented. In early 1914, Lloyd George was actually pressing for a reduction in the naval estimates.

Germany at least deserved credit for the thoroughness of its preparations. When war broke out it was discovered that Germany had collected almost all her foreign debts while leaving her own international creditors waiting for payment. As a result the Bundesbank held record gold reserves.

In May 1914 the German and Austro-Hungarian chiefs of staff (Helmut von Molke and Conrad von Hotzendorf) had one of their remarkably rare meetings. They agreed that the time had come. But the Berlin foreign ministry insisted on waiting. Britain and Germany were engaged in discussions over the future of Mesopotamia and diplomats retained the hope that the government in London would choose to remain aloof from Europe. Gladstone had felt no obligation to rally to the defence of France in 1870. Why should his successor feel any differently in 1914? Molke knew better. The Schlieffen Plan involved German troops invading Belgium on their way to France. Britain, he had no doubt, would feel an obligation to defend the sovereignty of so small a nation. He pressed for an earlier start and a quick finish so that the war in Europe would be over before the British naval blockade began to take effect. France and Russia – not realising that the first casualty would be Belgium – felt less certain that Britain would come to their aid. The Czar expressed his concern about the Russian state of readiness and the Duma agreed to raise the strength of the army from 1,240,000 to 1,700,000 men. Europe had reached the position in which the preparedness for war made war inevitable.

President Woodrow Wilson, in office for a year, exhibited the instinct which made him pioneer the League of Nations. He sent a personal (and secret) emissary, Colonel House, to Europe. In Berlin, House found the German army determined to go to war. London remained sceptical. British ministers retained their confidence in the German ambassador's good faith.

Asquith also had Ireland on his mind. Carson was at his most vociferous and the Army remained anxious about what role it would play if Ulster did rebel. The Prime Minister felt less of an obligation to Belgium than Molke imagined. 'The Cabinet', he told the King, 'consider this matter . . . one of policy rather than legality.'[21] And his ministers were bitterly divided. He judged (correctly) that Burns and Haldane would go if Britain joined the war and that Grey would only stay if war was declared. The rest of the Cabinet, in typical British spirit, hoped it would not happen.

On 28 June 1914, the Archduke Ferdinand, heir apparent to the throne of the Austro-Hungarian Empire, was assassinated during a state visit to Sarajevo, the capital of Bosnia. The assassins were Austrian, but there was no doubt that they were motivated by the desire to end Vienna's influence over Serbia. The *causus belli*, for which the German and Austrian general staff had waited so impatiently, had at last been created.

On the day that the news of the Sarajevo assassinations reached Britain, London papers printed two special editions. One reported the murder of the Archduke and Archduchess. The other recorded the death of Joe Chamberlain. He had been paralysed and virtually mute for eight years as the result of a stroke which he had suffered two days after he had celebrated his seventieth birthday with the people of Birmingham. But since then – incredibly, even by the standards of the time – he had twice been returned to Parliament unopposed. He was incapable of signing the register, so, on his last visit to the House of Commons, he was carried into the chamber at the end of a day's business when all other Members had left. 'For a moment he sat, piteously but proudly motionless, while his eye slowly surveyed the empty benches and galleries and then he indistinctly repeated the oath to the clerk. To sign the roll was, for him, a physical impossibility but Austen [his son] guided his hand sufficiently for him to make a shaky cross.'[22] Despite the eight-year silence (and the widespread animosity which had prompted him to tell Winston Churchill that 'if a man is sure of himself', abuse 'only sharpens him and makes him more effective'), [23] his death was marked by the expression of almost universal sadness. The people knew that a chapter of British history had closed.

There were new men ready and anxious to complete the new chapter which was about to begin. Amongst them was Winston Churchill, the minister who one day was to hold Britain's destiny in his hand. In the summer of 1914 (as at many other moments of his career) he was blessed with unreasonably good fortune. In the middle of the year the fleet had been congregated in the home ports to take part in a 'trial mobilisation' in place of the usual manoeuvres. The exercise had been planned as an economy measure. Ships in port are less expensive than ships firing shells at sea. The presence of so many capital ships in and about the Channel meant that, during the crisis which followed the assassination, the Navy was ready to go into action. In fact, when the news from Sarajevo reached London, some of the smaller ships had already left port – but Prince Louis of Battenberg, the First Sea Lord since 1912, stopped the dispersal without consulting higher authority. Churchill immediately endorsed his action. His first stint as First Lord was to end with the disaster of the Dardanelles. It began with the success that only Providence can provide.

It was the one happy chance in a miserable month for a Cabinet which was almost united in its detestation of war and the thought of war. On 3 August, when Germany demanded what it described as 'free passage' through Belgium, even Lloyd George, who had been the most senior advocate of continued neutrality, accepted that the government now had no choice. Grey issued a rival British ultimatum to Germany. Unless Berlin made clear, by midnight, that an invasion of Belgium was neither planned nor contemplated, a state of war would exist between the two nations.

The third of August was a clear English summer's day. Crowds gathered in London and cheered the Prime Minister on his way to Parliament. He expressed his loathing for the levity and quoted Robert Walpole. 'Now they ring the bells but soon they will wring their hands.'[24] As eleven o'clock approached (midnight by Berlin time), Whitehall was packed with a cheering crowd. At eleven-thirty, Asquith invited Lloyd George to join him in the Cabinet Room. When he arrived, he found Grey and McKenna (by then Home Secretary, having exchanged jobs with Churchill) were already there. So was Mrs Asquith. Grey was still not sure that war was inevitable. Then he received a message that the British Ambassador to Berlin had left the Embassy and was on the way home.

The crowd outside Downing Street went quiet as the hour struck. In the Cabinet Room, the Prime Minister and his guests sat in silence for several minutes. Then 'Winston dashed into the room'. Margot Asquith recorded the scene. Churchill was 'radiant, his face bright, his manner keen and he told us – one word pouring out on the other – how he was going to send telegrams to the Mediterranean, the North Sea and God knows where! You could see that he was really happy.'[25]

Winston Churchill was just forty. He had already held one of the Great Offices of State, as well as two other Cabinet posts, and had confirmed his reputation as a 'coming man' by the uninhibited enthusiasm with which he had charged at every task. That night in Downing Street his Cabinet colleagues, not surprisingly, thought his brash exuberance wholly out of place. They could not possibly have anticipated the horrors of the First World War. But they were, instinctively as well as intellectually, opposed to war itself for reasons which went far beyond their abhorrence of the death and destruction which were bound to be its consequence. War would disturb the established order and change the world from the steady state which Edward Grey, the Foreign Secretary, had worked so hard to maintain. Only once, in a hundred years, had Britain fought on the continent. And the campaign, far away in the Crimea, had ended in disaster. Yet in August 1914, the lights were going out all over continental Europe and the darkness was spreading across the Channel. Nothing would ever be quite the same again and few people – perhaps not even the eternally optimistic Winston Churchill, believed that the world would be changed for the better.

The pessimists were wrong. The inexorable march of progress continued. The course of improvement did not run smooth - the slaughter of 1916 and the slump of 1929 lay ahead. But fifty years on life was far better for the average family than it had been in 1914 – just as it was better in 1914 than in 1864. But the real error, shared by the solemn ministers assembled in Downing Street that night, was the belief that the world was about to be turned upside down. The political, social and cultural revolution had already happened. Modern Britain was born in the opening years of the twentieth century. It is the legacy of the Edwardians.

NOTES

Part One: 'Anxieties for England'

Chapter 1: *A Cloud Across the Sun* (pages 7–17)

1. *Daily Telegraph*, 4.2.01.
2. Rennell. *The Last Days of Glory*, p. 268.
3. *Daily Telegraph*, 5.2.01.
4. Rennell. *The Last Days of Glory*, p. 227.
5. *Ibid.*
6. *Westminster Gazette*, 5.2.01.
7. Lawrence (ed.). *Collected Letters of Bernard Shaw*, p. 216.
8. *Daily Chronicle*, 7.2.01.
9. Rennell. *The Last Days of Glory*, p. 197.
10. *Ibid.*, p. 198.
11. *Daily News*, 28.1.01.
12. Gilmour. *Curzon*, p. 234.
13. *Ibid.*
14. *The Times*, 6.2.01.
15. Kaplan. *Henry James*, pp. 180-1, p. 350.
16. Victor Cavendish diaries, 23.1.01.
17. Rennell. *The Last Days of Glory*, p. 287.

Chapter 2: *The Spirit of the Age* (pages 18–41)

1. Heffer. *Power and Place*, p. 21.
2. Foot (ed.). *The Gladstone Diaries*, p. 123.
3. Royal Archives, R229, Windsor Castle.
4. Heffer. *Power and Place*, p. 35.
5. Royal Archives, Z449/94, Windsor Castle.
6. *Ibid.*, 449/69.
7. *Ibid.*, 449/74.
8. *Ibid.*, 449/80.
9. *Ibid.*, 449/86.

10. Rowland Evans diaries, 24.6.02.
11. Fisher. *Joseph Lister*, p. 315.
12. *Ibid.*
13. *Ibid.*
14. Magnus. *King Edward VII*, p. 268.
15. Priestley. *The Edwardians*, p. 65.
16. Heffer. *Power and Place*, p. 50.
17. Magnus. *King Edward VII*, p. 267.
18. Cecil. *Life in Edwardian England*, p. 111.
19. Magnus. *King Edward VII*, p. 274.
20. Cecil. *Life in Edwardian England*, p. 8.
21. Cardigan, Countess of. *My Recollections*, p. 174.
22. Portland, Duke of. *Men, Women and Things*, p. 227.
23. Athlone, Countess of. *For My Grandchildren*, p. 30.
24. Magnus. *King Edward VII*, p. 123.
25. *Ibid.*, p. 315.
26. Lee. *Edward VII*, p. 153.
27. Magnus. *King Edward VII*, p. 301.
28. *Ibid.*, p. 313.
29. *Ibid.*

Chapter 3: *The Powers Behind the Throne* (pages 42–63)

1. Royal Archives, 42/61, Windsor Castle.
2. Mackay. *Balfour*, p. 40.
3. Gordon. *The Victorian School Manager*, p. 207.
4. Churchill. *Great Contemporaries*, p. 183.
5. *Ibid.*, p. 45.
6. Mackay. *Balfour*, p. 124.
7. Greenville. *Lord Salisbury and Foreign Policy*, p. 421.
8. Mackay. *Balfour*, p. 124.
9. Gilmour. *Curzon*, p. 185.
10. *Ibid.*, p. 186.
11. *Ibid.*, p. 428.
12. *Ibid.*, p. 166.
13. Churchill. *Great Contemporaries*, p. 71.
14. *Ibid.*, p. 9.
15. Rhodes James. *The British Revolution*, p. 154.
16. Churchill. *Great Contemporaries*, p. 1.
17. *Ibid.*, p. 7.
18. Jenkins. *Asquith*, p. 259.
19. Indian budget debate 1907.
20. Magnus. *King Edward VII*, p. 308.
21. *Ibid.*

22. Royal Archives, 45/59, Windsor Castle.
23. *Ibid.*, 45/72.
24. Heffer. *Power and Place*, p. 224.
25. *Ibid.*
26. Esher papers, 10/57, Churchill College, Cambridge.
27. Heffer. *Power and Place*, p. 285.
28. *Ibid.*, p. 216.
29. *Ibid.*, p. 213.
30. Massie. *Dreadnought*, p. 406.
31. *Ibid.*, p. 457.
32. Churchill. *Great Contemporaries*, p. 266.
33. Magnus. *King Edward VII*, p. 346.
34. Royal Archives, George V, AA 24/31, Windsor Castle.
35. Magnus. *King Edward VII*, p. 348.
36. *Ibid.*, p. 260.
37. *Ibid.*, p. 386.
38. Lee. *Edward VII*, p. 180.
39. Royal Archives, George V, AA 24/42, Windsor Castle.
40. Royal Archives, R27/21.
41. Magnus. *King Edward VII*, p. 353.
42. *Ibid.*, p. 348.

Chapter 4: *The Condition of England* (pages 64–82)

1. Masterman. *The Condition of England*, p. 17.
2. Haggard. *Rural England*, p. 536.
3. Drummond and Wilbraham. *The Englishman's Food*, p. 403.
4. Johnson (ed.). *Twentieth-Century Britain*, p. 23.
5. Altimrah. *Economic Elements of Pax Britannica*, p. 37.
6. Johnson (ed.). *Twentieth-Century Britain*, p. 24.
7. Hawkins. *The Death of Rural England*, p. 8.
8. Johnson (ed.). *Twentieth-Century Britain*, p. 65.
9. Ashworth. *An Economic History of England*, p. 3.
10. Bourke. *Dismembering the Male*, p. 13.
11. Kershen. *Henry Mayhew and Charles Booth*, p. 105.
12. Davis. *Life in an English Village*, p. 45.
13. Rowntree and Kendall. *How the Labourer Lives*, p. 312.
14. Dundee Social Union. *Report on Housing and Industrial Conditions 1905*, p. 24.
15. John. *At the Works*, p. 11.
16. Gazeley. *Poverty in Britain*, p. 10.
17. Bowley. *Wages and Income since 1860*, p. 42.
18. Reeves. *Round About a Pound a Week*, p. 114.
19. *Ibid.*, p. 65.

20. *Report upon the Study of the Diet of the Labouring Classes in the City of Glasgow*, 1911.
21. Reeves. *Round About a Pound a Week*, p. 149.
22. *Ibid.*, p. 210.
23. John. *At the Works*, p. 47.
24. Thane. *Old Age in English History*, part III, p. 292.
25. Johnson (ed.). *Twentieth-Century Britain*, p. 95.
26. Davies (ed.). *Maternity: Letters from Working Women*, p. 60.
27. Gazeley. *Poverty in Britain*, p. 19.

Part Two: 'Enough of this Tomfoolery'

Chapter 5: *Unfinished Business* (pages 85–103)

1. Thomas. *Rhodes: The Race for Africa*, p. 234.
2. Rhodes James. *The British Revolution*, p. 175.
3. *Ibid.*, p. 192.
4. *Ibid.*, p. 173.
5. *Ibid.*, p. 182.
6. *Ibid.*, p. 189.
7. *Ibid.*, p. 194.
8. *Ibid.*, p. 189.
9. Jenkins. *Asquith*, p. 114.
10. *Ibid.*
11. *Ibid.*
12. Rhodes James. *The British Revolution*, p. 197.
13. Grigg. *The Young Lloyd George*, p. 262.
14. Rhodes James. *The British Revolution*, p. 198.
15. *Ibid.*
16. Mackay. *Balfour*, p. 82.
17. Thomas. *Rhodes*, p. 343.
18. Grigg. *The Young Lloyd George*, p. 258.
19. *Ibid.*
20. *Ibid.*, p. 201.
21. Rhodes James. *The British Revolution*, p. 260.
22. Grigg. *The Young Lloyd George*, p. 264.
23. Jenkins. *Asquith*, p. 119.
24. Rhodes James. *The British Revolution*, p. 203.
25. Grigg. *The Young Lloyd George*, p. 270.
26. Jenkins. *Asquith*, p. 121.
27. Rhodes James. *The British Revolution*, p. 277.
28. Jenkins. *Asquith*, p. 128.
29. Grigg. *The Young Lloyd George*, p. 286.

Chapter 6: *A Preference for Empire* (pages 104–26)

1. Joseph Chamberlain Papers. University of Birmingham, note by J. S. Sanders, 16.10.28.
2. Cabinet papers, 41/28, No. 4, letter 10.3.03, Public Record Office.
3. Balfour. *Essays and Addresses*, p. 139.
4. Mackay. *Balfour*, p. 137.
5. Cabinet papers, 41/29, No. 8, 12.5.03, Public Record Office.
6. Balfour papers, 49770, H66741, 27.8.03, British Library.
7. *Annual Register*, 1903
8. Fitzroy. *Memoirs*, p. 143.
9. Hansard, 28.5.03, column 123.
10. Mackay. *Balfour*, p. 146.
11. *Ibid.*, p. 149.
12. Cabinet papers, 41/28, No. 19, 15.8.03, Public Record Office.
13. Gollin. *Balfour's Burden*, p. 153.
14. Devonshire mss, series 340, 2902, Chatsworth House, Derbyshire.
15. *Ibid.*
16. Fitzroy. *Memoirs*, p. 152.
17. Holland. *Life of Spear Compton*, pp. 342ff.
18. Royal Archives, R23, No. 85, Windsor Castle.
19. Gollin. *Balfour's Burden*, p. 162.
20. Victor Cavendish diaries, 18.9.03.
21. Holland. *Life of Spear Compton*, p. 352.
22. Gollin. *Balfour's Burden*, p. 172.
23. *Ibid.*, p. 174.
24. *Ibid.*
25. *The Times*, 18.8.07.
26. Royal Archives, R23, No. 100, 1.10.03, Windsor Castle.
27. Churchill. *Great Contemporaries*, p. 194.
28. Holland. *Life of Spencer Compton*, p. 369.
29. Fitzroy. *Memoirs*, p. 150.
30. Gollin. *Balfour's Burden*, p. 182.
31. Royal Archives, R23, No. 103, 4.10.03, Windsor Castle.
32. Gollin. *Balfour's Burden*, p. 184.
33. Jay. *Joseph Chamberlain*, p. 257.
34. Fraser. *Evolution of the British Welfare State*, p. 257.
35. Cabinet papers, 41/30, No. 10B, 21.3.05, Public Record Office.
36. Fraser. *Evolution of the British Welfare State*, p. 261.
37. Mackay. *Balfour*, p. 251.
38. *Ibid.*, p. 213.
39. *Ibid.*
40. *Ibid.*, p. 215.
41. *Ibid.*, p. 226.
42. Jenkins. *Asquith*, p. 148.

Chapter 7: *Uniting the Nation* (pages 127–49)

1. Cabinet papers, 41/30, No. 5B, 28.2.05, Public Record Office.
2. *Ibid.* No. 30, 1.8.05.
3. *Ibid.*
4. Webb. *Our Partnership*, p. 322.
5. Fraser. *Evolution of the British Welfare State*, p. 173.
6. Royal Commission on Poor Law, 1902, Minutes of Evidence, Q 2230.
7. Hollis. *Ladies Elect*, p. 250.
8. Rhodes James. *The British Revolution*, p. 240.
9. *New Review*, December 1903.
10. Webb. *The Diaries of Beatrice Webb*, 30.10.01
11. Addison. *Churchill on the Home Front*, p. 56.
12. *Ibid.*, p. 71.
13. Harris. *William Beveridge*, p. 139.
14. Cabinet papers 37/98/159, 30.11.09, Public Record Office.
15. Fraser. *Evolution of the British Welfare State*, p. 186.
16. *Ibid.*, p. 169.
17. Addison. *Churchill on the Home Front*, p. 74.
18. Fraser. *Evolution of the British Welfare State*, p. 109.
19. Addison. *Churchill on the Home Front*, p. 75.
20. *Ibid.*, p. 78.
21. Masterman. *The Condition of England*, p. 135.
22. Rhodes James. *The British Revolution*, p. 244.
23. Jenkins. *Churchill*, p. 147.
24. Soames (ed.). *Speaking for Themselves*, p. 21.
25. *Ibid.*
26. *Ibid.*
27. Addison. *Churchill on the Home Front*, p. 86.
28. *Ibid.*
29. *Ibid.*, p. 111.
30. Jenkins. *Churchill*, p. 179.
31. Addison. *Churchill on the Home Front*, p. 115.
32. *Ibid.*, p. 116.
33. Howard. *Rab*, p. 255.
34. Addison. *Churchill on the Home Front*, p. 114.
35. Jenkins. *Churchill*, p. 184.

Chapter 8: *Who Shall Rule?* (pages 150–72)

1. Jenkins. *Asquith*, p. 179.
2. *Ibid.*, p. 162.
3. Balfour papers, 49729, 31.3.06, British Library.
4. Jenkins. *Asquith*, p. 197, note 1.

5. Grigg. *The People's Champion*, p. 178.
6. *Ibid.*
7. *Ibid.*
8. *Ibid.*
9. Mallet. *British Budgets*, p. 298.
10. Fraser. *Evolution of the British Welfare State*, p. 177.
11. Pearce. *Lines of Most Resistance*, p. 249.
12. *Ibid.*, p. 246.
13. *Hansard*, 29.5.08, column 395.
14. Dangerfield. *The Strange Death of Liberal England*, p. 30.
15. *Ibid.*
16. Grigg. *The People's Champion*, p. 173.
17. *The Times*, 3.5.09.
18. *Ibid.*, 4.5.09.
19. Grigg. *The People's Champion*, p. 198.
20. Jenkins. *Asquith*, p. 406.
21. Grigg. *The People's Champion*, p. 198.
22. *The Times*, 16.6.09.
23. *Ibid.*, 17.7.09.
24. *Ibid.*
25. Addison. *Churchill on the Home Front*, p. 89.
26. Jenkins. *Asquith*, p. 160.
27. Addison. *Churchill on the Home Front*, p. 89.
28. *Ibid.*, p. 87.
29. *Ibid.*
30. Grigg. *The People's Champion*, p. 208.
31. Magnus. *King Edward VII*, p. 421.
32. Jenkins. *Asquith*, p. 200.
33. Grigg. *The People's Champion*, p. 233.
34. Jenkins. *Asquith*, p. 202.
35. Spender and Asquith, *Life of Lord Oxford and Asquith*, p. 261.
36. Grigg. *The People's Champion*, p. 234.
37. Jenkins. *Asquith*, p. 209.
38. Nicolson. *King George V*, p. 213.
39. Jenkins. *Asquith*, p. 218.
40. *Ibid.*, p. 221.
41. Nicolson. *King George V*, p. 221.
42. Blake. *The Unknown Prime Minister*, p. 69.
43. *Ibid.*

Part Three: 'The Force Majeure which Activates and Arms'

Chapter 9: *Ourselves Alone* (pages 175–96)

1. MacBride. *Servant of the Queen*, p. 295.
2. Kee. *The Green Flag*, p. 44.
3. MacBride. *Servant of the Queen*, p. 321.
4. *Ibid.*, p. 327.
5. *Ibid.*, p. 316.
6. Kee. *The Green Flag*, p. 458.
7. *Ibid.*
8. *Report into Housing Conditions of Working Class in Dublin.* Parliamentary Papers, 1914, vol. xix, p. 66.
9. Kee. *The Green Flag*, p. 491.
10. Greaves. *The Life and Times of James Connolly*, p. 23.
11. *Ibid.*
12. *Ibid.*, p. 133.
13. Kee. *The Green Flag*, p. 493.
14. MacBride. *Servant of the Queen*, p. 317.
15. *United Irishman*, 8.10.1899.
16. *Ibid.*, 6.4.03.
17. *Cork Examiner*, 3.8.03.
18. Jenkins. *Asquith*, p. 121.
19. *Ibid.*, p. 132.
20. *Ibid.*, p. 136.
21. Kee. *The Green Flag*, p. 455.
22. *Ibid.*, p. 22.
23. *Ibid.*
24. Hyde. *Carson*, p. 466.
25. *Ibid.*, p. 462.
26. Jenkins. *Asquith*, p. 276.
27. Hyde. *Carson*, p. 467.
28. *Ibid.*, p. 510.
29. Pearce. *Lines of Most Resistance*, p. 402.
30. Rhodes James. *The British Revolution*, p. 271.
31. Blake. *The Unknown Prime Minister*, p. 130.
32. Ensor. *England 1870–1914*, p. 359.
33. *The Times*, 16.3.14.
34. Hyde. *Carson*, p. 339.
35. Kee. *The Green Flag*, p. 479.
36. *Ibid.*, p. 483.
37. Greaves. *The Life and Times of James Connolly*, p. 248.
38. *Report of Dublin Disturbances Committee*, Parliamentary Papers, 1914, vol. xviii, p. 647.
39. Dangerfield. *The Strange Death of Liberal England*, p. 262.

Chapter 10: *Votes for Women!* (pages 197–221)

1. Gretton. *A Modern History of the English People*, p. 185.
2. *The Times*, 13.6. 1884.
3. Booth. *Life and Labour of the People in London*, p. 59.
4. Pugh. *The Pankhursts*, p. 82.
5. *Ibid.*
6. Lewis. *Eva Gore-Booth and Esther Roper*, p. 17.
7. *Ibid.*, p. 6.
8. Pugh. *The Pankhursts*, p. 93.
9. *Ibid.*, p. 107.
10. *Ibid.*, p. 101.
11. John Bruce Glazier, diaries 5.4.02, Sydney Jones Library, University of Liverpool.
12. *Labour Leader*, 14.3.03.
13. *Ibid.*, 30.5.03.
14. Pugh. *The Pankhursts*, p. 125.
15. Addison. *Churchill on the Home Front*, p. 48.
16. *Ibid.*
17. Pugh. *The Pankhursts*, p. 128.
18. *Ibid.*
19. *Ibid.*, p. 129.
20. Addison. *Churchill on the Home Front*, p. 49.
21. Jenkins. *Churchill*, p. 185.
22. Pugh. *The Pankhursts*, p. 137.
23. *Daily Mirror*, 2.3.06.
24. Pugh. *The Pankhursts*, p. 165.
25. *Ibid.* p. 167.
26. Pugh. *The Pankhursts*, p. 180.
27. *Ibid.*
28. *Ibid.*
29. Scott papers, 128/67/68, *Manchester Guardian*, 21.5.09.
30. Pugh. *The Pankhursts*, p. 185.
31. Scott papers, 128/87.
32. Pugh. *The Pankhursts*, p. 195.
33. Magnus. *King Edward VII*, p. 396.
34. *Ibid.*, p. 409.
35. Jenkins. *Asquith*, p. 246.
36. Jenkins. *Churchill*, p. 186.
37. Pugh. *The Pankhursts*, p. 213.
38. Scott Papers, 128/190.
39. Pugh. *The Pankhursts*, p. 230.
40. *The Suffragette*, 12.11.12.
41. Jenkins. *Asquith*, p. 249.

42. *Ibid.*, p. 250.
43. Pugh. *The Pankhursts*, p. 266.
44. *The Suffragette*, 7.8.14.
45. Jenkins. *Asquith*, p. 243.

Chapter 11: *United We Stand* (pages 222–42)

1. Pelling. *The History of the British Trade Unions*, p. 125.
2. Webb. *History of Trade Unions*, p. 568.
3. Dugan. *The Shipwrights*, p. 120.
4. Mortimer. *History of the Boilermakers Society*, p. 144.
5. Rhodes-James. *The British Revolution*, p. 162.
6. Dugan. *The Shipwrights*, p. 125.
7. Mortimer. *History of the Boilermakers Society*, p. 145.
8. Challinor. *The Lancashire and Cheshire Miners*, p. 225.
9. Cabinet papers, 41/29, No. 12, Public Record Office.
10. *Ibid.*, 41/29, N12/37.
11. *Ibid.*
12. Mackay. *Balfour*, p. 227.
13. Jenkins *Asquith*, p. 170.
14. *The Times*, 14.8.15.
15. Morgan. *Labour People*, p. 42.
16. Jenkins, *Churchill*, p. 408.
17. 'Colliery Disturbances in South Wales', parliamentary papers, lxiv, column 5568, 1911.
18. Addison. *Churchill on the Home Front*, p. 142.
19. Pelling. *The History of the British Trade Unions*, p. 129.
20. *Ibid.*, p. 131.
21. *Ibid.*, p. 133.
22. *Ibid.*, p. 138.
23. *Ibid.*, p. 140.

Chapter 12: *Useful Members of the Community* (pages 243–64)

1. Stephens. *Education in Britain*, p. 83.
2. *Ibid.*, p. 84.
3. *Ibid.*
4. *Ibid.*, p. 92.
5. *Annual Register*, 1890, p. 51.
6. Curtis. *Education in Britain since 1900*, p. 10.
7. *Royal Commission on Secondary Education*, 1895.
8. *Ibid.*, Minutes of Evidence, 492.
9. Lawson and Silver. *A Social History of Education in England*, p. 321.
10. Balfour papers, 49698, H b14, British Library.
11. Mackay. *Balfour*, p. 108.

12. Kekewich. *The Education Department and After*, p. 92.
13. *Hansard*, 96/1446, 9.7.01.
14. Mackay. *Balfour*, p. 95.
15. Balfour papers, 49765, British Library.
16. Mackay. *Balfour*, p. 90.
17. *Ibid.*, p. 91.
18. *Ibid.*, p. 93.
19. Rowland Evans diaries, 30.6.02.
20. Norman. *The English Catholic Church in the Nineteenth Century*, p. 368.
21. O'Neil. *Cardinal Herbert Vaughan*, p. 443.
22. Murphy. *Church, State and Schools in Britain*, p. 90.
23. Munson, J. E. R. 'The Unionist Coalition in Education 1800–1870', *Historical Journal*, volume xx, 1977.
24. Victor Cavendish diaries, 3.11.01.
25. Rowland Evans diaries, 4.2.07.
26. Mackay. *Balfour*, p. 105.
27. Alderson. *Universities and Elites in Britain since 1800*, p. 103.
28. Richards, C. *Education Journal*, issue 72, 2003.
29. *Ibid.*
30. Stephens. *Education in Britain*, p. 105.
31. Morgan. *Rise and Progress of Scottish Education*, p. 53.
32. Silver. *Education of the Poor*, p. 142.
33. Curtis. *Working Class Education in Britain*, p. 209.

Part Four: 'Everybody Got Down off their Stilts'

Chapter 13: *Ideas Enter the Drawing Room* (pages 267–90)

1. Wilson. *Edwardian Theatre*, p. 15.
2. Shaw. *Complete Plays of Bernard Shaw*, p. 179.
3. Jones, Arthur. *Life and Letters*, p. 434.
4. Trewin. *The Edwardian Theatre*, p. 31.
5. Magnus. *King Edward VII*, p. 172.
6. Wilson. *Edwardian Theatre*, p. 11.
7. Trewin. *The Edwardian Theatre*, p. 44.
8. Wilson. *Edwardian Theatre*, p. 45.
9. Holroyd. *Bernard Shaw*, volume 2, p. 378.
10. Trewin. *The Edwardian Theatre*, p. 89.
11. Wilson. *Edwardian Theatre*, p. 49.
12. *Ibid.*
13. *Ibid.*, p. 51.
14. *Ibid.*
15. *Ibid.*, p. 76.

16. *Ibid.*, p. 77.

17. *Ibid.*, p. 78.

18. Trewin. *The Edwardian Theatre*, p. 136.

19. *Ibid.*, p. 139.

20. *Ibid.*, p. 141.

21. *Ibid.*

22. Victor Cavendish diaries, 11.1.02.

23. *Ibid.*, 13.1.02.

24. *Ibid.*, 17.4.02.

25. Rowland Evans diaries, 26.2.07.

26. *Ibid.*, 28.4.07.

27. *Ibid.*, 12.5.07.

28. Kate Jarvis diaries, 3.10.04.

29. *Ibid.*, 4.11.08.

30. Priestley. *The Edwardians*, p. 234.

31. Pearsall. *Edwardian Life and Leisure*, p. 238.

32. Lawrence. (ed.). *Collected Letters of Bernard Shaw*, p. 13.

33. *Ibid.*, p. 707.

34. Holroyd, *Bernard Shaw*, one-volume edition, Chatto & Windus, 1997, p. 378.

35. *Ibid.*, p. 379.

36. Lawrence (ed.). *Collected Letters of Bernard Shaw*, p. 850.

37. Wilson. *Edwardian Theatre*, p. 195.

38. Trewin. *The Edwardian Theatre*, p. 92.

39. Lawrence (ed.). *Collected Letters of Bernard Shaw*, p. 352.

40. *Ibid.*, p. 907.

41. Agate. *A Short View of the English Stage*, p. 79.

42. Portland. *Men, Women and Things*, p. 156.

43. *Ibid.*

44. Trewin. *The Edwardian Theatre*, p. 84.

Chapter 14: *Literature Comes Home* (pages 291–314)

1. Millard. *Georgian Poetry*, p. vii.

2. Maas (ed.). *Letters of A. E. Housman*, p. 125.

3. Yeats (ed.). *Oxford Book of Modern Verse*, preface.

4. Millard. *Edwardian Poetry*, p. ii.

5. *Ibid.*, p. 8.

6. *Ibid.*, p. 10.

7. *Ibid.*, p. 174.

8. Eliot. *Selected Prose*, p. 202.

9. Maddox. *George's Ghosts*, p. 41.

10. Kaplan. *Henry James,* p. 467.

11. *Ibid.*, p. 468.

12. *Ibid.*, p. 527.
13. Camp. *Edwardian Fiction*, p. xii.
14. McConkey. *The Novels of E. M. Forster*, p. 215.
15. Furbank. *E. M. Forster*, p. 27.
16. *Ibid.*
17. Wells. *The New Machiavelli*, p. 149.
18. Foot. *The History of Mr Wells*, p. 54.

Chapter 15: *The End of Innocence* (pages 315–37)

1. Johnson (ed.). *Twentieth-Century Britain*, p. 121.
2. *Ibid.*, p. 188.
3. Cecil. *Life in Edwardian England*, p. 200.
4. Pearsall. *Edwardian Life and Leisure*, p. 217.
5. Birley. *A Social History of English Cricket*, p. 178.
6. *Ibid.*
7. *Ibid.*
8. *Ibid.*
9. *Ibid.*
10. Arlott. *The Oxford Companion to Sport and Games*, p. 32.
11. *Punch*, 12.5.04.
12. Birley. *A Social History of English Cricket*, p. 203.
13. *Ibid.*
14. *Ibid.*, p. 191.
15. *Ibid.*, p. 199.
16. Mason. *Sport in the British Isles*, p. 95.
17. *District Times*, 28.7.11.
18. Lampton. *Men and Horses I Have Known*, p. 241.
19. *The Winning Post.*
20. Longrigg. *The History of Horse Racing*, p. 278.
21. Arlott. *The Oxford Companion to Sport and Games*, p. 32.
22. Mason. *Association Football and English Society*, p. 226.
23. Sassoon. *The Memoirs of a Fox-Hunting Man*, p. 101.
24. Ridley. *Fox Hunting*, p. 130.
25. *Ibid.*
26. *Ibid.*, p. 135.
27. *Ibid.*, p. 139.
28. Sassoon. *The Memoirs of a Fox-Hunting Man*, p. 116.
29. *Ibid.*, p. 122.

Chapter 16: *Gerontius Awakes* (pages 338–60)

1. Humphreys. *Tate Companion to British Art*, p. 168.
2. Young. *Elgar O. M.*, p. 86.
3. *Ibid.*, p. 88.

4. *Ibid.*, p. 308.
5. *Manchester Guardian*, 5.10.00.
6. Mundy. *Elgar*, p. 87.
7. *Ibid.*, p. 94.
8. Young. *Elgar O. M.*, p. 99.
9. *Ibid.*, p. 89.
10. Service. *Edwardian Architecture and Its Origins*, p. 344.
11. Riley. *The Architect and His Wife*, p. 222.
12. Service. *Edwardian Architecture and Its Origins*, p. 297.
13. *Ibid.*, p. 299.
14. *Ibid.*, p. 413.
15. Avery. *Victorian and Edwardian Architecture*, p. 24.
16. Service. *Edwardian Architecture and Its Origins*, p. 234
17. Humphreys. *Tate Companion to British Art*, p. 166.
18. *Ibid.*, p. 151.
19. Priestley. *The Edwardians*, p. 140.
20. Spalding. *Duncan Grant*, p. 98.
21. *Ibid.*
22. MacCarthy, D. 'The Art-Quake', *The Listener*, February 1945.
23. *Ibid.*
24. Woolf. *Roger Fry*, p. 123.
25. Spalding. *Duncan Grant*, p. 100.
26. 'Post Impressionists and the Art of the Insane', *Nineteenth-Century Magazine*, February 1911.
27. Woolf. *Roger Fry*, p. 124.
28. *Ibid.*, p. 147.
29. Spalding. *Duncan Grant*, p. 100.
30. *Ibid.*
31. Humphreys. *Tate Companion to British Art*, p. 175.
32. *Ibid.*, p. 178.

Part Five: 'Full of Energy and Purpose'

Chapter 17: *Would You Believe It?* (pages 363–85)

1. Harrod. *The Life of John Maynard Keynes*, p. 75.
2. Holroyd. *Lytton Strachey*, single volume edition, p. 207.
3. Skidelsky. *John Maynard Keynes*, p. 56.
4. Harrod. *The Life of John Maynard Keynes*, p. 76.
5. Scruton. *Modern Philosophy*, p. 325.
6. Frazer. *The Golden Bough*, p. 273.
7. Peel. *The Future of England*, p. 2.
8. Masterman. *The Condition of England*, p. 75.

9. Hylson-Smith. *The Churches in England*, volume 3, p. 144.
10. *Ibid*.
11. *Ibid*.
12. O'Neil. *The Life of Cardinal Herbert Vaughan*, volume 2, p. 314.
13. Purcell. *The Life of Cardinal Manning*, p. 354.
14. *The Tablet*, 9.4.32.
15. *The Organisation of the Church in Large Centres of Population with Special Regard to the Church in Saint Pancras*. London, 1900.
16. Bell. *Randall Davidson*, volume 1, p. 406.
17. Lloyd. *The Church of England*, p. 53.
18. *Ibid*., p. 63.
19. *Ibid*., p. 90.
20. *Ibid*.
21. Kate Jarvis diaries (various dates).
22. *Hibbert journal*, 11.4.11.
23. *Ibid*., 7.7.11.
24. Lloyd. *The Church of England*, p. 103.
25. *Ibid*., p. 105.
26. Kavanagh (ed.). *The Paradoxes of Christianity*, p. 282.
27. Hylson-Smith. *The Churches in England*, volume 3, p. 16.
28. Lloyd. *The Church of England*, p. 35.
29. *Ibid*.
30. *Ibid*., p. 138.
31. Bell. *Randall Davidson*, volume 1, p. 459.
32. Norman. *Church and Society in England*, p. 222.
33. *Ibid*., p. 127.
34. *Ibid*., p. 222.
35. Masterman. *The Condition of England*, p. 221.
36. Campbell. *The New Theology*, p. 70.
37. Kent. *The Unacceptable Face*, p. 121.
38. Begbie. *William Booth*, volume 2, p. 209.

Chapter 18: *Hardihood, Endurance and Courage* (pages 386–407)

1. Huxley. *Scott of the Antarctic*, p. 4.
2. *Ibid*., p. 20.
3. *Ibid*., p. 19.
4. *Ibid*., p. 34.
5. Huntford. *Shackleton*, p. 137.
6. Begbie. *Shackleton: A Memory*, p. 6.
7. Fisher. *Shackleton*, p. 40.
8. Huxley. *Scott of the Antarctic*, p. 88.
9. Huntford. *Shackleton*, p. 58.
10. Huxley. *Scott of the Antarctic*, p. 97.

11. *Ibid.*, p. 98.
12. *Ibid.*, p. 105.
13. Huntford. *Scott and Amundsen*, p. 165.
14. Huntford. *Shackleton*, p. 69.
15. Huntford. *Scott and Amundsen*, p. 404.
16. *Ibid.*, p. 263.
17. Gilmour. *Curzon*, p. 275.
18. *Ibid.*
19. Walker. *Auriel Stein*, p. 123.
20. Stein mss 36, 15.6.07, Bodleian Library, Oxford.
21. Huxley. *Scott of the Antarctic*, p. 151.
22. *Ibid.*
23. Huntford. *Shackleton*, p. 109.
24. Huxley. *Scott of the Antarctic*, p. 156.
25. Huntford. *Shackleton*, p. 225.
26. Fisher. *Shackleton*, p. 225.
27. Huntford. *Shackleton*, p. 256.
28. *Ibid.*, p. 210.
29. *Ibid.*, p. 216.
30. *Ibid.*, p. 217.
31. Huntford. *Scott and Amundsen*, p. 49.
32. Huxley. *Scott of the Antarctic*, p. 180.
33. Huntford. *Scott and Amundsen*, p. 461.
34. Huxley. *Scott of the Antarctic*, p. 191.
35. *Ibid.*, p. 21.
36. *Ibid.*
37. *Ibid.*, p. 236.
38. *Ibid.*, p. 249.
39. *Ibid.*, p. 254.
40. *Ibid.*, p. 255.
41. Huntford. *Scott and Amundsen*, p. 385.

Chapter 19: *Halfpenny Dreadful* (pages 408–30)

1. *The Times*, 10.5.10.
2. Taylor. *The Great Outsiders*, p. 24.
3. *Ibid.*
4. Herd. *The March of Journalism*, p. 228.
5. *Ibid.*, p. 223.
6. *Ibid.*, p. 239.
7. Pemberton. *Lord Northcliffe*, p. 30.
8. *Ibid.*, p. 28.
9. *Ibid.*
10. *Ibid.*, p. 32.

11. Harmsworth. *The Romance of the* Daily Mail, p. 17.
12. Jones. *Fleet Street and Downing Street*, p. 138.
13. *Ibid.*, p. 37.
14. Taylor. *The Great Outsiders*, p. 59.
15. *Ibid.*
16. *Ibid.*, p. 70.
17. *Ibid.*, p. 112.
18. Spender. *Life, Journalism and Politics*, p. 171.
19. *Daily Mail*, 16.9.03.
20. *Ibid.*, 21.10.03.
21. Gollin. *The* Observer *and J. L. Garvin*, p. 22.
22. *Ibid.*, p. 294.
23. Brendon. *Eminent Edwardians*, p. 24.
24. *Ibid.*
25. Taylor. *The Great Outsiders*, p. 88.
26. *Ibid.*, p. 89.
27. Gollin. *The* Observer *and J. L. Garvin*, p. 24.
28. Fyfe. *Sixty Years of Fleet Street*, p. 128.
29. *Ibid.*, p. 128.
30. Portland. *Men, Women and Things*, p. 183.
31. Brendon. *Eminent Edwardians*, p. 33.
32. Wickham-Steed (ed.). *History of* The Times, p. 52.
33. *Ibid.*, p. 540.
34. Grigg. *Lloyd George: The People's Champion*, p. 214.
35. *Ibid.*
36. *Ibid.*, p. 125.
37. Taylor. *The Great Outsiders*, p. 141.
38. *Ibid.*
39. Herd. *The March of Journalism*, p. 286.
40. Taylor. *The Great Outsiders*, p. 142.
41. *Ibid.*, p. 119.
42. *Ibid.*, p. 120.
43. *Ibid.*, p. 122.
44. *Ibid.*

Chapter 20: *The Shape of Things to Come* (pages 431–59)

1. Burgess (ed.). *The Automobile*, p. 30.
2. *Ibid.*, p. 17.
3. *Ibid.*
4. *Ibid.*, p. 10.
5. Lloyd. *Rolls-Royce*, p. 5.
6. *Ibid.*, p. 6.
7. Montagu. *Rolls of Rolls-Royce*, p. 99.

8. *Ibid.*, p. 113.
9. Lloyd. *Rolls-Royce*, p. 19.
10. *Ibid.*, p. 14.
11. *Ibid.*, p. 34.
12. Montagu. *Rolls of Rolls-Royce*, p. 144.
13. Taylor. *The Great Outsiders*, p. 120.
14. *Ibid.*
15. Montagu. *Rolls of Rolls-Royce*, p. 178.
16. Taylor. *The Great Outsiders*, p. 122.
17. *Ibid.*, p. 121.
18. Montagu. *Rolls of Rolls-Royce*, p. 199.
19. *Ibid.*, p. 187.
20. Taylor. *The Great Outsiders*, p. 122.
21. *Ibid.*
22. *Ibid.*, p. 123.
23. *The Times*, 29.4.10.
24. Taylor. *The Great Outsiders*, p. 123.
25. *Ibid.*, p. 127.
26. Johnson (ed.). *Twentieth-Century Britain*, p. 40.
27. White Paper. *World Naval Expenditure*, 18.10.13, Public Record Office.
28. Hough. *The Big Battleship*, p. 14.
29. *The Times*, 25.6.1897.
30. *Shipbuilder*, November 1907.
31. Fisher. *Memories and Records*, p. 29.
32. Jenkins. *Asquith*, p. 252.
33. Jenkins. *Churchill*, p. 224.
34. Churchill. *Winston S. Churchill*, p. 555.
35. Nicolson. *King George V*, p. 210.

Epilogue: *The Summer Ends in August* (pages 460–81)

1. Rennell. *The Last Days of Glory*, p. 94.
2. *Ibid.*
3. Magnus. *King Edward VII*, p. 345.
4. *Ibid.*
5. *Ibid.*
6. *Ibid.*, p. 342.
7. Esher journals and letters, volume II, p. 25, Churchill College, Cambridge.
8. Magnus. *King Edward VII*, p. 419.
9. Temperley. British Documents vii, 602.
10. Massie. *Dreadnought*, p. 463.
11. *Ibid.*, p. 471.
12. *Ibid.*, p. 475.

13. *Ibid.*, p. 468.
14. Ensor. *England*, p. 399.
15. Massie. *Dreadnought*, p. 532.
16. *Ibid.*, p. 477.
17. *Ibid.*, p. 528.
18. *The Times*, 6.2.08.
19. Jenkins. *Asquith*, p. 241.
20. Balfour papers, 49779, f.18, 17.5.08, British Library.
21. Jenkins. *Asquith*, p. 225.
22. Clarke. *The Story of My Life*, p. 113.
23. Churchill. *Great Contemporaries*, p. 55.
24. Stanley. *Letters*, p. 150.
25. Clifford. *The Asquiths*, p. 224.

SELECT BIBLIOGRAPHY

Addison, P. *Churchill on the Home Front*. London: Jonathan Cape, 1992.

Agate, J. *A Short View of the English Stage*. London: Herbert Jenkins, 1926.

Alderson, R. *Universities and Elites in Britain since 1800*. London: Stephens, 1900.

Altimrah, P. *Economic Elements of Pax Britannica*. Oxford: Oxford University Press, 1956.

Arlott, J. *The Oxford Companion to Sport and Games*. Oxford: Oxford University Press, 1975.

Ashworth, W. *An Economic History of England 1870–1939*. London: Methuen, 1960.

Athlone, Countess of. *For My Grandchildren*. London: Evans Brothers, 1966.

Avery, D. *Victorian and Edwardian Architecture*. London: Chaucer Press, 2003.

Balfour, A. J. *Essays and Addresses*. Edinburgh: Douglas, 1893.

Begbie, H. *William Booth*. London: Macmillan, 1926.

—— *Shackleton: A Memory*. London: Mills & Boon, 1922.

Bell, G. K. M. *Randall Davidson: Archbishop of Canterbury*. Oxford: Oxford University Press, 1935.

Birley, D. *A Social History of English Cricket*. London: Aurum Press, 1999.

Blake, R. *The Unknown Prime Minister: The Life and Times of Andrew Bonar Law 1858–1923*. London: Macmillan, 1955.

Booth, C. *Life and Labour of the People of London*. London, 1903.

Bourke, J. *Dismembering the Male: Men's Bodies, Britain and the Great War*. London: Reaktion Books, 1996.

Bowley, A. L. *Wages and Income since 1860*. Cambridge: Cambridge University Press, 1937.

Brendon, P. *Eminent Edwardians. Four Figures Who Defined Their Age: Northcliffe, Balfour, Pankhurst, Baden-Powell*. London: Pimlico, 2003.

Burgess, D. (ed.) et al. *The Automobile: The First Century*. London: Orbis, 1983.

Campbell, J. R. *The New Theology*. London: Chapman and Hall, 1907.

Cardigan, Countess of. *My Recollections*. London: Everleigh Nash, 1909.

Cecil, R. *Life in Edwardian England*. London: Batsford, 1969.

Challinor, R. *The Lancashire and Cheshire Miners*. Newcastle upon Tyne: Frank Graham, 1972.

Churchill, R. *Winston S. Churchill: The Young Statesman 1901–14*. London: Heinemann, 1967.

Churchill, W. *Great Contemporaries*. London: Odhams Press, 1947.

Clarke, E. *The Story of My Life*. London: John Murray, 1920.

Clifford, C. *The Asquiths*. London: John Murray, 2003.

Curtis, J. *Working-Class Education in Britain*. Oxford: Oxford University Press, 1994.

Curtis, S. *Education in Britain since 1900*. London: Dakers, 1953.

Cyril, M. *The Haymarket Theatre: Some Records and Reminiscences*. London: 1904.

Dangerfield, G. *The Strange Death of Liberal England*. New York: Harrison Smith, 1935.

Davies, M. L. (ed.). *Maternity: Letters from Working Women*. London: Virago, 1978.

Davis, M. *Life in an English Village*. London, 1909.

Drummond, J. C., and Wilbraham, A. *The Englishman's Food*. London: Jonathan Cape, 1957.

Dugan, D. *The Shipwrights*. Newcastle upon Tyne: Frank Graham, 1975.

Egremont, M. *A Life of Arthur James Balfour*. London: Weidenfeld & Nicolson, 1998.

Eliot, T. S. *Selected Prose*. London: Penguin, 1953.

Ensor, *England 1870–1914*. Oxford: Oxford University Press, 1936.

Fisher, J. *Memories and Records*. New York: George H. Doran, 1920.

Fisher, M. and J. *Shackleton*. London: James Barrie, 1957.

Fisher, R. B. *Joseph Lister*. London: Macdonald and Jane's, 1977.

Fitzroy, A. *Memoirs*, volume 1. London: Hutchinson, 1925.

Foot, M. R. (ed.). *The Gladstone Diaries*, volume 7. Oxford: Oxford University Press, 1968.

Foot, M. *The History of Mr Wells*. London: Doubleday, 1995.

Foster, R. F. *W. B. Yeats: A Life*, volume 1. Oxford: Oxford University Press, 1997.

Fraser, D. *Evolution of the British Welfare State*. London: Macmillan, 1973.

Frazer, J. *The Golden Bough*. London: Macmillan, 1922.

Furbank, P. *E. M. Forster*. London: Secker & Warburg, 1978.

Fyfe, H. *Sixty Years of Fleet Street*. London: W. H. Allen, 1949.

Garvin, J. L., and Amery, J. *The Life of Joseph Chamberlain*. London: Macmillan, 1951.

Gazeley, I. *Poverty in Britain*. London: Palgrave Macmillan, 2003.

Gilbert, P. F. *Lloyd George: The Architect of Change 1863–1912*. London: Batsford, 1987.

Gilmour, D. *Curzon*. London: John Murray, 1994.

Gollin, A. M. *Balfour's Burden*. London: Anthony Blond, 1965.

—— *The* Observer *and J. L. Garvin 1908–1914: A Study in a Great Editorship*. Oxford: Oxford University Press, 1960.

Gordon, J. A. *The Victorian School Manager: A Study in the Management of Education 1800–1902*. London: Woburn Press, 1974.

Greaves, C. D. *The Life and Times of James Connolly*. London: Lawrence & Wishart, 1961.

Greenville, J. A. S. *Lord Salisbury and Foreign Policy*. London: Athlone Press, 1964.

Gretton, R. H. *A Modern History of the English People 1880–1922*. London: Secker & Warburg, 1930.

Grigg, J. *The Young Lloyd George*. London: Eyre Methuen, 1973.

—— *Lloyd George: The People's Champion*. London: Eyre Methuen, 1978.

Haggard, R. *Rural England*, volume 2. London: Longmans, Green and Co., 1902.

Harris, J. *William Beveridge*. Oxford: Oxford University Press, 1977.

Harrod, R. *The Life of John Maynard Keynes*. London: Macmillan, 1951.

Hattersley, R. *Blood and Fire: The Biography of William and Catherine Booth*. London: Little, Brown, 1999.

Hawkins, A. *The Death of Rural England*. London: Routledge, 2003.

Heffer, S. *Power and Place*. London: Weidenfeld & Nicolson, 1998.

Hepburn, G. (ed.). *The Letters of Arnold Bennett*. Oxford: Oxford University Press, 1986.

Herd, H. *The March of Journalism*. London: George Allen & Unwin, 1952.

Hibbert, C. *Queen Victoria: A Personal History*. London: HarperCollins, 2000.

Hill, J. A. (ed.). *Letters from Sir Oliver Lodge*. London: Cassell, 1932.

Holland, B. *Life of Spear Compton, Duke of Devonshire*, volume 2. London: Longmans, Green and Co., 1911.

Hollis, P. *Ladies Elect*. Oxford: Oxford University Press, 1987.

Holroyd, M. *Bernard Shaw*. London: Chatto & Windus, 1989.

—— *Lytton Strachey*. London: Vintage, 1998.

Hough, R. *The Big Battleship*. London: Periscope Publishing, 2003.

Howard, A. *Rab*. London: Jonathan Cape, 1987.

Humphreys, R. *Tate Companion to British Art*. London: Tate Publishing, 2001.

Huntford, R. *Scott and Amundsen*. London: Random House, 1979.

—— *Shackleton*. London: Hodder & Stoughton, 1985.

Huxley, E. *Scott of the Antarctic*. London: Weidenfeld & Nicolson, 1977.

Hyde, H. M. *Carson: The Life of Sir Edward Carson, Lord Carson of Duncairn*. London: Heinemann, 1953.

Hylson-Smith, K. *The Churches in England from Elizabeth I to Elizabeth II: 1833–1998*. London: SCM Press, 1966.

Jenkins, R. *Asquith*, London: Collins, 1964.

—— *Churchill*. London: Macmillan, 2001.

John, A. (ed.). *At the Works*. London: Virago, 1985.

Johnson, P. (ed.). *Twentieth-Century Britain*. London: Longman, 1994.

Jones, A. D. *Taking the Curtain Call: The Life and Letters of Henry Arthur Jones*. London: Gollancz, 1930.

Jones, K. *Fleet Street and Downing Street*. London: Hutchinson, 1919.

Kaplan, F. *Henry James: The Imagination of Genius*. London: Hodder & Stoughton, 1992.

Kavanagh, R. J. (ed.). *The Paradoxes of Christianity*, London: Bodley Head, 1985.

Kee, R. *The Green Flag: History of Irish Nationalism*. London: Weidenfeld & Nicolson, 1972.

Kekewich, G. *The Education Department and After*. London: Constable & Co., 1920.

Kemp, S., et al. *Edwardian Fiction*. Oxford: Oxford University Press, 1997.

Kent, J. *The Unacceptable Face: The Modern Church in the Eyes of History*. London: SCM Press, 1987.

Lampton, G. *Men and Horses I Have Known*, London: J. A. Allen, 1963.

Lawrence, D. H. (ed.). *Collected Letters of Bernard Shaw 1898–1910*. London: Max Reinhardt, 1972.

Lawson, J., and Silver, H. *A Social History of Education in England*. London: Methuen, 1973.

Lee, H. *Virginia Woolf*. London: Chatto & Windus, 1996.

Lee, S. *Edward VII*, volume 2. London: Macmillan, 1925.

Lewis, G. *Eva Gore-Booth and Esther Roper*. London: Rivers Oram Press, 1988.

Lloyd, I. *Rolls-Royce: The Growth of a Firm*. London: Macmillan, 1978.

Lloyd, R. *The Church of England 1900–1965*. London: SCM Press, 1966.

Longrigg, R. *The History of Horse Racing*. London: Macmillan, 1972.

Maas, H. (ed.). *Letters of A. E. Housman*. London: Hart-Davis, 1971.

Mackay, R. F. *Balfour*, Oxford: Oxford University Press, 1985.

Maddox, B. *George's Ghosts*. London: Picador, 1999.

Magnus, P. *King Edward VII*. London: John Murray, 1964.

Mallet, B. *British Budgets 1887–1913*. Oxford: Oxford University Press, 1971.

Masefield, J. *Ballads and Poems*. London: E. Mathews, 1910.

Mason, T. *Association Football and English Society 1853–1915*. London: Harvester, 1980.

—— *Sport in the British Isles: A Social Survey*. London: Harvester, 1988.

Massie, R. *Dreadnought: Britain, Germany and the Coming of the Great War*. London: Jonathan Cape, 1991.

Masterman, C. F. G. *The Condition of England*. London: Eyre Methuen, 1909.

MacBride, M. G. *Servant of the Queen: Reminiscences*. London: Gollancz, 1974.

McConkey, James. *The Novels of E. M. Forster*. Ithaca, New York: Cornell University Press, 1957.

Millard, K. *Edwardian Poetry*. Oxford: Oxford University Press, 1991.

Marsh, E. (ed.). *Georgian Poetry 1911–12*. London: Poetry Bookshop, 1913.

Montagu, Lord. *Rolls of Rolls-Royce*. London: Cassell, 1966.

Morgan, K. *Labour People*. Oxford: Oxford University Press, 1987.

Morgan, P. *Rise and Progress of Scottish Education*. Edinburgh: Oliver & Boyd, 1927.

Mortimer, J. *History of the Boilermakers Society*. London: George Allen & Unwin, 1973.

Mundy, S. *Elgar*. London: Midas, 1980.

Murphy, J. *Church, State and Schools in Britain 1800–1870*. London: Routledge, 1971.

Nicolson, H. *King George V: His Life and Reign*. London: Constable, 1984.

Norman, E. *The English Catholic Church in the Nineteenth Century*. Oxford: Oxford University Press, 1984.

—— *Church and Society in England*. Oxford: Clarendon Press, 1976.

O'Neil, R. *The Life of Cardinal Herbert Vaughan*. London: Burns and Oates, 1995.

Pearce, E. *Lines of Most Resistance*. London: Little, Brown, 1999.

Pearsall, R. *Edwardian Life and Leisure*. Newton Abbott. David & Charles, 1973.

Peel, G. *The Future of England*. London: Macmillan, 1912.

Pelling, H. *The History of the British Trade Unions*. London: Macmillan, 1954.

Pemberton, M. *Lord Northcliffe: A Memoir*. London: Hodder & Stoughton, 1925.

Portland, Duke of. *Men, Women and Things*. London: Faber & Faber, 1927.

Priestley, J. B. *The Edwardians*. London: Heinemann, 1970.

Pugh, M. *The Pankhursts*. London: Allen Lane, 2001.

Purcell, E. *The Life of Cardinal Manning*. London: Macmillan, 1896.

Reeves, M. P. *Round About a Pound a Week*. London: Virago, 1979.

Rennell, T. *The Last Days of Glory*. London: Viking, 2000.

Rhodes James, R. *The British Revolution 1880–1939*. London: Hamish Hamilton, 1976.

Ridley, J. *Fox Hunting*. London: HarperCollins, 1990.

Riley, J. *The Architect and His Wife: A Life of Edwin Lutyens*. London: Chatto & Windus, 2002.

Rowntree, B. S. and Kendall, M. *How the Labourer Lives: A Study of the Rural Labour Problem*. London: Thomas Nelson, 1913.

Sassoon, S. *The Memoirs of a Fox-Hunting Man*. London: Faber & Faber, 1928.

Schweitzer, A. *The Quest of the Historical Jesus*. London: A. & C. Black, 1910.

Scruton, R. *Modern Philosophy*. London: Sinclair Stevenson, 1994.

Service, A. *Edwardian Architecture and Its Origins*. London: Architectural Press, 1975.

Shaw, G. B. *Complete Plays of Bernard Shaw*. London: Odhams Press, 1934.

Silver, H. *Education of the Poor*. London: Routledge & Kegan Paul, 1974.

Skidelsky, R. *John Maynard Keynes*, volume 2. London: Macmillan, 1992.

Soames, M. (ed.). *Speaking for Themselves: The Personal Letters of Winston and Clementine Churchill*. London: Doubleday, 1998.

Spalding, F. *Duncan Grant: A Biography*. London: Chatto & Windus, 1997.

Spender, J. A. *Life, Journalism and Politics*, volume 2. London: Cassell, 1927.

—— and Asquith, C. *Life of Herbert Henry Asquith, Lord Oxford and Asquith*. London: Hutchinson, 1932.

Stephens, W. *Education in Britain, 1750–1914*. London: Palgrave Macmillan, 1998.

Taylor, S. J. *The Great Outsiders*. London: Weidenfeld & Nicolson, 1996.

Thane, P. *Old Age in English History: Past Experiences, Present Issues*. Oxford: Oxford University Press, 2000.

Thomas, A. *Rhodes: The Race for Africa*. London: BBC Books, 1996.

Trewin, J. C. *The Edwardian Theatre*. Oxford: Blackwells, 1976.

Walker, A. *Auriel Stein: Pioneer of the Silk Road*. London: John Murray, 1995.

Webb, B. *Our Partnership*. London: Longmans, Green and Co., 1948.

Webb, S. *History of Trade Unions*. London: Longman, 1894.

—— *The Diaries of Beatrice Webb*. London: Virago, 2000.

Wells, H. G. *The New Machiavelli*. London: Allen Lane, 1911.

Wilson, A. E. *Edwardian Theatre*. London: Arthur Barker Ltd, 1951.

Woolf, V. *Roger Fry: A Biography*. Oxford: Blackwell, 1995.

Yeats, W. B. (ed.). *Oxford Book of Modern Verse 1892–1935*. Oxford: Oxford University Press, 1936.

Young, P. M. *Elgar O.M.* New York: White Lion, 1973.

INDEX